The Industrialization of Rural China

The Industrialization of Rural China

Chris Bramall

OXFORD
UNIVERSITY PRESS

OXFORD
UNIVERSITY PRESS

Great Clarendon Street, Oxford OX2 6DP

Oxford University Press is a department of the University of Oxford.
It furthers the University's objective of excellence in research, scholarship,
and education by publishing worldwide in

Oxford New York

Auckland Cape Town Dar es Salaam Hong Kong Karachi
Kuala Lumpur Madrid Melbourne Mexico City Nairobi
New Delhi Shanghai Taipei Toronto

With offices in

Argentina Austria Brazil Chile Czech Republic France Greece
Guatemala Hungary Italy Japan Poland Portugal Singapore
South Korea Switzerland Thailand Turkey Ukraine Vietnam

Oxford is a registered trade mark of Oxford University Press
in the UK and in certain other countries

Published in the United States
by Oxford University Press Inc., New York

British Library Cataloguing in Publication Data
Data available

Library of Congress Cataloging in Publication Data
Data available

Typeset by Newgen Imaging Systems (P) Ltd., Chennai, India
Printed in Great Britain
on acid-free paper by
Biddles Ltd., King's Lynn, Norfolk

ISBN 0-19-927593-9 978-0-19-927593-9

10 9 8 7 6 5 4 3 2 1

For Sophie, Rosa and Kay

Contents

List of Figures

List of Tables

Acknowledgements

This book owes its inspiration to many people, but I should especially like to pay tribute to the work of Vivienne Shue, Marc Blecher, Carl Riskin, Gao Mobo and Han Dongping for insisting that we cannot neglect the Maoist past in analysing the Chinese present. I am most grateful to Bonnie McDougall, Catherine Schenk, Jane Duckett, Vivienne Shue, Rachel Murphy, Linda Yueh, Kun-chin Lin, Daniel Buck and to all the other participants, for their helpful comments in seminars at the Universities of Oxford and Edinburgh. The *Journal of Asian Business and Management* was kind enough to publish an earlier form of some of the ideas outlined in this book; I am grateful to its Editor, Harukiyo Hasegawa and to an anonymous referee of that journal for their comments.

Oxford University Press has, as ever, served me superbly in bringing this book to publication. I am grateful to Andrew Schuller for guiding me through the early stages of this project, and greatly indebted to Jennifer Wilkinson for her encouragement and advice. Carol Bestley, Joy Mellor and Joe Howarth worked superbly to ensure that the production process was rapid and efficient, and I thank all of them. I should also like to thank two anonymous referees for their invaluable comments.

My colleagues at the School of East Asian Studies at Sheffield University have contributed immeasurably by providing a stimulating and collegial environment in which to develop these ideas. In addition, I owe a personal debt of thanks to Tim Wright, Christopher Howe, Dic Lo, Bob Ash, Terry Byres, Marion E. Jones, Liu Minquan and Godfrey Yeung for their encouragement. My greatest debt is to Beate Müller for conceptualizing this book as the third in a series, and for much else besides.

Abbreviations

5YP	Five Year Plan
CBE	Commune and brigade enterprise
COE	Collectively-owned enterprise
Five small industries	Cement, chemical fertilizer, iron and steel, machinery, and power
GVA	Gross value-added, calculated using the SNA system
GVIO	Gross value of industrial output calculated using the MPS system
Household industry (*geti*)	Industrial enterprises employing fewer than eight workers
NBS	National Bureau of Statistics
NDMP	Net domestic material product or national income
NVIO	Net value of industrial output (the value-added version of GVIO)
Private industry (*siying*)	Industrial enterprises employing eight workers or more
SOE	State-owned enterprises. Includes all industries owned by jurisdictions at the county level and above
TFP	Total factor productivity
TVE	Township and village enterprises. Includes town, private, individual and joint enterprises

1
Introduction

An extensive literature on the extraordinary pace and pattern of Chinese rural industrialization after the death of Mao Zedong in 1976 already exists. All-China studies include Byrd and Lin (1990), Findlay et al. (1994) and Oi (1999), and these have been supplemented by a number of fine local studies (Blecher and Shue 1996; Ho 1994; Walder 1998; Whiting 2001; Oi and Walder 1999). These accounts see a shift in economic policy—the abandonment of Maoism and the adoption of the policy of *gaige kaifang* (reform and opening up)—as the catalyst for rural industrialization. To be sure, there is disagreement as to the decisive element in the new policy package. Some focus on the removal of restrictions on private entrepreneurship, both domestic and foreign. Others assign credit to fiscal decentralization. However, all are agreed that the explosive growth of rural industry was initiated by policy change. This central argument is supplemented by a geographical explanation of the spatial disparities that have subsequently emerged. More precisely, it is claimed that physical geography has prevented much of western China from fully exploiting the opportunities offered by policy change (Démurger et al. 2002; Bao et al. 2002). This type of geographical explanation is similar to that put forward to explain the failure of development in other parts of the world, notably sub-Saharan Africa. There, too, geography is said to be destiny (Sachs 2005). By contrast, the pace of growth was much faster along the Bohai rim, and in the deltas of the Pearl and Yangzi rivers because geography offered opportunities rather than imposing constraints.

There is much in this conventional wisdom which makes sense, and many of these fine studies illuminate the Chinese rural industrialization process. The electric pace of rural industrial growth is well recognized. So too the extent of regional diversity. The role played by local government, and the impact of the changing pattern of incentives faced by county and village officials, has been extensively documented and discussed. The impact of physical geography, and of foreign trade and investment, has been widely acknowledged. And few doubt that rural industrialization must assume centre stage in any proper account of the reduction in poverty which has taken place over the last two decades in the Chinese countryside, an achievement without historical precedent.

However, the conventional wisdom is problematic because it offers an explanation of Chinese rural industrialization which is devoid of proper historical content. Much of the literature, indeed, simply ignores historical factors. Oi (1999) devotes only four pages to history, and the volume edited by Findlay et al. (1994) does not discuss historical antecedents at all: post-1978 growth is explained purely by the changes in incentives and property rights introduced under Deng and his successors. It is hard to accept this cavalier disregard for the historical dimension. To be sure, the policy changes introduced after 1978 played an important part in driving the growth process. Indeed I should not wish to decry the importance of the 'reform' package for the growth of rural industry: it is hard to believe that the institutional changes of the Dengist era were anything other than pivotal. However, we need to recognize the possibility of continuity across the great historical divides of 1949 and 1978. Contemporary Chinese rural industry is not a sector without a past, and any proper account of its development must start with a recognition of that history.

Other scholars do take history much more seriously (Sachs and Woo 1994; Naughton 1988; Wong 1988, 1991a; Whiting 2001). But whilst this alternative treatment of history acknowledges that Chinese rural industry started to grow before 1978, it contends that the legacies of Maoism were a burden rather than a springboard. This, it is argued, is because the rural industries of the 1960s and 1970s were invariably state-owned and often militarily-orientated in their production, both of which made for chronic inefficiency. From this perspective, it was no accident that Wenzhou—the part of rural China which industrialized most rapidly of all—had no rural industrial base to speak of at the close of the 1970s; it had all the advantages of a late start. Of course the reasons which lie behind this tendency to dismiss the legacies of the Maoist era are not hard to fathom. Those who seek to identify the achievements of Maoism are typically dismissed as being little better than Holocaust deniers, and therefore one stands in harm's way in seeking to understand, let alone defend, aspects of Maoism. As Putterman (1997: 1640) points out, even to suggest that 'the roots of China's success . . . can be found in the policies and institutions of the Mao era would be risking ridicule from some quarters.' Of course there is much in the Maoist record to castigate. Even leaving aside the wider issues of the Great Famine and the suppression of human rights, the economic record is hardly one of untarnished achievement. Writers such as Wong (1991a) and Naughton (1988) have rightly documented the inefficiency of Maoist collective industry, and Third Front enterprises respectively. Whiting (2001) is undoubtedly correct in contending that the choices of the Maoist era constrained those of the 1980s and 1990s. But there is another, largely unexplored, side to the Maoist record. Even if rural industry was inefficient in terms of the levels of productivity attained, it is not hard to argue that Chinese workers and cadres alike learnt from the process, or that this learning in turn made possible the remarkable growth of the Dengist era. There is also the possibility that local government across China, but especially in Jiangsu, chose to remain on the collective road because such industries were much more efficient than their private cousins. If so, any notion of path dependency—in the sense of growth along an inefficient equilibrium path—has to be questioned. Furthermore, there is abundant international evidence suggesting that a protracted period of 'learning-by-doing' is necessary before a poor country can successfully develop rural industry. That seems to be the lesson from countries as diverse as Britain and Japan (neither developed rural industries out of nothing), and for South Korea and Taiwan (both of which struggled during the 1950s despite considerable US aid). Furthermore, the experience of both Vietnam and India over the last two decades appears instructive: neither country has found it easy to develop rural industry, and the absence of any tradition of modern rural industrialization has surely played a role.

Some scholars do offer an altogether more positive appraisal of the legacies of history (Blecher and Shue 1996; Putterman 1997; Perkins 1998). Lin and Yao (2001: 150), for example, are moved to acknowledge that 'The development of the commune and brigade enterprises in the 1970s laid a solid foundation for RE [rural enterprise] development in the 1980s.' However, this literature typically touches upon the role of history, rather than examining it in detail. There are exceptions, but these are local studies. Blecher and Shue (1996), for example, provide a superb discussion of the continuities between the Maoist and post-1978 eras, but their analysis is confined to a single Chinese county. And the valuable literature which addresses in passing the historical roots of rural industrialization in Jiangsu (Fei 1986; Li 1998) makes all-China generalization problematic. Moreover, not one of these micro studies uses statistical data in any methodical way to evaluate the causal links between prior industrialization, and the growth of the 1980s. That is not meant as criticism; these local accounts have illuminated the growth process in a way which no national study possibly could. However, we need some proper macro-economic analysis which makes full use of the available national data, gives due attention to provincial and regional variation, and which systematically addresses the question of causality.

Furthermore, those of us who have been more inclined to dwell on the positive legacies of China's Maoist past have been content with the *assertion* that history mattered. The link between the legacies of Maoism and the rural industrialization of the 1980s and 1990s is sometimes suggested, as it is in the writings of Putterman (1997) and Perkins (1998) on the Maoist era, or in those of Fei (1986) and Li (1998) linking Republican proto-industrialization to industrial growth in the 1980s. But there is little by way of systematic analysis of the causal link. For example, Perkins (1998: 26) argues that ' . . . the close relationship [between Maoist rural industrialization and that of the 1980s] . . . could probably be established statistically', but he himself admits to relying on 'anecdotal evidence' to make his case. Some of my own previous work (Bramall 1993) is also deficient in doing little more than asserting that the Third Front laid the foundations for post-1978 growth in Sichuan: *post hoc, ergo propter hoc.*

This sort of analysis will no longer do. The anti-Maoist tide noted by Putterman is flowing less strongly, and a good deal of local level evidence has now been published on rural industrial development in China, both in the *difang zhi* (local records) and in the plethora of post-1978 statistical publications. The time is therefore ripe to investigate more systematically the extent of the continuity between the Chinese past and its present. We need to move beyond correlation and anecdote to address the issue of causality.

The explanation for post-1978 rural industrialization proposed in this book is that historical legacies were a prime mover in the growth process, rather than a mere coda. More precisely, my explanation centres around what I have called the capability, or learning, hypothesis. This approach starts out from the premise that manufacturing capability depends upon possession of a stock of plant and equipment. However, such physical capital is ineffectual unless complemented by a skilled industrial workforce. Manufacturing capability is thus a function of both physical capital and skills. Skill acquisition in turn is critically dependent upon experience of industrial employment because it offers a vehicle for learning-by-doing whereby rural workers acquire the skills necessary to run manufacturing industry efficiently. Some skills can be learned from others, and here formal education and training have a role to play. However, there is no substitute for informal skills and tacit knowledge, and these informal skills can only be acquired via employment in modern industry. China's failure to invest heavily in plant and equipment in the early twentieth century was therefore doubly damaging because it left the economy bereft of both physical capital, and skills. The new Maoist regime was able relatively easily to rectify China's 'object gap' by creating an array of new factories and industrial enterprises. But the skills deficit was not so easily addressed. Precisely because learning-by-doing was so late to begin, the (infant) industries eventually set up during the 1950s, 1960s and 1970s were, for the most part, still inefficient by the close of the Maoist era. However, invaluable skills and competencies were gradually acquired during this long process of apprenticeship. These skills, once created, provided the basis for the absorption of new technologies from the cities and from abroad after Mao's death. During the 1980s and 1990s, the development of manufacturing capability during the Maoist era paid dividends. In these decades, China's infant industries grew up. By the time of Deng's death, China possessed a large and competitive rural industrial sector, and in the process millions of its citizens had begun their ascent from poverty.

In order to test this learning hypothesis, I adopt an approach which properly defines rural industry, and which makes use of spatial data. The first step is to recognize that the customary distinction between state-owned and *xiangzhen* (Township and village enterprises (TVE)) industry operating alongside each other in county towns in the Chinese countryside is artificial. Both types of industry were essentially rural, and should be treated as such. I therefore broaden the definition of rural industry to encompass state-owned and collectively-owned industry based in Chinese counties, as well as commune and brigade industries and their TVE successors. Once this definition is adopted, it is clear that the extent of rural industrialization that had been achieved by the close of the Maoist era was much greater than usually thought. And with this extensive rural industrialization went hand-in-hand an equally extensive process of industrial skill acquisition. In other words, manufacturing capability had developed apace in the late Maoist era.

Secondly, I use county-level data to test the hypothesis (provincial level data are no good because they include urban centres). If the learning hypothesis is correct, we would expect to find that those counties which inherited a higher level of capability from the Maoist era enjoyed faster rural industrialization—*ceteris paribus*—after 1978 than those which started from a weaker base. The central chapter of this book (Chapter 7) thus builds on the broader definition of the rural industrial sector by constructing and employing a dataset for each of China's 2,000 plus counties. We have data on total rural industrial employment rates in 1982 by county from the Population Census of that year; we can use these figures to proxy the extent of the Republican and Maoist skills legacy. We can estimate county-level GDP per head for 1982 using gross output data, and combine it with published data for 1999 and 2000 to produce county growth rates between 1982 and the end of the millennium. This massive dataset therefore allows a more systematic analysis of the link between the industrial legacies at the start of the transition era, and subsequent economic growth than offered in an earlier work of mine, which focused on a sample of 757 counties and restricted its time frame to the period 1982–97 (Bramall 2003). Of course we need to consider whether observed differences in rural growth rates reflect factors other than legacies, such as physical geography. Was, for example, the rapid growth of rural industry in Sunan a consequence of its Maoist and Republican legacies, or was it driven by nothing more than favourable geographical factors such as high yield agriculture and proximity to Shanghai? Proxies for geography are therefore a central part of the analysis.

I have supplemented this national-level statistical approach with three chapters offering more detailed provincial studies. In part this is because the national approach is constrained by the absence of time series data on industrial output for every Chinese county. The use of provincial data also in principle allows us to generate more robust estimates of industrial output growth based on proper time series data, and to test whether the results are sensitive to (for example) the truncation of the time series in 1996, the last full year before the Asian financial crisis. Provincial samples are important too for methodological reasons. It is much easier to show statistical significance in a large than it is in a small sample; accordingly, if a hypothesis which appears valid at a national level is also supported at a provincial level, we can be much more confident that it is robust. A provincial approach also allows a more thorough evaluation of the impact of historical legacies on growth rates. For example, if there is evidence that the human capital legacies of the past impacted upon post-1978 growth, it is worth asking which of the Third Front, the 'five small industries' programme, and the rural industrialization of the Republican era laid the foundations for the industrialization of the transition era. Fei Xiaotong, for example, has suggested that the growth of the 1980s and 1990s in Jiangsu was based upon the revival of the handicraft traditions which had flourished before 1949 and which were dormant during the Maoist era. Many of the skills, he argues, were passed on from generation to generation, allowing (say) the electronics industry of the post-Mao era to tap into a range of competencies and talents. If Fei's conjectures are correct, we need to see the industrialization of the 1980s as a triumph for proto-industrialization rather than a vindication of the late Maoist industrialization strategy.

Jiangsu is a natural provincial choice because there are especially rich data on its experience. As importantly, we know that Jiangsu was the heartland of the pre-1949 handicraft tradition in China. We also know that county, commune and brigade industry developed very quickly in the province under Mao. In principle, therefore, we can look to see whether post-1978 patterns of growth were conditioned more by Republican or by Maoist industrialization. But we also know that there was extensive migration within rural Jiangsu after the late 1970s, mainly from poor counties in Subei to relatively rich counties in Sunan. Was this migration on such a scale that it wiped out the initial human capital advantage enjoyed by its comparatively poor counties? Accordingly, Jiangsu provides a demanding test of the hypothesis that initial human capital levels were positively correlated with growth. Precisely because migration was so extensive into and within the province, we would expect a much weaker relationship between initial human capital conditions and growth. If, despite this labour migration, a relationship does exist, then that strengthens my hypothesis: if inherited skills mattered in Jiangsu, they probably mattered in virtually every other part of China as well.

The second province chosen is Guangdong. I have selected this province with some reluctance: far too much of the literature on the Chinese economy has dwelt on the experience of Guangdong at the expense of the provinces of the vast Chinese interior. However, its inclusion was ultimately dictated by the consideration that it provides the most demanding test of the manufacturing capability hypothesis and therefore ought not to be ignored. Guangdong provides a demanding test because its rural sector grew very quickly after 1978 despite, so it is generally argued, a very meagre inheritance from the Maoist era. Moreover, insofar as Guangdong's poor counties did inherit skills from the Maoist era, there is much to suggest that they were dissipated by an exodus of skilled labour to the special economic zones and to the Delta. All this suggests that the massive inflow of foreign technology, know-how and skilled managers from abroad offers a far more potent explanation of Guangdong's rural industrialization than its Maoist inheritance. If anything, therefore, Guangdong poses even more of a challenge for the learning hypothesis than does Jiangsu. Its experience seems to suggest that foreign skills and technology were able to serve as a substitute for prior industrialization and learning. This is the Sachs-Woo contention: coastal China grew so rapidly in the 1980s and 1990s precisely because it was under-industrialized. It was the absence of extensive negative Maoist legacies—in the form of inefficient state-owned enterprises—which made possible the rise of Guangdong, just as the scale of these same legacies in Manchuria condemned that region to decades of slow growth. Guangdong, so it is argued, enjoyed all the advantages of being a late starter. But rhetoric is no substitute for evidence. Is it really true that Guangdong gained little from the Maoist industrialization strategy? Could it be that Guangdong's meteoric growth owed at least as much to Maoist legacies as it did to inflows of foreign skills and capital, and that the prior development of manufacturing capability was a *sine qua non* for the attraction of inward investment?

The third province discussed is Sichuan, the focus of the Third Front programme (the quintessentially Maoist approach to the development of industry). Much of this construction occurred in rural western Sichuan, especially along the Anning river valley and at Dukou (Panzhihua). Many other rural areas were also affected: Deyang, to the north of Chengdu, is a good example. In other words, the Front was in most respects a programme of rural industrialization, even if those parts of the countryside most affected became urban by the end of the process. Accordingly, Sichuan's experience provides an excellent test of the capability hypothesis. Does the evidence suggest that defence-orientated industrialization—an integral part of the Third Front construction—was much less conducive to subsequent growth than other types of rural industrialization? Did the impact of Third Front construction trump the geographical handicaps suffered by the prefectures of western Sichuan? Insofar as geographically well-favoured prefectures within the Sichuan basin failed to catch-up, was that because the legacies of the Front imposed an insuperable handicap?

2

Rural Industrialization in the Maoist Era

It is conventional in the literature to define Maoist rural industry to mean the industrial enterprises owned and managed by Chinese communes and brigades. On the basis of this definition, the extent of rural industrial development by the close of the Maoist era appears meagre. This chapter considers whether such a narrow definition is appropriate, and the implications of using a broader definition for our perceptions of late Maoist industrialization.

2.1. Context: The Rationale for Rural Industrialization

The attitude of the Chinese Communist Party (CCP) towards rural industry was rather ambivalent for much of the Maoist era. Necessity dictated the development of industry in (predominantly rural) CCP base areas during the 1930s and 1940s, but the victorious conclusion to the Chinese civil war removed wartime pressures and hence the urgency for rural industrial development. To be sure, the development of industry continued to be seen as a way of raising rural living standards, but industrialization was also seen as diverting labour from the key agricultural sector. Furthermore, insofar as industrialization was promoted, the main priority was the development of heavy industry in poor areas. For example, the share of basic construction investment going to what were to be the Third Front provinces rose from 24 percent in 1952 to 34 percent in 1957 (Chen 2003).[1] That necessarily meant the neglect of traditional light industry, and some types of proto-industry undoubtedly declined; traditional paper-making in Sichuan is one example (Eyferth 2004). It also had spatial implications. Relatively affluent regions which had specialized in light industry in the Republican era were especially neglected: not one of the 156 major projects begun during the First **Five Year Plan** (5YP) was located in Guangdong, one of the traditional centres of light

[1] The Third Front provinces here are Sichuan, Guizhou, Yunnan, Shaanxi, Gansu, Qinghai, Ningxia, Henan, Hubei, Hunan and Shanxi.

industrial production. Within provinces, priorities were similarly skewed away from traditional centres of light industry, such as Sunan and the Pearl River Delta.

The first systematic attempt by the CCP to promote rural industry properly dates from the Great Leap Forward. The Chengdu meeting of the CCP in March 1958 encouraged the development of rural industry, and the spring and summer of that year saw the establishment of a large number of new factories (He 2004: 16). The failure of the Leap imposed a break on the process. In large measure, this was because the famine of the late 1950s and early 1960s was deemed to have been caused by the diversion of labour from essential farm tasks and towards the production of iron and steel. In policy terms, the 10th Plenum of the Eighth Central Committee in September 1962, which passed a resolution on the 'Regulations on the Work of the Rural People's Communes' (widely known as the Sixty Articles) was crucial. Article 13 explicitly limited rural industrial development, stating that 'The commune administrative committees shall generally not run new enterprises for years to come . . . ' (He 2004: 22). A further Central Committee pronouncement of 22 November 1962 made essentially the same point, banning the creation of both enterprises and specialist sideline teams by communes and brigades.

Nevertheless, the long run impact of Article 13 was slight, because Mao launched a new initiative to promote rural industry in April 1964 (He 2004: 24). This initiative was driven by two considerations. Firstly, it was increasingly obvious that the traditional agricultural 'package', based upon conventional seed varieties, abundant quantities of labour and the application of animal and human manure, had reached its limits. The only way, it was generally agreed, to raise yields was by means of agricultural modernization—the application of chemical fertilizer, the construction of large-scale water conservancy projects (which in turn required cement and steel), the development of new high-yielding varieties, and by mechanization.[2] All this had been obvious to the planners by the late 1950s; the Great Leap Forward, with its emphasis on labour mobilization, backyard iron and steel production and the expansion of irrigation networks, was a first attempt at agricultural modernization. The Leap of course failed, but its flaws were widely seen as being those of execution rather than conception. With better planning and less haste in the development of rural industry, there was every reason to expect the underlying strategy to succeed.

This desire to promote rural industry was given renewed urgency in the early 1960s by the deterioration in the military and strategic environment. Indeed Chinese industrial choices at that time were dictated far more by defence considerations than by the notional economic advantages conferred by the application of appropriate technology in rural areas, issues extensively discussed in the western 'choice of technique' literature of the 1970s.[3] China's isolation was important for agricultural policy because, in theory, agricultural modernization

---

[2] In retrospect, the focus on mechanization seems misconceived. The international evidence demonstrates that mechanization is generally labour-saving but yield neutral.

[3] Much of this literature is summarized in Ellman (1989).

can be achieved without small-scale rural industry. One solution would have been to set up chemical fertilizer plants in the well-established urban industrial centres of Shanghai and Liaoning, though the appeal of such a strategy was limited to some extent by the transport costs involved. An alternative (more radical) solution available in principle to a developing country would have been to abandon agricultural modernization entirely in favour of a development strategy based around grain imports.

The breakdown in Sino-Soviet relations in the early 1960s combined with growing American involvement in Indo-China altered the calculus completely. The threat of interdiction to supply chains forced the CCP to abandon both possible solutions to the problem of agricultural modernization. Modernization could not be based around imports of heavy industrial products; their supply could only be assured by increasing indigenous production. But it was not just import-based strategies which were closed off: China's isolation threatened industrial production more directly. Much of China's industrial capacity was located in Shanghai, the front line (*qianxian*) provinces along the coast and in Manchuria, and therefore highly vulnerable to attack. The ability of the economy of the People's Republic to survive any large-scale conflict with America or the Soviet Union was thus strictly limited. Accordingly, from a purely military point of view, it was essential to develop a new industrial base capable of meeting China's defence and other economic requirements in the hinterland. Furthermore, China's commitment to supporting Ho Chi Minh's insurgents in Vietnam dictated that many of the new industries should be established in western China in order to shorten supply lines. Additionally, the KMT's successful retreat to Chongqing as a means of resisting the wartime Japanese offensive was fresh in the minds of the Chinese leadership. And so the programme of large Third Front (*da sanxian*) construction in Sichuan, Gansu, Guizhou and Yunnan was born.[4]

Many of Mao's speeches and writings during the 1960s make clear these twin imperatives of agricultural modernization and defence industrialization. Two of the best examples are Mao's speech on the logic which under-pinned the Third 5YP, and at an enlarged Politburo meeting on March 20th 1966:

Moreover, we should consider war and make strategic plans. Party committees in various localities should not manage civil affairs alone and ignore the military, they should not manage money alone and ignore guns. As long as imperialism exists, there is always the danger of war. We must build up the strategic rear . . . This does not mean that we no longer care about the sea coast which must also be well guarded so that it can play the role

---

[4] The Cultural Revolution itself may also have helped the process. The suspension of production in urban factories under the auspices of the slogan *tingchan nao geming* ('stop production, make revolution') forced communes to produce the goods themselves. Gongxian in Henan is one such example. Some of its communes needed agricultural tools and irrigation equipment, and decided to produce the goods themselves in 1966 (HNXZ 1995: 180). See also SSDSB (1997: 7); HNQH (1989: 83); Mo (1987: 122).

of supporting the construction of new bases . . . Two fists and one rear end. Agriculture is one fist, and national defense is another fist. To make the fist strong, the rear end must be seated securely. The rear end is basic industry.

(Mao 1964)

At present, grain is being shipped from the south to the north and coal from the north to the south. This will not do. (Premier Zhou, the national defense industry should also be returned to the local areas. In general, this industry should be given to the lower levels and not to the upper levels. The central government should handle only important matters). The aircraft factories still have not been relocated. In time of war, even rifles cannot be supplied. Every province must have a small iron and steel plant. There are several hundred thousand people in a province. A hundred thousand tons of steel is not enough. A province must therefore operate several dozen steel plants.

(Mao 1966*a*)

It is also clear that Mao envisaged small-scale collectively-run industry, not merely county-level SOEs, as one of the solutions. Initial attempts to promote rural industrialization during the Great Leap Forward may have failed, but Mao saw this as no more than a temporary setback. And, given the perceived external threat as well as the apparent stagnation of agriculture, the need for rural industrial development had increased rather than diminished. By the mid-1960s, as Mao's letter of 7 May 1966 to Lin Biao, makes clear, he envisaged commune-managed industry as an integral part of rural industrialization:

The communes do their main agricultural work (including forestry, fishing, animal husbandry and subsidiary trades), but they must also learn military affairs, politics and culture. When circumstances allow, they should collectively set up small-scale factories and take part in criticizing the capitalist class.

(Mao 1966*b*)

In concrete terms, defence industrialization and the modernization of agriculture were to be achieved by the development of defence-focused Third Front industry in certain selected regions, and by the expansion of rural industrial production across the whole of China. This latter involved the development of county-owned enterprises as well as enterprises owned by communes and production brigades. Given the twin imperatives of agricultural modernization and defence industrialization, it is not surprising that the programme focused on the output of a narrow range of heavy industrial goods, the products of the famous 'five small industries'.

2.2. The Third Front

The Third Front programme was launched in 1964–65 (Naughton 1988; Wei 2000a: 77–83; Chen 2003). It continued to dominate economic policy-making until the late 1970s and, in purely economic terms, the Front was much more

11

important than the Cultural Revolution. One aim of the Front was to create new civilian industries in western China, and in relatively mountainous regions within the coastal provinces (the small Third Front). More importantly the pro-gramme aimed to expand the production of weapons and ordnance, primarily in western China but also in the interior of the coastal provinces.

More precisely, the Third Front comprised three distinct components. Firstly, the development of industries in Gansu, Guizhou and Sichuan. This first phase began in the mid-1960s and it revolved around three projects: the building of a new steel plant at Dukou (later renamed Panzhihua) in south-western Sichuan, the establishment of a new coal base at Liupanshui in Guizhou, and an ambi-tious programme of railway construction designed to link together the three provinces of Sichuan, Guizhou and Yunnan (Chen 2003: 127–33). The second phase of the programme, which spanned the years between 1969 and 1976, maintained the high level of investment in the south-west but also extended the reach of the Front to the mountainous western interior of Hunan and Hubei provinces. The third element of the Front, which began in the mid-1960s, was the creation of 'little' Third Front regions within China's coastal provinces; for example, Shaoguan was designated as Guangdong's little Third Front region.[5]

2.2.1. Third Front Programmes in Western China

Third Front investment was directed primarily towards western China (the big Third Front or *da sanxian*). In absolute terms, Sichuan was the largest single beneficiary, especially during 1964–67 (Gu 1985; Gao 1987; Yang 1990: 134–51; Yang 1997: 162–86). The key Front projects there were the creation of a steel plant at Dukou (Panzhihua), the development of a missile testing and launching centre at Xichang, the building of a weapons base at Chongqing, and the con-struction of a railway linking Chengdu with Kunming. However, although the absolute level of investment in the Front in Sichuan was large, per capita invest-ment was barely above the national average because of its large population. In fact, per capita basic construction in the *da sanxian* provinces (45 *yuan*) was barely above the national average (42 *yuan*) for the period 1965–76 (see Table 2.1). The north-western provinces actually received the greatest per capita allocation. This is not entirely surprising because they were so sparsely popu-lated; Golmud city, one centre of Third Front construction in Qinghai, had a population of only 23,000 in 1964.

The centrepiece of the Third Front was the steel plant of Panzhihua, where construction began in the early 1960s. Its completion was, in Mao's eyes, not merely an economic issue but a matter of strategic importance (LYZW 1993: 36). This was because, when linked to Chengdu to the north and Kunming to the south by the Chengdu-Kunming railway (completed in 1970), the plant would

[5] A useful list of the main Third Front projects is provided in Chen (2003: 253–329).

serve to promote the industrialization of the entire south-western region. The enterprise was established on what was then a green field site on both banks of the Jinsha river out of the counties of Yanbian and Huili in Sichuan, and Yongren and Huaping in Yunnan (Pu 1986: 556). Its location was selected because the surveys of the 1950s had revealed large iron ore and coal deposits (Yang 1990; Shapiro 2001): 'The enormous iron ore deposit there can be mined in the open-cut fashion . . . There is a good prospect for developing the heavy industry in this district' (Sun 1960: 323). The region would probably have been developed in any case, and its industries were growing rapidly even in the 1950s; secondary GVA tripled between 1952 and 1957. However, there is not much doubt that the Front provided great impetus to economic development. Per capita current price GDP in Panzhihua was only 101 *yuan* in 1957 even despite the industrialization of the 1950s. By 1965, as construction got under way, this figure rose to 290 *yuan*, and by 1978 it had reached 851 *yuan* (Panzhihua tongjiju 2001: 58). The population data tell the same story of expansion; between the Population Censuses of 1964 and 1982, the municipality's population rose from 289,000 to over 815,000 (Liu 1988: 175). Panzhihua thus offers an excellent example of the way in which the Third Front transformed a rural site by means of industrialization. In 1962, agriculture accounted for 64 percent of GDP, but by 1978 this was down to a mere 7 percent—a remarkable transformation by any standard.

Two other regions within Sichuan benefited. The first was Chongqing city itself, which became the focus for the construction of a conventional weapon industrial base (*changgui bingqi gongye jidi*). Around 46,000 workers were brought into the municipality during 1964–65 to work on Third Front projects, and many of them were employed in Chongqing city proper (CSJW 1991: 108–10). However, much of the expansion took place in rural areas to the north of the city. Front construction also took place in Deyang-Mianyang region, a predominantly rural area to the north-east of Chengdu.[6] The focus in Deyang and nearby Jiangyou was on the production of pig iron, steel and ferrous alloys, and the development of a heavy engineering industry (Yang 1990: 205–10). Production of steel and pig iron increased from nothing in the mid-1960s to 74,000 and 11,000 tonnes respectively by 1978, and the output of the heavy engineering subsector increased 18 fold between 1965 and 1978, a period during which total GVIO increased only by a factor of 6 (SCZL 1990: 346–7).

In the neighbouring province of Guizhou, Front projects included the development of a ballistic missile industry at Kaili, and the expansion of coal production in the western part of the province at Liupanshui to service the Panzhihua complex. More generally, defence industry flourished along a corridor linking

---

[6] None of the four jurisdictions which made up Deyang municipality in the 1980s—Deyang itself, Shifang, Guanghan and Jiangyou—were classified as urban at the time of the 1964 Population Census (TJJ 1988: 367).

Guiyang with Anshun (which was upgraded from county to city status in 1966) via Liupanshui, and along the railway corridor linking Guiyang via Zunyi with the defence base at Chongqing to the north (GZSQ 1986). The Kaili project was driven by the transfer of some 2,000 workers from Beijing, Tianjin and Shanghai (Chen 2003: 423). More significant was the Liupanshui coal base, the name of which was derived from those of its three component special districts (Liuzhi, Panxian and Shuicheng). This project was singled out as one of three major projects in the south-west (Panzhihua and the construction of three railways linking Sichuan, Guizhou and Yunnan being the other two). The most rapid industrialization occurred in Panxian, where GVIO rose by a factor of 19 between 1965 and 1978, mainly because of an increase in coal production from 80,000 to 2.6 million tonnes (GZSQ 1986: 230, 822–3). Some idea of the overall impact of the Third Front in Guizhou is apparent from the scale and nature of industrial production. Between 1965 and 1978, the value of industrial production in the province increased from 930 million *yuan* to 4.09 billion *yuan*; over that same period, output value in the coal industry increased tenfold and that of machinery by a factor of 11. Still more remarkably given that Guizhou was perhaps China's poorest province—and therefore in desperate need of consumer goods—the share of heavy industry rose from 42 percent in 1965 to an unbelievable 71 percent in 1971 (GT 1984: 179, 183–4), at a time when the national share was only 57 percent (TJJ 1990*b*: 10).

In some ways, however, the most dramatic part of the Third Front programme centred on Gansu, where investment peaked in 1970. The sectors prioritized were metallurgy in the mid-1960s, and machine tools in the early 1970s (GSSQ 1988: 269–70, 275–6). The geographical centre of industrial expansion was Lanzhou, the provincial capital. By the early 1980s, Lanzhou alone accounted for over 50 percent of provincial GVIO, a much higher figure than for most provincial capital; Nanjing, for example, contributed only 15 percent of Jiangsu's industrial production (World Bank 1988: 213). But *rural* industrialization also featured prominently in Gansu, beginning in the early 1960s. One centre was around Yumen-Jiayuguan-Jiuquan (Zheng 1987; GSSQ 1988). At Jiuquan, a large integrated iron and steel company was established, partly in order to facilitate the development of the various plutonium, iron alloy and oilfield complexes at Subei and Yumen (Lewis and Xue 1988: 111; Naughton 1988: 361; World Bank 1988: 252).[7] A second major project was the Baiyin Non-Ferrous Metal Company, producing copper. Some of this industrialization took place in urban areas; Yumen, for example, was already a city in 1964. But neither

---

[7] The plant turned out significant quantities of pig iron fairly early on, but its record on steel production was rather mixed (Naughton talks of 'colossal failure'). It finally began to produce steel only in 1985, by which time it had fixed capital of 860 million *yuan* and a workforce of 26,000 (GSSQ 1988: 183; Naughton 1991: 377). By the mid-1990s, however, its production had reached respectable levels; in 1996, it produced 1.2 million tonnes of steel, and 0.7 million tonnes of steel products (GSNJ 1997: 125).

Subei nor Jiuquan were cities, and Baiyin's elevation to city status in 1958 lasted only until 1963, and was not restored until 1985 (Chen and Wang 1986: 173).

Tianshui municipality was another region within Gansu singled out for Front construction. In large measure, this was because Tianshui was located astride the main trunk railway linking Shanghai and Urumqi (the section linking Lanzhou with Shanghai, and running through Tianshui, was completed in 1954; that between Lanzhou and Urumqi was finished in 1965). It became home to a large number of state-owned and **PLA** industrial enterprises specializing in the production of machine tools; Tianshui produced 69 percent of Gansu's machine tools by the early 1980s (Zheng 1987: 287). Its development was deemed so successful that it was lauded as a 'developing industrial city' in *Renmin Ribao* in March 1974 (Tianshui shi tongjiju 1989: 27). These developments at Tianshui were complemented by the construction and expansion of a range of machine-building industries in the Baoji-Hanzhong region of Shaanxi (Tang 1988: 168–70; Chen 2003: 264–5). Particularly noteworthy here was the development of aircraft production at Hanzhong (Chen 2003: 293–4, 426).

The second phase of the Third Front programme was launched in the early 1970s, this time focusing on the under-developed western prefectures within Henan, Hubei, Shanxi and Hunan. In Hubei, much of the focus was on the development of lorry production at the greenfield Second Automobile works in Shiyan, part of Yunyang prefecture (HBGK 1984: 36–7). Lorry production was necessarily integral to the 'big' Third Front programme, and its expansion was largely successful; output was running at over 70,000 lorries per annum by 1984, second only to the scale of production in the First Automobile works in Changchun (TJJ 1985: 307). Shiyan was carved out of what was Yunxian county in the early 1960s and it therefore offers a further interesting example—rather like Panzhihua—of rural industrialization leading to the creation of an urban centre. Xiangfan, a key railway junction, was also developed as a Front centre. GVIO increased almost ninefold between 1965 and 1978 (TJJ 1990*a*: 233). Unusually though, the mainstay of the economy was light industry, principally textiles (HBGK 1984: 45–7).

Within Hunan, the centre of Front construction was the western prefecture of Xiangxi. Development there was launched during 1965–67, but the real acceleration occurred after 1969. The emphasis was on the development of machine production, but that in turn required an initial major investment in electricity generation (notably the construction of a hydroelectricity complex at Fengtan) and in railway construction (Liu 1990: 163–4).[8] As with Third Front programmes elsewhere in China, the effect was to transform rural landscapes. In the particular cases of Huaihua and Hongjiang, it led ultimately (in 1979) to the upgrading of rural to urban jurisdictions.

---

[8] Across the province, hydroelectricity output approximately quadrupled between 1965 and 1970 (HNSQ 1989: 125).

2.2.2. The Third Front in Eastern China

The components of the Front discussed above focused on western China. However, an integral part of the programme was also the construction of 'little Third Front' (*xiao sanxian*) centres in each of China's provinces. As Naughton (1988: 352) notes, this was the way in which the term 'Third Front' was first used by Lin Biao in 1962 when he talked of a withdrawal from Shanghai to Suzhou (the Second Front) and ultimately to Huangshan in Anhui (the Third Front) if necessary. The overall aim was to make each province self-sufficient in the production of basic weaponry (Wang 1993: 70–1). Most of these Front enterprises were set up in mountainous districts. Shanghai's Third Front industries were transferred to the counties of Huangshan in Anhui. In Guangdong, Front construction focused on the relatively mountainous northern prefecture of Shaoguan. Some of the industries of the Pearl River Delta were transferred there in the 1960s, and industrial production across the prefecture was dominated by heavy industry (Vogel 1989: 229–32; Bachman 2001). In Jiangsu, 'little Third Front' construction in the late 1960s and early 1970s focused on the Subei region. In Zhejiang, some 50 percent of all basic construction investment went into little Third Front projects in 1970 (Shang 1989: 522). Most of this investment was concentrated on developing heavy industry in the western prefecture of Jinhua, and many of the industries were established in rural areas such as Jiangshan county (Lin 1992: 221). In that the little Third Front diverted some state investment to poor areas within otherwise comparatively affluent and industrialized provinces, it operated to offset the regional inequality caused by the growth of CBEs in peri-urban areas.

2.2.3. Outcomes: The Expansion of Industrial Production in Third Front Regions

Assessments of the impact of the Third Front have focused on whether it narrowed *provincial* income disparities during the late Maoist era. They have concluded that the gap between west and east was largely unchanged, and by implication that the Third Front failed. This conclusion varies somewhat depending on the treatment of the central municipalities, the output indicator, and upon the measure of dispersion used. Nevertheless, the overall trends are clear enough. Shanghai, for example, lost ground; its share in national GVIO fell from 18 percent in 1965 to 13 percent in 1978. Yet the poor western provinces gained little. Sichuan's share rose by only 0.6 percentage points (to 5.3 percent in 1978) and Gansu's share rose by 0.5 percent between 1965 and 1978. The biggest gains were actually made by Jiangsu (1.8 percentage points and Shandong (2.3 percentage points) (TJJ 1985: 145). The data on industrial value-added also suggest that Gansu and Sichuan made little relative progress; they increased their shares in the national total by only 0.4 and 0.7 percentage points respectively over the 1965–78 period (TJJ

1999: 3, 677, 794). Given the under-developed state of the infrastructure in the Third Front provinces, their large resident populations, the relatively hostile environment, and the fact (previously noted) that Front investment barely exceeded the national average, it was almost inevitable that the Front provinces failed to close the gap between themselves and the rest of China.

However, this provincial approach is too aggregated to tell us much about the effect of the Front *per se*. Many parts of western and central China were not singled out for Third Front construction; much of Sichuan, for example, was unaffected. Conversely, parts of eastern China—such as Guangdong—were included. A two-way comparison between Sichuan and Guangdong therefore tells us little about the impact of the programme. A direct comparison of Front and non-Front municipalities provides more insight (Table 2.1), showing that Front municipalities such as Tianshui, Baoji, Xiangfan, Liupanshui, Shaoguan and especially Panzhihua all grew faster than non-Third Front urban centres. The picture is not entirely consistent, but that reflects a number of special factors. The data for Chongqing tend to underestimate the impact of the Third Front both because they exclude many types of secret military production and, more prosaically, because the municipality included a number of backward

Table 2.1 Growth of industrial output in Third Front regions

	GVIO per capita in 1965 (current *yuan*)	GVIO Index in 1978 (comparable prices; 1965=100)
Third Front centres:		
Panzhihua	26	11,477
Liupanshui	17	781
Xiangfan	35	890
Tianshui	21	1,346
Shaoguan	96	559
Chongqing	220	240
Baoji	148	503
Deyang	61	571
Other centres:		
Shanghai	2,110	287
Shenyang	1,098	235
Guangzhou	698	291
Nantong	137	402
Wuxi	355	465
National	193	367

Notes: The data refer to the entire jurisdiction (city proper plus subordinated counties). The GVIO figures probably exclude brigade and sub-brigade industry, but the sources are rarely specific. Note that the GVIO data for the municipalities in which brigade industry grew most quickly—Nantong and Wuxi—do include all types of industrial production. In the other jurisdictions, brigade-level industry was far less important than SOEs and COEs owned at the county level and above, and therefore the comparison between Third Front and other regions is fair.

Sources: TJJ (1990a: 104–5, 228–9, 232–3); SCZL (1990: 336–7, 338–9, 342–3); Tianshui tongjiju (1989: 521–2); Shaoguan SZ (2001); GZSQ (1986: 821–4).

areas which were largely (and deliberately) unaffected by the programme. Wuxi's rapid growth reflected the development of commune and brigade industry at a pace which was unusual by Chinese standards; as will be seen, the Third Front was by no means a necessary condition for rapid rural industrialization. Of course most Front areas began their industrialization from a low base level of per capita output and that helped to ensure that the rate of industrial growth was rapid. But that was the point; the very purpose of the Third Front was to generate industrial growth in relatively under-developed areas.

These aggregated data on Third Front regions tell us little directly about the pace of *rural* industrialization because the (local) centre of a Front programme was often an urban jurisdiction such as Chongqing and Lanzhou where existing infrastructure could be readily exploited. However, a conscious effort was also made to urbanize the countryside by creating new cities, and by locating new industries within existing counties because urban centres were deemed vulnerable to aerial attack. The Third Front was therefore a programme of both rural and urban industrialization. For example, Tianshui's programme focused on Tianshui city, and Guangdong's little Third Front was centred on Shaoguan city.

Nevertheless, the data presented in Table 2.1 provide a useful indirect impression of the rural compass of the Front. This becomes apparent in those instances where more disaggregated data are available. Take Tianshui. In a strict sense, it provides an example of urban industrialization. Tianshui was designated a city in 1950, and the bulk of industrial output was provided by factories located within the city proper. That was certainly true of industries owned by Gansu province and the Beijing-based ministries, but it was also true of the location of local enterprises (enterprises owned by Tianshui municipality or by its constituent counties). In 1978, for example, 85 percent of the GVIO produced by local enterprises originated in the urban core. Nevertheless, industrial growth in Tianshui's counties was rapid: the GVIO of county-level enterprises in the municipality increased almost sixfold between 1965 and 1978 (Tianshuishi tongjiju 1989: 528–9). This rate of increase was certainly lower than for the whole municipality, in which industrial output increased by a factor of 13 between 1965–78; it is therefore right to conclude that the urban core was the principal beneficiary of the Front. However, even the sixfold growth rate of industrial production achieved by Tianshui's counties was much faster than the 3.8 fold increase achieved on average across Gansu (TJJ 1999: 805). Given that Gansu's overall rate of industrialization was itself slightly above the national 3.7 fold rise during this 13 year period, the rate of industrialization in rural Tianshui was an impressive achievement. The Shaoguan evidence, discussed in more detail in Chapter 10, shows an even more striking pattern. There, the median growth rate of industrial production in the counties equalled that achieved in the city proper between 1965 and 1978.

It is plain from this brief examination of the experiences of Tianshui and Shaoguan that the Front had a genuinely transformative effect on rural areas. This conclusion is strengthened when we look at industrial growth rates in those regions which were almost entirely rural at the time of its inception. As Table 2.2 shows, Dukou's industrial output grew at a staggering rate during the late 1960s and 1970s. In 1965, there were only 46 industrial enterprises operating in the whole of what was to become Dukou city proper, and the two counties of Miyi and Yanbian; they produced output to the tune of 9 million *yuan* (measured at 1980 constant prices). By 1978, there were 357 enterprises, producing no less than 1.036 billion *yuan* (SCZL 1990: 342–3). The development of Dukou is thus a clear example of rural industrialization leading to the creation of an urban settlement. Deyang municipality, also in Sichuan, provides another example of industrialization in a rural setting: Deyang itself did not become a city until 1984 and even then its constituent jurisdictions were still counties. The Liupanshui (Guizhou) evidence points in the same direction. Growth there was not as fast as in Panzhihua, but the rate of increase was nevertheless much faster than in non-Third Front areas. Again this is an example of rural industrialization; Liuzhi, Panxian and Shuicheng, the three jurisdictions which made up the new Liupanshui municipality, were all counties at the time of the 1964 Census. A final example is provided by Qiandongnan prefecture, a very poor region in south-western Guizhou. Per capita output there was very low in 1965 but the Third Front led to a fivefold increase in industrial production between 1965 and 1978 (GZSQ 1986: 915), and resulted in Kaili—the regional centre but only a county in 1964—being accorded city status.

In short, much of the Front's focus was on the expansion of industrial production in under-developed *rural* areas. Maoist rural industrialization is often perceived as being centred around commune and brigades, and this perception is given substance by the fact that some Front investment was directed towards existing urban areas. But the Front was about developing rural as well as urban jurisdictions, and it was in regions that were rural in the early 1960s that its impact was most felt. It is therefore not wrong to think of the Third Front as above all else a programme of rural industrialization.

2.3. County, Commune and Brigade-level Rural Industries, 1962–78

The rural industrialization programmes of the late Maoist era went well beyond the Third Front. By the mid-1960s, the fear that any promotion of rural industry would precipitate a repetition of famine had begun to recede, and this led to the beginnings of a programme of rural industrialization that was much more all encompassing than the Third Front.

2.3.1. Policy

The initial step was taken in 1964 when local governments acquired the power to create their own independent industrial sectors (Naughton 1991: 165–6).

To accelerate the process, local enterprise development received a large central government subsidy in 1970, and new enterprises were allowed to retain a substantial proportion of their profits. These initial steps to promote industrial development focused on the creation of industries owned by county governments.

After 1970, however, the emphasis of rural industrial policy shifted firmly towards the development of the five small industries by communes and brigades (Riskin 1971, 1978*a*, *b*, 1987; Sigurdson 1977; He 2004: 26–32). According to Riskin (1987: 214): 'The high growth phase for county-run industry began in the late 1960s and tapered off around 1972. Thereafter, it was industry run by the communes and brigades that experienced rapid growth'. The focus was very much on the exploitation of local resources, and indeed CBEs were expected to adhere to the 'three locals' (*sanjiu de yuanze* or *sanjiu fangzhen*) meaning local production, use of local inputs, and the sale of output to local markets.

This shift in industrial policy was evident in the structure of production in the 1970s. According to Liu and Wu (1986: 362–3):

. . . under state patronage, 1970 saw a vigorous development of the 'five small local industries.' In this very year, nearly 300 counties and municipalities in the country had set up their own small iron and steel plants; over 20 provinces . . . had built up factories making walking tractors, small motor works and plants making small farm implements and their parts. About 90 percent of counties in the country had set up their own factories producing or repairing farm machinery.

Admittedly some of the new enterprises were agricultural in orientation, engaged in either planting (*zhongzhi qiye*) or breeding (*yangzhi qiye*). Yet whereas rural industry had previously focused on the production of farm-related outputs such as machinery, fertilizer and processing, the enterprises established in the early 1970s increasingly focused on electricity generation and on the production of iron and steel (Riskin 1978*a*: 87). Between 1969 and October 1976, 1,225 small-scale fertilizer plants were set up across China (Yang and Tao 1988: 56).[9] Zhejiang's experience is typical. During the 1970s, more than 400 factories producing agricultural tools, and more than 80 small-scale chemical fertilizer plants, were created. By the time of Mao's death, small-scale plants were supplying two thirds of the province's chemical fertilizer and 70 percent of cement. Simultaneously, the development of 'little Third Front' enterprises in western Zhejiang proceeded apace (Shang 1989: 421–2).[10]

[9] Sichuan was something of an exception, probably because of the focus on Third Front construction. The development of small-scale industry was not neglected; by 1971, 62 of the counties in the province had steel furnaces, 193 counties had facilities for agricultural tool production and repair, 122 had small cement plants and over 40 percent of coal output came from small mines (Yang 1997: 207). But the key element in the rural development strategy was probably the 1973 decision to import key producer goods because this made two large chemical fertilizer plants—one set up in Chengdu and the other in Luzhou—available to the province.

[10] For a useful discussion of the expansion of chemical fertilizer production at the county level in the late 1970s, see Wong (1991*b*).

Various factors came together to promote CBE expansion. Among those identified in Hunan's case were the disruption to urban production during the last throes of the Cultural Revolution (which created a market for rural industrial products), and the 'sending down' to the countryside of cadres, workers and technicians. But policy change also seems to have played an important part. In 1970, for example, the slogan 'Construct an Industrialized Province within Ten Years' was promulgated, and 1972 saw the creation of a commune and brigade industry bureau (HNQH 1989: 23, 82). However, the pivotal national event was probably the North China Agricultural Conference of 1970, which actively promoted the development of the five small industries. This conference is widely mentioned in both the western (Zweig 1997: 255) and Chinese literature as having played a vital role in accelerating industrial CBE development. The National Conference on Rural Mechanization of September 1971, which declared that a key purpose in developing rural industry was to further the cause of agricultural mechanization over a ten year period and which made rural industry eligible for bank loans and fiscal support, was also important (He 2004: 28).

The whole process was facilitated by bank lending to the CBE sector. In Mianyang prefecture (Sichuan), lending to collective industries increased by 58 percent in 1970, and by a further 75 percent in 1971; between 1969 and 1978, the total increase in lending was 5.7 fold (MSJZB 1993: 141). In Tonghu (Zhejiang), banking lending to CBEs increased more than sixfold between 1976 and 1979 (Tonghu XZ 1991: 385). In Linhai (Zhejiang), lending to CBEs soared between 1976 and 1978 (Linhai XZ 1989: 475). The data for Kunshan show most clearly the surge in lending in the 1970s, which rose from a mere 3,000 *yuan* in 1971 to 112,000 *yuan* in 1974, and to 5.55 million *yuan* in 1978 (Kunshan XZ 1990: 433).

Nevertheless, the development of rural industry did not follow a linear course. For one thing, production in many county-level enterprises was disrupted by worker involvement in the Cultural Revolution. For another thing, there was a continuing tension throughout the era between the desire to promote rural industry and a simultaneous concern to expand levels of agricultural production; the two activities were often viewed as substitutes in terms of their demand for labour, land and capital. The fear of famine had receded, but it had not disappeared, and very often those who advocated rural industrial development were accused of *zhinong zhuan gui* ('deviating from the path of supporting agriculture'). The other problem for the advocates of rural industry was that it was highly profitable, and therefore often viewed as inherently capitalist. Moreover, cadres were often appointed to manage rural industries because the appointment took them away from their power base in production teams and brigades. According to Siu (1989: 259) 'The official explanation for the appointments was that the retiring cadres could no longer carry their weight in the fields. Underlying the transfers, however, was an unspoken political objective: The Maoists were more than happy to remove the old cadres from their bases in the villages.'

The inconsistencies in Chinese policy towards the development of rural industry is reflected in the volatility of the output data, with years of very slow or even negative growth punctuated by years when output grew by more than 20 percent. One example is provided by Hunan province (HNQH 1989: 28); the contrast between 1971 (a 26 percent fall) and 1972 (a 26 percent rise) is especially stark. In general, brigade and team-level output was more volatile than that of communes because these small enterprises were viewed (in some cases no doubt correctly) as much more akin to private enterprises than the larger commune ones.

2.3.2. The Growth of the Commune and Brigade Subsector

It is apparent that rapid CBE growth began very late in some of China's provinces. To see this, we can compare the year in which industrial CBEs regained the level of output achieved at the peak of the **Great Leap Forward** (**GLF**); only when output exceeded that level can we think of provinces embarking upon a new phase of rural industrialization.[11] Using this criterion, rural industrialization began late in Jiangxi and Xinjiang (which regained their GLF peak only in 1977), and in Sichuan and Anhui (both devastated by famine in the late 1950s); there, previous peak output was re-attained only in 1978 and 1980 respectively.

However, the experiences of Anhui, Sichuan, Jiangxi and Xinjiang were unusual. Most Chinese provinces regained their 1958 peak by the mid- or late 1960s and, even if the Leap peak was sometimes slow to be re-attained, there can be no doubting the general acceleration in the pace of CBE development during the late 1960s and 1970s (Table 2.2). The provinces included in Table 2.2 cover many of China's main producers but are not entirely representative: the median growth rate during 1962–71 for the 12 provinces is considerably higher than the national average, whereas that for 1971–78 is somewhat lower. This is partly because the twelve province sample excludes the north-east, where the expansion of larger SOEs was the primary aim. It is also because of the exclusion of most of the poor western provinces, where CBE production was slow to start in the 1960s; there were only 661 commune industrial enterprises in the whole of Guizhou in 1970 compared with 155 in Wuxi county alone (GZSQ 1986: 202; WXG 1990: 28). Even amongst the provinces included in Table 2.2, the pace of industrial growth varied considerably. The output of industrial CBEs in Jiangxi, oddly enough, grew most rapidly in the 1960s, but this was very much the exception. For the whole sample, the median growth rate was at its slowest between 1962 and 1971, and Jiangxi was the only province in which growth was faster during 1962–71 than it was between 1971 and 1978.

[11] The published data for the Leap used here (from TJJ 1990b) almost certainly exaggerate the true value of output in 1958–60 even though they have been much revised since they were first published. In that sense, the comparison used in the text is rather a demanding one.

Table 2.2 Growth of commune and brigade industrial output, 1962–78 (percent per annum; 1980 prices)

	1962–71	1971–78
Province:		
Fujian	4.7	12.1
Guangdong	5.1	24.1
Hebei	18.2	27.8
Henan	21.4	28.7
Hubei	4.7	16.6
Hunan	11.5	13.9
Jiangsu	17.5	30.6
Jiangxi	22.1	11.0
Ningxia	5.5	16.4
Shanxi	9.5	17.4
Sichuan	17.0	18.7
Zhejiang	13.7	21.1
Sample median	12.6	18.1
All China:		
Commune	15.8	30.1
Brigade	2.8	17.4
All CBEs	5.9	23.5

Notes: (a) Growth rates are based on GVIO data. These data typically exclude all types of sub-brigade industry, including private and individual enterprises; systematic national data for pre-1984 do not seem to exist for these categories (see for example Nongye bu 1989: 294–5). (b) There are no systematic data on brigade industrial production in Jiangsu for pre-1965, seemingly because the brigade sector was extremely under-developed before the mid-1960s (Mo 1987: 98–9); the growth rate given here for 1962–71 is actually for 1965–71. (c) The Fujian and Guangdong (excluding Hainan) data are for brigade and below industries only. (d) Jiangxi's high growth rate for the 1960s does appear to be correct, at least in the sense that the data given in TJJ (1990b) are the same as those in the provincial statistical yearbook (JXTJNJ 1990: 47). (e) There are no reliable indices for trends in CBE value-added or prices during the 1960s and 1970s. The retail price index for industrial goods selling in rural areas—which is a fair price proxy—shows a decline of about 8 percent in total between 1961 and 1970 (and 2 percent between 1970 and 1978) so the data in this table understate somewhat the true growth rate between 1962 and 1971.

Sources: TJJ (1990b); SCZL (1990: 23); GDFZ (1990: 10–15); He (2004: 24, 28, 31 and 38).

The provincial data thus show a clear pattern of accelerating output growth, and this appears even more apparent in the all-China data, which show sustained growth in the 1960s. The very fact that the output of commune-run industry grew at nearly 16 percent during the period 1962–71 demonstrates that rural industrialization never entirely lost its momentum despite the setback imposed by the Leap. After 1971, the rate of increase rose dramatically to reach nearly 24 percent, a phenomenal pace for the rural sector of an LDC. During that period, the commune subsector led the way, but (in contrast to the 1960s) brigade-owned industry also grew very rapidly. The pattern of trend acceleration is therefore apparent enough. After a period of slow growth in the 1960s, the commune and brigade sector began to grow rapidly after 1970–71 in most parts of rural China, and this pace of advance accelerated in 1975–76. Thus any notion that rural industrialization only began after 1978 is self-evidently contradicted by the CBE figures. There is therefore much to be said for Jack Gray's view (1974, 2006) that the Leap was no more than a temporary setback in the development of commune and brigade industry.

2.4. Bringing the Evidence Together: Aggregate County-Level Output Growth, 1962–78

The data on commune and brigade industry when viewed in isolation provide an inadequate guide to the pace and pattern of rural industrial growth. For one thing, they exclude state and collective industries located in Chinese counties but owned by higher levels within the administrative hierarchy. These types of industries were more important in quantitative terms than commune and brigade enterprises during the 1960s and 1970s, especially in Third Front areas. Sichuan is a good example; there, rural industrialization was driven much more by county-level rural industry and the Front than by CBEs until the mid-1970s. The same is true of the Manchurian provinces, where the focus was on the development of local state-owned industry in the 1960s and 1970s. The commune and brigade measure of rural industrialization is also unsatisfactory because it includes industries operating in *qu* (districts) within urban areas. Many of these were to be found in the suburban districts; in Chengdu's Jinniu district, for example, brigade level industry and below accounted for 34 percent of industrial output in 1978 and combined commune and brigade output for no less than 83 percent (SCZL 1990: 475). Jinniu was probably unusual, but there is clear evidence elsewhere of commune and brigade production in urban areas. Five percent of industrial output in Changsha city was contributed by TVEs in 1986 (HNTJNJ 1987: 474) and they accounted for 6 percent of industrial output in Nanjing city even in 1992 (Jiangsu tongjiju 1992: 81). There is thus a strong case for identifying rural with total industrial production in Chinese counties, rather than with the output of the commune and brigade sector (see also Appendix 4).

This type of measure poses problems of its own. Firstly, data on GVIO often exclude brigade and sub-brigade industry. This type of production was included in agriculture before 1984 and, though some of the industrial totals have been adjusted retrospectively, many have not. This omission means that county industrial growth rates often understate the true growth rate. The second problem is that it is difficult to document county industrial growth with precision because comprehensive national data do not exist for the Maoist era. Nevertheless, although the task of documenting county-level industrialization is difficult, it is not impossible. One especially useful source is *Forty Years of Urban China* (TJJ 1990*a*) because it provides time series data on a number of municipalities. Whilst the municipal total for industrial production include both cities and counties, the source also provides data on industrial output in the city proper for some jurisdictions, which allows us to calculate county industrial output as a residual. Of course these data are affected by boundary changes but, by expressing industrial output in per capita terms, we can avoid the worst of these problems. Proceeding along these lines generates a sample of county data for 28 municipal-level jurisdictions in 1952, 1957, 1965 and 1978. The total population of these counties was 70 million in 1978 and, as the sample covers 17 provinces, it provides a useful insight into the national trend. However, the source does not provide data on any of the poor western provinces of Sichuan, Gansu, Guizhou, Yunnan and Ningxia. It is therefore spatially rather unrepresentative. For that reason, I have supplemented it with data from two jurisdictions located in Guizhou province, which raises the total population covered to about 75 million.

The results for these counties are shown in Table 2.3, which also provides comparative data on the cities located within each municipality.[12] The county data show a clear upward trend: current price GVIO grew by 10 percent per year in 1965–78. Rural industrialization, then, was a feature of the late Maoist era, and it is particularly interesting that the rate of industrialization was faster than in urban areas after 1965—leading to a marked narrowing of the urban-rural industrial gap from 28 to 1 in 1965 to 17 to 1 in 1978, and in turn undermining some of the more exaggerated claims of urban bias in that era.

Still, these results cannot be seen as conclusive. For one thing, many of the GVIO data exclude brigade, team and private industry, and therefore understate both the true level of county output by 1978 and the growth rate between 1965 and 1978. Secondly, and even despite the inclusion of a pair of Guizhou prefectures, the sample is biased towards comparatively well-off eastern jurisdictions. Thirdly, and perhaps most significantly, the growth rates are based entirely on the endpoints of 1965 and 1978. They would be much more reliable if based upon proper time series data for the whole 1965–1978 period. To gain a better understanding of Maoist rural industrialization, we need more detailed data which allow us to investigate whether there is any evidence of a break in the series in the late 1960s or early 1970s, and to provide more broadly-based evidence than for the jurisdictions in Table 2.3. Later chapters look in detail at the experiences of Sichuan, Guangdong and Jiangsu provinces. However, there is a wealth of information in the *County Records* and provincial compilations which allows us to chart county industrial growth with a fair degree of accuracy. To these materials I now turn.

---

[12] The use of 1980 constant price data would revise the growth rates upwards to 14.8 percent per year for 1952–57 and to 11.3 percent for 1965–78. This is because industrial prices declined in the late Maoist era as production increased.

Table 2.3 Growth of GVIO per capita in some Chinese counties, 1965–78 (county data grouped by municipality)

Municipality	Province	GVIO per capita (current *yuan*)		Growth of GVIO per capita (percent per annum) 1965–78
		1965	1978	
Wuhu	Anhui	29	120	11.4
Huainan	Anhui	28	94	9.9
Hefei	Anhui	18	56	9.0
Fuzhou	Fujian	40	79	5.5
Guangzhou	Guangdong	148	262	4.5
Nanning	Guangxi	42	122	8.6
Liuzhou	Guangxi	28	99	10.2
Harbin	Heilongjiang	258	287	0.8
Jiamusi	Heilongjiang	45	118	7.6
Qiqihar	Heilongjiang	40	116	8.5
Zhengzhou	Henan	27	228	17.8
Anyang	Henan	33	115	10.1
Xiangfan	Hubei	25	118	12.8
Zhuzhou	Hunan	30	173	14.4
Suzhou	Jiangsu	164	646	11.1
Wuxi	Jiangsu	110	580	13.6
Nantong	Jiangsu	88	256	8.5
Jingdezhen	Jiangxi	71	237	9.7
Nanchang	Jiangxi	28	100	10.3
Jilin	Jilin	37	277	16.7
Fushun	Liaoning	17	134	17.3
Baotou	Nei Menggu	22	84	10.8
Hohot	Nei Menggu	11	76	15.6
Baoji	Shaanxi	61	145	6.9
Shijiazhuang	Shandong	44	236	13.7
Qingdao	Shandong	26	203	17.1
Changzhi	Shanxi	51	160	9.2
Ningbo	Zhejiang	95	316	9.7
Tongren	Guizhou	23	42	4.7
Anshun	Guizhou	25	28	0.9
County median		35	128	10.5
City median		995	2159	6.1
City: County per capita ratio		28:1	17:1	

Notes: GVIO data are at current prices and are for all counties located in each municipality. A direct comparison between 1965–78 and 1952–57 (not shown here) would show that rural industrial growth was actually faster in the 1950s and that, although the urban–rural industrial gap narrowed between 1965 and 1978, the gap in 1978 was still above that for 1957 (15:1 for this sample). However, inferences drawn from a comparison of early and late Maoist periods are not reliable because of various problems with the 1950s data. Firstly, the data for rural industrial production are problematic because many of the industries involved were handicrafts and therefore it was very difficult to estimate output. The first post-1949 survey of handicraft production was not even carried out until 1954; estimates for 1952 thus required a degree of backward projection. More generally, there was a strong incentive to under-report 1952 production at a local level because that tended to make for a lower 1957 plan target. In the light of these considerations, it is revealing that the Liu and Yeh's (1965: 102, 156) estimates of handicraft value-added suggest a per capita increase based on the size of the agricultural population of about 20 percent between 1952 and 1957. This is well below the 74 percent increase between 1952 and 1957 generated by the TJJ (1990a) data. To be sure, the counties benefited from the development of modern industry and therefore the handicraft growth rate under-states the true county growth rate. However, we know that the bulk of modern industry was established in urban rather than rural China in the 1950s, and therefore modern industrial development in rural areas ought not have raised the growth rate very much. Accordingly, the official estimate of a 74 percent increase seems far too high.

Source: GZSQ (1986: 1163–81, 1268–86); TJJ (1990a: 104–7, 228–31).

2.4.1. Rural Industrialization in Southern China

Rural industrial growth appears not to have accelerated everywhere in southern China during the 1970s. As previously noted, Jiangxi provides one such example, and Yunnan may be another, though the data for the commune sector are very incomplete. If we take the data that are available (ZYSWZY 1986: 396; TJJ 1990*b*) and interpolate where necessary, it appears that the sector's output grew at 7.9 percent in 1962–69, a figure which would be much higher still if we took into account the massive surge in brigade output during 1970. However, there is little sign of acceleration thereafter; the growth rate during 1971–78 was only 7 percent.

But Jiangxi and Yunnan were the exceptions. For the rest of China's southern provinces, the evidence of accelerating rural industrialization is unmistakable. In Zhejiang, the level of rural industrial output achieved at the height of the Great Leap Forward was regained by 1965, and thereafter the province did not look back: there was no decline in commune and brigade output in any year during the 1970s. By 1976, 86 percent of communes and 49 percent of brigades had set up rural industries in Zhejiang, even though a provincial CBE management bureau was not established until August 1978 (Shang 1989: 270). More detailed evidence on all types of county industry comes from the experience of Wenzhou (Table 2.4).

These Wenzhou data are especially interesting because the municipality has been portrayed so generally as a region where growth accelerated only after 1978 because of the development of private industry. The data here certainly show acceleration in the 1980s, but they suggest a turning point in the early 1970s even for relatively poor counties such as Wencheng and Taishun.[13] Thus the

Table 2.4 Growth of rural GVIO in Wenzhou municipality, 1962–88 (annual growth rates; 1980 constant prices)

	1962–70	1970–78	1978–88
Rui'an	3.8	9.8	19.9
Dongtou	27.8	21.5	24.7
Yueqing	5.4	10.7	28.2
Yongjia	−1.3	13.1	27.3
Pingyang/Cangnan	3.1	11.1	25.6
Wencheng	1.5	6.2	11.6
Taishun	−2.8	9.7	18.5
Rural total	3.4	10.8	24.2

Notes: The data here cover county, collective, and CBE industry located within the counties of Wenzhou. Individual and private industry is included from 1984 onwards. The city proper of Wenzhou (including Ouhai county, which was incorporated into Wenzhou city in the early 1980s) is excluded from the totals.

Source: Chen (1989).

[13] The data in the remainder of the paragraph are for GVIO at 1980 prices for *rural* Wenzhou, defined here as the municipal total minus industrial output in Wenzhou city proper (Chen 1989: 122–3, 256). Ouhai county was not incorporated into Wenzhou city until the early 1980s and is included in the rural total.

overall industrial growth rate in rural Wenzhou rose from 5 percent in 1962–71 to 9.5 percent between 1971 and 1978. The data also point to a much bigger role for county-level industries than usually acknowledged. The share of SOEs undoubtedly declined in the 1960s and 1970s, falling from 63 percent of GVIO in 1962 to 26 percent in 1978; GVIO in 1976 was about half its level in 1972, reflecting the impact of the Cultural Revolution. However, this state sector decline was more than offset by the growth of its collective industrial sector, which grew at about 12 percent per year over the whole 1962–78 period. Output growth in CBE industry was even faster, averaging over 19 percent per year between 1971 and 1978, but it was from a very low base. Without the rapid growth of county-level collectives, Wenzhou's overall growth rate would not have accelerated. The inference to be drawn from Wenzhou's experience is therefore unmistakable. Its industrial growth started to accelerate well before 1978, and it was driven by county-owned collectives as much as the commune and brigade sector. Private industry contributed immeasurably to the process after 1978, but late Maoist growth was driven by the public sector.

In Jiangsu, the Great Leap peak level of commune and brigade output was regained by 1969, and the next ten years saw rapid growth of rural industrial production. In Sunan (restricted here to the counties of Suzhou and Wuxi municipalities), the surge in rural industrialization was especially dramatic (Table 2.5). The growth rate during the 1960s had been by no means slow, averaging about 9 percent between 1962 and 1970. However, the rate was almost twice as high between 1970 and 1978. Further acceleration occurred during the 1980s, but the true turning point long pre-dated the notional 1978 watershed.

Table 2.5 Growth of GVIO in the counties of Sunan, 1962–88 (annual growth rates; 1980 constant prices)

	1962–70	1970–78	1978–88
Jiangyin	14.2	17.1	27.2
Yixing	7.6	18.4	28.0
Wuxi County	12.3	24.8	30.6
Changshu	6.3	16.5	27.4
Zhangjiagang	6.7	24.4	32.8
Taicang	5.8	13.9	26.8
Kunshan	5.0	11.6	31.9
Wuxian	4.2	17.9	27.2
Wujiang	7.5	12.9	25.8
Total	9.1	17.7	28.6

Notes: The data here cover county, collective, and CBE industry located within the counties of Suzhou and Wuxi (as defined in the early 1980s). Individual and private industry is included from 1984 onwards. The cities proper of Wuxi and Suzhou are excluded from the totals.

Sources: JSB 1989; WXG (1990); Taicang XZ (1991); Jiangyin XZ (1992); Shazhou XZ (1992); *Wuxian zhi* (1994); Suzhou tongjiju (1996); Wuxi tongjiju (1997).

The specific instance of Wuxi county demonstrates the contribution of the various subsectors to the growth process (WXG 1990). County-run industries dominated industrial production in absolute terms during the 1960s. In part, this was because the growth of Wuxi's CBE sector was put back by the Leap; commune output did not regain its 1960 peak until 1971. Nevertheless, industrial CBE production began to grow quickly in the mid-1960s. In 1966 alone, output increased by a factor of 27, and for the 1961–70 period the sector grew annually by 53 percent (compared with 7 percent per year in the county sector). Brigade-level industrial production began only in 1964, but it too grew spectacularly, recording an annual rate of 36 percent between 1964 and 1970. Thereafter, growth was much more consistent, with commune and brigade industrial production registering annual rises of 35 and 34 percent respectively during the 1970s, whereas the state sector increased its production by a mere 16 percent. In the 1980s, the TVE sector again dominated, with a growth rate of more than double that achieved by county-level enterprises. Wuxi's experience thus shows that the CBE sector was the engine of growth after the early 1960s. County-run industry contributed enormously to the growth process, but it was led by CBEs. The experience of neighbouring Wuxian was similar to that of Wuxi. In Wuxian, the peak level of output achieved during the Leap (in 1960) was not regained until 1971. Nevertheless, insofar as output was on a rising trajectory during the 1960s, it was the CBE sector which led the way. Thus, although the combined output of county-run enterprises (county collectives and county SOEs) rose by 2.8 percent per year between 1961 and 1970, CBE output increased annually by 9.5 percent. The gap between 1970 and 1978 was almost equally large, with the CBE sector's 28.5 percent growth rate dwarfing the 12.4 percent achieved in county-run enterprises. To a considerable extent, this differential in the 1960s and 1970s reflected the much higher base level of output in the county-run sector. By 1978, however, the CBE subsector was actually larger and this helped to ensure that the growth rates of the two sectors converged. Admittedly this is not apparent from the data, which show the TVE sector growing at 31 percent per annum between 1978 and 1990 compared with 17.1 percent in the county sector. However, this is because the growth of TVE output was inflated by the re-definition of the coverage of the TVE sector in the mid-1980s (Wuxian GZ 1993: 5–7).

Evidence from other southern provinces also points to an acceleration in the rate of industrial growth in the late 1960s and early 1970s. In Jinjiang county (Fujian), CBE output rose from 3.8 million *yuan* in 1965 to 42.1 million *yuan* in 1978. By 1978, there were already 1,141 CBEs operating in the county employing close to 52,000 workers (Jinjiang SZ 1994: 304, 306–7). In Songjiang, one of the counties of Shanghai municipality, the GVIO of CBEs rose by 27 percent per year between 1970 and 1978. Employment tripled over the same period, reaching 40,000 by 1978. The gross output value of county-owned industrial enterprises climbed by just under 5 percent per year between 1962 and 1970, but by 11 percent annually between 1970 and 1978 (Songjiang XZ 1991: 426, 454–5). In Hunan province, the impetus for accelerating rural industrialization appears to have come from the establishment of rural industrial bureaux in 1972 at the provincial, prefectural and county levels (HNQH 1989: 23; HNTJNJ 1989: 77; Liu 1990: 336–7; HNTJNJ 1989: 77). Certainly the growth rate picked up very markedly thereafter. In Ningyuan county, TVE gross income rose almost ninefold between 1971 and 1978 (Ningyuan qing 1993: 99).

Despite this overwhelming evidence of accelerating rural industrialization across southern China, some writers continue to claim that Maoist industrial development left the southern coastal region largely untouched (Bao et al. 2002). Nothing could be further from the truth. Between 1952 and 1976, the share of the primary sector fell from 51 to 33 percent, whereas that of the secondary sector rose from 21 to 45 percent. In supposedly unindustrialized Guangdong, the share of the primary sector fell from 49 percent in 1952 to 30 percent in 1978, by which time the share of industry had increased from 23 to 47 percent (TJJ 2004: 13, 405). The driving force behind this process was the development of rural industry. As demonstrated in Appendix 3, the growth of rural industrial production averaged 10 percent per year during the period 1952–78 in Guangdong, a staggering rate by international standards. The bulk of Guangdong's labour force continued to be employed in agriculture, but Bao's claim that its 'economic basis . . . remained basically unchanged' is simply unconvincing.

2.4.2. Rural Industrialization in North China

The pace of rural industrialization also accelerated across northern China after the mid-1960s. In Shandong, 1969 was the turning point. In that year, the province, in the national frontline (*qianxian*) on the Pacific seaboard, was instructed to make the two 'big efforts' (*daban*) and fight the 'two battles' (*huizhan*). These two big efforts focused on the development of agriculture and national defence, and resulted in the construction of irrigation systems in the Huang-Huai-Hai river basin, and vastly increased output of steel, chemical fertilizer and agricultural tools in rural areas (ZSDSWY 1989: 113–15). For example, chemical fertilizer production soared from about 400,000 tonnes in 1969 to 1.9 million tonnes in 1973 (TJJ 1990*b*: 509).

In 1974, Henan's Second Bureau of Light Industry (responsible for handicraft industry) decided to establish a CBE management office, which presided over an impressive surge in rural industrial production (Zhang and Hou 1990: 599). A good example is provided by the experience of Gongxian. Urban production was halted in many factories in 1966, and so the county responded by developing its own industry; commune and brigade GVIO rose from 0.66 million *yuan* in 1965 to 9.67 million in 1966. Thereafter, production rose steadily, reaching 21.7 million *yuan* in 1970 and 224.8 million *yuan* in 1978. The annual growth rate between 1965 and 1978 was no less than 43 percent, by which time the CBE sector was contributing over 50 percent of the county's total industrial production. Gongxian was not alone; gross income from CBEs in Henan's Anyang county increased by a factor of 19 between 1966 and 1978 (HNXZ 1995: 179–84, 196).[14]

In Shanxi, rural industrialization was more fitful before the mid-1970s. Between 1964 and 1970, brigade output (at 1980 prices) almost tripled, whilst that of the commune sector declined (SXTJNJ 1985: 102; TJJ 1990b: 167). But brigade output hardly increased at all in the first half of the 1970s, whereas commune output was more than four times higher in 1975 than it had been in 1970. Only after the mid-1970s, in fact, does output appear to have increased steadily in both commune and brigade sectors. In Pingding county, for example, 1973–74 was the clear turning point. Only 500 workers were employed in the CBE sector in 1973 but that leapt to 4,900 in 1974 as 39 new enterprises were established, 36 of them at the brigade level, as part of the five small industries programme. By 1978, total CBE employment had reached 10,362 workers. Total GVIO, the bulk of which was produced by the TVE sector, soared from just below 46 million *yuan* in 1970 to 126 million *yuan* by 1978 with the state sector growing almost as fast as its collective cousin (Pingding XZ 1992: 145–52). To be sure, the growth of both output and employment continued after 1978, but it is evident that take-off began in the early 1970s.

In Gansu, as we have seen, much of the Third Front investment focused on urban centres like Lanzhou, Tianshui city and Jiuquan. Nevertheless, the pace of industrialization was by no means slow in rural areas. The counties of Tianshui municipality and Zhangye (in the Hexi corridor to the north-west) illustrate the point (Tianshui shi tongjiju 1989: 528; ZGZ 1993: 62, 89). In this six county sample, the median growth rate of GVIO in the 1960s exceeded 13 percent, and it rose to 16 percent between 1970 and 1978 as Front construction quickened. These rates of growth were of course achieved from a low base, but there can be no denying that the process of industrialization had been well and truly launched even in rural Gansu by the close of the 1970s.

Inner Mongolia provides another example of the accelerating pace of rural industrial development. Systematic data on the output of CBEs appear to be unavailable—see for example TJJ (1990b) and Nei Menggu tongjiju (1999)—but some indication of the trend in rural industrial production is shown by the 2.8 fold increase (at 1970 prices) in the GVIO of the collective sector between 1970 and 1978 (TJJ 1990b: 197). This upsurge is confirmed by examining trends in total GVIO for a sample of the province's counties (Table 2.6). These data show that the median rate of growth of industrial production was just over 7 percent per year between 1962 and 1970. This rate more than doubled to reach 16.3 percent per

[14] Other Henan counties where TVE development was rapid before 1978 were Xinxiang and Huixian (HNXZ 1995: 4).

year between 1970 and 1978, where it remained during the 20 years after the Third Plenum. Only three of the 18 counties show a decline in the growth rate during the 1970s, a clear sign of trend acceleration in the pace of rural industrial growth.

Anhui's experience is also interesting. Much has been written about the province's seemingly poor rural performance in the late Maoist period; Anhui's slow rate of growth, so it is argued, was a key factor in encouraging early decollectivization in counties such as Fengyang. But whatever the performance of agriculture, the county-level evidence suggests extensive rural industrial growth after 1965: in fact, the median county growth rate for GVIO was 11 percent during 1965–78 (AHSQ 1987). Even though this growth rate is calculated between the endpoints of 1965 and 1978 only, it suggests that, far from stagnating, industrial output was on a rising trajectory well before decollectivization. Even in Fengyang, GVIO (at 1970 prices) increased 2.8 fold between 1971 and 1978, an annual growth rate of over 15 percent (Fengyang XZ 1999: 237). Boxian, also in Anhui and one of the counties hardest hit during the famine of the early 1960s, enjoyed a similar industrial trajectory; GVIO rose by more than 13 percent per year during 1971–78 (Bozhou qing 1993: 130–1).[15]

All in all, then, the evidence on north and south China demonstrates a pronounced acceleration in the pace of rural industrial growth during the late

Table 2.6 Growth of GVIO in rural Inner Mongolia, 1962–98 (percent per annum; 1990 constant prices)

	1962–70	1970–78	1978–98
Aohan	3.7	17.2	17.4
Ar Horqin	0.8	16.6	13.5
Bairin LB	3.8	13.4	18.4
Bairin RB	0.8	21.4	15.2
Butha	7.1	14.7	7.4
Darhan	8.2	−0.5	20.6
Guyang	7.7	9.8	21.7
Harqin	17.9	18.6	15.3
Hexigten	4.5	14.8	12.7
Horinger	14.0	17.3	16.8
Linxi	1.2	16.0	15.5
Ningcheng	5.4	27.4	13.9
Ongniud	1.3	19.9	15.1
Qingshuihe	15.2	14.1	18.3
Togtoh	16.2	15.3	28.2
Tumd LB	12.2	21.6	22.9
Tumd RB	7.0	18.9	22.7
Wuchuan	12.5	13.3	15.0
Median	7.1	16.3	16.2

Source: Nei Menggu tongjiju (1999).

[15] The 1960 crude death rate was 146 per 1,000, far above the provincial average (69). Only three Anhui counties recorded higher 1960 crude death rates (AHSZ 1995: 99–101).

1960s and early 1970s even in areas outside those included in the Third Front programme. In much of Jiangsu and Zhejiang in particular, the pause in the industrialization process which followed the Great Leap Forward was comparatively short. By the end of the 1960s, the losses of the early 1960s had been more than made good, and rural industrialization was in full flow. Yet even in less prosperous parts of the People's Republic, there is no doubt that rural industrialization was well under way by early 1970s.

2.5. The Growth of Urban Jurisdictions

An alternative approach to judging the joint impact of the Third Front and the development of county, commune and brigade industry is in terms of the growth of urban jurisdictions in the late Maoist era.

This jurisdictional approach provides a useful way of measuring the extent of industrialization because successful rural jurisdictions were invariably upgraded to city status. It is of course hardly an infallible guide. Urbanization was driven in part by population growth, and much industrialization occurred in previously-established urban centres. The Daqing oilfield was developed within the existing urban jurisdiction of Anda and even the Third Front programme was as much about the expansion of existing industrial centres in western China as it was about the creation of new ones. In Yunnan, for example, the focus of Front construction was urban Kunming. There was also a good deal of reluctance to up-grade jurisdictions during the late Maoist era because of concerns over its impact on agricultural production. One response to the famine of the early 1960s, for example, had been to reduce the number of cities from 208 in 1961 (well up on the 1957 figure of 176) to 169 in 1974.

Nevertheless, due largely to rural industrialization, the number of urban jurisdictions had risen to 188 by 1976. The total then rose very quickly in the late 1970s and early 1980s as recognition was accorded to the extent of urbanization which had occurred in the 1960s and 1970s; by 1982, the number of cities stood at 245 (Chen and Wang 1986: 203–4). By way of comparison, whilst the number of cities increased from 169 in 1965 to 245 in 1982 (a 45 percent rise), the number of counties rose by only eight (a 0.4 percent increase). Not all parts of China were equally affected and indeed more recognition appears to have been given to Third Front centres than to concentrations of commune and brigade industry. It was more than a little paradoxical that not a single new city was created in Jiangsu—the centre of rural industrialization in the late Maoist era—between 1964 and 1982. Zhejiang did little better. There, the six cities of 1957 were reduced to three in 1963 (Hangzhou, Ningbo and Wenzhou), and did not increase again until 1980 (TJJ 1990a: 21). For all that, the emergence of new cities such as Dukou/Panzhihua, Deyang and Mianyang (Sichuan), Liupanshui, Duyun, Kaili and Anshun (Guizhou), Shiyan (Hubei), Huaihua and Hongjiang

(Hunan), and Jinchang and Jiayuguan (Gansu) provides a clear indication of the success of the rural industrialization programme.

2.6. Rural Industry in China at the Close of the Maoist Era

The results of the process of late Maoist rural industrialization are evident from the national data, although it is not easy to quantify the size of the sector in the 1970s with any precision. Of the 75 million workers employed in state-owned enterprises across China in 1978, 24 million were employed in county-level enterprises (TJJ 1989: 40). However, this figure includes all types of enterprises and not just industrial enterprises. It also includes employment in an array of institutions; industrial employment accounted for less than half the SOE national total (the county-level SOE industrial total is not available). CBEs employed a further 28 million workers (Nongye bu 1989: 292). However, the CBE figure is for commune and brigade enterprises only (we do not have precise data on village, team and private employment) and also covers all types of enterprises. To correct for these opposing biases, we can use the results of a survey of 222 villages drawn from 59 counties across China (Yu 1989: 19). That gives rural industrial employment in the countryside in 1980 (excluding county-level enterprises) in all types of sub-county industrial enterprises as amounting to 9.1 percent of the rural workforce, which is 28 million (by coincidence the same figure as for all CBE enterprises). A further 12 million workers were employed in industrial **collectively owned enterprises (COEs)**, though many of these were resident in urban districts rather than county towns (TJJ 1989: 75).

A more precise accounting can be obtained by using the data on occupational categories collected during the 1982 Population Census. Industry was defined for the purposes of that Census as the sum of manufacturing, mining, utilities and construction (Population Census Office 1987: xxii; TJJ 1988).[16] If we take county to be synonymous with rural for the reasons outlined in Appendix Four, the number employed in industry in China's counties (as defined by the jurisdictional boundaries of 1982) was as set out in Table 2.7.

The 1982 data exaggerate the industrialization of the Chinese countryside in 1978 because we know that the private and individual sectors expanded quite rapidly between 1978 and 1982. Nevertheless, the distortion is not too grave because we know that private and individual employment was still rather limited in 1982 and because we know that the 'readjustment' policies of this period checked the growth of the state and the (state-owned) TVE sector. These 1982 figures therefore show two things. Firstly, the overall degree of rural industrialization was not insignificant at the dawn of the 1980s. According to the definition of

[16] Rather oddly, the *national* total given for industry (Population Census Office 1987: xxii) excludes construction from the definition of industry, but the county total for industrial employment include construction.

Table 2.7 Industrial employment rates in China, 1982 (percentages of total employment; provinces ranked by county industrial employment rates)

	Cities	Cities and counties	Counties
Shanghai	64.6	51.1	37.1
Zhejiang	37.4	27.9	25.9
Beijing	50.3	41.1	25.2
Liaoning	61.7	36.6	20.8
Tianjin	57.9	46.3	19.5
Jiangsu	61.2	24.1	19.1
Heilongjiang	57.9	30.3	17.6
Jilin	53.1	27.1	16.8
Fujian	42.5	18.1	14.4
Guangdong	41.4	15.5	11.6
Jiangxi	42.5	15.7	11.5
Shanxi	52.9	17.4	9.7
Nei Menggu	49.9	16.1	8.6
Shaanxi	44.6	13.5	8.4
Shandong	39.9	12.3	8.4
Hunan	45.1	11.9	8.2
Xinjiang	39.5	14.6	8.2
Qinghai	53.5	15.5	7.4
Hubei	57.2	13.6	7.2
Ningxia	46.5	14.5	7.1
Hebei	55.7	13.3	7.0
Anhui	42.0	10.7	6.7
Chongqing	51.3	11.1	6.1
Sichuan	34.2	8.8	5.8
Gansu	53.6	10.1	4.8
Guangxi	44.2	7.2	4.3
Yunnan	43.0	7.4	4.2
Henan	46.4	8.3	4.1
Guizhou	28.3	7.2	3.5
All China	49.3	16.0	9.9

Notes: Data on county-level jurisdictions are based on the classifications of cities and counties used in the 1982 Population Census. The figures cover employment in all industrial enterprises, including both TVEs and centrally-owned SOEs and COEs. The *county*-level 1982 Census data include construction within industry (in addition to manufacturing, mining and utilities; this is clear from comparing the sum of all county and city industrial employment by province with the totals published in the various provincial *renkou fence* (population volumes) on the 1982 census results.

Source: TJJ (1988).

rural used in this book, 43.456 million workers were employed in rural industry across China out of a national industrial workforce of 83.3 million in 1982. Although the rural industrial employment rate of 10 percent was significantly lower than the urban rate (49.3 percent), it nevertheless indicates that Maoist programmes had brought a considerable level of industrial development to the countryside. And of course the rural industrial employment rate here tends to under-state the impact of Maoist rural industrialization because those rural areas which were transformed by industrialization, and therefore upgraded to city status between 1964 and 1982, are excluded from the rural total.

Putting the 1982 figures in proper historical perspective is hard because we lack good data on the Republican era; even the reconstruction undertaken by Liu and Yeh (1965: 182), distinguishes only between the non-agricultural and the agricultural population. Still, Buck's estimates for 1929–31 are useful in this context. Even though his farm surveys were biased towards more prosperous localities, Buck's estimates put the percentage of males in rural areas engaged exclusively in either home industries or manufacturing at no more than 2.1 percent; for women, the figure was 2.8 percent (Buck 1937: 372). An alternative approach is to use the data from the 1954 handicraft survey, which suggests a rural handicraft employment total of perhaps 4.9 million (Liu 1993: 49–50). No more than about 6 million workers were employed in 1954 in all types of modern industry (including mining and utilities), whether in rural or urban areas (Liu and Yeh 1965: 194). Accordingly, there cannot have been more than 10 million workers employed in all types of rural 'industry' in 1954, and that figure must be regarded as a maximum; total industrial employment for that year is officially estimated as only 18.8 million (LDNJ 1997: 9). If we accept the rural estimate, the implication is that rural industrial employment more than quadrupled between 1954 and 1982. This amounts to a rise from 5 to 10 percent of the rural workforce.[17]

A second feature of Table 2.7 is the spatial inequality it shows. The counties located close to the metropolitan centres of Beijing, Tianjin and Shanghai were comparatively industrialized. So too the counties of Manchuria, the heartland of Chinese industry. The other concentration of industry was in the coastal provinces. Both Fujian and Guangdong had experienced considerable industrialization, but the levels attained were much greater in Jiangsu and especially in Zhejiang, which was by some distance the most industrialized part of the Chinese countryside. At a higher level of aggregation, the data show that the share of industry in rural employment was generally higher in north than in south China; Gansu was the only northern province with a comparatively low level of rural industry. This outcome was driven in part by the north's relatively lower level of agricultural fertility. Precisely because farm yields were low, more of an effort had been made to take advantage of north China's comparatively abundant mineral resources and develop rural industry as a substitute for agriculture. By contrast, rural industry was comparatively under-developed in the more fertile south and south-west. All the south-western provinces had very low levels of rural industrialization by the early 1980s, the figures for Guangxi, Yunnan and Guizhou being especially low. Perhaps more surprisingly, rural industrialization had also progressed comparatively little on the north China plain; under-development was particularly apparent in Hebei, Anhui and (especially) Henan, where rural industrial production was almost as rare as it was in

[17] The CCP definition of the rural population of course excludes those employed in state enterprises operating in rural areas, but the distortion thus caused is fairly small for the early 1950s.

Guizhou. One consequence was that per capita rural income levels were also depressed; there is no question that under-industrialization was a major reason for the persistence of poverty at the close of the Maoist era.

A third characteristic of rural industrialization under Mao was that the promotion of the five small industries led to regional convergence of production in those sectors. Take electricity generation. In 1952, Jilin, Liaoning and Shanghai together produced 52 percent of China's electricity. By 1978, that share was down to about 23 percent. In the case of pig iron, Liaoning's share declined from 59 percent of the national total in 1952 and 50 percent in 1965 to only 28 percent in 1978. The dispersion of cement production also declined markedly. Liaoning's share was down from 39 percent in 1952 to only 9 percent by 1978. Admittedly Shanxi's place as China's premier coal-producing province did not change, but then its share of national output in 1978 was only 16 percent (TJJ 1985: 166, 168, 169 and 172). Of course these provincial data are misleading as a guide to *rural* industrial production because it was often new centres of urban—rather than rural—production which displaced older urban centres. For example, the decline of Liaoning as the centre of Chinese iron and steel production was partly due to the growth of steel production in the urban centre of Wuhan. Indeed much of the decline in Liaoning's share in the national total occurred prior to 1965, well before the initiation of the five small industries programme. But for all that, there is little doubt that rural industrialization went some way towards mitigating spatial inequalities in overall industrial production.

2.7. The Limitations of Late Maoist Rural Industrialization

The evidence above demonstrates unequivocally the rapid growth of the rural industrial sector during the 1960s and 1970s. This nevertheless leaves open two questions. Firstly, to what extent was rural industry efficient? Secondly, can we reasonably conclude that rural industrial growth had taken-off before 1978? For if so, that implies that the policy changes of post-1978 were unnecessary.

2.7.1. The Inefficiency of Rural Industrial Enterprises

Few direct attempts have made to judge the efficiency of late Maoist rural industry.[18] One of the reasons is the absence of reliable measures of productivity. Chinese industries, especially those officially designated as SOEs (it was much less true of commune and brigade industries), provided a wide range of social

---

[18] The discussion here makes no attempt to define 'efficiency' in any precise sense because all conceivable definitions point to the same conclusion. Whether one uses profitability, productivity or a more macro-economic definition (see the next chapter), most Maoist rural industry was inefficient.

services such as education, health care and housing to their workforce and dependents; it is therefore hard to estimate the number of workers directly engaged in production. The measurement of capital is equally problematic because the data on the capital stock include housing and some types of military facilities (Chen et al. 1988). In addition, assessments of productivity are sensitive to the prices used, and it is anything but clear whether plan prices are the appropriate shadow prices for the valuation of output and inputs. A comparison between world and plan prices tells us little useful because of world market failure and the presence of pervasive externalities. Should, for example, the shadow price for Chinese steel be set below the world price (low quality), or at a level far above the world price (China's isolation in the 1960s gave steel products an almost incalculable value to both military and civilian sectors)?

An alternative way to assess rural efficiency is to look at financial flows between sectors to see if rural industry was genuinely self-reliant (and by implication efficient). For Wong (1988, 1991a: 195), the clearest sign that rural industry was inefficient was its reliance on central government subsidies; for example, about two-thirds of the investment in small nitrogenous fertilizer plants between 1958 and 1979 came from budgetary allocations, and about 50 percent of investment in farm machinery plants between 1966 and 1978 came from the same source. Thus:

... "easy money" fed excessive growth in the program such that, by the mid-1970s, rural industries had expanded beyond optimal scales and local supply capabilities, creating enormous technical, supply and financial problems.

(Wong 1991a: 185)

Wong's analysis appears well-founded.[19] The rural industries that were established across China in the 1960s and 1970s benefited from two types of subsidy. Firstly, rural industries received technical assistance and seconded personnel from urban industries; much of the assistance given to CBEs came from state-owned enterprises operating in the same county (Leeming 1985: 115–18; Huang 1990: 318; Naughton 1995: 149–58; Whiting 2001: 53–62). Using the definition of 'rural' employed in this book, such transfers would be classified as rural-rural, but clearly the CBEs involved were not self-sufficient in any real sense. Secondly, and more importantly in financial terms, the intersectoral terms of trade worked in favour of industry. Industrial product prices exhibited little trend decline in the Maoist era despite big increases in labour productivity which, in a market economy, would have translated into large reductions in the price of industrial inputs used by agriculture. Conversely, and by virtue of its

---

[19] However, this book takes issue with her claim that subsidies were required because state ownership is *necessarily* inefficient. I shall argue below that rural industrial subsidies were needed in the Maoist era because the enterprises were infants; Maoist subsidies thus counteracted the capital market failure of the Republican era. By the 1980s, many of them had grown up and no longer needed subsidies.

monopsony power, the Chinese state was able to hold down the prices of farm products sold to industrial enterprises and their workers. The result was a process of unequal exchange, whereby the Chinese industrial sector—irrespective of its location—was able to rack up large profits.[20] To be sure, some of the surplus extracted was returned to the agricultural sector; as county-level fiscal data reveal, there were large *gross* transfers from the centre to the counties. However, a large proportion of these flows amounted simply to the return of funds which had been collected as taxes by the counties on behalf of the central authorities in the first place, or which had been extracted by the centre via the internal terms of trade. These flows clearly were not subsidies from the centre in any real sense but rather transfers from agriculture to industry. After all these transactions had taken place, there was thus a *net* flow of resources from agriculture to industry within each county, with a part of the resources extracted by the state from agriculture being used to finance urban development outside the county. The extent of these flows was such that the only conclusion to be drawn is that most Maoist rural industry was inefficient; it would not have needed subsidies otherwise.

A rather different, and much more contentious, efficiency argument is advanced by Whiting (2001), who suggests that the process of resource extraction from agriculture under Mao privileged some *regions* over others. In particular, Whiting argues that the rapid development of rural industries in the Yangzi Delta only occurred because the region received favourable fiscal treatment from central government:

... in Wuxi and Songjiang, commune and brigade industry received substantial state support through budgetary grants, bank loans, and direct and indirect inclusion in state plans.

(Whiting 2001: 70)

Wuxi is the most egregious example; without such subsidies, its rapid industrialization would not have occurred. However, the very act of providing subsidies ensured that the recipient industries would be inefficient. The absence of a hard budget constraint made that inevitable. By implication, the extensive industrial base which had been established in places like Wuxi was an encumbrance rather than an advantage in the post-Mao era because the industries had absorbed scarce capital and labour. Its rate of rural industrial growth may have been faster than the national average in the late Maoist period, but in the long run Sunan was locked into path dependent development by its legacy of state-subsidized industries.

---

[20] This argument is controversial because of its counterfactual basis; the actual trend in the terms of trade is being compared against a counterfactual in which the price of industrial products falls over time because of rising productivity. If we focus our attention on actual movements in the terms of trade, there is no doubt that the extent of unequal exchange declined significantly over time and that the agricultural sector was a net recipient by the 1970s (Ishikawa 1967, 1988; Karshenas 1995). In the text here, I follow the argument advanced by Sheng (1993) and most Chinese economists, and concentrate on the double factorial internal terms of trade.

By contrast, Wenzhou's Yueqing county fared badly in the Maoist era for two reasons according to Whiting. Firstly, the development of small-scale private industry in Yueqing was ruled out by central government decree. Secondly, it was constrained by shortages of capital. Yueqing lacked a prosperous agricultural sector (in contrast to Sunan) and therefore there was no indigenous investible surplus for investment in industry; Yueqing also (again in contrast to Sunan) received few subsidies from central government. More generally: '[Wenzhou] . . . was truly "self-reliant"—in many ways closer to the Maoist ideal than Wuxi or Songjiang. As a result, however, Wenzhou's growth rate during the Maoist period was slower than those of . . . other research sites' (Whiting 2001: 70). Much of this is borne out by Whiting's data. Industrial output stagnated in Yueqing in the 1960s, and even declined during the 1970s (Whiting 2001: 54–5 and 70). Per capita GVIO in the county was only 111 *yuan* in 1978. The more rapid industrial development of Sunan as compared with Wenzhou during the Maoist era therefore reflects a differential process of subsidization. Sunan was privileged by central government, whereas Wenzhou was discriminated against.

Whiting's argument is based around two empirical contentions. Her first is that the rate rural industrialization was much faster in Sunan than in Wenzhou in the late Maoist era. On this point she appears to be correct. If we define Sunan as comprising all the rural jurisdictions located within Suzhou and Wuxi municipalities in 1982, and Wenzhou as the municipality less the Wenzhou city proper and neighbouring urban Ouhai (incorporated into Wenzhou city in the 1980s), the pattern of industrial development during the Maoist era is as charted in Table 2.8. These data show a considerable differential between Sunan and Wenzhou at the beginning of the Maoist era, with per capita industrial output in Sunan almost three times greater than in Wenzhou. That ratio had changed little by 1965, as industrial development proceeded at a similar (slow) pace in the two. Between 1965 and 1978, however, Sunan surged ahead. As a result, the gap between the two had increased to well over 5:1 by the close of the Maoist era.

Table 2.8 Per capita GVIO in rural Wenzhou and Sunan, 1952–78 (*yuan*; 1980 constant prices)

Region	1952	1965	1978
Wenzhou	26	43	107
Sunan	73	141	558
Ratio	2.8:1	3.3:1	5.2:1

Notes: GVIO includes village-owned industry which was officially incorporated into agriculture before 1984. Sunan here comprises those jurisdictions officially classified as counties in 1982 in Suzhou (Changshu, Zhangjiagang, Taicang, Kunshan, Wujiang and Wuxian) and Wuxi (Jiangyin, Yixing and Wuxi).
Sources: Chen (1989); JSB (1989).

Whiting's second contention is that the industrial divergence of Sunan and Wenzhou reflected differences in the level of central government subsidies; Suzhou grew rapidly only because it was in receipt of large subsidies. This argument seems much less well-founded. It is true that Wenzhou appears to have been a net contributor to the national exchequer in 1978 (Wenzhou tongjiju 2001: 396–9). However, the surplus was only modest and four of Wenzhou's counties were actually net recipients of funds in 1978; even now, Taishun and Wencheng counties are very poor by the standards of eastern China. More significantly, Wenzhou was a clear net recipient in the mid-1970s; budgetary data suggest that the municipality received very large bank loans in 1975 and 1976 because those years saw revenue collapse. In 1975, budgetary revenue met only 33 percent of expenditure, and in 1976 its contribution was 43 percent (Chen 1989: 90). This deficit, caused by a big fall in income from state-owned enterprises (itself a product of political disruption to production—Forster 1998), was filled by bank lending. It does not seem to be much of a leap to suggest that these loans were a crucial factor in promoting the region's take-off in the 1980s, thus calling into question the notion that Wenzhou provides an example of self-sufficient rural industrialization.

The fiscal circumstances faced by the counties of rural Sunan were precisely the reverse. Whereas Wenzhou was a net recipient of finance in the 1970s, Sunan made a very substantial net contribution to the national exchequer. In 1978, for example, revenue generated by the counties of Sunan was about four times greater than expenditure (JSB 1989). The region's counties were levying high rates of taxation and transferring the bulk of this revenue to higher level authorities. Of course Wuxi and Suzhou *cities* were making even more of a contribution; as is well known the bulk of the funds used to subsidize Third Front construction and the development of western China more generally were provided by the cities of eastern China. Of course Chinese public finances during the Maoist period—as well as post-1978—are extraordinarily involved (Blecher and Shue 1996). Budget flows tell only a part of the story; extrabudgetary and other sources of revenue contributed massively to the finances of Chinese local government. And industrial profitability reflected at least as much the relative price structure as it did underlying enterprise efficiency. Nevertheless, it is hard to believe that analysis of these flows would contradict the budgetary story. Counties able to make large budgetary transfers to the centre would in general also be able to collect large extrabudgetary sums. Thus the right conclusion should surely be that Sunan's counties were not receiving net transfers from other regions.

The counties of Sunan were hardly alone. If we analyse those parts of China where county-level rural industry prospered during the 1970s, we see that the areas were generally prosperous, well-favoured by geography—and wholly reliant upon their own resources. Guanghan, one of the counties in Sichuan which pioneered rural industrialization, is a case in point. Budgetary revenue raised there amounted to about 10 million *yuan* in 1973, rising to about 21 million *yuan* by 1978. However, total expenditure in 1973 was only around 5 million, rising to less than 8 million *yuan* in 1978 (Guanghan XZ 1992: 306, 312). In Hunan, too, the counties around the provincial capital and in the Xiang river valley where rural industrialization was most advanced by the end of the 1970s were generally net contributors to the exchequer in 1978. By comparison, the under-industrialized western and south-western prefectures of (running from north to south) Xiangxi, Qianyang, Shaoyang and Lingling were generally net recipients (HNTJNJ 1987: 533–7).[21]

In fact, the relative success of rural Sunan and those other parts of China where rural industries developed quickly in the late Maoist period seems to have owed very little to 'cheap money'; those regions where rural industry developed most quickly appear to have been net contributors to the national exchequer. Indeed the fiscal pressure placed on the counties of rural Sunan by central government resource extraction may have helped to ensure that the industries they developed during the late 1960s and 1970s were comparatively *efficient*. Deprived of state handouts, the counties of Sunan were forced to develop efficient county-run enterprises, and probably reacted to their circumstances by putting pressure on communes and brigades to develop efficient enterprises as a means of generating extra-budgetary revenue to finance a range of local expenditures. That in turn implies that the decisions made by local government to continue along the collective road after 1978 may well have reflected—as Oi (1999), and Blecher and Shue (1996) suggest—a recognition that public ownership was a wholly appropriate vehicle for the development of efficient rural industry within a decentralized fiscal system.

All this suggests that we need to distinguish carefully between inter-regional and inter-sectoral financial flows. Whiting and Wong, in common with many other scholars, are surely right in claiming that agriculture provided subsidies to rural industry during the Maoist era; the notion of industrial self-reliance is undoubtedly a myth. But the data on the public finances of Sunan suggest that those regions of rural eastern China which industrialized quickly did not do so on the back of central government subsidies. Conversely, there is precious little evidence that Wenzhou provides an example of self-reliant industrialization. The most plausible explanation of regional divergence is that Sunan's industries were increasingly more 'mature' by the end of the 1970s and therefore no longer in need of the sort of subsidies required by infant industries in Wenzhou and other poor parts of China. Sunan's maturity in turn owed much to a combination of factors: its long history of industrial production, its more favourable geography (which undoubtedly contributed to the former) and the more active role played by local government in promoting rural industrialization. The

---

[21] Spatial differences in rural CBE development in Hunan in the 1970s and 1980s are discussed in HNQH (1989: 25–7, 48–64, 85–9).

relative significance of these factors will be explored in later chapters. But it is clear that, despite large subsidies, Wenzhou made much less progress in developing rural industry than Sunan in the late Maoist era. In that respect, Wenzhou had much in common with the rest of rural China; rural industry undoubtedly developed in the 1960s and 1970s, but it did so slowly and needed central government subsidies.

It is possible—a systematic study of the subject is lacking—that industry across Sunan (both urban and rural) was still being subsidized by the region's agricultural sector via the internal terms of trade well into the 1970s. It is hard to be certain because, although the budgets of urban and rural Sunan jurisdictions show a net surplus, the source of these surpluses remains unclear: was it the underlying efficiency of enterprises which generated the surpluses, or was it extraction via a distorted relative price structure? Similarly, recorded flows of funds from industry to agriculture tell us nothing about the net position; how much of the apparent transfer from industry to agriculture was generated by agriculture in the first place? But there is nothing in the record to suggest that rural Sunan as a *region* was being subsidized by central government. Self-reliance at a regional level—more precisely, being required to make a net contribution to the national exchequer—was the norm for most prosperous regions in the late Maoist era. It was poor regions like Wenzhou that were net recipients and which still found it hard to develop industry.

2.7.2. Third Front Inefficiency

The inefficiency critique of late Maoist industrialization is strongest when it comes to Third Front enterprises. Many of these firms, it is argued, caused enormous environmental damage (Shapiro 2001), and were hopelessly dependent for their very survival upon large financial subsidies: '. . . many of the Third Front factories are simply not economically viable, and are unlikely to be economically viable for a long time' (Naughton 1988: 383). In part, the problems of Third Front enterprises are attributed to their state ownership, but much of the literature focuses on the particular problems caused by the military orientation of the programme.

One problem for many Front enterprises was their location. The great Panzhihua steel complex was built close to the Chengdu–Kunming railway. However, that railway was often closed even in the 1990s because of landslides and, railway notwithstanding, the plant was still far removed from the great urban centres where steel demand was large. Thus Panzhihua's profitability was heavily compromised by the high transport costs incurred in shipping finished steel products to the east. Similar problems confronted the enterprises located along the railway in the Gansu corridor. More generally, the sites for Third Front enterprises were chosen with military rather than efficiency goals in mind. The driving slogans were *fensan yinbi kaoshan* (dispersed, concealed and near mountains) often abbreviated as *shansandong* (mountains, dispersed, in tunnels) and *dafensan xiaojizhong* (great dispersion, little concentration). The logic was to make the enterprises less vulnerable to aerial attack.[22] The policy was clearly demonstrated in Hunan, where virtually all Front investment was channelled into the Tujia autonomous prefecture of Xiangxi, traditionally the poorest part of the entire province because of its mountainous topography (Liu 1990: 162–70). The editors of *Henan sheng qing* (Henan yanjiushi 1987: 283) bemoaned the fact that most of the province's defence industries were located in 'mountainous or remote mountainous areas'. And Guangdong's small Third Front region was designated as Shaoguan prefecture, in the relatively mountainous northern part of the province on the border with Hunan.

Related to the problem of location was that of scale. As a result of the emphasis on dispersion, most Front enterprises were small, yet highly vertically integrated. It was therefore difficult for them to exploit economies of scale, which in principle were enormous given that many of the enterprises were engaged in manufacturing producer goods. This intrinsic difficulty was compounded by the fact that construction of many of the enterprises had not even been completed by the late 1970s, when the programme ran out of steam.

The most obvious supporting evidence for the inefficiency of the Front is provided by a direct comparison of productivity in the Panzhihua steel complex (Pangang) with productivity in other steel plants across China; by looking at productivity in the same industry, we normalize for most of the differences in product type. Furthermore, Pangang was very much the flagship of the Third Front programme; if Pangang was not efficient by Chinese standards, there is every reason to suppose that other Front industries were even less efficient. Data on Pangang's relative productivity are presented in Table 2.9. They show that Pangang certainly was not the most inefficient of China's main producers in the 1980s (and the smaller plants were far worse). However, given that Pangang was

Table 2.9 Labour productivity in the Chinese steel industry, 1984

	Workers (thousand)	GVIO (million 1980 *yuan*)	GVIO per worker (thousand 1980 *yuan*)
Angang (Liaoning)	137	3,789	28
Shougang (Beijing)	61	1,872	31
Wugang (Hubei)	72	2,479	34
Magang (Anhui)	42	834	20
Baoshan (Inner Mongolia)	40	724	18
Pangang (Panzhihua)	32	819	26

Source: TJJ (1985: 271–3).

[22] See CSJW (1991: 108).

a recently-built plant, this record was not very impressive, and it appeared even less so after the construction of the new Baogang plant at Baoshan (on the out-skirts of Shanghai), an enterprise which was to be four or five times more efficient than the rest—not least because of its use of best practice foreign tech-nology and skills.

Even if we accept the underlying Maoist assumption that China was threat-ened militarily by the USA and by the Soviet Union, it is moot whether the development of heavy industries in western China, especially in mountainous or desert regions, made strategic sense. The programme certainly can be ration-alized if one assumes that there was a high probability of a long conventional war between China and either of its main rivals in the 1960s and 1970s, but it is entirely reasonable to wonder whether China would have been better served by concentrating on the development of its own nuclear weapons programme and the requisite delivery vehicles.

2.7.3. Late Maoist Rural Industrial Take-off?

The second obvious limitation of the late Maoist rural industrialization pro-gramme was that there is little indication of 'take-off', meaning a process of rapid and self-sustaining growth, even during the late 1970s.

The evidence here is compelling. As we have seen, many of China's counties and indeed provinces were slow to regain the peak level of industrial output achieved during the Great Leap Forward. Leap output levels were vastly exagger-ated in contemporary accounts, but that was much less true of the statistical publications of the 1980s, many of which heavily revised the original Leap estim-ates. Accordingly, the very fact that industrial output did not regain these levels until the mid or late 1970s in some of the poorer regions of China indicates the fitful nature of industrial growth in the late Maoist era.

It is also apparent that the rate of growth of CBE industrial production was higher in the 1980s than it had been in either the 1960s, or in the period 1971–78; the contrast is especially apparent in the cases of Sunan and Wenzhou. In a sense, this is not surprising: the disruption caused to industrial production at the height of the Cultural Revolution (1966–68) served to depress the growth rate. However, this is much less true for the 1970s. Although output was badly affected in some parts of China in 1975–76 (Wenzhou provides one such example), the industrial sector as a whole was much less affected than during the late 1960s. Furthermore, and more importantly, growth began from an extremely low base. The scope for rapid catch-up growth was at its apogee in the 1960s, and that is therefore the decade in which we might have expected to see growth rates reaching their peak, rather than during the 1970s or 1980s when the level of production was much higher. The very fact that growth accelerated after 1978 therefore suggests that, for most parts of the countryside, the 1980s were the years of rural industrial take-off.

Thirdly, the term 'take-off' carries with it the notion of self-sustaining growth. However, as we have seen, much Chinese industry was not self-reliant. Almost irrespective of whether one looks at the Third Front programme, county-owned state industries or commune and brigade enterprises, the picture painted is one of inefficiency. To be sure, many of these industries did make profits. However, that reflected more the distorted relative price structure of the 1970s than it did high levels of productivity or indeed any real capacity to meet the demand for industrial products. Although I will argue in subsequent chapters that the absence of efficiency should not be regarded as a sign of rural industrial failure in the late Maoist era (far from it), it equally cannot be seen as indicative of industrial take-off.

2.8. Conclusion

It is widely recognized that the beginnings of rural industrialization in China long pre-date the political watershed of 1978. Nevertheless, it is a characteristic of much of the literature that this industrialization is downplayed.[23] The industrial enterprises of the pre-1949 era are dismissed as mere proto-industries. Maoist rural industrialization is portrayed as essentially fitful, its development immeasurably retarded by the nationalization of the 1950s, the Great Leap Forward and the Cultural Revolution. It was thus only because rural industrialization was so *shallow* under Mao that a vast army of under-employed farm workers were available for employment in the new privately-run enterprises of the 1980s and 1990s. And this depiction of pre-1978 Chinese rural industrialization is partially accurate. Rural industrial development was in its infancy at the time of Mao's death; agricultural production dominated the economies of most Chinese counties. Secondly, there is little real evidence that a process of rural industrial take-off was underway during the 1970s. Thirdly, and relatedly, it is hard to resist the conclusion that the rural industries of the 1970s were inefficient and in many cases incapable of self-sustained growth in the short term.

Yet we do well not to under-estimate the extent of pre-1978 rural industrialization. Too much of the existing literature continues to do that. In part this is because of an ideological aversion towards all forms of state ownership and, relatedly, a belief that state ownership must necessarily bring inefficiency in its train. The second reason why Maoist rural industrialization tends to be discounted is that industry is defined as being no more than the commune and brigade sector. By adopting such a narrow definition, the true extent of Maoist rural industrial development goes unappreciated. This chapter has adopted a more encompassing approach: it has looked at the development of *all* types of

---

[23] This is less true of the older literature, which properly recognized the extent of rural industrialization during the 1960s and 1970s (Sigurdson 1977; Riskin 1978*a*, *b*; Riskin 1987).

industry operating within Chinese counties, not least because strenuous efforts were made during the 1960s and 1970s to expand these types of industries. More precisely, rural industry during the late Maoist era has been defined to cover all types of industrial enterprises which developed, or were newly established, in jurisdictions designated as counties at the time of the 1964 Population Census. This definition thus includes industries owned by *zhen* (town) governments based within counties and, much more importantly, the full range of state and collectively-owned industries located within each county, irrespective of whether they were owned by the county, a central ministry or an intermediate level of government (see also Appendix 4).

Once rural industry is defined in this broad fashion—as it should be—it becomes apparent that industrial growth accelerated markedly in the Chinese countryside during the 1960s and 1970s, and that rural industrial production was substantial in many regions by the time of Mao's death. It is admittedly difficult to document this rural industrialization with any degree of precision. There are abundant data in the *County Records* and provincial publications, but no comprehensive time series figures exist for the national pattern of rural industrialization. Nevertheless, by using the available data on the Third Front Programme and the five small industries (iron and steel, chemical fertilizer, machine-building, coal mining and cement), and (in later chapters) by looking at a number of provinces in more detail, we can delineate rural industrial expansion with a fair degree of success. This evidence will confirm the conclusion of this chapter that rural industrialization was well and truly underway by the early 1970s.

3

Rural Industrialization After 1978

Rural industry was well-established in China by the close of the Maoist era, and the growth rate of rural industrial output accelerated during the 1970s. That much is clear from the previous chapter. Compared, however, with what was to follow in the years after 1978, this was merely a prelude.

3.1. Government Policy Towards Rural Industry after 1978

Four clearly demarcated post-1978 government policies are discernible in respect of rural industries (by which, as in previous chapters, I mean the totality of enterprises operating within county boundaries, whether state, collective, TVE, private or individual). Firstly, the Chinese state embarked upon what became known as the readjustment programme, an attempt to increase the efficiency of CBEs and state-owned enterprises operating in both urban and rural areas. Secondly, a succession of policies were introduced during the 1980s and 1990s which were designed to reform the system of SOE governance, but which culminated in the extensive privatizations of the late 1990s. Thirdly, local governments sought to create new TVEs in order to generate employment and an enhanced revenue stream. but ended up privatizing the majority of them in the late 1990s. Finally, controls on industrial ownership were liberalized, thus allowing the emergence of a private industrial sector across China.

3.1.1. The Significance of the Readjustment Programme

During 1978–81, CCP industrial policy focused on investment re-allocation across sectors rather than upon ownership change; aside from some limited experiments with family farming in mountainous parts of Anhui and Sichuan, collective farming and state-ownership of industry continued. The readjustment programme thus centred around structural rather than systemic change. This programme was a final attempt to make Leninist socialism work. To that end, the state sought to restore the patterns of investment seen during the 'golden age' of the 1950s when China pursued what many in the party (notably Chen Yun) saw as the correct (Leninist) transitional path to socialism (Xu 1982; Sun 1995). Accordingly, Hua Guofeng's 'foreign leap forward' was brought to an end. Investment in the Third Front, metallurgy, machine-building and heavy industry was curtailed. Investment in light industry, the subsectors of heavy industry which served agriculture (notably chemicals and chemical fertilizer), transport, energy and construction surged. In the process, it was hoped, the perceived heavy industry and urban bias of the late Maoist era in the countryside (as much as in the cities) would be reversed.

The readjustment programme in the countryside focused on the closure of agricultural CBEs and the transfer of their assets to households as part of the more general process of decollectivization. The result was that the number of workers employed in agricultural CBEs fell from 6.08 million in 1978 to 3.44 million in 1982 (Nongye bu 1989: 292). By contrast, employment in the industrial subsector rose, though less quickly than output. The net result was a marked rise in labour productivity, which more than doubled in agricultural enterprises and rose by a still impressive 57 percent in industrial CBEs. However, the industrial sector also experienced re-structuring. The share of building materials in CBE industrial output declined from 30 percent in 1978 to less than 21 percent in 1980, and that of electrical machinery fell from 33.5 percent to 26 percent (XZNJ 1989: 44, 56, 59). The transformation was rather less marked in those provinces where CBEs were well established. In Jiangsu, for example, the share of electrical machinery declined by only 4 percentage points (from 32 to 28 percent). But even there, the structure of industrial output altered: one sign of this was the rise in the share of the textile sector from 11 percent in 1979 to 19 percent in 1981 (Mo 1987: 192).

Few economists believe that the readjustment programme played a critical role in the subsequent expansion of the town and village enterprise (TVE) sector. The consensus is that readjustment certainly helped; in Christine Wong's (1982, 1988) early work, for example, the programme was assessed as important because it led to the closure of the more egregiously-inefficient state, commune and brigade enterprises. Readjustment therefore placed rural industrialization on a much healthier footing by ensuring that scarce investment and skilled labour was not diverted to exceptionally inefficient enterprises.

Nevertheless, Wong's more recent work, in common with that of other scholars, has tended to portray the effects of the readjustment policies as transitory rather than permanent. To be sure, the provincial data show a diminution in the share of heavy industry in total industrial production during 1978–81; in every province, the share of light industry rose significantly during that period. However, the increased share of light industry brought about by readjustment was merely temporary. This is most easily demonstrated using the national data. These show a light industry share of 42 percent in 1978, which had risen to 49 percent by 1981 as a result of readjustment. By 1985, however, the light industry share was back down again to 47 percent (TJJ 1990*b*: 10). Secondly, the absolute change in the share achieved between 1978 and 1981 was rather small. Some heavy industries were closed down in rural China in these years, but the burden of readjustment within the TVE sector fell upon agricultural enterprises, whose fate paralleled that of the communes. Thirdly, it was not so much the change in the share of light industry that was important for subsequent rural industrialization but rather the absolute size of the subsector in 1981. It is surely no accident that Zhejiang, Fujian, Guangdong and Jiangsu were the provinces in the van of the rural industrial revolution of the 1980s. In all of them, the light industry share exceeded 60 percent in the early 1980s, a figure far in excess of the national average. Conversely, the very small light industry shares observed in Guizhou, Heilongjiang, Liaoning and especially Ningxia and Gansu, surely help to explain the fitful pace of rural industrialization in these provinces in the post-Mao era. The shallow light industrial basis which was the norm in these provinces at the start of the 1980s made it well nigh impossible for them to compete with (say) Zhejiang in meeting the soaring consumer demand of the 1980s and 1990s. In short, and although there is no doubt that readjustment did take place between 1978 and 1981, it is hard to hang an argument for rural industrialization after 1978 on foundations as frail as these. If we are to emphasize policy change as the prime mover in the rural industrialization process, we must look elsewhere.

3.1.2. The Reform and Restructuring of the State Sector

However, the centrepiece of post-1978 Chinese industrial policy was not readjustment but a sustained attempted to improve the efficiency of SOEs by governance reform. As initially conceived, this policy aimed to transfer power to factory directors, and to create an elaborate structure of incentives for managers and workers alike. Over time, and in response to the perceived failure of these early initiatives, policy became increasingly radical. Although these policies are usually conceived of as attempts to reform urban industry, they applied with equal force to county-level enterprises.

Three types of governance reform were attempted in the 1980s (Naughton 1995; Chai 1998). Firstly, enterprise directors were given much more autonomy in respect of labour hiring, wage payments, material purchasing and investment decisions. The idea was to hand decision-making from those who were 'red' (Party officials) to those who were 'expert' (factory directors). With economic criteria thereby much more to the fore in the decision-making process, it was expected that enterprise productive efficiency would rise. Secondly, the incentive structure was changed such that enterprises were allowed to retain a greater proportion of their profits. This, it was hoped, would spur directors and workers to raise profitability. The introduction of stock markets in Shenzhen and Shanghai in 1992 was a variant on this theme; the threat of takeover would force listed companies to pay more attention to maximizing shareholder value.

Thirdly, the central government expected the emergence of the non-state sector to make the Chinese marketplace more competitive, which would in turn force SOEs to boost their performance in order to pay the higher wages and salaries needed to retain workers and managers. Thus ownership liberalization was conceived as a way of promoting improvements in SOE performance; and foreign companies, the emerging private sector and TVEs were all enlisted in pursuit of this grand design. In that privatization featured nowhere on this agenda, Chinese industrial policy was a world removed from the orthodoxy encouraged by the Washington institutions and the majority of academic economists across the world, and implemented in much of Eastern Europe, the former Soviet Union and Latin America.

From the mid-1990s onwards, however, Chinese policy towards SOEs became much more orthodox in response to a growing perception that governance reform had failed. The aim was nothing less than the wholesale restructuring or *gaizhi* (reform of the ownership system). The key slogan was *zhuada fangxiao* ('seize the large, let go the small'), which featured prominently in Li Peng's 'Report on the Work of Government' for 1996 delivered to the 8th National People's Congress in March 1997.[1] The policy was given further emphasis by Zhu Rongji in the same year when he decreed that loss-making SOEs were to turn around their performance within three years (*sannian tuokun*), a policy formally adopted by the 15th Party Congress in September 1997. The more efficient and larger SOEs were increasingly merged to form larger companies and enterprise groups (*jituangongsi*); initial re-structuring focused on 57 groups and the number was expanded further to 120 in 1997 (Li 1997: 10). In this process, the profitability of the SOE sector undoubtedly improved.[2] However, a substantial number of SOE employees were laid-off in the process.

Smaller SOEs were privatized or simply closed on the grounds that they were too small ever to be efficient.[3] In part at least, this policy of closure and privatization was driven by the growing number of small SOEs which were revealed to be loss-making even when the Chinese economy revived after the cyclical trough of 1989–91. The privatization of small SOEs, predominantly at the county level, was well under way before the mid-1990s. Counties appear to have moved more quickly than the larger cities in this regard. A good example is Yibin county in

---

[1] According to Li (1997: 10): 'In recent years, some localities have revitalized a large number of these [CMB: small SOEs] enterprises through reorganization, association, merger, joint stock partnership, leasing, contract operation and sell-off. This year we shall quicken the pace of reform in this regard'.

[2] In Liaoning, restructuring and/or privatization were not simply-achieved options because many of the industrial enterprises were relatively old and large. Nevertheless, the restructuring process helped to increase profits from 1.3 billion *yuan* in 1999 to 11.7 billion in 2000 (Lin 2002: 34).

[3] As well as companies officially designated as private, it is clear that those called cooperatives, joint ownership units and limited liability corporations were private enterprises in all but name.

Sichuan which started to privatize as early as 1992, and perhaps (the sources disagree) even in 1990. Moreover, many provinces appear to have privatized 50 percent or more of their small SOEs by the end of 1996 (Garnaut and Song 2003; Imai 2003; Garnaut et al. 2005; Cao et al. 1999). Thus China under Jiang Zemin increasingly embraced the orthodox prescriptions embodied in the Washington consensus. By the time of Hu Jintao's accession in 2003, the focus of Chinese industrial policy was on the creation of a comparatively small number of large industrial enterprises, many of which were either private or joint ventures.[4] In this process, small-scale SOEs and COEs operating in the Chinese countryside were the main losers.

Not surprisingly, the bulk of the privatizations were 'insider' privatizations: they took the form of management buyouts or management–employee buyouts. Instances of privatization via auction or IPO—whereby outsiders were allowed to bid for shares—were comparatively rare. The problem here, of course, was the small size of the privatized sector. As a result, there were very few private sector entrepreneurs able and willing to purchase SOEs (Imai 2003; Mako and Zhang 2003). But, and irrespective of the nature of privatization, the net result was that the number of workers in county-level SOEs fell from 43.01 million in 1996 to 31.11 million by 2002, of whom almost one million were officially off-post (LDNJ 1997: 217; 2003: 269, 271).

3.1.3. The Expansion of Township and Village Enterprises

The transition era also saw a concerted attempt at various levels of government to improve the productivity and profitability of TVEs. Following the initial readjustment of the CBE sector, three main phases of evolution are identifiable.[5]

The first phase, running from 1982 to 1988, was one of expansion. Most controls on the number of CBEs were lifted and restrictions on bank lending to the sector were also removed. The demise of the commune also led to a name change; the CBEs of the late Maoist era were re-named TVEs and the coverage of the term was expanded to include private and individual enterprises in 1984. The number of township and village enterprises rose from the re-adjustment nadir of 1.34 million in 1981 to 1.59 million in 1988. More significantly, the number of sub-village enterprises increased from 4.42 million in 1984 (the year in which data first become available) to 17.29 million in 1988 (NYTJZL 1988: 206–7; Nongye bu 1989: 290). These years also saw further significant restructuring of the TVE sector. The building materials and machinery sectors experienced a decline in their share of total TVE industrial output of 3.3 and

---

[4] For example, Konka—one of China's leading non-state producers of TVs—received a loan from the Bank of China of 4.2 billion *yuan* in 1998–99, which was upped to 5 billion in 2000 (Saha 2000: 4240).

[5] This three phase chronology (four phases if the readjustment of CBEs is included) is quite commonplace in much of the Chinese literature, though the precise dates adopted differ somewhat; see for example SDFGJYK (2001).

1.7 percentage points respectively during 1980–87. The main gainer was textiles, which increased its share from only 6.8 percent in 1980 to 14.3 percent by 1987 (XZNJ 1989: 44).[6] Many breweries and distilleries were also established during this period. Nevertheless, most TVEs were still very much community enterprises, not least in that they closed during the summer period to allow their workers—most of whom were still members of households engaged in farming—to collect the harvest. Moreover, and despite the growing significance of consumer good production, TVE output of producer goods was still significant relative to the national total. In 1987, for example, TVEs contributed 32 percent of coal production, 25 percent of cement and more than 80 percent of small agricultural tools (XZNJ 1989: 31). In that sense, the Maoist roots of the TVE sector remained very visible.

The second phase of TVE development began in 1989 with a process of restructuring, but culminated in the breakneck growth of 1993–94. The economic slowdown of 1989 and 1990 led to a fall in the number of township enterprises from 424,000 in 1988 to 382,000 in 1991; over the same period village-level enterprise numbers fell from 1.17 million to 1.06 million. The growth of the number of smaller TVEs also slowed, though the number still climbed from 17.29 million in 1988 to 17.65 million in 1991 (TJNJ 1994: 361). However, this period of TVE stagnation was brief. As Chinese economic growth began again in 1991 and 1992 (when it was given renewed energy by Deng's *nanxun*), so the TVE sector revived. By 1994, the number of township and village enterprises had eclipsed the 1988 level (1.65 million enterprises compared with 1.59 million in 1988). Over the same period, sub-village enterprise numbers rose from 17.29 million to 23.30 million (TJNJ 1997: 399). By the mid-1990s, the structure of TVE industrial production was very different to that of the late 1970s. Zhejiang offers one example. In 1980, the output value of textiles was only 85 percent of that of building materials, and 62 percent of that of electrical machinery. By 1994, however, textiles was the largest single sector. It accounted for over 27 percent of total output, significantly greater than the share of electrical machinery (24 percent) and vastly greater than that of building materials (8 percent) (ZJJ 1997: 205–6). For Jiangsu, the pattern of industrial change was not dissimilar. By 1995, the share of building materials was down to 5 percent compared with 19 percent for textiles and 21 percent for machinery (Jiang 1998: 145–6). This evidence suggests that the TVE sector was more consumer-orientated. Nevertheless, the producer goods subsectors which dominated in the late 1970s were still important, and this testifies to the growing sophistication of industrial production; one would expect to see relatively mature industrial economies producing large volumes of machinery, and so it was in China.

In retrospect, 1994 marks the apogee of the TVE sector. Thereafter, it entered a phase of wholesale restructuring marked by the privatization of many township

---

[6] These data are for township- and village-level enterprises only.

and village enterprises. In part this was driven by the policy of *zhuada fangxiao*, which affected the TVE sector in much the same way as small-scale SOEs. At least as importantly, the recentralization of the Chinese fiscal system under Zhu Rongji in 1994 placed increasing pressure on the budgets of townships and villages. The effect of this recentralization, in combination with growing pressure on Chinese banks to restrict their lending to TVEs, was to increase the share of budget revenue accruing to central government. As a result, local government budget revenue fell from 339 billion *yuan* in 1993 to 231 billion in 1994 (TJJ 1999: 18). Some of central government's revenue was of course returned to local government, but the effect of the 1994 recentralization was to force local governments to look for additional sources of revenue in the form of unofficial off-budget funds. The pressure on local government was further intensified by the 'Budget Law' of 1995 which forbade the monetization of fiscal deficits and even restricted the extent to which local and central governments could resort to bond-finance. The main response to the fiscal pressure induced by the changes of 1994 and 1995 was the privatization of TVEs to raise revenue (discussed further below). In the process, a number of closures were inevitable. By 2002, the number of TVEs stood at 21.33 million (XZNJ 2003), well down on the 1994 figure of 24.95 million enterprises (TJNJ 1997: 309).

3.1.4. The Emergence of the Private Sector

A further element in Chinese industrial policy after the late 1970s was ownership liberalization, which affected rural as well as urban areas (Odgaard 1992; Young and Yang 1994; Zhou 1996). Official sanction was given to the growth of household (*geti*) enterprises by a State Council decree of 1 March 1984, which re-defined and expanded the scope of the TVE sector.[7] By that time, the individual sector was well established, not least because the *zhuanyehu* (specialized households)—often portrayed as a key element in the surge of agricultural production—were in many cases private industrial enterprises operating in the countryside.

The data for 1984, in which household enterprises appear as part of the TVE sector for the first time, show that there were 6.07 million TVEs of all types across China. Of these, no less than 3.30 million were *geti* enterprises, contributing about 7 percent of TVE gross output value (Nongye bu 1989: 291, 294–5). Even this probably under-estimates the significance of the private sector because it takes no account of household sideline income, a considerable proportion of which was derived from the production of industrial handicraft products

---

[7] See 'Report on the Initiation of A New Phase for Commune and Brigade Enterprises' in Nongye bu (1985: 450). This announcement legalized enterprises employing less than seven workers, but not larger 'private' enterprises (*siying qiye*). These latter were legalized at the Seventh NPC in March–April 1988 when Article 11 of the Constitution was amended to include the statement: 'The state permits the private sector of the economy to exist and develop within the limits prescribed by law' (Zong 1989: 251).

(*nongmin jiating jianying shougongye*).[8] In 1984, production of these handicrafts was worth a further 9.8 billion *yuan*, a year in which all types of *geti* enterprises generated output value to the tune of a further 11.7 billion *yuan* (Nongye bu 1989: 118, 295). In that same year, GVAO (including village industry) was some 379 billion *yuan*, suggesting that the non-agricultural private sector was providing a significant—though by no means overwhelming—contribution to peasant incomes. Further impetus for the growth of the private sector came from the formal recognition of non-state enterprises employing 8 workers or more in 1988 and, much more importantly, from the privatizations of the mid-1990s (Bowles and Dong 1999; Han and Pannell 1999; Dong et al. 2002; Ho et al. 2003).

3.2. Outcomes: The Growth of Rural Industrial Output and Employment

The impact of these policy changes on the pace and nature of post-1978 rural industrial development is controversial. However, the remarkable rate of expansion achieved across the whole sector during the 1980s and 1990s is not in doubt, nowhere more so than in the TVE sector.

3.2.1. The Expansion of the TVE Sector

The output of the TVE sector grew at just under 19 percent per year during 1978–2004; the overall rate of growth was such that real value-added in 2004 was no less than 54 times greater than it had been in 1978 (Table 3.1).

The prime mover in this growth process was the industrial sector. With output growing annually at 20.5 percent between 1978 and 2004 (the growth rate is little different before and after the Tian'anmen divide of 1989), the industrial subsector increased its share in TVE production from 59 to 85 percent over the period.[9] To be sure, growth slowed to about 10 percent per annum in real terms between 1997 and 2004, but that testifies more to the maturity of the sector than to any failure. These data are of course unreliable in any absolute sense. The series breaks in 1984 (as is well known); thereafter, the data include smaller rural enterprises as well as those run by the new township and village governments. And censuses of both industry and tertiary sectors have revealed considerable evidence of over-reporting. Nevertheless, there is no doubt that the picture painted—that of a sector growing extremely rapidly—is broadly accurate. Even the data collected during the Industrial Census of 1995 show that TVE industry

---

[8] Household handicraft sidelines remained part of the agricultural sector for statistical purposes when brigade and sub-brigade industrial enterprises were shifted from agriculture to industry in 1984. Rather confusingly, the sector continued to be called *shou gongye* (handicraft industry) even though it was classified as part of agriculture (Nongye bu 1989: 118–19).

[9] The current price shares were respectively 77 and 70 percent in 1978 and 2002 (TJNJ 2003: 449).

Table 3.1 Growth of TVE value-added, 1978–2004 (billion *yuan*; 1990 prices)

	All TVEs	Industrial TVEs	Industry share
1978	37.8	22.3	59
1979	40.1	24.2	60
1980	48.2	28.8	60
1981	53.2	33.5	63
1982	62.0	37.3	60
1983	66.9	41.3	62
1984	98.8	55.9	57
1985	109.4	66.3	61
1986	118.3	72.6	61
1987	182.7	127.2	70
1988	200.3	142.6	71
1989	220.1	159.7	73
1990	250.4	185.5	74
1991	278.4	216.0	78
1992	389.6	309.9	80
1993	607.0	479.0	79
1994	691.4	566.9	82
1995	815.9	676.3	83
1996	931.9	756.4	81
1997	1,086.1	868.2	80
1998	1,190.5	981.5	82
1999	1,365.7	1,134.5	83
2000	1,476.5	1,211.5	82
2001	1,577.5	1,310.3	83
2002	1,744.7	1,471.1	84
2003	1,934.9	1,643.4	85
2004	2,058.8	1,757.9	85

Notes: Pre-1984 data are for commune and brigade enterprises only. The share of industry in total TVE output in 1978 is much lower at 1990 prices than at current prices. This is due to much greater price inflation outside the industrial sector in the 1980s. The underlying cause was the difference in productivity growth; industrial product prices grew slowly because of the subsector's faster productivity growth.

Sources: Current price value-added data from He (2004: 218), and Xiangzhen qiyeju (2005) for 2003 and 2004. These are converted to constant prices by using the all-China GDP deflator for all TVEs, and the all-China industry deflator for industrial TVEs (TJNJ 2005: 55–4).

accounted for 42.5 percent of industrial production, well up on the figure of 17.7 percent recorded for 1985, and implying an annual growth rate (current prices) between 1985 and 1995 of 29.7 percent.

The growth of TVE employment was equally relentless, rising from 28 million in 1978 to no less than 139 million by 2004 (XZNJ 2003: 7, 473; He 2004: 217; TJNJ 2005: 121). This growth was driven by the expansion of the industrial, construction and tertiary subsectors; agricultural TVEs employed 4 million fewer workers in 2002 than they had done in 1978. Most significantly of all, the contribution of the TVE sector to total rural employment tripled between 1978 and 2004. Indeed the only period of stagnation was between 1989 and 1992. This reflected the contraction of the sector during the period of very slow overall economic growth in the aftermath of the inflationary boom of the late 1980s. During these years, agricultural employment expanded rapidly as workers moved out of TVEs and back into farming. Between 1985 and 1988, agricultural employment rose in total by 11 million workers, but 1989 alone saw a comparable increase and in 1990 the figure shot up by about 50 million. Nevertheless, this 'return to the farm' was short-lived; agricultural employment fell back in both aggregate and percentage terms during the boom of the mid-1990s. These trends thus suggest that the farm sector provided a 'reserve army of labour' for TVEs in the 1990s. Changes in farm sector employment reflected not structural changes in the farm sector itself, but rather variations in TVE growth.

When looked at in broader perspective, the growth of China's TVEs (both in respect of output and employment) during the 1980s and 1990s was extraordinary in two senses. Firstly, the rate of growth was exceptionally fast by international standards. Nothing comparable has been seen in South Asia, sub-Saharan Africa or Latin America; insofar as modernization has occurred in these regions, it has been primarily an urban phenomenon. Secondly, the growth rate of the rural non-agricultural sector was unprecedented by Chinese historical standards—and therefore unexpected. Even the Party leadership was surprised. As Deng ([1987] 1994: 236) admitted in: 'In the rural reform our greatest success—and it is one we had by no means anticipated—has been the emergence of a large number of enterprises run by villages and townships . . . this result was not anything that I or any of the other comrades had foreseen; it just came out of the blue'.

As for the structure of the TVE sector, there is as yet little sign that the growth of employment has proceeded so rapidly that the sector has matured to the point where deindustrialization is beginning. It is true that employment in industrial TVEs has stagnated since 1995, but then so too has total TVE employment, the result being that the industry share has changed very little. It is also true that the TVE sector has become more diversified during the 1990s, as subsectors such as tourism, catering and finance have begun to develop, but the industrial subsector continues to be the engine of growth. All this suggests that any notion of deindustrialization in the Chinese countryside is premature. Agriculture has been progressively displaced by industry in rural China over the last 20 years, but there is as yet little sign of the emergence of a post-industrial economy. The main structural change was in fact the growing significance of the non-public TVE sector. By 1985, this subsector already accounted for some 45 percent of total TVE employment according to recent data, a much higher figure than previously thought and much more in line with the argument made by Zhou (1996) that many of the supposedly 'collective' enterprises of the 1980s were fakes. Its expansion was given a further boost by the privatizations of the 1990s; private employment tripled between 1995 and 1996 alone.[10] By 2002, approaching three quarters of all TVE workers were employed in the non-public sector, a dramatic transformation of the situation which prevailed only two decades previously.

---

[10] The numbers given for *geti* employment in many pre-2003 publications are significantly different from those in more recent sources. For example, a 1985 *geti* figure of 18.81 million workers is given in the well-known Nongye bu (1989: 293). And big changes have been made between

3.2.2. Output and Employment in County SOEs and COEs

Employment in county-level SOEs and COEs also expanded during the 1980s and 1990s. As Table 3.2 shows, county-run SOEs increased their employment

Table 3.2 Employment in the state sector, 1978–2004 (millions)

	Central Ministries	Provincial Government	Prefectural Government	County Government	Total	County Share (%)
1978	7.97	22.81	19.71	24.02	74.51	32
1979	n.a.	n.a.	n.a.	n.a.	n.a.	n.a.
1980	11.49	23.14	18.63	26.93	80.19	34
1981	n.a.	n.a.	n.a.	n.a.	n.a.	n.a.
1982	n.a.	n.a.	n.a.	n.a.	n.a.	n.a.
1983	n.a.	n.a.	n.a.	n.a.	n.a.	n.a.
1984	n.a.	n.a.	n.a.	n.a.	n.a.	n.a.
1985	19.71	19.38	23.89	26.92	89.90	30
1986	20.31	19.70	25.23	28.09	93.33	30
1987	20.63	19.87	26.59	29.45	96.54	31
1988	20.79	20.11	27.83	31.11	99.84	31
1989	21.03	20.32	28.37	31.37	101.10	31
1990	21.69	20.82	28.99	31.97	103.50	31
1991	22.51	21.06	29.70	33.38	106.70	31
1992	23.04	18.14	32.86	34.85	108.90	32
1993	23.21	20.24	27.63	37.81	108.90	35
1994	23.16	18.32	27.91	39.41	108.80	36
1995	n.a.	n.a.	n.a.	n.a.	n.a.	n.a.
1996	23.30	17.94	28.10	43.01	112.40	38
1997	23.07	17.77	26.69	42.77	110.44	39
1998	18.69	15.22	19.75	36.76	90.58	41
1999	17.58	14.39	18.19	35.43	85.72	41
2000	16.21	13.58	16.99	34.10	81.02	42
2001	14.85	12.93	15.71	32.71	76.20	43
2002	13.78	12.15	14.21	31.12	71.63	43
2003	n.a.	n.a.	n.a.	n.a.	n.a.	n.a.
2004	12.70	11.36	12.75	30.03	67.10	45

Notes: (a) These categories refer to level of ownership; in some cases, management responsibility was delegated to a lower level administrative authority. (b) The data include all types of sectors, including agriculture and services. The data also cover all state-owned units, including institutions (*shiye*) and organizations (*jiguan*). They therefore include workers employed in government agencies, scientific research, education and health care, as well as in enterprises. In 1996, for example, of the 1.502 million SOEs of all types across China, 552,000 were institutions of government and education, and a further 342,000 were government and Party agencies. There were in fact only 75,019 SOEs engaged in manufacturing in that year (LDNJ 1997: 217–18). (c) Provincial level includes the provincial-level municipalities of Beijing, Tianjin, Shanghai and Chongqing. Prefectural level includes provincial-level municipalities. County-level includes county-level cities. (d) The totals include laid off (*xiagang*) workers; the total number of laid-off workers across the state sector was officially put at 2.4 million in 2002 (LDNJ 2003: 269–71).

Sources: LDNJ (1989: 40; 1990: 79; 1997: 217; 2002: 255; 2003: 269; 2005: 311); TJNJ (1991: 109; 1992: 111; 1993: 111; 1994: 90; 1995: 90).

the publications of 2001–02 and 2003. For example, the 1991 household figure is given as 17.3 million (TJJ 2001; TJNJ 2002: 121) compared with 41.1 million in the more recent series (TJNJ 2003: 448). Most significantly, the figures for private (*siying*) employment has been revised upwards very substantially. The series published in 2002 (TJNJ 2002: 121) put private rural employment at 1.16 million in 1991, whereas the series published in 2003 increases it to 7.27 million (TJNJ 2003: 448). Whether this latter is better remains moot. For example, the collective from around 24 million in 1978 to 43 million by 1996.[11] After 1996, largely as a result of the policy of *zhuada fangxiao*, employment fell back across the state sector. However, the county-run sector was apparently less affected than other subsectors; it shed around 10 million workers between 1996 and 2002, but still increased its share in the state total from 38 to 43 percent.

Of course, output and employment in county SOEs grew far less quickly than in non-agricultural TVEs which, as we have seen, increased their workforce by over 110 million workers over the same period. As a result, whereas TVE and county SOE employment was approximately equal in 1978 (22 and 24 million employees respectively), the TVE sector was some three times bigger by 1996. Indeed, in those parts of rural China where the TVE sector had expanded most rapidly (and perhaps because of early SOE privatization), county-run SOEs had almost disappeared by the mid-1990s. In Jiangyin, Yixing and Xishan—the three rural jurisdictions within Wuxi municipality which had been re-classified as cities by that time—the shares of the state sector in GVIO was only 4.1, 5.0 and 4.9 percent respectively. But Sunan was not typical of China. In Yancheng municipality in northern Jiangsu, the figures were far higher. Xiangshui's state sector accounted for 29 percent of the county total and the figure was 30 percent in neighbouring Binhai. Further to the west, state industry provided 45 percent of industrial output in Lianshui county (JSTJNJ 1997: 370-4). In the much poorer province of Gansu, the role of the state sector was still greater. In some of the counties of Tianshui municipality, figures of over 70 percent were recorded in 1996; in Linxia and Gannan prefectures, almost all of industrial production was contributed by the state sector (GSNJ 1997: 671-3). We therefore ignore the state sector at our peril in analysing the pattern of rural industrialization in poor regions (the majority) of China in the 1980s and 1990s.

Data on output and employment in county-level COEs are much more difficult to obtain.[12] One source shows that COEs employed 10.9 million workers in subcounty enterprises (those located in market towns within counties), and that a further 22.4 million workers were employed in collective enterprises located in county towns or urban districts in 1985 (LDNJ 1990: 249). We need, however, a rather more precise accounting because many of these workers were employed in urban jurisdictions, including the big metropolitan centres. This type of breakdown is available for a number of provinces (Table 3.3). Here rural industry is roughly approximated as the sum of county-owned and industrial TVEs (some

category includes a range of joint collective-private TVEs, as well as foreign-invested TVEs (XZNJ 2003), and the *geti* category includes nearly 32 million workers employed in 'other' TVEs and only 27.9 million in 'pure' *geti* enterprises.

[11] The SOE total for 1978 exaggerates the extent of non-farm employment because a significant proportion of county SOEs were involved in agricultural production. It is probably fair to say that employment levels in the two were remarkably similar at the end of the 1970s.

[12] For example, the *Statistical Yearbooks* of the early and mid-1990s disaggregate the state sector by level in the administrative hierarchy but not the collective sector.

Table 3.3 The structure of GVIO in selected provinces, late 1980s (million *yuan*; 1980 prices)

Level of ownership	Jiangxi	Sichuan	Gansu
County SOEs	3,692	7,764	691
County COEs	786	3,248	404
Township	2,100	7,150	325
Village and below	3,732	11,088	420
Town	444	1,060	90
County-owned share (%)	42	36	57

Note: The county share here is county SOE and COE output as a percentage of all the categories. Data are for 1988 except for Gansu (which is 1985).
Sources: SCZL (1990: 24); JXTJNJ (1990: 200); GSSQ (1988: 166, 182).

industrial enterprises within county boundaries were owned by higher level jurisdictions, but the bulk of these enterprises were located within cities).

Township and village enterprises together dominated industrial production in Sichuan and Jiangxi provinces by 1988. However, county-owned COEs and SOEs together still accounted for 40 percent of industrial production. In Gansu, admittedly for a rather earlier year, the county share was no less than 57 percent. To be sure, the contribution of county-owned COEs was less in coastal provinces; the importance of the state sector tended to be inversely proportional to the level of development. But even in the developed coastal provinces, county COEs were by no means unimportant. In Fujian, the output of county COEs was nearly 57 percent of that of township enterprises. In more affluent Jiangsu, county COEs still contributed the equivalent of 27 percent of township GVIO by 1987 and the Zhejiang figure was 32 percent (GFYZ 1992: 200, 211, 248). Similarly at the county level. In Wuxian county in Sunan, county-level industries provided 20 percent of industrial output in 1988 (Wuxian GZ 1993: 7). Even in nearby Wuxi, one of China's richest counties, county-level industries still supplied 10 percent of industrial output in 1988, well down on the 35 percent of 1978 but manifestly by no means trivial (WXG 1990: 29–31). Of Wenzhou's collective industrial output in 1980, township level collectives contributed about 175 million *yuan*, rather less than either the 402 million *yuan* generated by firms owned by Wenzhou city proper or the 259 million *yuan* attributable to county-owned collective enterprises. Even adding in the production of village-run industrial enterprises (200 million *yuan*), it is apparent that the GVIO of the TVE sector was not much bigger than that of county-level collectives in the early 1980s (Wenzhou tongjiju 1985: 62, 125).[13]

---

[13] For Yunnan, the GVIO of TVEs was 0.9 billion *yuan* in 1984 compared with 2.5 billion *yuan* in county SOEs and COEs combined (ZYSWZY 1986: 328, 399). In Hunan, county level gross industrial output (including that of county-level cities) was 8 billion *yuan* in 1985, compared with about 5 billion in the TVE sector (Hunan tongjiju 1991: 143).

To be sure, county-run industrial COEs became a less important component of the rural industrial sector as the transition era progressed. In extensively-studied Zouping in Shandong, county collective GVIO accounted for about 10 percent of all county GVIO even in 1993 (Walder 1998: 10). In Chongqing municipality the share in 1996 was similar: county-level collectives produced (gross) output to the value of 4.3 billion *yuan*, compared with 7.8 billion *yuan* in county-level SOEs and 33.5 billion *yuan* in all industrial TVEs (CQTJNJ 1997: 109). In the most industrialized parts of rural China, the figures were much lower. Sunan is a case in point. In Xishan (formerly Wuxi county), the county collective share was less than 3 percent in 1996, and in neighbouring Jiangyin and Yixing the shares were 3.9 percent and 1.6 percent respectively (Wuxi tongjiju 1997: 132, 137–41). Nevertheless, as the 1995 Industrial Census revealed, Sunan was not typical. In that year, 58.6 million workers were employed in collective industries of all types across China. Of these, 40.9 million were employed in township and village enterprises or in rural cooperatives. But 6.85 million were employed in county-run COEs, and these enterprises contributed slightly over 10 percent of GVIO. In Jiangsu alone, 0.84 million industrial workers (7 percent of the total industrial workforce) were employed in county-owned COEs (GYPC 1997: 1, 17).

In short, we cannot ignore county-run COEs even in the mid-1990s. Indeed, taken together, county-run industrial COEs and SOEs were more important as sources of output and employment than the TVE sector in many parts of rural China well into the 1990s. Even in Wenzhou (and excluding the city proper), non-TVE GVIO averaged 24 percent of the total as late as 2000 (Wenzhou tongjiju 2001: 98, 188–9 and 209).

3.2.3. Total Rural Non-agricultural Employment in China after 1978

If 'rural' is defined to mean all types of enterprises operating within Chinese counties (the approach advocated in the previous chapter and discussed in Appendix 4), around 60 to 70 million workers were employed in some form of rural non-farm enterprise at the end of the 1970s. They were distributed more or less evenly between SOEs, COEs and CBEs, and the bulk of these workers were employed in industry. More precisely, we know that some 43.27 million workers were employed in industrial enterprises located in China's counties, almost exactly 10 percent of the rural workforce. With a further 7.4 percent of the rural population employed in the tertiary sector, this made for a non-agricultural workforce of about 17 percent or 75 million out of the 440 millions working in county-level jurisdictions.

By the time of the 1995 Industrial Census, the rural industrial sector was larger still. Total rural industrial employment in China reached 92 million, some 62 percent of the national industrial total and double the 1982 figure (GYPC 1997: 1). The share in output (55 percent) was somewhat less, reflecting the relatively greater size of non-rural industrial enterprises. Nevertheless, the significance of the rural industrial sector by the mid-1990s is plain to see and demonstrates the rapidity of industrialization across the Chinese countryside.

Trends since 1995 are difficult to establish with any precision. We know that employment in industrial TVEs stood at 76.7 million in 2002. However, employment in industrial COEs and SOEs is difficult to estimate because very few data are now published, in no small measure because of a shift away from classifying enterprises by ownership towards a size-based classification on the part of the statistical authorities. A further problem is caused by the creation of shareholding enterprises, many of which (but not all) are essentially SOEs by a different name; in only a small number of cases did the state not have a controlling share in the early years of the new millennium. We can, however, approximate employment in industrial COEs and SOEs (including shareholding companies) from the number of staff and workers, which covers all types of non-private enterprises. Across the whole of China, there were 5.4 million in mining, 29.8 million in manufacturing and 2.9 million in construction. In order to estimate the county-level component of this total, we can use the share of county employment in all SOE employment; this was 31.1 million workers out of 71.6 million in the entire state sector (LDNJ 2003: 169, 269). Applying this ratio (0.43) to the combined staff and worker figure for mining, manufacturing and construction gives a figure for employment at the county level in all types of non-private industrial enterprises of 16.4 million. Combined with the TVE figure of 76.7 million, this gives a grand total of about 93 million workers in 2002, little different to the Census figure for 1995.

3.3. Regional Variation in the Rural Industrialization Process

Rural industrial development occurred in many parts of China after 1978, but there was considerable variation in its pace. Take TVEs. In Jiangsu, they provided 46 percent of rural employment, and the figure was 52 percent in Zhejiang. In Sichuan, however, the TVE contribution was only 19 percent, and it was a mere 12 percent in Guizhou (TJNJ 2005: 121). Furthermore, the underlying causal process differed across Chinese regions. In some areas of the countryside, foreign investment and remittances played an important role. In other places, the private sector was especially important. Elsewhere, virtually all industry was owned and controlled by local government. The structure of production also varied. In some regions, the emphasis was on the development of producer goods, whereas other regions emphasized the production of textiles and garments. We can in fact identify a number of distinctive models of rural industrialization.

3.3.1. The Sunan Model: Manufacturing Industry Owned by Local Government

The heartland of public TVEs in China for many years was Sunan (the southern part of Jiangsu and the northern part of Zhejiang).[14] Public TVEs existed across China in the 1980s and early 1990s.[15] However, their expansion was most rapid in Sunan, and hence the term 'Sunan model' has been applied to this type of state-led rural industrialization.

In fact, as we have seen, commune and brigade industries were already well-established in the Sunan region by the late 1970s. In Jiangsu as a whole, industrial CBE production amounted to 6.2 billion *yuan* in 1978, almost 20 percent of provincial GVIO (JSB 1989: 137). However, TVE industrial production accounted for fully 65 percent of GVIO in Wuxi county, the heartland of Sunan. Although the private sector did expand rapidly there in the 1980s, its share by 1988 was only slightly more than 1 percent even if all household enterprises are classed as private. By comparison township and village-owned industry together contributed 89 percent of GVIO (WXG 1990: 29–31). Even in 1996, when the privatization of TVEs was well advanced in many parts of China, collective production continued to dominate. In Jiangyin, Yixing and Wuxi, the three counties which made up Wuxi municipality, township and village industry contributed 84, 83 and 89 percent respectively of total GVIO (Wuxi tongjiju 1997: 132).[16] The picture was little different in neighbouring Suzhou. In Taicang, township and village industry contributed 78 percent of county GVIO, and the figures were 60, 64, 71, 77 and 81 percent in the counties of Changshu, Kunshan, Zhangjiagang, Wuxian and Wujiang respectively (Suzhou tongjiju 1996: 134–5). For the entire Sunan region, the non-public sector (*geti* and joint enterprises combined) contributed only 9 percent of TVE industrial output in 1997. Even in Subei, where the public component of the TVE sector was less developed, the private share was still only 32 percent. The employment data for Jiangsu tell the same sort of story. In 1997, the private sector employed only 24 percent of all workers employed in the TVE sector (JSXZ 2000: 23, 81, 86). In other words, Wuxi and Suzhou, along with much of Jiangsu, remained 'on the collective road' long after the climacterics of 1978 and 1994.[17]

---

[14] The Chinese terminology of the late 1990s, in which the TVE sector is partitioned into public (*guoyou*) and non-public (*fei guoyou*) or private, is used here in preference to the misleading collective and non-collective distinction.

[15] Another celebrated example of this approach—at least until the imprisonment of Yu Zuomin, its Party secretary, in 1993—was Daqiuzhuang in Tianjin. The rapid growth of output in this village owed much to the creation of four new factories by Yu between 1977 and 1982 (Gilley 2001).

[16] In all these cases, total GVIO includes county-run COEs and SOEs as well as TVEs. Wuxi county had been renamed Xishan by this time.

[17] Sunan has of course been heavily criticized for its failure to embrace private entrepreneurship much earlier (Sachs and Woo 1994; Wu 2005). The extensive legacy of CBEs from the Maoist era is seen as responsible for its path-dependent development after 1978 (Whiting 2001), as discussed in the next chapter.

Jiangsu was not typical of China: in other provinces, the development of local public sector enterprises was much slower. As a result, Jiangsu actually increased its share of national township and village-owned GVIO from 12 percent in 1971 to 25 percent by 1985 (Mo 1987: 321–2). As the province was home to no more than 6 percent of the Chinese population, this shows a remarkable degree of dominance, and testifies positively to the underlying dynamism and competitiveness of its local public industries. It was this Sunan model which predominated during the 1980s and into the early 1990s across China. To be sure, there was a large number of sub-village enterprises even in Sunan, but these were typically small in scale and hence contributed only a fraction of output and employment. In 1984, when the data include the non-public sector for the first time, the share of township and village enterprises in output was 84 percent (Nongye bu 1989: 295). Despite the expansion of private and household enterprises, the public component of TVE output in Jiangsu stood at 49 percent as late as 1994, and even this calculation probably exaggerates the size of the non-public sector because it classifies all sub-village enterprises as private.

3.3.2. The Pingding Model

Rural industrialization in northern China has followed a very different path. To be sure, collective industries has been as important as in Sunan, but in north China industrialization focused on the exploitation of natural resources. This made sense given that population densities were rather lower and the mineral base much more extensive. Pingding county in Shanxi offers one of the best examples of this type of resource-based development. The county has a long history as a centre of coal mining and metallurgy. According to von Richthofen, iron production there was running at around 50,000 tons per year in the 1870s, and a similar figure was reported for output during the Republican period (Wagner 1995: 150). Iron production in turn depended upon coal, and this was being produced by a myriad of small mines in Pingding prior to the depression of the 1930s; coal output was in the order of 80,000 tons in the 1910s (Wright 1984: 64). Between 1952 and 1978, industrial growth resumed with GVIO increasing at annual rate of just over 14 percent between 1952 and 1978 (Pingding XZ 1992: 152).

After 1978, output grew at the same sort of rate; between 1978 and 1990, GVIO from all types of industries grew by 13.6 percent per year. The TVE sector was the mainstay, contributing 91 percent of output value in 1990 compared with 58 percent in 1978. Over the same period, TVE industrial employment—mainly in village-level enterprises—rose from 10,362 to 46,273 workers (Pingding XZ 1992: 145, 151–2). Heavy industry dominated; in 1985, light industry contributed only 8 percent of output value, whereas mining alone contributed 53 percent. Indeed total coal production was running at around 3 million tonnes per annum, vastly greater than the prewar figure (Chen 1988: 142–3).

The building materials sector, based around quarrying (especially limestone) was also very large and its share of output was growing during the early 1980s, mainly because it was a highly profitable sector—much more so than mining.

Taken as a whole, then, Pingding county had a very different industrial structure to that characteristic of any of the other TVE models. However, this approach to industrialization was not just common in parts of northern China; it has also been widely promoted across the rural parts of western China. Much of Gansu's industrial production was based around mining, and so too in many Third Front counties in Sichuan (such as Shimian) or Guangdong's Shaoguan prefecture. In addition, some mountainous parts of western China sought to industrialize by developing their lumber industry. It was thus heavy industry which was the key to industrialization in all these regions. In Sichuan's three ethnic minority prefectures of Aba, Ganzi and Liangshan heavy industry accounted for 81, 77 and 60 percent of GVIO in 1988, exceptionally high figures for what were very poor areas. This was very different to the structure of industrial production in Deyang on the Chengdu plain, which followed much more closely the Sunan model; as a result, heavy industry accounted there for only 51 percent of production (SCZL 1990). In Wenzhou (including Wenzhou city), the heavy industry share was 43 percent (Wenzhou tongjiju 1989: 126).

3.3.3. Private and Household Industry: The Wenzhou Model

In Wenzhou, however, the private sector was far more important, and that municipality has acquired fame outside China for this very reason. Indeed it was commonplace by the end of the 1980s to use the phrase 'Wenzhou model' (*Wenzhou moshi*) to characterize a process of TVE expansion which centred on the growth of private enterprises (Dong 1992), and the Wenzhou model has come to be seen in many quarters as superior to the Sunan approach precisely because it was based around private enterprise (Wu 2005: 200–2).[18]

Most Chinese sources date the beginning of this industrial transformation in Wenzhou to the late 1970s (He 1987; Nolan and Dong 1990).[19] Nevertheless, there is considerable evidence that the private sector never completely disappeared in the late Maoist period. Family farming continued to be practised between 1966 and 1973, and household industry certainly existed in the mid-1970s (Liu 1992: 307–8). It therefore seems reasonable to argue that the rise of

[18] The Gengche model (a township in northern Jiangsu's Suqian county) features in some accounts but it is evident that its emphasis on private industry differed little from that in Wenzhou. Although Gengche's industrial structure was arguably more diversified than that found in rural Wenzhou, the private (*geti*) sector accounted for 38 percent of GVIO and 75 percent of industrial employment, very high figures by Chinese standards (Chen 1988: 123). Furthermore, most of Gengche's production centred on simple processing and handicrafts, again little different from Wenzhou.

[19] According to Li Shi, one of the CASS team which visited Wenzhou in 1986, 'The rapid rise of household industry, however, took place after about 1980' (Nolan and Dong 1990: 108).

private industry properly dates from the demise of the Gang of Four in 1976, which gave a green light to those cadres favourably disposed towards promoting the expansion of the private sector. Thereafter, private sector industry developed apace in Wenzhou. By 1988, of the 462,000 workers employed in TVE industry, 260,000 were working in sub-village enterprises (Wenzhou tongjiju 1989: 62–3). By 2000, when the data on employment in the non-public sector are rather more precise, the private sector (*geti* and *siying* combined) accounted for 426,000 of the 918,000 workers employed in industrial TVEs.[20] For Wenzhou's TVE sector as a whole, private employment amounted to 440,000 out of a total of 946,000, or some 47 percent (Wenzhou TJNJ 2001: 100).

The growth of industrial output in the municipality was very rapid during the 1980s and 1990s. Total industrial value-added for Wenzhou's counties rose at over 20 percent per year in real terms over the post-1978 period, and the growth rate of township and village enterprises was even faster, running at about 30 percent per year (Chen 1989: 122–3; TJJ 1999; Wenzhou tongjiju 2001: 53–5, 98, 206–17).[21] By any standard, international or Chinese, this was a remarkable pace of industrialization. Moreover, growth was widely shared within Wenzhou. Even Wencheng and Taishun, its poorest counties, saw big increases in real industrial output value during the 1980s; in Wencheng, output increased threefold and in Taishun the increase was almost eightfold between 1978 and 1988 (Chen 1989: 400, 420). This growth did not eliminate poverty in the two; both were on the list of poor counties drawn up by the Office of the Leading Group for Poverty Reduction in 1988 (OLG 1989: 26), Wencheng and Taishun being two of only three Zhejiang counties so designated. Nevertheless, the very fact that the two were able to industrialize so speedily seems to confirm the view expressed by Dong Fureng that the Wenzhou model based around labour-intensive small-scale industry was particularly well-suited to the task of promoting industrialization in poor areas.

Now there is little doubt that the prime mover in the rural industrialization process in Wenzhou was the private sector, but it is hard to be sure about its size in Wenzhou or anywhere else in China during the 1980s. According to Zhou (1996), private entrepreneurs across China disguised their enterprises as collectives; these enterprises were thus *jia jiti* (fake collective) enterprises. The rationale was undeniable; by maintaining a low profile, entrepreneurs avoided being labelled 'capitalist roaders', a charge that continued to resonate across

[20] Of these 426,000 workers in private enterprises, 225,000 had jobs in enterprises employing eight workers or more.

[21] The all-industry data are for the counties of Wenzhou only (Ouhai is included in Wenzhou city for all time periods here). Total industrial output value includes state-owned, village and sub-village enterprises. Pre-1978 data are deflated using the all-Zhejiang industrial value-added deflator. 1978 and after data for all industry and TVE industry are deflated using the Wenzhou (including Wenzhou city proper) industrial value-added deflator. Value-added ratios (GDP basis) are derived from the ratio of gross output value to industrial value added for Zhejiang pre-1978 and for Wenzhou (including Wenzhou city proper) post-1978. The figure for TVE growth for 1971–78 is based on output value measured at 1980 constant prices. 1962–71 TVE growth is at 1980 prices and is for village and below industries only.

China during the 1980s.[22] If we accept this line of argument, the segment of industry officially designated as private under-states the true extent of private ownership, and we are thus in danger of under-estimating the true contribution of the private sector to rural industrialization.

One way to resolve this problem is to estimate an upper bound estimate for the size of the private sector by classifying all village enterprises as non-public.[23] Using this definition, Wenzhou's private sector contributed about 10 percent of GVIO in 1978 (Wenzhou tongjiju 2001: 203). This is a plausible enough figure if we accept the usual discourse on Wenzhou in which the liberalization process began after the arrest of the Gang of Four in the autumn of 1976.[24] Clearly, then, the public sector dominated at the commencement of the era of *gaige kaifang*. By 1985, when many of the restrictions on private enterprises had been removed, the non-public sector had its expanded its share to 25 percent, a noteworthy pace of advance. Modest further progress was made up to 1991, no doubt reflecting the national slowdown in the pace of reform during the economic retrenchment and political repression of the late 1980s. After Deng re-launched the reform programme during 1991–92, however, Wenzhou's private sector developed exceptionally swiftly. From a share of some 31 percent of industrial output in 1991, the non-public sector increased in size to claim no less than 90 percent by 2000. In other words, the development of the private sector in Wenzhou seems to have occurred primarily during the 1990s. Much progress was made during the 1980s, but private sector industry really took off only after 1991.

Ironically, the surge in private sector growth in the 1990s coincided with an attempt by Wenzhou's government to play a more interventionist role. Perhaps because of this, the private sector actually grew more quickly in other parts of Zhejiang in the 1990s. The provincial data show that 57 percent of all TVE workers were privately employed as early as 1998. In Lishui prefecture the figure was 89 percent, 83 percent in Jinhua, 72 percent in Quzhou and only 46 percent in Wenzhou (ZJTJNJ 1999: 253). This Wenzhou figure was much closer to the figures evident in Jiaxing (52 percent), historically part of Sunan. Nevertheless, Wenzhou's fame rests on the pioneering role it played in developing private industry.

3.3.4. The Open Door: The Guangdong and Jinjiang Models

In many parts of south-east China, the development of the TVE sector centred around the development of labour-intensive manufacturing production by

---

[22] The traditional Chinese expression for this sort of behaviour is *ren pa chuming zhu pa zhuang* (people fear fame for the same reason that pigs fear becoming fat).

[23] It makes little sense to argue that township-level enterprises were largely private because these enterprises were much larger and better regulated.

[24] 'Public' is the combined share of the state sector, urban collectively-owned enterprises and rural township-level enterprises. The non-public sector includes private enterprises based in Wenzhou city proper and it therefore overstates the share of the non-public sector in rural Wenzhou.

private enterprises. However, and in contrast to the Wenzhou model, much of the production was aimed at foreign markets, and a significant proportion of the finance came from foreign sources, much of it provided by overseas Chinese.[25] The Wenzhou model was one of industrialization driven by indigenous entrepreneurship whereas the Guangdong model conceded centre-stage to the foreigner.[26]

As is well-known, coastal South China's engagement with the world economy centred on the four special economic zones of Xiamen, Zhuhai, Shantou and Shenzhen, and the three Pearl River (Zhujiang) Delta cities of Foshan, Zhongshan and Jiangmen. This involvement was so extensive that Shenzhen, an essentially greenfield site at the end of the 1970s, was transformed by foreign trade and by foreign investment.[27] However, all these jurisdictions were officially designated as urban areas right from the start of the transition era. Accordingly, it is not appropriate to regard these as exemplars of *rural* industrialization.

But the open door affected many rural parts of Guangdong and Fujian as well. In the Pearl River Delta, the counties of Nanhai, Shunde, Gaoming, Sanshui, Xinhui, Kaiping, Enping, Heshan, Taishan, Zengcheng, Bao'an and Doumen all developed TVEs on the back of foreign capital. Dongguan is perhaps the classic example of rural industrialization in Guangdong. It was still officially classified as a county in September 1985, but its very success in export processing led to it being accorded city status. The record shows why: Dongguan attracted 12 percent of all foreign investment in Guangdong between 1980 and 1997, and 3.4 percent of all investment in China over the same period (Yeung 2001: 46, 84–5). No county received more FDI than Dongguan during the late 1980s and early 1990s (GDZL 1991). This was a remarkable achievement given that Dongguan's population, even including migrants, was only about 3 million in 1997. This

---

[25] Chen (1988) distinguishes between the Zhujiang model implemented in parts of Guangdong (where FDI played a key role) and the Jinjiang model (Fujian province), whereas overseas Chinese remittances were more important. The Zhujiang model is also sometimes referred to as the Nanhai model (G.C.S. Lin 1997), and the Jinjiang model is often referred to as the Quanzhou model, the prefecture in which Jinjiang is located (Tong 1997: 195). However, in that reliance on the open door differentiated both 'models' from other parts of China, and because the open door was relatively more important in Guangdong than in Fujian, it seems more appropriate to consider the two together as a single 'Guangdong model'. This last phrase has tended to have growing currency since 1992, when Guangdong's development accelerated markedly following Deng's *nanxun*. See, for example, Cheng (1998).

[26] Some accounts even suggest that Guangdong's growth slowed in the late 1990s because of its sluggishness in reforming SOEs and promoting private enterprise (Wu 2005: 203).

[27] Even here, however, we need to be chary of attributing all the credit to the open door policy. In fact, Shenzhen benefited enormously from state investment in basic infrastructure (Kleinberg 1990). There seem, therefore, to be clear parallels with Wenzhou. Even if private entrepreneurship and the open door were the prime movers in Wenzhou and Shenzhen respectively, it is more than likely that growth would have been much slower without state infrastructural investment. Démurger (2001) echoes this point, arguing that one of the main reasons for the failure of western China to catch-up has been its weak infrastructural base.

foreign investment was crucial because, as Potter and Potter (1990: 317–19) have pointed out, many communes seem to have been unable to make the transition out of traditional handicraft industries in the late 1970s. The open door allowed villages like Zengbu to break out of this development trap by enabling them to attract investment and entrepreneurship from Hong Kong as early as 1979–80 and this transformed the employment prospects of the workforce, especially those of young women. On the back of FDI, Dongguan's growth rate soared; between 1978 and 1997, current price GDP increased by a factor of 48 (Yeung 2001: 246). Over the same period, national GDP increased by a factor of only 20 (TJNJ 2003: 55). Even allowing for higher inflation in Dongguan, it is evident that output in that municipality increased about twice as fast as the national average.[28] By 1998, total GVIO in Dongguan was just under 60 billion *yuan*. Of the 48 billion *yuan* produced by large companies, no less than 41 billion *yuan* was produced by foreign-owned (including Hong Kong, Taiwan and Macao) firms based in the area (GDTJNJ 1999: 339, 639).

Dongguan received more FDI than any other Guangdong county, but it was not alone in being affected by the open door. The Zhujiang Delta in particular received large inflows. Of the ten counties which received the most foreign direct investment during 1986–1990—which serves as a reasonably proxy for the entire period between the launch of the open door and the Asian crisis—only Xuwen was located outside the Delta.[29] These Delta counties seem to have benefited very substantially in terms of industrial growth. All of them experienced per capita NVIO growth rates between 1980 and 1996 which exceeded the median for Guangdong's counties (itself a remarkable 23.5 percent). The Delta median was in fact about 28 percent per annum. By contrast, not one of the ten counties which received the least FDI—most were located in mountainous areas, primarily in Shaoguan and Meixian prefectures—managed to achieve the provincial median (GDZL 1991; GDTJNJ 1992, 1994 and 1997). More systematic analysis is needed to isolate the precise effect of FDI when geography and other initial conditions are controlled for; that is the subject of Chapter 10. However, the evidence here strongly suggests that FDI played a significant role in spurring industrialization.

Further north, counties like Jinjiang—located not far from the Xiamen special economic zone and virtually opposite Taipei—in Fujian also owed much of their rural industrialization to the agency of overseas Chinese, whether based in

---

[28] Again, as with Shenzhen, we cannot explain the transformation of Dongguan exclusively in terms of the open door. The municipal government also invested heavily in infrastructure and in education; by the late 1980s, Dongguan had more miles of paved road than any other county in the province (Vogel 1989: 179). It is also worth observing that Dongguan's industrial base was already well-established by 1978. In that year, the secondary sector contributed 44 percent of the county's GDP, little different from the national average of 48 percent (Yeung 2001: 246; TJNJ 2003: 55).

[29] Xuwen, located in the extreme south of Guangdong, was attractive as a location because of its close proximity to Hainan island.

Taiwan or in Singapore, Indonesia or Malaysia. Here the TVE sector grew rapidly on the basis of the development of labour-intensive manufactures produced by *lianhu* (joint households, often translated in the Jinjiang context as business partnerships). In 1983, the county was home to 2,271 enterprises, of which 714 were *lianhu*. By 1986, however, this had risen to 4,329 out of 5,418 and accounted for 68 percent of TVE employment (Zhang and Ming 1999: 34); a lower figure of about 50 percent for 1988 is given in the County Records. *Lianhu* enterprises tend to be included in the private category in the official Chinese data, and there is no doubt that the Jinjiang approach was rather closer to the Wenzhou model than to that which was the norm in Sunan. Furthermore, the Jinjiang model was highly effective in generating output and employment growth. In Jinjiang itself, TVE employment rose more than fourfold between 1978 and 1988. Over the same period, TVE income increased by a factor of 34, an implied annual rate of 42 percent at current prices (Jinjiang XZ 1994: 307). Both rates of increase were significantly above the Fujian TVE averages. By 1995, Jinjiang was one of only six Fujian counties where TVE gross output value exceeded 10 billion *yuan*. Of the total income generated by the TVE sector, around 10 percent was produced by the county's 145 *sanzi* TVEs (Tong 1997: 189–92, 306 and 601). The value of the county's exports in 1988 was 178 million *yuan*. Jinjiang's record was replicated by Quanzhou prefecture as a whole. Although the prefecture was home to only seven of the province's 60 plus counties, it accounted for about one third of the gross output value and the exports of the provincial TVE sector in the mid-1990s. Of the 107 townships in which output value exceeded 100 million *yuan* in 1995, no less than 37 were to be found in Quanzhou. One consequence of all this was a rapid rate of poverty reduction. In 1985, 1.22 million people (26 percent of the rural population) lived below the poverty line in Quanzhou but by 1995 that figure had fallen to 70,000 or 1.3 percent (Tong 1997: 192–4, 424).[30]

3.4. Conclusion

It is abundantly clear that the death of Mao was a climacteric in both a quantitative and qualitative sense for China's rural industrial sector. The pace of industrialization accelerated after 1978, the pattern of ownership became much more diverse and, perhaps most importantly of all, rural industrialization led the ascent from poverty. Given the significance of rural industrialization for poverty reduction, a central challenge for any political economist is to explain why the pace of rural industrialization accelerated after the death of Mao. However, almost equally important is the need to develop a theory capable of explaining

---

[30] A detailed discussion of economic development in Quanzhou's Anxi county is offered in Lyons (1994).

why the pace of rural industrialization was spatially uneven. In many coastal areas, and around large cities, the rural industrial growth rate was very high. But in much of western China, and especially in many Third Front regions, the pace of industrialization was glacially slow. And for precisely this reason, the rate at which poverty was reduced was also slow. Accordingly, we need a theory capable of explaining not only the increase in the *average* rate of industrialization, but also the *spatial variation* in that rate. To what extent can such spatial variation be seen simply as a reflection of the adoption of different models of rural industrialization, and to what degree were growth rates determined by geographical and historical factors?

4

The Role of Policy Change

We saw in the previous chapter that the pace of rural industrial development accelerated in much of China after 1978. This process brought in its wake a reduction in rural poverty without precedent in either Chinese or world history. Given the obvious instrumental significance of rural industrialization, it is not surprising that a variety of explanations have been offered. All of these focus in one way or another on the role played by policy changes introduced after 1978. This chapter considers these explanations, and their limitations.

4.1. Orthodox and Revisionist Explanations: An Overview

Although the extent of pre-1978 Chinese rural industrialization documented in Chapter 2 has been under-stated in the literature, it is well understood that the process began in the late Maoist era (Lin and Yao 2001; Whiting 2001). Even Sachs and Woo (1997: 34) acknowledge that: 'The foundation for collectively-owned rural industrial enterprises was laid during the decade-long Cultural Revolution . . . ' To argue, therefore, that most Western scholarship ignores the development of rural industry under Mao would be quite wrong, even if the more ideologically-driven pieces are less careful on this point.[1]

4.1.1. The Orthodoxy

Nevertheless, the two most widely cited explanations of rural industrialization play down the contribution of Maoism. The first of these explanations (the orthodoxy) is associated in particular with the writings of Wong (1991a); Sachs and Woo (1994); Lin and Yao (2001); Whiting (2001); and Wu (2005). These writers acknowledge that rural industry had emerged in some parts of China by the late 1970s, though there is some disagreement as to the role played by state subsidies in the birth of rural enterprises. Wong, Whiting and Wu tend to emphasize the importance of state protection even in regions like Sunan.

---

[1] One example is provided by Bao et al. (2002: 96).

Others, like Lin and Yao, argue that its growth and development was driven far more by the accident of geography than by the agency of the state. Where geography was favourable, state subsidies were largely unnecessary. Where geography was unfavourable, the state was powerless (Lin et al. 1996: 190–1). The work of Lin and Yao (2001: 150) is representative of this sort of approach. The Maoist era '. . . laid a solid foundation . . . [and] . . . the commune system . . . resulted in considerable investment in rural infrastructure . . . Nevertheless, the strongest factor determining the geographic distribution of rural enterprises in the 1970s was the endowment of land and labor, as shown by their concentration in the coastal provinces'.

One matter on which orthodox scholars are united is in their portrayal of Maoist rural industry as chronically inefficient. Even where geography was conducive to rural industrial development, the industries were invariably inefficient precisely because they were state-owned. Wong (1991*b*: 25) comments on the expansion of chemical fertilizer production that 'In economic terms, the programme was disastrous, which also makes it typical of Maoist programmes.' Similarly, Wirtschaffer and Shih (1990) have documented the inefficiency of small electricity-generating plants. These failures arose because the soft budget constraints introduced by state ownership removed competitive pressure. As a consequence, the enterprises which had been established by the close of the Maoist era were incapable of providing the basis for sustained industrial growth, and this became obvious by the 1990s even in geographically-favoured areas such as southern Jiangsu, the cradle of local state-owned rural industry. Prior industrialization actually impeded subsequent growth because inefficient state-owned industries absorbed labour—skilled and unskilled—and capital which could have been better used in other sectors of the economy. In consequence, those areas where industrialization had proceeded furthest were trapped in an inefficient equilibrium because the pay and conditions enjoyed by (local) state sector employees made them reluctant to abandon these sinecures to take up the riskier jobs on offer in the private sector. By contrast, regions where the bulk of the workforce was still employed in agriculture at the end of the 1970s were at an advantage because this 'surplus' labour could easily be mobilized by the new and private (hence efficient) industries which sprang up in the countryside in the 1980s and 1990s. Agricultural labour, in contrast to the employees of local state enterprises, had little to lose by hitching its fortunes to the burgeoning private sector. Sachs and Woo (1994: 116) were amongst the first to make this sort of argument: 'We offer a "Russification" hypothesis: preceding industrialization (along Soviet lines) was a hindrance, not a help, to economic growth in the 1980s'.

That 1978 was a climacteric in the development of rural industry is very clear in the literature. For example, the sections discussing rural industry in the *Encyclopaedia of Chinese Agriculture (Zhongguo nongye quanshu)*, which includes a volume for every Chinese province, include only a cursory discussion of the pre-1978 process of rural industrialization. The various *Sheng qing* (*Provincial Situation*) volumes and supposed histories of rural industry (such as SXQS 1988) take the same approach; it is very rare to find time series data on the production of rural industry for the pre-1978 period. Reading these volumes, it is as if the TVE sector has no history.[2] The English-language literature is not so very different; almost invariably, the Dengist restoration is portrayed as the turning-point in the development of rural industry (Byrd and Lin 1990; Wong 1991*a*; Findlay et al. 1994; Sachs and Woo 1994; Zhou 1996; Oi 1999; Whiting 2001).

1978 did mark a turning-point because it ushered in a series of policy changes which were decisive in transforming Chinese rural industry. In part, the argument here is simply that *gaige kaifang* (reform and opening up) led to a faster rate of growth than under Mao because it allowed access to foreign technology, and because it re-invigorated agriculture (the rural surplus available for industrial investment therefore increased). There was thus a step-change in the process of growth after 1978. According, for example, to Lin and Yao (2001: 151): 'The period 1984 to 1988 was the take-off period of China's rural industrialization and witnessed the fastest growth of rural enterprises'. Without these changes, the rural industrialization process begun under Mao would not have been self-sustaining.

More fundamentally, however, *gaige kaifang* was important because it removed controls on industrial ownership, and hence made possible the development of a dynamic private sector. This is exactly what happened: the rural industrialization of the post-1978 era was driven by the newly-emerging private and foreign sectors. *Gaige kaifang* thus caused a *qualitative* transformation of rural industrialization. By deregulating relations with the outside world, the People's Republic was able to attract foreign capital and skills into its rural industrial sector. The removal of ownership controls was also important because it allowed the emergence of a vibrant and dynamic private sector, not least in relatively poor areas where limited supplies of capital were adequate only to establish household industry. It was thus the removal of controls on private and foreign ownership in the eyes of orthodox scholars which was decisive because it allowed the gradual displacement of an inefficient state sector in the Chinese countryside by a more efficient array of privately-owned enterprises.

Nevertheless, policy change did regions like southern Jiangsu little good in the short run. State-owned enterprises could provide no lasting basis for rural industrialization precisely because they were state-owned and hence inefficient. Moreover, although *gaige kaifang* made private ownership possible, a private sector could not develop in Sunan because surplus agricultural labour has already been absorbed by the inefficient state sector: private and foreign-owned

---

[2] Yet these same volumes make plain the sheer number of TVEs which already existed across China by 1978 even in some of the poorest provinces. The Henan volume (Henan yanjiushi 1987: 171) reports the existence of 76,000 enterprises and there were almost 25,000 enterprises in Gansu (GSSQ 1988: 166). The Yunnan volume is only marginally better, taking the story back as far as 1976, by which time 12,800 enterprises had been established (ZYSWZY 1986: 325).

enterprises were therefore crowded-out. Even though state-owned enterprises were widely recognized as inefficient after 1978, Sunan persisted with them because the costs of closure (especially in terms of unemployment) were greater than the short term benefits. Under-industrialized areas such as Wenzhou were by contrast at a great advantage because they had no legacies to constrain them; there were no costs to set against the putative benefits of private industry. Only in the late 1990s, and in the face of spiralling losses, was it rational for governments across Sunan to abandon state ownership and embrace the private enterprise model pioneered in Zhejiang (Whiting 2001; Wu 2005: 200–2).

4.1.2. The Revisionist Explanation

The second (revisionist) approach to explaining rural industrial success also focuses on the role played by policy change.[3] However, revisionist scholars argue that policy change invigorated the rural state sector, transforming it from the inefficient behemoth of the Maoist era into an altogether more dynamic and flexible engine of growth. In this account, it is the reformed state sector—not private enterprises—which is cast in the starring role.

More precisely, revisionist scholars see fiscal decentralization, rather than the liberalization of ownership, as the catalyst for growth. This approach, associated with Susan Shirk but more especially the writings of Jean Oi (1999), accepts that 1978 was the watershed date in the development of Chinese rural industry. However, argues Oi, the important contribution of the *gaige kaifang* programme was not so much that it allowed private and foreign ownership, but that it initiated a thorough-going programme of fiscal decentralization. Fiscal decentralization changed the incentive structures faced by local government in such a way as to encourage them to establish efficient state-owned industrial enterprises. Thus the lion's share of those rural industrial enterprises established after 1978 were established under the aegis of local government, rather than by private or foreign entrepreneurs. By hardening the budget constraints faced by local government, efficient local state-owned enterprises were created.

4.1.3. Contrasting Visions and Common Ground

Orthodox and revisionist scholars share a common view of the inefficiency of late Maoist rural industry. This view seems well-founded, as we saw in Chapter 2. The orthodoxy and revisionist approaches are further united in seeing policy change as the decisive factor behind the emergence and rapid growth of an efficient rural industrial sector in the 1980s and 1990s. It is change, rather than continuity, which explains successful Chinese rural industrialization over the last two decades in the eyes of both schools.

[3] The approach deserves the epithet 'revisionist' because it offers a more positive appraisal of the efficiency of state-run industries than is the norm in the economics literature.

Beyond this, however, there is little common ground. The orthodoxy argues that the engine of growth was the private sector. Liberalization was thus the decisive policy change because it allowed domestic and foreign entrepreneurs to establish industries which were private and therefore necessarily efficient. Those industries which continued to be owned by government, whether central or local, continued to be inefficient by virtue of their public ownership and their continued existence handicapped those regions, like Sunan, which inherited a large public sector in the late 1970s. The short term costs of closing these inefficient enterprises were very high, and therefore Sunan became locked into a path dependent process of rural industrial growth.

By contrast, the revisionists deny that public sector was inefficient in Sunan, at least when enterprises were managed and owned by local government. For them, fiscal decentralization was the key post-1978 policy change. By tightening the budget constraints faced by the localities, central government unwittingly forced rural jurisdictions to develop industrial enterprises which were efficient and which contributed to local revenues. To be sure, private and foreign entrepreneurs contributed to the growth process, but this contribution was small. For the revisionists, the engine of rural industrial growth was the public sector, not private entrepreneurship. Furthermore, although Sunan and other parts of China privatized their rural industries in the late 1990s, the fact of privatization in itself tells us nothing about the underlying efficiency of the industrial sector. It is all too easy to see the cyclical problems of the late 1990s as emblematic of structural weakness.

There are thus three main areas of disagreement between orthodox and revisionist writers. Firstly, what was the contribution of the private sector to the rural industrialization process? Was it the engine of growth, or is that title more properly accorded to the public sector? Secondly, did the efficiency of state-owned rural industries improve after 1978, or did these industries remain as inefficient as they had been under Mao? Thirdly, what precisely was the contribution of fiscal decentralization to the growth process?

4.2. The Contribution of the Private Sector

As has been seen, the re-emergence of private industry is integral to the orthodox explanation of rural industrial growth. Pioneered in regions such as Wenzhou, private enterprise was quick to spread to other Chinese regions and played the decisive role in their industrial transformation. Precisely because the budget constraint faced by private entrepreneurs, whether indigenous or foreign, was hard, private enterprises were forced to be efficient. This superior efficiency enabled them to out-last their public sector rivals; these latter were ultimately privatized by bankrupt local government which, by the 1990s, could no longer afford to subsidize persistently loss-making enterprises. The private sector was also successful, it is argued, because much of it was small-scale. According to Dong Fureng (Nolan and Dong 1990; Dong 1992), the Wenzhou model of household industry was well-suited to poor areas where capital was at a premium, and where economies of scale were difficult to exploit because of limited markets.

4.2.1. The Limits to Private Entrepreneurship: The Wenzhou Fable

The evidence certainly supports the orthodoxy's contention that the private sector established itself first in comparatively poor areas. In Jiangsu, the development of the private sector was very slow in the early 1980s; total employment in household industries increased from 290,000 in 1984 to 'only' 1.12 million in 1990. However, household industry was quick to develop in northern Jiangsu, historically a much poorer region than Sunan. By 1990, employment in private industry totalled 118,000 in Sunan, compared with 312,000 in Suzhong and 692,000 in Subei (JSXZ 2000: 45). After that time, private rural industries developed quickly across the whole of Jiangsu. By 2001, township and village enterprises accounted for only 25 percent of total TVE employment, the balance being provided by the private (42 percent) and individual (33 percent) sectors (JSTJNJ 2002: 170). Much of the impetus for this came from the privatizations of the 1990s. This surge in private sector production during the 1990s was replicated in other provinces. The share of the non-public sector in Sichuan—the source here combines *siying* (private) and *geti* (household) enterprises—in total TVE employment was no less than 81 percent by 2001 (SCTJNJ 2002: 311).[4] This figure for 2001 was only a little higher than that for 2000, when non-public enterprises contributed 76 percent of TVE employment, of which household enterprises contributed 55 percentage points and private enterprises the remaining 21 points. Much of the growth appears to have been driven by privatization, which began in earnest in 1995 (Jie and Wang 2001: 28). In other comparatively poor areas, the privatization process was also well-advanced by the end of the millennium. In Chongqing, a provincial-level municipality after 1997 but with a large rural hinterland encompassing the poor counties centred around the Yangzi Gorges, the share of private enterprises in TVE employment rose from 27 percent in 1997 to 54 percent by 2000 (CQTJNJ 2001: 337).

Orthodox scholars further contend that recently-released Chinese data, which offer a more reliable measure of the scale of the private sector than earlier statistical series, show that the displacement of the public by the private sector began earlier in the transition era than previously thought (Table 4.1).[5] The private sector is thus cast in the leading role much earlier than in previous accounts, which

[4] Very different figures are given TJNJ (2002: 121) for employment in household and private enterprises in Sichuan and Jiangsu for 2001, although the TVE totals match. The provincial yearbook figures are probably more reliable. Given these discrepancies it seems very likely that the national figure is a substantial under-estimate.

[5] It has been suggested that the data released in the early 1990s were even more misleading than those of the late 1980s because of extensive secret privatizations across the countryside in the early 1990s (Woo et al. 1997: 25). The new data seek to avoid these and other pitfalls, and

Table 4.1 Employment in TVEs by ownership category, 1978–2004 (millions)

	Township and village	Private	Household	Total	Non-public share (percent)
1978	28.27	0	0	28.27	100.0
1979	n.a.	n.a.	n.a.	29.09	n.a.
1980	n.a.	n.a.	n.a.	30.00	n.a.
1981	n.a.	n.a.	n.a.	29.70	n.a.
1982	n.a.	n.a.	n.a.	31.13	n.a.
1983	n.a.	n.a.	n.a.	32.35	n.a.
1984	n.a.	n.a.	n.a.	52.08	n.a.
1985	41.52	4.75	23.52	69.79	40.5
1986	n.a.	n.a.	n.a.	79.37	n.a.
1987	n.a.	n.a.	n.a.	88.05	n.a.
1988	n.a.	n.a.	n.a.	95.45	n.a.
1989	47.20	8.84	37.63	93.67	49.6
1990	45.92	8.14	38.58	92.65	50.4
1991	47.69	7.27	41.18	96.09	50.4
1992	51.76	7.71	46.78	106.25	51.3
1993	57.68	9.14	56.64	123.45	53.3
1994	58.99	7.30	53.88	120.17	50.9
1995	60.60	8.74	59.27	128.62	52.9
1996	59.53	24.64	50.91	135.08	55.9
1997	53.27	26.25	50.99	130.50	59.2
1998	48.29	26.20	50.87	125.36	61.5
1999	43.69	28.51	54.84	127.04	65.6
2000	38.33	32.53	57.34	128.20	70.1
2001	33.72	36.94	60.20	130.86	74.2
2002	31.52	41.52	59.84	132.88	76.3
2003	28.78	46.01	60.94	135.73	78.8
2004	n.a.	n.a.	n.a.	138.66	n.a.

Notes: (a) The main problem in interpreting the primary data is that a variety of different aggregation methods are used. If one wishes to use only the three categories of collective, private and household (the approach taken in TJNJ 2003), problems arise over the categorization of cooperative TVEs, joint TVEs, limited liability TVEs, shareholding TVEs, 'other' TVEs and foreign-invested TVEs. The approach taken in TJNJ 2003 (as XZNJ 2003 makes clear) is to include cooperative, joint, limited liability and shareholding TVEs in collective, 'other' (including team enterprises) in household, and foreign-invested enterprises in the private category. By way of comparison, XZNJ (1989: 574) includes employment in team enterprises within the village total for 1985, whereas the table above includes this category in the household total (Nongye bu 1989: 293). (b) 'Non-public' in this table is the sum of private and household. 'Private' includes foreign-invested enterprises (including those which were Hong Kong, Macao or Taiwan-owned); 'township and village' includes collective, cooperative, joint, limited liability, and shareholding TVEs. 'Household' is geti (individual) and 'other'. It can certainly be argued that it is better to maintain the disaggregation than to create the three aggregate categories use in TJNJ (2003). That said, no plausible method of aggregation would reduce the share of the private TVE subsector. In that sense, the figure for employment in private TVEs given above must be regarded as a lower bound. (c) Many of the Chinese publications adopt differing approaches in the way they present data on rural employment (see for example TJNJ 2002: 121). Despite what is often implied in these publications, private and individual enterprises are usually included in the TVE total (as they should be according to the official definition of the TVE sector). Several of the provincial yearbooks make this clear; see for example JSTJNJ (2002: 170) and SCTJNJ (2002: 311). The total for private employment includes both private employees and employers (or 'investors' as they are often styled); see LDNJ (2001: Table 7.4).
Sources: TJNJ (2003: 448); NYNJ (2005); TJNJ (2005: 117).

certainly generate much higher estimates than in the older publications. For example LDNJ (1997: 7) gives a total for private and household employment in rural China of only 56.6 million in 1996, well below the 75.5 million given in Table 4.1. In general, however, comparisons across sources are problematic because some of the totals quoted do not make clear whether the private and household sector figures include the self-employed (17.7 million in rural household enterprises and 0.3 million in private rural enterprises in 1996) as well as employees (5.51 million in the rural private sector and 33.1 million in the household sector).

tended to emphasize the initial dominance of state-owned TVEs. These data show that the share of the non-public sector in employment reached 40 percent as early as 1985, and seem to support Zhou's (1996) view that many of the collective industries which dominated the old data for the 1980s were actually private enterprises in disguise. By 1990, despite the pause in the liberalization process after 1988 associated with the Tian'anmen massacre, the private sector share had climbed past the 50 percent mark. By 2003, the size of the public sector had dwindled to less than 30 million out of the 136 million strong TVE workforce.

As for the provincial data, they reveal that the collective share in employment exceeded 20 percent by 2002 in only five cases (XZNJ 2003). If one strips out the big cities of Beijing and Tianjin as well as Tibet, there are only two deviant provinces (Shanxi and Hubei) and there the figure was only barely above the 20 percent mark. In a handful of provinces, the foreign sector accounted for a significant proportion of the remainder; in Guangdong, Shanghai and Fujian, the foreign share was 10 percent or more. In every province, however, the private sector had comfortably eclipsed both collective and foreign sectors, and in no less than 23 provinces the private sector's share exceeded 80 percent.

For all this evidence, the case made by the orthodoxy depends critically on the assumption that the contribution of the private sector is best measured by its share in TVE employment. If we instead measure the private sector share in TVE value-added, its contribution appears much smaller. The share of the non-public TVE sector in employment reached 50 percent as early as 1989, but estimates of value-added suggest that the public sector continued to dominate long into the transition era (TJNJ 2003: 449). In fact, the non-public share in value-added only rose above 40 percent when the privatizations of the mid-1990s began. Indeed in the ten years between 1985 and 1995, there was comparatively little growth in the share of the private sector. Furthermore, in counties like Wujin (Jiangsu), private enterprises accounted for only 30 percent of TVEs (and much less in terms of value added) even on the eve of privatization in 1996 (Ho et al. 2003: 13). The high employment share of the private sector did not translate into a high output share because of its technological backwardness, low levels of productivity and low wages. For all the criticisms made of the efficiency of the public sector, labour productivity in the collective TVE sector averaged 31,746 *yuan* per worker in 2002, compared with 25,180 *yuan* in privately-owned TVEs and only 19,218 *yuan* in the household sector (by calculation from TVE value-added and employment). These statistics strongly suggest that the public sector was the prime mover in the rural industrialization process until the mid-1990s—and therefore that it is the growth of the *public* sector after 1978 which really needs to be explained. As Oi (1999: 62–3) says:

In the 1980s, much of China's post-Mao rapid rural industrialization occurred in *local government-owned enterprises at the township and village levels.* This fact is sometimes forgotten . . . [the orthodoxy] . . . misrepresents the character of these enterprises and misidentifies the pivotal actors in the process of China's rural industrialization.

(Original emphasis)

79

This conclusion that the public sector was crucial is reinforced when we recognize that rural industry encompassed county-run SOEs as well as TVEs. These industries were privatized rapidly after the mid-1990s but before then they remained in public hands, and enjoyed considerable expansion. In 1996, in fact, county SOEs still employed over 43 million workers, earning a total of just over 200 billion *yuan* (LDNJ 1997: 217). If we use this as an estimate of county SOE value-added and add it to the collective TVE total above, that alone would raise the share of the rural public sector by around 4 percentage points for 1996. Given that earnings represent a very conservative estimate of value-added and that even this calculus excludes county-run collectives, it must be concluded that the share of the public sector across rural China could hardly have been less than 70 percent of value-added even in 1996. Applying the same procedure to the data for 2002, when county SOE earnings totalled 314.3 billion *yuan* (LDNJ 2003: 269), would raise the share of the public sector to well over 40 percent. The privatizations of the 1990s certainly altered the shares of the respective sectors, but we do well to remember that the privatization process in the countryside was still only partially complete by the time of Hu Jintao's accession in autumn 2002.

A second problem with the orthodoxy is the way that it interprets the experience of Wenzhou, its exemplar of private entrepreneurship. The rapid growth of the private sector in this Zhejiang municipality after 1978 is not in doubt. However, this evidence alone falls well short of making the case for private industry as the *sine qua non* for Chinese rural industrialization in the 1980s. For one thing, many parts of rural China were able to achieve equally rapid rates of industrialization without significant recourse to private industry.[6] Table 4.2 brings together data on Wenzhou and six other rural regions during the period 1978–88: the prosperous counties of Suzhou and Wuxi (in southern Jiangsu), Yancheng (a poor coastal region in Subei), Huaiyin (a poor inland region within Subei), the counties around Kunming (Yunnan province), the Chengdu plain (Sichuan), and the counties of the Xiang river valley in eastern Hunan. None of these regions is mountainous and all have relatively good communication links. It is therefore reasonable to suppose that there was no insuperable barrier to industrialization in any of them (in contrast to the situation in much of western China). Wenzhou apart, all these regions were dominated by public sector rural industry during the 1980s.

Now at first glance, the data in Table 4.2 suggest a clear casual link between growth rates and a large private sector share in output; the potency of the private sector as a vehicle for rapid rural industrialization is suggested by the clear gap between the growth rate in Wenzhou and the growth rates achieved in (say) the

---

[6] Guangdong, a province in the vanguard of reform in many areas, did not develop private industry especially quickly. The data for 1995, for example, show the *geti* sector as contributing only 28 percent of TVE gross income (GDTJNJ 1999: 309).

Table 4.2 Growth of rural industrial output in seven Chinese regions, 1978–88 (1980 constant prices)

	Per capita GVIO, 1978 (*yuan*)	Growth rate of GVIO, 1978–88 (percent per annum)
Suzhou-Wuxi (Jiangsu)	558	28.6
Wenzhou (Zhejiang)	107	24.2
Huaiyin prefecture (Jiangsu)	121	19.8
Chengdu plain (Sichuan)	212	19.7
Yancheng prefecture (Jiangsu)	201	17.3
Xiang river valley (Hunan)	146	11.4
Kunming region (Yunnan)	265	10.2

Notes: (a) Data cover all types of county industrial output; jurisdictions designated as cities at the time of the 1982 Census are excluded. The Xiang river valley data are for 1978–87. (b) One of the advantages of looking at the 1978–88 sub-period rather than the whole post-1978 period is that data consistently valued at 1980 constant prices are more readily available. In addition, it normalizes for the impact of foreign direct investment, which was almost insignificant in most parts of China during the 1980s (it took off only after Deng's *nanxun* in 1992).

Sources: Suzhou-Wuxi, Huaiyin and Yancheng—JSB (1989); Wenzhou—Chen (1989); Chengdu plain—SCZL (1990); Xiang river valley—HNTJNJ (1982, 1986, 1987); Kunming—YNTJNJ (1990).

Xiang river valley, and around Kunming. The best to be said for the collective model is that private industry was not a necessary condition for rapid growth; the rates achieved away from Wenzhou were, by LDC standards, extremely rapid.

However, closer inspection reveals a more ambivalent picture. For one thing, Wenzhou was out-performed by Sunan despite the prevalence of public owner-ship there (the public contribution to TVE output exceeded 90 percent even in 1997; JSXZ 2000: 81, 86), and its much higher base level of output in 1978. The only way to reverse this verdict is to argue, as Whiting does, that Sunan's collect-ive sector was much less efficient than the private sector which dominated in Wenzhou. The implication of this statement is that Sunan would have grown 'even faster' with private ownership, but it is not really sensible to claim that a growth rate of close to 29 percent per annum in real terms constitutes some sort of failure. In fact, there are real grounds for doubting whether Sunan is an example of path dependency at all. Just as many of the classic stories of path dependency are open to question—it has for example been argued that VHS displaced betamax because it was the more efficient technology, and the same been said of the qwerty keyboard (Lewin 2002)—so too with Sunan. The very dynamism of the region surely suggests that Sunan was on an efficient growth path during the 1980s and 1990s.

The other problem with the orthodoxy's treatment of Wenzhou is that it res-olutely ignores three special factors which worked in the municipality's favour. Firstly, the remarkable acceleration of growth after 1978 was driven as much by capital inflows as by private entrepreneurship. In 1980, only 2.2 percent of Wenzhou's GNP was attributable to capital inflows. By 1988, however, this figure had risen to 9 percent, an extremely high figure by international standards. The significance of 'foreign' capital was even more important in some of Wenzhou's counties. In Yongjia, for example, net property income from abroad accounted for 15 percent of GNP in 1988. In Yueqing, the figure was even higher at 21.5 percent, itself slightly down on the 1987 figure of 24.8 percent (Wenzhou tongjiju 1989: 34–8).[7] Some of this inflow came from Taiwan (the main external source of capital) but most came from Wenzhou residents working elsewhere in China (Oi 1999: 69). However, that does not alter the point that Wenzhou was exceptional in enjoying such large capital inflows and being a net exporter of labour. By contrast, the counties of Wuxi and Suzhou experienced net outflows of capital by the late 1980s as workers recruited from other provinces remitted a part of their income to their home village.[8] Furthermore, there appears to have been a close temporal relationship between patterns of growth in Wenzhou, and capital inflows. In 1991, foreign investment in the municipality was worth US$18.8 million. In 1992, however, this soared to US$243.7 million and it reached US$354 million in 1993. Industrial output soared during these years; the GVIO of TVEs rose by 68 percent in 1992 and 94 percent in 1993. When foreign investment levels fell back in the late 1990s—to US$46 million in 1999 and US$67 million in 2000—so too did industrial growth; between 1998 and 2000, it averaged around 14 percent per year (Wenzhou tongjiju 2001: 99 and 384). Causality is difficult to prove, but there is much to suggest that inward investment, not private entrepreneurship, was the prime mover in the growth process in Wenzhou during the 1990s.

Secondly, the development of Wenzhou's household industry was driven by the exploitation of child labour. This was made possible in part by the age structure of the population. At the time of the 1982 Population Census, the proportion of the population aged 14 or younger was 36.3 percent, well above the provincial (29.3 percent) and national averages (33.6 percent). Only in Guizhou (40.9 percent) was the Wenzhou figure exceeded amongst China's provinces, and there the development of any form of industry was hampered by a range of other factors (Wang 1988: 238; RKNJ 1986).[9] We cannot be sure how many of

[7] These figure for net capital inflow are given as the difference between GDP and GNP in the *Wenzhou Statistical Yearbook* (Wenzhou tongjiju 2001). The phrase used to describe the origin of the inflow is *guo (diqu) wai*.

[8] It is rare for provincial data on gross national product (or gross national income) to be published. Recent data for Jiangsu are for gross domestic product, and (where it is stated) gross national product is simply given as identical to GDP. Part of the problem is the terminology involved; it is odd in both English and Chinese to talk of *provincial* gross *national* product. Nevertheless, attempts were made in the late 1980s and early 1990s to distinguish between GDP and GNP at a provincial level. For example, Jiangsu's GDP was some 8.7 billion *yuan* larger than its GNP; compare JSB (1989: 17) with TJJ (1999: 367). The net material product data for the 1980s show the same pattern. For Jiangsu, *guomin shouru* (national income) is usually greater than *guomin shouru shiyong'e* (national income utilized). The reverse is the case for poor provinces such as Guizhou, which received net inflows from workers employed outside the province (TJJ 1990*b*).

[9] The relative abundance of child labour reflected the high rates of fertility amongst Wenzhou's population even in the mid-1970s, as a result of which the municipality's population was growing almost twice as fast as the provincial average at that time.

these children were put to work in service of the miracle, but scattered evidence suggests that Wenzhou exploited its opportunity to the full. According to Chen, for example, child labour accounted for not less than 20 percent of hired workers in the municipality in 1984 (Nolan and Dong 1990: 141).

Thirdly, local government initiative played a greater role in the Wenzhou growth process than is often admitted; within-budget state investment, for example, increased by no less than 94 percent in 1977 compared with 1976 (Li 1988: 21-2). Furthermore, the share of state fixed investment in GVAIO rose significantly. It reached a nadir of 0.6 percent in 1974, and was little higher in 1975 and 1976 (0.8 and 0.6 respectively). Thereafter, however, the share increased substantially, reaching 1.3 percent in 1978, 2 percent in 1979 and 2.6 percent by 1982 (Chen 1989: 80, 151). This 1982 figure was still small, but it may well have been enough to kick-start the process of industrialization. More generally, local government played a key role in promoting industrialization in Wenzhou throughout the 1980s and 1990s, creating the physical structures needed for markets, port facilities and housing for the workforce (Nolan and Dong 1990). In fact, the role played by the state in Wenzhou was not so dissimilar to that played by the local state in Shulu (Hebei), a role which Blecher has called 'developmental' (Blecher 1991). There is of course a distinction between direct state management of industry, and state investment in infrastructure combined with regulation of industrial development; this is the basis of Blecher's distinction between the entrepreneurial local governments which operated in Guanghan (Sichuan) and Sunan, and the developmental state of Shulu. But in both stories the state remains critical to the industrialization process, and so it was in Wenzhou.

The claim that the private sector was the engine of rural industrialization in China during the 1980s and 1990s therefore rests on flimsy foundations. Its share in value-added did not exceed 50 percent until the late 1990s; before then, it was the public sector which was overwhelmingly dominant. And although Wenzhou's industrial sector grew quickly after 1978, it is hard to see this as evidence of private sector efficiency. The municipality's growth rate was slower than that of public sector-dominated Sunan despite starting from a much lower base and, even in Wenzhou, local government played a key role in assisting the growth process. Most importantly of all, and contra Whiting, Wenzhou was not self-reliant but dependent upon massive inflows of foreign and domestic capital and the ruthless exploitation of child labour. It is at least arguable that Wenzhou would have grown faster still if state-owned local government enterprises had played a greater role in the process.

4.2.2. The Limited Reach of the Open Door

In the eyes of orthodox scholarship, the opening-up of China's borders to foreign trade and capital flows in the 1980s was almost as important as the development of an indigenous private sector in driving the rural industrialization process.

The argument here has two dimensions.[10] On the one hand, trade and FDI had a powerful and direct effect on the economies of Guangdong and Fujian, and to a lesser extent the coastal provinces of Zhejiang, Jiangsu and Shandong. The need to be competitive at home and abroad forced domestic firms to increase their productive efficiency, and the availability of world markets in turn allowed labour-intensive TVEs to exploit economies of scale in the classic Smithian fashion. Foreign direct investment raised output directly, both as a net addition to the capital stock, and because foreign capital was on average more productive than domestic capital; the productivity of workers employed in the foreign sector was therefore higher than in the domestic sector.

The second dimension of the argument is that foreign trade and FDI had significant spillover effects. This is important because it implies that the benefits of the open door were not confined to the coastal provinces but were more general. Several channels are envisaged. Firstly, competition from MNCs forced domestic firms in that sector to innovate and to raise productive efficiency. Secondly, there were important spillover effects in the labour market. Those workers recruited by MNCs acquired new skills, and labour turnover ensured that these skills were disseminated widely; the MNCs were not able to fully appropriate the cost of their investment in training and therefore spillovers occurred. Insofar as a considerable proportion of the workers recruited by MNCs were from the Chinese interior, and insofar as they returned to their home towns and villages, a clear process of technological spillover was set in train. In addition, the impact of remittances from migrant workers to the interior provinces should not be ignored. Thirdly, FDI generated demonstration effects. MNCs are usually keen to encourage the transfer of technology to their own suppliers, and therefore vertical transfers were highly significant. Taken as a whole, argue orthodox scholars, these spillover effects were very important in China. According to Démurger et al. (2002: 447):

> ... FDI had an impact on economic growth that went beyond an addition to the capital stock: it also provided competition to domestic firms and hence forced them to raise their productivity, generated demonstration effects that enabled domestic firms to improve their operations, and provided a training ground for future managers of domestic firms in the same industries.

Now the orthodoxy's claim that there were powerful direct effects from the open door is hard to deny for Guangdong or Fujian. The importation of capital goods represents in principle an important channel for technological diffusion, as well as a means to supplement the domestic capital stock; it is not, for example, unreasonable to argue that postwar growth in Japan, South Korea and Taiwan was based upon a protectionist regime which imposed high tariffs on consumer goods but low tariffs on capital goods. The same has been true of Guangdong

[10] There is an extensive general literature on the impact of trade and FDI which includes Blomstrom and Kokko (1998), Saggi (2002), and Gorg and Greenaway (2004).

and Fujian. Counties such as those located in Quanzhou prefecture in Fujian, the heartland of the Jinjiang model, did especially well out of the process because it made possible, as we have seen earlier, the adoption of a strategy based around the production of labour-intensive manufactures for export. Tom Lyons, writing of Anxi's experience, is in little doubt as to the impact of the open door:

> The record leaves little doubt that the sources of Anxi's recent growth are intimately tied to changes in policy—and, specifically, to abandoning the autarkic stance characteristic of Maoism and accepting a greater degree of interdependence with other regions of China and with the rest of the world.

(Lyons 1994: 117)

The Pearl River Delta in particular and Guangdong in general also benefited enormously from the open door. Of course the special economic zones received the lion's share of inward investment, but counties such as Shunde and Dongguan were also very significant beneficiaries (Chapter 10).

The central issue, however, is not whether the open door policy benefited Guangdong and Fujian, but whether it can be used to explain the development of TVEs across China. The problem here for the orthodoxy is that foreign trade and FDI were very limited elsewhere. By the late 1990s, as Table 4.3 shows, exports provided the most important market for a number of China's coastal provinces, Guangdong and Fujian in particular. However, TVE exports from the interior western provinces, represented here by Guizhou, Sichuan and Gansu, were far lower. Even the national figure of 29 percent recorded as late as 2002 was not especially high. SOEs and COEs operating within Chinese counties were far less export-orientated than the TVE sector (mainly because their output was more geared towards producer goods in which China had little by way of comparative advantage), and therefore the national reach of the open door during the transition era was decidedly limited.

This conclusion is even stronger when we look at the role played by FDI and by foreign entrepreneurship—as opposed to export markets—in the rural growth

Table 4.3 Value of TVE exports, 2002 (provinces ranked by value of exports)

	Exports (million *yuan*)	TVE Value-added (million *yuan*)	Export Share (percent)
Guangdong	238.2	278.3	86
Zhejiang	211.8	381.1	56
Jiangsu	134.5	334.7	40
Fujian	82.8	154.1	54
Sichuan	2.8	114.2	2
Guizhou	0.6	25.3	2
Gansu	0.4	23.6	2
China	922.5	3238.6	29

Source: He (2004: 234, 226).

process. Foreign-owned and invested companies certainly contributed to growth; by the mid-1990s, FDI contributed 15 percent of Guangdong's GDP. But the national figure even for the mid-1990s was much lower, standing at perhaps 5 percent of GDP. In the 1980s it was lower still, barely 1 percent of national GDP (Bramall 2000: 370–2). Moreover, these data are for the economy as a whole; the contribution of FDI and foreign ownership to *rural* industrialization was even less. These numbers alone make it extremely hard to argue that FDI was a key factor behind rural industrialization. This conclusion is confirmed when we look at the record of regions which experienced rapid rural industrialization in the 1980s. For example, Jiangsu's realized FDI in 1985—when rural industry was expanding rapidly—was a very modest US$11.9 million. This rose to US$103 million in 1988 (JSN 1989: 165), but in the same year the Guangdong municipality of Dongguan alone attracted US$241 million (Yeung 2001: 248, 281). Even as late as 1996, the value of actual FDI in Wuxi municipality—the heartland of rural industry in Sunan—was only US$915 million, some 9 percent of GDP (Wuxi tongjiju 1997: 46, 281). The total received was comparable to that attracted by Dongguan in the same year, but Wuxi's population was some 50 percent larger. And between 1986 and 1990, when Wuxi attracted total FDI worth US$47 million, Dongguan attracted close to US$1 billion. In short, during the crucial decade of the 1980s when rural industry was being established, the contribution of FDI in southern Jiangsu was almost negligible. If anything, its contribution to rural industrialization in Zhejiang was even less. In 1988, FDI in the whole of that province was a mere US$30 million (ZJTJNJ 1989: 257). Even by 2002, the contribution of the foreign-funded enterprises sector to TVE growth was minuscule in most of China. The foreign sector contributed upwards of 20 percent of TVE value-added and employment in Guangdong and in the counties surrounding the city of Shanghai (XZNJ 2003). However, the foreign contribution was less than 10 percent even in the relatively open province of Fujian, and nationally, the contribution of foreign TVEs to the total was 1 percent or less in no fewer than 22 of China's provinces. Even allowing for the presence of non-TVE foreign companies in the Chinese countryside, one is hard put to argue that the *direct* contribution of the foreign sector to rural industrialization was very large.

Orthodox scholars must therefore demonstrate that FDI and foreign trade had powerful indirect (spillover) effects if they are to show that the open door had *general* effects on TVE development across China. But here too the empirical evidence is against them. For one thing, the international evidence on technological spillovers via trade and (especially) FDI is decidedly equivocal. Few doubt that FDI is desirable because of its effects on the capital stock, and in raising the productivity of workers employed in MNCs, but the spillover argument often deployed by governments to justify subsidies to encourage FDI does not seem to hold. In fact, many of the direct studies have either found little concrete evidence of spillovers taking place, or are problematic because of the endogeneity and sample selection problems encountered in empirical research (Saggi 2002; Görg and Greenaway 2004). There are probably three explanations. Firstly, there is a negative effect on the profitability of incumbent firms caused by the entry of MNCs which are much more competitive because of their higher productivity. Such destructive competition erodes the profits needed to finance investment in research and development, and in new equipment embodying more advanced technology. Secondly, the extent to which foreign firms are willing to allow horizontal spillovers is a limiting factor. If spillovers are perceived to help local firms which are producing the same type of goods, the foreign firm will inevitably be reluctant to allow catch-up. In the longer term, labour turnover will make some diffusion inevitable but the time horizon involved may be rather long. Thirdly, reverse engineering in LDCs is limited by patents and by licensing agreements. The partial excludability conferred by patents clearly slows the rate of technological diffusion, even if the patent encourages innovation in rich countries in the first place (and therefore raises the global stock of knowledge which LDCs can access). Free trade in itself therefore offers no guarantee of technological diffusion.

The evidence on spillovers from FDI in China is equally equivocal. Certainly some occurred. The jobs created by FDI and the expansion of trade attracted migrants from many poor parts of China; of Dongguan's total population of 2.9 million in 1997, some 1.4 million were migrants, mainly from poor parts of southern China (Yeung 2001: 243). In this way, FDI helped to alleviate poverty. Furthermore, the skills acquired by returning migrants help to promote the modernization of the Chinese countryside (Murphy 2002). Nevertheless, there is not much evidence that these FDI and trade spillovers have had a *significant* impact on growth in the Chinese interior. Even Guangdong's interior prefectures of Meizhou and Shaoguan gained little from the integration of the Zhujiang Delta into the world economy to judge by their rather modest growth rates after 1978. More generally, the absence of significant spillovers from the coastal region to the interior is demonstrated by the growth of regional inequality, which suggests that the coastal provinces have benefited far more from the open door (Brun et al. 2002). In no small measure, this is because China's growing integration into the world economy has been accompanied by a reduction in inter-regional trade (Kumar 1994*a*, *b*; Young 2000), although the literature on this is not entirely conclusive (Naughton 2001). Labour migration and remittances by migrant workers helped the Chinese interior, but the flows involved were not significant enough to transform its prospects. In Guizhou's case, for example, net income from outside the province (measured here as the difference between provincial GDP and GNP) amounted to only about 1 percent of GDP in 1996 (Guizhou tongjiju 1997: 18). By way of comparison, Pakistan's net property income from abroad (mainly from migrant workers in the Gulf states) was about 6 percent of GDP in the late 1990s (World Bank 2000). This conclusion that spillover effects were weak is echoed in the econometric literature on

China (Li et al. 2001; Zhang 2001; Hu and Jefferson 2002; Liu 2002). Spillovers did occur, but they were generally weak. For example, Hu and Jefferson (2002: 1075) are largely dismissive of short run effects, and even in respect of the long run their conclusion is hedged with qualification:

... we find negative and statistically significant spillover effects of industry FDI on domestic firms in the electronics industry ... Our long-run results ... [suggest] that in some industries, some domestic Chinese firms—those that are able to survive in the face of competition from FDI firms seem able to capture some of the technology and know-how that are introduced to the industry from abroad.

In sum, it seems that foreign trade and FDI did much to promote rural industrial development in the coastal regions of Guangdong and Fujian. However, precisely because FDI and trade were regionally concentrated, and because the spillover effects appear to have been weak, it is hard to see the open door as an adequate explanation for the development of rural industry across China as a whole. We are therefore surely entitled to conclude that the public sector, not private industry or foreign entrepreneurship, was the engine of rural industrialization.

4.3. The Efficiency of Rural Industry

This conclusion that the public sector was the motor for rural industrial growth after 1978 assuredly undermines the orthodoxy. However, at one and the same time, it increases the potential significance of the orthodoxy's contention that public sector industry continued to be inefficient even after 1978. For if an inefficient public sector dominated production, it follows that the inefficiency of rural industry as a whole cannot be in doubt. This contention, if true, brings with it the conclusion that the Chinese post-1978 rural industrialization process failed. It served simply to replace the inefficient but small rural industrial sector of the Maoist era with a much larger, diverse but equally inefficient industrial sector which, by virtue of its very expansion, imposed even more of a long run constraint on the rural development process. This contention puts the orthodoxy on a direct collision course with revisionist scholars, who argue that fiscal decentralization transformed the inefficient publicly-owned rural industries of the Maoist era into an efficient public sector by the late 1980s and early 1990s.

The main post-1978 problem faced by public sector industry in the eyes of the orthodoxy was the continuing absence of secure property rights. This discouraged outsider investment in public industries (thus limiting capital availability) as well as entrepreneurship and technical progress, and invited political interference. As a result, even in Zhejiang and Jiangsu where industries owned by local government were most developed, the public sector was inefficient (Woo

1997: 170–1; Sachs and Woo 1997). This inefficiency did not prevent state-owned industries from developing because of path dependency effects: inefficient institutions (in this case state-owned firms) and technologies persisted because the (short run) costs involved in their elimination were too high. Much of the Chinese rural industrial sector therefore evolved along an inefficient equilibrium growth path. The rapid rural development of the last 20 years in Sunan can thus be seen as similar in character to that enjoyed by the Soviet Union in the 1950s and early 1960s; growth was rapid, but ultimately it was unsustainable because of enterprise inefficiency.

4.3.1. Path-dependent Rural Industrialization in Sunan and Third Front Regions

The path dependency argument is articulated most convincingly in the Chinese context by Whiting (2001). For her, public industries in Sunan (she focuses in particular on the example of Wuxi county) continued to make a significant contribution to Chinese growth after 1978. However, their growth could not disguise their inefficiency:

The fact that they [collective enterprises (CB)] were buttressed by access to soft bank credits and cushioned by softness in their tax obligations through the mid-1990s meant that these firms were not perfectly efficient 'first-best' alternatives to the large, state-owned enterprises that had dominated the planned economy. Nevertheless, they contributed significantly to China's economic growth . . .

(Whiting 2001: 295)

The continuing growth of rural industry in Sunan reflected the ability of the sector to generate local government revenue, inefficiency notwithstanding. In large measure this was because Wuxi in particular, and Sunan in general, enjoyed first mover advantage. There was massive excess demand for consumer goods in rural China in the early 1980s, and Sunan was one of the few regions with the industrial capability to meet it. Accordingly, Sunan accrued very large rents (profits) even though its enterprises were inefficient (in terms of productivity). The rents generated were smaller than they would otherwise have been, but they were large enough to appease local government, which was therefore most reluctant to close down low productivity enterprises. Wuxi could have privatized its rural industry in the 1980s (or at least made more of an effort to develop private industry); other parts of China did so. But Wuxi did not do so because, especially in the short run, widespread industrial restructuring would have adversely impacted on its revenue base; it was far easier to extract revenue from comparatively inefficient state-owned industry than to gamble on creating—and being able to tax—a myriad of private enterprises. Only in the mid-1990s, under pressure from central government, did the counties of Sunan finally embrace privatization.

For Whiting (2001: 257, 263, 295fn), fiscal decentralization and the other policy initiatives of the early 1980s did not help because these initiatives did not fully harden the budgets faced by local government. More importantly, they did not address the problem of soft budget constraints at the firm level.[11] The budget constraints faced by local government were still far too soft even in those relatively affluent parts of China which had developed collective industry by the late 1970s, and this encouraged inefficiency until the mid-1990s: 'It is difficult to explain the first wave of privatization in the mid-1990s if we assume, following Oi, that budget constraints at the township level had been hardened more than a decade earlier' (Whiting 2001: 266). To be sure, the fiscal decentralization of the early 1980s did not discourage the creation of rural industries. In that the marginal rate of return (in terms of tax revenue) to local government from any new industry was higher under the new system, Wuxi's officials had a greater incentive to promote rural industrialization (the substitution effect). In principle, this could have been offset by the income effect; the lower rate of central 'taxation' on the local economy following increased fiscal decentralization left Wuxi's government with a greater surplus and therefore with less need to develop new industries to provide public services and finance cadre wages. That the income effect did not dominate presumably reflects the fact that Wuxi, though affluent by Chinese standards, was still poor in global terms. The work-leisure trade-off for Wuxi officials was therefore still firmly in favour of the work involved in establishing and regulating new industries.[12]

In fact, argues Whiting, the continued softness of the budget constraint it faced, combined with the expansion of the revenue base by fiscal decentralization, to ensure that local government in Sunan lacked the incentive to abandon the relatively inefficient 'collective' industries of the Maoist era. This only changed in the mid-1990s because budget constraints were hardened (as central government tried to restore its own revenue base), and because of the deteriorating financial performance of many Sunan enterprises. This forced local governments in Wuxi and across the region to take a more aggressive stance towards their loss-making enterprises, either closing or privatizing them. Up to the mid-1990s, by leaving Wuxi, and the counties in Sunan with a greater proportion of revenue, the fiscal reform of the early 1980s hindered the creation of an efficient industrial sector—but helped accelerate the pace of rural industrial growth; the losses run up by existing firms could be offset by setting up new

[11] This point applies with even more force to SOEs located to rural areas but owned by higher levels of government. These enterprises, which were rural according to the definition adopted in this book, remained an integral part of the state plan and therefore the recipients of within-budget transfers where needed.

[12] Oi (1999: 31–2) discusses the likely response of poor areas to continued subsidies during the 1980s, and concludes that they retained a strong incentive to revenue maximize. Indeed industrial output grew faster in those parts of North China which receive state subsidies. One would expect the income effect to have been stronger in Wuxi precisely because that county was more affluent, but still not strong enough to discourage TVE development.

profitable firms. The perpetuation of an inefficient form of industrial production in Wuxi thus parallels those classic examples of path dependency in technological choice. As with the examples of the qwerty keyboard and the VHS
video recorder, an inferior choice was made in Wuxi not because of a rigidity—
though political considerations precluded wholesale privatization in the
1980s—but because there was no clear incentive to adopt the more efficient
form of industrial organization.

The significance of budget constraints in influencing performance, whether
the constraints faced by enterprises or those faced by local government, is
confirmed for Whiting by the experience of Songjiang county, part of the
municipality of Shanghai in the 1980s and 1990s (Whiting 2001: 213–15).
Shanghai was required even after the early 1980s to finance other regions in
China. It also inherited a significant number of loss-making enterprises from
the Maoist era which needed to be subsidized. This forced the Shanghai government to monitor, supervise and restructure TVEs much more closely in order to
maximize the revenue they produced. The net result was that Shanghai's rural
industry was much more efficient than in neighbouring Jiangsu.

Whiting's analysis echoes the ideas outlined in earlier work. Ho (1994) argued
that many of Sunan's local SOEs and TVEs were inefficient, whilst Sachs and
Woo (1994, 1997) and Woo (1997) took the view that the Sunan model was not
sustainable. Local government-led industrialization had generated rapid
growth in the 1980s, but the limits to that growth were being reached by the
early 1990s. The main problem, according to Sachs and Woo (1994: 130–1), was
that property rights were muddled, thus encouraging corruption and wasteful
investment. As a result,

Until the 1990s, the Jiangsu model was considered the best TVE form because it was closest
in its adherence to traditional socialist concepts. However, like the traditional SOEs, the
Jiangsu-type TVEs soon ran into financial problems . . . China would be ill-advised to
continue to base its rural industrialization on collective ownership.

(Sachs and Woo 1997: 35, 81)

Furthermore, the extensive privatizations of the mid and late 1990s have often
been interpreted as a consequence of declining profitability, and as a sign that
the whole programme of local SOE and TVE expansion had run out of steam
(Park and Shen 2003: 500, 509; Eyferth 2004).

From a path dependency perspective, there is an obvious parallel between
Sunan and Britain's relative decline in the late nineteenth century. Like Wuxi in
the 1990s, Britain in the 1870s was suffering from the legacy of its early start (Crafts
1985). In the British case, too many industries were inadequate in size, hampered
by location and producing the wrong types of products for the markets of the late
nineteenth century. The costs likely to be incurred in scrapping the coal mines
and textile mills of the first industrial revolution outweighed the benefits from
new industries, with all the setup costs necessarily involved in making the

transition. Given relatively short time horizons, it was therefore a rational decision for Britain to retain its existing industrial structure. And so it was for rural Sunan.

For Whiting, Sachs and Woo, the failure to privatize early cost China dear. The continuing inefficiency of rural industry even after the 1978 climacteric hindered the industrialization process in two respects. On the one hand, the inefficient rural enterprises absorbed labour. As a result, less skilled and unskilled labour was available to develop the new efficient private sector enterprises which emerged after 1978. Of course labour could in principle be re-deployed from old to new industries, but workers were in general very reluctant to abandon their existing wages, benefits and terms of employment. In addition, the inefficient rural industries of the late Maoist era constrained subsequent industrialization by absorbing scarce capital. Precisely because TVEs, locally-owned SOEs and Third Front industries were heavily dependent upon subsidies, local governments were short of the funds needed to develop local infrastructure after 1978. They therefore faced the unenviable choice of either neglecting education and transport, or raising extra-budgetary funds by imposing a range of taxes and levies on the private sector.

If Wuxi had only privatized earlier, so Whiting argues, it could have used its skilled labour and scarce capital much more efficiently in the private sector. With an efficient private sector, Wuxi and the entire Sunan region would have been able to make even better use of its geographical advantage. By implication, Wuxi's rural growth would have been still faster, and its industry much more profitable and efficient.[13] From a dynamic perspective, therefore, the failure of the Sunan region to achieve its (first best) potential rate of growth is testimony to the continued inefficiency of the rural public sector even after 1978. Sunan still experienced rapid rural industrialization but, from an orthodox perspective, it ought to have done better still in the transition era.

The orthodoxy also adopts a path dependent approach to the analysis of industrialization in Third Front regions, which were if anything more disadvantaged by the legacies of the past than Sunan. Thus one of the key reasons that provinces such as Gansu, Guizhou and Sichuan grew relatively slowly after 1978 was because Front enterprises located within their borders continued to absorb scarce investment funds and skilled labour. Paradoxically, the attempt to abandon the dualist approach of the Maoist era (whereby Third Front enterprises operated outside the control of local government and were funded centrally) intensified the burden on provincial and sub-provincial governments in western China still further. Of course Front industries could be re-located to coastal provinces or to more promising sites within Third Front provinces, thus relieving the burden on the local exchequer. But re-location was an expensive process

---

[13] Lin and Yao (2001: 160) agree that collective industry was less efficient than private industry: 'Entering the 1990s . . . rural public firms began to share the same soft-budget constraints as their urban counterparts . . . They also shouldered other functions such as employment generation. As a result they operated much less efficiently than private firms. These problems provided the impetus for the privatization programs'.

(Brömmelhörster and Frankenstein 1997: 138). Left *in situ*, these enterprises had little hope of becoming efficient in the long run because the combination of their location and the nature of their output.

The problems faced by western China were further compounded by obstacles to factor mobility. The fact that the *gaige kaifang* was incomplete in the sense that barriers to mobility were not demolished after 1978 (regional protectionism tended to offset the impact of growing labour mobility) did the provinces of western China little good. That provinces such as Guizhou and Gansu were able to retain more 'skilled' labour and capital than they might otherwise have been able to do had the reform strategy created a genuinely competitive market system was of scant benefit because this human and physical capital was of such low quality. By limiting the extent of competition, technology transfer and inward investment, rigidities in western China unambiguously hindered—so it is claimed—the process of rural economic growth. A key piece of evidence used here by the orthodoxy is that of regional differences in productivity. Dong and Putterman (1997) found that location in a coastal province raised productivity by between 27 and 60 percent compared with the central provinces, and that productivity in Gansu was 40 percent lower still. A study by Fleisher and Chen (1997: 220) reached a similar conclusion: 'We find that total factor productivity is roughly twice as high in the coastal provinces . . .' Even the raw data show the same pattern. According to the figures assembled by Hare and West (1999: 480), gross output value per worker in TVE manufacturing enterprises located in the coastal region averaged 81 percent more than in the interior. As interesting is their finding that that labour productivity gap cannot be explained in terms of different degrees of capital intensity, a conclusion echoed in the writings of Fleisher and Chen.[14] In short, the provinces of western China needed above all intensified competition and marketization to rid themselves of the rigidities and legacies of the past. For orthodox scholars, the *gaige kaifang* strategy did not go far enough in fully overcoming the legacies of the Maoist and Republican past. The poor provinces of western China were the main losers.

Nevertheless, despite the operation of these powerful path dependency mechanisms in both Sunan and western China, the continued existence of inefficient public sector industry did not prevent rapid rural industrialization in the transition era. This was because pre-1978 rural industrialization was simply too limited to act as a binding constraint. As Sachs and Woo have pointed out, the main difference between China and Russia at the start of the transition process was that industrialization had proceeded very much further in the latter than in the former. In those parts of China where Maoist industrialization had progressed rapidly, post-1978 growth was slow because the state sector crowded-out the

---

[14] As they say, higher labour productivity in the coastal region could in principle have reflected a higher capital-worker ratio. If true, the policy implication would have been that western China needed a massive injection of investment to raise its capital-worker ratio, rather than privatization.

scarce labour and capital needed by the fledgling foreign and private sectors. But outside Manchuria, Sunan and Third Front areas, rural industrialization had barely begun. The overall rate of industrial employment in China's counties was barely 10 percent in 1982, and in many parts of western China—despite the Third Front—it was much less. Moreover, there were even geographically-favoured parts of China where rural industrialization under Mao had left little impression. The provinces of Shandong and Hebei in the north registered employment rates of less than 10 percent at the time of the 1982 Population Census, whilst the two favourably-located south-eastern provinces of Guangdong and Fujian were scarcely more heavily industrialized. As Zhou (1996: 108) notes, the spatial limitations of Maoist industrialization were obvious in the late 1970s: 'Prior to 1978, the scale of rural industries was small and relatively concentrated in a few provinces, Jiangsu and Zhejiang in particular. Despite its rapid growth, the rural share of industrial production was only 7 percent in 1978'. From this orthodox perspective, it was fortunate that Maoist rural industrialization had not proceeded very far. In consequence, there were still ample reserves of labour which could be re-deployed for use in the private and foreign sectors after 1978. The historic contribution of *gaige kaifang* was to unlock this potential.

4.3.2. Re-thinking Efficiency in Developing Countries

The problem with the orthodox critique of post-1978 Chinese rural industry on efficiency grounds is that the measures of efficiency used—industrial TFP and profitability—are extremely dubious.

Even if it is true (as often claimed) that profitability declined between 1978 and the mid-1990s, it is not clear that this reflected a deterioration in efficiency. For one thing, the decline was driven by increasing competition as the monopoly position of the state sector was eroded. Secondly, the decline was driven partly by cyclical factors—a conclusion reinforced by the *rise* in profitability across the entire industrial sector during the cyclical up-turn of 1996–2004.

The data on productivity are equally hard to interpret. Trends in total factor productivity show relatively poor performance but TFP is a thoroughly unreliable guide because of a range of conceptual and measurement problems. For example, shifts in the production function are indistinguishable from movements along the function because increases in the capital stock go hand-in-hand with improvements in technology. We therefore cannot separate the accumulation of factors of production from technical progress: observed increases in labour productivity usually reflects technical progress, not simply capital accumulation (Solow [1970] 1988; Scott 1989; McCombie and Thirlwall 1994; De Long and Summers 1993; Kaldor 1957, [1961] 1989). As Kaldor (1957: 595) put it:

The use of more capital per worker . . . inevitably entails the introduction of superior techniques which require 'inventiveness' of some kind . . . On the other hand, most, though not all, technical innovations which are capable of raising the productivity of labour require the use of more capital per man—more elaborate equipment and/or more mechanical power . . . A society where technical change and adaptation proceed slowly, where producers are reluctant to abandon traditional methods and to adopt new techniques is necessarily one where the rate capital accumulation is small . . . the rate of shift of the production function due to the changing state of 'knowledge' cannot be treated as an independent function of (chronological) time, but depends on the rate of accumulation of capital itself. Since improved knowledge is, largely, if not entirely, infused into the economy through the introduction of new equipment, the rate of shift of the curve will itself depend on the speed of movement along the curve, which makes any attempt to isolate the one from the other the more nonsensical.

(Kaldor [1961] 1989: 263)

In sharp contrast to TFP trends, the data on labour productivity suggest a thoroughly impressive performance; TVE labour productivity rose annually at a rate of 12 percent between 1987 and 1991, and by 15 percent per annum between 1991 and 2002. On this basis, the efficiency of the TVE sector is surely not in doubt.[15]

The more fundamental critique of the orthodoxy is that neither profitability nor productivity offers a true guide to *macroeconomic* efficiency. The assumption implicit in the literature discussed above is that the object of development should be to raise the efficiency of the industrial sector; the absolute size of the industrial sector is not regarded as an issue. Thus the implicit counter-factual is that China could increase its GDP per person by transferring capital and labour from the (low productivity) state sector to the (high productivity) private and foreign sectors.

A better way, however, to think about this issue of how to promote Chinese development is to start from the definition of industrial efficiency offered by Ajit Singh in 1977:

. . . an 'efficient' manufacturing sector must be able to provide (currently and potentially) sufficient net exports to meet the country's overall import requirements at socially acceptable level of output, employment and exchange rate. It is in this important sense that, in spite of the growth in productivity, there is evidence that the UK manufacturing sector is becoming increasingly inefficient.

(Singh 1977: 136)

This is of course an essentially macro-economic definition of efficiency, and that is its great merit.[16] Singh's approach recognizes an essential truth: that the

---

[15] These estimates are based on current price value-added data (He 2004: 218). The data are converted to constant 1990 price data by deflating current price value-added by the all-China GDP and industry deflators (TJNJ 2003: 55, 58). The TVE employment used as the denominator in the calculation is from He (2004: 217).

[16] This definition does not of course imply that industrial expansion *per se* is desirable; the industrial sector has to be competitive as well. If its outputs are of low quality, imports and

policy objective for governments in developing countries ought to be the maximization of *per capita output*. If that is the goal, the obvious policy solution is to put surplus labour to productive use in order to raise output and to provide wage incomes. If the industrial sector of the LDC can absorb surplus labour rapidly, the growth rate of per capita output will be more closely associated with the growth rate of industrial output than with the level or growth rate of industrial productivity, and this underlies Singh's approach. To be sure, an increase in industrial labour productivity will help to raise per capita output. However, an exclusive focus on raising the productivity of the labour force employed in industry may not be an especially sensible objective because the employed labour force in a poor country in the early stages of development is likely to be only a small subset of the economically-active population. Taken to the limit, a focus on productivity implies that an economy based around a single high productivity oil refinery would be a desirable outcome even though such a country would be characterized by massive unemployment.

The issue here is one of second best. In a fully-employed economy, productivity gains are a *sine qua non* for higher per capita output; by definition, that is the only way to raise per capita output. However, in an economy out of general equilibrium (or in an inefficient equilibrium), the calculus must be altogether different. For a poor country, it is more realistic to aim for an outcome which ensures that the labour force is fully employed, rather than one which focuses on maximizing the productivity of the employed subset of the working population; productivity gains are almost irrelevant in an economy characterized by surplus labour. To put it another way, Singh's approach suggests that industrial efficiency rises if industrial output *per capita* rises, even if industrial output *per worker* falls. Unless marginal labour productivity in industry is zero (or negative), an increase in employment will raise per capita output even if it depresses output per worker. Even if worker productivity is less than the private sector norm for a particular plant, low productivity workers in China's state sector, by virtue of being employed, raise per capita industrial output and therefore contribute to raising living standards.[17] In a sense, there is a trade-off. If an economy cannot achieve both full employment and first-best levels of labour

inflation will rise because domestic industry is unable to satisfy consumer demand. This is why the test of efficiency incorporates balance of payments and inflation constraints; it is not enough for the industrial sector to be capable of ensuring full employment. We should also incorporate income distribution into the definition: industrial expansion is not worth having if bought at the expense of the agricultural sector. Thus the expansion of per capita industrial output achieved by China during the Great Leap Forward was not efficient because it was associated with the collapse of agriculture. Singh's approach therefore suggests the following strategy for government: maximize the growth of the industrial sector, subject to the achievement of low inflation, balance of payments equilibrium, and a socially acceptable distribution of income (where acceptability depends primarily upon the levels of agricultural output and the level of employment).

[17] Of course the socially efficient outcome would be to close plants down if productivity was zero, unemployment costs not withstanding.

productivity—and by definition that is the problem for developing countries—it is better to aim for full employment because that has the more positive effect on per capita output. The policy implication is clear: the industrial sector needs to be large enough to meet the full employment demand for manufactures. If the industrial sector is too small, an economy will encounter balance of payments difficulties or inflationary problems because that is the only way excess demand can be accommodated. In a dynamic context, an efficient industrial sector is therefore one capable of generating rapid growth in per capita output and employment.[18]

Applying this approach to China, the conclusion appears to be that efficiency improved only slowly during the Maoist era. Per capita industrial output (excluding construction) grew in real terms at over 16 percent per annum during 1952–57. Thereafter, however, the rate of growth declined, averaging only 6.4 percent during 1957–78. By 1978, the share of industry (the sum of manufacturing, mining and construction) in total employment was 17 percent, well up on the 7 percent recorded in 1952 (Table 4.4). But although this was a creditable achievement, the Chinese industrial share was still far below the figures recorded by OECD countries at the height of their industrialization. In the USA for example, the rate peaked at around 38 percent in 1955, and in Japan at 37 percent in 1973. In West Germany, however, it climbed to 48 percent in 1966, a figure attained in the UK in 1955.

Of course one might argue that it is unrealistic to expect Chinese industrial employment rates to reach the levels recorded in the OECD. In the postwar era,

Table 4.4 Industrial employment shares in China and the OECD (percentage of total employment)

	China	Japan	UK	Germany	USA
1952	7 (1950)	23	47	42	37
1957	9 (1955)	25	48	46	38
1965	8 (1966)	33	46	48	36
1978	17 (1973)	37	43	48	33
1988	22 (1981)	35	36	44	30
1998	23 (2002)	29	24	31	22
2002	21				

Notes: The industrial sector is defined here as industry plus construction and mining. German data are for West Germany for 1981 and earlier. The 2002 data for the OECD countries are a simple average of male and female rates.

Sources: LDNJ (2003: 7–8); Rowthorn and Wells (1987: 358); World Bank (2004: 46–8).

---

[18] Using this criterion, the slowdown in the growth of Soviet GDP per capita after the 1960s should be interpreted as showing that Soviet industrial efficiency was increasing less quickly. The standstill in growth in the early 1980s denotes stagnation. These perspectives, based purely on per capita growth, seem to accord well with other evidence on the fate of the Soviet Union; we do not need data on TFP.

both West Germany and Britain had limited arable area and limited supplies of raw materials, and therefore were relatively heavy importers. Furthermore, the greater capital intensity of production by the 1980s across the world (driven by labour-saving technical progress) reduced the need for industrial enterprises to use labour as intensively as in the 1950s and 1960s. On the other hand, China's arable area is also limited relative to its population, and its mineral resources (though extensive) are not easily exploited. It therefore seems reasonable to conclude that China in 1978 was a long way short of achieving industrial efficiency; its industrial sector was still far too small.

The inadequate size of the Chinese industrial sector by the time of Mao's death is also evident from its inability to meet the demand for manufactures even though per capita incomes were low. That much is clear from the extent of repressed inflation and widespread rationing of consumer and producer goods. This problem was not resolved in the short run by the revival of agriculture in the late 1970s and early 1980s. Indeed higher agricultural incomes increased the demand for manufactures. However, the longer run implication of the rise in agricultural productivity was the creation of surplus labour, and this in turn established the preconditions for much faster industrial expansion.[19] China's overwhelming need by the mid-1980s was to use this labour surplus to develop her industrial sector at a rate that was fast enough to ensure full employment and meet the rising demand for manufactures without the country having to resort to large-scale imports.

As for the efficiency of Chinese industry in the three decades after Mao's death, the evidence indicates that, applying Singh's definition, China still had far to go. Levels of overall industrial employment tell part of the story: the shares achieved even in the late 1990s were low by postwar OECD standards. More significantly, the inadequate size of the Chinese industrial sector is apparent from the macroeconomic problems encountered. True, the balance of payments problem was kept in check, but this reflected the continuing use of tariff barriers; even in the early 1990s, the average tariff rate exceeded 30 percent. But the persistence of inflationary pressures, especially during 1985–86, 1988–90 and 1993–95, demonstrated China's continuing industrial weakness. On each occasion, the failings of the industrial sector compelled the Chinese government to reduce aggregate demand, leading to rises in unemployment. In this way, and especially in the late 1990s, inflation was eliminated, but China's industrial working class bore the burden of adjustment.

---

[19] Low labour productivity in agriculture was the root cause of industrial under-development in the Maoist period, as is clear from the events of the late 1950s. The Great Leap Forward did succeed initially in raising industrial output and employment; by the end of 1958, indeed, industrial employment had soared to nearly 27 percent of the national total. However, because there was little increase in farm labour productivity, the effect of this diversion of labour was to crowd-out agricultural production, thus contributing to the catastrophic famine of 1958–62.

Nevertheless, rural industrialization ensured that China's industrial sector was far *more* efficient by the late 1990s than it had been in 1978. For one thing, it was rural industrial growth which increased China's overall per capita industrial growth rate from the 6.4 percent of the late Maoist era to the 10.8 percent figure averaged during 1978–2002. TVEs were instrumental in this process, expanding their workforce by over 100 million since 1978; by virtue of its very expansion, China's TVE sector has gone some way towards creating the sort of efficient industrial sector that the country requires. Indeed the growth of the TVE sector was absolutely instrumental in meeting growing Chinese home demand for manufactures and thus preventing the full-blown inflationary and balance of payments crises which have afflicted the larger Latin American countries for much of the postwar era.

Secondly, the growing efficiency of China's industrial sector is evident from its rising share in world markets after 1978, a point emphasized by Sanjaya Lall (1992, 2001; Lall and Albaladejo 2004). To be sure, this type of definition ducks the question of absolute competitiveness, but it is not clear that the question of absolutes is a very sensible one to ask. Chinese industry may not be operating on the world production frontier, but one would hardly expect that of a developing country; indeed the expenditure on R & D required by such a strategy would constitute a colossal mis-allocation of resources for a poor county. More fundamentally, it is not clear that China's absolute industrial inefficiency matters given that the country's industrial sector has been able to support a growth rate of per capita output which exceeds that of almost all developing countries. To be sure China is able to exploit its 'cheap labour' but then it would be an odd poor country which did not; why develop high technology industries when one does not need to in the short and medium term? Of course one can always pose the neoclassical counterfactual: China would do even better if it privatized its industrial sector (just as it has been claimed that Japanese industrialization in the 1960s would have been even faster without MITI). However, it is not clear that this type of counterfactual makes sense given that there is no actually-existing market driven economy capable of emulating, let alone surpassing, China.

Applying Lall's approach, the growing efficiency of Chinese rural industry is demonstrated by the way in which it was able to increase dramatically its exports over the course of the 1980s and 1990s, thus generating the foreign exchange needed to finance the modernization of the entire industrial sector. In 1986 (the first year for which we have plausible data), the export value of the TVE sector amounted to only 9.9 billion *yuan*, a mere 209 *yuan* per industrial worker. Thereafter, TVE exports soared. Between 1986 and 1997, the growth rate averaged well over 40 percent per annum and, even after 1997 when global conditions were much less favourable, the rate exceeded 10 percent (He 2004: 217, 221).

The application of this Singh-Lall approach to efficiency also suggests that China's industrial closure programme of the late 1990s was mis-conceived. Some of the enterprises involved may have been subtracting value, and accordingly their closure made sense. But given that China's industrial employment share in the late 1990s was still very low by postwar OECD standards, it is doubtful that the reduction in industrial employment was well advised. Reducing secondary sector employment by 8.2 million jobs (5 percent) between 1998 and 2002 may have increased output per worker, but it did little to promote the growth of per capita industrial output, the true measure of industrial efficiency.[20] For all the (predictable) plaudits accorded in the literature to the privatization programmes of this era, it is far from clear that they have taken China in the right direction. The strategy which closed down county-level SOEs and TVEs during the late 1990s simply on the grounds that they were operating below the production possibility frontier was foolish because of the unemployment implications. Privatization has therefore failed to raise macro-economic efficiency in the Chinese countryside in a true sense because it has failed to generate the full employment of labour.

The central argument being advanced here centres on learning. To be sure, private and foreign-owned companies have set up and operated successfully in some sectors across China; the skill deficit is by no means universal. In the main, however, such enterprises operate in sectors where low wages compensate for low skills (and hence low levels of productivity), or where transport costs are very low (along the Pacific Rim). By contrast, the workers of western and central China lack the skills to produce heavy industrial goods successfully. As a result of a long and extended process of learning, the skills deficit by the 1990s was much less than it had been in the late 1950s: the infant industries of the 1960s and 1970s have matured. Nevertheless, the skills base remains inadequately developed, and skill transfers from east to west remain problematic because few workers, whether foreign or Chinese, want to live and work in the Chinese interior. Even in much of eastern China, the rural skills base remains underdeveloped because so few skilled workers wish to live in the countryside. As a result, many of the state-owned industries operating in rural China remain immature in the sense that a large proportion of their workers are relatively unskilled. The rural industries of western China in particular have moved some way along the learning curve since the 1960s, but they still have far to go. In other words, many of these industries are inefficient by world standards, and compared with some of the industrial enterprises operating in eastern China. But this is not an argument for closure. The industries are infants and they need more time to mature. Closing down these industries would create mass unemployment and lead to a decline in living standards in many parts of China. To criticize these industries for being inefficient in terms of productivity or profitability in any absolute sense is therefore besides the point if the objective is—as it should be—to raise rural living standards. Much of rural China needs more industry rather than less in order to develop its skills base via learning.

[20] The trajectory of manufacturing employment during these years is not entirely clear because of definitional changes which have re-classified some manufacturing jobs as services.

In sum, Chinese rural industry remains absolutely inefficient in the sense that it is operating below the world technological frontier. Nevertheless, if we think of efficiency in broader macro terms as the ability to raise per capita output at a satisfactory rate, the sector has made dramatic progress in the last 30 years. This is shown by its growing share in world markets (despite falling subsidies), and by its ability to meet rapidly rising domestic demand for manufactures. Whereas late Maoist rural industry was extremely inefficient—the sector was too small to meet more than a fraction of the full employment demand for manufactures, and its ability to gain market share was limited—the industrial sector which had been established by the end of the 1990s was a different beast entirely. By the new millennium, the infants of the late Maoist era had grown up.

4.4. The Role of Fiscal Decentralization

The evidence considered above points towards a rejection of the orthodoxy for two reasons. Firstly, China's public sector was the engine of growth in the rural industrialization process. Secondly, when efficiency is properly defined in terms of sectoral size and international competitiveness, China's rural industrial sector made impressive progress in the period after 1978. The analytical problem is therefore to explain how the inefficient industries of the Maoist era became the efficient enterprises of the transition era.

4.4.1. The Revisionist Hypothesis

The explanation for this transformation offered by revisionist scholars is that the improvement in efficiency was brought about by policy change. More precisely, it was the element of fiscal decentralization embodied in the *gaige kaifang* package which was decisive (Oi 1992; Shirk 1993; Huang 1996; Oi 1999; Lin and Liu 2000), even if it may also have played a role in creating inflationary pressures (Brandt and Zhu 2000; Feltenstein and Iwata 2005) and created adverse distributional effects (Park et al. 1996; Wang and Hu 1999, 2001).[21]

Now there is no doubt that the Chinese fiscal system changed after Mao's death. In particular, pressure from some of the main contributing provinces ('playing to the provinces' as Shirk calls it), persuaded central government to introduce a new system of 'eating in separate kitchens' (*fen zao chifan*) in place of the old system of *chi daguo fan* ('eating out of the same big pot'). Under this new approach, richer regions retained more of their surplus, and the position of poorer regions was protected, a circle squared only by central government

---

[21] Useful discussions of the Chinese fiscal system are offered by Wong et al. (1995), Wong (1997) and Brean (1998). For a critical account of fiscal decentralization, see Zhang and Zou (1998).

acceptance of a declining share in total tax revenue. Fiscal decentralization (*fangquan rangli*) was pioneered in Jiangsu in 1977, where the introduction of *guding bili baogan* (fixed rate contact) specified that the province could retain 42 percent of revenue raised over the following four years. The key national reform did not occur until 1980. That year saw a lump sum system introduced in Guangdong and Fujian, a fixed rate system (based on the Jiangsu model) put in place for the great metropolitan centres, whilst all the remaining provinces operated a system under which specific types of revenue were shared between province and centre (Shirk 1993: 166–8).

The scale of the decentralization is apparent from the provincial public finance data (TJJ 1999). Richer provinces like Jiangsu and Liaoning continued to be net contributors, but the scale of their contributions fell significantly; in Liaoning's case, the ratio of revenue to expenditure halved between the 1970s and 1982–88. Shanghai is a further example of this. Indeed many would argue that fiscal decentralization has been a key element in the revival of the city's fortunes after the late 1980s because its greater ability to retain revenue provided it with the surpluses needed to modernize obsolete urban infrastructure.

Further fiscal reforms followed during the 1980s. The 1988 reform, for example, treated fast-growing provinces even more favourably by specifying that a certain proportion of 1988 revenue would be handed over to central government but that a smaller proportion of any additional revenue would be remitted (Shirk 1993: 192–3). This *shouru dizeng baogan* system was designed to provide provinces with the incentive to increase revenue by reducing the marginal remittance rate. The system which had evolved by the early 1990s had two distinct elements: contracted transfers and earmarked transfers (Wong et al. 1995: 90–8; Wong 1997: 48–57). On the one hand, all China's provinces had agreed a fiscal contract which specified either the remittance of a certain amount to the centre (rich provinces), or that they received an agreed subsidy (poor provinces). In addition, every province received earmarked transfers from central government. Some of these earmarked subsidies were for capital construction. However, no less than 59 percent of all earmarked grants took the form of price subsidies (Wong 1997: 53). These necessarily benefited affluent, urbanized, areas. Thus Guangdong's 1990 contracted remittance of 5.2 billion *yuan* was partially offset by an earmarked inflow of 1.24 billion *yuan* (Wong et al. 1995: 98).

The fiscal reforms of 1994 engineered by Zhu Rongji partially reversed the trend towards decentralization. The new tax-sharing system (*fengshuizhi*) operated by assigning the revenue from all the various forms of taxation to either central or to local government, thus in effect guaranteeing certain types of revenue to each level of government (Wong 1997: 31–8). But the system has been at best only a partial success (Naughton 1997: 259–65). It has, to be sure, increased the central government share of tax revenue, but only rather modestly. The main reason is that the physical process of tax collection remains in the hands of local government, which has little incentive to collect revenue which are simply handed over to central government. And local governments have been able to camouflage their success in raising revenue by ensuring that the revenue is collected in the form of extra-budgetary levies rather than formal taxation. Furthermore, the central government was only able to persuade the provinces to accept the new system by agreeing to provide a large tax rebate based upon provincial ability to raise revenue for the centre. As a result, fast-growing coastal provinces have tended to receive very substantial rebates (Lee 2000: 1013–20). Although the central government has continued to provide subsidies to the western provinces, these subsidies have grown only modestly. Furthermore, the provinces of *central* China have tended to do badly because they have no claim on central fiscal resources on either ethnic or frontier grounds.

How did this decentralization promote rural industrialization? According to Jean Oi, the changes introduced after 1978 were critical because they hardened the budget constraints faced by local government. In particular, local governments concluded revenue contracts with central government which were much more binding than had been the case in the Maoist era (Oi 1999: 47–8). As a result, the revenue-sharing arrangements of the 1980s and 1990s involved a credible commitment on the part of central government, giving local government much more certainty as to its revenue stream. This served in effect to lower the marginal (central government) rate of taxation on the profits made by local industries, and thus provided local government with an incentive to create profitable rural industries. It was therefore fiscal decentralization which led directly to the creation of an *efficient* rural industrial sector and which ensured that what Oi (1999: 62) calls the '. . . the dismal performance of the state in managing economic development during the Maoist period . . .' was not repeated. As the revenue-sharing contracts stipulated that each level of government received a fixed share of locally-raised revenue, local government had a clear incentive to increase its revenue base. The system was not lump sum (though some levels of government did negotiate such agreements), but it still provided localities with a strong incentive to develop profitable local enterprises. Thus the 'five small industries' of the Maoist era, with their focus on heavy industrial output and assisting the development of agriculture, were quickly abandoned in favour of labour-intensive light industries producing a range of consumer goods. Just as the 'easy money' of the Maoist era induced all manner of wasteful investment and duplication, so the 'tight money' of the post-Mao era encouraged more efficient investment decisions. Even though many of the new rural enterprises were state-owned, they still operated relatively efficiently. The industries themselves did not face a hard budget constraint but local government did, and it was this which induced efficient investment decisions. As a result, rural industry blossomed.

For Oi and others (Cao et al. 1999; Lau et al. 2000; Wu 2005), the twin characteristics of rural industrialization after the 1978 watershed were that it was state-led and that the industries in the van of the process were increasingly efficient:

In the 1980s, much of China's post-Mao rapid rural industrialization occurred in *local government-owned enterprises at the township and village levels*. This fact is sometimes forgotten ... [the orthodoxy] ... misrepresents the character of these enterprises and misidentifies the pivotal actors in the process of China's rural industrialization ... it was the institutions inherited from the pre-reform period that provided local governments with the basic tools to foster the rapid growth of rural industry. The Maoist system was plagued by economic inefficiency but once modified to allow for local initiative ... this system became the basis of a new and efficient form of local state-led development ...

(Oi 1999: 62–3, 95–6; original emphasis)

As Oi also stresses, decentralization only worked because officials were motivated by material incentives after 1978. Indeed the behaviour of local government officials changed after the late 1970s. Before that time, decision-making was heavily influence by political and ideological constraints, as dictated by the Maoist slogan 'politics in command'. As a result, local officials had little incentive to develop successful rural industries; local revenue was guaranteed by central government, and 'politics in command' meant that the ideological commitment of officials was far more important than their economic competence. According to Oi (1999: 6):

For China the issue was not whether its bureaucracy was *capable* of generating economic growth but whether it had the *incentive* to do so ... During the Maoist period, the constraints of the state plan and the fiscal system provided localities with little inducement to generate additional revenues ... China's bureaucrats could be mobilized to action, but Maoist ideology distorted incentives.

(emphasis added)

After 1978, as is well known, the CCP increasingly downplayed the importance of adherence to ideological and political norms for local government officials. China was deemed to be in the 'primary stage' of socialism, and therefore rapid economic development was the main aim. Instead, promotion prospects, as well as pay and conditions of employment, were increasingly linked to economic success. Local economic development therefore assumed instrumental significance for government cadres in a way it had not done in the late Maoist era. Linking the promotion, pay and conditions of employment of local government officials to economic success necessarily provided them with a powerful incentive to revenue-maximize. But this in itself would not have been enough to spur local economic development because, under a centralized system, local officials could only have increased the revenue available to them by bargaining more effectively with the centre. Fiscal decentralization closed off this option. Only by means of economic development could local officials create the surpluses necessary to finance both rapid growth, and improvements in pay and conditions. In short, the process of fiscal decentralization gave the local bureaucracy the incentive it needed for efficient industrial production (Oi 1999: 56).

As importantly, (although the argument is given comparatively little emphasis by Oi), fiscal decentralization had powerful income effects on local government budgets in many cases. In particular, decentralization had the effect of transferring a significant part of the re-investible surplus from central to local government, thus providing the localities with the resources needed to finance the programme of industrial expansion. This worked in two ways. On the one hand, it allowed local governments to invest directly in locally state-owned enterprises of various kinds thus providing the foundation for the expansion of the local state sector. On the other hand, it allowed local government to invest in infrastructure, which was important because it facilitated the expansion of the private sector and served to encourage inward investment (Brandt and Zhu 2000; Feltenstein and Iwata 2005).

4.4.2. The Interplay of Geography and Fiscal Decentralization

Not the least of the attractions of Oi's hypothesis that fiscal decentralization played a critical role in spurring rural industry is that it helps to explain regional differences across China in the rural industrialization process. These regional differences were considerable. In the coastal provinces, especially in southern Jiangsu and northern Zhejiang, the growth rate was relatively rapid after 1978. However, in central provinces such as Henan or Anhui, the pace of growth was considerably slower. And in the western provinces, especially within their least geographically-favoured prefectures, growth was slower still. In view of this evidence, it is a simple matter to link together fiscal decentralization with the size of the local tax base to provide a coherent explanation of differences in regional growth rates.

Take Sunan. In that region, precisely because its geography was so favourable, the investible surplus was large, and fiscal decentralization thus placed a large surplus in the hands of local officials. As Wang and Hu (1999) point out, fiscal decentralization played into the hands of well-favoured parts of China such as Jiangsu, Zhejiang and Guangdong. By contrast, the challenge for the poor counties of western China was to create *any* sort of rural industry because successful rural industrialization depended upon more than just incentives. For many poor counties, the problem was the inadequacy of resources to finance the establishment of rural industry in the first place: locally-raised revenue typically fell short of expenditure in the early 1980s.[22] In the case of Guizhou province, locally-available revenue financed only about one third of state expenditure.

---

[22] Under the Chinese system, profits made by SOEs owned by central government operating within a given province were transferred to central government ministries. Much of the revenue raised via the industrial and commercial tax also accrued to the centre. This necessitated large transfers of resources back to the areas where the revenue had been collected in the first place.

For the period 1982–88, however, the local contribution had risen to 60 percent indicating a greater degree of decentralization. The deficit in Guizhou, as in other provinces, was financed principally by two types of state subsidies, fixed (or quota) subsidies and earmarked subsidies. In the case of Gansu, there was a revenue shortfall of 762 million *yuan* in 1985 (TJJ 1999: 799). This was closed by means of a fixed subsidy from the centre of 246 million *yuan* and earmarked subsidies to the tune of a further 541 million *yuan* (GSSQ 1988: 359; Wong 1997: 54). Of this latter, 250 million was paid for poverty relief in the 66 counties identified as poor in that year. In Shaanxi's case, the 1985 revenue shortfall of 720 million *yuan* was covered by a fixed subsidy of 270 million *yuan* and earmarked subsidies of 560 millions (Park et al. 1996: 755).

The problem for these poor provinces was that their subsidies, if not absolutely 'fixed', rose only slowly. Gansu's fixed subsidy was 199 million in 1983 and 1984, and rose to 246 million in 1985 (GSSQ 1988: 359). However, it remained at 246 millions in 1986 and 1987 (Wong 1997: 51). Given relatively high inflation, the real value of this subsidy therefore declined significantly over time. To be sure, earmarked subsidies varied from year to year in response to changes in provincial income. For example, Gansu's subsidy for poverty relief in poor counties rose from 136 million *yuan* in 1983 (when 59 counties were identified as poor) to 250 million *yuan* in 1985 (when there were 66 poor counties). However, the link between provincial income and earmarked subsidies was not a precise one and therefore the province often faced a shortfall. In 1988, for example, expenditure exceeded income by 1.14 billion *yuan* (TJJ 1999: 799) and the province received only 126 million in fixed subsidies and 627 million in earmarked subsidies (Wong 1997: 51, 54). The remaining deficit—387 million *yuan*—had to be financed from extrabudgetary sources, miscellaneous levies or by borrowing.

In such circumstances, there was a clear incentive to create additional sources of revenue by developing rural industries. There was also a good deal of pressure to cut investment to meet current expenditure needs (Park et al. 1996: 777). A second side effect was that poor counties have often been tempted to follow the Sunan model and develop rural industries even when conditions have not been suitable.[23] In the immediate aftermath of the agricultural miracle of the early 1980s, a small number of affluent locations in eastern China already enjoyed 'first mover' advantage because they possessed a comparatively well-developed rural industrial base. Their position was further enhanced by

[23] According to Wong (1997), and Nyberg and Rozelle (1999), the governments of poor Chinese regions should favour infrastructure construction over manufacturing enterprises because economic geography fatally constrains manufacturing production: 'Instead of focusing on revenue generation, poverty alleviation strategies should focus on removing the resource disadvantages that most commonly cause poverty. Improving infrastructure by investing in both physical and human capital is essential. Such investments are more likely to increase fiscal capacity in poor areas in the long run than government-directed investment in rural enterprises' (Wong 1997: 328).

decentralization because it allowed them to make full use of the surplus created by agricultural growth. These supply-side advantages interacted with chronic excess demand for consumer products across China in the early 1980s to ensure that many eastern regions secured large rents. By the 1990s, when poor regions attempted to shift out of agriculture and into industry, these rents not longer existed because of growing competition. In many respects, therefore, it was a perfectly rational choice on the part of banks and other financial institutions not to lend money for TVE development in western China. The long run social rate of return may have been high, but the short run private rate of return was not. Fiscal decentralization has therefore disadvantaged poor regions and this explains much of the regional differential in the pace of rural industrialization (Wang and Hu 1999, 2001).

4.4.3. Timing: Fiscal Decentralization Before 1978

The fiscal decentralization argument has a compelling logic about it. Not only does it explain rapid rural industrial growth but also it is able to explain regional differentiation. However, there is a problem over timing.

Oi and others have argued that the process was in its essentials a post-1978 phenomenon. Yet the evidence points towards a relatively decentralized system well before Mao's death. For the twin imperatives of defence industrialization and agricultural modernization in the late Maoist era spawned not merely the Third Front, but also a programme of fiscal decentralization designed to promote rural industrialization. Whereas the Third Front focused on the development of heavy industry in a limited number of locations, fiscal decentralization aimed at the China-wide promotion of rural industry. This was because only industrial self-sufficiency would ensure that agricultural modernization could not be halted by the interdiction of transport links, an obvious potential bombing strategy for any aggressor in the event of the bulk of agricultural producer goods being produced in Shanghai, Manchuria and Beijing-Tianjin. The logic was impeccable. Military considerations alone made it foolish to assume that policy could be devised and carried out from Beijing; the localities had to be given both the freedom and the resources to create independent industrial kingdoms. As Mao (1966a) argued at an enlarged meeting of the Politburo in March 1966: 'When war starts, will it be possible to issue *Renmin Ribao*? It is necessary to pay attention to the division of power. Do not empty the pond to catch fish. At present, there is no one to administer things at the top. At the lower levels there is no one who has the authority to administer things. At present, fighting for one's independence is permitted. There must be independence against bureaucracy.' In 1970, Mao is alleged to have gone still further, arguing that '. . . decentralization is a revolution and the more decentralization the greater the revolution' (Shirk 1993: 160; Wu 2005: 53).

More importantly, the CCP went well beyond a mere articulation of the rhetoric of decentralization in the Maoist era. In November 1957, partial control of the revenue streams of state-owned enterprises was transferred from central to local government. To be sure, the system was gradually recentralized between 1959 and the mid-1960s, but a new process of decentralization began following the meeting of the Forum for National Planning in February 1969. By the end of September 1969, the nine central ministries had transferred no fewer than 2,237 of their 3,082 enterprises to local government; those affected by the transfer included Anshan Steel, the Daqing oil company and the great Changchun lorry-producing factory (Liu and Wu 1986: 364). In 1970, in an explicit attempt to promote rural industry, a special fund was set up and local government was allowed to keep 60 percent of the profits made by the five small industries in the first three years (Liu and Wu 1986: 362). Given that rural industrial take-off did not occur in the 1970s, the very fact that fiscal decentralization was so extensive in the late Maoist era suggests that decentralization was not by itself enough to generate rural industrial growth. This implies that it was the removal of some other form of binding constraint on rural industrialization after 1978 which was decisive, not the fiscal decentralization process itself.

The main counter-argument to this rather negative appraisal of the decentralization hypothesis is implicit in the extensive literature on the issue of centralization and decentralization in the late Maoist fiscal system (Donnithorne 1967, 1972, 1976; Lardy 1976, 1978; Riskin 1987; Hsiao 1987; Oksenberg and Tong 1991; Wei 2000b). This literature, though it does not address the specific issue of rural industrialization, is important because much of it concludes that the decentralization drives of 1957 and at the end of the 1960s were more notional than real. Lardy (1978), for example, concluded that the Chinese system was much less 'cellular' than argued by Donnithorne; whatever the notional degree of decentralization, massive re-distribution between the localities was achieved by central government in the late Maoist era.

This debate has to some extent been resolved by the release of a range of financial data for the 1960s and 1970s. These data make it clear that the late Maoist system combined elements of re-distribution with elements of fiscal decentralization. On the one hand, it is abundantly clear that the fiscal system was never fully decentralized. The central government continued to re-distribute funds from rich to poor provinces or, to use the Chinese term, provinces 'ate out of the same big pot'. Thus poor and ethnic minority provinces such as Xinjiang, Tibet, Qinghai, Yunnan, Guizhou and Guangxi were net recipients, whereas the metropolitan centres (Beijing, Shanghai and Tianjin) and more industrialized provinces such as Liaoning and Jiangsu were net contributors (Oksenberg and Tong 1991; Shirk 1993; Wang and Hu 1999).[24] As Wong rightly notes, central

[24] Gansu—though a poor province in terms of per capita rural income—was actually a net contributor to the national exchequer in the late 1970s. This reflected high levels of revenue generated by industrial enterprises which at that time were under provincial control (see World Bank 1988: 14–15; TJJ 1999). In fairness, Gansu was not a particularly poor province if measured by its per capita GDP. This reflected the exploitation of its extensive mineral resources via state investment in heavy industry in the Maoist period.

government attempted to play a key role in developing rural industry in backward regions which lacked the resources for purely self-sufficient development. Local jurisdictions were to be self-reliant in the long run, but much of the *initial* funding came from the central government budget, and much of the equipment from urban state-owned enterprises. For example, in order to compensate for the 'weak' industrial base in China's backward provinces and autonomous regions, Shanghai's factories were instructed to produce 100 sets of small-scale equipment for the production of nitrogenous fertilizer each year for three years, starting in 1970 (Yang and Tao 1988: 56).

On the other hand, it is clear that fiscal re-distribution was circumscribed because a part of locally-raised revenue was retained and invested locally. This is suggested by trends in spatial inequality: the data show that per capita GDP rose faster in rich provinces than it did in poor provinces in the late 1950s and, after declining in the aftermath of the Great Leap Forward, rose steadily during the late 1960s and throughout the 1970s. Wei's (2000*a*: 28) data, for example, show the provincial coefficient of variation for per capita national income rising from a little less than 0.9 in 1963 to well over 1.2 by the late 1970s. A simple two-way comparison between Guizhou and Jiangsu provinces makes the same point. The ratio of per capita GDP (current prices) for the two stood at 1.72 to 1 in Jiangsu's favour in 1963, but by 1978 it had risen to 2.46 to 1. The pattern is little different if GDP is measured at constant prices; per capita GDP in Jiangsu rose by 137 percent in real terms between 1963 and 1978 but by only 74 percent in Guizhou (TJJ 1999: 367–8, 700–1). These spatial differentials could not have occurred if the fiscal system had been highly re-distributive because such a system would have denied rich provinces the investible surpluses needed to finance rapid growth. Thus although the Maoist system may have aimed to reduce inequality, the evidence points strongly in the direction of a process of cumulative causation, at least at the provincial level, after the early 1960s. The initial advantages enjoyed by coastal provinces in terms of their inheritance and their innate physical geography seem to have increased over time because part of their investible surplus were retained locally.

An alternative and more direct insight is offered by fiscal and investment flows after the 1970 decentralization. For China as a whole, the local government share in total budgetary revenue was 68 percent in 1964–66, but by 1972–74, its share had risen to 85 percent. To put this another way, local government revenue rose by 39 billion *yuan* between 1968 and 1974, whereas central government revenue rose by only 2.7 billion *yuan*. The effect of decentralization is even more apparent if we make a Jiangsu-Guizhou comparison. Between 1969 and 1978, gross capital formation in Guizhou increased by a factor of 2.3 whereas in Jiangsu it rose by a factor of 3.7, indicating the substantially greater surplus available in the richer coastal province (TJJ 1999: 18, 370, 703).

The sub-provincial data tend to confirm that the fiscal system embodied a considerable degree of decentralization during the late Maoist period, especially during the 1970s. In general, three sources of revenue can be identified. Firstly, counties were allocated funds as part of the state budgetary process. Revenues raised within a county were remitted upwards within the government hierarchy and then a portion was returned to the county. In the case of poor counties, these return flows were much greater than the initial revenue remitted upwards but for rich counties budgetary income remitted upward always exceeded budgetary expenditure. Expenditure totals were carefully negotiated between the county and upper levels of government, and accordingly counties had little control over expenditure patterns; in this sense, the system was highly centralized. Nevertheless, as the detailed study by Blecher and Shue (1996) makes clear, central government put in place an incentive structure to ensure that counties met their budgetary revenue targets. The revenue the counties received from this incentive system went into the extrabudgetary fund under the county's control (Blecher and Shue 1996: 48–9, 85–6). Shulu's experience does not seem to have been very different to that of other counties. For example, both Guanghan (Sichuan) and Tonglu (Zhejiang) received a significant portion of extrabudgetary income from county-run enterprises (Touglu XZ 1991: 351; Guanghan XZ 1992: 307).

Secondly, a proportion of the stream of revenue generated by industries reporting to central ministries was retained within Chinese counties. These retained profits were at the disposal of local ministry officials (not the county government), but in practice their decision-making was heavily influenced by the wishes of county officials. Accordingly, counties had a clear incentive to promote the development of these sorts of industries. Blecher and Shue (1996: 56, 76–80) give the example of the Second Light Industry bureau in Shulu, which was allowed to retain a large proportion of the profits made by its collective enterprises between 1968 and 1986. These retained profits (the rest was transferred upwards to the ministries), equivalent to some 6 percent of county budgetary income in 1979, could be used by the Bureau and by the collective industries themselves to finance industrial expansion because investment decisions, though subject to approval by the prefectural authorities, were essentially made at a local level. These county-level COEs were thus both inside and outside the plan. Some of their profits accrued centrally, but a significant part was available for local use.

The third revenue stream for the county was its extrabudgetary income. As already noted, the incentive system established as part of the budgetary process contributed to the extrabudgetary fund. There were, however, other important sources of extrabudgetary income. One was a share in the profits made by the five small industries which counties were explicitly encouraged to set up and run (as county-owned SOEs) after 1970. In Guanghan, some 60 percent of profits made by county-run enterprises could be retained by the county for the first three years after investment, a figure which was lowered to 50 percent in 1976 and raised to 80 percent in 1977 (Guanghan XZ 1992: 304). As for other Sichuan counties, exactly the same ratios were applied in Pengxian (Peng XZ 1989: 516), though somewhat lower retention rates were allowed in Shehong (Shehong XZ 1990: 445) and Wushan (Wushan XZ 1991: 284). In Nanchong, a 50 percent rate was allowed in 1976, and this increased to 60 percent in 1978 (Nanchong XZ 1993: 418). In all these cases, the explicit aim was to promote the development of the five small industries.

Blecher and Shue (1996: 57, 82–6) note a number of other extrabudgetary sources for Shulu. For example, revenue was raised via surtaxes on the industrial and commercial tax, and on the agricultural tax and increasingly from the profits of industrial CBEs themselves. Even more importantly, the county was able to raise revenue from extrabudgetary enterprises—county-owned SOEs whose revenue stream after the payment of income tax fell *outside* the state budget. Also important in Shulu was the enterprise depreciation fund (*zhejiu jijin*), and this was very significant as a source of extrabudgetary revenue in Zhejiang's Linhai county (Linhai XZ 1989: 459) and in Jiangshan. This fund was typically split between the enterprise, the county and the prefecture in varying proportions; in Jiangshan (Jiangshan SZ 1990: 295), the fund provided over a quarter of extrabudgetary revenue in 1978. The county component could be shifted from enterprise to enterprise to promote growth.[25]

A precise breakdown of extrabudgetary funds are not available for Shulu (Blecher and Shue 1996: 82), but they do exist for some counties. In Guanghan, for example, retained profits from county-level enterprises contributed 39 percent of total extrabudgetary income in 1975, and 56 percent in 1978 (Guanghan XZ 1992: 307). The comparable ratios for Shehong were 29 percent in 1974 and 42 percent in 1978 (Shehong XZ 1990: 451).

4.4.4. The Limits to Revisionism: Pre-1978 Industrial Failure and Fiscal Decentralization

The evidence reviewed above suggests that the late Maoist fiscal system combined elements of both fiscal re-distribution from rich to poor localities, and a decentralized structure which encouraged county governments to develop profitable rural industries. By so doing, localities could raise a significant volume of extrabudgetary funds which could be used to finance expenditure. In that sense, it seems reasonable to conclude that Maoist fiscal decentralization was real, and not merely notional.

Nevertheless, the real analytical challenge is to assess the significance of fiscal decentralization. Oi argues that fiscal decentralization before 1978 meant little for rural industrial development for two reasons. Firstly, the extrabudgetary fund was not large, and even where the funds existed, they were still subject to tight central control (Oi 1999: 38–9). Secondly, pre-1980 fiscal contracts were

---

[25] A good discussion of this fund is provided by Hsiao (1987: 93–4). The Ministry of Finance issued regulations in 1973 which stipulated for its use in this way (Mianzhu XZ 1992: 502).

not very credible and therefore, uncertain of the resources likely to be available, localities were reluctant to commit to a programme of long run industrial expansion:

For a residual to be effective in generating local economic growth there must be credible commitment on the part of the principal, the central state . . . The Mao period fiscal policies failed to provide such commitment to the localities . . . localities had little assurance that they would benefit from increased revenues. Pre-1980 fiscal contracts were valid for only one year. No clear limits applied to the central share; that left uncertain the residual for the localities. Use of what little surplus revenue remained at the local levels required upper-level approval.

(Oi 1999: 48)

However, the evidence is more difficult to interpret than Oi implies. As far as the credibility argument is concerned, it is arguable, at least on the basis of those data which do exist, that extrabudgetary revenue from enterprise profits was not especially volatile. To be sure, the (de facto) marginal tax rate levied by central government was subject to annual re-negotiation during the 1970s, and the data for Guanghan and Shehong do show considerable fluctuation (Table 4.5). Nevertheless, it is clear that county governments could count on a significant annual revenue stream—provided they could successfully develop profitable industrial enterprises.[26]

Table 4.5 County extrabudgetary income from industrial enterprises in Sichuan (million current *yuan*)

	Guanghan county	Shehong county
1974	0.29	0.53
1975	0.52	0.32
1976	0.30	0.50
1977	0.29	0.56
1978	1.45	0.61
1979	0.36	0.70
1980	0.44	1.09
1981	0.94	0.98
1982	1.03	0.85
1983	1.27	0.81
1984	2.35	1.67

Sources: Guanghan XZ (1992: 307); Shehong XZ (1990: 451–2).

[26] The microeconomics of Oi's argument are also more ambivalent than is often realized. The fiscal decentralization of which she writes is properly regarded as a cut in the marginal tax rate faced by local government. However, as is well known, cuts in marginal tax rates have income as well as substitution effects. To be sure, the tax cut provided an incentive to create new and profitable enterprises (the substitution effect). However, it also increased the revenue stream enjoyed by local government from existing enterprises. It is therefore by no means impossible that the fiscal decentralization process might have discouraged rural industrialization; that

Secondly, although local expenditure may have required central government approval, the evidence suggests that local governments did use those resources available to them to help foster rural industrial development. Guanghan in Sichuan is a case in point. Its accounts explicitly report that extrabudgetary spending on investment in local industries rose from around 150,000 *yuan* per annum at the start of the 1970s to over 900,000 *yuan* by 1978, which amounted to 50 percent of all extrabudgetary spending (Guanghan XZ 1992: 313). Total within-budget spending for the county for all purposes was only 7.7 million, so this evidently amounted to a very significant contribution. Shehong county also recorded a big increase in extrabudgetary enterprise investment in the 1970s. In 1978, over 75 percent of extrabudgetary spending was deployed in this way, equivalent to about 8 percent of all budgetary spending (Shehong XZ 1990: 460–1).

Nevertheless, the pattern was far from universal. The experience of Songjiang county on the outskirts of Shanghai is revealing. CBE gross output value rose by a spectacular 27 percent per year in the county between 1970 and 1978. However, this seems to have owed little to extrabudgetary expenditure. Extrabudgetary income rose by only 36 percent between 1970 and 1978, and in the latter it accounted for only 3 percent of budgetary income. Furthermore, little county income was spent directly on rural industrialization. Extrabudgetary expenditure data do not include industrial spending as a separate category and show rather that the bulk of spending was on agriculture. And budgetary investment in the five small industries was typically less than 0.5 million *yuan* in the mid-1970s, far below the 1.7 million *yuan* invested in the sector in 1958 (Songjiang XZ 1991: 655, 659–60 and 663). This evidence is not decisive; we cannot be sure whether the county was raising and spending large sums which were simply not recorded in the extrabudgetary category. But there is little here to suggest that CBE growth was being propelled by fiscal decentralization. In short, the evidence on the impact of fiscal decentralization on rural industrialization prior to 1978 is ambivalent. In some areas, like Shulu, Guanghan and Shehong, extrabudgetary expenditure on CBEs does seem to have been important. In other counties such as Songjiang, it was apparently much less significant. The evidence does not refute Oi's contention, but neither does it properly support it.

A third weakness in Oi's argument is that the county-level data, though by no means entirely consistent, suggest that the significance of extrabudgetary income rose steadily well before the 1978 climacteric. If we consider a selection

would certainly be the outcome if the income effect outweighed the substitution effect. Just as tax cuts may lead workers to work less hard, so too the effect of fiscal decentralization on local government. In regions such as Sunan where the rural industrial sector was already well-developed in the early 1980s, local governments may well have responded to fiscal decentralization by *reducing* investment in rural industry: why invest in risky new industries when the revenue stream from established industries was large enough to finance most key government expenditure objectives? It is also worth noting that some empirical studies have concluded that fiscal decentralization.

of Zhejiang counties, the ratio of extrabudgetary to budgetary spending in the late 1970s were 10 percent in Tonglu (Tonglu XZ 1991: 350–1), 28 percent in Jiangshan (Jiangshan SZ 1990: 292, 295), 18 percent in Haiyan (Haiyan XZ 1992: 493), 13 percent in Jiashan (Jiashan XZ 1995: 548–9) and 44 percent in Haining (Haining SZ 1995: 577–8). If we look at Sichuan, Guanghan's 1978 figure was 12 percent (Guanghan XZ 1992: 306–7). In Mianzhu, the corresponding figure was 14 percent (Mianzhu XZ 1992: 491, 503). In Pengxian, it averaged over 10 percent in the late 1970s (Peng XZ 1989: 510). The county-evidence also shows that extrabudgetary revenue rose quickly during the 1970s (and of course was further enhanced as commune and brigade industry started to develop). In Jiangshan, extrabudgetary income rose fivefold between the early 1970s and 1978 (Jiangshan SZ 1990: 295). In Guanghan, it increased about fourfold (Guanghan XZ 1992: 307). In Mianzhu, it increased by 2.7 fold between 1975 and 1978 (Mianzhu XZ 1992: 503). In Shehong, the increase between 1978 and 1970 was 3.4 fold (Shehong XZ 1990: 451). Again, this evidence points towards the conclusion that many observers over-state the degree to which the emergence of extrabudgetary revenue was a phenomenon which post-dated the 1978 climacteric. There is universal agreement that they grew rapidly in the 1980s, but it is evident that this growth had begun in the 1970s.

In fairness, the county-level data do not suggest a uniform picture. In Deqing (Zhejiang), extrabudgetary revenue as a percentage of budgetary revenue was less than 5 percent in 1978 (Deqing XZ 1992: 331, 334). They were also negligible in Pinghu county until 1978 when the county was allowed to retain 30 percent of SOE profits for extrabudgetary purposes (Pinghu XZ 1993: 485). In Songjiang, the 1978 figure for extrabudgetary income was only 3 percent of budgetary income (Songjiang XZ 1991: 655, 663). Nevertheless, taken as a whole, this evidence suggests that Oi's claim that extrabudgetary revenue in the 1970s was 'minimal at best' goes too far. In many counties, extrabudgetary income appears to have been substantial and growing in the late 1970s.

In summary, the evidence suggests that Oi over-states the extent to which the death of Mao was a watershed in the evolution of the process of fiscal decentralization. Extrabudgetary income stream were sizeable in the 1970s, and they were stable enough to allow at least a degree of long run industrial planning. There is therefore a strong case for considering the fiscal decentralization of 1970 to have been the turning point, rather than any event during the late 1970s or early 1980s. This evidence is of great significance because it tends to undermine any fiscal explanation of rural industrialization. If, as Oi claims, fiscal decentralization was the prime mover in the industrialization process because of its incentive effects, and given that fiscal decentralization pre-dated 1978, rural industrial development ought to have taken off in the 1970s. But it did not. Industrial growth was rising, but there is no obvious discontinuity—the opposite of what one would expect if the fiscal decentralization of 1970 was so important. Furthermore, much of the growth which did occur before 1978 reflected the contribution of the Third Front and the development of county-level SOEs in the 1960s—the opposite of what one would expect if decentralization was so important. And the notion that fiscal decentralization led to the creation of efficient industries is contradicted by the extensive evidence on poor industrial performance in the 1970s. My reading of all this evidence is therefore that fiscal decentralization dates from 1970 rather than 1978, but that it did not ignite rural industrial take-off. It seems, therefore, that we might do better to regard decentralization and rural industrialization as essentially independent processes.

4.5. Conclusion

Both orthodox and revisionist scholars offer an explanation for the pace and pattern of rural industrial growth which incorporates geography, historical legacies and policy change. In the eyes of both, it is policy change which provides the essential growth dynamic. The orthodoxy stresses the removal of constraints on private ownership, both foreign or domestic. The revisionists point to the role played by fiscal decentralization in providing an incentive for efficient local government management of industrial enterprises. Nevertheless, there is agreement between orthodox and revisionist scholars that it was the death of Mao and the accession of Deng Xiaoping which marks a watershed in the rural industrialization process: it made policy change possible.

As for the regional pattern of rural industrialization, the literature suggests that policy change interacted with geography and historical legacies to produce spatial disparities. In the eyes of the orthodoxy, Sunan's geographical advantages were offset by the very extent of Maoist industrialization, which left a vast array of inefficient enterprises as its most enduring legacy. Precisely because these enterprises had absorbed labour, skilled and unskilled alike, they ensured that the region's growth was path-dependent. The growth rate was by no means slow in the 1980s, but ultimately the extensive Maoist industrial legacy was ruinous because it delayed the development of efficient private sector industries. By contrast, the Pearl River Delta and Wenzhou fared extremely well after 1978. Their coastal geography made the regions attractive to foreign investment, and they had little inherited industry to hold them back. Revisionist scholarship focuses on the interaction of geography with fiscal decentralization. Thus Jiangsu did so well after 1978 precisely because, as a geographically well-favoured region, it was capable of generating a large surplus which the new fiscal regime allowed it to retain. By contrast, the regions of the arid north-west, the Himalayan plateau and the foothills of south-west China fared badly; fiscal decentralization put an end to the Third Front and to the financial transfers they had enjoyed from the coastal provinces during the Maoist era. Much of the Chinese rural hinterland was thus thrown back on its own resources which, precisely because geography was adverse, were meagre indeed. The removal of controls on the private sector was no panacea for the problems caused by the limited size of the surplus.

Nevertheless, neither the orthodox nor the revisionist approach is fully convincing. Orthodox scholarship exaggerates the contribution of the private and foreign sectors to the rural industrialization process. Its central charge that rural industry continued to be inefficient after 1978 is undermined by its overly narrow definition of efficiency. As for revisionism, its main weakness is that the Chinese fiscal system already incorporated a powerful element of decentralization before 1978. Revisionism is therefore unable to explain either the existence of inefficient rural industries, or the absence of take-off, in the last decade of Maoist rule. For all that, the main charge against both revisionism and the orthodoxy is that the explanation they offer centres far too much on the role played by policy change. In so doing, they neglect the contribution made by the development of skills during the Maoist era to subsequent rural industrialization. This alternative learning hypothesis provides the focus for the discussion in the next two chapters.

5

The Learning Hypothesis

For all the force and elegance of revisionist and orthodox theorizing, both over-state the contributions of policy change and geography to the rural industrial-ization of the transition era. Theirs is quintessentially a sin of omission: they neglect the contribution of history. In this chapter and in the next, I shall argue that we cannot explain post-1978 Chinese rural industrialization without refer-ence to the extended process of learning which occurred during the Maoist era.

5.1. Pre-requisites for Manufacturing Capability

The persistence of world poverty at root reflects the under-development of manufacturing industry. Manufacturing is important for four main reasons: there is an almost infinite demand for manufactured goods; there is great scope for technological progress ('dynamic economies of scale'); its extensive forward and backward linkage effects; and manufactured outputs are tradeable. It is thus manufacturing which is the engine of growth in the early and middle stages of development (Lewis 1954; Kaldor [1966] 1989; Cornwall 1977; Rowthorn and Wells 1987; Rowthorn and Coutts 2004). It is less important in mature economies, and a small number of countries have prospered without following this 'classical' British path to development, but these are the exception rather than the rule. Successful economic development therefore usually requires the creation of an efficient (in the sense discussed in the previ-ous chapter) manufacturing sector. This in turn requires both the development of manufacturing capability, and the establishment of an incentive structure which will ensure that manufacturing capability is effectively utilized. Capability by itself will not be enough for growth in the absence of incentives to utilize it effectively, but capability is without doubt a necessary condition for that growth.

The pre-requisites for the development of manufacturing capability are twofold. Firstly, new technology and ideas are required to raise labour produc-tivity to a level such that the manufacturing sector is competitive given the level of real wages. The technologies required to enhance productivity need either to be created or (more likely) acquired via the diffusion of pre-existing foreign, or (especially in the case of rural areas) from more advanced urban centres. In both cases, the technology has to be embodied in capital. In part, poor areas are simply deficient in physical capital: they suffer from what Romer (1993) has called an object gap. However, the distinction between an ideas and an object gap is not especially useful. The ideas gap can only be bridged by embodying the new ideas in the form of physical capital, and in practice any additions to the capital stock will embody new technology.[1] But none of this is straightforward, not least because of obstacles to the diffusion of knowledge to rural areas.[2] Self-evidently, the diffusion of knowledge will be accelerated by the transfer (either temporarily or permanently) of urban personnel (technicians, teachers and managers) to rural areas, and by making available textbooks, manuals, books of blueprints and the like. Return migration, whereby rural workers move temporarily to urban centres, acquire knowledge and then return to their rural home, will also help the process. Migration from urban to rural areas is therefore essential for the diffusion of knowledge.

The second pre-requisite for the development of manufacturing capability is an ability to utilize new technologies. Possession of the technologies is not enough; the capacity to absorb and utilize new technologies is not given, but needs to be created. That in turn means that poor areas need to pay close attention to the enhancement of the education and skills of their workforces. Insofar as knowledge is codifiable, the expansion of education and training programmes in rural areas will be necessary to ensure that the newly available 'books of blueprints' are read and understood: knowledge has to be acquired by the rural population through a formal process of learning. The expansion of education will help, but it will not be enough. That is because much knowledge is tacit: it can only be acquired via a process of learning-by-doing. Most obviously, poor rural areas need to create an industrial proletariat accustomed to the pace and rhythms of factory life out of the farm workforce; in the words of E. P. Thompson (1968), the 'making of a working class' is a required. Once this process is completed, a long phase of industrial learning-by-doing based upon output expansion and the production of new goods may be necessary before learning has progressed to such a level that labour productivity in rural industries approaches world levels.

[1] The problem for an under-developed area is that it has little capital per worker (measured in value terms) and this reflects both a lack of volume and the low level of technology embodied in that capital. In more neoclassical terms, we cannot easily distinguish between movements along a production function, and a shift in that function.

[2] I focus here on the development of manufacturing capability in rural areas. Even if a state emphasizes the expansion of urban areas, that process still requires that the economies of peri-urban (rural) districts are re-orientated away from farming and towards industrial production. The very fact that diffusion will occur more rapidly between urban cores and peri-urban districts than between core and peripheral rural areas provides a justification for policies designed to expand existing urban areas.

Let us discuss each of these pre-requisites for the development of manufacturing capability in more detail.

5.2. The Diffusion of Knowledge

A central premise in the traditional neoclassical paradigm is that knowledge is a public good, and therefore freely available to all countries and to all regions within any given country. Knowledge creation is therefore not an issue. According to Mankiw (1995: 301):

. . . theories of the creation of knowledge may be of little help in explaining international differences in growth rates. Knowledge, as opposed to capital, travels around the world fairly quickly. State-of-the-art textbooks are available in the poorest countries . . . For understanding international experience, the best assumption may be that all countries have access to the same pool of knowledge.

The 'new growth' literature has taken the notion of information imperfections much more seriously, in no small measure because of the work of Paul Romer (1986, 1990). Much of this literature in turn owes a debt to the well-developed heterodox tradition, which has stressed the extent to which growth is based on 'catch-up'. One thinks here of both the path-breaking theoretical studies (such as Abramovitz 1986), and the empirical work of (for example) Amsden's (1989), who famously explained development in South Korea in terms of 'industrialization by learning'.

One area of common ground in the growth literature is that those countries which put effort into sending students abroad to learn new ideas, which encourage inward investment and which are outward-looking are likely to grow quickly (Rogers 2004). Thus technological diffusion in heterodox and new growth models, as well as in more sophisticated neoclassical models (Parente and Prescott 1994), is usually seen as dependent upon the intensity of trade and the extent of FDI. Of course inward-orientated countries are perfectly capable of developing new knowledge. Maoist China was able to develop a range of new technologies and competencies despite being relatively isolated; its successful development of high-yielding varieties of wheat, rice and cotton, or the pioneering use of artemisinin against malaria, are obvious examples of the success of late Maoism in this regard. It may also be that internationally-available technology is not suited to the particular conditions which are prevalent in the under-developed area; this type of argument is advanced by Sachs et al. (2004: 137) in explaining the limited application of HYVs in sub-Saharan Africa. Furthermore, countries can acquire new technology via industrial espionage without much by way of formal trade. Thus the result that there are substantial benefits to poor countries from R & D expenditure in rich countries (Helpman 2004: 81–5) does not of itself make the case for free trade. In some ways the classic example is provided by the Soviet Union, which was able to base at least some of its cold war-era growth on technology developed originally in the USA (Sutton 1973) despite comparatively little international trade.

Although internationally-available technology and trade offer no simple panacea for the problem of technological backwardness, it is evident that the exploitation of ideas, technologies and processes already developed elsewhere in the world will be less expensive than if an inward-looking country seeks to develop new technologies from scratch, or relies entirely on industrial espionage. For example, there is little doubt that China closed the knowledge gap far more quickly after 1978 when the People's Republic was more open. It therefore seems fair to conclude that barriers to international trade and to FDI will limit technological diffusion and hence the catch-up process. To be sure, the precise channels by which technological diffusion remain uncertain, there will be lags in the diffusion process, and the Helpman-type result is weakened by its reliance on the neoclassical growth accounting framework. Nevertheless, it is hard to deny the existence of widespread technological diffusion via trade and FDI over comparatively short time horizons. In principle, therefore, there is widespread scope for developing countries to grow rapidly by taking comparatively simple steps to promote technological diffusion.

Rather less well studied, at least in the economics literature, is the diffusion of technology from urban to rural areas. However, it is evident that the issues involved are fundamentally the same as those relating to international technology flows: the countryside will be able to grow quickly by exploiting technologies and ideas already developed in the cities. Several insights follow from this. The first is that poor countries should pay close attention to the promotion of the transfer of knowledge from urban to rural areas. These transfers could be accomplished in various ways. For example, urban teachers might be encouraged to live in the countryside or, conversely, rural teachers might be granted a subsidy in order to allow them to spend some time in urban areas. Another obvious approach would be to encourage cooperation between urban and rural-based firms, perhaps by the promotion of vertically-integrated enterprises. In all such cases, however, a key requirement would be to ensure that those sent to urban areas did indeed return to the countryside for at least long enough to pass on their newly-acquired knowledge. Secondly, links between the domestic and the international economy might be developed in such a way as to help rural areas. For example, subsidies might be granted to foreign companies willing to locate in relatively backward rural areas. In that way, the closing of the skills gap could be accomplished more readily than simply relying upon knowledge transfers to urban areas in the first place. Thirdly, we would expect urban proximity to accelerate the pace of technology transfer. Those rural areas within a developing country located close to large cities, and still more so for villages close to urban centres which are outward-looking, would tend to enjoy much more rapid diffusion of ideas than more distant parts of the countryside. In a world of imperfect information, location matters for the diffusion of technology.

5.3. Learning and the Absorption of Knowledge

The second reason for limited manufacturing capability is the under-development of the capacity to absorb and apply more advanced knowledge ('absorptive capacity'). Poor areas which lack this capacity will fare badly. Conversely, those abundantly supplied will prosper; thus the scope for catch-up will be greatest when a country '. . . is technologically backward but socially advanced' (Abramovitz 1986: 388). A key pre-requisite for an escape from the poverty trap is therefore the enhancement of the skills of the labour force. Firms can be globally competitive on the basis of low wages despite low productivity. However, development—in the sense of rising per capita income—necessarily requires the payment of high wages, and that in turn requires increased labour productivity. Productivity levels are positively related to knowledge. This is partly because knowledge allows higher output per unit of capital for a given level of technology and for a given range of goods. But human capital also matters because it allows an economy to use new technologies and produce new types of goods more efficiently. In other words, the process of catch-up for a poor country depends upon having the human capital base to be able to absorb and utilize new technologies and ideas. It is not enough for textbooks, books of blueprints or experts (all of which are sources of knowledge) to be available in under-developed areas. The knowledge embodied in these various forms needs also to be transferred to the workforce. Mankiw's view of knowledge as a public good which is freely available may be implausible, but there is no doubt that he is right in arguing that knowledge will not be fully utilized in all countries because of a lack of human capital (Mankiw et al. 1992; Mankiw 1995).

The more general version of this type of skill deficiency argument in which LDCs are portrayed as lacking the capacity to absorb new technologies and ideas goes under the name of 'social capability', which is used more or less interchangeably with absorptive capability in the literature. The phrase seems to have been used originally by Ohkawa and Rosovsky (1973), and is typically now used to encompass not only educational and skill levels but also institutional quality (Abramovitz 1986; Fagerberg 1994; Abramovitz and David 1996; Temple and Johnson 1998). As Abramovitz (1986: 390) puts it:

Countries that are technologically backward have a potentiality for generating growth more rapid than that of more advanced countries, provided their social capabilities are sufficiently developed to permit successful exploitation of technologies already employed by the technological leaders.

Social capability changes only slowly. Countries find it much easier to acquire new technology than to enhance their social capability in such a way as to enable them to apply effectively the new technology. Accordingly, the absence of sufficient social capability may give rise to path dependency or hysteresis: countries are unable to escape from their poverty trap in the short or medium term

(Abramovitz and David 1996: 34). Nevertheless, it is evident that the incorporation of institutional factors into its definition make social capability a distinctly slippery concept to operationalize for empirical work.[3] Whilst a number of attempts have been made to develop proxies for the quality of institutions, it is understandable that much work has focused on the human capital dimension of social capability as the binding constraint on successful technological diffusion.

In this regard, one of the interesting features of the literature on the impact of FDI in poor countries is its conclusion that the extent of technological diffusion is limited by the absorptive capacity of the LDC (Cantwell 1995; Borensztein et al. 1998; Xu 2000; Saggi 2002). More concretely, LDCs benefit far less, and perhaps not even at all, from FDI if their human capital is under-developed. They simply do not have the skill base to make use of the more advanced technology. As Borensztein et al. (1998: 9) say: 'The main regression results indicate that FDI has a positive overall effect on economic growth, although the magnitude of this effect depends on the stock of human capital available in the host economy'. Indeed they found that countries where human capital is grossly under-developed did not gain at all. This type of finding has especial relevance to under-developed rural regions *within* LDCs. Just as poor countries encounter difficulties in absorbing technology from abroad, so a rural area with an under-developed skill base will find it hard to absorb more advanced technology from urban areas within the same country.

That said, it is hard to test these sorts of ideas precisely because even human capital is such an all-embracing concept (and also because of endogeneity problems in the sense that FDI often induces local government to invest heavily in developing human capital). Nevertheless, the evidence on two dimensions of human capital, namely formal education and training on the one hand, and learning-by-doing on the other, does provide some pointers.

5.3.1. Education and Training

It is self-evident that the diffusion of new ideas to rural areas within a developing country is not enough by itself to generate rapid growth unless the workforce has the skills necessary to apply these new ideas and technologies productively.

(A) THEORY

One obvious way of acquiring the requisite skills is by means of formal education and, not surprisingly, an emphasis on the role played by education in promoting growth features in much of the theoretical literature (Schultz 1960; Nelson and Phelps 1966; Abramovitz 1986; Aghion and Howitt 1998). Here, two

---

[3] Abramovitz (1986: 388) recognized the problem very clearly: 'The trouble with absorbing social capability into the catch-up hypothesis is that no one knows just what it means or how to measure it . . . judgements about social capability remain highly problematic'.

rather different approaches may be distinguished: one focuses on educational levels (a short and medium term focus), and the other on educational changes (which is more of a long run argument).

The first approach posits the existence of a relation between the *level* of education and the rate of output growth via innovation and diffusion. Implicit here seems to be the standard catch-up idea that poor countries will enjoy rapid catch-up growth as they exploit their existing human capital stock; the argument is therefore about transitional dynamics. The underlying idea is straightforward enough. According to Barro (2001: 14): 'First, more human capital facilitates the absorption of superior technologies from leading countries. Second, human capital levels tend to be more difficult to adjust than physical capital'. A country with a better-educated population will be in a far superior position to introduce and adapt imported technology—the foundation of modern factory industry—than a country where the bulk of the population is illiterate. Even basic education provides a range of transferable skills which firms are unlikely to provide for their employees. It has further been noted that there may be an element of increasing returns to the production of educated workers. That is, countries or regions which have a high level of education are likely to attract highly-educated immigrants; the absolute wage paid to skilled workers is thus much higher in developed than in under-developed countries. This tendency for the rate of return to education to be higher in rich countries than in poor countries reflects skill complementarities. One might expect *a priori* that a shortage of skilled labour in a poor country ought to make the rate of return higher, but skill complementarity produces the reverse. The clear implication is that developing regions will find it very difficult to catch-up simply by increasing their educational spending (in the absence of barriers to emigration). Moreover, there seems to be widespread acceptance that a high initial level of education will ensure the catch-up in the short and medium term. Thus the successful catch-up of East Asia economies was based not just upon technology transfer but on the development of local capability; even many of those who are otherwise sceptical of the significance of education for the growth process acknowledge this point (Easterly 2001: 76–7). In the absence of technological change, education may count for very little, but Pack's (2001: 214) argument along such lines is hardly relevant for most poor areas because there the scope for catch-up is usually enormous. Even within a closed economy, there will almost certainly be abundant opportunities for catch-up for poor regions, especially by acquiring more advanced technology from cities.

The second approach to education accords more emphasis to *changes* in human capital, and hence posits that there is a relationship between the growth of human capital and the growth of output (Lucas 1988; Mankiw et al. 1992). The argument here is about the long term; it is more about moving along an equilibrium growth path than about transitional dynamics. The country in question is assumed to have already achieved the potential level of output implied by its level of education; there is no scope for catch-up. Output growth therefore depends upon raising the level of education, rather than making effective use of the existing level of attainment.

In this conceptualization, human capital is treated as just another input into the productive process; it is increasingly conventional for growth accounting to include human capital in the production function alongside physical capital. However, there is a good deal of debate about the nature of long run returns to education and hence about the specification of the production function. Some researchers in the endogenous growth tradition have argued that returns to investment in human capital are non-diminishing (Lucas 1988). However, most researchers have not been persuaded by this idea. For example, most neoclassical formulations have entered human capital into the production function in the same way as physical capital, such that the essential Solowian result—that the long run growth rate of per capita output depends only on technical progress—is retained; investment in human capital is thus assumed to be subject to diminishing returns. This approach reflects a body of evidence suggesting that the (social) returns to tertiary education are lower than those to other types of education in most countries. Paul Romer's emphasis on investment in ideas as a source of non-diminishing returns has thus been viewed by most as being the more plausible endogenous mechanism for under-pinning growth. More generally, there remains the question as to whether education improves labour force quality (Becker 1974), or whether it merely provides a signal to would-be employers of motivation (Spence 1976). The private rate of return to (say) tertiary education is considerable, but the size of the social rate of return is much more questionable.

(B) EMPIRICAL EVIDENCE

As far as the evidence on the relationship between education and growth is concerned, the best that can be said is that it is mixed. Few would deny the intrinsic value of education; in that sense, one can reasonably define development to include education, as of course the United Nations Development Programme does. But the instrumental significance of education for the growth process remains a matter for conjecture. One problem is to establish causality; is it the case that education drives growth or does the growth of output (by increasing incomes and hence the demand for education) drive educational attainment? Both causal processes are highly plausible, and it is difficult to separate out the two. It is partly to circumvent this endogeneity problem that so many researchers have focused on the initial level of education in their econometric analysis.

The famous Mankiw et al. (1992) study certainly found that human capital accumulation helped to explain a large part of economic growth, and other studies have reached the same conclusion (Benhabib and Spiegel 1994; Barro and Sala-i-Martin 1995; Barro 2001). Furthermore there is evidence that education is important for agriculture as well as for industry. And many studies have concluded that education was a crucial ingredient in the postwar success of East Asia, whereas South Asia was hampered by its low literacy rate (Drèze and Sen 1995). For example, the Krugman-Young literature, whilst relatively dismissive of the role played by productivity growth in the East Asian miracle, gives great weight to the role played by the accumulation of human capital.

However, there is also a considerable weight of evidence pointing in the other direction. The Mankiw et al. result, for example, seems to have been driven by the use of secondary education as a measure of educational attainment; broader measures of education produce much more equivocal results (Easterly 2001: 78–80). The significance of primary education has also been questioned (Barro 1997: 19–22). For example, a high level of educational development was not necessary for the development of proto-industry in the eighteenth and nineteenth centuries: many regions across the world experienced rapid proto-industrialization despite very low levels of literacy (Ogilvie and Cerman 1996; Ogilvie 1997). Studies based on postwar data, and which have looked at the relationship between output growth and changes in years of attainment (Barro and Sala-i-Martin 1995: 425–6 and 437), or changes in adult literacy rates (Dasgupta and Weale 1992), have found that they are not significant either. Others have tended to concur, including Easterly (2001: 84): 'Despite all the lofty sentiments about education, the return to the educational explosion of the past four decades has been disappointing.' The experience of the Indian state of Kerala also casts doubt upon the importance of education as a means of promoting industrial growth. Despite human capital indicators which are far more impressive, Kerala's level of per capita manufacturing value-added lags well behind that of China (Thomas 2005: 763). For Pritchett (2001), this contrary evidence was so compelling that he even posed the question: 'where has all the education gone?'

Pritchett offered a number of answers to his own question. Firstly, there is a divergence between social and private rates of return (education is often state-subsidized, and workers use their new education to engage in socially unproductive activity). This type of argument has been elaborated by Easterly (2001), who argues that educational expenditure has largely failed in the Third World because of flawed incentive structures across the whole economy. For example, excessive state intervention (by implication, industrial policy of one form or another) persuades educated workers to engage in rent-seeking rather than productive activity. Secondly, there are demand side problems (inadequate demand for educated labour); skilled workers in poor countries thus find themselves in jobs where their skills cannot be fully utilized. Thirdly, Pritchett raises the possibility that the quality of education is low (such that years of schooling in add nothing to skills).

There are other possible reasons why education may be less important than sometimes argued. One is that, once education has reached some threshold value, further increases generate little by way of additional return. Bowman and Anderson (1963) put forward the view that a literacy rate of 30 percent was the critical threshold value, and it is noteworthy that this seems to have been enough for England and Japan to launch their respective industrial revolutions. Indeed some have argued that there is little to suggest that educational expansion contributed to England's Industrial Revolution (Mitch 1993), not least because there is considerable evidence that the literacy rate may have declined during the early nineteenth century (Sanderson 1991; Nicholas and Oxley 1993). Implicit here is the idea that, once opportunities for catch-up have been exhausted—in other words, once a country has reached the world technological frontier—further educational expansion reaps little reward.

A second line of argument stems from the recognition that education involves opportunity costs. Insofar as an expansion of education diverts teenagers from factory jobs to the school room, it may harm industrial development. This is no trivial consideration in many poor countries where children make up a significant fraction of the population. Of course the long run benefits from education may outweigh the short run costs, but much depends on the extent of learning-by-doing. Consider a country in which education is growing rapidly. Then those entering the workforce after completing a full secondary education will on average be better educated than their predecessors, who necessarily did not have the opportunity to acquire an education. Yet the international evidence suggests overwhelmingly that older workers will be paid vastly more on average than younger workers, despite their inferior educational qualifications. For some jobs, nimbleness, manual dexterity, excellent eyesight and even small physical size are crucial, and in all these respects youth commands a premium over age. But in general, there is a high seniority premium in industrial employment. This reflects the gains in terms of productivity that derive from experience. This type of argument becomes still stronger if one argues that many skills are more readily acquired when young; a 14-year-old learns faster than somebody in their late 20s. If the crucial teenage years are spent in school rather than in learning-by-doing on the factory floor, it may prove much harder to acquire the skills later in life once formal education is completed. Of course developing countries will require a significant cadre of well-educated workers; that is not the issue. Rather, the question centres on just how large this cadre needs to be, and therefore how much emphasis should be placed on developing (say) tertiary education.

There is no suggestion in this section that education is anything other than desirable on intrinsic grounds. Rather, the argument is that if one wishes to make the case for educational expansion, it is much easier to do it on intrinsic rather than instrumental grounds. There is undoubtedly some sort of instrumental link between education and economic growth, but the sum of the research to date suggests that the nature of that link is elusive.

5.3.2. Learning-by-Doing

As we have seen, knowledge can be acquired via the process of learning associated with formal education. In addition, it can be acquired by reading manuals which explain how to operate a particular type of machinery. However, a large number of scholars have argued that an important part of knowledge is tacit and not readily codifiable; it can only by acquired by a process of on-the-job learning. The acquisition of the knowledge needed to operate manufacturing processes successfully therefore depends upon learning-by-doing. As Lall (1992: 166) puts it:

Technological knowledge is not shared equally among firms, nor is it easily imitated by or transferred across firms. Transfer necessarily requires learning because technologies are tacit, and their underlying principles are not always clearly understood. Thus, simply to gain mastery of a new technology requires skills, effort and investment by the receiving firm, and the extent of mastery achieved is uncertain and necessarily varies by firm according to these inputs.

(A) THE THEORY

The first formalization of learning-by-doing is usually attributed to Arrow (1962). He advanced three principal lines of argument. Firstly, knowledge plays a key role in increasing output, such that differences in output per person across countries cannot be explained simply in terms of differences in the ratio of physical capital to labour. Secondly, the acquisition of knowledge (learning) depends upon experience:

. . . one empirical generalization is so clear that all schools must accept it, although they interpret it in different fashions: Learning is the product of experience. Learning can only take place through the attempt to solve a problem and therefore only takes place during activity . . . I advance the hypothesis here that technical change in general can be ascribed to experience . . .

(Arrow 1962: 155, 156)

This conclusion was based upon the experience of a range of plants in which productivity rose over a period of time in the absence of new investment. Total learning is therefore a function of the cumulative volume of goods produced, or (Arrow's preferred formulation) cumulative gross investment. This latter preference stems from Arrow's third insight: learning diminishes rapidly at the margin from the repetition of the same type of production. Maintaining a high rate of learning in an economy over time thus requires either that new types of good are produced, or the introduction of new types of capital equipment. The scope for learning from a single process is therefore limited. By implication, cumulative hours worked in industry will not be a good measure of learning in the absence of product or process innovation.[4]

---

[4] The usual modern formulation is to assume that the accumulation of physical capital leads to learning. A typical production function is therefore written as $Y = F(K, AL)$, where A is the stock of knowledge, Y output, K physical capital and L labour (Barro and Sala-i-Martin 1995: 146-7). An increase in capital has an impact on output over and above the increase in K; it increases the quality of labour as well by increasing A.

Since the publication of Arrow's work, his insights have been developed in a number of ways. One extension is that learning is more rapid in manufacturing than in other types of industry. This is one of the key reasons for the emphasis placed by Kaldor on manufacturing as the engine of growth, and it reflects the relatively greater scope for innovation in that sector. Secondly, Lucas (1993) cites interesting studies of the learning process in the building of Liberty ships during World War II. Many of these ships were produced over a number of years using an identical blueprint by the same yard; the evidence thus normalizes for a range of other influences and provides unambiguous evidence of learning. It is therefore especially noteworthy, as Lucas says, that these yards increased output per man-hour by 40 percent per year over the period December 1941 to December 1944 on the basis of learning. This suggests that learning effects can be very powerful indeed.

A third extension is that experience of agricultural production is not of much use for industrial production; learning needs to begin anew for workers transferred from agriculture to industry. In its essentials, the argument is that prior experience of factory work is important: farm work is qualitatively different to that on an assembly line in being outdoor, seasonal, and characterized by the absence of close supervision. The working habits acquired by farm workers are hard for manufacturers to break, and the transition from farm to factory is a profoundly alienating experience for those involved. Accordingly, an extended process of learning and habituation is essential before farm workers are able to achieve high levels of productivity. Alexander Gerschenkron (1962: 9) understood this central point. For him, the primary obstacle to the development of poor countries was a shortage of skilled labour, and it was no simple matter to create an industrial workforce out of the ranks of the peasantry:

. . . the overriding fact to consider is that industrial labor, in the sense of a stable, reliable and disciplined group that has cut the umbilical cord connecting it with the land and has become suitable for utilization in factories, is not abundant but extremely scarce in a backward country. Creation of an industrial labor force that really deserves its name is a most difficult and protracted process . . . The advantages inherent in the use of technologically superior equipment were not counteracted but reinforced by its labor-saving effect.

Note here the point that labour is not merely a 'factor of production'. Labour differs from capital in needing to be motivated and disciplined if it is to work effectively in a factory context. In that sense, governments need to give attention to the process whereby an industrial working class is formed because there are costs involved for agricultural workers attempting to make the transition from farm to factory. Development is therefore not the simple process set out in the famous Lewis model in which surplus labour released by agriculture is costlessly absorbed into factory industry. Of course we need to think about the creation of an industrial labour force in the most general sense to encompass workers, technicians and managers, a point emphasized in some of the writings of Nurkse (1953). Indeed the creation of a cadre of skilled managers is even more important than the training of factory workers themselves in the early stages of development. Nevertheless, Gerschenkron's central point remains valid: shortages of skilled labour will serve as a constraint on development.

Much recent work has focused on spillovers and the production of new goods (Stokey 1988; Young 1991). Learning generated by the production of one good will allow improvements in productivity in other sectors as the skills and competencies acquired are used in the production of other goods. It follows that rates of economy-wide learning will depend in part upon the extent to which diffusion takes place. This clearly provides a compelling argument for the creation of industrial clusters to maximize spillover effects, and more generally for a 'big push' industrialization strategy along the lines suggested by Rosenstein-Rodan (1943). However, if learning effects from the production of any one good are bounded, it follows that the introduction of new goods is essential if learning is to continue. For example, it has been suggested that Kerala's failure to diversify away from the chemical industries which were established in Travancore in the 1930s have hampered its long run industrial development (Thomas 2005). The general conclusion is therefore that the mix of goods produced will have an effect on the extent of learning. A heavy industrialization strategy, emphasizing the production of new capital intensive goods instead of traditional light industrial products, may thus have an important role to play in accelerating the growth rate if the gains from the traditional sector have largely been exhausted. A further implication of recognizing the pivotal role of new goods is that international trade (but not necessarily free trade) may have an important role to play in promoting productivity growth. A country with a comparatively mature industrial sector may, by abandoning an autarkic industrialization strategy, be able to enhance its productivity growth by producing new goods (or old goods using new types of capital). This is because the act of opening-up will create new learning opportunities insofar as domestic firms are willing to compete in markets involving the sale of new goods, whether at home or abroad. By shifting labour away from the production of old goods (where continuing scope for learning is low) and towards the production of new goods (where the scope for learning is extensive), country-wide productivity growth can accelerate as the knowledge acquired in the production of the new good spills over to other sectors.

(B) THE LEARNING-BY-DOING PROCESS

Country studies tend to suggest that a long and protracted period of learning is needed before productivity will be high enough to allow industries to compete effectively in domestic and overseas markets. Here the historical experience of successful western economies is instructive. Industrial Revolution Britain provides one such example (Thompson 1968; von Tunzelmann 1978; Mokyr 1985). There, at least if we accept Crafts' (1985) estimates of TFP growth, productivity growth was low in the early nineteenth century by almost any measure, and only began to rise quickly in the middle of the century. Part of the reason was that it took time for employees to learn the new skills required. This was certainly true in the iron and coal industries, but it was even more so in the cotton sector. Admittedly, someone brought up in a mill took only about 3 months to learn how to operate a mule (von Tunzelmann 1994: 275). However, this in itself demonstrates the importance of on-the-job learning; such workers, having spent their childhood in the mills of Lancashire, had effectively served a long apprenticeship which allowed them to pick up all manner of tacit knowledge. For outsiders, the learning process was much longer; it took a year and a half to two years to learn how to operate the mule effectively in Britain, and this was one reason why the Japanese cotton industry preferred to use ring spinning technology (Tsurumi 1990: 111). The steam engine was in use early on in the most advanced sectors of the British economy, but its adoption by most British companies did not occur until the middle of the nineteenth century (von Tunzelmann 1978). It is not hard to see this as a consequence of a slow process of learning spillovers from the most dynamic industry (cotton) to other sectors of the economy.

The experiences of Meiji and interwar Japan (Tsurumi 1990) and 'the Rest', Amsden's (2001) term for those countries in Latin America and Asia which have successfully developed modern manufacturing production since 1945, are also instructive. The growth of the Japanese textile industry provides a good example. Much of the know-how developed in the Lancashire cotton mills (and especially by Platt Brothers of Oldham) was available to Japan as early as the 1870s. As a result, the first modern mill was founded at Osaka in 1882 and began operation in 1884 (Crawcour 1988: 425; Francks 1992: 180–6). As far as silk is concerned, the modern Tomioka steam-filature plant was established in 1872; French technicians were employed to provide training to the workforce (Tsurumi 1990: 26). The process of technological diffusion was further enhanced by the employment of foreign advisors, some 4,000 of whom were engaged by Japan during the Meiji period (Beasley 1990: 88). However, if we look at measures of competitiveness, it is significant that Japan did not displace British cotton textiles in the China market until the 1920s, and even that owed much to the re-orientation of the British manufacturing sector to meeting the demands imposed by World War I.[5] In other words, Japan's experience seems to show that a long period of learning is necessary successfully to attain world-best levels of productivity even in circumstances where technological diffusion is comparatively rapid.

Part of the reason why learning was so protracted in Japan was that the peasant labour force found it hard to adjust to the pace and pattern of factory life. The Tomioka silk filature provides a good example; even though the filature offered excellent conditions of employment, it proved extremely difficult to recruit female workers from the countryside. Tsurumi (1990: 27) explains why:

Europeans drank red wine and cooked with lard, but the country people thought they were drinking human blood and cooking with human fat. It was widely believed that the

[5] By 1926, Japan had 67 percent of the China market, compared with 20 percent in 1913; over this period, Japan had successfully displaced British cotton, which supplied only 24 percent of the market in 1926 compared with 53 percent in 1913 (Yamazawa 1990: 75).

government's eagerness to recruit young girls and send them to Tomioka was to provide the Europeans there with fresh supplies of blood and fat. Despite the national government's repeated calls for young women 'between the ages of fifteen and twenty five' and its denunciations of 'foolish rumors and idle talk' that spread misunderstandings about the French at Tomioka, not a single volunteer came forward.

The very fact, indeed, of being asked to travel long distances to work amongst strangers was alienating enough: 'In the eyes of those whose lives had been totally within or close to the environs of their own villages, young strangers from distant prefectures were almost as foreign as the French instructors at Tomioka' (Tsurumi 1990: 27). The experience of the Tomioka workforce may have been unusually alienating because of the presence of French technicians, but it gives a flavour of the adjustment problems typically ignored in many of the economic models of labour migration from field to factory.

In the contemporary Asian context, China's success in developing rural industry after 1978 can be contrasted with Vietnam's failure. China and Vietnam pursued similar ('gradualist') transition policies. In the latter, however, industrial policy under socialism was highly centralized (most industrial production was incorporated into the plan) and focused on urban industry in combination with mineral extraction in rural areas (Fforde and de Vylder 1996; Perkins 1998; O'Connor 1998; van de Walle and Cratty 2004).[6] Rural industry was almost non-existent. As a result, the rural industrial base on the eve of transition was very weak and therefore the strategy of the 1990s failed to generate rapid growth; the learning process in Vietnam had simply not progressed far enough to make possible rapid rural industrialization.

Much less clear from the historical record is whether *proto-industry* provides an adequate basis for the sort of learning-by-doing needed for modern industries to be internationally competitive.[7] Now a number of scholars have certainly argued that proto-industry did facilitate learning. In the Japanese case, for example, it has been suggested that the proto-industrial development of the Tokugawa period helped to lay the foundation for modern economic growth by creating the disciplined and obedient labour force emphasized as a *sine qua non* for development by Gerschenkron. According to Smith:

My argument is that the growth of the modern textile industry was made possible by the specific skills, attitudes, roles, capital accumulations, and commercial practices brought into being mainly during the period of 'premodern growth' . . . The preindustrial values incorporated in the emergent factory system were not immemorial. Insofar as they included willingness to work for long periods off the farm for wages and were associated with industrially useful skills, they were mainly the product of the Tokugawa period, and

---

[6] Even in the late 1990s, the share of GDP contributed by manufacturing in Vietnam was well below that in China.

[7] Proto-industry is usually defined as industry selling to a national or international market using essentially pre-modern technology. Being able to sell goods on the world market based on relatively high wages helps to solve the realization problem that would otherwise result from the payment of low wages to home workers.

of its last century especially. Modern Japanese industry took over these new preindustrial values, changing them in the process, although—as many observers have noticed—less than one would think.

(T.C. Smith 1988: 44)

But others have tended to look at the Japanese experience and conclude, contra Smith, that pre-modern skills were of little use in the modern factories of the late nineteenth and early twentieth centuries. Indeed, to judge by indicators such as the turnover rate, interviews with textile workers carried out at the time and the data on productivity, the Japanese textile workforce was anything but the disciplined, skilled and highly-motivated workforce sometimes suggested (Taira 1978; Tsurumi 1990; Francks 1992).[8] There is no doubt that the Tokugawa era saw the rapid growth of cotton spinning and sericulture, a development which served to displace linen from the consumption bundles of many households (Hayami et al. 2004: 344–5). However, the transformation of Japanese industry occurred after 1868 as opening-up created new markets for reeled silk exports (with spillover effects on sericulture) and cotton spinning technology from Lancashire destroyed the native cotton spinning industry (Saito and Tanimoto 2004). The impact of opening-up may have been less important than argued by Huber (1971), but some work suggests that it was nevertheless substantial (Bernhofen and Brown 2005: 208–25).

This rather negative outlook on the legacies of proto-industrialization is the norm in much of the literature on Europe (Mendels 1972; Ogilvie and Cerman 1986; Ogilvie 1997). Now there is no doubt that it is perfectly possible to create a competitive industrial sector purely on the basis of low wages. Low unit labour costs are the prime determinant of competitiveness, and it is self-evident that this can be achieved either by keeping wages low or by raising labour productivity. Proto-industry is a classic example of a form of industrialization which relies upon low wages, and this sort of industry has a long and venerable history. For example, proto-industry in prewar economies was often able to survive the onslaught of competition from foreign imports, especially in cotton weaving but only by cutting wages and relocating to the rural hinterland. However, this type of proto-industry provides no intrinsic basis for modern development because there is a logical contradiction between development (which necessarily requires high wages) and its achievement on the basis of an industrial sector paying low real wages. Indeed the path-breaking work of Mendels showed that a transition from proto-industry to modern industry was not inevitable, and his insight has been confirmed by two decades of research on proto-industrialization in Europe, where it seems that few centres of proto-industry made the transition from handicraft production to what Marx called 'machinofacture'.

---

[8] The US had exactly the same problem. Its ante-bellum cotton industry was much inferior in terms of its productivity to that of Britain, and it therefore depended heavily on tariff protection to survive (Amsden 2001: 46).

British proto-industry in the eighteenth century, for example, centred on the east Midlands, yet modern industry developed in Lancashire and Yorkshire. Often, in fact, proto-industry was a hindrance rather than a help to factory industrialization. The social institutions typical of proto-industry (such as guilds) hampered the setting-up of factories. The illiteracy of the bulk of the European proto-industrial workforce made it hard to develop modern factory industry, just as Meiji Japan's cotton and silk magnates preferred to recruit young, untrained, 'factory girls' in preference to proto-industrial workers whose traditional skills needed to be first unlearned if they were to become proficient power loom operatives; skills mattered for modern industrial production, but not those of the traditional variety.

In general, as Amsden (2001) has argued, pockets of proto-industry in prewar economies were able to survive the onslaught of competition from foreign imports, especially in cotton weaving. But proto-industry survived only by cutting wages and relocating to the rural hinterland. It was not able to generate productivity increases based upon technical progress—the hallmark of modern manufacturing production.

Despite a revisionist literature that romanticizes the handloom weaver and resuscitates his (India) or her (China and the Ottoman Empire) bones from the bleached plains where Karl Marx left them, 'the rest's' artisans were tragic figures. They competed by cutting their own wages and retreating to geographically inaccessible low-income regional markets. There is no evidence of 'flexibility' or inventiveness on their part, traits typically attributed in the 1990s to small-scale firms.

(Amsden 2001: 50)

In other words, *modern* industrial development requires learning in a factory-orientated environment characterized by the use of machinery rather than traditional proto-industrial technologies. Amsden (2001: 101–6) argues that this is exactly what happened in the prewar period in Korea and Taiwan. Korea benefited extensively from Japanese colonialism. Taiwan also benefited from its colonial legacies, though for Amsden emigration from China in the wake of the 1949 Revolution was much more important. These legacies were not, argues Amsden, sufficient in themselves to guarantee modern economic growth but the development of a 'new elite of managers and engineers' (Amsden 2001: 121) was crucial for their future development, as it was for other parts of Asia and Latin America which were comparatively successful in developing manufacturing in the postwar era. Amsden further argues that size matters. Those poor economies which developed successfully after World War II did so by developing large enterprises (Taiwan was the exception which proved the rule). Although Amsden says little about the reasons for this, there is little doubt that large firms can benefit more from learning because much knowledge is tacit or proprietary to firms; in more modern jargon, it is partially excludable, especially in the short term. In order, therefore, to acquire this type of knowledge, firms have to generate it themselves and therefore the scale of production matters. Small firms simply do not produce enough, employ enough workers or use sufficient capital to fully exploit the learning opportunities associated with a particular type of technology.

5.4. Manufacturing Capability and the Role of the State

The development of manufacturing capability can of course be left to the market, and that has been the approach of many poor countries. This approach has been largely unsuccessful precisely because market failure and rigidities are pervasive in a capitalist economy. It is on the premise of such failure that the case for state intervention rests. In fact, it is now commonplace amongst economists to think of under-development as a low level equilibrium or poverty trap. This notion of poverty as equilibrium has two dimensions. On the one hand, the under-developed area lacks a number of the key pre-requisites for economic growth. On the other hand, these pre-requisites are absent because of the existence of rigidities and market 'imperfections'. It is these rigidities which make poverty an equilibrium state. More concretely, it is the existence of imperfections which prevent the development of manufacturing capability, either by limiting the diffusion of knowledge and technologies, or by limiting the development of manufacturing skills.

It is not hard to think of imperfections which hamper the development of manufacturing capability. One approach comes close to geographical determinism. Here under-developed areas are poor because they face geographical obstacles which are almost impossible to overcome; these obstacles might be topographical (rich mountainous areas are rare) or climatic (many tropical counties are poor). This is the argument offered by Sachs et al. (2004) and Sachs (2005) for the problems of the tropical sub-Saharan Africa. For them, factors such as high transport costs, disease, and low productivity agriculture impose an all but binding constraint on development; only massive development assistance from the rich countries offers a way out of the impasse.

An alternative approach is to think of the low level equilibrium trap as the product of a coordination failure which can only be resolved by government intervention. From this perspective, manufacturing does not develop and poverty persists because there is little incentive for rational firms or workers to invest in physical and human capital, or in the acquisition of new technology and knowledge.[9] An increase in productive capacity by one firm may not be profitable because the increase in production will not be matched by a

---

[9] The 'poverty trap' and vicious circle terminology here is associated with the writings of Nelson (1956), Leibenstein (1957) and Myrdal (1957). For more recent approaches in the literature, see Bloom et al. (2003) and Sachs (2005).

proportionate increase in demand for the firm's product. The problem is effectively one of excludability; the firm cannot require its workers (who receive a higher wage as a result of the increase in production) to spend their increased wage exclusively on its own products, nor can it capture the external benefits that other firms will receive from increased supplies of the product in question. An increased supply of (say) machinery by one firm will raise the profits of all firms which use the machinery, but there is no guarantee that the producing firm will benefit. Only if all firms increase production will the demand for the output of any single firm increase proportionately. Similarly firms will not invest in training because they cannot fully capture its benefits. Investment in training by a firm generates positive externalities for other firms because some of the newly-trained workers will leave for other firms and other regions. Equally, there is little incentive for a worker to invest skills unless the general demand for skills within the economy also rises. This is because firms will switch to a more sophisticated method of production requiring higher skills only if *all* the workers involved have those higher skills. In effect, the sophistication of the production method is determined by the least-skilled member of the labour force because there are complementarities between labour inputs, such that the lack of any one will have devastating effects.[10] Thus skilled workers earn more in rich countries than in poor countries because, even though their specific skill is less scarce in the rich country, they benefit from the complementary skills of other skilled workers. Only if all firms and all workers increase their supply will demand for any individual firm or worker rise proportionately. The only way to resolve what is essentially a coordination failure is by means of a 'big push' initiated by government. This is the argument advanced by Rosenstein-Rodan (1943) and Nurkse (1953), and formalized more recently in the writings of Murphy et al. (1989), Krugman (1995) and Fujita et al. (1999).

There is also a case for subsidies which are explicitly linked to skill creation because of the inherent tension between skill creation and skill diffusion. Firms will be able to capture only a part of the neo-Schumpeterian rents generated by training because some workers will migrate to other firms once their training is complete. The process of migration promotes skill diffusion but it discourages firm-level investment in skills because of the impossibility of full excludability. Accordingly, there will often be a justification for government subsidies to firms to encourage high levels of investment in skills precisely because such investment generates powerful externalities. In the absence of subsidies, firms resort to a mixture of incentives (the payment of efficiency wages; the provision of factory dormitories) and compulsion (the withholding of wages; physical obstacles, such as fences, to prevent workers from leaving the factory compound) to reduce turnover rates.

---

[10] This is often called the O-ring theory of labour productivity. The space shuttle 'Challenger' exploded because of the failure of a single key component, the O-ring (Kremer 1993).

The older literature focuses more on the interaction of economies of scale with capital market failure. Infant industries are unprofitable in the short run because learning takes time and because the scale of operation is small (such that economies of scale cannot be exploited). Risk-averse capital markets are typically unwilling to subsidize these short run losses because there is too much uncertainty over the learning process, especially where a new technology is involved. Precisely because the future is uncertain, firms and financial institutions are typically reluctant to provide capital to infant industries, and this provides a *prima facie* case for state intervention. This was the base for Keynes' (1936: 164) view that 'I expect to see the state, which is in a position to calculate the marginal efficiency of capital goods on long views and on the basis of the greater social advantage, taking an ever greater responsibility for directly organising investment . . .' Without state intervention, poor countries will be characterized by low levels of investment in manufacturing, and this creates an equilibrium trap by inhibiting the process of learning-by-doing and thereby depressing short term profitability in the infant industry still further.

This example is an obvious case of market failure driven by imperfect information, and there is every reason to expect it to be widespread. Only when the infant reaches maturity (by implication, when the returns to learning are small) can the subsidy be withdrawn. Learning-by-doing thus provides a justification for the protection of infant industries in developing countries, the policy advocated in the classic accounts offered by Mill, List and Hamilton.[11] There is an abundance of evidence which demonstrates that infant industry protection played a pivotal role in the economic development of Britain, American and Germany in the nineteenth century, and Japan in the twentieth (Eatwell 1982; Chang 2002).[12] Trade therefore has the potential to promote productivity growth by promoting learning-by-doing if properly managed.

A fourth instance of market failure relates to labour migration. The presence of increasing returns creates a process of cumulative causation. There will be a persistent net flow of skilled labour from poor to rich areas because the presence of external returns to scale means that there is no tendency for the marginal productivity of labour to stagnate, still less decline. Poor areas are therefore handicapped by an exodus of skilled labour and therefore some sort of regional policy may be needed to reverse that decline (Kaldor 1970; Krugman 1991). In addition,

[11] The extensive literature on the precise circumstances in which protection (I use the word here in the broad sense to encompass subsidies, tariffs and non-tariff barriers) for infant industries is justified, and on the most appropriate form of protection, include *inter alia* Baldwin (1969), Krueger and Tuncer (1982) and Succar (1987). In general terms, the case for a subsidy is much stronger than that for tariffs (essentially because tariffs will hamper firms who might use the imported good as an input into production as well as reducing consumption), although the problems involved in raising the revenue needed by the subsidy alter the calculus somewhat.

[12] Though the notion that the state played a key role continues to be denied by most economists; see, for example, the list of reasons given by Sachs (2005: 33–5) for Britain's successful Industrial Revolution.

there is some recognition that the learning process may actually slow as workers are transferred from the production of old to new goods. As Lucas (1993: 263–4) says '. . . . shift of workers from old goods with low learning rates to new goods with high rates involves an initial drop in productivity: people are better at familiar activities than they are at novel ones'. This also provides a justification for some degree of state intervention to speed the process of labour transfer from one industry to another.

All these arguments provide a powerful case for state intervention. Nevertheless, such government intervention may simply replace market failure with state failure. In particular, the notion that learning should be promoted by some form of protection is controversial. The title of Kemp's (1960) paper *The Mill-Bastable Infant Industry Dogma* undoubtedly gives the flavour of much of the literature, and much of the empirical work on the specific issue of industrial policy carried out over the last twenty years has also tended to conclude unfavourably. That market failure occurs is universally recognized, but it is a leap from there to the conclusion that industrial policy is the solution.[13] In a stylized neoclassical world of perfect information and zero transaction costs, the sort of rigidities that under-pin the low level equilibrium states described above could not exist. But even in a world of imperfect information, non-trivial transaction costs, capital market failure and pervasive increasing returns to scale, the case for a national technology policy still has to be made. As Paul Krugman (1993*a*, *b*, 1996) has rightly pointed out, even if we accept the desirability of increasing economy-wide productivity (as an end in itself rather than a means to simply increasing 'competitiveness'), it is still not obvious that state intervention is the best solution. The main problem is political. According to Krugman (1993*b*: 161), 'Much, probably most, actual industrial policy continues to be based on economically irrational criteria. In addition, the political economy of industrial policy remains very problematic, with the risks of capture by special interest groups very high'. For Sachs (2005) too, industrial policy has no role to play in 'making poverty history' across the globe. The case for economy-wide or non-selective intervention is of course more easily made than that for industrial policy (selective intervention) precisely because the informational requirements and monitoring costs are much less. But even developing an adequate non-selective technology policy is by no means an easy task, and countries with weak states may do better to focus on 'getting prices right' rather than spending heavily in an attempt to enhance education and skills.

There are a number of responses to all this. Firstly, there is now a well-articulated body of theory which provides a justification for state intervention to develop manufacturing capability. The evolutionary approach, with its emphasis on the need for learning and state industrial policy, attempts to do exactly that (Nelson and Winter 1982). There is also a good deal of evidence from East Asia

---

[13] A useful general discussion of the issues can be found in Lall (1992, 2001).

which supports the contention that industrial policy can work (Amsden 1989; Wade 1990; Lall 2001). Secondly, on the specific issue of infant industry protection based on capital market failure, Krugman (1993a: 135) has claimed that '. . . many infant industries in developing countries are made up of subsidiaries of multinational firms, which presumably have little problem of access to capital, and even domestic firms often have close links to banking groups that could presumably finance them if the prospect of future profitability were fairly high'. But it is hard to see that this has much relevance to the situation faced by many small and medium-sized firms located in rural areas in developing countries, still less countries which were necessarily closed as in the case of Maoist China. The second best policy here is likely to be government subsidies to the infant industries concerned. Of course Krugman is right in saying that 'institutional reform' will help in many cases, but that will not tackle the fundamental problem of imperfect information and uncertainty over when learning will have proceeded far enough to allow profits to be made. Even in countries with financial sectors as well-developed as those of Britain and the USA, shortage of finance for the small-scale sector and more general short-termism on part of financial institutions is a problem of long-standing (Zysman 1983; Hutton 1995; Pollin 1995; Kitson and Michie 2000). It was first officially identified as long ago as 1931 by the Macmillan committee. Thus Kitson and Michie (1996: 47) concluded that even, after financial liberalization under Thatcher, the Britain of the 1990s needed '. . . an investment bank for small and medium-sized enterprises, not only to help start-ups, but to facilitate the growth of small firms and the creation of a competitive Mittlestand sector'.

Thirdly, we must not expect too much of poor countries in terms of the development of technological capability in manufacturing. We need in particular to distinguish between two types of capability: the capability to innovate, and the capability to absorb and apply existing world technologies. For a poor country, the immediate task is to develop the latter rather than the former because the benefits are so much greater than the costs. It is of course true that growth on the basis of the diffusion of knowledge is likely to be of comparatively short duration, at least if we regard several decades as falling within the compass of 'short'. As the late-starter approaches the world technological frontier, so its growth rate is likely to slow as the scope for catch-up diminishes and it is forced to deploy increasing resources to research and development. In the long run, then, there is no alternative but to develop an indigenous innovation capability. Nevertheless, this long run problem is not an issue which confronts most poor countries, for whom the essential problem is to start rather than to sustain the development process. To berate China for failing to develop innovatory capability and for reliance on cheap labour, as does much of the literature bemoaning the absence of globally competitive firms in China, is rather beside the point. The very fact that output, employment and profitability have grown so more quickly than under any plausible counterfactual points strongly to the conclusion that China has been remarkably successful. If we are to make international comparisons, the right one is between contemporary China and the textile-orientated Japan of the 1920s and 1930s, rather than with the Japan of the 1950s, when MITI presided over the shift towards heavy industry.

Ultimately, however, these questions are empirical. And as will be argued in the next chapter, the experience of Maoist China supports the evolutionary/revisionist approach: that is, China was comparatively successful in developing its technological capability because it followed an explicitly interventionist strategy. The picture which will be painted is not one of uniform success. Nevertheless, there are good reasons for concluding that late Maoist China was generally very successful in enhancing its manufacturing capability in rural areas, and that this enhancement of capability laid the foundations for the rural industrial expansion of the 1980s and 1990s.

5.5. The Learning Hypothesis

Let me summarize the argument. There is a wealth of international evidence and economic theory which suggests that convergence of per incomes between rich and poor countries is neither a simple nor a mechanistic process. Rather, successful industrialization requires a long and protracted process of learning. To be sure, developing economies will speed the catch-up process if they are receptive to new ideas. But ideas themselves are not enough. Poor countries need also to apply those ideas effectively, and such a capability can only be acquired via learning-by-doing. The very process of learning itself requires an extensive programme of investment in physical capital; many skills are acquired by a process of learning-by-doing in a factory environment. For that very reason, one cannot expect newly-created industries to be efficient. It is a simple enough task to create new factories, but it takes time before infant industries grow up to become efficient enterprises.

Furthermore, there is every reason to believe that learning will occur only slowly—and perhaps not at all—in a market-driven economy. Precisely because of capital market failure and the existence of increasing returns, the case for infant industry subsidies is extremely powerful. Indeed it is hard to think of a country which has successfully industrialized—certainly not the USA, Germany, Japan or South Korea—without extensive state intervention, whether in the form of industrial subsidies or tariff protection. It is because infant industries are unprofitable in the short and perhaps even medium term that subsidies are essential.

More precisely, the discussion in this chapter suggests the following hypothesis. Rapid growth in poor countries depends primarily upon raising economy-wide productivity by the application of more advanced technology (catch-up). Successful catch-up in turn depends upon three factors. Firstly, and self-evidently, the scope for catch-up will be much greater in countries or regions which are technologically backward. The counties of rural China were of course far from the world technology frontier at the close of the Maoist era and therefore in principle could exploit the advantages of backwardness. Secondly, successful catch-up growth can only be realized if a poor country has access to more advanced technology. Of course countries can innovate themselves, but the costs involved will in general be greater than if they are willing to learn from abroad. This does not imply that a country must implement a free trade regime; strategic or managed integration, focusing on the import of capital goods embodying new technologies, will be enough. But there is little doubt that (for example) China's ability to attract FDI in the 1980s and 1990s helped the process of technology transfer. The third necessary pre-condition for rapid catch-up is a well-developed human capital base. Unless a country has a sufficiently well-developed absorptive capacity, it will not be able to make much use of imported technology. Some skills and competencies are readily codifiable and can be acquired via education or by simply reading a book of blueprints. But an important element in skill acquisition is a more informal process of learning-by-doing because that is the only way to absorb tacit knowledge. The development of absorptive capacity therefore seems to depend not only upon the expansion of the educational base, but also upon an experience-based process of learning-by-doing. Employment in manufacturing industry provides the context for such learning.

6

Learning to Industrialize in the Maoist Era

The conventional wisdom explains Chinese rural industrialization in the 1980s and 1990s in terms of either fiscal decentralization or liberalization. Such an approach allows in *principle* for the possibility that the enhancement of manufacturing capability in the Maoist era eased the path of the reformers, but in practice little such enhancement is said to have occurred: 'The economic basis of the coastal regions remained basically unchanged from the prerevolution period' (Bao et al. 2002: 96). Insofar as skills and ideas were important for post-1978 industrial success, indigenous learning-by-doing during the Maoist era proved much less important than the know-how provided via the open door. There is an important kernel of truth in this sort of story. For example, the coastal region benefited significantly from the open door, and many export-orientated industries were established on the back of foreign know-how. Maoist skill legacies may therefore have been less important for some of the coastal provinces than skills acquired from abroad. A region deficient in management skills can substitute foreign for indigenous managers, and it is arguable that this is what transpired in parts of Guangdong and Fujian.

However, there is an alternative way to conceptualize Chinese rural industrial success. As discussed in the previous chapter, an extensive process of learning-by-doing in the industrial sector was the norm in many countries during the early stages of their economic development. In both nineteenth century Britain and post-1868 Japan, a long period of learning was needed before either country was able to establish industries characterized by high levels of labour productivity. In each case, industrial policy facilitated learning: it is one of the more enduring myths of Britain's industrial revolution that it was brought about by a regime committed to laissez faire. The historical applicability of the Lewis model—in which unlimited supplies of unskilled labour glide almost effortlessly from agriculture to industry in response to a surge in the investment rate—is in fact very limited. It was not shortages of unskilled labour which constrained industrialization but a lack of essential skills.

From this perspective, it seems entirely plausible to view the rapid development of manufacturing in the Chinese countryside after 1978 as the culmination of a long process of learning. More precisely, it was the diffusion of skills from urban core to rural periphery, and the learning-by-doing in the primitive rural industries of the Maoist era, which ensured that China entered the 1980s with the workforce needed for rapid industrial expansion. By 1978, an extensive manufacturing capability had been created in rural areas.

6.1. Rural Industrialization and Learning-by-Doing

Many of the skills which made possible the rapid industrialization of the transition era were acquired via a process of learning-by-doing under Mao. The vehicle for learning-by-doing was the rural industry established under the aegis of the Third Front, and the county and CBE programmes of the 1960s and 1970s. This process of rural industrial expansion was documented in Chapter Two. As a result, China already possessed a large rural industrial workforce by 1978. These workers had made the difficult transition from farm to factory, and most had gained invaluable experience of factory employment. They had learned by doing.

One of the attractions of this learning-by-doing hypothesis is that it explains the *gradual* acceleration in the growth of rural industrial output during the late 1970s. If policy change had been critical to the process, a much more abrupt discontinuity in the pace of the growth in the early 1970s (following fiscal decentralization) or in the early 1980s (as a result of liberalization of controls on ownership) would be observed. In fact, however, the change was much more gradual. The growth rate began to accelerate, and continued to do so during the 1970s and the 1980s, in most parts of China. The process, in other words, was one of trend acceleration. This evidence seems in accord with the notion of a gradual process of learning-by-doing which generated steadily rising levels of rural industrial output.

In a sense, however, the need for a protracted process of learning-by-doing is demonstrated by the *failure* of the attempts at rural industrialization during the Great Leap Forward. The experience of a county like Zhangye in northern Gansu was fairly typical. GVIO there soared from 5.7 million *yuan* in 1957 to 27.6 million *yuan* in 1960, but then plummeted to a mere 3.4 million *yuan* in 1963 as the gains from the Leap were reversed (ZGZ 1993: 62, 89). The only places where the programme was even relatively successful already had an established rural industrial base. As Wagner (1995) points out, the skills acquired in traditional iron-making in the Dabieshan region of Shanxi helped to make the Great Leap Forward work. In Wuxi, too, the industrial inheritance appears to have ensured that industrial output did not collapse after 1960. However, there is little evidence that the Leap helped to push forward the pace of industrialization. At its

1963 trough, GVIO stood at 43 million *yuan*—approximately half the level achieved at the apogee of the Leap in 1960—and the 1960 level was not re-attained until 1969 (WXG 1990: 25–7).

The main problem was that the Leap strategy over-emphasized heavy industry. In Wuxi, for example, the share of light industry declined from 93 percent in 1957 to only 65 percent in 1960, an impossibly rapid pace of attempted structural transformation. In Zhangye, the problem was the expansion of iron production. This led to excessive and premature exploitation of the county's large coal reserves, so much so that coal production—which reportedly touched 328,000 tonnes in 1959—did not regain its 1957 level of production of 48,000 tonnes until 1970 (ZGZ 1993: 104). The Great Leap Forward might well have been much more successful (at least in the short run) if it had emphasized expansion of existing industries rather than diversification. It could, for example, have focused on the sorts of light industry which made more use of the traditional proto-industrial and handicraft skills which did exist in most parts of the countryside. One thinks here of textiles, garments, the traditional paper-making discussed by Eyferth (2003, 2004) and food processing. It therefore seems reasonable to conclude that the type of rural industrialization attempted during the Great Leap Forward was premature. Rural China simply lacked the capability to develop modern industry in the late 1950s.

Nevertheless, some of the legacies of the Leap were long-lasting. For one thing, many of the rural enterprises which existed in rural China by the late 1970s had been initially established during the Leap. In Huancheng commune in Xinhui county (Guangdong), for example, five of the fifteen enterprises operating in 1980 had been set up in 1958 (Siu 1989: 253). The same was true of Zhangye's coal mines (ZGZ 1993: 102–3). As importantly, many lessons were learnt from the failure of the Leap, the most obvious of which was the need to proceed more slowly in developing rural industry. This is reflected in the relatively measured approach to industrialization adopted during the 1960s and 1970s. Thus the programmes of the 1960s focused on developing Third Front industries in Sichuan and the north-west, and on state-owned industries. Only in the 1970s did the focus of the industrialization programme shift to Third Front programmes in western Hubei, Henan and Hunan, at the same time as intra-county emphasis shifted to commune and brigade enterprises. Furthermore, much more emphasis was placed on developing a more diversified rural industrial sector. Whereas the strategy adopted during the Leap focused almost exclusively on iron and steel, the programmes of the 1970s—as the very name 'five small industries' makes clear—was much broader in its conception and much more successful as a result.

The existence of learning-by-doing also meant that the losses made by the rural industries of the late Maoist era was not necessarily a good argument for their closure. Whereas Wong, Whiting and others portray these losses as a sign of failure (an inevitable consequence of state ownership as an instrument of industrialization), one can equally well argue that the losses reflected the infant status of the industries. The learning curve faced by these rural industries was still steep even in the 1970s and accordingly, evaluated in either neoclassical terms or in terms of global competitiveness, much Maoist rural industry was still inefficient. But the medium term gains in respect of the acquisition of more advanced general skills were high. In that sense, the very fact that the Maoist rural industrialization strategy placed so much emphasis on the production of new goods was a great advantage. The scope for learning in the production of iron and steel, chemical fertilizer, cement etc was much greater than that in the production of traditional textiles and food products. Proto-industry, precisely because it involved the production of traditional goods using non-mechanized techniques, provided a much more limited range of skills to its workforce. Regions with an extensive tradition of proto-industrial production still had an advantage over regions without such a tradition in terms of absolute productivity levels but, if it is assumed that the gains from learning-by-doing are bounded, their scope for further gains must have been limited by the 1970s.

6.2. The Diffusion of Skills and Educational Expansion in Rural Areas under Mao

Learning-by-doing was central to the development of industrial skills in rural China. However, the creation of a skills base in the countryside by the close of the 1970s also owed a great deal to two other late Maoist programmes: the diffusion of skills from urban to rural areas, and the expansion of rural education.

6.2.1. From Urban Bias to Walking on Two Legs: Policy Imperatives in the Maoist Era

The late Maoist era was characterized by an unparalleled process of skill diffusion from urban to rural areas. This diffusion process centred around the Third Front programme and the sending down of cadres and educated youth to the countryside. It was preceded, however, by an altogether different approach to the problem of development.

In retrospect, the industrialization strategy adopted during the First 5YP—the years characterized by Chen Yun as a Leninist golden age—was a classic example of urban bias. The famous 156 large-scale projects launched during this period with Soviet assistance were located predominantly in urban areas, albeit mainly in interior rather than coastal provinces. And the rate of agricultural growth lagged substantially behind that of the industrial sector: grain output grew by only about 2 percent per year if one accepts the view of Liu and Yeh (1965) that the official data for the 1950s under-state production in 1952, and therefore exaggerate the growth rate during the First 5YP (Bramall 2004). Even the official data show agricultural value-added growing at only 4 percent per year between 1952 and 1957, well below the 19 percent growth achieved in industry (TJJ 1999). To be sure, the base level of industrial production was much lower in 1952, but the mis-match between agricultural and industrial growth is still striking. Thirdly, and perhaps most significantly, the pattern of intersectoral flows shows that the net outflow from the agricultural to the industrial sector was greater during the 1950s than at any other time during the post-1949 era (Sheng 1993; Ishikawa 1967). Finally, as noted earlier, there was little attempt to use rural industry to close the urban-rural gap: as Riskin (1987: 118) says, 'little attention was actually paid to local industrialization during the First Plan period'.

A proper characterization of China's post-1957 development strategy is more difficult. Until at least the late 1970s, Mao's 1956 speech on the 'Ten Great Relationships' and the subsequent promulgation of the slogan 'walking on two legs' were widely seen in the West as signalling a genuine shift towards a more rural-orientated development strategy, and hence a break from the Stalinist model employed in the Soviet Union. Some continued to hold this view into the new millennium (Gray 2006). However, most scholars revised their view during the 1980s because newly-released data revealed the extent of the famine of the early 1960s and the stagnation of per capita grain output during the 1960s and early 1970s at its 1957 level of about 306 kgs (TJJ 1999: 79). By the 1990s, the academic consensus was that the Maoist commitment to rural development had been more notional than real. Rural material living standards increased only slowly as a result of enforced collectivization, the suppression of rural sidelines and continuing extraction of resources from the rural sector via the internal terms of trade.

Such revisionism has gone too far. It ignores the systematic under-statement of production levels by the official data for the 1970s, and the evidence pointing to trend acceleration in the growth of agricultural production in that decade driven by the trinity of irrigation, chemical fertilizer inputs and the growing availability of new high-yielding crop varieties. The conventional wisdom also underplays the many efforts that were made to develop the rural sector in the late Maoist era. Policy may have been biased against *agriculture*, but it is much less clear that it was biased against the *rural* sector as a whole because of the increasing emphasis given to developing industry in the countryside. Rural industrialization was given priority in 1958, and so it was again after 1965: much of the focus was on expanding the output of producer goods for use in the agricultural sector. There continued to be a net outflow of resources from agriculture, but its extent was undoubtedly less than it had been in the 1950s. And Maoist attempts to expand the irrigation network were very real, and brought lasting benefits. All this continues to distinguish Maoism from the strategies adopted across most of the developing world.

Most importantly for our purposes, much effort went into enhancing rural technological capability via the development of education and skills in the late

Maoist era. These efforts fall conveniently into three categories. Firstly, the Third Front programme of defence industrialization was predicated upon skill transfers from the urban sector. Secondly, the *xiafang* campaign, which provided the foundation for the nationwide expansion of county SOEs and commune and brigade enterprises. Together these two amounted to a programme of urban to rural skill diffusion and can conveniently be discussed together. The third element in promotion of rural development was the expansion of rural education.

6.2.2. The Diffusion of Skills to the Countryside

One key element in this post-1960 process of capability enhancement was the transfer of skilled workers and urban youth to the countryside. Some of these skill transfers occurred during the 1950s. For example, 50,000 skilled workers were moved into Maoming county in Guangdong in 1958 to establish an oil refinery (Maoming SZ 1997: 113). However, the bulk of the transfers took place during the 1960s as an integral part of the programmes of Third Front construction, and the sending-down to the countryside of urban youth and skilled urban workers.

(A) THE THIRD FRONT

Of the three regions singled out for the big Third Front (*da sanxian*), the southwest received the largest influx of labour. Sichuan was of course the focus. The number of workers employed in its basic construction teams increased from 200,000 in 1964 to 845,000 in 1966, and the total number of those involved during the high tide of 1964–65 was 2 to 3 million; many of these workers were mobilized to construct the Kunming-Chengdu railway and the steel complex at Panzhihua. Critical to this process was an influx of plant, research institutes and skilled workers from outside the province. For example, 90 enterprises were re-located to Sichuan from the first front between the middle of 1964 and 1967, and a further 27 were re-located during 1970–71 (Yang 1997: 166–8). These enterprises were re-located from coastal regions and from established industrial centres, and thus skill diffusion followed in their wake. In all, perhaps 400,000 workers were moved into Sichuan as part of the Third Front (Liu 1988: 150).

One particular focus for Third Front programmes within Sichuan was the city of Chongqing. Chongqing had been developed as an armaments base by warlords in the 1920s and 1930s, and was expanded further during the second Sino-Japanese war (Howard 2004), and Front planners sought to build upon this skills base. 46,000 workers were moved in to the Chongqing weapons base during 1965–65 alone, mainly from Beijing, Shanghai and Nanjing, and the provinces of Liaoning and Guangdong (CSJW 1991: 108–10). Many of these workers went to Chongqing city itself, but a significant proportion went to outlying counties within Chongqing municipality.

Sichuan was not the only western province selected as a centre for Front construction. Guizhou, for example, received an influx of about 100,000 workers, who were deployed in coal (over 20,000), metallurgy (5,000), machinery (5,000), chemicals (2,500) and hydropower. The largest contingent (36,000) joined various military construction brigades (Pan 1988: 172–7; Shen and Tong 1992). Many of these workers were transferred from relatively advanced industrial centres like Shanghai and Liaoning. The north-west was also targeted as a centre for Third Front construction. Gansu received a large influx of workers from Guangxi, Liaoning and Jiangxi provinces, and steel workers sent from the Ma'anshan and Shoudu plants were instrumental in developing steel production in the province (Su 1988: 165). Qinghai and Ningxia also benefited (Shen and Tong 1992: 161–2).

During the second stage of *da sanxian* construction, the focus shifted more towards central China and there the aim was to develop weapons production in the western prefectures of Hunan, Hubei and Henan (Wang 1993: 68–72, 396–7). In Hunan, the decision to develop the province's Xiangxi prefecture as a Front centre led to a reported influx of 2 million workers and cadres from other parts of the province (Liu 1990: 163). Other workers came from outside Hunan; some 15,000 skilled workers were despatched from Henan, Shanxi and Shandong to develop coal production, and the transfer of 40 enterprises and nearly 29,000 workers to Xiangxi was designed to establish the weapons base itself. All this had the effect of increasing the share of the machinery industry in GVIO from less than 6 percent to 23 percent by the mid-1970s (Mao 1987: 171–2). The mountainous western region of Henan benefited from a similar process when Front construction was stepped up there in the early 1970s (Zhang and Hou 1990: 157–8). And the decision to build the Second Automobile plant at Shiyan led to a big influx of skilled workers into Hubei (Shen and Tong 1992: 163).

As important in promoting the diffusion of skills to the countryside were the 'little' Third Front projects launched in China's eastern provinces. The decision to develop a Huanan heavy industrial base in Shaoguan in northern Guangdong—the province's little Third Front programme—led to the transfer of whole factories as well as their personnel to counties such as Lechang (Lechang XZ 1994: 201). Shanghai contributed some 262,000 workers to Third Front construction between 1966 and 1979, the bulk of whom went to 'little' Third Front projects in Anhui (Shanghai's designated Third Front region), Jiangxi and Shandong (Hu 1987: 146). Indeed inflows of workers from Jiangsu and Liaoning ensured that Anhui's electrical machinery industry developed very quickly after 1970 (Zheng and Gao 1987: 169).

(B) *XIAFANG*: TRANSFERS OF EDUCATED YOUTH AND CADRES

The skills base in rural China was also expanded by the policy of *shangshan xiaxiang* ('up to the mountains and down to the countryside'), which returned many cadres and workers to rural areas, and sent many urban-educated young people to the same destinations. The *xiafang* (sending down) process occurred in two phases. The first, running from approximately 1961 to 1965, was aimed at reversing the 'premature' urbanization of the Great Leap Forward which was partially blamed for the famine. During these years, some jurisdictions which had become cities were demoted to county status, and a large number of migrants were returned to their former home village. In Zhejiang, about 1 million people experienced some form of *xiafang* between 1961 and 1966. Of these some 36,000 were sent to state farms, and a further 30,000 were allocated to the PLA's Production and Construction corps. But the majority were either returned to their home village (811,000), or sent to some other production team (Wang 1988: 153). In Jiangsu, the numbers were much smaller; only 153,000 were affected (Du 1987: 151). In Hunan, the pre-1965 figure was 78,000 (Mao 1987: 182). The second phase of the *xiafang* process was launched during 1967-68. The scale this time was much larger, partly because of a perceived need to disperse the large number of Red Guards who had wreaked havoc in the cities during the early years of the Cultural Revolution. By the time this second phase was brought to an end in 1977-79, no less than between 16 and 18 million people had been displaced (Bernstein 1977; Shen and Tong 1992: 187; He 2004: 27).

The usual destination for those subject to *xiafang* was a neighbouring county within the same province; many of Shanghai's Red Guards went no further than Chongming and Hengsha islands in the mouth of the Yangzi river. Wuxi county, nicknamed 'little Shanghai' before the Revolution because of its industrialization and its close links with the municipality, was also a frequent destination. Further afield, the story was often the same. Workers and young people were exiled, but often not very far; for example, much of Jung Chang's (1991) exile was spent in Deyang, close to Chengdu.

However, there was certainly some inter-provincial migration. Shanghai sent over half a million educated youth to work outside the municipality (Hu 1987: 146); of these, no less than 151,000 ended up in Anhui (Zheng and Gao 1987: 180). In 1970 alone there were 371,000 permanent emigrants, compared with only 59,000 immigrants (TJJ 1988: 237). Jiangsu rusticated 23,000 to Xinjiang, Nei Menggu and Northern Shaanxi (Du 1987: 146, 151). Yunnan's Xishuangbanna was an especially frequent destination because it had been designated a rubber base and therefore required a larger workforce. Shanghai, for example, sent some 48,000 young people to Yunnan during 1967-77 (Zou and Miao 1989: 210). The *xiafang* programme also sent large numbers to the Sanjiang region of Heilongjiang province, the 'Great Northern Wilderness'. Heilongjiang received at least 400,000 educated youth, of whom 170,000 were sent from Shanghai, 67,000 from Tianjin and 104,000 from Beijing (Shen and Tong 1992: 189). Its permanent population increased by over 200,000 in 1970 solely due to in-migration (TJJ 1988: 236).[1] In both the Sanjiang region and in Xishuangbanna, the educated youth found themselves working on quasi-militarized state farms, rather than as members of

---

[1] It is not entirely clear whether this figure refers simply to *hukou* migration (to those who permanently changed their place of registration) or also includes temporary population movements.

production teams. Still others ended up on state farms in the border provinces of Xinjiang and Inner Mongolia.

The numbers affected by these programmes were not small. The estimates cited in the literature vary somewhat, partly because of differences in the time periods selected, and depending upon whether cadres are included in the numbers. In Guangdong, for example, some 580,000 young people were sent down in to the countryside between 1962 and 1974 along with 29,000 cadres between 1966 and 1970 (GDRKZ 1995: 67–8). Yunnan's *xiafang* programme involved 216,000 persons between 1967 and 1977 (Zou and Miao 1989: 225), and Zhejiang sent down about 0.5 million in the post-1966 period (Wang 1988: 153). Gansu sent down 1,760,000 workers and cadres in 1968 alone; a further 204,000 were dispatched between 1973 and 1977 (Su 1988: 171–2). Not surprisingly, the numbers involved for the more populace provinces were much greater. Jiangsu's *xiafang* programme involved 861,000 between 1963 and 1979 (Du 1987: 151), and Hunan's *xiafang* programme affected 636,000 between 1962 and 1979 (Mao 1987: 184). The officially-reported Shanghai figure for rustication was about 600,000 between 1968 and 1976 (Hu 1987: 146). However, the population counts suggest that the outflow was even larger.

The *xiafang* programme had its limitations as a strategy for the promotion of rural industrialization. For one thing, the period spent in the countryside was comparatively short and this must have limited the extent of diffusion. For example, many of Shanghai's exiles returned in the late 1970s; there was net return migration of well over 250,000 in 1979 alone. Secondly, and although the experience of urban youth in the countryside varied (Jiang and Ashley 2000), there is no doubt that many came to loathe their enforced rural exile (Chang 1991), and not just those sent there unwillingly (R. Yang 1997). This alienation inevitably inhibited the process of skill diffusion. In any case, few of the rusticated brought with them especially valuable industrial skills. Furthermore, many of the educated youth ended up working on state farms, and thereby contributing to the expansion of agricultural production via land clearance and involvement in drainage projects, rather than contributing to industrial development. The rustification programmes also led to very considerable environmental damage in sensitive regions like as Xishuangbanna or Hainan island, another centre for rubber production (Shapiro 2001).

Nevertheless, and despite these limitations, the *xiafang* programmes did much to promote skill diffusion. Urban youth often lacked industrial skills, but their education enabled them to take on key book-keeping and managerial roles in both production teams and in small-scale industrial enterprises. Many production teams also exploited the contacts of their educated youth and rusticated cadres to acquire technology, specialist skills and access to the markets of the big urban centres (He 2004: 27). Wuxi county, which developed close links with Shanghai, offers a good example. Wuxi was able to develop these links because a significant number of Shanghai's cadres had been 'sent down' to that county; it received about 33,000 workers during the 1960s, and further 2,400 cadres as a result of *xiafang* during the 1970s (Leeming 1985; Mo 1987: 123; WXG 1990: 10).[2] Similarly, Wuxian county was able to exploit both its geographical proximity and historical ties with Suzhou city (Wuxian GZ 1993). More generally, one of the key reasons for the successful development of commune and brigade industry in Sunan was the forging of close links between cities and rural areas (Mo 1987: 155–6). Retired workers played a crucial role in this process, accounting for a third of Wuxi's technicians in 1970 (Zhu R. 1992: 275). Across Sunan, in fact, counties appear to have benefited as much from an influx of retired urban workers as they did from rusticated youth (Ho 1994: 129–30).

Sunan provides the best example of skill diffusion but its experience was far from unique. Sichuan's counties adopted a dual strategy of both attracting outsiders to provide knowledge, and in sending technicians of their own to urban centres to acquire skills (Enos 1984: 232–3). In Zhejiang, stoppages of production at the height of the Cultural Revolution allowed cadres and technicians from SOEs to help establish silk cloth production in the countryside (Zhu 1992: 275). Xinhui county in Guangdong offers an equally good example; communes there forged successful links with SOEs in the urban centre of Jiangmen (Siu 1989: 245–72). The significance of these exchanges is reinforced by accounts from those provinces where skill transfers were less extensive. For example, a lack of rural skills was seen in Hunan as a key constraint on the development of rural industry (HNQH 1989: 94–5).

To be sure, all these programmes of skill diffusion could have been managed better, and there is no denying the coercive element in many (though not all) of the labour transfers to the Chinese countryside. However, the fact remains that this process of urban to rural diffusion was without parallel in the developing world. It is hard to believe that the rural industrial explosion of the 1980s would have occurred in its absence. As the experience of countries such as Vietnam has demonstrated, the development of industry in the countryside requires much more than incentives.

6.2.3. The Expansion of Rural Education

An integral part of the late Maoist development programme was the expansion of education, a field in which Chinese policy differed significantly from that adopted by India and in most other developing countries (Drèze and Sen 1995). Whereas most countries focused their development efforts on the expansion of urban education during the postwar era, China prioritized its rural sector during the late Maoist era and many scholars have argued that the expansion of rural education was one of the main achievements of the Cultural Revolution (Gao 1999; Han 2000, 2001).

---

[2] Mo (1987: 122) gives a figure of 1,300. Note that Wuxi city also developed close ties with Shanghai. However, the focus in this paragraph is on Wuxi county.

Chinese policy had not always focused on meeting the needs of the country-side. The May Fourth movement advocated the modernization of China's educational system, but it was the needs of China's urban centres that were accorded priority in the Republican era, and there was continuity across the 1949 divide in that the elitist Soviet approach was followed slavishly during the 1950s. Admittedly the first decade of CCP rule had seen considerable efforts to make primary education universal, but rural secondary education was accorded low priority on the grounds that peasants needed no more than a basic education. In consequence, fewer than 40 percent of primary graduates enrolled in lower middle schools and only 30 percent of this cohort ended up enrolling in upper middle schools (Pepper 1996). Only as late as 1958 was any real attempt made to change this system. Although there was some initial success (the upper middle school enrolment rate jumped from 29 to 50 percent between 1957 and 1958), the collapse of the Great Leap Forward and the famine of the early 1960s saw the restoration of the Soviet system. In 1965, as a result of modest enrolment rates in conjunction with high drop-outs rates, only 450,000 of the 1953 cohort of 13 million 6-year-olds enrolled in upper middle school (JYNJ 1997: 1001, 1021).

All this changed during the Cultural Revolution when the elitist model was abandoned in favour of mass secondary education. After the initial disruption of 1967–68, when many schools were closed, enrolment rates soared (JYNJ 1984: 1001, 1021). By 1976, the year in which the radical approach reached its apogee, enrolment rates for lower and upper middle school were respectively double and triple the levels of 1965. The 1964 Population Census recorded 19.7 million children aged seven (TJJ 1988: 400); of these, 4.5 million entered upper middle school in 1973. Of the 14 million children aged four in 1964, 8.6 million entered upper middle school in 1976.

However, the rise in enrolment rates does not tell the full story of Chinese education during the Cultural Revolution. Some of the severest critics have been those who suffered directly during the process. Admittedly much of this criticism is rooted in little more than prejudice. Rusticated 'intellectuals' and cadres saw peasant literacy as a threat to their standing, and it is evident from autobiographical accounts of the period that perceptions of the countryside were derived from a notion of native place hierarchy in which, for the Delta-born intellectual, Shanghai stood at the apex and rural Tibet at the foot. Nevertheless, the educational system suffered from real deficiencies. One acute problem was the low quality of many rural teachers; the policy of sending-down educated youth to rural China in the late 1960s, and employing them as teachers, was at best a partial remedy. Furthermore, the development of education in ethnic minority provinces proceeded slowly. Although illiteracy rates in provinces like Gansu, Yunnan and Guizhou were well down on the pre-revolutionary figures of 85–90 percent, the rates still averaged around 55 percent in the early 1980s. The main reason was the low primary school enrolment rates. Even in 1984, when the national enrolment rate for 7- to 11-year-olds was 95 percent, the rates for these three poor provinces were only 86 percent in Gansu, 92 percent in Yunnan and 84 percent in Guizhou (RKNJ 1986: 311).

Others have offered a more general critique. Seeberg (1990), for example, argued that literacy rates improved only modestly under Mao, and stood at little more than about 30 percent at the end of the 1970s. Glen Peterson (1994a) has offered a somewhat more sophisticated critique. One problem, he argues, was that the criterion for literacy—a knowledge of 1,500 characters—was set at a low level and tended to discourage further learning.[3] Furthermore, whilst noting that collectivization acted as an important stimulus to anti-illiteracy drives (not least because a degree of literacy and numeracy was necessary to draw up production team accounts), the emphasis placed in the late Maoist era on *functional* literacy acted as a constraint on upward mobility through the educational system. By teaching such a narrow curriculum and thereby neglecting general education, the *minban* schools of the Maoist era effectively condemned the rural population to second class status. According to Peterson (1994a: 117): 'The village schools inculcated a basic, poorly funded and limited literacy program. Their economic and social uses terminated at the production team gate'.

For all that, Han Dongping and Gao Mobo are surely right to stress the transformative effect of education in the countryside. Firstly, higher enrolment rates translated into lower illiteracy rates; the 1982 Population Census revealed that only 23 percent of men and women aged 15 or over were illiterate, a vast improvement when contrasted with pre-1949 illiteracy rates of between 70 and 80 percent (Lavely et al. 1990). The criterion for literacy may have been low, but more Chinese were surmounting that hurdle than ever before during the 1960s and 1970s. Moreover, the age structure of illiteracy points to the success of the new educational system. Although the illiteracy rate for the population aged 60 and over was 79 percent (95 percent for women), the rate for those aged between 12 and 19 was less than 10 percent—and this despite the disruption caused by the Cultural Revolution (RKNJ 1986: 618). In the face of these Census data on the age structure of illiteracy, it is hard to accept Seeberg's analysis. Even Peterson (1994b: 120) accepts that China's progress was noteworthy.

Secondly, even if the emphasis of the programmes launched during the Cultural Revolution was on developing functional literacy, we ought not to under-estimate the popularity of education amongst the peasant population (Gao 1999). There may have been initial doubts about its utility (Peterson 1994a), but the peasantry appear to have become much more positive, so much so that there was considerable resistance to the closure programmes of the late 1970s (Pepper 1996). Part of the reason was the obvious correlation between earnings and the level of education. Whether education was functionally necessary for many industrial jobs or whether it served mainly as a signal to employers

---

[3] The 1,500 character benchmark (2,000 for the urban population) was set by the State Council in March 1956 (JYNJ 1984: 895–7).

is moot; one way or another, education helped peasants to gain access to industrial employment. This link between occupational mobility and education is very apparent from the results of the 1982 Population Census. These show that the educational level of those employed in industry was considerably higher than that of those employed in agriculture: 36 percent of agricultural workers were illiterate in 1982, compared with only 8 percent of those employed in industry and transport (RKNJ 1985: 658–9). Furthermore, the link between access to industrial employment and educational attainment appears to have held across Chinese provinces. In every one of the provinces included in Table 6.1 (and the sample is undoubtedly representative), the illiteracy rate amongst the manufacturing workforce was far below that of agricultural workers. Indeed in most of these provinces, the proportion of the agricultural workforce which was illiterate was some 4 to 5 times greater than the proportion in manufacturing. Little had changed by the end of the millennium. By 2002, only 7.8 percent of the total workforce was illiterate. However, of those working in agriculture, 11.7 percent were illiterate compared with only 1.3 percent of workers in manufacturing. Amongst employees in township enterprises, only 2.5 percent of workers were illiterate (LDNJ 2003: 48–53, 67). In other words, literacy was an important entry qualification for employment in manufacturing industry in the early 1980s and beyond.[4]

Thirdly, there is little evidence that the fruits of education in poor and middle-income areas were dissipated by out-migration. During the late Maoist period, of course, the extent of migration was severely constrained by government

Table 6.1 Illiteracy rates by occupation, 1982 (percent; provinces ranked by overall illiteracy rate)

	All Occupations	Agriculture	Manufacturing
Yunnan	48.8	55.5	11.1
Guizhou	48.8	55.5	9.2
Anhui	47.0	55.1	12.4
Jiangsu	32.0	43.3	10.3
Sichuan	30.5	35.4	6.7
Nei Menggu	27.2	36.8	8.1
Zhejiang	24.9	32.0	16.0
Hebei	22.8	27.9	5.7
Guangxi	21.3	24.3	4.8
Jilin	11.8	17.8	4.8
Liaoning	7.7	12.3	3.6
All China	28.2	35.9	7.5

Sources: RKNJ (1985: 654–5); Cao (1987: 276–7); Du (1987: 250); Song N. (1987: 300); Song Z. (1987: 234); Wang (1987: 337); Zheng and Gao (1987: 290); Huang (1988: 260); Liu (1988: 270); Pan (1988: 297–9); Wang (1988: 263); Zou and Miao (1989: 371–3).

[4] The illiteracy rate for manufacturing workers in Zhejiang shown in Table 6.1 is rather anomalous, a point to which I shall return.

legislation. But even after 1978, when migration increased dramatically, education *per se* was not a decisive factor in determining migration decisions. Young educated peasants were much more likely to migrate than older less educated members of the rural community; Du's (2000) study of out-migration from Anhui and Sichuan shows this very clearly. Furthermore, educated migrants tended to earn higher wages than non-educated migrants. In Dongguan, where migrants were likely to find jobs in industry, the return to education was much higher than in areas where migrants typically found jobs in construction (Meng 2000). Nevertheless, multivariate analysis shows that age was the critical factor in influencing migration decisions: education is not even significant in many migration studies (Rozelle et al. 1999; Mallee 2000: 53). In other words, increasing the educational level of the population did not of itself raise the propensity to migrate, and it did bring lasting benefit to local communities.

6.3. The Link Between Skills, Education and Rural Industrial Expansion

The evidence discussed in the preceding sections points towards the conclusion that both the rural skills base, and the size of the educated rural population, expanded apace during the Maoist era. However, although it is not hard to make a case for the intrinsic importance of either, to what extent did the development of skills and education play the instrumental role of promoting rural industrialization?

6.3.1. The Contribution of Rural Education

The econometric evidence on the instrumental significance of education for earnings and for growth is actually rather ambivalent for China. Byron and Manaloto (1990) found that the return to education was lower than in many LDCs. Knight et al. (1999: 79, 87) found in their analysis of migrants to four Chinese cities that the return to having a senior secondary school education was only 8 percent greater than having a primary education or worse. They concluded that wage differentials in their sample were primarily down to discrimination rather than to differences in human capital. Ho and Kueh (2000: 60–5) found that education was important in influencing employers to hire a worker in the first place, but that it played little role in determining the structure of earnings. However, others have argued that the returns were much higher. Heckman (2003: 789) argues that the social return was much higher than the private return, because labour market distortions ensured that earnings did not fully reflect marginal productivity. He concludes that the true rate of return in terms of output rather than wage earnings (excluding intangible externalities) was in the order of 30–40 percent. Moreover, some more recent studies suggest that the private return is not especially low; Liu (2003: 828) concluded that the return to education in the urban sector was in the order of 2.5 percent per year in 1988.

This ambivalent evidence is echoed in what we know of rural growth patterns in the 1980s and 1990s. These show that there was no clear correlation between literacy rates and the growth of rural GDP. Rural Fujian, Jiangsu and Zhejiang, three of China's fastest-growing provinces, all entered the 1980s with literacy rates which were modest by Chinese standards.[5] Yet these provinces enjoyed average per capita GDP growth of a distinctly immodest 10 percent per year or more between 1982 and 1999. By contrast, counties located in Shanxi, Hunan, Guangxi and the three Manchurian provinces, where literacy rates averaged over 70 percent in 1982, grew much less quickly. We can go further. One striking feature of the occupational data in Table 6.1 is that illiteracy was so high in the manufacturing sector in Jiangsu and Zhejiang, both affluent provinces. In Jiangsu, the manufacturing illiteracy rate of 10.3 percent was significantly higher than the national average, whilst that for Zhejiang (at 16 percent) was the highest of any of the provinces included in the sample. Yet, and as we know, rural industry grew faster in Zhejiang and Jiangsu than almost anywhere else in China in the 1980s and 1990s. The clear inference is that literacy was not necessary for the successful development of manufacturing.

What then was happening in Jiangsu and Zhejiang? At one level, the answer is simple: the illiteracy rates were higher in the two provinces because of the greater share of the rural sector in manufacturing employment. Whereas urban manufacturing dominated in both rich provinces like Liaoning and in poor provinces like Guizhou or Sichuan, rural manufacturing was much more important in Jiangsu and Zhejiang, and in that subsector literacy rates were generally lower. An additional contributing factor was that children were working on the factory floor instead of the classroom in disproportionate numbers. Direct data on this are hard to find, but it is interesting to look at the 1982 Census records for those aged between 15 and 19 because we would expect workers aged under 15 to be included in this category. This is because employers and workers alike had an incentive to exaggerate the age of their youthful workers and the obvious thing to do was to categorize 13- and 14-year-olds as being aged 15 or more. On this point, the Census data reveal that 14.6 percent of those employed nationally in manufacturing fell into the 15–19 year category, whereas for Zhejiang the figure was no less than 22.6 percent (RKNJ 1985: 650; Wang 1988: 262). As these child labourers were necessarily unable to complete their education, it is not surprising that occupational illiteracy rates were relatively high.

---

[5] Literacy rates averaged 61, 62, and 68 percent respectively in the *counties* of these provinces in 1982. By contrast, rural rates were about ten percentage points higher in Manchuria (TJNJ 1988).

This evidence for Zhejiang and Jiangsu seems to suggest that an industrial apprenticeship (begun in childhood) was more important than literacy for certain *types* of industrial production. In particular, the sort of small-scale industry successfully developed in the rural hinterland of the coastal provinces did not require much by way of an educated workforce. Wenzhou municipality is in some respects the classic example. It developed all manner of relatively simple industrial products—badges, labels, shoes, plastic bags, simple electrical appliances—in the 1980s and 1990s. Its literacy rate was low; the median literacy rate for Wenzhou's nine counties was only 59 percent, almost 10 percentage points below the Zhejiang rural average of 68 percent (TJNJ 1988). Yet per capita real GDP grew annually by 20.5 percent, fully 8 percent points *higher* than the provincial average.[6] Wenzhou was not alone. Other parts of Zhejiang adopted a similar approach, and even those plants which had set up in Guangdong on the basis of extensive FDI seem to have managed with a comparatively uneducated workforce (Yeung 2001).

It is also worth noting that there is little correlation at the provincial level between *changes* in literacy rates over the period 1982–2000, and growth rates. It is true that Gansu and Guizhou did badly in terms of both output growth and literacy improvement in the 1980s and 1990s. Yet output growth was slow in Guangxi and Hunan provinces even though both achieved big reductions in illiteracy between 1982 and 2000. Zhejiang and Anhui achieved comparable rates of reduction in illiteracy, but output growth was much faster in the former than in the latter (TJJ 1992; TJNJ 2000: 94, 110).

All in all, therefore, the national and provincial data on the relationship between output per head and literacy tell an ambivalent tale for the instrumental significance of education. The safest conclusion from this evidence is that Maoist educational programmes and their successors during the 1980s and 1990s were of intrinsic rather than instrumental significance, at least in the short run. Nevertheless, this is only an interim conclusion. The analytical method used thus far has violated the usual *ceteris paribus* assumption: it leaves unanswered the question of whether the true impact of education on growth is being disguised by the operation of other factors. For example, might the growth of Hunan and Shanxi have been lower still but for their high rate of literacy? A more definitive conclusion on the growth-literacy relationship therefore requires more systematic econometric analysis, a challenge taken up in Chapter 7.

6.3.2. The Significance of Skills for Rural Industrialization

As for the effects of the expansion of the skills base in rural China under Mao, doubts have also been expressed. Sachs and Woo (1994, 1997) are sceptical of the

[6] Wenzhou's success cannot be explained in terms of foreign direct investment; its most explosive growth occurred in the 1980s at a time when the municipality attracted only negligible quantities of foreign investment.

significance of prior industrialization on two counts. Firstly, they argue, labour absorbed by the inefficient industries of the late Maoist period was hard to re-deploy for use in the more efficient private sector even when controls on sectoral labour mobility were lifted in the 1980s because quits were discouraged by the loss of welfare entitlement. An inheritance of skilled labour was therefore irrelevant because it could not be released. Secondly, Sachs and Woo question the importance of skilled labour for development in a country such as China. For them, it is a simple matter to set up and run a new industry using labour fresh from agriculture. There is no need for a long period of apprenticeship or learning-by-doing for such firms and their labour force; low productivity is offset by low wages. This sort of view is of course rooted in one reading of the Lewis model of economic development with unlimited supplies of labour. The Sachs-Woo contention is that the primary requirement for the development of industry in many rural areas across China was an abundance of *unskilled* labour. In particular, those Chinese regions which were industrially under-developed by the time of Mao's death (Guangdong or Zhejiang are usually mentioned in this context) but geographically well-favoured, were in the best position to exploit the opportunities of the transition era. Precisely because such predominantly rural provinces had available a large under-employed farm population, they enjoyed a great advantage over regions (such as Manchuria) where the bulk of the work-force was already employed in inefficient state-owned enterprises. These latter could in principle be transferred into privately-owned enterprises, but they were less likely to be tempted than farm workers because of the loss of pension and welfare rights they enjoyed within SOEs. A large pool of underemployed farm labour was thus the best guarantor of industrial success. The Sachs-Woo view is widely held. Lin and Yao (2001: 179) offer a positive view of the rural infrastructural programmes of the Maoist era but accord little significance to its industrial legacies. According to their econometric analysis '. . . the initial size of the RE [rural enterprise] sector is shown not to matter very much . . .'

However, this sort of analysis tends to ignore two aspects of the Chinese labour market. Firstly, the industrial labour market was segmented. State-imposed barriers were one hurdle; the *hukou* system posed a formidable obstacle to sectoral and geographical migration, and therefore workers remained tied to their place of birth. At root, however, the labour market would have been highly segmented even if the labour market had been 'free' of government interference (as had been the case before 1949). Under-employed farmers, for example, were of little use to industrial employers unless they had the sort of background that would allow them to be integrated into the existing workforce; only after a long period of habituation would 'outsiders' come to be accepted. Segmentation was along the lines of geography, gender, age and party membership. Piek (1998: 128–9), for example, notes that the most important background qualification for those setting up enterprises in Santai and Qianwei counties in Sichuan in the 1980s was party membership because of the connections that conferred.

However, widespread labour market discrimination directed against geograph-ically-determined 'outsiders' was the more general problem. This phenomenon was commonplace in the pre-1949 labour market; outside workers recruited to the Nantong cotton mills in the Republican era were referred to as *chongzi* (worms) (Köll 2003: 97). By contrast, the arsenals of wartime Chongqing tended to discriminate against native Sichuan workers in the early years. Wartime pres-sures admittedly induced a reduction in segmentation in the arsenals of Chongqing, where initial prejudice against Sichuanese workers broke down in the face of labour shortages and escalating costs (Howard 2004: 83–122). Nevertheless, segmentation offers a useful way to explain the absence of class solidarity amongst the Republican workforce (Honig 1992, 1996; Finnane 1993).

The significance of geographical background as an obstacle to employment has also been recognized in the context of the newly-emerging labour markets of the 1980s and 1990s (Wang 1998; Knight et al. 1999; Solinger 1999; West and Zhao 2000). For these scholars, 'insiders' (the local population) had a much bet-ter chance of obtaining a job in a given rural industry than an 'outsider', even if the outsider had a higher skills level. A survey of the origins of workers employed in rural enterprises in the early 1980s found that the proportion of those recruited from outside the province was typically less than 5 percent of the total (Meng 1990: 303). Wu (1994: 121) noted that about 80 percent of employees in any given enterprise came from the village in which the enterprise was located. These findings have been duplicated by most subsequent surveys; lack of *guanxi* was as much a factor in preventing employment in high wage-high status jobs as lack of skills *per se* (Zhang and Li 2003). During the 1980s, the definition of out-sider was a very parochial one; for example, there was a good deal of hostility even between those born in northern Jiangsu and those living in the southern part of the province (Honig 1992; Finnane 1993). In Wuxi, discrimination against outsiders was rampant. Kinship and patronage appear to have been the key factors in determining access to well-paid jobs (Ma 2000). Localism was also very much the norm in Shenzhen, where the Yangzi river and the ability to speak Mandarin were basic dividing lines when it came to categorizing workers (Lee 1995: 384–6). Even when migration did take place, wage payments were tied closely to the worker's place of origin. Workers from Sichuan typically occupied the lowest rung in the hierarchy and were usually relegated to jobs in agri-business (Chan et al. 1992: 304–7).

Labour market segmentation certainly declined as the transition era pro-gressed. In southern Jiangsu, Guangdong and Zhejiang in particular, the pace of growth led to a tightening of labour markets. As real wages rose, so employers looked further afield for cheap labour. The Delta counties of Guangdong started to import labour in the early 1980s; in Dongguan, for example, local workers often found jobs in Shenzhen and even in Hong Kong, and had to be replaced by workers hired in from other provinces (Potter and Potter 1990: 317–23; Meng 2000; Yeung 2001). Jiangsu also became a significant importer of labour from

Anhui province (Ho 1994; Ho and Kueh 2000). By the mid-1990s, some 50 per-cent of the industrial workforce across Sunan consisted of migrants (Wang 1998: 199). Transition-era China thus provides a classic example of the way in which capitalism breaks down traditional cultural and social barriers.

Nevertheless, the central point is clear. For most parts of China during the bulk of the transition era, it was no easy matter for an outsider to find industrial employment because firms had a clear preference for the recruitment of 'inside' workers. Those firms which already employed an abundant and well-integrated workforce at the start of the transition era, even if its productivity was low, were at a great advantage over firms starting off anew.

The second weakness in the Sachs-Woo approach is that it exaggerates the value of unskilled workers to industrial enterprises. There is no doubt that *some* indus-trial employers preferred to recruit relatively unskilled and inexperienced workers. The 1991 survey discussed by Wu (1994: 135–7) found that around 68 percent of the workers in his sample had less than three years of experience in their previous enterprise.[7] A study of applicants for jobs in Chengdu, Nanchong and Suining in 1995 noted that only 21 percent had experience of three years or more (Ho and Kueh 2000: 52). Knight et al. (1999: 78) found that only 10 percent of migrants to Beijing, Wuhan, Shenzhen and Suzhou were skilled and that 61 percent came from an occupational background in farming. In fact, many firms—especially those operating in the Pearl River Delta—were happy to recruit young unmarried women workers (who by definition lacked experience and skills) because they were seen as relatively docile, lacking family commitments (and therefore not needing much time off) and having a high degree of manual dexterity. This made them well-suited to employment on assembly lines used for the production of tex-tiles, apparel and electronics (Lee 1995; Fan 2003; Fan 2004a).[8] Indeed young women were often seen as the ideal type of worker.[9] For one private employer, the ideal white collar worker was male, college-educated, married and aged between 30 and 35, but the perfect blue collar employee was an unmarried woman under the age of 25 (Wang 1998: 279). According to Fan (2003: 33):

Labor recruitment is often driven by the widely accepted correlation between youth and productivity . . . Employers in urban areas target young single migrant women who are perceived to be meticulous to detail, efficient, easy to control and capable of handling delicate work.

[7] Though the sample was deliberately biased towards studying the rural textile and apparel industry, where many of the workers were young and unskilled women (Wu 1994: 146).

[8] One factory studied by Fan (2003: 33) even took the view that deteriorating eyesight made the employment of women aged over 20 as problematic. A partial solution to the problem of unskilled labour was to adopt the Smithian/Fordist approach and to break down a process into its component parts, thus requiring a worker to acquire expertise in a very narrowly-defined type of work.

[9] However, marriage was by no means the barrier to migration sometimes suggested. As a study of out-migration from Sichuan and Anhui shows, '. . . counter to commonly held views, these rural women do migrate in substantial numbers after marriage. The sense that marriage ends migration for them is simply not correct' (Lou et al. 2004: 216).

This preference for young female workers seems to have been true not only of Guangdong (on which many of the studies focus) but also of some firms in Zhejiang and Fujian. For example, only 15 percent of the 1,109 in-migrants to Zhejiang included in the 1986 survey were aged over 35, and most of Zhejiang's in-migrants (84 percent) were destined to work in industry. In Fujian, only 22 percent were aged over 35 (Yu 1989: 102-3, 126-7). Employers in Chengdu, Nanchong and Suining did not in practice recruit workers aged over 40 (Ho and Kueh 2000: 63-5).

Nevertheless, many migrant workers, especially those who migrated outside the *hukou* system, were only able to find employment in *non-industrial* occupations (Chan 2004; Fan 2004b). Systematic data collected in a survey of almost 27,000 out-migrants in 1986 (part of a survey of 189,000 rural workers) shows that 8,597 of them found work in the low skill construction sector compared with the 4,593 of them who found work in industry (Yu 1989: 17). Smaller-scale surveys confirm this. The jobs typically undertaken by male migrants were carpentry, portering, loading or to be found in the construction sector. Many female migrants were only able to find jobs as street sellers, waitresses or housemaids. Even if we control for age, sex, education, ethnicity and marital status '. . . [migrants] concentrated on a few selected occupations within each broad occupational category. In particular the jobs required low skills and were potentially health hazardous and labor intensive' (Yang and Guo 1996: 785).

Furthermore, even though unskilled workers sometimes found it possible to gain industrial employment, productivity tended to rise with work experience, and most employers had a clear preference for skilled workers. Here the evidence on the Republican era offers an *indirect* guide to the factors determining the demand for labour in Chinese markets during the transition era. Even during this period, when many industrial jobs required a rather basic array of skills, a premium attached to skilled and experienced workers. Experience mattered because the productivity of a new factory entrant was typically very low due to the profoundly alienating nature of the transition from farm to factory (Hershatter 1986; Honig 1986, 1992; Köll 2003). Many newly-recruited workers were new to manufacturing, and lacked familiarity with the work practices required. The informal and tacit skills which derived from experience of factory work were crucial to achieve high levels of industrial productivity because the rhythms of farming—outdoor, seasonal, the absence of close supervision—were hard for manufacturers to break. Accordingly, an extended process of learning and habituation was necessary before farm workers were able to achieve high levels of productivity. Once workers had gone through this process of habituation, their productivity was much higher. Prior experience of factory life therefore commanded a wage premium.

The attainment of high productivity also required a skilled workforce; thus the Chongqing arsenals of the 1940s required that workers completed a two or three year apprenticeship, and passed a series of examinations as a condition of employment in many skilled occupations. Contrary to some of the more extreme claims made for the significance of geographical segmentation, 'Genuine skill remained essential to armaments production in China . . . Recruiters considered provincial origins *per se* less important than the amount of skill and experience in arms manufacturing a worker brought to the job' (Howard 2004: 106, 107). Of course the Chongqing arsenals were unusual in terms of the skills they required. However, we should not under-estimate the skills needed by workers employed in textile mills. The pre-1949 Nantong cotton mills of Jiangsu province offer a particularly interesting example because this is an example of industrialization in an essentially rural environment on the north bank of the Yangzi estuary. The Nantong mills did use unskilled workers but only for simple tasks. Moreover, a plethora of rules and regulations were drawn up to enforce discipline and standards, clear evidence that unskilled workers had to be carefully supervised and controlled in order to ensure even minimally acceptable levels of productivity (Köll 2003: 81–122). More skilled workers had to be recruited from Ningbo and from parts of Sunan; the decision to set up a Textile School at Nantong was another attempt to address the problems caused by a lack of skilled labour (Köll 2003: 96). The difficulties encountered by Jiangsu's peasant workforce in making the farm to factory transition are clear from the fact that semi-proletarianization was commonplace. Many Nantong workers continued to work their farmland as well as working in the factories, partly as insurance against the effect of factory closure but also because of a recognition that alienation was so intense amongst the workforce that exit (whether by quit or by dismissal) was a likely outcome.

If skills and experience mattered for high productivity in the Republican era, they were more important still after 1978. The evidence here is extensive. One example is provided by the Kelon refrigerator company (Huang 2003: 183–8). Kelon, a township enterprise in Guangdong's Shunde county, became China's largest producer of refrigerators by 1991. Wang Guodan, its founder, had considerable experience of running a transistor-producing firm on behalf of a Hong Kong company before starting to produce fridges in 1984. The 4,000 workers he recruited were not farmers but came primarily from factories producing MSG, rice cookers, and parts for cars. For Wang and for Kelon, experience clearly counted, and the reasons for this become apparent when we consider the problems experienced by firms employing migrant workers with little or no experience of factory work. Yeung (2001: 183–8), in his study on Dongguan, noted the relatively low level of attention paid by migrants to sanitation, cleanliness and safety regulations (though it is evident that insider technicians and managers had an attitude that was nearly as lax). Potter and Potter (1990: 321), in analysing the attitudes of Dongguan's rural population, noted the strong preference for non-factory jobs where these offered a comparable rate of remuneration. Lee (1995) shows how migrant workers regarded the regime in Shenzhen factories as despotic because of the way in which managers controlled their specific place of work within the factory (including lavatory access), the temporal discipline, and the imposition of fines for taking 'unauthorized' leave. Furthermore, they reacted against such discipline:

The rigid compartmentalization of the factory property into areas for different ranks of workers contracted with their former freedom to roam the countryside at will. Thus new recruits to the factory often staunchly and openly resisted management's transfer instructions . . . [CB: from one assembly line to another] . . . Very often compliance was exacted only with the personal appearance of the supervisor or manager on the shop floor

(Lee 1995: 383)

There is also evidence of employer preference for experienced workers. Amongst employers recruiting in Chengdu, Nanchong and Suining in 1995, 61 percent wanted applicants to have some experience of the job applied for, and 19 percent insisted on three years of relevant work experience. This same survey found that wages, especially in the electronic industry, were strongly correlated with experience and that both age and education were very much secondary considerations (Ho and Kueh 2000: 59–60, 63–5). Moreover, skills and experience even trumped place of origin on occasion. Ma (2000: 318) gives the example of an immigrant from Anhui who successfully landed a job as an accountant in a Wuxi factory despite lacking *guanxi*. The migrant in question had no less than 12 years of education and four years of experience as an accountant.

More generally, we need to distinguish between *hukou* migration (where migrant workers change their official place of residence) and non-*hukou* or unofficial migration because there were important differences between these two classes of migrants. Non-*hukou* migrants tended to be relatively uneducated, drawn from rural backgrounds, and likely to end up in rural jurisdictions (the counties of eastern China rather than the cities). *Hukou* migrants often moved to urban centres in eastern China and were usually much more skilled and educated than non-*hukou* migrants (He and Pooler 2002; Chan 2004: 232–4; Fan 2004*b*: 247–50). Many of the more dynamic and advanced industrial firms based in urban centres, in other words, were very happy to employ *hukou* migrants where possible.

The age profile of recruits, and the relationship between age and wages, also tells us a great deal about the premium attached to skills and experience. Women in their late teens (i.e. unskilled women), for example, were not often recruited in the 1980s. The 1986 survey shows that 78 percent of out-migrants (21,122 out of 26,993) were male, and that 9,881 of the combined total (37 percent) were aged 36 or more (Yu 1989: 17). Other evidence suggests that about 50 percent of migrants were aged over 25 in 1988 and 1995 (Rozelle et al. 1999). Of a sample of 655 in-migrants to Jiangsu in 1986 42 percent were aged over 35, which certainly suggests a preference for older workers (Yu 1989: 80).[10] This may

[10] Survey evidence reported by Knight and Song (1999: 299) for the rural area around Handan in Hebei shows that 27 percent of those who had not looked for non-farm work did so because they perceived themselves as lacking skills.

be because the sort of work on offer in Jiangsu was rather different to that required of young women in the electronic assembly factories in parts of Guangdong, Fujian and Zhejiang. If we assume that age went hand-in-hand with greater skills and experience, this does tend to suggest that employers recognized the importance of employing a cadre of skilled workers.

It is also interesting that wages tended to increase in line with age and experience in rural industry. In Zhejiang's Dongyang county, a seven year period of training (three years as an apprentice and four as a journeyman) were regarded as essential training for the traditional woodcarving industry (Cooper 1998: 50-1). In late Maoist Dongguan, a three year apprenticeship and five wage grades based primarily on seniority was the norm in rural industries. The failure of communes to diversify industrial production outside the traditional industries of tile and brick manufacturing into plastics etc. was blamed on lack of knowledge, skills and understanding of markets (Potter and Potter 1990: 138–42, 150-1). In Meishan county in Sichuan, wages amongst workers were directly related to seniority, and to skills (Ruf 1998: 143). More generally, as Knight and Song (1993: 179–81) point out, wages across the TVE sector were strongly correlated with age.[11] The 1988 sample they use shows that the wages of those aged 56–60—the peak earning cohort—were some 20 percent higher than the wages of workers aged between 21-5. And Liu (2003: 828) uses the same data to conclude that an additional year of experience (measured as age minus years of education) raised earnings by between 2.2 and 3 percent.

To be sure, this evidence on the apparent relationship between age and experience on the one hand, and wages on the other, does not constitute decisive evidence on the relationship between experience and productivity. For that to be the case, we would also have to show that wages serve as a reliable proxy for productivity, and on this point the data are open to different interpretations. The household survey used by Knight and Song (1993) is not representative and, as they point out, the link between age and wages does not necessarily reflected the impact of human capital. Culturally-mandated preferential treatment for the elderly within China is another plausible explanation, and that interpretation is strengthened by the relatively non-competitive nature of factor markets in the early 1980s. As a result, wages are not necessarily a guide to marginal labour productivity. Still, Knight and Song probably under-state the impact of market influences within the TVE sector. The shortages of skilled labour in much of China by the mid-1980s was such that firms were more than willing to pay (efficiency) wages which were well above the notional market-clearing level in order to prevent voluntary quitting by skilled labour. Moreover, there is some direct evidence that earnings tended to understate true productivity. According to Heckman (2003: 799), unskilled workers were paid

---

[11] The correlation is even more marked for SOE employees (Knight and Song 1993: 221-31).

their marginal product but skilled workers received only about 10 percent of their true marginal productivity.

Taken together, all this evidence suggests that unskilled workers may have been able to gain *entry* to a wide range of jobs, but *productivity* nevertheless increased with age and experience. Chinese firms could produce profitably by using essentially unskilled migrant workers. However, they were only able to do so in a relatively restricted range of markets using a restricted range of technologies, and by paying very low wages. In the long run, this was not a viable development strategy as, for example, Wenzhou municipality discovered as the 1990s wore on. The long run prosperity of the Chinese industrial sector depended upon raising productivity, and that in turn meant that firms increasingly turned their attention towards the recruitment and retention of skilled workers.

Management skills also mattered. In this regard, the late Maoist era was a good incubator. According to Dwight Perkins (1998: 26, 28):

> The localities learned during the early 1970s and to some extent earlier how to manage a small industrial firm . . . technicians were sent out from city enterprises to help the local people to master the technology and to set up a business organization and train the managers and workers. Local people also went into the city to gain relevant experience, and it was not just the managers and workers that learned how to operate these firms. The cadres in the commune and brigade administration also learned about what it took to make a rural industry successful . . . If there had not been a rural small-scale industry programme earlier, it is unlikely that the response to these incentives would have been anywhere near as rapid. There was no such response to similar reforms in Vietnam.

Furthermore, it is not difficult to argue that learning-by-doing was as important for managers and entrepreneurs as for ordinary workers. Even when Maoist industrial CBEs were inefficient and unprofitable at the close of the 1970s, their workers and cadres acquired valuable 'skills' and these provided the foundation for the growth of the 1980s and beyond. According to Putterman (1997: 1642): 'Contrary to the image of rural cadre status as a reward for revolutionary service implying no managerial competence, there are grounds for believing that the ranks of local government and Party institutions became a relatively effective school of entrepreneurship'. In fact, the successful establishment of CBEs in the 1970s depended upon entrepreneurs with good contacts (to raise the necessary finance from the Agricultural Bank and to ensure both adequate supplies of inputs and market access) and key skills. Where these were available, a lack of skilled labour seems to have been less important (Endicott 1988; Potter and Potter 1990; Chan et al. 1992; Ruf 1998).[12]

---

[12] We should also recognize that private entrepreneurs, almost by definition, were skilled. A survey carried out in Wenzhou found that the background of the overwhelming majority of the managers of 'big labour-hiring households' (*de facto* private enterprises) fell into one of four categories: ex-army, skilled craftsmen, cadres and educated youth sent down into the countryside in the 1960s and 1970s (Nolan and Dong 1990: 143).

6.4. Proto-industrialization and Learning

Industrial skills were acquired across rural China under Mao via learning-by-doing. This process took place in the vast array of rural factories established by the Third Front, county-owned enterprises and the five small industries, the creation and expansion of which was documented in Chapter 2. Previous sections of this chapter have taken the argument a stage further by showing that Maoism contributed further to this process of learning by the promotion of skill diffusion from urban to rural areas (the Third Front and *xiafang* programmes), and by the expansion of education in the countryside. It has also been demonstrated that skills mattered for productivity and industrial expansion after 1978; China's rural industrialization was erected upon an edifice of skilled labour. From this it is a small step to the conclusion that the creation of a skilled labour force was the historic contribution of the programmes of rural development launched across China during the 1960s and 1970s. By recruiting and training previously unskilled farm workers, Maoism laid the foundations for the expansion of industrial production in the decades ahead. Insofar as the Maoist development strategy helped to provide China with a cadre of skilled rural workers, it laid the foundations for long run rural prosperity.

Acceptance of all this nevertheless leaves open the possibility that many of the skills which facilitated post-1978 industrialization were in fact the product of the development of small-scale rural industry during the Republican era. Maoism may have contributed, but the decisive contribution was that of Republican rural industrialization. If true, this implies continuity writ large: the climacterics of both 1949 and 1978 would both have to be set aside. Seen in such a perspective, contemporary industrialization in the Chinese countryside serves as a tribute to the enduring impact of proto-industrialization, rather than to the potency of the state-led industrial development programmes of the Maoist era.

There is no doubt that a wide range of proto-industries had developed across China by 1949 despite insecure property rights, and the absence of any coherent state-sponsored infant industry programme. Nowhere was this proto-industry more permanently established than in Jiangsu, and on this basis many have suggested that the rapid rural industrialization experienced in southern Jiangsu after 1978 had its origins in the prewar era (Fei 1986; Gates 1996; Li 1998). The argument has also been made for parts of Zhejiang. According to Cooper (1998: 53–5), Dongyang's success during the 1980s in developing its woodcarving industry owed much to its tradition in this sphere. The cadre of workers who had acquired skills either before 1937, or during the 1950s (when the revival of industry was deliberately promoted by government) was the base for the development of the industry from the late 1970s onwards.

However, the proto-industrial argument is not very convincing in the Chinese context. The enormous effort expended on identifying the 'sprouts of capitalism' in the nineteenth century has signally failed to show that China was on the verge of 'take-off' in 1839. Moreover, insofar as the economy was poised ready for take-off a century later (as Rawski and others have claimed), the essential dynamic was being provided by the modern industrial sector. The problem with proto-industry was that it locked China into an involutionary process: it allowed output and population to grow at the same rate but provided no basis for per capita output growth (Huang 1990). Moreover, because involutionary growth was characterized by semi-proletarianization (rural households spent some of their time working in handicraft industry, but did not abandon their ties to the land), the process hampered the emergence of the genuine proletariat needed for the development of modern industry. This type of analysis has been argued especially persuasively by Xu (1988) in the context of the cotton spinning. Semi-proletarianization may have helped handicraft producers to ward off competition from western imports in the late nineteenth century, but it did little to further the growth of a modern cotton-spinning industry. These producers only survived by subsidizing handicrafts out of the profits of farming, not by raising productivity. According to Xu (1988: 32): 'Chinese cotton handicrafts were able to offer stubborn resistance to the large-scale machine industry . . . We can safely say that such resistance was, by nature, the ultimate obstacle to the birth and development of modern domestic industry . . .' The contrasting rates of technological dynamism exhibited by the silk-reeling sectors of prewar Japan and China is also illuminating. Ma's (2004) estimates of TFP are not convincing because of both data and methodological problems, but it is hard to take issue with the contrast he draws between a dynamic Japanese and a listless Chinese sector. On the basis of this sort of evidence, writers such as R. Wong (1997) have emphasized the parallels between the processes of proto-industrialization in England, Europe, Japan and pre-1949 China. In all these cases, proto-industrialization led nowhere; only where the sector was revolutionized by modern technology was output growth rapid, and even then (as in the case of cotton weaving) the days of the proto-industries were numbered.

In any case, and whatever the merits of the proto-industrial legacy for industrialization in China during the Republican era, it is difficult to argue that proto-industrial legacies did not atrophy after 1949. The fact that the location of TVE production in the 1980s is correlated with that of pre-1949 rural industry arguably points to the underlying importance of physical geography (the availability of natural resources, low transport costs and proximity to markets) rather than to the significance of skill legacies. There is also recognition, even amongst those who have written about the social costs produced by the decline of proto-industry after 1949, that the preservation of traditional industry was not a viable long run development strategy. According to Eyferth (2003: 54):

It is possible . . . that temporary de-industrialization in the countryside was a price worth paying for China's generally successful transition to industrial modernity. A look at states that protected their craft industries and performed poorly compared with China, such as India, can only reinforce the view that China was right to phase out 'obsolete' industries.

For all that, we cannot entirely dismiss the legacies of traditional industries. China's pre-1949 proto-industry may not have provided the country with an anvil on which to forge an industrial revolution, but it is hard not to conclude that those areas with a proto-industrial heritage enjoyed an advantage over those regions which did not. For example, and as will be discussed in Chapter 8, Shengze's success in developing silk textile production undoubtedly owed something to its favourable location on the Yangzi Delta. However, its history of silk production was probably much more important; after all, there were many other counties in eastern China that were at least as well favoured in terms of their physical geography. The issue of proto-industrial legacies is therefore discussed in more detail in respect of Jiangsu, Guangdong and Sichuan in subsequent chapters.

7

The National Evidence

The Maoist state created a rural manufacturing sector which was large but inefficient. This inefficiency arose partly because political imperative often over-rode economic calculation. But the main reason for industrial failure was that policy activism could not transcend the constraints imposed by the limited development of manufacturing capability in the Chinese countryside. As a result, the rural industrialization campaign of the late 1950s, the cornerstone of the Great Leap Forward, foundered on the rock of skill deficiency. So, too, the Third Front and the 'five small industries' programme of the 1960s.

By the time of Mao's death, however, conditions were altogether more propitious. For all its weaknesses, late Maoist industrialization had set in train a process of learning which expanded the rural skills base. This process of 'learning-by-industrializing' was the crucial element in the development of manufacturing capability. Cadres and workers alike had acquired a range of skills during the abortive industrialization of 1958, and also from the more successful (though limited) industrial development of the 1960s and 1970s. The industries so established were inefficient, but their workers learned by doing and in the process manufacturing capability was created even in some of the unlikeliest corners of the Chinese countryside. By the dawn of the 1980s, efficient rural industrialization was altogether more feasible than it had been during the late 1950s: by then many of China's infant industries had grown up. It was the historic role of *gaige kaifang* to unlock this potential. For policy change did matter: the removal of controls on the private sector promoted industrial growth, as did fiscal decentralization. But these changes provide only an incomplete explanation without some recognition of the role played by the Maoist state in developing rural manufacturing capability.

The acid test of this capability hypothesis is provided by the spatial evidence. If manufacturing capability mattered, we would expect those parts of the People's Republic which inherited an extensive skills legacy to have grown much more quickly than those regions where human capital was still relatively under-developed at the end of the 1970s. We need of course to normalize for the impact of other factors, notably geographical influences on growth. But once that has been done, it ought to be possible to trace a causal connection from initial skills to subsequent growth.

7.1. Trends in County-Level Per Capita Output

As argued previously, there is a strong case for viewing counties as rural jurisdictions. If the manufacturing capability hypothesis is correct, we would expect to find a marked correlation between inherited levels of capability in the late 1970s, and the pace of industrial growth at the county level during the transition era.

7.1.1. Measuring Industrial Output Growth

The biggest problem inherent in this approach is the absence of national data for county-level *industrial* output in the early 1980s, let alone the 1970s. Data on the combined gross output value of agriculture and industry (GVAIO) by county have been published, but data on GVIO (gross industrial output value) are much harder to find. Even where GVIO data are available, village-level (and below) industrial production is usually included within agricultural output before 1984. As a result, published GVIO data under-state the true extent of rural industrialization. The type of national disaggregated data needed to correct for this problem do not exist, and therefore we cannot analyse directly national trends in industrial production at the county level.[1]

---

[1] There are three possible sources for GVIO data at the county level: the *County Records*, provincial compilations and national compilations. However, all three types of materials are problematic. One could in principle use the *County Records* (*xian zhi*) to compile data on industrial output in the 1970s. However, the *xian zhi* rarely contain complete data; it is much more usual to find point estimates for 1965, 1978 and perhaps for 1975 than to find a complete time series. Furthermore, the *xian zhi* are not consistent. Some use constant prices, whereas others give output value in current prices. Some include CBE industrial output in the totals, but others do not.

Similar problems affect the provincial compilations. A number of provincial sources provide county-level GVIO data for 1978; these include AHSQ (1987), HBGK (1984), and YNTJNJ (1990). However, there are no reliable county-level value-added data, and it is often unclear whether the prices used are current or constant. Even more significantly, the provincial compilations typically exclude village and sub-village industry from GVIO. This is not surprising because the official definition of GVIO was expanded to include village and sub-village industrial output only in 1984 (previously, village industry was included in agricultural output). Some provinces have changed the historical data retrospectively and published the results (e.g. SCZL 1990), but this is very much the exception. This problem is compounded by the recently-adopted NBS practice of excluding the output of all small-scale industry from estimates of GVIO. This component of output was usually included in GVIO in most county compilations in the late 1980s and early 1990s, but some recent retrospective revisions have taken to excluding it from all years; for example, the county-level time series data published for 1978 to 1996 in Anhui tongjiju (1997) exclude all industry below the township level.

National compilations are equally problematic. The results of the 1985 Industry Census show GVIO by county, but these too exclude village and sub-village industry. A compilation produced by the Ministry of Finance (Caizheng bu 2000) purports to provide GVIO data for every county

However, this problem can be circumvented by converting GVAIO to GDP (better a measure of valued added than one of gross output), and then using GDP as a proxy for industrial production. By combining data on gross agricultural and industrial output value with those for the occupational composition of the population in 1982, we can estimate county-level GDP in the early 1980s (full details of the methodology used are provided in Appendix 1). Data for county-level GDP at the end of the 1990s are readily available. By averaging the figures available for 1999 and 2000, we can eliminate some of the year-on-year fluctuation and ensure a relatively complete dataset.[2] We can then combine the per capita GDP figures for the end of the millennium with the 1982 estimates to calculate the growth rate of per capita GDP by county between 1982 and 1999–2000. This approach gives us GDP per capita growth rates for each of 2,010 counties out of the 2,059 county-level jurisdictions for which gross output data for 1982 have been published. These estimates provide the basis for the discussion in the remainder of this chapter.

The use of GDP estimates in this way to proxy industrial growth is open to a number of objections, but none of them are compelling. Of course GDP is not the same as industrial output. However, we know that rural GDP increases were driven primarily by rises in industrial production; neither agriculture nor services were leading sectors in the growth of the 1980s and 1990s, and especially not after the surge in agricultural production in the early 1980s. Accordingly, rapid GDP growth serves as a good proxy for rapid industrial growth especially if sustained over a period as long as 1982–2000. The second problem is that a large number of assumptions are needed to estimate 1982 GDP from GVAIO (Appendix 1).[3] County GDP data have, however, been published for some

and city for 1996, but the results are very odd: the data show convergence of GVIO per head between the counties of Anhui and Guangdong, a completely implausible result (the provincial aggregates show that Guangdong's industrial sector grew much faster). Again this is probably because of the exclusion of small-scale industrial enterprises. By contrast, many of the publications of the Ministry of Agriculture (NCGY 1989 and later) suffer from the opposite bias: they exclude township industry and higher.

[2] More recent NBS compilations do not give GDP data by county; see for example XSNJ (2003).

[3] One of the quirks of using GVAIO to estimate GDP is that GVAIO must first be disaggregated into its agricultural and industrial components for the purpose of calculating value-added. The implication is that we could in principle use the estimates of industrial output instead of GDP. However, the estimates of industrial value-added for 1982 are not reliable enough to use in their own right to measure industrial growth because I have calculated them as residuals. That is, GVAIO is disaggregated by first calculating 1982 gross agricultural output; this is estimated on the basis of 1985 per capita agricultural output data (which are available by county), and the resulting figure for 1982 GVAO is then subtracted from GVAIO to produce GVIO. Industrial output is thus the residual, and errors in the estimation of agricultural production show up as biased estimates of industrial production. These biases do not matter too much for the estimation of GDP in 1982 because industrial production was typically only a small component of GDP for most Chinese counties, but the errors are very large as a proportion of industrial output precisely because it was often so small in rural China at that time. It therefore does not make much sense to attempt a direct comparison of industrial output by county in 1982 and 1999/2000.

provinces (such as Jiangsu) and by comparing these 'true' figures with our estimates, it is apparent that the GVAIO-based estimates are comparatively reliable.

A third problem is that some county boundaries changed significantly between 1982 and 1999/2000, and it is impossible to correct for these directly.[4] By calculating the growth of *per capita* GDP, however, the impact of boundary changes can be minimized because (say) under-statement of GDP is offset by a similar—though not of course identical—under-statement of population. Fourthly, county-level price deflators are unavailable. But provincial deflators do exist, and using these (the approach adopted in this chapter) at least corrects for differences between the more inflation-prone provinces (such as Guangdong and Fujian) and those of the interior. Finally, any calculation of growth rates which relies solely on endpoints is problematic because of the potentially distorting effects of local 'shocks' e.g. flooding. The use of data for both 1999 and 2000 does, however, reduce this problem. Moreover, sensitivity analysis suggests that the results are not dependent on the choice of end year. To check this, I experimented with data from the respective provincial *Statistical Yearbooks* for Guangdong in 1998 (GDTJNJ 1999), Zhejiang in 1995 (ZJTJNJ 1996), and for Gansu, Jiangsu, Guizhou and Sichuan for 1996 (GSNJ 1997; JSTJNJ 1997; Guizhou tongjiju 1997; SCTJNJ 1997). In each case, the results essentially replicated the findings outlined below. The overall results are further confirmed by analysis of trends in Jiangsu, where (unusually) time series data on GDP are available in the provincial *Statistical Yearbooks* by county for every year during the 1980s and 1990s.

7.1.2. County-Level Trends: Provincial Aggregation

A useful first step in making sense of the county growth rates for 1982–2000 is to average these estimates for each province. By aggregating county-level data by province, we arrive at much better estimates of *rural* industrial growth than if we use the provincial totals published in (say) the *Chinese Statistical Yearbook*. That is because the county-based methodology excises all cities (as classified at the time of the 1982 Census) from the provincial totals.

The results are shown in Table 7.1. It provides average county per capita GDP growth rates for the period 1982–1999/2000, and juxtaposes them against the level of GDP per head in 1982 and two proxies for industrial capability: the literacy rate, and the rate of industrial employment at the time of the 1982 Population Census. These data show a broadly positive relationship between rates of industrial employment in 1982, and subsequent growth rates; all but one of the fastest-growing five provinces has an industrial employment rate well

---

[4] One consequence of boundary changes in the 1980s and 1990s is that some peri-urban counties have been absorbed into the adjacent city of the same name. For example, the 1982 jurisdiction of Bao'an has been absorbed into Shenzhen, and Laoshan (Shandong province) has been absorbed by Qingdao. As a result, although data exist on these jurisdictions for 1982, they do not for 1999/2000. Accordingly, these counties have been omitted from the analysis.

above the average, and all but one of the slowest-growing five provinces has a below-average industrial employment rate. Nevertheless, the relationship between growth and initial industrial employment is certainly not tight. Hebei, Shandong and Henan all experienced rapid rural growth despite low industrial employment rates in the early 1980s. By contrast, the highly-industrialized Manchurian provinces grew slowly despite high rates of industrial employment; this is especially apparent for Heilongjiang. Using literacy rates to explain provincial variation does not help. The data show very little relationship between literacy and rural growth with only one (Guangdong) of the fastest-growing eight provinces having an especially high rural literacy rate. Indeed Jiangsu, Fujian and Zhejiang grew very rapidly despite rather ordinary rural literacy rates at the start of the 1980s.

To be sure, the impact of rural industrialization becomes more apparent when we normalize for the initial level of GDP per capita (on the grounds that we

Table 7.1 Growth of real GDP per capita by county and initial conditions (provinces ranked by growth rate)

	Growth of GDP per Capita (%)	Industrial Employment (%)	GDP per Capita (yuan)	Literacy (%)
Zhejiang	11.5	25.9	492	67
Jiangsu	10.9	19.1	505	62
Hebei	10.3	7.0	344	68
Fujian	10.0	14.4	413	61
Guangdong	9.7	11.6	456	76
Shandong	9.5	8.4	443	61
Henan	9.4	4.1	275	62
Anhui	8.3	6.7	319	54
Jilin	8.3	16.8	431	77
Hubei	8.2	7.2	379	66
Nei Menggu	8.0	8.6	424	66
Chongqing	7.7	6.1	270	68
Liaoning	7.6	20.8	499	80
Shaanxi	7.1	8.4	279	61
Gansu	6.9	4.8	298	47
Hunan	6.8	8.2	352	73
Guangxi	6.7	4.3	294	71
Jiangxi	6.7	11.5	372	66
Sichuan	6.7	5.8	329	59
Shanxi	6.5	9.7	408	72
Xinjiang	6.4	8.2	374	68
Guizhou	6.2	3.5	240	51
Ningxia	6.2	7.1	366	52
Heilongjiang	6.1	17.6	526	76
Yunnan	5.7	4.2	302	49
Qinghai	3.5	7.4	476	41
All Rural China	7.9	9.9	373	64

Notes: All data are for 1982 except the growth rate, which is for 1982–1999/2000. Aggregates by province are for all jurisdictions identified as counties in 1982. Guangdong includes Hainan.

Source: TJJ (1988); Appendix 1.

would expect provinces which were relatively prosperous in the early 1980s to have grown less quickly because of their higher base). Thus the comparatively high levels of per capita GDP attained in Heilongjiang, Liaoning and Jilin by 1982 help to explain why the three grow slowly despite otherwise favourable endowments of human capital. But GDP per capita, even in conjunction with industrial employment levels, can only go so far in explaining the pattern of growth. Most obviously, Zhejiang and Jiangsu entered the post-Mao era with level of rural GDP far above the provincial average, yet still managed to grow very quickly.

These results imply that the pace of rural growth was conditioned by factors not included in Table 7.1. Geography is one prime candidate. Rural Hebei, for example, must have benefited considerably from its proximity to the great urban centres of Tianjin and Beijing. Conversely, the Manchurian provinces were far removed from the centres of inward FDI, which was concentrated around Shanghai and along the coasts of Fujian and Guangdong. And whilst Manchuria had gained from its proximity to centres of Soviet industry in the 1950s, it enjoyed no equivalent benefit in the 1980s and 1990s because of the collapse of the Russian economy. Other provinces which also must have lost out because of their relative isolation and adverse physical geography were Xinjiang, Ningxia and Qinghai in the north-west and Yunnan, Guizhou and Sichuan in the south-west.

7.2. The Regression Framework: An Overview

The descriptive statistics summarized in Table 7.1 make possible a number of heady generalizations about the effect of inherited levels of industrial employment on rural growth rates in the 1980s and beyond. However, we need a more systematic analysis to tease out the precise nature of the relationship between human capital levels in the early 1980s and subsequent rural growth. The approach adopted in the previous section has a further limitation in that it focuses on provincial aggregates. Although Chinese provinces are well-understood spatial categories, they contain extremely diverse geography. For example, the promotion of economic development is altogether more challenging in mountainous Shaoguan prefecture in northern Guangdong than it is in the Pearl River Delta, or on the loess plateau north of Yan'an in Shaanxi province as compared with the Guanzhong plain around Xi'an. These considerations suggest that we need to abandon the province as an analytical unit in favour of the county, and that we should employ an approach based around regression analysis to isolate the precise determinants of rural per capita growth rates.

The regression approach adopted here follows this course. It uses the data on county-level output growth, literacy, GDP per head in 1982 and 1982 rates of industrial employment summarized in the previous section and combines them with a number of geographical variables to create a county-level dataset.[5] The justification for the inclusion of these variables is discussed in the next two sections.

7.3. Regression Proxies for Learning

The central hypothesis advanced in the preceding chapter is that rural industrialization after 1978 was made possible by the prior expansion of human capital in the Maoist era. There were two elements to this process: industrial learning-by-doing and formal education. Those counties which pioneered industrialization before 1949, and again during the 1950s and 1960s, acquired a considerable skills base in the process. The costs were high, but the development of an extensive industrial base by the end of the Maoist era gave a county a great advantage, and this initial advantage was locked in by continuing barriers to the migration of skilled labour. It is therefore hypothesized that there was a correlation between the extent of rural industrialization at the close of the Maoist era, and the rate of growth during the 1980s and 1990s.

An additional factor to consider is the level of formal education. As we saw in the previous chapter, the link between formal education and industrialization in rural China appears ambiguous. It is reasonable to assume that very low literacy rates (say below 50 percent) hampered industrial growth. For many firms, however, it appears that youth and dexterity were far more desirable attributes in selecting workers than their level of formal education, and there is an extensive body of literature that views education as providing a signal, rather than skills *per se*. Nevertheless, there are enough doubts about these questions to make it worthwhile still to consider the precise impact of literacy, not least because of the very scale of educational expansion under Mao, and for which China has often been praised (Drèze and Sen 1995). Measures of both skills and education therefore need to be included in any regression analysis.

7.3.1. Industrial Employment Rates as a Skills Proxy

It is difficult to evaluate the role played by prior learning-by-doing in any direct manner because of the absence of county-level data on skills: the 1982 Population Census data provide information on formal educational qualifications such as literacy and the number of university graduates by county, but not on (say) the number of technicians per county. In order, therefore, to evaluate the importance of learning-by-doing, I proxy the rural skills base by the share of industrial

---

[5] Foreign direct investment is excluded from the list of variables considered, partly because it is endogenous (FDI is attracted to fast-growing areas in an economy in which transport costs are non-negligible), partly because there was so little FDI in many parts of China, and partly because of data problems. However, and as will be seen in the later provincial chapters, it was of great importance in some of the coastal provinces.

employment in total employment at the time of the 1982 Census. The logic here is that those counties where the bulk of the workforce was still employed in agriculture were disadvantaged because their cadres and workers had acquired few industrial skills via experience of industrial work. By contrast, it is hypothesized that counties where industrial employment rates were high entered the transition era with a well-developed skills base which was exploited over the following two decades. Sunan's counties provide the best example.

The 1982 Census data on employment are not ideal. For one thing, the national compilations which publish industrial employment data for each county include both mining and construction within industry. Secondly, it would be better to have data for the late 1970s, the end of the Maoist era. Nevertheless the 1982 Census data have two great advantages. Firstly, they are relatively reliable precisely because they were collected as part of the 1982 Census. Secondly, they appear to cover all types of rural industrial employment—*guoying* (state owned), *jiti* (collective), *shedui/xiangzhen* (township and village), *geti* (individual or self-employment) and *siying* (private) enterprises (NBS 1988).

By using these 1982 industrial employment data, the learning-by-doing hypothesis is amenable to testing. If the contrasting Sachs-Woo hypothesis—that surplus labour was the key to rapid growth, and that an industrial inheritance was an obstacle to growth—is correct, we would expect to see an inverse relationship. Counties with large industrial sectors would grow slowly because of the prior absorption of scarce labour by inefficient industry. Workers employed in such inefficient industries would be reluctant to abandon their jobs because exit would necessarily incur a penalty in the form of lost welfare benefits, and because of the risk involved in 'entering the sea' (*xia hai*) of labour market competition for private sector employment.

7.3.2. Literacy Rates

I proxy formal education by the literacy rate at the time of the 1982 Population Census. Other measures could be used, but because literacy rates were still comparatively low in many parts of rural China even at the close of the 1970s, it seems more appropriate to use the literacy rate rather than (say) the proportion of the population who had attended university. Basic education was probably more relevant for industrialization in the context of rural China than higher level academic qualifications. We therefore might expect to see counties with high literacy rates in the early 1980s growing quickly thereafter, and vice versa.

7.4. Normalization

It is not enough to include skills and education in the regression analysis. Human capital certainly expanded in the Maoist era, but manufacturing capability was enhanced in other respects too. Population density was much higher, and this helped to ensure that larger markets for industrial goods were available in rural areas. Rural infrastructure was more developed, and therefore the transport bottlenecks which had crippled industrialization in the 1930s were much reduced. Unless these variables are included in the analysis, the coefficients on human capital will be biased.

We need also to take into account the impact of the initial level of GDP per head on growth rates. China's poorest counties enjoyed the advantages of backwardness. *Ceteris paribus*, we would therefore expect them to have enjoyed more rapid growth than richer counties, irrespective of their human capital endowment. We must also consider the possible impact of geographical factors because a good *prima facie* case can be made for the proposition that geographically well-favoured counties grew faster than those which were not when other factors are held constant. In assessing, the 'true' impact of human capital endowments on growth rates, we therefore need to normalize for the effect of geography.

7.4.1. The Level of GDP Per Head

As with other growth regressions, the initial level of GDP per head is included here as an independent variable. The expectation is of course that growth rates will be inversely related to the initial level of output. Rich regions are expected to grow less quickly than poor countries, either because of the impact of diminishing returns to the application of capital and labour inputs (Solow [1970] 1988), or because of greater scope for the application of first-best technology in poor countries (Abramovitz 1986).[6] Poor regions by contrast enjoy the advantages of backwardness: if the level of per capital output is low but initial conditions are otherwise favourable, growth will be faster than in a rich region. This is the conditional convergence prediction of neoclassical growth theory; during convergence to the long run equilibrium growth path determined by the (exogenously given) rate of technical progress, the transitional growth path of the poor region will be very steep.

Nevertheless, there will only be an inverse relationship between growth rates and the initial level of per capita output if other initial conditions are favourable. In fact, many poor countries are caught in a low level equilibrium trap in which per capita output is low because the supply of capital per worker is inadequate. Thus sub-Saharan Africa has all the potential advantages of backwardness, but its problem lies in realizing that advantage because so many of the countries in that region are so poor that they are unable to generate the surplus needed to finance a higher rate of investment. Sub-Saharan Africa has thus become trapped in an

---

[6] As Thirlwall (2002) rightly points out, the existence of an inverse relationship between the growth rate and the base level of per capita output is compatible with either diminishing returns to capital or labour, or with declining scope for catch-up.

equilibrium characterized by a low capital-labour ratio. In a very real sense, therefore, poverty begets poverty. Expressed in more neoclassical language, countries may be members of convergence clubs; equilibrium states differ across countries and therefore there is no reason to expect (absolute) convergence across the world. Thus poor countries will converge on their low level equilibrium and rich countries on their high level equilibrium, but there will be no tendency for the poor countries to catch up with the rich country club. It also should be observed that there is a long established tradition within economics which is sceptical of the entire notion of catch-up. For scholars such as Myrdal, Young and Kaldor, and for 'new growth' theorists such as Romer and Lucas, the growth process is often one of cumulative causation based around economies of scale. In the absence of diminishing returns to one factor or other, or countervailing state intervention, there is no reason to expect convergence at all.

As far as China is concerned, it is unclear *a priori* whether the initial level of output was a help or hindrance to growth. Some have argued that there is evidence of convergence at a provincial level, although this finding is sensitive to model specification. For example, the case for convergence is stronger if urban centres are included in the sample because many of China's largely rural provinces—most obviously Jiangsu, Zhejiang, Guangdong and Fujian—have grown faster than the great urban centres of Shanghai, Tianjin and Beijing.[7] Others have argued that many of China's poor counties have become trapped in a low level equilibrium by fiscal decentralization: the weakening of the process of re-distribution from east to west has deprived the poor counties of western China of the very resources they need to initiate growth. The only way to tease out the contribution of the initial level of output is therefore to include per capita GDP in county-level regression analysis.

7.4.2. Geography

The case for the inclusion of geographical variables when looking at spatial data is so obvious that it needs little adumbration. However, it has proven extremely difficult to distinguish between the respective contributions of geography and institutions in global growth processes.[8] In part, the difficulty lies in accurately measuring the two. Institutional quality is impossible to capture in any simple numerical fashion, but geography too is so multi-faceted that it is hard to avoid ambiguity. It is especially hard to identify which elements of geography are truly exogenous and therefore in some sense prior to institutions; grain yields, for example, depend upon both physical geography and institutional structures.

---

[7] Although even this is subject to the time period chosen; the revival of Shanghai during the 1990s brought a slowing-down, and perhaps even a halt, to the process of convergence.

[8] It is of course true that both are important. However, if geography is far more significant than institutions, the policy conclusion is rather stark: much less attention should be given to institution-building and much more to the promotion of labour emigration from geographically-disadvantaged areas.

177

It is to avoid these sorts of problems that much of the literature has used exogenous instruments such as distance from the sea, latitude or distance from the equator to proxy geographical conditions.[9]

Much recent work on China has also viewed geography as fundamental to any explanation of growth.[10] But here too the measurement of geographical advantage has proven difficult. We can all agree that the favourable geography of the coastal region has played an important (prior) role in attracting FDI; this latter is in no sense an exogenous variable. However, the precise nature of the geographical advantage enjoyed is not easily quantified. Rural Hebei is close to the coast and is relatively flat, but water shortages impose real constraints on industrial and agricultural development. Rural Heilongjiang is comparatively close to the coast (at least by way of comparison with western China), and is relatively low lying, yet its winter temperatures are extremely low. And the Chengdu plain is far from the coast, yet blessed with favourable growing and transport conditions. Where does the balance of geography advantage lie between these regions?

We are therefore left with a choice either of employing rather imperfect geographical proxies, or of dispensing with geography entirely for regression purposes. This latter is superficially attractive, but it is bound to lead to biased estimates of the contribution of learning to the rural industrialization process. And given geography's potentially grave importance, it is hard to argue that we should ignore its contribution entirely. It therefore seems best to employ imperfect proxies rather than nothing at all. Accordingly, I have used the grain yield and the distance of counties from urban centres as geographical instruments.

(A) THE GRAIN YIELD

The grain yield undoubtedly captures a large part of the impact of climate and elevation: those parts of China typically seen by most scholars as geographically advantaged had high grain yields at the start of the 1980s and vice versa. Counties located on the Tibetan plateau and across the north-west have low grain yields, whereas the counties found along the coast, on the Chengdu plain and around Dongting lake had high yields.

Of course the grain yield is an imperfect measure. The main problem is that it is partly endogenous. Rainfall, average daily temperature and elevation all affect yields, but they also depend upon policy variables and institutions. For

---

[9] The literature has concentrated mainly on cross-country comparisons; see for example Bloom and Sachs (1998); Acemoglu et al. (2001, 2002); Bosworth and Collins (2003); Bloom et al. (2003); Rodrik (2003); and Rodrik et al. (2004). The work of Krugman (1991, 1995) on regional issues has, however, served to revitalize the whole field of economic geography. Nevertheless, firm empirical conclusions remain elusive. Many, like Rodrik and Krugman, reject any notion of 'geography as destiny', but others are less convinced. For example, Sachs et al. (2004) explain Africa's poverty trap largely in terms of geography.

[10] For some of the China literature, see Fleisher and Chen (1997); Hare and West (1999); Démurger (2001); Bao et al. (2002); and Démurger et al. (2002).

example, high levels of labour productivity are largely independent of geography but exert a significant effect on yields. Yields in the 1980s were also influenced by the availability of chemical fertilizer. Furthermore, and even more importantly, the quality of irrigation system varied very substantially across the People's Republic. Counties with high quality institutions and leadership were better able to develop irrigation systems even in adverse geographical circumstances; Dazhai (at least according to one reading of the evidence) provides the classic example. One might, for example, argue that north-east China's low yields in the early 1980s reflected not adverse geography, but low population densities (such that there was less need to maximize yields). Conversely, although some of the oasis counties of the north-west did manage high grain yields, few would argue that they were geographically advantaged. One further point needs to be made. Even if we accept that the grain yield provides important information on geographical determinants of growth, it is difficult to find a dataset which is not distorted by weather. I have not been able to find national data for 1982, which would be the best year to use in order to ensure consistency with other data drawn from the Population Census. Data do exist for 1980 and 1985, but in both cases yields were severely affected by poor weather in many parts of China. I have therefore chosen to use the grain yield data for 1987 as the best proxy.[11]

(B) URBAN PROXIMITY

I have also looked at whether Chinese rural growth has been conditioned by the 'tyranny of distance', as measured by the proximity of a county to a large urban centre. The underlying idea is that transport costs are a key constraint on the development of manufacturing production. Distance thus raises both the unit cost of acquiring the means of production, and the cost incurred in transporting finished outputs to markets. As a very crude approximation, elevation (and hence unit transport cost) rises as one travels from east to west within China, and therefore distance from the coast offers a measure of geographical advantage. Nevertheless, this distance measure is problematic: much of Manchuria is close to the coast, but North Korea hinders access. More prosaically, it is the proximity of a port which is more important than sheer physical distance. That causes difficulties for empirical work because it then requires an assessment of the quality of port facilities.

I have therefore chosen to use other distance measures in this chapter. The first measures the proximity of a county to the nearest of Beijing-Tianjin, Shenzhen or Shanghai.[12] The logic here is that these three were far more important in economic terms than other Chinese urban centres. Beijing is the

---

[11] The more detailed analysis in subsequent chapters tests the sensitivity of the results for Jiangsu, Guangdong and Sichuan to the use of yield data for other years.
[12] Given that Tianjin is so close to Beijing, there is little virtue in looking at its impact separately.

national capital (and Tianjin a part of this massive conurbation), Shanghai the heartland of Chinese industry, and Shenzhen the major conduit for investment and foreign trade because of its proximity to Hong Kong. We would expect proximity to one of these great urban centres to have promoted rural industrialization in several ways. Firstly, as a market for the goods produced in rural industries. In this respect, Hong Kong was as important as a source of demand as either Shanghai or Beijing-Tianjin. Secondly, as a source of skills and technology. Many accounts emphasize the way in which fledgling rural industries were set up using equipment purchased from a metropolitan centre, or how a rural community was able to use its proximity to Shanghai or Beijing-Tianjin to gain access to skills and technologies. And of course proximity to Hong Kong facilitated access to foreign skills and technology. Thirdly, metropolitan proximity meant employment opportunities for rural labour. This out-migration in turn facilitated rural mechanization, skill transfer and generated remittance income, all of which would have encouraged rural industrial development. Fourthly, all three centres were vital conduits for foreign trade and investment. Shenzhen was especially important in the 1980s after it had become a special economic zone, but Beijing-Tianjin was important throughout the post-1978 period and, as is well known, Shanghai's significance as a trade centre increased dramatically during the course of the 1990s. It is therefore not unreasonable to see proximity to one of these three centres as a good trade/FDI proxy. Of course data on foreign trade and FDI by county for the whole of China would be better still, but they are not available. Better, therefore, a distance proxy than nothing at all; the open door was probably of limited significance as a factor determining Chinese growth in the aggregate during the post-Mao era but its local importance was undoubtedly great.

These same arguments suggest that we also need to look at the proximity of counties to provincial capitals, and this is the second measure of distance employed in this chapter. Proximity to (say) Wuhan may not have been as important as proximity to Shanghai; Wuhan is a less important urban centre in terms of both industry and population. And the smaller provincial capitals, such as Shijiazhuang or Yinchuan, have still less economic significance. Nevertheless, precisely because even small urban jurisdictions are centres of demand for products and for labour, source of skills and new technology, and conduits for foreign trade/FDI, we would expect a county located nearby to be advantaged. I have therefore included distance to the provincial capital as a variable in the regression analysis.

One further point needs to be emphasized about urban proximity. There is no doubt that China enjoyed scope for catch-up as a result of its links with the Soviet Union in the 1950s, by beginning to import technology from the West in the early 1970s and by the open door policy of the 1980s and beyond. However, the absorptive capacity of the Chinese countryside was limited because of the under-development of human capital. China's cities, Sunan, the Bohai rim and the Pearl River Delta could absorb overseas technology readily enough, but the bulk of the Chinese countryside was too far behind. For rural China, catch-up could best be achieved on the basis of the application of the technologies already available in many Chinese cities. Closing the technological gap thus *required the absorption and application of the intermediate technologies available in urban areas.* Most technology available from abroad was simply too advanced, and it is in this sense that the relevance of the open door for much of rural Chinese industrialization must be called into question. It could be much more easily modernized by the application of intermediate urban technology, without any need for more advanced foreign technology.

Perhaps the most important implication of this approach is that those Chinese counties close to urban centres—not just counties which were in a position to benefit from the open door—were at a great advantage in terms of access to both markets and technology. We would therefore expect urban proximity to provide a potent explanation for spatial inequalities in the pace of Chinese rural industrial growth. Indeed casual empiricism alone shows that some of the most dynamic regions across rural China were those near to important urban centres. Obvious examples include the counties on the Chengdu plain (close to Sichuan's provincial capital), the Pearl River Delta counties (close to both Guangzhou and Hong Kong) and the counties of Sunan (close to Shanghai). Ultimately, however, the extent of learning is an empirical matter and that is the justification for its inclusion in the regression.

7.4.3. Demographic Variables: Population Density and the Dependency Rate

Geography is important, but we cannot neglect demographic variables either. One of the main changes which occurred in China during the 1960s was the acceleration in the rate of population growth. To be sure, growth was not slow during the 1950s, but it was after 1962 that China became a country of truly high population density. Whereas the national population increased by only about 88 millions (15 percent) between 1952 and 1962, it rose by a further 38 percent over the next 12 years as nearly 250 million more people were added. It is not, therefore, surprising that Chinese population policy changed rather dramatically at the end of the 1960s.

The effects of this surge in population for Chinese economic development are not easily identified. For one thing, the scholarly community is deeply divided. Population pessimism has traditionally focused on the constraints imposed by fixed factors of one form or other. Thus the growth of per capita income is constrained by the limited availability of cultivated area (Malthus) or by the capital stock, at least if one assumes that the savings rate is exogenous. Coale and Hoover (1958), perhaps the best known example of population pessimism, also stressed the implications of the rising dependency ratio implied by either rising fertility (more government expenditure required for education and childcare) or falling mortality (rising health care costs for the elderly). In both cases, the growing number of dependents within the population crowds out productive investment. This theme has been re-iterated in much of the more recent literature (Birdsall et al. 2001). Thus population growth driven by in-migration is less likely to be harmful because immigrants are typically younger and better educated than the resident population. Population structure is important because a 'gift' phase (a period characterized by a low dependency ratio) will follow the initial 'burden' phase (in which the dependency ratio rises). From this perspective, the East Asian 'miracle' of the 1960s and 1970s was a partial consequence of the gift phase of population growth in which a large number of able-bodied workers were available for employment (Bloom and Williamson 1998). Not only did this increase the size of the (potential) labour force but also it increased the average savings rate. The outcome, according to Williamson (2001: 111–12), was as follows:

As East Asia graduated from demographic burden to gift, the youth dependency burden decreased and the proportion of working-age adults increased. The result was an acceleration of the growth rate abetted by demographic forces. These transitional demographic forces helped to push the growth rate far above its pre-1970 level to the 'miraculous' rates of the past quarter century.

Conversely, Japan might be portrayed as entering a burden phase from the late 1980s onwards, with deleterious effects on its growth rate. What matters, then, is not the rate of growth of population *per se*, but the growth of working age population—which has a significant positive effect on the growth rate of the economy (Williamson 2001: 115–16).

Yet other scholars take a more optimistic stance on population. The Solowian one sector neoclassical model, still very much the workhorse of modern growth theory, predicts that the equilibrium growth rate of per capita income is independent of population growth; an acceleration in population growth reduces the level of per capita income because of capital shallowing in the manner of Coale and Hoover, but long run income growth depends only upon the rate of technical progress. Writers such as Boserup (1981) have gone still further, noting the way in which higher population density facilitates the development of irrigation and transport infrastructure, increases the supply of genius and gives rise to endogenous technical progress ('necessity is the mother of invention').[13]

---

[13] An alternative approach emphasizes the absolute size of the population (Simon 1981; Kremer 1993; Bosworth and Collins 2003). The underlying logic is that an increase in population size increases the number of inventions and ideas, and because ideas are non-rival goods, they give rise to powerful externalities. One implication is that, *ceteris paribus*, large countries will grow faster than small countries; as Frankel puts it, small countries trade extensively because international trade is no more than a substitute for the absence of a large population. It is moot whether any of this is convincing. Some economists (Barro 1997) have seen the implication that country size matters as an unwelcome complication in growth theory. There is some evidence to support it (Kremer 1993; Bosworth and Collins 2003), but the underlying premise seems weak. If a larger population increases the stock of genius, does it not also increase the stock of Eichmanns? I have therefore chosen to focus on population density rather than absolute population size in this and subsequent chapters.

Furthermore, one of the conclusions of the new economic geography is that high population density confers advantage. If we assume non-trivial transport costs and economies of scale in production, firms will concentrate production (to exploit economies of scale) close to or within densely-populated areas (because transport costs associated with selling outputs are much greater than those associated with purchasing inputs and therefore locating close to markets is the preferred option).[14] Even if labour costs are lower in the periphery, transport costs will still be the decisive factor in encouraging industrial location in densely-populated core regions. In addition, an argument long associated with Alfred Marshall, high population density is said to generate externalities in terms of the supply of skilled labour. Firms located in densely-populated areas are more readily able to access a pool of highly skilled labour. As the existence of these firms creates more skilled labour via 'learning-by-doing' and on-the-job training, new firms will want to locate in the same areas, thus setting in train a process of increasing returns. There is thus an argument for the promotion of industrial clusters of the type seen in many parts of the OECD countries.

In the Chinese context, there is also a case for arguing that population growth generated environmental damage, which in turn has hampered economic growth (Smil 1993; Qu and Li 1994; Shapiro 2001; World Bank 2001*b*). And it is easy to point to over-grazing in Inner Mongolia (Jiang 1999), a falling water table on the North China plain, and deforestation in Yunnan, Hainan and the 'Great Northern Wilderness' (Wu 1993; Yang 1997), as supporting evidence.

But the rapid population growth of the 1960s generated benefits as well as costs. China's dependency ratio (measured as the sum of those aged 14 and under, and 65 and over, as a percentage of the total) was improving by the late 1960s and 1970s. Between 1953 and 1964, the dependency ratio rose from 40.7 to 44.3. Thereafter the rate declined, reaching 39.6 by 1975; this was mainly as a result of the falling birth rate in the 1960s (RKNJ 1985: 871; TJNJ 2001: 93). As a result, dependency was much less of a problem in China than it had been at the beginning of the Maoist period, the big increase in the total population notwithstanding. Moreover, the late Maoist figure was not especially high by international standards. The data for 1980, for example, put China below the averages for low and middle income countries, which were 44.8 and 40.9 respectively (World Bank 2000: 278–9). Some of the common perceptions about population pressures in China in the late Maoist period are therefore rather misleading.

Furthermore, if we follow the conclusions of the new economic geography, the high population densities increasingly experienced by eastern China in the 1960s and 1970s may have helped to promote economic growth. Indeed the very fact that there were considerable barriers to internal trade in the late Maoist era

---

[14] If transport costs are very high, concentration of manufacturing will not tend to occur because then the transport costs involved in shipping goods even short distances become prohibitively high.

and beyond (Kumar 1994*a*, *b*; Young 2000) tends to reinforce the notion that population density helped growth. By raising transport costs still further, barriers to factor mobility increased the advantage for a company of location in regions with very high population densities. Access to the large, well-developed, markets of Shanghai and the lower Yangzi was far more important than access to the cheap labour, minerals and raw materials of central and western China, especially in the 1980s when key inputs could be imported.[15]

High population density also had a more direct effect in the Chinese context. By the late 1970s, the man-land ratio was extremely high in parts of eastern China. One consequence, as documented by Huang (1990), was low marginal labour productivity in agriculture. This in turn meant that, in the presence of state-imposed constraints on out-migration, communes and brigades were strongly motivated to use their surplus labour to develop the non-farm sector. Such 'push' factors are a staple of the Chinese literature on the development of CBEs (Mo 1987; SXQS 1988; HNQH 1989). Du's (1990: 48) view on Wuxi's growth is representative: '. . . the growth of TVP [CB: township, village and private] industry has been in inverse proportion to the amount of rural arable land per person and the number of surplus agricultural laborers'. This surplus agricultural labour had to be educated, and in those parts of China where yields were low, labour productivity was still positive: labour inputs into farming needed to be maximized to achieve even subsistence levels of consumption. But in comparatively prosperous regions, there was a strong argument for using surplus labour for the development of industrial production, thus allowing a step change in the level of per capita output.

In sum it is plausible that rapid population growth in China during the 1960s, followed by the marked slowdown in the 1970s, was conducive to post-1978 rural industrial development. The high population densities attained by the late 1970s may well have promoted long run growth because of the positive effects of high density—in the presence of non-trivial transport costs—on both market size and the pool of labour. The slowdown in China's population growth rate in the 1970s, combined with the large number of births in the 1960s, meant that China's dependency rate was falling in the 1980s and 1990s. This ensured a large number of persons of working age, and little need to divert scarce investment resources to education and health care. Post-1978 China was thus in the 'gift' phase of the demographic transition, provided of course that the burgeoning supply of labour could be employed.

Ultimately, however, the impact of population density on rural industrialization in China is an empirical matter. We therefore need to include some measures of the impact of population growth in the regression analysis. Fortunately, this is a relatively straightforward matter because county-level data are readily

---

[15] Industry will tend to locate in 'core' regions because '. . . access to markets outweighs production costs as a determinant of location' (Krugman 1991: 97).

available from the 1982 Census; the county data for 1982 include information on both the percentage of the population under the age of 15, and the percentage aged 65 or over. We can therefore assess directly the impact of both population density and dependency rates on rural industrialization with a high degree of confidence.

7.4.4. Infrastructure

A final factor to consider is the impact of the development of infrastructure on subsequent growth rates. The late Maoist era was characterized by its high level of investment in transport infrastructure and in particular railways. Much of it occurred as part of the programme of Third Front construction initiated after 1964. This period saw (*inter alia*) the construction of a railway line linking Chengdu and Yunnan across the Daliang mountains in south-west China via the newly-built city of Dukou and completed in 1970. Even before that, however, the vital 1,892 km link through the Hexi corridor between Urumqi and Lanzhou was completed in 1965. Perhaps most interesting is that most of the railway construction of the Maoist era—no less than 75 percent—occurred in western China, previously all but isolated from the Zhonghua nation.

It is easy to see how this infrastructure construction was a great boon for rural China in the decades after 1978. According to Lin and Yao (2001: 175), the density of railways and paved roads had a positive and significant effect upon the size of the rural enterprise sector; for them, the development of transport infrastructure was the single most important economic consequence of Maoism. Nevertheless, caution is in order. As Démurger (2001) points out, transport costs were still extremely high in western China during the 1980s and 1990s despite the investment of the Maoist era. These transport costs combined with low population densities meant that western China's cheap labour was not enough to give it a locational advantage. In other words, even Maoist investment in transport infrastructure was probably not enough to generate the sort of critical mass needed for take-off and self-sustaining economic growth in western China. We also do well to recall the extensive literature on the social savings generated by railway construction across the world. This literature has tended to conclude that railway construction raised GDP but that the increase was less than previously suspected, essentially because the canal age had already significantly reduced transport costs. Railways drove down costs still further, and in the process impoverished the owners of canal boats. But the railway age did not bring about any step change in transport costs.

It may be that the experience of western China was different. Its mountainous topography was such that the scope for water-based transport was limited outside the central riverine zone of the upper Yangzi river and therefore—at least in principle—railway construction may have had a dramatic impact. We should also note Huenemann's (1984: 241–2) view that, even before 1949, the contribution of the railway was far from trivial. For all that, we await a detailed cliometric analysis of the social savings generated by the Maoist railway programme. We also lack the detailed county-level data on infrastructure which might allow us to resolve these sorts of questions by including some sort of infrastructural proxy in the regression analysis. All we can therefore do is to conclude that the impact of Maoist infrastructural construction on rural industrialization remains uncertain.[16]

7.5. The National Evidence

Table 7.2 provides a first look at the role played by these various initial conditions in determining county-level growth. It provides three types of summary information. Firstly, the average value in each category for China's 2,010 county-level jurisdictions. Secondly, the typical initial conditions which prevailed in the fastest-growing one hundred counties. Thirdly, and conversely, the initial conditions experienced by the slowest growing one hundred counties.

Table 7.2 China's fastest- and slowest-growing counties, 1982–2000 (mean values; data are for 1982 unless stated)

Variable	Unit	Top 100 Counties	All Counties	Bottom 100 Counties
GDP per capita	yuan	475	373	442
Grain yield, 1987	kgs	290	228	145
Population density	per km^2	482	251	67
Dependency rate	percent	37	41	43
Industrial employment rate	percent	19	9	7
Agricultural employment rate	percent	74	82	83
Literacy	percent	71	64	54
Growth of real GDP per capita, 1982–2000	percent	14.4	7.7	2.0

Notes: These data cover the 2,010 county-level jurisdictions identified at the time of the 1982 Population Census. The top ten counties comprised four counties from Sunan (Wuxi, Zhangjiagang, Kunshan and Jiangyin), the Pearl River Delta counties of Huiyang and Huaxian (now Huadu city), two counties in Fujian (Jinjiang and Fuqing, both industrial centres and recipients of substantial overseas Chinese investment), the tobacco county of Yuxi (Yunnan) and Shanshan, an emerging gas and oil centre in Xinjiang. This list would be rather different were separate (and consistent) data available on those peri-urban counties which merged with their neighbouring city in the 1980s and 1990s. Growth rates are calculated here between 1982 and the average for 1999/2000.

Source: See Appendix 1.

[16] That said, there is a case for arguing that we can proxy transport infrastructural development by using distance from the nearest of Beijing, Shanghai and Shenzhen on the grounds that infrastructural size and quality deteriorates monotonically as one moves from east to west China.

It is immediately evident that growth rates varied dramatically across rural China during the 1980s and 1990s. The fastest-growing one hundred counties achieved annual per capita GDP growth rates of more than 14 percent per year, a remarkable record by any standard. By contrast, the slowest-growing hundred experienced a much more modest 2 percent increase and, for some, there was no increase at all. This 12 percentage point growth gap between the top 100 and the bottom 100 counties of course reflected differences in the rate of industrialization. In almost every case, manufacturing was the engine of growth, and where that engine faltered, the overall growth rate was apt to fade and die.

Inspection of Table 7.2 suggests that differences in the growth trajectory of China's counties were firmly related to contrasting initial conditions. The top 100 counties enjoyed a much higher grain yield in 1982 than both the average and the bottom hundred. In other words, the greater agricultural prosperity—more generally the geographical advantage—enjoyed by the top 100 seems to have translated into a faster rate of growth, and vice versa. Even more striking is the difference in population density between the two sub-samples. Whereas the slowest-growing hundred counties averaged only 67 persons per square kilometre, the fastest-growing sub-sample of counties enjoyed population densities which were about seven times larger. Larger market size (as proxied by population density) thus appears to have translated into more rapid economic growth. Additionally, a higher dependency ratio appears to have been associated with slower subsequent growth. Admittedly the difference in dependency ratios between the two sub-samples is much less striking but it is still significant.

More importantly from the viewpoint of the capability hypothesis, both literacy and industrial employment levels in 1982 were positively correlated with growth. The average literacy rate for the top hundred counties was fully 18 percentage points higher in 1982 than that for the bottom hundred; the gap between the bottom and top ten was even higher (20 percentage points). The 1982 industrial employment rate was also much higher (19 percent) in the fast-growing counties than in the slow-growing hundred (7 percent). This suggests that a well-developed industrial sector at the dawn of the 1980s was a boon, rather than an obstacle to growth. Indeed, amongst the fastest-growing ten counties, the mean 1982 industrial employment rate was 21 percent; only two of them (Shanshan and Huiyang) were industrially backward in the early 1980s. Thus, although Shanshan and Huiyang demonstrate that prior industrialization was not a necessary condition for industrial growth, it was the industrially *developed* areas which enjoyed the lion's share of success after 1982. This contradicts the proposition advanced by Sachs and Woo that over-industrialization was a handicap to growth because it tied labour to inefficient enterprises.

Proximity to one of Shanghai, Beijing or Shenzhen also appears to have been growth-promoting. Although this is not shown directly in Table 7.2, the provincial composition of the fastest and slowest-growing counties points to the importance of metropolitan proximity. Of the fastest-growing hundred counties, no fewer than 77 were drawn from just six coastal provinces (15 in each of Zhejiang and Jiangsu, 14 in each of Hebei and Guangdong, 10 in Shandong, and 9 in Fujian); all of these were close to one of the three great urban centres. Not a single one of the bottom hundred were located in any of these provinces, suggesting that location had a powerful influence on rural growth rates. Indeed, of the bottom one hundred, 20 were located in Qinghai, 14 in Yunnan, 10 in Xinjiang, 10 in Heilongjiang and 9 in Sichuan, all provinces far removed from China's Pacific seaboard and its great cities.

Taken together, these results suggest that initial conditions exerted a powerful influence on growth rates. Urban proximity and a high grain yield (the geographical variables), high population density (one of the demographic variables) and both literacy and industrial employment (the measures of formal education and prior learning) were all factors making for more rapid growth. Nevertheless, more formal statistical analysis is required in order to determine the significance of the variables identified. Are these variables significant for the whole sample, as well as for the bottom and top ends of the distribution? Is the correlation identified in Table 7.2 statistically significant? For example, if we normalize for the impact of literacy, population density etc., was initial industrial employment still a significant factor influencing the growth rates? Furthermore, some of the results summarized in Table 7.2 are ambivalent. Most obviously, for example, *both* the fastest-growing hundred and the slowest-growth hundred countries enjoyed initial levels of GDP per head in 1982 which exceeded the sample average. It is not clear from this whether initial prosperity was a factor which promoted or hindered growth. Only by regression analysis can we shed light on some of these questions.

7.6. Regression Results

In order to isolate further the impact of the hypothesized variables upon the growth rate, I have used the county data to estimate an equation of the form:

$\Delta[\ln(\text{GDPpc})] = f[\ln(\text{GDPpc}), \ln(\text{population density}), \ln(\text{dependency}), \ln(\text{literacy rate}), \ln(\text{industrial employment rate}), \ln(\text{grain yield}), \ln(\text{proximity urban metropolis}), \ln(\text{proximity to provincial capital})]$

where Δ indicates the annual percentage growth rate, and $\ln$ the natural log. The log approach is preferred here because it reduces the distorting effect of outliers and also because slope coefficients can then be read as elasticities.

7.6.1. Regression Set-up: Growth Fundamentals and the Proximate Sources of Growth

Before discussing the results, it is worth saying a number of things about the regression set up. Firstly, the regression approach includes two measures of initial industrial conditions: the industrial employment rate, and the level of GDP per capita. It is hypothesized here that GDP per head is negatively related to GDP per growth: a county with a high initial level of GDP per head is expected to grow less quickly (*ceteris paribus*) because of limited scope for technological catch-up. At the same time, it is expected that a county with a workforce experienced in manufacturing production would be at an advantage because that experience facilitated the absorption of technology. Thus the ideal for a county was technological backwardness (hence abundant scope for raising output via technological catch-up), allied to a workforce with extensive industrial experience (and hence skills). Technological backwardness alone does not facilitate growth; a purely agricultural workforce is not able to exploit the opportunities available for catch-up. This is of course the essence of the analysis offered by Abramovitz (1986: 390). To conceptualize the point slightly differently, per capita GDP measures short run output, whereas the skills base is a measure of manufacturing capability and hence the industrial potential of a county. Not a few Chinese counties achieved comparatively high levels of per capita industrial output (and hence GDP per head) by using capital-intensive technologies to develop industry, whilst simultaneously retaining the bulk of their labour force in agriculture. But precisely because so few of their workers had acquired experience of manufacturing, they were ill-positioned to develop manufacturing industry in the 1980s and 1990s.

Secondly, the regression set-up omits a number of important variables and thus differs greatly from the usual 'sources of growth' approach that dominates the literature. The approach taken in this chapter focuses on the underlying determinants of growth—the *growth fundamentals*—rather than the proximate variables.[17] These latter are the variables typically included in growth accounting exercises, namely the growth of the capital stock (including foreign direct investment), the growth of the labour force, and the growth of human capital. By *definition*, the growth of these variables (along with technical progress, economies of scale and externalities, the staple fare of the residual) must fully explain the growth of output. Even if, however, we accept the extremely dubious neoclassical methodology involved—it makes little sense from a Kaldorian perspective to distinguish between technical progress and capital accumulation because of the need for embodiment, an issue discussed in Chapter 4—little real insight is gained from this sort of exercise. To say that rapid capital accumulation played a key role in China's rural industrialization tells us something, but it does not tell us why some counties were far more successful than others in this regard. For example, is a high observed investment rate a consequence of geography, institutions, policy or perhaps even culture?[18] For these reasons, the

[17] This chapter is therefore an exercise in growth regression, rather than in growth accounting. For a useful summary of the literature, see Bosworth and Collins (2003).

[18] Trade has an intermediate status. It clearly has no place in an accounting framework, but it is hard to see it as a growth fundamental because it in turns depends upon policy and geography.

approach adopted here focuses on the fundamentals of historical legacies and geography.

The econometric focus on fundamentals is also dictated by considerations of endogeneity. Is, for example, a high average investment rate sustained over a period of time a cause, or a consequence, of rapid economic growth? The growth of literacy rates since the early 1980s in China is partly a cause of GDP growth but also its consequence: a rise in GDP raises both disposable income and government revenue, both of which are sources of educational funding. Self-evidently, causation is in both directions, and it is impossible to isolate the dominant direction in any unambiguous way. For that reason, much empirical work has focused on initial conditions, rather than growth rates of inputs (Bosworth and Collins 2003; Rogers 2004), and that is the approach taken here. In order to focus on growth fundamentals and to avoid problems of multicollinearity, the regression analysis adopted focuses on the relationship between growth of GDP per head (our industrialization proxy) between 1982 and 2000, and initial conditions—that is, *level* variables for the late 1970s and early 1980s.

Of course this approach does ignore one obvious growth fundamental, namely the contribution of institutions (in particular variation in the quality of county-level and sub-county level institutions).[19] The cadre evaluation system certainly helped to ensure that local government leaders in China at the county level were more 'developmental' and less 'predatory' than in other countries because that system emphasized growth promotion (Edin 1998, 2003). Nevertheless, these cadres could not always enforce the writ of the county at the township and (especially) village level (Mood 2005). As a result, differences in county growth during the transition era in part reflected differing degrees of local compliance. Thus those Chinese counties which possessed high quality institutions enjoyed both high rates of investment, and a much more growth-promoting pattern of investment. By contrast, we would expect to see counties with weak institutions exhibiting low rates of investment, and pervasive misallocation of capital across sectors. It is not possible, however, to proxy the quality of county-level institutions, not least because of the extent of variation in village behaviour. Even data on investment rates are simply unavailable for the early 1980s, and the rates for the late 1990s show such year-on-year volatility that point estimates cannot serve as proxies for average investment rates over the entire post-1982 period.[20]

---

[19] I use the word 'institutions' here in a loose sense to mean organizations and leadership, rather than the rules of the game (as in the new institutional economics), or as a short hand for the *system* of government (Glaeser et al. 2004 in essence use 'institutions' to denote whether a system of government is democratic or not, but that approach is not of much use here).

[20] One consequence of omitting instruments for policy change and institutional quality is that the R^2 in the equation is comparatively low at 0.36. It is well-known, however, that a high R^2 should usually be treated with suspicion, because it reflects a high degree of multicollinearity or because the equation being estimated is little more than an identity. Given that the R^2 here is respectable enough, it is much more important to see if the individual variables are themselves significant determinants of growth.

7.6.2. Statistical Significance

The regression results obtained using the framework discussed in previous sections are summarized in Table 7.3. If it is the 'significance' of the individual coefficients which 'matters' (I use both words advisedly for reasons which will be discussed), it is encouraging that so many of the coefficients here are indeed statistically significant at the 5 percent level in equation (1).

To start with, the initial level of GDP has the expected (negative) sign and is significant. This result resolves the puzzle identified in Table 7.2: a high level of initial (1982) income was disadvantageous for growth when the full sample—as opposed to the top and bottom ends—is analysed, and when other variables are included. Thus counties which were poor in 1982 were, *ceteris paribus*, much more likely to grow quickly over the next two decades than those which were affluent in 1982. For example, the average growth rate of the ten richest in 1982 was only 5.4 percent, well below the average for all 2,010 counties. We can thus interpret the coefficient on GDP per capita as a measure of either diminishing returns to factor inputs, or the scope available for technological catch-up. That

Table 7.3 Regressions results for county per capita GDP growth (Independent variable is real per capita GDP growth, 1982–2000)

Variable	Equation (1)	Equation (2)		Equation (3)
		Unstandardized Coefficients	Standardized Coefficients	
GDP per capita, 1982	−0.016	−0.016	−0.216	−0.023
	(−8.76)	(−8.76)		(−13.82)
Population density, 1982	0.001			
	(0.83)			
Industrial employment	0.007	0.007	0.226	0.007
rate, 1982	(8.74)	(8.70)		(8.82)
Dependency rate, 1982	−0.063	−0.065	−0.220	−0.036
	(−8.54)	(−9.37)		(−5.56)
Literacy rate, 1982	0.010	0.010	0.087	0.014
	(3.72)	(3.83)		(5.13)
Grain yield, 1987	0.003	0.004	0.083	0.004
	(3.38)	(4.21)		(4.80)
Proximity to Shanghai,	−0.011	−0.011	−0.281	−0.014
Beijing-Tianjin or	(−11.70)	(−13.34)		(−17.41)
Shenzhen				
Proximity to provincial	−0.006	−0.007	−0.116	−0.004
Capital	(−5.16)	(−6.04)		(−4.76)
Adjusted R²	0.36	0.36	0.36	0.31
Number of counties	2,010	2,010	2,010	2,226

Notes: t statistics in parentheses. All variables here are in log form. As is usually the case, this log-linear specification performs better than the linear version of the equation. Equations (1) and (2) cover China's 2,010 counties. Equation (3) includes 216 urban jurisdictions in the sample as well to see if the results are sensitive to the particular definition of 'rural' used here. Equation (2) addresses the issue of economic significance, and is discussed in section 7, below. The standardized coefficients reported here for that equation re-base the variables such that, in each case, the mean is 1 and the variance is zero. Note that population density, as discussed in the text, is dropped from equations (2) and (3) because of its insignificance in equation (1).

Source: See Appendix 1.

many poor counties failed to grow by exploiting this technology gap (i.e. by exploiting their advantages of backwardness) only goes to show that they lacked some of the other essential capabilities for modern industrialization. The coefficient on initial GDP per head also implies that some of the literature about the impact of fiscal decentralization on poor counties is mis-directed. It is often claimed that decentralization has penalized poor counties because their revenue base is too small to finance industrialization. Given that the revenue base is a function of per capita GDP, this implies the existence of a clear positive correlation between the level of per capita GDP in 1982, and subsequent growth. The regression results here suggest that, on the contrary, *high* GDP per capita was much more of a disadvantage for growth than *low* GDP per capita. In other words, the advantages of backwardness in terms of marginal returns to capital and scope for technological diffusion appear to have outweighed the revenue disadvantages.

The conclusion that backwardness *per se* generated few disadvantages is contradicted to some degree by the evidence that grain yields were positively and significantly related to economic growth. This finding suggests that agricultural prosperity was a favourable pre-condition for rural industrialization and it accords with casual empiricism; rural industrialization was often most rapid in fertile parts of China such as Sunan, the Pearl River Delta, and the Chengdu plain. Thus the surge in agricultural output, which began in the early 1970s following the introduction of the green revolution package of high yielding varieties, irrigation and chemical fertilizer, may well have been crucial in triggering rural industrialization. Given that few counties were able (or willing) to rely upon imported grain (whether from elsewhere in China or from overseas), it may even be that agricultural prosperity was of greater importance for industrialization in China than in other countries. Indeed the regression result suggests that any notion that agricultural backwardness acted as spur to industrialization is not compelling. Some agriculturally-backward parts of China have successfully developed rural industry; Wenzhou is perhaps the most obvious example. Nevertheless, the regression results here suggest that Wenzhou might have grown even faster had it possessed a high-yielding agricultural sector.

The precise causal link from agricultural prosperity to industrialization is necessarily unclear from the regression. However, it might reasonably be conjectured that high yields enabled a county to redeploy its labour out of agriculture and into industry without incurring a significant fall in agricultural production. Alternatively, rising incomes from farming increased the demand for industrial goods. However, there is nothing to rule out the possibility that the grain yield term in the regression is doing no more than capturing the impact of a range of geographical factors instead of the impact of agricultural prosperity as such. Thus the positive coefficient on the grain yield may simply be showing that a favourable climate and low elevation is generally conducive to industrial development because it implies an absence of any serious geographical obstacles. Thus the mountainous counties of south-western China found it hard to develop industry not so much because their grain yields were low *per se*, but because these low yields reflected adverse physical geography, which in turn made for high transport costs.

As for the demographic variables, the dependency ratio in equation (1) of Table 7.3 is significant and has the expected negative sign. Evidently, high dependency ratios depressed Chinese rural growth rates. This suggests that the rural China of the 1980s and 1990s, characterized as it was by falling dependency rates in the aftermath of slowing population growth, enjoyed the 'gift' phase of the demographic transition. Yet demography was not destiny. Population density, for instance, was not a statistically significant determinant of growth even though, as previously noted, population density in the top 100 counties was substantially higher than that in the slowest-growing one hundred. This result, combined with the evidence on the advantages of urban proximity (discussed below), suggests that it was access to large urban population concentrations which was much more important than population density within the counties themselves. This might be because a large proportion of county residents were simply too poor to provide a large market for manufactured goods. A more likely explanation, however, is that transport modernization had proceeded so far that any core-periphery distinction had diminished to the point where access to non-local rural markets was not a problem for most rural manufacturers. As a result, the demand for rural manufactures was no longer dependent upon the size of the population in the immediate vicinity of the enterprise. Whatever the reason, population density is clearly insignificant, and I have therefore dropped it from equations (2) and (3).[21]

By contrast, the literacy rate has the expected (positive) sign, and emerges as a statistically significant determinant of growth. This suggests that the extent of formal basic education attained at the close of the Maoist era was a factor in making possible the explosive economic growth of the 1980s and 1990s. The finding supports the view of writers such as Han (2000, 2001) and Gao Mobo (1999) that one of the most important and positive legacies of the Cultural Revolution was the expansion of primary and secondary education in the countryside because it expanded the horizons and opportunities open to China's rural population. A 'first-glance' examination of the regression results thus suggests that the Maoist expansion of education had an instrumental value for economic growth over and above its undoubted intrinsic value, implying that there

---

[21] Experimentation reveals that population density is highly significant if the geographical variables—urban proximity and grain yields—are dropped from the equation. This suggests that it serves as a proxy for other geographical factors, rather than being important in its own right.

is no trade-off between spending on basic needs and on the promotion of economic growth.

As far as the urban proximity variable is concerned, the results shown in Table 7.3 are striking. The coefficient on proximity to one of Shanghai, Beijing-Tianjin or Shenzhen has the expected (negative) sign and is highly significant. This suggest that being located close to one of the three great urban centres was of enormous significance for rural growth; whether via skill transfers, the spread effects of foreign trade and FDI, out-migration, or access to large urban markets, the proximity of a metropolitan centre was a boon for Chinese counties. This explains why so many of the fastest-growing one hundred counties identified in Table 7.2 were to be found close to the Beijing-Tianjin conurbation (the 25 found in Hebei and Shandong), Shanghai (the 29 located in Zhejiang and Jiangsu) and Shenzhen (the 23 counties of the top hundred located in Fujian and Guangdong). Conversely, many of the slow-growing counties were located in the provinces of Xinjiang, Qinghai and Heilongjiang, far removed from China's key urban centres. The distance of a county from the provincial capital is also revealed to be strongly significant: counties close to provincial capitals grew quickly, and vice versa. This finding suggests that even comparatively small urban centres served to promote rural growth via supply and demand side effects. Taken together, the evidence on urban proximity points to the signal importance of urban centres in the Chinese rural growth process of the 1980s and 1990s.

Nevertheless, the statistical significance of the urban proximity variables lends itself to a number of interpretations. To be sure, market access is one of the great advantages enjoyed by peri-urban Chinese counties. It may be, however, that the proximity variables are picking up the effects of the superior transport infrastructure rather than urban access *per se*. Although county-level infrastructural data are not readily available, there is no doubt that the transport infrastructure of eastern China was far more developed than that of the western hinterland. For example, the rail network was more extensive in eastern than in western China at the time of the 1949 Revolution, and the Maoist building programmes served only to reduce rather than to eliminate the differential. In addition, there are comparatively few navigable waterways in western China. Furthermore, there is no question that the transport infrastructure enjoyed by counties located in the core of macro-regions was greatly superior to that of counties located in the periphery. Rural manufacturers may have been able to access markets outside their own county but urban proximity was still (*ceteris paribus*) an advantage. In short, location undoubtedly affected growth rates in the 1980s and 1990s, but it remains unclear as to which aspect of 'location' was crucial and what exactly is being picked up by the 'urban proximity' variables in the regression.

This leaves us to consider the role of initial industrial employment, which is being used here as a proxy for manufacturing capability and prior learning-by-doing, and the evidence in Table 7.3 suggests that it did have a positive and significant effect on rural growth rates. That is to say, those counties which had industrialized to a considerable extent by 1982, whether as a result of Maoist industrialization programmes or because of the skills acquired prior to the 1949 Revolution, seem to have been able to exploit their industrial inheritance, and industrialize still more rapidly in the 1980s and 1990s. Certainly there is little here to support the notion that prior industrialization was a handicap. On the contrary. Those counties where the industrial base was shallow in the early 1980s seem to have found it most difficult to industrialize in the post-Mao era when we normalize for other factors.

This finding that prior industrial development helped, rather than hindered, rural growth is reinforced if we carry out a more direct test of the Sachs-Woo (1994) hypothesis that surplus agricultural labour was the most useful inheritance from the Maoist era. If Sachs and Woo are correct, we would expect to see those counties where the agricultural workforce was proportionately larger in the early 1980s growing faster than those counties where agricultural employment was much smaller. Regression analysis, however, provides no support for this proposition. If we use county-level rates of agricultural employment instead of industrial employment in the regression, we find a significant but *negative* relationship between agricultural employment and growth; the coefficient on the rate of agricultural employment is -0.022 with a t statistic of -6.15. That is, high rates of agricultural employment are associated with slower rates of growth. An alternative test is to compare the average agricultural employment rates of fast and slow-growing counties. For the slowest-growing ten in the sample, the agricultural employment accounted for 89 percent of all employment. By contrast, the rate was only 63 percent for the fastest-growing ten counties. In other words, there is nothing here to support the contention that an abundance of agricultural labour at the close of the Maoist era served to promote subsequent growth.

The third equation reported in Table 7.3 (equation (2) is discussed in the next section) tests whether the results obtained in equation (1) are affected by the particular definition of 'rural' adopted by the Chinese authorities at the time of the 1982 Population Census, and the difficulty (as previously noted) of distinguishing between urban and rural jurisdictions in *desakota* regions. Whereas equation (1) covers only officially-designated rural jurisdictions, equation (3) expands the sample to include every jurisdiction, irrespective of whether it was officially-designated urban or rural by the Chinese authorities in 1982; it thus includes the cities of Shanghai, Beijing and Tianjin. In fact, the addition of these 216 jurisdictions does not have a major effect on the results. The R^2 falls somewhat, and there are lower coefficients on both dependency and on distance from the provincial capital. The other variables, however, increase their level of statistical significance, strikingly so in the case of initial GDP per head, and distance from the nearest of Beijing, Shanghai and Shenzhen. None of this is surprising. We would expect small cities to grow faster if they were close to one of the great growth poles of the Chinese economy, and the adverse effect of a high level of initial GDP per head becomes all the more apparent once small cities are included; most of these (one thinks of Wuxi or Suzhou) were both affluent in 1982 and grew slowly thereafter. In short, the inclusion of urban centres tends to strengthen the results obtained in equation (1). Once we normalize for geography and the initial level of GDP per head, cities across China (as with counties) grew comparatively quickly *ceteris paribus* if they had a high initial level of industrial employment. Their measured growth rates were low, but that was little more than a reflection of their very prosperity at the dawn of the 1980s. They would have grown more slowly but for their favourable geography and the high levels of industrial skills they had built up during the Maoist era.

7.7. Interpreting the Regression Results

The results discussed in the previous section suggest the existence of a statistically significant relationship between a range of initial variables and output growth. Most interestingly, at least from the perspective of the learning hypothesis advanced in previous chapters, the results show a clear statistical relationship between inherited human capital and subsequent rates of rural industrialization.

7.7.1. Statistical Versus Economic Significance

However, we need to consider the question of economic significance as opposed to merely statistical significance. As McCloskey reminds us, the two concepts of significance are not the same (McCloskey 1985, 2002; McCloskey and Ziliak 1996; Ziliak and McCloskey 2004). An independent variable may be statistically significant but still have comparatively little by way of explanatory power. In this context, an initial condition may have contributed positively to the growth rate but, at the same time, its impact may have been so small that its usefulness as an explanation of rural industrialization is very limited. Conversely, the absence of statistical significance does not necessarily imply any lack of economic or substantive significance. To give a medical analogy, a trial may reveal that a new drug saves the life of only two out of a hundred at-risk patients. The effect of taking the drug is therefore statistically insignificant; it may just be a fluke that two patients were saved. But the drug is still worth prescribing just on the off-chance that lives may be saved, at least if we assume that the costs involved in production and prescription are not prohibitively high.

The 'significance' issue here is whether initial conditions had a major impact on the pace of post-1982 growth, or whether they were of trivial importance. If the latter, we would draw two conclusions. Firstly, the costs inflicted by the

Maoist industrialization programme (in terms, for example, of low investment in agriculture or urban industry) were far greater than the benefits generated. Secondly, although the legacies of the Maoist era were helpful to post-1978 rural industrialization, their impact was far less than the policy changes introduced after 1978. If initial conditions exerted only a small influence, we would then be justified in viewing policy change as decisive, and in therefore concentrating on such changes in explaining growth.

At first glance at least, the regression results seem to suggest a comparatively limited role for both history and for geography as determinants of growth. Taken together (and accepting the data at face value for the moment), history and geography seem to explain only about a third of the variation in rural industrial growth, leaving two thirds to be explained in terms of policy and institutions. In fact, we can go further by looking at the impact on the value of R^2 if we omit each of the independent variables in turn. This provides an insight into the explanatory power of each variable.[22] Such an approach reveals that the distance of a county from the closest of Beijing, Shanghai or Shenzhen was by some way the most important of the variables considered here; if distance is omitted, the R^2 falls by some 16 percent. The omission of the grain yield has very little impact on the R^2 even though it is statistically significant. Distance from the provincial capital is also comparatively unimportant in explaining variations in growth rates. By contrast, the omission of the initial level of GDP per head has more of an impact, but even here the effect is to reduce the R^2 by only 7 percent.

To do this type of exercise more systematically, we need more than just elasticities. This is because the coefficient of variation for (say) industrial employment is much greater than the coefficient of variation for (say) GDP per head. Even comparatively small differences in industrial employment rates are meaningful, whereas those in GDP per capita are not. A direct comparison of unstandardized coefficients therefore provides an unreliable guide to the relative (substantive) significance of each independent variable. To circumvent this problem, we need to look at standardized coefficients, which can be calculated by re-basing each variable such that its mean is zero and its standard deviation is one. The results are show here by the standardized coefficients given under equation (2) of Table 7.3.

One immediate conclusion from an examination of the standardized coefficients is that, although the literacy rate is statistically significant, its economic significance was much less than that of the other variables considered.

---

[22] This procedure is problematic in a strict sense because the omission of a variable leads to its effect being picked up in part by another variable. For example, if distance from Shenzhen/Shanghai/Beijing is dropped, there is a significant increase in the dependency coefficient—suggesting that dependency is closely correlated with distance from these urban centres. Nevertheless, this stepwise procedure does offer an important insight into the economic significance of the variables considered here.

A one standard deviation rise in the literacy rate increases the standard deviation of per capita output growth by less than a tenth (about 0.2 percentage points), barely a third of the effect of a one standard deviation fall in GDP per capita. In other words, the literacy rate was not an important determinant of growth. Further examination of the data reveals the processes at work: literacy is only statistically significant in the all-China regressions because of the low literacy rates that were the norm in the western provinces. We can demonstrate this by re-running the regression, but this time excluding the counties of Gansu, Ningxia, Xinjiang, Qinghai, Nei Menggu, Guizhou, Yunnan and western Sichuan (the prefectures of Aba, Ganzi, Liangshan and Ya'an). The result for the sub-sample is that literacy is not even statistically significant; the coefficient has the wrong sign and a t value of only -0.25. In other words, differences in literacy rates do not help to explain differences in per capita growth rates for the provinces of central and eastern China. Taken together, this evidence suggests that there was little benefit to economic growth once the literacy rate had climbed above the 50 percent mark. It suggests that the development of literacy—irrespective of its intrinsic value, or instrumental value in terms of life expectancy—did little to promote industrialization. Given the hypothesis advanced in this book, that the Maoist era was critical for rural industrial growth after 1978 because of its development of human capital, this is an important conclusion.

By contrast, the dependency ratio was much more important. Its standardized coefficient shows that a one standard deviation rise in the dependency rate served to reduce the growth rate by about 0.6 percentage points. This suggests that rapid growth depended to a significant extent upon the availability of a large labour force, a proposition that makes great sense: a pool of labour was essential for growth in a relatively capital-scarce economy such as the China of the 1980s. This fits in well with some work on the growth of the East Asian region, which suggests that the growth of the labour force was as important as capital accumulation in much of the postwar era (Bloom and Williamson 1998).

The standardized coefficients also show that the grain yield—the proxy used here for agricultural fertility and the most obvious indicator of physical geography—was comparatively unimportant for growth. As with literacy, a one standard deviation rise in the grain yield produces only a 0.2 percentage point rise in per capita output growth. There is thus little here to suggest that an agricultural revolution was a necessary condition for rural industrialization. Rather, the growth of rural industry seems to have been largely independent of the surge in farm production between 1977 and 1984. At the same time, the standardized coefficients suggest that other aspects of 'geography' were important for rural industrial development. A one standard deviation increase in the distance of a county from the provincial capital reduced its growth rate by about 0.3 percentage points. This comparatively low figure suggests that provincial centres were not especially important catalysts for rural growth. That is perhaps as one might expect. Although some provincial capital were vital industrial centres (such as

Wuhan), many of them were essentially administrative, cultural or transport centres; Shijiazhuang is the most obvious example. The proximity of a county to one of the great metropolitan centres was by contrast far more important for growth. A one standard deviation increase in the distance to Shanghai, Shenzhen or Beijing-Tianjin appears to have lowered the growth rate by almost a quarter of a standard deviation, or over 0.6 percentage points. Access to metropolitan markets and sources of technology was evidently of no little importance to the rural industrialization process.

Yet geography was not the only important factor at work. That backwardness conferred advantage by allowing scope for rapid catch-up growth is evident from the standardized coefficient on per capita GDP in 1982. This shows that a one standard deviation increase in GDP per head reduced the average county growth rate by almost a quarter of a standard deviation, or about 0.6 percentage points. In other words, rich counties grew less quickly (*ceteris paribus*) than poor counties. At least as importantly, skills—as proxied by the initial level of industrial employment—mattered too. As the standardized coefficients show, the level of industrial employment in 1982 was almost as important as any other initial condition in conditioning the pace of growth. At 0.23, the standardized coefficient on industrial employment in equation (2) was second only to that on proximity to a metropolitan centre as a determinant of growth.

In concrete terms, this means that the rapid growth of (for example) the counties of southern Jiangsu in the post-Mao era was certainly conditioned by the proximity of Shanghai. But Sunan's inherited industrial base was almost as important, and certainly much more so for growth than either the region's agricultural prosperity or its literacy rate. More generally, we can say that the county most likely to grow quickly after 1978 was one which, in the early 1980s, had a low level of GDP per head (and hence a low level of industrial production per capita), but a high level of industrial potential (as measured by its industrial employment rate), a large labour force and which was close to a great metropolitan centre. It was thus the mis-match between realized industrial output and industrial potential or capability which provided the conditions for explosive growth. And given what is revealed by equation (2) about the importance of skills in determining industrial potential, these results provide a powerful affirmation of the learning hypothesis advanced in previous chapters.

This conclusion that the initial level of skills mattered in both a statistical and economic sense is especially interesting because of what we know about the extent of post-1978 labour migration. In the presence of labour migration, inherited levels of human capital ought to matter less. To put this another way, one of the reasons why initial levels of human capital emerge as highly significant in cross-country regression analysis for the post-1960 period is the limited extent of international labour migration. Labour does of course migrate between countries, but its extent is far lower than within most countries. As a result, a poor country which enjoyed a high level of human capital in 1960 saw little dissipation of that human capital inheritance over the following decades; its initial advantage was locked in by international barriers to labour migration.

Similarly in China under Mao. During that era, labour market rigidity stemmed from deliberate state-imposed restrictions on labour migration, especially between rural and urban areas. As a result, a county which was successful in enhancing its capital stock reaped the full benefits of its investment because skilled labour was prevented from leaving. After 1978, however, a skills-rich but income-poor country derived less benefit from its skills inheritance. Instead, its human capital resources were dissipated by an exodus of skilled workers, attracted by the higher wages on offer in the richer counties. The skilled labour so laboriously created in poor parts of China migrated to the richer coastal region, and in the process undermined the foundations for subsequent rural industrialization in the periphery. Conversely, a high wage county did not have to rely upon its own stocks of skilled labour after 1978. Instead, it could exploit the potential provided by an influx of migrants, whose migration was driven by the wage gap between the high wage county and its low wage competitors. These considerations suggests that, in an economy characterized by extensive labour migration, initial differences in the endowments of mobile factors of production ought to matter comparatively little. Some sort of market imperfection is needed for initial conditions to have long-lasting effects. It is the assumption of such a rigidity which provides the theoretical basis for existence of the sort of path dependency discussed by Myrdal (1957), Kaldor (1970), David (1985), Arthur (1989) or, for that matter, Whiting (2001).[23]

This analysis is highly relevant in the post-1978 Chinese context because we know that labour migration has increased. We know too that the direction of migration has been from relatively poor and slow-growing areas to relatively rich and fast-growing areas. And we also know that the bulk of those migrating have held a non-agricultural *hukou* (Fan 2004*b*: 251): skilled industrial workers have been much more likely to migrate than unskilled farm workers. The net result is that low wage areas have suffered from an exodus of skilled workers since the late 1970s; any human capital legacy acquired from the Maoist era has been dissipated. By contrast, high wage (often coastal) regions in eastern China have benefited from an influx of skilled workers, which has added to their stock of human capital.

Yet despite all this migration, the econometric analysis shows clearly that the initial stock of human capital was still a major influence on the per capita rural

---

[23] In neoclassical terms, the 1982 Chinese equilibrium was inefficient in the sense that skilled labour was mis-allocated between high wage eastern China and low wage western China. Labour migration after 1982, it is argued, increased efficiency. It narrowed (*ceteris paribus*) the wage gap between the two regions, and increased total output both by reducing the deadweight loss and by raising profits (via lower modern sector wages) and hence investment in the coastal region. The obverse of the improvement in national efficiency was a more unequal distribution of income as poor counties suffered an exodus of the skilled labour needed to fashion an industrial base.

growth rate. This finding seems to suggest that the impact of labour migration on the pace of industrial growth was rather less than is suggested in much of the literature. There are probably three reasons for this. Firstly, the sort of return migration identified and analysed by Murphy (2002) was of national significance: that is, migrants acquired skills and capital from their host county or city, and then returned with both to their native village instead of migrating permanently. Any loss of skills was therefore only temporary. Secondly, the very fact of labour market discrimination against 'outside' labour, partly on social grounds, ensured that there was a premium attached to locally-available skilled labour and entrepreneurship in the late 1970s and early 1980s; cities and rich counties faced significant social obstacles to the absorption of migrant labour, and that hampered their growth. In other words, the Lewis-type model of economic development with unlimited supplies of labour does not easily apply when the process of labour migration is spatial (as opposed to merely intersectoral within the same county) because it ignores the absorption problems which need to be overcome by the modern sector. Thirdly, the barriers to internal labour migration during the early and mid-1980s were still formidable in many parts of China. It was often easy enough to migrate, but it was much harder to gain either permanent *hukou* status or the full benefits of citizenship because of state-imposed restrictions. These barriers served as a formidable disincentive to labour migration until well into the 1990s, and we therefore do well not to exaggerate the degree of labour migration in the first decade and more after Mao's death.

A further implication is that the regression coefficients understate the *overall or all-China* contribution of Maoist investment in human capital in the transition era. The general hypothesis advanced in previous chapters is that the inherited levels of human capital from the Maoist era helped to speed up the pace of rural industrialization after 1978; the policy changes embodied in the slogan *gaige kaifang* would not in themselves have produced such spectacular growth. The *specific test* adopted in this chapter is a spatial one: did areas which inherited more human capital experience faster rural industrialization (*ceteris paribus*) than rural regions with less developed human capital?

The specific test, however, of the human capital hypothesis used here is ambiguous. The test would only be unambiguous if there had been no factor mobility—in particular no labour migration—in rural China during the 1980s and 1990s. Then the initial employment level in industry would provide a good indication of the stock of skilled labour in a county. In the presence of labour migration, however, the human capital levels of 1982 provide a biased estimate of human capital availability at the county level during the post-Mao period.[24] The

---

[24] This bias is of course not true of many of the other initial conditions. For example, the geographical advantages enjoyed by much of eastern China in the early 1980s or by counties located close to sizeable cities, were permanent rather than temporary. These advantages should have affected the pace of industrialization almost as much ('almost' because the pattern of urbanization did change over the course of the 1980s and 1990s) in the late 1990s as they did in the early 1980s.

1982 levels of industrial employment overstate the human capital available to slow-growing counties, which lost skilled labour because of out-migration. Inherited human capital in many of these counties *was* extensive at the close of the 1970s, but this dwindled as out-migration of skilled workers occurred. Conversely, the 1982 employment levels under-state the true availability of skilled labour in fast-growing counties, which gained skilled labour via in-migration.[25] The net effect is to under-state the true contribution of the learning which occurred during the Maoist era. This is very obvious from experimentation. Suppose we assume that in-migration was directly proportionate to the growth rate of output, and that we adjust the level of human capital accordingly so that the initial level of industrial employment is increased for fast-growing counties, and reduced for slow-growing counties. The resultant migration-adjusted stock of human capital becomes a much more significant determinant of growth.

We could of course do this more formally by using the *growth* of industrial employment at the county level in the regression (instead of its level in 1982), and establish the degree to which there is a correlation between it and the growth of output. That, however, causes problems of its own. Firstly, the data on migration flows are not very reliable. Secondly, there is a problem of endogeneity: does the growth of human capital cause output growth, or does output growth cause human capital expansion? Clearly causation is two way, and it is impossible to measure the precise extent of the causal link from human capital to output. It is for this very reason, as we have seen, that some growth econometrics has focused on initial conditions (which are necessarily exogenous) instead of the growth of inputs. Thirdly, the inclusion of the growth of human capital makes the exercise much closer to one of growth accounting. Any relationship thus identified between output and human capital growth becomes definitionally true because the measurement of human capital requires the use of the wage rate for aggregation purposes; we end up regressing the growth of GDP on one of its components (the growth of labour income). For all these various reasons, we must content ourselves with a qualitative conclusion: the existence of labour migration masks the true significance of the human capital inheritance for post-1978 rural growth rates.

These considerations serve to ensure that the specific spatial test employed in this chapter understates the true contribution of human capital to rural industrialization. Our primary concern is with the effect of inherited human capital on Chinese rural growth as a whole, not on the effect of human capital accumulation in any specific region. The fact that Sunan benefited after 1978 from human capital accumulation in (say) Guizhou during the Maoist era *supports* the

---

[25] The analysis assumes here that migration flows were driven primarily by the growth of labour demand (reflected in both wage and employment growth) rather than by the absolute average wage differential. This assumption seems reasonable given that the counties best able to attract migrant workers were those like Dongguan in the Pearl River delta which had comparatively low average wages but offered high wages at the margin.

underlying hypothesis, rather than refuting it. Guizhou may have captured few of the benefits from the development of human capital in the 1960s and 1970s, but that is not the same as saying that there were no benefits for rural China as a whole. Labour migration serves simply to make the central hypothesis much more difficult to test. The very fact that the coefficients are still significant in the presence of migration testifies to the strength of the relationship.

The regression analysis also under-estimates the absolute significance of skills (though not the impact of the Maoist skills inheritance) for growth. This is because knowledge which otherwise would have had to be generated via learning-by-doing was partially supplied in coastal provinces (especially in the case of Guangdong) by an influx of foreign workers and managers. Thus the omission of trade and FDI instruments, though justified on the grounds of data and endogeneity problems, does cause biases. A region seeking to develop manufacturing in the absence of significant Maoist industrialization could in principle have exploited the substitution possibilities inherent in international skills transfers. This might explain why southern China was able to develop rural industry quite quickly despite its limited Maoist industrial inheritance. A Maoist skills legacy thus helped growth, but it was not a necessary condition provided that a county could acquire skills from abroad. For most Chinese counties, of course, this type of growth was out of the question because of their location, and even for well-located counties there must be doubts about the extent which FDI led to a skills transformation.[26] Nevertheless, we must not exaggerate the importance of the Maoist inheritance. Other factors mattered as well, and the open door was certainly one.

7.7.2. Skills and Investment in Physical Capital

An additional problem with the regression approach adopted here is that it may well be mis-specified. We know that China was relatively successful after 1978 in maintaining a rate of investment in physical capital which, at close to 40 percent of GDP, was the envy of most developing countries. We also know that the provinces of coastal China, especially Guangdong and Fujian, were especially successful in attracting foreign direct investment. It is at least arguable that such FDI and domestic investment interacted with the skills inheritance. For example, FDI was often attracted only because a well-established skills base already existed. Similarly, those parts of the Chinese countryside which possessed a large skilled workforce probably attracted much more domestic investment than counties whose workforces lacked essential skills. In other words, investment interacted with skills to generate rapid growth. If this is true, it

---

[26] The 'FDI as a bringer of skills' argument becomes more powerful if one takes the view that it was the supply of management and entrepreneurship, rather than the size of the ordinary skilled workforce *per se*, that was the critical ingredient for industrial success. That is because it was far easier to import a small number of foreign and overseas Chinese managers than a large number of skilled workers.

implies that the coefficient on industrial employment may under-estimates its true significance. If we had included investment in physical capital in the regression, the reported return to skills might well have emerged as much greater still.

There is nothing useful to be done about this at a national level using county-level data (however, the issue is taken up in the chapters on Jiangsu and Guangdong below). Neither good estimates of the capital stock, and changes therein, nor county-level data on FDI for the whole of China, exist. All that we can do is simply note that our estimates probably under-estimate the role played by inherited levels of human capital in driving the growth process.

7.8. Qualifications

It has been argued in the previous section that there are good reasons for assigning much of the credit for post-1978 rural growth to the human capital legacies of the Maoist period. The coefficient on the level of industrial employment is significant in both economic and statistical senses. If anything, its economic significance is under-stated in the regression because that takes no account of the impact of labour migration, nor of the joint effect of inherited skills and high levels of investment in physical capital.

All this having been said, we need to recognize that our analysis has other limitations. One difficulty stems from the size of the sample used in this chapter. It has sometimes been argued that almost any variable becomes statistically significant if the sample becomes large enough (McCloskey and Ziliak 1996). The logic here is that, as sample size rises, so too the likelihood of finding falsely-significant results. In this chapter, the 'sample' of Chinese counties is virtually the whole 'population'; those few county-level jurisdictions omitted owe their exclusion to inadequate data. It is therefore quite possible that the sample includes a number of 'rogue' cases, the effect of which is to generate a statistical relationship between two variables where none exists. If, therefore, we are to claim that the results summarized in Table 7.3 are robust (i.e. that inherited industrial skills were a critical factor in explaining post-1978 growth), it is important to show that the relationship holds for smaller samples as well.

An obvious way to address this concern is to consider the results for individual provinces, and to identify the proportion of the provinces in which inherited human capital is significant. These results are summarized in Table 7.4. They tend to suggest that the national-level data are not robust. To be sure, the finding that initial levels of human capital had a positive and significant effect on growth is not contradicted. However, it is revealing that industrial employment is statistically significant in only ten and literacy in only nine of the 26 provincial cases.[27] We seem to be left with the conclusion that the statistical

[27] The two variables have the 'correct' sign in 24 and 19 cases respectively.

Table 7.4 Regression results for 1982–99/2000 by province

Variable	Number of provinces where the coefficient is statistically significant (at the 5 percent level) and has the expected sign
GDP per capita	11
Industrial employment rate	10
Dependency rate	2
Literacy rate	9
Grain yield	5
Proximity to Shenzhen, Shanghai or Beijing	4
Proximity to provincial capital	9

Notes: The regression set-up is as for Table 7.3. The dependent variable is the growth rate of GDP per capita between 1982 and 1999/2000. 26 provinces are covered here; the heavily urbanized metropolitan centres of Beijing, Shanghai and Tianjin are omitted, as is Tibet. Guangdong includes Hainan and Sichuan includes Chongqing.

Source: See Table 7.3.

significance of initial levels of human capital as a determinant of future growth is open to question.

The evidence provided by Table 7.4, however, is certainly not decisive. Large samples assuredly cause problems of their own, but small samples—county data aggregated for individual provinces—pose problems of their own because the results can easily be distorted by the experience of a small number of exceptional counties i.e. a provincial sample may be non-random. Additionally, dubious data for a handful of counties can have a very serious impact within the confines of a small sample. This suggests that, if we are to use small samples, we should assemble and 'clean' the data very carefully before jumping to any conclusion.

Two types of cleaning are worth considering. Firstly, it makes sense to use data on industrial production, rather than GDP, because the latter is much more subject to a range of influences which have nothing to do with industrial performance e.g. a natural disaster affecting agriculture. Secondly, it would be useful to assemble complete time series data on industrial output, instead of just relying upon point estimates of output in 1982 and 1999/2000 as has been done above. This is because the use of point estimates, though it economizes on data, runs the risk of basing a conclusion on data which have been distorted by special factors in the year in question e.g. short run demand fluctuations; unusually flawed data collection.

7.9. Conclusion

In sum, the results generated in this chapter are certainly interesting in that they suggest an important role for an array of initial conditions in influencing the rural growth process in China after 1978. Proximity to large urban centres, the dependency rate and initial GDP per head all appear to have exerted a powerful impact, much more so than population density, literacy, grain yields or proximity to a provincial capital. Most importantly of all, the hypothesis advanced in previous chapters that inherited industrial skills helped to promote growth is supported in both a statistical and a substantive sense. Whatever the impact of policy change, it should not be allowed to overshadow the contribution of both geography and history. Location mattered. But so too did prior learning—and in a much more positive sense than much of the path dependency literature allows. Nevertheless, we must regard the results as still being inconclusive at this stage. We need to supplement the national data on GDP growth between the endpoints of 1982 and 1999/2000 with time series data on the growth of industrial output in a number of key provinces before reaching any final conclusions. Such an approach is adopted in the remaining chapters of this book.

8

Jiangsu

Few Chinese provinces have attracted as much scholarly attention as Jiangsu.[1] In no small measure, this is because the province is one of the most prosperous in China. Yet Jiangsu's rise is a recent phenomenon. To be sure, extensive industrialization had occurred in Jiangsu under Mao, but the focus of pre-1978 Chinese industrialization was not the Yangzi Delta, but the north-east, and the greater Third Front provinces. It was to be the rural industrialization of the 1980s and 1990s which transformed the prospects of the province. The Jiangsu of 1978 was therefore much more typical of China than is commonly realized.[2] The province merits study for two other reasons. Firstly, Jiangsu's post-1978 development trajectory brought in its wake a pattern of regional inequality not dissimilar to the national one. Just as there is a well-defined difference in growth between China's coastal 'core' and its western 'periphery,' so there is a clear north-south divide between rural Sunan and impoverished Subei.[3] Secondly, there is an abundance of good quality data for the province during the Maoist era even at the county level. With GDP and other value-added data available, we need not rely upon GVAIO measures, especially for the analysis of the post-1978 period.[4]

[1] The extensive literature on Jiangsu's post-1978 rural industrial development includes Mo (1987); Tao (1988); Ginsburg et al. (1991); Ho (1994); Jacobs and Hong (1994); Rozelle (1994); Zhou (1994); Cao and Shen (1997); Brown (1998); Liu et al. (1998); Jacobs (1999); Smyth (1999); Ho and Kueh (2000); JSXZ (2000); Marton (2000); Wei (2000b); Wei and Fan (2000); Long and Ng (2001); Whiting (2001); Wei and Kim (2002); Keng and Chen (2005).
[2] Jiangsu's 1978 per capita GDP was 430 *yuan*, only about 13 percent above the national average (TJJ 2004). By 2004, and measured at current prices, per capita GDP in Jiangsu averaged 20,705 *yuan*, almost double the national figure of 10,561 *yuan* per person (TJNJ 2005: 51, 61).
[3] This is a simplification. More recently, the Jiangsu government has divided the province into three; Sunan comprises Suzhou, Wuxi and Changzhou municipalities, the municipalities of Nanjing, Zhenjiang, Yangzhou and Nantong are assigned to Suzhong, and the rest are assigned to Subei (JSJJZ 1999). Jacobs (1999) and Fei (1986: 88–9) take a similar approach.
[4] A key data source is JSB (1989), which gives historical data at the county level for many of the years between 1952 and 1988. This can be combined with the county data given in successive editions of the *Jiangsu Statistical Yearbook* to create long time series. JSSXGK (1989) is also a very useful source for the late 1970s and 1980s. The Jiangsu Statistical Bureau has made available much web-based data (at http://www.jssb.cn), but its reliability is limited because of a tendency to link together datasets (without explanation) to form an apparent time series even where the

Figure 8.1 The municipalities of Jiangsu in the late 1980s

Perhaps most importantly of all, Jiangsu's experience is important because it offers a demanding 'test' of the learning hypothesis advanced in previous chapters. This is because the province's labour force was highly mobile by Chinese standards (Fei 1986: 106–7; Bakken 1998: 35, 82). Extensive out-migration of skilled workers from Subei after 1978 would have rapidly dissipated the region's human capital inheritance and reduced its growth potential. Conversely, the counties of Sunan would have been able to grow much faster than implied by their inherited manufacturing capability because in-migration would have supplemented their already ample resources of skilled labour. In other words, their human capital inheritance ought to have been less important for Jiangsu's counties than for those of other provinces. If the learning hypothesis still holds in Jiangsu in the face of such labour mobility, we may fairly assume it is robust.

sets involved use very different definitions. This apart, the Jiangsu value-added data are generally good. Accordingly, there is little justification for continued use of GVO data in assessing output and spatial inequality (the approach taken by Marton 2000, and Wei and Kim 2002). This type of work is misleading because of differences in value-added between locations and between sectors, the share of agricultural GVA is much higher than that of industrial GVA in gross output value, and the same is true of heavy as opposed to light industry.

8.1. Proto-industrial Legacies

One of the interesting issues in the context of Jiangsu is the role played by proto-industrial legacies in driving the growth of the 1980s. Precisely because Jiangsu possessed such an extensive light industrial base in the 1930s, there is a very real possibility of industrial continuity running from the Republican to the post-Mao era.

This notion of a causal link between the growth of industry during the Republican era and the rural industrialization of the 1980s has certainly found favour in the literature.[5] For example, Hill Gates (1996) has suggested that small-scale household industry or 'petty capitalism,' has been the motor for Chinese economic growth over the last thousand years. By contrast, she argues, the Chinese state—not least during the Maoist era—has been predatory. Its intervention has served mainly to inhibit the inherent dynamism of the handicraft sector. Li (1998: 178–9) is still more explicit: '. . . it is these not (sic) well-educated peasants who constitute the economic miracle in Jiangnan. If we want to trace their talents, which seem to be innate, we have to admit that these talents are rooted in Jiangnan traditional culture'. A similar explanation has been offered for the meteoric growth of the silk centre of Shengze, located in Sunan's Wujiang county. According to Fei (1986: 22), 'The family-based textile industry served not only as the foundation for Shengze's development but also for the development of Suzhou and Hangzhou areas'. Ju and Wu (1986: 303–4) go much further:

Many weavers come from well-known silk-making families, having acquired the traditional weaving skills from their parents in their youth . . . The traditional silk weaving techniques which Shengze has evolved over the course of the past 500 years have been handed down from generation to generation, and has become the town's common heritage.

Thus traditional skills, not those acquired in the development of heavy industries and the 'five small industries' of the Maoist period, have provided the basis for post-1978 rural industrialization.

Of course there is no doubt that extensive industrialization occurred across Jiangsu during the 1920s and 1930s. The centre of modern industrial production in the Yangzi Delta was the great metropolis of Shanghai, which employed (inter alia) 65,000 workers in cotton spinning, 48,000 in silk reeling and 16,000 in cigarette manufacture during the early 1930s (BFT 1933). Nevertheless the extent and variety of rural industry across Jiangsu was extraordinary. At the end

---

[5] In what follows, the terms 'pre-modern' and 'proto' industry are used to describe handicraft industry selling goods to non-local markets. Modern or factory industry refers to mechanized production. The literature on pre-1949 industry in Jiangsu includes BFT (1933); Fei ([1939] 1980); Ju and Wu (1986); JSK (1987); Huang (1990); JNSZ (1991); Li (1998); Bell (1999); Walker (1999); and Köll (2003).

of 1932, some 146,000 workers were employed in modern factory industry in the province (JSK 1987: 432–78).[6] Jiangsu's modern cotton spinning sector employed 40,000 workers, and cotton weaving a further 12,000; modern silk filatures also employed some 40,000 workers. Much of the province's modern industry was concentrated in Wuxi city ('little Shanghai'), where 64,000 workers were employed at the end of 1932; 14,000 workers were employed in cotton spinning and no less than 37,000 in steam-powered silk filatures in the early 1930s (BFT 1933; Bell 1999; Fei [1939] 1980). Other important industrial centres employing more than 4,000 factory workers in late 1932 were Nanjing (nearly 10,000), Jiangyin (8,000), Wujin (9,000), Wuxian (8,400), Zhenjiang (4,700) and Nantong (12,500) (JSK 1987). Nantong was the home of the Dasheng Spinning Factory which had been founded by Zhang Jian in the late 1890s, and which rose to become one of the most successful native prewar cotton spinning companies (Walker 1999). Although silk and cotton textiles were the principal modern industries, other modern industries included oil and flour milling, the knitting industry and towel manufacture; in all four, modern factories existed alongside handloom production.

Jiangsu's proto-industrial sector was even bigger, and large-scale non-mechanized production was commonplace. That was especially true for cotton; although the cotton spinning sector was in decline in the early twentieth century, handicraft cotton weaving flourished as producers turned increasingly to machine-spun yarn (Xu 1988). For example, handicraft industry in Nantong used machine-spun cotton yarn produced in Shanghai and Japan to weave cotton cloth sold in the markets of northern China (Walker 1999). And although handicraft-based silk weaving was also in steep decline because of tariffs on exports to Korea and competition from rayon, many peasant households were still engaged in it as a sideline occupation. It is also worth noting the diversity of Jiangsu's rural industry. Mat weaving employed over 1,000 workers in some counties (e.g. Wuxian) and 20,000 workers were involved in grass cloth (ramie) production in Kunshan during the 1920s. Furthermore, the development of modern industries in turn helped the growth of proto-industries in other counties in the Yangzi Delta; Nantong yarn facilitated the growth of handicraft cotton production in Haimen and Chongming counties, and raw silk from Wuxi's filatures provided the basis for silk weaving in Danyang. Over 30,000 workers were employed in the silk weaving industry in Suzhou, Nanjing, Wuxian and Danyang during its zenith at the end of World War I. In 1936–37, there were 2,100 power looms and 500 handlooms operating in Suzhou's silk industry, and a further 4,300 handlooms were operating in Danyang (JNSZ 1991: 124). It is admittedly difficult to gauge the size of the handcraft sector in Jiangsu.

---

[6] I am grateful to Tim Wright for alerting me to this source. The data were collected as part of the national survey supervised by D. K. Lieu in 1932–33, which is generally regarded as the best pre-Revolution industrial survey; see Liu and Yeh (1965).

However, if we accept the figure of 146,000 factory workers and the Liu-Yeh ratio of about 8 to 1 for handicraft to factory workers nationally, that would put handicraft employment at perhaps 1.2 million out of Jiangsu's population of 35 million (Liu and Yeh 1965: 69 and 178). The figure was almost certainly much larger during the 'golden age' of the 1920s. By way of comparison, about 48 percent of Jiangsu's GVIO was produced by its predominantly rural handicraft sector in 1949 (Ho 1994: 13).

The significance of this proto-industrial inheritance receives confirmation from the vibrancy of the traditional sector after 1978. The production of cotton cloth rose by 23 percent per year between 1978 and 1988 in Wuxi (WXG 1990: 22–3) and the output of silk goods in Suzhou municipality increased by 14 percent annually between 1978 and 1995 (Suzhou tongjiju 1996: 21). For Jiangsu as a whole, the share of the textile sector in provincial GVIO rose from 22 percent in 1978 to 28 percent in 1981 (JSB 1989: 139). In that light industry did at least partially displace heavy industry during the re-adjustment of the early 1980s, Sunan can be seen as going 'back to the future' after the 'aberration' of the Maoist era. And it is hard to believe that 'traditional' industry would have developed so quickly after 1978 but for its long history of successful development across the province.

Perhaps most interestingly of all, there is direct evidence of such continuity between Republican and post-1978 rural industrialization. Shengze was one of the main centres of silk weaving in the 1920s and 1930s; 8,000 handlooms and 1,100 power looms were in operation within its precincts in 1936–37 (JNSZ 1991: 124). The industry provided the principal source of income for some 20,000 families (BFT 1933: 406). After 1978, its fortunes rapidly revived. Silk production in county-run factories doubled in value between 1978 and 1982, and some of these skills must have been inherited from the Republican era. A survey of 268 households found that 57 percent of households had worked in the silk industry for two generations, and 6 percent had worked in it for three. The survey also discovered that young women entering the industry with a silk weaving family background acquired the necessary skills some four or five times faster than the norm (Ju and Wu 1986: 305). It is therefore hardly fanciful to argue that the skills and knowledge acquired before 1949 facilitated the revival of production after 1978. In fact Fei (1986: 22) claims that an (unidentified) visitor to the region (during an unspecified year) made a prediction along these very lines: 'Once a foreign friend, amazed by the dexterity of Suzhou girls, remarked to me that their skills might well be applicable in the modern electronics industry, which requires highly accurate and precise work'.

On balance, however, the beguiling possibility of continuity between Jiangsu's industrial present and its Republican past, does not really measure up to critical scrutiny. For one thing, the development of modern industry in the province before 1949 was largely an urban phenomenon, whereas the industrialization of the transition era centred on traditionally rural areas. As we have seen, of the 146,000 factory workers employed in 1932, no fewer than 90,000 were employed in the urban centres of Nanjing, Nantong, Zhenjiang and (with the lion's share) Wuxi. Only Jiangyin, Wujin and Wuxian amongst Jiangsu's counties employed more than 7,000 each. Precisely because modern manufacturing barely existed in rural Jiangsu before the war, it is hard to argue that it provided much by way of a foundation for post-1978 rural industry. Prewar urban industrialization assuredly assisted the development of urban industry in the Maoist era, but it can have done little directly to promote rural industrialization in the years after 1978.

A second reason for scepticism is that the notion of proto-industrial legacies takes scant account of the development of heavy industry in Jiangsu in the Maoist era, and the central importance of that sector in driving growth after 1978. Indeed, the numbers needed to demonstrate that light industry was the engine of growth *par excellence* after 1978 simply do not add up. Precisely because the heavy industrial sector was so large at the end of the 1970s and the cutbacks of the early 1980s so minor, it follows that a large proportion of post-1978 growth must, as a matter of arithmetic, have been due to the expansion of the heavy industrial sector. The significance of heavy industry is also clear from the county-level evidence. There were, for example, no chemical and machinery industries in Jiangyin county during 1935; no less than 57 percent of the county's 11,000 workers were employed in textiles. By 1985, however, machinery and chemicals accounted for 29 percent and 11 percent of industrial output respectively (JSSXGK 1989: 159-61). In Wuxi county, 83 percent of industrial output was supplied by the food processing sector in 1949, and heavy industry accounted for only 3.5 percent of production. By 1957, the heavy industry share was still only 8 percent, but thereafter it increased quickly, reaching 19 percent in 1965 and the dizzy heights of 72 percent by 1979. Steel production, almost unknown before 1970, was running at 13,000 tonnes per annum by 1977, and chemical fertilizer production—only 1,000 tonnes in 1966—was close to the 19,000 tonne figure by 1978 (WXG 1990: 20-1, 24-9). The provincial aggregates make plain the importance of heavy industry during the transition era. In 1978, heavy industry accounted for 47.6 percent of GVIO; by 1998 the share was actually slightly higher. Even when heavy industry reached its nadir in 1981, it still accounted for 39 percent of GVIO (JSTJNJ 1999: 168). Jiangsu's heavy industry also played a key role in promoting the development of modern light industry. For example, many of the powered looms used in silk weaving in the early 1980s were produced by the electrical machinery industry of Wujiang county, the development of which was a product of the Maoist era; this heavy industry alone accounted for some 19 percent of industrial product in the county in 1985 (JSSXGK 1989: 514).

Thus heavy industry located in rural areas was instrumental to Jiangsu's post-1978 growth, a point recognized even by so ardent an advocate of traditional light industry as Fei Xiaotong. Although Fei was convinced that rural living standards were unduly depressed in the Maoist era by the neglect of (traditional) light industry, he does not seem to have regarded small-scale industry as offering any simple panacea for the problem of under-development. Reviewing his assessment of Kaixian'gong village in the 1950s, he concluded that:

Owing perhaps to a certain lack of clarity in my argument, and to an overly zealous emphasis on the position of such small-scale light industry in the national economy, I was taken as a bourgeois thinker during the thought-reform period and severely criticized. Now, thinking about it in a calmer period, my though of that period was not without error. The error lay in neglecting heavy industry, something which ought to have been criticized.

(Fei 1983: 169)

A third reason for doubting the long run significance of Republican proto-industry is that the light industries which led rural industrialization after 1978 were far removed from the handicraft workshops of the Republican era. Whereas food processing and textiles were the leading sectors in the 1930s, electronics, plastics and other 'modern' consumer good industries were in the vanguard of transition-era growth. In Wuxi municipality, the 1952 share of heavy industry in GVIO (for township enterprises and above) was a mere 3 percent. By 1978 that had soared to 36 percent, and it reached 55 percent by 1996 (Wuxi tongjiju 1997: 131). This figure of course exaggerates the importance of heavy industry because it excludes much small-scale rural industry, but even so there is little evidence of proto-industrial revival in Wuxi. The same is true even of Suzhou, the centre of the prewar textile industry. There, the share of heavy industry measured at 1990 prices (and including sub-*xiang* industry) stood at 39 percent by 1995 (Suzhou tongjiju 1996: 135). To be sure, the rural textile sector also grew quickly in the immediate aftermath of the 1978 watershed, but it did so by using modern, rather than handicraft, technology. Shengze became the pre-eminent centre of silk weaving after 1978 not by using prewar traditional technology, but by employing water- and air-jet looms imported from Japan (Ho and Kueh 2000: 99). Furthermore, and even more significantly, those industries producing traditional goods were plagued by over-capacity in the mid-1990s. There was scope for local specialization within Jiangsu (as indicated by the experience of Shengze), and the output of traditional products such as knitted silk continued to rise. But cloth production was 36 percent down on its 1995 peak by the late 1990s, and silk production by almost 50 percent (JSTJNJ 1999: 208). Indeed, the number of spindles fell by 810,000 in 1998, very much in line with the national plan to reduce over-capacity in the textile sector. It was therefore modern manufacturing, not traditional industry, which led rural Jiangsu into the 1990s and beyond.

That the renaissance of proto-industry in Jiangsu after 1978 was either short-lived or non-existent is not surprising because the 'golden age' of the 1920s was the product of a unique set of circumstances. Proto-industrial growth was not simply a response to the unfettered operation of market forces. Rather, the golden age of the Republican era resulted from the peculiar conditions which prevailed in the world economy (Bergère 1989). On the demand side, World War I created an unexpected opportunity for handicraft producers in South Asia, Latin America, Japan and China itself. On the supply side, the technologies required for successful production were simple and therefore required no very sophisticated labour force. But the return of peace to Europe, and the gradual revival of the North Atlantic economies, heralded the end of China's golden age. For example, silk weaving collapsed in Jiangsu because of the high tariffs in its export markets, and competition from rayon. Production peaked in the early 1920s, and thereafter fell back in Wuxian, Danyang and Nanjing leading to widespread structural unemployment (BFT 1933: 402–14).[7] The suffering of the silk and cotton industries is well-known, but the fate of more traditional industries was little different. In Kunshan county, for example, grass cloth (ramie) production peaked at 19.2 million feet in 1919, but by 1931 output was down to only 850,000 (BFT 1933: 470). Patterns of consumer demand had also changed irremediably by the 1980s, as a result of which there was no future for Kunshan's grass cloth industry, or mat-weaving in Wuxian. Thus Kunshan county based its transition-era growth on an initial move into cotton and silk production—both of which were virtually non-existent in the golden age (Kunshan XZ 1990: 277)—rather than upon a revival of the grass cloth industries which had flourished in the 1920s. The experience of Shengze, where the tradition of silk-weaving was re-born, was therefore the exception rather than the rule. Accordingly, the removal of state-imposed restrictions on the scope and scale of rural industry in the 1980s was not by itself enough to generate a proto-industrial revival.

We can in fact address the issue of pre-revolutionary industrial legacies more systematically by looking at the relationship between the level of per capita GVIO in 1952, and post-1978 growth. The GVIO data (we have no reliable information on value-added) show that pre-1949 industrial development in Jiangsu was concentrated in Sunan and in urban areas; urban GVIO per head was over 10 times higher there than in rural areas (364 *yuan* compared with 30 *yuan*). That rural industrialization was so limited in 1952 would lead one to expect that it was of little significance for post-1978 growth—that is, the prewar rural industrial base was simply too small. That presupposition is supported by the econometrics; the coefficient on 1952 per capita GVIO is not significant as a determinant of post-1978 growth if we enter it into the regressions of Table 8.6. To be sure, this negative result is not entirely decisive; employment data (which are unavailable) would be more useful than GVIO data. Nevertheless, the result

---

[7] More generally, the Bureau did little to play down its pessimistic view of the prospects for the silk industry: 'Inspite of its past glorious history, the Chinese silk industry is today in a deplorable state' (BFT 1933: 370).

does suggest that, even if traditional industry was of great importance in Jiangsu during the late 1920s, the destructive effects of recession, Japanese occupation and civil war were so enormous that the prewar industrial base was beyond revival by the early 1950s.

The extent of structural change within Jiangsu's industrial sector wrought by war, civil war and the Maoist era therefore means that any 'continuity' hypothesis must rest not on the revival of *specific* proto-industries, but upon the notion that prewar proto-industry provided enduring informal skills and experience. It must be shown that handicraft skills could readily be applied in the modern manufacturing which increasingly characterized transition-era Jiangsu—in other words, that the skills retained by the small group of 'survivors' from the industries of the Republican era provided the basis for the education of a new cohort of industrial workers after 1978. But this type of argument is not very compelling. Inter-generational skills transfers cannot have been very significant given the interval of time which had elapsed between the 1940s and 1978. In fact, only 4 percent of Jiangsu's manufacturing workforce was aged 55 and over in 1982, and therefore had even potential direct experience of handicraft production in the prewar period (Du 1987: 244). Moreover, much of the economic literature on the impact of unemployment in Europe during the 1980s and 1990s has demonstrated the operation of hysteresis: de-skilling occurs rapidly, and a consequence of the process is that the long term unemployed face great difficulties in re-entering the labour market when the demand for labour improves (Layard et al. 1991). By implication, Jiangsu's proto-industrial skill base was almost impossible to re-build once lost. Even if it is accepted that the skills acquired in knitting, hand-weaving, grass cloth and mat production were useful in producing modern industrial goods such as refrigerators, washing machines and fans—and such a claim is surely a stretch—the best that can be said of the inter-generational skills transfer hypothesis is that it is weak.

None of this is to deny the proposition that the industrialization of the Republican era yielded some important proto-industrial legacies. Shengze's growth after 1978 probably would not have been so rapid in its absence, and the imprint of pre-revolutionary industrialization is still to be seen in parts of the Jiangsu countryside. However, there is a strong suggestion that proto-industrialization was no more than a minor contributory factor, and that we should look elsewhere to develop a learning argument. On *prima facie* grounds, it is to the Maoist era to which we should look.

8.2. Maoist Industrialization in Jiangsu

The level of per capita industrial output in rural Jiangsu was very low in 1952; GVIO in the median county (at 1980 prices) was no more than 16 *yuan*

(JSB 1989: 381–4, 393–6). In part, this reflected the concentration of prewar modern and proto-industry in urban centres; per capita industrial output was over 17 times higher in Jiangsu's cities than in the countryside. But it also owed much to more general under-industrialization; in 1952, agriculture contributed no less than 53 percent of GDP, and industry only 16 percent (TJJ 2004: 270), the typical structure of an under-developed region. By 1978, much had changed. The industry share in GDP was up to 47 percent (TJJ 2004: 270) and GVIO per head in Jiangsu's median county had climbed to 235 *yuan* (Table 8.4, below). This transformation was based upon an annual industrial growth rate of about 10 percent (JSB 1989), a pace of growth which bears comparison with the rates of industrialization achieved in the most successful East Asian economies in the postwar era.

8.2.1. The Expansion of Heavy Industry

Central to the Maoist development programme in Jiangsu was the expansion of heavy industry. The slogan *youxian fazhan zhonggongye* ('give priority to the development of heavy industry') was adopted during the First 5YP (JSJJZ 1999: 231), and the effects of this emphasis were quickly apparent. In 1952, heavy industry contributed only 6 percent of Jiangsu's GVIO. This had climbed to 15 percent as early as 1957 and it reached the dizzy heights of 31 percent in 1960 (JSJJZ 1999: 231–3; TJJ 1990*b*: 347). By 1965, the figure was back to a more sustainable 25 percent, but thereafter it climbed once more, reaching 48 percent in 1978 (JSB 1989: 137).

Even within the CBE sector, heavy industry played a key role. By 1978, it contributed 45 percent of commune and brigade GVIO, little different to its share in state sector output. The machine-building subsector alone contributed 34 percent of the CBE total, whilst chemicals contributed a further 12 percent. By comparison, the contributions of textiles and apparel, and food processing, were only 15 and 3 percent respectively. These data dispel any notion that CBEs focused on light industrial products. Moreover, and despite its reputation for light industrial products, Sunan's CBE sector was actually more heavy industry-orientated in 1978 than Subei's; 50 percent of GVIO came from heavy industry in Suzhou compared with only 37 percent in Subei (JSXZ 2000: 73, 79, 85).[8]

8.2.2. The Growth of County-Level Industrial Enterprises

It is an often neglected fact that Jiangsu's rural industrialization was initially driven by the creation of county-owned enterprises. Commune and brigade

---

[8] This source defines Subei as comprising Xuzhou, Huayin, Yancheng and Lianyungang; no data are given for the central Jiangsu (Suzhong) municipalities of Nanjing, Nantong, Yangzhou and Zhenjiang. The figures here include cities in the regional and prefectural totals.

enterprises certainly played a role (as will be seen), but it was the county sector which was the mainspring of industrialization in the Jiangsu countryside for much of the Maoist era.

In the pre-1957 period, the expansion of the county-level sector was based around the nationalization of existing private and handicraft enterprises. This seizure of the 'commanding heights' took the share of the state sector across the whole province (rural and urban areas combined) from 17 percent in 1952 to 74 percent by 1957, and in 1958—at the height of the Leap—state-owned industry accounted for nearly 88 percent of all industrial output (JSJJZ 1999: 219–23). The remaining 26 percent was owned by the collective sector, and nascent commune industry contributed about 5 percent of the combined state-collective total (JSB 1989: 137).

The dominance of state enterprises in rural Jiangsu was equally marked by 1970 (Table 8.1). Although the GVIO aggregates are not always comprehensive in coverage (it is rarely specified whether all brigade and sub-brigade output is included in the GVIO total for each county), the picture is clear enough: the state sector contribute less than 50 percent of GVIO only in Danyang, Hanjiang and Jiangyin (marginally) amongst the counties in this sample. State sector

Table 8.1 State sector GVIO in rural Jiangsu, 1970

Region/County	GVIO of county SOEs (m *yuan*, 1980 prices)	Total GVIO (m *yuan;* 1980 prices)	SOE share in GVIO (percent)
Sunan			
Jiangyin	112.4	230.2	49
Wujiang	119.6	149.9	80
Taicang	74.7	92.2	81
Wuxian	83.0	132.1	63
Dantu	16.2	38.2	42
Danyang	74.8	103.0	73
Wuxi	73.1	113.0	65
Kunshan	76.2	87.0	88
Changshu	142.7	209.0	68
Subei			
Donghai	18.8	24.0	78
Gaoyou	35.6	48.5	74
Guannan	8.5	13.0	65
Haimen	117.7	142.0	83
Hanjiang	9.0	40.1	22
Jinhu	11.8	13.0	91
Jiangpu	8.7	14.0	62
Taixing	56.4	122.0	46

Note: In some cases, the GVIO totals differ from those given in JSB (1989) because the *xian zhi* data are at current prices, or exclude brigade industry and below.

Sources: Changshu XZ (1990: 323); Gaoyou XZ (1990: 264–5); Kunshan XZ (1990: 255); WXG (1990: 29); Taicang XZ (1991: 261); Danyang XZ (1992: 304); Jiangyin XZ (1992: 340–1); Dantu XZ (1993: 283–4); Wuxian GZ (1993: 6); Donghai XZ (1994: 194); Jinhu XZ (1994: 302); Wujiang XZ (1994: 252); Guannan XZ (1995: 238–9); Hanjiang XZ (1995: 257–8); Jiangpu XZ (1995: 213); Haimen XZ (1996: 308).

dominance reflected the expansion of the sector during the 1960s. In Wuxi, Wuxian and Kunshan, for example, state sector GVIO measured at 1980 prices was between 75 and 100 percent higher in 1970 than it had been in 1957 (Kunshan XZ 1990: 255; Wuxian GZ 1993: 5-6; WXG 1990: 25, 29). Over the entire 1952-78 period, the rate of expansion of state sector industrial output was if anything faster in poorer than in rich counties. In Jinhu and Guannan, for example, growth averaged over 20 percent per year between 1962 and 1978. In Jiangpu and Taixing, also in Subei, the rate was about 13 percent. By contrast, the average growth rate in more developed counties such as Changshu, Danyang, Taicang, Wuxi, Wuxian and Kunshan was only about 7 percent. In other words, a process of convergence between Subei and Sunan was clearly at work, one driven by the expansion of the state sector in the north of the province.

8.2.3. The Growth of Commune and Brigade Industry

The level of industrial production outside the formally-designated state sector was typically very low in the early 1950s. In large measure, this was because proto-industry developed mainly in urban centres like Wuxi, Nantong and Suzhou in the decades before the Revolution. The aggregate data make this plain: township (later commune) industry produced output to the value of 163 million *yuan* in 1952, about 6 percent of provincial GVIO (JSB 1989: 137).[9]

Thereafter, the evolution of Jiangsu's township industry followed the national trend. Output grew during the 1950s, and surged (at least when measured at current prices) between 1958-60 during the campaign to develop iron and steel production. In 1958, Jiangsu's metallurgy sector out-produced both food processing and textiles, a remarkable transformation compared with the early 1950s when metallurgy was almost non-existent (Mo 1987: 90). The 1958 data (as released by Jiangsu's Statistical Bureau at the time) show the commune sector employing over 1 million workers and producing GVIO to the tune

---

[9] Provincial sources typically distinguish only between 'commune' and 'brigade and below' industries for the purpose of presenting time series data for 1952-84. In the early 1950s, the industries included in the commune category were private rural handicraft enterprises (*nongcun geti shougongye*) and household sideline industries (*nongcun jiating fuye*). After these industries were taken over by townships in the 1950s, they were referred to as township industries (*xiang zhengfu bian de gongye*) until the communes were established in 1958; then they became commune industry (JSXZ 2000: 22, 24). The term 'brigade and below' as used in recent statistical publications typically refers to cooperative industry when applied to the early 1950s, and after 1958 to those industries owned by the production brigades and teams (JSXZ 2000: 29-30). However, there seems to be no consistency in this distinction between commune and brigade industry. In Wuxi municipality, for example, the prefectural yearbook attributes all non-SOE and COE industrial production to the brigade sector before 1962 (Wuxi tongjiju 1997: 131). For Suzhou, too, all small-scale rural industry seems to be lumped together as brigade level industry and below (Suzhou tongjiju 1996: 131). In this section, the terms 'township' and 'village' denote the industries of the 1950s, and 'commune' and 'brigade' the industries which operated between 1958 and 1984.

of 1.479 billion *yuan* in that year, about 5 times more than in 1957 (Mo 1987: 87–8, 94). More recently published statistical compilations revise these figures downwards; the 1958 figure is put at no more than 298 million *yuan* (JSB 1989: 137), or 255 million *yuan* in 1957 prices (TJJ 1990b: 356). Nevertheless, there is no doubting the short-lived surge in industrial production in the Jiangsu countryside during the late 1950s.

Commune-level industrial production fell after the Leap as the labour force was diverted back to concentrating on farm production; in Danyang, for example, 40 of the county's 97 commune-level industries ceased production in 1962 (Danyang XZ 1992: 331–2). By the end of that year, there were only 1,673 enterprises across the whole province, compared with 39,000 in 1958 (JSXZ 2000: 25), and the number fell to 841 in 1963 (Mo 1987: 97).[10] The sector languished during the rest of the decade. In Wuxian, for example, commune GVIO fell from 5.2 million in 1962 to 1.2 million *yuan* in 1968 (Wu XZ 1994: 468). But there was no uniformity; commune GVIO rose steadily in Jiangyin between 1962 and 1968 (Jiangyin XZ 1992: 340–1). 1969 marks a clear watershed in the history of Jiangsu's township and village industry. In that year, commune-level industrial production rose by about 70 percent in real terms, finally regaining the level reached in 1957. Thereafter, growth was very rapid, averaging about 37 percent per year in real terms between 1968 and 1978, well up on the rate of 6 percent achieved between 1962 and 1968. By 1978, commune-level industry contributed about 11 percent of provincial GVIO at current prices, double its 1952 share (JSB 1989: 137–8; JSJJZ 1999: 24–9).

It is more difficult to chart the development of village (later brigade) industry in Jiangsu before the mid-1960s, largely because of definitional problems. No province-wide data seem to exist for the village sector before 1965; there are no village data for pre-1963 even for a prosperous county like Wuxi (WXG 1990: 27). The data for the entire Jiangsu handicraft sector, including both private and cooperatively-owned handicrafts, show GVIO (at 1957 prices) rising from 776 million *yuan* in 1952 to only 1,065 million *yuan* by 1957 (Mo 1987: 81), although the usefulness of this information is limited by the inclusion of what were to become both brigade and commune enterprises. Prefecture- and county-specific data are equally opaque. The Suzhou evidence shows that village production declined as a share of GVIO from 7 percent in 1952 to less than 1 percent in 1957 (Suzhou tongjiju 1996: 131). Although this decline probably reflects little more than the re-classification of industries from the village to the township level, the decline recorded in household (*geti*) industry in Wuxi (WXG 1990: 25) almost certainly reflected the suppression of the private sector in the wake of collectivization, a process commented on unfavourably by Fei Xiaotong and others. By contrast, other scattered county-level data suggest a more substantial village sector. For example, village GVIO in Yixing accounted for

---

[10] Mo (1987: 96) gives a figure of 66,000 enterprises in 1958 and 13,036 in 1959.

about 6 percent of total GVIO by 1957 (JSXZ 2000: 30). Probably the only safe conclusion to be drawn is that village-level industry grew slowly in the 1950s.

The fortunes of the village sector during the Leap are even more uncertain, mainly because of the absence of any clear distinction between industry owned by the commune and industry owned by Jiangsu villages. There is something in the record to suggest explosive growth (JSB 1989: 393) but even if true there is no doubt that the surge was short-lived. Thereafter, the picture gradually becomes a little clearer. Certainly the evidence points to a revival from the nadir of 1962. Output in the re-named brigade sector were well up on its 1963 level by 1965 in Jiangyin, Taixing, Yancheng and Yangzhong counties (Jiangyin XZ 1992: 340; JSXZ 2000: 32). In Zhangjiagang (then called Shazhou county), brigade industrial output (probably at current prices) increased from 9 million *yuan* in 1962 to 339 million *yuan* by 1965 (Shazhou XZ 1992: 341). In both Baoying and Danyang counties, the trend was also upward (Danyang XZ 1992: 331; Baoying XZ 1994: 304). But, as with the commune sector, there was no uniformity; in Dantu, for example, brigade output fell by two thirds between 1962 and 1965 (Dantu XZ 1993: 283). At the height of the Cultural Revolution (1966–68), this upward trend came to a halt. Production seems even to have fallen somewhat in real terms during these years; the index of brigade GVIO was only 98 in 1969, down on the 100 and 105 recorded in 1965 and 1966 respectively (JSB 1989: 138). In Suzhou municipality, for instance, brigade output was lower in 1967 and 1968 than it had been in 1966 (Mo 1987: 100). Yet even during 1966–68, some counties experienced rapid expansion. Hanjiang's village-level GVIO increased sevenfold between 1965 and 1970 compared with a provincial increase of 29 percent (Hanjiang XZ 1995: 257). In Wuxi county, brigade GVIO doubled between 1965 and 1968 (WXG 1990: 27).

During the 1970s, brigade-level industrial output undoubtedly increased substantially. Whereas 1969 marks the turning point for Jiangsu's commune industry, 1970 was the turning point for the brigade sector. For Jiangsu as a whole, the real GVIO of brigade industry grew at 31 percent per year between 1970 and 1978, far above the rate of 3.3 percent achieved between 1965 and 1970 (JSB 1989: 138). The rate of growth was especially rapid in some of the poorer parts of the province. The net result of these efforts was that a large and vibrant brigade-level industrial sector was eventually established across the province by 1978. Together with commune-level enterprises, brigade enterprises contributed no less than 18 percent of total provincial GVIO by that time. Jiangsu's rural private sector may have been suppressed, but its contribution was more than offset by the emergence of the CBE sector. By the mid-1970s, it was the CBE rather than the county-owned sector which was the engine of rural industrialization.

8.2.4. Industrial Convergence Across Jiangsu

One of the features of the Maoist era was a reduction in the extent of spatial inequalities in industrialization. As the data in Table 8.2 show, industrial output

Table 8.2 Growth of per capita industrial output in rural Jiangsu, 1952–78 (municipalities ranked by growth rates)

Municipality	Location	GVIO per capita (*yuan*; 1980 prices)		Growth rate of GVIO per capita (percent per annum)
		1952	1978	1952–1978
Zhenjiang	Sunan	6	413	14.7
Huaiyin	Subei	6	114	13.7
Xuzhou	Subei	4	109	13.3
Lianyungang	Subei	6	115	12.8
Nanjing	Sunan	14	240	10.5
Yangzhou	Subei	21	290	10.3
Changzhou	Sunan	20	256	9.2
Wuxi	Sunan	40	662	8.2
Nantong	Subei	36	253	8.0
Yancheng	Subei	21	220	7.9
Suzhou	Sunan	100	562	6.5
Aggregates:				
Rural Subei		13	201	10.4
Rural Sunan		40	430	8.2
Rural Jiangsu		16	235	10.2
Urban Jiangsu		276	3,069	9.4

Notes: Growth rates calculated here by extrapolation between 1952, 1957, 1965, 1970, 1975 and 1978. The municipality figure is in each case that of the median county. The GVIO data include industrial CBEs. All jurisdictions designated as urban in the early 1980s are excluded from the municipality figures; the cities so excluded are Nanjing, Changzhou, Suzhou, Wuxi, Zhenjiang, Xuzhou Nantong, Lianyungang, Yancheng, Yangzhou, Taizhou and Huaiyin. Figures for rural Subei, rural Sunan, rural Jiangsu as a whole and urban areas are medians of county-level jurisdictions.

Source: JSB (1989).

per head grew by over 2 percent more in Subei than in Sunan, and this made a big difference when cumulated over 26 years, reducing the differential between the two regions from 3 to 1 in 1952 to 2 to 1 by 1978.[11] The development of commune and brigade industries in even the poorest parts of Jiangsu during the 1970s was one factor making for convergence. Another factor was the low base level of industrial production in the countryside, which gave rural areas great scope for catch-up. However, it appears that government played a critical role in realizing catch-up potential. The development of state-owned industry at the county level was the key equalizing force. The rate of expansion was certainly rapid, and the state sector was undoubtedly more important in the north than in the south of the province: in Sunan, state-owned industry contributed about 37 percent of all GVIO, whereas in Subei it contributed some 48 percent (JSSXGK 1989). But Subei's growth was not based around the rapid expansion of an otherwise chronically inefficient state sector. Labour productivity, as measured by GVIO per employed worker, was only 8 percent higher in the counties of Sunan

[11] Note, however, that the use of 1980 prices in Table 8.2 gives a high weight to slow-growing light industry, and a low weight to fast-growing heavy industry (heavy industry prices fell much more quickly between 1957 and 1980). This tends to penalize Suxichang; its large light industrial sector grew rather slowly after 1949 and this depressed its overall growth rate. The use of 1957 prices to value output would reduce the extent of convergence.

221

than in those of Subei by 1978. Value-added ratios in the two regions were very similar in the mid-1980s (we have no useful data before 1985), and therefore it seems fair to assume that value-added per worker was only marginally in Sunan's favour in the late 1970s. Such efficiency helped to ensure that per capita output in Subei increased over tenfold between 1952 and 1978, a growth rate which bears testimony both to the success of the state in promoting industrialization even in comparatively backward regions, and to the importance of county-level SOEs in that process.

Nevertheless, there was no uniformity to the process: rural Suzhou, for example, grew less quickly than urban areas across Jiangsu even though its industrialization level was lower. The reason seems to have been that the advantages conferred on rural Suzhou by its low base was offset by the disadvantages associated with the heavy industry orientation of the provincial development strategy. In fact, traditional light industry-orientated centres lost out across Jiangsu. The well-developed textile, garment and food processing industrial sectors of Wuxi and Changzhou, and Nantong—the centre of cotton production before 1949—all lost out. Nevertheless, the counties of Suzhou fared especially poorly; by 1978, their level of per capita industrial production had been surpassed by rural Wuxi, and the counties of Zhenjiang were also catching-up quickly.

Still, despite this process of state-led convergence, Sunan entered the Dengist era with a much more developed industrial base than Subei. Both history and geography played their part. Sunan benefited from its proximity to Shanghai, whereas Subei was handicapped by the flooding caused by the Huai river, low quality soils, poor irrigation, under-developed transport infrastructure and limited mineral resources. Subei's 'inferior' culture has also been blamed for its poverty, though Jacobs' interviewees suggested that a limited inheritance of human capital was perhaps more important: '. . . Subei lacks many types of human resources. It lacks scientists and technicians. It lacks managers. It lacks enlightened cadres. And it lacks a skilled workforce' (Jacobs 1999: 129). Maoist rural development programmes narrowed this gap but could not eliminate it: 'As northern Jiangsu's rural industry was started late, its collectively-owned enterprises have a weak foundation' (Fei 1986: 113). As previously discussed, Fei probably over-states the case for proto-industrial legacies, but there is no doubt that a tradition of rural industrialization gave Sunan's counties an advantage that was not easily eroded.

In sum, the Maoist era saw an accelerating process of rural industrialization across Jiangsu. Led in the 1960s by county-managed firms, and accelerating due to the expansion of commune and brigade enterprises in the 1970s, industry developed at a pace that was rapid by international standards even in northern Jiangsu, so much so that the gap between Subei and Sunan narrowed appreciably. There is no doubt that an extensive industrial skills base had been established across the province by the end of the 1970s. For all that, the impact of Maoist industrialization on rural Jiangsu should not be exaggerated. Even 25 years of breakneck Maoist industrialization was not enough to eliminate Jiangsu's north-south gap. Moreover, it is hard to argue convincingly that rural industrial *take-off* pre-dates 1978. In part this is because the growth rate of late Maoist industrial CBE output was about 28 percent per year, little different from the rate achieved after 1978. Given that the growth of the transition era began from a much higher base level of output than in (say) 1965, it is difficult to portray the late Maoist growth rate as indicative of take-off—it is the sustaining of that rate after 1978 which is truly extraordinary. Other evidence points to the same conclusion. Even in Sunan, where the base level of output was especially high by the late 1970s, industrial output grew more quickly after 1978 than it did in the late Maoist era. And across Jiangsu, the commune and brigade sector was still heavily reliant upon subsidies, hardly a sign of self-sustaining growth. It is important to emphasize the essential continuity in the rural industrialization process across the 1978 divide, probably more so in the case of Jiangsu than for other provinces—but there is little evidence of rural industrial take-off in the Maoist era.

8.3. Education in Rural Jiangsu under Mao

Alongside the development of rural industry in the Jiangsu countryside went the expansion of rural education. It is of course true that rural primary education programmes pre-dated the 1949 Revolution in Jiangsu. As Table 8.3 shows,

Table 8.3 Primary school enrolments rates in Jiangsu, 1952–80

Municipality	County	Enrolment rates (percent)		
		Early 1950s	Mid 1960s	Late 1970s
Nanjing	Lishui	28 (1951)	41 (1965)	99 (1980)
Wuxi	Yixing	48 (1949)	96 (1965)	99 (1976)
Suzhou	Taicang	56 (1952)	85 (1965)	100 (1980)
Changzhou	Jintan	50 (1952)	86 (1965)	98 (1978)
Zhenjiang	Dantu	65 (1952)	93 (1965)	99 (1979)
Taizhou	Jingjiang	58 (1952)	85 (1965)	99 (1980)
Suqian	Suqian	55 (1949)	88 (1965)	92 (1978)
Lianyungang	Donghai	19 (1952)	69 (1965)	95 (1978)
Huaiyin	Lianshui	13 (1949)	66 (1965)	98 (1978)
Nantong	Haimen	76 (1952)	96 (1965)	99 (1980)
Xuzhou	Tongshan	28 (1947)	75 (1965)	95 (1980)
Yangzhou	Baoying	49 (1952)	70 (1965)	96 (1980)
Yancheng	Xiangshui	n/a	92 (1966)	98 (1978)

Notes: Although comprehensive county data on education are available in JSSXGK (1989) for 1965 and 1980, the *xian zhi* figures are used here wherever possible to ensure consistency with the 1950s data. Municipality boundaries are those of post-1983. Before that date, Jiangsu's counties were grouped into prefectures (seven in 1980).

Sources: Lianshui XZ (1990: 517–18, 753); Yixing XZ (1990: 621); Taicang XZ (1991: 676–7); Jingjiang XZ (1992: 625); Dantu XZ (1993: 722–3); Jintan XZ (1993: 616–17); Tongshan XZ (1993: 710–11); Baoying XZ (1994: 730–1); Donghai XZ (1994: 645–7); Haimen XZ (1996: 695–6); Suqian SZ (1996: 768–9); Xiangshui XZ (1996: 599–600); Lishui XZ (1997: 753). Additional data for Lishui, Taicang, Changshu, Nantong, Tongshan and Baoying (for 1980) and Jingjiang, Haimen and Tongshan (1965) are taken from JSSXGK (1989).

enrolment rates were by no means insignificant even in the 1930s. In Taicang county the enrolment rate was 40 percent by 1937 (Taicang XZ 1991: 676), and it was about 38 percent in Kunshan (Kunshan XZ 1990: 145, 615). In Jintan, the rate reached 29 percent as early as 1931 (Jintan XZ 1993: 615). The data on illiteracy by age collected during the 1982 Population Census also testify to rising enrolment rates during the Nanjing decade. Of those born in 1922 and earlier, 80 percent were illiterate in 1982. But of those born in Jiangsu between 1923 and 1927—and who therefore received their primary education during the 1930s— the illiteracy rate was 'only' 69 percent in 1982 (Du 1987: 341). To be sure, some of this cohort may have been educated either during World War II or after 1949, but that is true of all the pre-1949 cohorts. The very fact that the literacy rate was significantly higher for the 1923–27 birth cohort compared with previous cohorts suggests real improvement in primary education during the 1930s.

Nevertheless, we should not exaggerate the educational legacies of the Republican era. For one thing, girls benefited little from the expansion of the 1930s. Buck's famous *Land Utilization* survey found that only 49 percent of males and a mere 3 percent of females had received any form of schooling, whether modern or traditional, in South China (Buck 1937: 373). Given that Buck's sample was biased towards richer villages, this certainly suggests very limited educational development. Even in an 'advanced' Subei county such as Haimen, the proportion of girls entering primary school in 1933 was only 9 percent, compared with 50 percent of boys (Haimen XZ 1996: 695). The illiteracy rate amongst women born between 1928 and 1932 across Jiangsu was no less than 88 percent at the time of the 1982 Census (Du 1987: 341). Furthermore, given that only 100,000 children were enrolled in secondary schools even in 1952, it is fair to say that secondary education in rural Jiangsu was under-developed. Fei's ([1939] 1980: 38–40) account of education in Kaixian'gong village during the 1930s also offers less than euphoric assessment. In it, he notes that attendance rates were much lower than notional rates of enrolment, both because the literary education on offer was seen by many villagers to be of little value, and because of the failure to integrate the school and agricultural calendars; for example, the school was closed during the slack season of July-September. More positively, some technical schools did exist e.g. the Sericulture School for Girls near Suzhou (Fei [1939] 1980: 203–4), but these sorts of schools were rare.

When this Republican evidence is set against what is known of the level of education development attained by the end of the 1970s, it seems reasonable to suppose that Jiangsu's educational progress occurred mainly during the Maoist era. This supposition is borne out by the post-1949 enrolment data. There were 3.4 million children enrolled in primary schools in 1952. This figure rose to 4.1 million in 1957, and to 6.3 million in 1960.[12] After declining in the early 1960s, it

---

[12] These same figures are given in TJJ (1999: 386). Slightly different figures for the 1950s are given in JYNJ (1984: 1027), but they do not alter the conclusions drawn above.

was back to 7 million by 1965 and reached 9.3 million in 1975, after which the number declined as the impact of a falling birth rate began to be felt (JSJYZ 2000: 1301-4). These data translate into enrolment rates of less than 50 percent in the early 1950s, rising to 63 percent in 1956, 87 percent in 1960, 75 percent in 1965 and 98 percent in 1976 (JSJYZ 2000: 163-6). It is of course true that primary school completion rates were lower—especially during the early years of the Cultural Revolution—but enrolment trends portray accurately the expansion of primary education.

Trends in secondary enrolments show steady expansion over time. In 1952, only about 100,000 children were enrolled in secondary schools in the whole of Jiangsu, and even by 1965 the figure was less than 700,000.[13] By 1970, however, the number was up to 1.5 million and it exceeded 4 million in 1977 before falling back to around 2.9 million in the early 1980s (JSJYZ 2000: 1301-4). Expressed in percentage terms, the enrolment rate of primary school graduates in secondary schools increased from about 40 percent in the early 1950s, to 60 percent in the late 1950s and early 1960s, and to about 90 percent at the end of the Maoist era. As with primary school rates, secondary enrolment and completion rates fell sharply during the Cultural Revolution, but the scale of the long run expansion of secondary education—much of it in rural areas—is undeniable.

There was, however, considerable spatial variation in both enrolment rates and in levels of attainment across the Jiangsu countryside. Subei in particular lagged behind, and this educational inequality hints at a possible explanation for disparities in rural industrialization rates after 1978. To be sure, spatial variation in enrolment rates was much diminished by the end of the 1970s. In every one of the Jiangsu counties listed, the enrolment rate was close to universal by 1980. But as the data also show, this was a recent phenomenon. In the early 1950s, many of the counties of Sunan recorded enrolments rates of over 50 percent, whereas the counties of Subei languished far behind. By the mid-1960s, the gap had closed substantially, but there was still many counties like Donghai, Lianshui and Baoying where enrolment rates were up to 20 percentage points lower than in Sunan. For the 14 county sample considered in Table 8.3, the Sunan median was 87 percent in 1965 compared with 80 percent in Subei, and this probably under-states the true gap: more comprehensive data for 17 Sunan counties and 34 counties located in Subei show a gap of 12 percentage points in 1965 (87 to 75 percent) (JSSXGK 1989). Only in the late Maoist period was the enrolment gap closed. These differences in enrolment translated into substantial variations in attainment. At the time of the 1982 Census, the median county literacy rate for northern Jiangsu was only 59 percent, compared with 71 percent in rural Sunan, and 84 percent in the urban centres (TJJ 1988). Much higher levels of literacy had been attained in Subei

[13] Somewhat different data are given in TJJ (1999: 386), which gives a figure of 270,000 in 1952 and 1 million in 1965. The figures for the 1970s are, however, the same.

than in China's western provinces, but Subei's human capital was still under-developed at the time of Mao's death.

It is also worth noting that Jiangsu was hardly unusual by Chinese standards in its level of educational attainment by the late 1970s. In fact, the literacy rate of the median Jiangsu county by 1982 was only 62 percent, rather lower than the national median of 66 percent. There was a similar gap (67 to 64 percent) if we compare the Jiangsu with the national median for rural and urban jurisdictions combined. Even in rural Suzhou, the heartland of post-1978 rural industrialization, the median literacy rate was only 68 percent (TJJ 1988). From this evidence at least, there is little basis for arguing that the rapid rural industrialization of the province as a whole in the 1980s and 1990s reflected an unusually well-educated rural population. That does not, however, preclude the possibility that educational legacies had a positive influence on growth rates in those counties where education was especially well-developed, but it puts Jiangsu's educational inheritance in its proper perspective.

8.4. Rural Industrialization after 1978

Previous sections have documented the expansion of education and industrial capability across Jiangsu in the Maoist era. The time has now come to consider whether this inheritance played a key role in driving the rural industrialization of the transition era.

8.4.1. The Growth of Rural Industrial Production in Jiangsu

It is now well appreciated that the pace of industrialization in the Jiangsu countryside was electric between 1978 and the mid-1990s (when the rate of growth slowed as the TVE sector was restructured). The most comprehensive indicator is the trend in county-level industrial value-added because this includes all types of industry. Using the 64 county jurisdictions of 1982 to delineate the countryside, Jiangsu's rural industrial growth rate averaged 16.4 percent per year between 1978 and 2002 in real terms, and 15.8 percent per capita. In the halcyon days of 1992–93, the rate of expansion was much faster, perhaps in the order of 30 percent per year.[14] The data on township and village industry, the more

---

[14] The series is taken to 2002, although the Jiangsu data for post-1996 are problematic because of the impact of the 1997 Asian crisis, the re-definition of industrial output in 1995–96 (following the results of the 1995 Industry Census), changes to county boundaries (in particular the incorporation of counties into cities), and growing under- and over-reporting issues (Rawski 2001). The 1992–93 figure of 30 percent growth also seems remarkably high. However, there are two points to be made on the other side of the argument. Firstly, NBS revisions to the national and provincial growth rates of the late 1990s (and published in 2005–06) have tended in general to revise output upwards. Secondly, NBS publications—and the NBS is more than aware of some of the questions that have been asked about Chinese industrial statistics—show value-added

conventional way to conceptualize the rural industrial sector, show a rather faster growth rate. TVE value-added grew at about 26 percent per year between 1978 and 2002 compared with the 16 percent growth rate achieved by all types of rural industry; the difference is probably explicable in terms of the slower growth of the county-run SOEs (partly because they started from a much higher base). Further disaggregation generates a TVE growth rate of 27 percent for 1978–88, and 25 percent for 1988–2002 (JSTJNJ (1997: 43–5, 210; 1999: 169; 2002: 154; 2003, 54–6, 190).

Rates of rural industrialization varied across Jiangsu, but there was no simple north-south dichotomy (Table 8.4). The extreme northern municipalities of Xuzhou and Lianyungang in fact grew more quickly than anywhere else in the province, reflecting the growth of trade (both domestic and international) along the Xuzhou-Lianyungang railway, the development of mineral resources, and their very low base level of industrial output. Nevertheless, precisely because the region was so industrially under-developed in 1978, its rapid growth thereafter was not enough to alter its relative standing as the least industrialized of any Jiangsu region. The four municipalities of central Jiangsu by contrast grew more slowly even though this region entered the transition era with a low level of industrialization. Central Jiangsu was undoubtedly hampered by its geography; the soils of Yancheng suffer from salinization, and the western municipality of Huaiyin has a long history of flooding, as well as being next to the poor province of Anhui. Across the region, transport infrastructure is under-developed and mineral resources few. But whether geography was the decisive factor is more problematic, as will be seen shortly.

Southern Jiangsu fared much better. This was of course the most industrialized part of the province in the late 1970s and, even though its growth rate was lower than those achieved in Xuzhou and Lianyungang, it comfortably maintained its position of dominance in 2002. Indeed the gap between Jiangsu's most industrialized (Suzhou) and its least industrialized municipality (Huaiyin) in 2002 was substantially wider than it had been in 1978, a measure of the cumulative impact of a modest growth differential sustained over a 25 year period. Herein lies one of the great paradoxes of the transition era. The very success of *rural* industrialization in Sunan in the 1980s and 1990s narrowed the gap between the southern Jiangsu countryside and traditional southern urban centres such as Wuxi and Suzhou. At the same time, this success widened the gap between rural Sunan and rural Subei, thus reversing the trend during the late Maoist era.

growth for all types of industry in Jiangsu as averaging 20 percent in real terms in *each year* during the Eighth Five Year Plan period, which ran from 1991–95 (TJJ 2004: 279). If the surge of 1992–93 is thought of as a recovery from the trough of the late 1980s, it is not implausible that the growth rate would have been especially high in those two years. In any case, whatever the detail, it is very hard to dispute the general contention that industrial growth was rapid in rural Jiangsu after 1978.

Table 8.4 Growth of rural industrial GVA in Jiangsu's municipalities, 1978–2002 (municipalities grouped by region)

Municipality	Industrial GVA per capita		Industrial GVA pc growth
	1978 (*yuan*)	2002 (*yuan*)	1978–2002 (percent per year)
Lianyungang	30	1,384	19.2
Xuzhou	42	1,402	18.4
Huaiyin	52	1,095	14.5
Yancheng	104	2,151	13.7
Nantong	116	2,591	13.3
Yangzhou	128	2,588	14.6
Nanjing	96	3,934	18.2
Zhenjiang	185	6,260	16.4
Changzhou	186	6,733	16.1
Suzhou	287	14,150	17.0
Wuxi	291	12,554	16.3
Jiangsu	158	3,869	15.8

Notes: Industrial GVA data and growth rates are at 1990 prices. The municipalities here are those which existed between 1983 and 1996; they exclude all jurisdictions officially designated as urban in 1982. Before 1983, the province was divided into seven prefectures and seven cities; of these latter, Nanjing was the only one to incorporate counties. After 1996–97, the large municipalities of Huaiyin and Yangzhou were reduced in size by creating the new municipalities of Suqian and Taizhou. Since then, Huaiyin has been re-named Huai'an, and a number of counties have been incorporated into the neighbouring municipal seat: Nanjing city now includes Jiangning, Jiangpu and Luhe counties, Wuxi city includes Xishan (the old Wuxi county), Suzhou city includes Wuxian, Changzhou city includes Wujin and Huai'an city now includes Huai'an county and Huaiyin. The 1996–97 changes cause little difficulty because the number of counties was left almost unchanged (I have incorporated Suyu into Suqian). Thereafter, it is more problematic because county-level data have no longer been given in the provincial yearbooks on those counties incorporated into cities. Their growth rate are proxied by that for the municipality as a whole. These changes necessarily ensure that these time series data are not entirely consistent, but the distortions caused are small.

Sources: As for Table 8.5.

Yet the most striking feature of Table 8.4 is the rise of rural Nanjing. In 1978, this was very much an under-industrialized rural region; per capita industrial output was actually lower than in many of the municipalities of central Jiangsu. It may even be that its counties made little progress in the first decade after Mao's death because of the backwash effects generated by Nanjing city itself (Veeck 1991: 168-9).[15] But all that changed in the 1990s, a decade during which the municipality enjoyed very rapid growth and experienced a convergence of its industrial output levels on those attained elsewhere in southern Jiangsu; growth was especially rapid (at over 20 percent per year) in Jiangning county.

8.4.2. Sources of Post-1978 Growth: A First Glance

The central question provoked by these data on industrialization is the relative contribution of Maoist industrial and educational legacies, and other factors, to

[15] This is supported by the data. Industrial output growth in rural Nanjing averaged about 15 percent per year between 1978 and 1985; only three other Jiangsu municipalities grew less rapidly, and Wuxi was growing at around 23 percent per year at this time.

post-1978 growth. The answer offered in the literature on Jiangsu emphasizes the role of geography and post-1978 policy changes. Smyth (1999) is fairly representative. For him, rural Sunan enjoyed all the benefits of surplus labour, low wages and excess demand for consumer goods that were the norm across China, as well as a number of specific advantages: easy access to the urban skill centres of Wuxi, Suzhou and Changzhou, and the proximity of Shanghai (Smyth 1999: 192–3, 202). The legacies of Maoism barely rate a mention.

One limitation of these types of accounts is that they are essentially anecdotal. But their most serious limitation is that they barely engage with history at all. This neglect makes little sense because the pre-eminent feature of rural industrialization in Jiangsu, as has been seen, is that it long pre-dates the supposed climacteric of 1978. In fairness, one can hardly accuse Wong (1988, 1991a) or Whiting (2001) of ignoring history. Their analysis is more sophisticated in that they see Jiangsu's long history of industrial development as a burden rather than a springboard; the experience of the province in the eyes of Whiting offers a classic example of path dependency. However, Whiting and Wong are perhaps too ready to dismiss the Maoist legacies. As the evidence in Table 8.5 shows, there is a clear correlation between the initial levels of industrial employment and subsequent growth. Subei entered the post-Mao period with little industrial employment and a comparatively low rate of literacy; its rate of industrial

Table 8.5 Rural industrialization and initial conditions in Jiangsu

	Subei	Sunan	Fastest-growing ten counties	Slowest-growing ten counties	Cities
Industrial employment rate, 1982 (percent)	12	28	27	9	63
Literacy rate, 1982 (percent)	59	71	67	57	84
Industrial GVA per head, 1978 (*yuan*)	81	245	98	95	2,078
Per capita industrial GVA growth, 1978–2002 (percent per annum)	14.4	17.4	18.7	11.5	6.0

Notes: The basis for the estimation of industrial GVA by county between 1978 and 1996 is GVIO data in 1978–88, 1991, 1993 and 1996. This is converted to GVA using 1998 county-specific ratios of GVIO to GVA adjusted by the provincial industrial GVA trend between 1978 and 1996. Post-1996 industrial GVA by county is given in the *Jiangsu Statistical Yearbooks*. Industrial GVA data are at 1990 prices. To obtain a consistent GVA series in 1990 prices, the provincial price deflator has been used to convert 1980 to 1990 prices for the GVIO data for 1978–88, and to convert current to constant prices thereafter. County-specific deflators for the 1990s are too unreliable; see for example JSTJNJ (1997), in which the series supposedly at 1990 constant gives GVIO estimates which are far too high. Linear interpolation generates GVA estimates for missing years, and allows the calculation of a time trend. The jurisdictional definitions are those at the time of the 1982 Population Census; even though many of these have subsequently acquired city status (e.g. Kunshan), they are referred to as counties throughout this chapter. The fastest-growing ten counties were (in order) Jurong, Jiangning, Kunshan, Tongshan, Ganyu, Wuxian, Lishui, Dantu, Donghai, and Wuxi county. The slowest-growing ten (slowest first) were Suqian, Lianshui, Xinghua, Yancheng, Rugao, Siyang, Rudong, Jingjiang, Taixing and Binhai.
Sources: JSB (1989); JSSXGK (1989); Jiangsu tongjiju (1992); Suzhou tongjiju (1997); JSTJNJ (1994, 1997, 1998, 2002, 2003); Wuxi tongjiju (1997); TJJ (1988).

growth over the next two decades was slow.[16] By contrast, Sunan seemingly grew more rapidly because of its more developed human capital stock. And the comparison between the fastest and slowest-growing Jiangsu counties shows clearly that the fastest rates of growth were associated was high levels of human capital, and vice versa. The fastest-growing ten counties entered the post-Mao era with a rate of industrial employment which was about three times greater than that of the slowest-growing ten.[17] To be sure, the cities grew more slowly despite their high levels of industrial employment in 1982, but this was largely as a result of their very high base level of output in 1978. All this evidence seems to fit in with Jacobs' (1999: 129) summary of the views offered by Jiangsu officials and scholars that Subei lacked a skilled workforce.

By contrast, the link between inherited literacy rates and rural growth seem rather tenuous. Slow-growing Subei certainly entered the transition with a lower rate of rural literacy than Sunan. However, the gap between the literacy rates attained in the fastest and slowest-growing ten counties was a relatively modest 10 percent points in 1982, surely not enough to explain the large growth differential. Perhaps more significantly, the top ten inherited a literacy rate that was actually lower than the Sunan average even though their rate of rural industrial growth was higher. In other words, an industrial inheritance appears to have been more important than schooling.

8.5. Human Capital and Rural Industrialization After 1978: Regression Results

Regression analysis makes possible a more sophisticated analysis of the data summarized in Table 8.5. The approach adopted here follows in the footsteps of the previous chapter in terms of the selection of independent variables. However, greater availability of data for Jiangsu means that industrial output can be measured directly instead of having to use GDP as a proxy. The better data also mean that grain yield data for 1978 (a fairly representative year in terms of weather) can be used in preference to those for 1987, a procedure which is clearly preferable in that our analytical focus is the role played by initial conditions.[18] A large number of assumptions still need to be made to calculate time series data

---

[16] All the Jiangsu counties located north of the Yangzi are classified as being in Subei for the discussion here, a procedure which divides Nanjing municipality in two.

[17] Most of the fastest-growing counties were in Sunan (seven). The other three (Tongshan in Xuzhou municipality, and Ganyu and Donghai counties in Lianyungang) benefited from the development of heavy industry along the Xuzhou-Lianyungang rail corridor. The slowest-growing ten counties were all located in Subei.

[18] No data on sown area by county are readily available for 1978, and therefore the 1980 data are used instead. However, the regression results are not sensitive to the choice of year in this context; neither 1978 not 1987 grain yields are statistically significant.

for industrial GVA in each Jiangsu county and city (as outlined in the notes to Table 8.5). We lack reliable, county-specific, time series data on prices and value-added, no trivial matter given the inflation of the late 1980s and mid-1990s, and the changing shares of heavy and light industry in county production (which has a big effect on value-added ratios; value-added is generally higher in heavy industry).[19]

One important difference between the approach adopted here, and that of the previous chapter, is the inclusion of foreign direct investment. This is because good data seem to exist, and because the role played by foreign capital in Jiangsu was more important than in many other provinces. Although much of the inward investment flowed to Fujian or to Guangdong in the 1980s, Jiangsu was also an increasingly important recipient by the 1990s. Kunshan is the best example: it attracted massive inward investment from Taiwan mainly directed towards the production of laptop computers (Keng and Chen 2005). In 2002, the county received over US$1 billion worth of foreign investment, or about US$1,700 per head (JSTJNJ 2003: 572–4, 595). Zhangjiagang, labelled 'Sunan's Siberia' in the early 1980s but now more often called 'Sunan's Singapore' according to a typically fanciful piece in *Beijing Review* (Liang 1996), successfully attracted heavy European inward investment in textiles. In 1995, it received about US$600 million, more even than Kunshan (Suzhou tongjiju 1996: 271). These figures were well above the Guangdong average (US$171 per head) and much greater even than the average for Foshan municipality in the Pearl River Delta (US$290 per head) (GDTJNJ 2003: 436, 541, 552). Kunshan was of course exceptional, but rural Suzhou as a whole attracted very large inflows in the late 1990s; none of its counties (as defined in 1982; all were cities by 2002) received less than US$350 million. Per capita 2002 figures for Changshu and Zhangjiagang were US$468 and US$565 respectively. By way of comparison, the best total achieved by any Zhejiang county (using the 1982 definition) was Yuyao's US$158 million. Even Wenzhou city managed only US$64 million (ZJTJNJ 2003: 621–2). By contrast, inward investment in Jiangsu was simply too important to ignore.[20]

Admittedly the inclusion of FDI in the regression is not without pitfalls. The most obvious is the problem of endogeneity: was foreign capital a genuinely independent variable, or whether it was driven by the growth of industrial output itself? Still, the likelihood is that the dominant direction of causality was from FDI to output growth. This is because most FDI flowed into China to take

---

[19] Nevertheless, the regression results appear generally robust. Whether one uses GVA data for 1978–96 (instead of the 1978 to 2002 time series) or the narrower concept of NVIO (net industrial output value)—estimated here by applying to county GVIO data in every year the average of 1985 and 1991 ratios of NVIO to GVIO—the regression results change little. The results are also insensitive to the use of 1978 instead of 1982 as the base year for industrial GVA per head. In fact, as discussed below, the results are much more sensitive to the treatment of urban areas and Suxichang than to changes in value-added concepts or time periods.

[20] The omission of the FDI variable greatly reduces the fit of the regression equations.

advantage of low labour costs; the projected growth of world demand was the determining factor, rather than the growth of the domestic Chinese market. In addition, insofar as FDI was driven by domestic demand, it was the size and growth of the domestic market as a whole which was crucial, not the growth of industrial output in the host county. The notion of a powerful causal link running from industrial output to FDI therefore seems unlikely.

One continuing omission from the regression is the share of SOEs in industrial output as an independent variable. Its inclusion as a proxy for the size of the state sector has been the usual practice in most empirical work on Jiangsu, but it is misconceived. This is because, as discussed in earlier chapters, SOEs comprised only a part of the state sector; properly measured, the state sector comprised the totality of SOEs, collective and CBEs in the late 1970s, and thus amounted to almost 100 percent in virtually every Jiangsu county in 1978. Previous work has determined that the coefficient on the SOE share in GVIO 1978 is both significant and negative; that result is replicated if GVA data are used (the findings are not shown here). But it is not surprising that the coefficient is significant and negative. It merely shows that, because SOE productivity was well above the average in the state sector at the end of the Maoist era, there was less scope for increasing it after 1978 than in the less efficient collective and CBE sectors. Jurisdictions with a large SOE sector therefore grew less quickly (*ceteris paribus*) than other jurisdictions simply because they enjoyed fewer of the advantages of backwardness (for which read inefficiency).[21]

The regression results obtained based on all these assumptions are summarized in Table 8.6. Equation (1) includes every Jiangsu jurisdiction classified as a county at the time of the 1982 Population Census (the other equations are discussed below). It is clearly disappointing from the perspective of the learning hypothesis because neither literacy nor initial industrial employment rates are statistically significant. The adjusted value of R^2 is also rather low (admittedly not necessarily a cause for concern), and even initial industrial output per head is only barely significant—an unusual result for a growth regression. These results are odd to say the least when compared with the national results discussed in the previous chapter, and this alone suggests that we should view them with some suspicion. There are two possible explanations. One centres on the definition of urban and rural adopted in the Jiangsu case. The other focuses on the distortions to output value caused by the price structure of the late 1970s.

---

[21] County-level data on fixed investment have been published for Jiangsu even for the early 1980s (JSB 1989) but the data appear too unreliable and too volatile from year to year (partly because they necessarily include investment in sectors other than industry e.g. housing; infrastructure). The data for the 1980s are especially problematic because they exclude rural investment (including investment by TVEs), and many of the county data for 1993 (from JSTJNJ 1994) appear to suffer from the same defect. No attempt is therefore made to include fixed investment rates in the regression.

Table 8.6 Regression results for Jiangsu, 1978–2002 (dependent variable is growth of industrial GVA per capita)

Variable	Equation and coefficients				
	(1)	(2)	(3)	(4)	
				Unstandardized	Standardized
Industrial GVA per head, 1978	−0.018	−0.021	−0.035	−0.037	−1.294
	(−2.08)	(−2.20)	(−6.73)	(−7.56)	
Population density	−0.024	−0.019	−0.017	−0.018	−0.360
	(−3.42)	(−2.49)	(−3.33)	(−3.80)	
Industrial employment rate	0.013	0.024	0.019	0.024	0.485
	(1.33)	(2.20)	(2.01)	(3.42)	
Foreign capital inflow, 1996	0.012	0.009	0.011	0.012	0.617
	(5.52)	(3.13)	(5.48)	(6.92)	
Distance to Shanghai	0.009	0.036	−0.007		
	(0.76)	(2.10)	(−0.93)		
Literacy rate	0.011	0.007	0.020		
	(0.40)	(0.28)	(0.76)		
Grain yield, 1978	−0.002	0.007	0.006		
	(−0.16)	(−0.42)	(0.43)		
Dependency ratio	0.024	−0.032	0.035		
	(0.49)	(−0.55)	(0.82)		
Adjusted R^2	0.36	0.33	0.76	0.77	0.77
Number of counties	64	52	75	75	75

Notes: (a) t statistics in parentheses. All variables are in logarithmic form. The data on independent variables are for 1982 unless otherwise specified. (b) Equation (1) is for all rural jurisdictions (as defined in the 1982 Population Census). Equation (2) excludes the twelve counties of rural Suxichang (Jiangyin, Yixing, Wuxi, Wujin, Jintan, Liyang, Changshu, Zhangjiagang, Taicang, Kunshan, Wuxian and Wujiang). Equation (3) includes Jiangsu's eleven cities (as defined in 1982) and all of its 64 counties. Equation (4) tidies up equation (3) by excluding statistically insignificant variables. (c) 'Distance to Shanghai' is the straight line distance of each county from Shanghai. (d) 'Dependency rate' is the proportion of the population aged under 15 and over 64. (e) 'Grain yield' is output in 1978 divided by grain sown area in 1980. (f) 'Population density' is persons per square kilometre. (g) 'Industrial employment rate' is the proportion of the population employed in all types of industry as a percentage of the total workforce. (h) 'Literacy rate' is for the population aged 12 and over. (i) Industrial GVA per head is at 1990 prices and for 1978. It includes all types of industry after 1983, but omits (as with most Chinese data) sub-village industries for 1983 and earlier; however, production in the sub-village subsector was small during that period. The method used to estimate GVA is outlined in the notes to Table 8.5, above. (j) These data use the jurisdictional boundaries and classifications in use at the time of the 1982 Census. (k) The data on capital inflows include all flows (not just FDI) and refer to actual rather than contracted values.

Sources: As for Table 8.5; and NCGY (1989); Shouce (1987); JSTJNJ (1997).

8.5.1. The Biased Relative Price Structure

The first possible explanation for the poor fit of equation (1) centres on the impact of the relative price structure on estimated industrial GVA. The data which underlie the regression analysis for 1978–88 in Table 8.6 are for GVIO at 1980 prices.[22] However, 1980 relative prices were state-imposed, and were designed to maximize profits rates in the light industrial sector, rather than to reflect market forces. In practice, this meant that the relative price of raw materials (coal is the classic example) was low, whereas the relative price of consumer

---

[22] These are then re-based to 1990 prices for 1978–88 using the provincial, rather than county-specific, price deflator. The use of 1990 prices therefore does not alter the relative standing of counties in terms of per capita industrial output in the late 1970s and 1980s.

goods was high. Given that raw materials were scarce in the late 1970s, it is hard to justify this sort of price structure in terms of demand and supply conditions, and many Chinese economists argued that prices had diverged substantially from embodied labour value by the late 1970s:

In the past ten years or more, unreasonable prices have appeared because of the shortcomings and errors in our work . . . Some of the light industrial goods made from agricultural raw materials, such as cotton cloth and sugar, yield fairly large profits . . . The prices of goods from heavy industry are also far from being reasonable. Generally speaking, the prices of raw materials especially mineral products, are too low while those of processed goods are too high . . . It is necessary to raise the price of coal and other minerals and lower the prices of processed goods . . . Coal is in short supply and, because of its low price, many coal mines have been losing money for years. engineering goods have been overstocked for a long time . . . Many commune-run factories are charging too much for the engineering goods because state controls over such goods is so strict or the procedure for getting them is so complicated that users have to buy them wherever they can . . .

(Xue 1981: 147, 149, 150, 159, 160)

In Jiangsu, these distortions meant that the prices of light industrial products in 1980 was 5.6 percent lower than they had been in 1957, whereas those of heavy industrial goods were no less than 32.5 percent lower (TJJ 1990b: 357).[23] Sectoral profit rates tell a similar story. In a well-functioning market economy without significant barriers to entry, we would expect to see similar rates of profit across sectors because of the impact of competition. However, this was not true of China at the end of the Maoist era (Zhang 1988: 174, 248–51). Profit rates were high across the board, reflecting the quasi-monopoly status of many of China's SOEs. However, rates were exceptionally high in the oil, food processing and textile subsectors, and very low in metallurgy and coal. Only after the price reforms of the 1980s do we see convergence occurring (Naughton 1995: 236–8).

These price distortions have important implications for the regression analysis because of differences in the structure of production across Jiangsu's regions. The case of Suzhou municipality is particularly instructive. There, industrial production in the late 1970s and early 1980s was dominated by the high price-high profit textile sector. If we look at TVEs, the textile sector accounted for 35 percent of GVIO (and 26 percent of industrial employment) in Suzhou during 1985, compared with only 20 and 18 percent in neighbouring Wuxi and Changzhou respectively (Tao 1988: 55, 70). If we consider all types of industrial enterprises, textiles accounted on average for 25 percent of output across Jiangsu in 1985. In rural Suzhou, however, the figure was much higher. In Taicang, for example, textiles accounted for 35 percent of GVIO in 1985 and in Changshu, Zhangjiagang and Wujiang the figures were 38, 45 and 49 percent

[23] The comparison with 1957 is especially interesting because estimates of intersectoral flows have often portrayed that year as the one in which the Chinese economy was close to being in equilibrium (Ishikawa 1967, 1988).

respectively (JSSXGK 1989: 440, 457, 471 and 513). Suzhou was not alone. In fact, profits rates were high in other parts of Suxichang, but this time because of the dominance of the high profit machine-building subsector. In fact, the machine-building subsector in Wuxi and Changzhou was even more profitable than in Jiangsu as a whole because it was strongly geared towards the production of machinery for textiles and the production of consumer goods—Xue Muqiao's engineering goods—for the rural market.

The significance of this is that the dominance of high price industrial subsectors in Suxichang served not only to inflate profit rates but also to raise the value of industrial output relative to other parts of Jiangsu. By contrast Subei's industry was dominated by the presence of low price-low profit raw material subsectors, which served to reduce the value of recorded industrial output. In consequence, as measured by the official data, GVIO in Suxichang was too high at the start of the transition era, and hence industrial GVA as well.[24] Given that the initial level of GVA per head occupies a central role in the regression, price distortions distort the regression results. More precisely, initial GVA per head is too low in some of Jiangsu's counties (mainly those located in Subei) and too high in others (primarily those located in Suxichang).

If the value of industrial production in Jiangsu in the 1980s were to be re-calculated using shadow market prices, it would have the effect of reducing industrial GVA per head in Suxichang in 1978. This would also have the effect of raising the industrial growth rate between 1978 and 1988 (post-1988 output value, derived as it is from market prices, would remain unchanged). The effect in terms of the regression is to increase the significance of the initial level of industrial employment because the high employment Suxichang region now has a considerably faster growth rate. For example, if we reduce output value in the counties of Suxichang by 50 percent in 1978, 45 percent in 1979, and so on until we make no adjustment to the 1988 figure (by which time much of China's price reform had been completed), the t statistic for initial GVA per head rises to above 4 and that for industrial employment to 1.82, which is significant at the 10 percent level (the adjusted R^2 rises in the process to 0.54). In short, once we adjust for the distortions caused by the use of 1980 relative prices, the Jiangsu regression results become much more plausible.[25]

---

[24] The valuation problem becomes much less in the 1990s because most prices were by then largely market-determined.

[25] The argument being made here is not that Suxichang was dominated by heavy industry in 1978. For one thing, it is factually incorrect. In Wuxi county, heavy industry accounted for fully 69 percent of GVIO (WXG 1990: 29). For Suxichang as a whole, heavy industry accounted for no less than 46 percent of output in 1978 (Zhou 1994: 157). Secondly, many subsectors within heavy industry were highly profitable, machine building (as we have discussed) being one example. Rather, the argument is that Suxichang had little by way of industrial processing of raw materials (e.g. coal) compared with other parts of Jiangsu; this was the subsector where profits and prices were especially low.

8.5.2. The Urban–Rural Divide

An alternative explanation for the poor fit of equation (1) in Table 8.6 is the problematic definition of 'urban' used in Jiangsu in the early 1980s. For although the province was much more heavily industrialized than the norm, comparatively few of its jurisdictions were designated as urban. Instead, centres of industrial production continued to be amalgamated with farming communities to form counties. The discrimination inflicted on Jiangsu in this regard is clear from the evidence. Of China's 167 cities in 1964, 11 (6.6 percent) were located in Jiangsu. By the time of the 1982 Population Census, the national total had risen to 245 as many centres of industrial production were granted urban status. Yet Jiangsu's allocation remained the same; as a result, the share of its eleven cities in the national total of urban jurisdictions declined from 6.6 percent to only 4.5 percent. This was the result of a deliberate government policy designed to limit the number of cities that Jiangsu was allowed to create (Jacobs 1999: 118). This outcome is very hard to justify given the pace of population growth and, more importantly, the pace of rural industrialization across the provinces in the 1960s and 1970s.

The significance of this anti-urban bias becomes apparent when we experiment with adding or excluding jurisdictions from the regression on the grounds that the urban-rural distinction is particularly arbitrary for Jiangsu. A particularly telling illustration is provided by removing the twelve counties of Suxichang, an exclusion which is logically very appealing because, by most Chinese standards, the region in 1982 had much more in common with officially-designated urban areas even though it was officially classified (the cities of Wuxi, Suzhou and Changzhou aside) as rural. One example using 1990 data for Wuxian county (adjacent to Suzhou city) demonstrates the point. In that year, many of Wuxian's townships and towns recorded levels of TVE industrial output which were as high as those achieved by relatively advanced *counties* in other provinces. Fengqiao town, for instance, recorded a 1990 level of TVE industrial output of 305 million *yuan*, measured at 1980 prices (WXG 1990: 46–7). By contrast, the GVIO of all types of industry in the entire county of Emei in Sichuan province was only 513 million *yuan* in 1989 (SCTJNJ 1990: 555). Yet despite its relative industrial under-development, Emei was a city and Fengqiao a mere town.

The statistical consequence of the amalgamation of areas of industrial production with their rural hinterland in Jiangsu is a flattening out of the dispersion of per capita industrial production. Whereas the coefficient of variation for county GVIO per head in Jiangsu in 1978 was 0.63, it was 0.89 in Sichuan, reflecting the existence in the latter of a substantial number of small counties with quite high levels of industrial production.[26] If Suxichang's county

[26] The Sichuan data here exclude the counties of Aba, Liangshan, Ganzi and Guangyuan prefectures, and the industrial processing district of Jinkouhe. Most of these counties had high level of industrial output per head (based on mineral extraction and lumber). Their inclusion would raise the Sichuan coefficient of variation even further.

boundaries are re-drawn to create a number of additional counties out of heavily industrialized towns, the effect is to add a number of counties which combined high initial industrial GVA with slow growth to the rural sample—which in turn (as will be seen) markedly alters the regression results.[27]

A second justification for excluding Suxichang overlaps with the first. Areas of industrial and agricultural production were bundled together as county-level units in Suxichang not just because of central government discrimination but also because it was virtually impossible to distinguish between rural and urban areas in this part of Jiangsu.[28] It is for this very reason that the concept of *desakota* has been coined by McGee to describe regions which are neither truly urban nor truly rural. For McGee, *desakota* regions have six characteristics: a large share of the population engaged in rice cultivation, rapid growth of non-agricultural production, a highly mobile population, mixed but highly intensive land use, a high female participation rate in the non-farm sector and comparatively weak central government control (Ginsburg et al. 1991: 16–17).[29]

Suxichang fits McGee's conceptualization very well (Ginsburg et al. 1991; Ho 1994; Marton 2000). For example, a large proportion of the female population is employed in the textile and apparel sector. In Wujin county, 49 percent of the industrial workforce employed at the time of the 1990 Population Census was female. In the textile sector, the 30,163 women employed accounted for 71 percent of workers (Wujin pucha 1992: 388). Rice is of course the key farm product, migration (both geographical and occupational) is extensive, and the expansion of the non-farm sector is the key characteristics of the region's development since the late 1960s. Furthermore, the extent of integration between farm and non-farm sectors is apparent. Many farm workers are employed part-time in the industrial sector, a type of working aptly summarized in the phrase *litu bu li xiang* (leave the farm but not the countryside), and different members of the same household typically work in farming and industry; the equally well-known phrase 'the men farm whilst the women weave', which is often used to describe traditional Sunan practice, characterizes this type of intra-household specialization. Industrial companies often employ a significant number of farm

---

[27] By contrast, there were few towns and few concentrations of industrial production in northern Jiangsu, especially in the early 1980s (Fei 1986). It is Suxichang that distorts the Jiangsu picture.

[28] There were other reasons. Some Jiangsu counties did not want urban status, largely because of concerns about losing independence; the seat of Wuxi county, for example, was located within the boundaries of Wuxi city and this discouraged the county from seeking urban status until the late 1990s (Marton 2000: 185). Wuxian, adjacent to Suzhou, faced much the same problem.

[29] Some Chinese scholars have argued along similar lines that the Chinese economy is properly conceived of as comprising three sectors (*sanyuan jingji jiegou*)—urban, rural, and a rural industrial sector—rather than the two sectors which feature in much western scholarship on developing countries.

workers (for example Ho 1994: 146), which leads to a marked blurring of occupational and sectoral employment distinctions. As Veeck (1991: 158, 174) says:

. . . *kotadesasi* regions may be difficult to delineate in Jiangsu, but there can be no doubt that a new type of place is evolving that is somehow different from the urban-rural transitional zones . . . The lack of a distinct urban-rural dichotomy in Sunan—at least from the perspective of per capita income—lends support to the kotadesasi model.

Fei (1986: 50) argues along similar lines that Sunan has seen the emergence of a large cadre of 'peasant workers' who '. . . live in the countryside, work in the small factories run by production brigades in normal times, look after household sideline occupations in their spare time and do farm work during the busy season'. The scale of the problem is evident from the 1990 census returns for Jiangsu. Wujin, for example, had an agricultural workforce of 448,000 according to a sectoral definition but only 358,000 according to an occupational definition (Wujin pucha 1992: 15–16).[30] The Chinese government deliberately encouraged this type of blurring in the early 1980s by promoting the development of small towns in counties, in preference to the expansion of cities (Fei 1986).

Suxichang was thus very different to the rest of Jiangsu. Even in the early 1980s, it was heavily industrialized, and its profusion of small towns meant that it had at least as much in common with Jiangsu's cities-proper as with the counties of Subei. By the mid-1990s, the process had progressed much further. By then, industrial GVA in Jiangyin and Xishan (the old Wuxi county) was larger than in Wuxi city, output in Wujin dwarfed that of Changzhou city, and Zhangjiagang was more heavily industrialized than Suzhou city. If we look at trends in per capita GDP, we see a similar process of convergence. By 1996, per capita GDP in Xishan was almost as large as in Wuxi city, and the same is true if we compare Wujin with Changzhou city. And Suzhou city itself had been overtaken by most of its hinterland. Every one of the six Suzhou jurisdictions which had been counties in 1982 had been promoted to city status by 1996, and it was not undeserved—in contrast to changes of status conferred on other jurisdictions across China, where city status had been given in order to promote development, rather than in recognition of what had actually been achieved. In five out of the six counties (Wuxian was the exception), per capita GDP was actually higher than in Suzhou city itself; in Zhangjiagang, it was no less than 50 percent greater (Wuxi tongjiju 1997: 405–7). This absolute convergence between those areas designated rural and urban in the early 1980s stands in contrast to developments in other Chinese provinces, where the dominance of provincial capitals has not been challenged.

---

[30] The agricultural workforce was supplemented during the busy summer period (when the Census was taken) by a large number of 'workers' whose occupation was non-agricultural. This explains why the sectoral definition is so much larger than the occupational one.

The effect of excluding Suxichang from the Jiangsu regression is considerable (equation (2) of Table 8.6).[31] Taken as a whole, this new equation fits far better (although the coefficient on distance from Shanghai suggests very strong backwash effects). It is also revealing that the industrial employment level is now significant as a determinant of growth, a result which appears robust. For example, industrial employment remains a statistically significant determinant of growth if we exclude Zhenjiang municipality (in Sunan) as well as Suxichang, and it is also significant if we confine the scope of the regression analysis to Subei alone. In short, inherited industrial employment is only insignificant when anomalous regions are included in the Jiangsu regression. Of these regions, Suxichang is by far the most extreme example, being neither truly urban nor truly rural in the early 1980s. There is therefore a strong argument for excluding it from the regression if we are interested in the determinants of rural industrialization. An alternative regression solution to the ill-defined nature of the urban-rural divide in Jiangsu in the 1980s and 1990s is to include *all* jurisdictions, whether officially urban or rural. The results obtained using this approach are summarized in equation (3). This provides by far the best fit of any of the equations in Table 8.6, with an adjusted R^2 of 0.76. Not only is the coefficient on industrial employment significant, but so too are those on initial industrial output per head, population density and foreign capital inflow. The Shanghai coefficient is not significant, suggesting that spread and backwash effects cancel out once urban centres are included in the sample.

Taken together these results imply that the jurisdictional distinctions used at the time of the 1982 Census in the case of Jiangsu are especially misleading in their distinction between urban and rural areas. Once this false dichotomy is eliminated, we can identify far more clearly the underlying determinants of industrial growth in Jiangsu. The significance for subsequent rural industrialization of learning-by-doing in the Maoist period (as proxied by industrial employment) then becomes plain.

None of the changes in sample size or urban definition discussed in the previous sections are sufficient to rescue literacy as an explanatory factor in the growth process. The Jiangsu data are characterized by a number of counties where rapid growth of industrial output went hand-in-hand with a high initial (1982) industrial employment and a low educational attainment. Literacy is insignificant in every regression specification, and the same is true of other measures of formal education. This suggests that a workforce with experience of industrial employment prior to 1982 may have been a necessary condition for

---

[31] An alternative procedure would be to include a Suxichang dummy, but the trouble with this is that quantitative variables have already been included in the equation to try to capture as much as possible of Suxichang's exceptionalism (grain yields, proximity to Shanghai and capital inflows). If the dummy variable approach is taken, logic dictates that all these proxies should be excluded from the equation and the dummy should be allowed to capture the special characteristics of the region. This is surely too blunt an approach and it has not been adopted here. For what it is worth, the simple addition of a Suxichang dummy generates a significant coefficient on the dummy, and other variables are largely unaffected.

rural industrialization, but formal education was much less important. For all its desirability on social grounds, a workforce with a high level of education does not appear to have been necessary for rapid growth in rural Jiangsu. In fact the two were evidently (and not surprisingly) close substitutes. In those counties where workers entered the mill in their mid-teens—rather than continuing with their secondary education—the industrial employment rate rose but levels of educational attainment stagnated. The numbers employed were by no means small. In Wujin county, for example, the 1990 Census returns show that 62,732 of those aged 15–19 were employed, whereas only 42,084 were still in school. It is also evident for Wujin that young women tended to enter the workforce earlier than men, who were more likely to continue in school: 2.6 percent of 15 year old males were employed in industry compared with 7.3 percent of 15 year old females, but at age 17, 24.5 percent of men worked in industry compared with no less than 42.6 percent of women (Wujin pucha 1992: 204, 340–4, 554–5). Young women thus played a key role in Wujin's industrialization, and it may well be— certainly the regression results suggest this—that the county's growth rate would have been less rapid had they remained at school.

8.5.3. Interpreting the Regression Results

Equation (4) takes full account of the considerations discussed in the previous section by including all Jiangsu's rural and urban jurisdictions (for the reasons outlined above), and by eliminating the insignificant variables like education. Standardized coefficients are also shown for this equation, thus allowing identification of the economic significance of initial variables.

The coefficients in equation (4) suggest that both FDI and population density had powerful effects on the rural industrialization rate. A one standard deviation rise in the former was enough to raise industrial growth by around 0.6 of a standard deviation, and a similar increase in the latter reduced growth by a non-negligible 0.36 of a standard deviation. FDI appears to have interacted with human capital (as proxied by industrial employment). Even if the analysis is limited to those jurisdictions officially classified as rural in 1982, the coefficient on industrial employment is higher when FDI is included than when it is excluded. When we take on board the *desakota* argument and include both urban and rural jurisdictions in the sample, foreign capital emerges as significant in both economic and statistical senses. This result suggests that industrial skills were a valuable inheritance in part because they helped to attract foreign capital. By contrast, those counties which lacked a skilled workforce seem to have found it difficult to attract FDI, setting in train a process of cumulative causation.[32]

---

[32] This is conjectural. Some studies have found no correlation between FDI and labour force quality (Cheng and Kwan 2000), although there is some evidence that labour force quality became more important as a factor in attracting FDI by the late 1990s (Gao 2005).

As importantly, the regression shows that the effect of a one standard deviation rise in the initial level of per capita output was to reduced growth by a stunning 1.3 standard deviations. This shows that Jiangsu's cities (where initial per capita industrial output was highest) were greatly disadvantaged by their prosperity. Wuxi and Suzhou cities demonstrate the point particularly clearly. In both cases, per capita industrial output grew by only 6 percent per annum, less than half the provincial average, between 1978 and 2002. But when one remembers that the level of per capita industrial output in 1978 was 2,084 *yuan* in Suzhou and 3,001 *yuan* in Wuxi whereas the provincial average was a mere 124 *yuan*, their slow growth is hardly surprising. By contrast, poor counties enjoyed all the advantages of backwardness; they could exploit the abundant opportunities available for catch-up growth. The Jiangsu evidence demonstrates that most took advantage.

Most importantly of all, industrial employment exerted an effect on the rate of industrialization which was significant in both an economic and a statistical sense. According to equation (4), a one standard deviation rise in industrial employment increased the rate of industrial growth by about half a standard deviation. Although less important an influence than initial per capita output, the economic significance of inherited industrial employment (and hence the size of the skills base) is undeniable. Indeed, taken together, these results suggest that the presence of a large but low productivity industrial sector was more conducive to rapid growth in Jiangsu after 1978 than anything else. The large industrial workforce meant that a county entered the transition era with an extensive skills base. A low level of industrial productivity, as proxied by output per head, meant that there was abundant scope for skills to be better utilized. Backwardness by itself was not enough: Jiangsu counties fared best when their skill base was wide and when industrial productivity was low. Those Jiangsu counties where industrial employment was low at the close of the 1970s were thus disadvantaged. They simply lacked the manufacturing capability to take advantage of the market opportunities available in the post-Mao era.

The results generated by equations (3) and (4) are equally interesting for what they tell us about the limited impact of geographical factors on the pace of growth. As we have seen, neither the grain yield, nor proximity to Shanghai, is a robust statistically significant factor in determining growth; too many counties close to these metropolitan centres have failed to share in the rapid industrialization of Suxichang. Although it may seem odd that proximity to Shanghai failed to confer economic advantage, this reckons without three factors. Firstly, none of Jiangsu's counties was located very far from the great metropolitan centre. One might therefore conclude that *all* gained from Shanghai's relative proximity, in sharp contrast to (say) counties in the mountain fastness of Gansu. Secondly, Jiangsu is an unusual province in having multiple urban centres, each of which serves as a growth pole. Of course Shanghai exerted a good deal of influence on Jiangsu's development, but it was even more important as a growth pole for Zhejiang. Furthermore, although Nanjing was a significant economic centre, the impact of Suzhou and Wuxi cities on the countryside was at least as great in the early 1980s. Combined industrial GVA there in 1978 was about equal to that of Nanjing, and this position was maintained into the mid-1990s. Thirdly, it is also possible that backwash effects were quite powerful; it is hard to explain the relative under-development of counties close to Nanjing without some reference to a drain of skills and capital from these rural areas to the provincial capital.

To be sure, we can not discount geographical factors entirely. The coefficient on FDI is significant, and Jiangsu was able to attract more FDI than most precisely because of its location. Furthermore, high population density had a significant negative effect on growth rates, and it is not unreasonable to regard density as partially determined by geographical factors. The negative coefficient here suggests that the costs of large population—in terms of necessary in health, housing and educational spending—offset any advantages conferred by market size. This is as one might expect in Jiangsu's case. A large local market for a county's products was probably not very important given the low transport costs which characterized the whole province: it was a simple matter for a county to sell its output in Shanghai, or elsewhere in Jiangsu. By contrast, the national evidence discussed in the previous chapter suggests that density was unimportant, perhaps because, in the presence of high transport costs, a large local population was important to provide a market.

Ultimately, however, the regression evidence suggests that 'history' (as measured by the extent of backwardness and the level of manufacturing capability) was much more important than geography at the county level in Jiangsu. This in turn implies a clear causal connection between the industrialization of the Maoist era, and the breakneck growth of the 1980s and 1990s. It was the expansion of manufacturing capability, itself the product of an extended process of learning, which made possible the successful industrialization of the transition era. Jiangsu's present is intimately linked to its industrial past.

8.6. Conclusion

In sum, and despite the existence of significant labour mobility across the province after 1978, the Jiangsu evidence points to a key role for Maoist learning-by-doing in powering the industrialization of the transition era. The learning hypothesis seems to hold up in Jiangsu in part because the scale of labour migration was rather less than much of the literature implies. Ho (1994: 162), for example, observes that migration was actually relatively limited (at least in the 1980s) given the extent of the wage differential between Subei and Sunan partly because of the continuing operation of the *hukou* system. Perhaps more importantly, there is much to suggest that migrant destinations were often unable (and unwilling) to absorb outsiders, so much so that migrants returned home after only a short sojourn. In no small measure, this transient quality to migration reflected widespread discrimination against migrant Subei workers across Sunan. That is, location acted in Jiangsu in the same way as ethnicity in other contexts—migrants were discriminated against on the basis of geographically-defined identity (Honig 1992; Finnane 1993). In consequence, Subei may have lost out in the sense that its *unskilled* labour was unable to find jobs in the south (and hence were not able to remit north part of their income), but this was offset by its ability to retain its *skilled* workers.

Whatever the reason, the Jiangsu evidence discussed in this chapter broadly supports the learning hypothesis. The evidence is veiled by the regional impact of product price distortions in Suxichang, and the artificiality of the urban-rural divide in much of southern Jiangsu in the early 1980s. But once this veil is lifted, it becomes apparent that the learning hypothesis is as applicable to Jiangsu as it is to other parts of China.

9

Sichuan

Sichuan offers a very demanding test of the industrial legacies hypothesis. This is because the province was the focus for Third Front construction, the archetypal Maoist industrialization programme, and therefore it might be expected that the Front's legacies in Sichuan were less potent than those of an equivalent degree of more civilian-orientated industrial development.[1] If there is evidence of positive industrial legacies in this province, there were almost certainly positive legacies in other parts of rural China as well. Sichuan is also interesting because in many ways its experience after 1949 encapsulates the full impact, for good and ill, of Maoism across China. Due in no small part to the ill-conceived radicalism of Li Jingquan, the Party secretary, as many as 15 million of Sichuan's citizens (more than in any other province) perished during the Great Leap Forward and its aftermath. Fighting was commonplace in the streets of its cities at the height of the Cultural Revolution. Agriculture, even in those counties watered by the famous Dujiangyan, languished until its revival under Zhao Ziyang in the late 1970s; farm output grew at over 13 percent per

---

[1] For the purposes of this chapter, Sichuan excludes the prefectures of Chongqing, Fuling and Wanxian, which were combined to create the provincial-level municipality of Chongqing in 1997 ('prefecture' is used for simplicity throughout to encompass both prefectural-level municipalities and autonomous minority prefectures). The area covered by this new municipality of Chongqing, historically part of Sichuan, is excluded from the analysis because of data problems. The growth rates of industrial production in many of its counties after 1978 have been distorted by the impact of the Sanxia dam project, especially in Wanxian and Fuling prefectures. Secondly, estimates of industrial production vary substantially depending on the source used; compare the SCZL (1990) data with those in Chongqing tongjiju (1989). This divergence probably reflects the treatment of Chongqing-based industrial enterprises owned by China's central ministries. The output of these enterprises is often omitted from Chinese county-level data, which has an especially distorting effect where the number of such enterprises is large. Thirdly, Chongqing was an important centre of weapons production during the Maoist period and thereafter (Gao 1987; CSJW 1991: 104–17; Yang 1997: 162–213; Wang 1993; Hessler 2001; Chen 2003). For example, many warship components were produced in the Chongqing weapons base, and the policy of *shansandong* ('in mountainous areas, dispersed and in caves') adopted during the 1960s and 1970s meant that production was dispersed. This type of production (though not that part of the output of military factories classified as civilian production) is usually omitted from the data, and therefore the presence of weapons production across so many counties causes a good deal of data distortion.

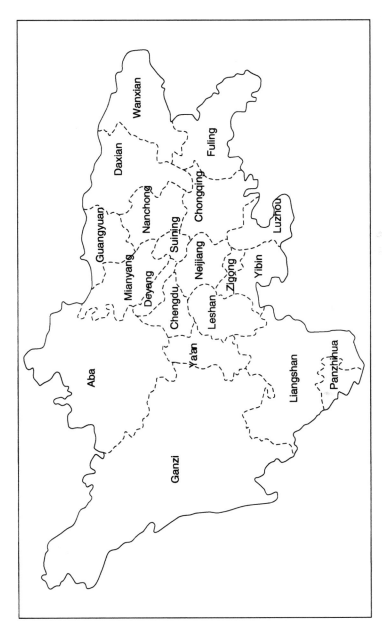

Figure 9.1 The prefectures of Sichuan in the late 1980s

annum between the cyclical troughs of 1976 and 1980. And yet the pace of industrialization was rapid, and life expectancy increased dramatically in the long run. Maoism even gave birth to the new city of Panzhihua, a potent symbol of modernity on the banks of the Jinsha river.

For all that, the transformative impact of Maoism in Sichuan was necessary limited by geography. Industrial development on the high Himalayan plateau west of Chengdu (the old province of Xikang) was limited. So too along the periphery of the Sichuan basin. These spatial variations are a boon for scholars interested in the sources of post-1978 rural industrial development. They enable us to tease out the interplay of industrial legacies and geography in a way which is not possible in the study of China's coastal provinces, where topographical variation is more muted. In addition, the available data on Sichuan's economic development are relatively good; there are few systematic county-level data for the pre-1978 era, but the materials taken as a whole are abundant enough to allow a proper assessment of the manufacturing capability hypothesis.

9.1. Maoist Industrialization in Sichuan

Sichuan's industrial development during the Maoist era was characterized by two features.[2] Firstly, the pace of industrialization. Secondly, a profound change in the industrial geography of the province.

9.1.1. The Pace of Industrialization

Sichuan's pre-1949 industrialization was less negligible than often assumed.[3] A heavy industrial base had been established around Chongqing by warlordism in the 1920s and 1930s, and by the KMT during the second Sino-Japanese War. As a result, the share of heavy industry in provincial GVIO was no less than 43 percent in 1952, significantly above the national share of 36 percent. But Sichuan's light industrial sector was under-developed. A substantial light industrial sector had grown up along the central riverine zone (the Yangzi and its tributaries) based on textiles, tong oil and salt, but by Chinese standards it was decidedly primitive. Moreover, the very under-development of light industry meant that

---

[2] The literature on Sichuan's economic development is enormous. Much of it is summarized in Bramall (1989, 1993); more recent studies cover agriculture (Bramall 1995; Pennarz 1998), Maoist rural industry (Piek 1998; Eyferth 2004), Meishan county (Ruf 1998), and prewar industrialization in Chongqing (Howard 2004). For an introduction to economic development in the province, see Hong (1997, 2004) and McNally (2004). Hessler (2001) provides an engaging account of life in Fuling in the 1990s. The most useful Chinese studies on Sichuan's industrial and economic development include SCJJDL (1985), SXQS (1988), Yang (1990), Zhang and Zhang (1990) and Yang (1997). For recent studies of the Third Front in Sichuan, see Chen (2003) and Shapiro (2001).

[3] Its implications for post-1978 growth are discussed in the final section of this chapter.

even the high heavy industry share in Sichuan translated into a level of per capita output that was low by national standards (10 *yuan* compared with 22 *yuan*). At 24 *yuan* per head, the overall level of industrial production in Sichuan in 1952 was well below the national figure of 61 *yuan* (SCZL 1990: 18; SCTJNJ 1990: 57; TJNJ 1993: 16, 103).

After 1949, the pace of industrial development quickened in the province: GVIO at comparable prices increased at a heady 8.7 percent per annum between 1952 and 1978 (SCZL 1990: 19). Industrial GVA grew more slowly, but the rate of increase of 5.9 percent per year (Hsueh and Li 1999: 484), was extraordinary by historical standards, and respectable when compared with the rates achieved in other poor countries. However, these impressive headline figures disguise the fact that the provincial growth rate was well below the national average of 9.9 percent. Furthermore, industrial production was also highly volatile in the late Maoist period. That had not been the case before 1962; although the great famine was particularly intense in Sichuan (Bramall 1997), the amplitude of the cycle of rapid industrial growth and collapse in 1958–62 broadly conformed to the national pattern. Thereafter, however, the extent of industrial fluctuation was much more extreme; industrial production collapsed in the province during 1961–2, 1967–8, 1971, 1974 and 1976, before soaring during 1976–8.

For all that, Sichuan's industry was transformed under Mao. This is most apparent from the changing composition of production. In 1952, the structure of provincial industry was very traditional (albeit less so than nationally, as previously noted); food processing and textiles together accounted for over 50 percent of production. During the Maoist era, however, they lost out, along with other more traditional products such as timber, garments, paper and 'other' (which in 1952 covered a range of proto-industrial products). By contrast, the production of chemicals and machinery rapidly increased. These two contributed only about 10 percent of output in 1952, but their combined share was up to 40 percent by 1978 if measured at 1970 prices, and to no less than 57 percent if measured at 1952 prices. The metallurgy sector also gained ground (though the increase was perhaps less than might have been expected given the emphasis on the development of iron and steel production in the Maoist years). In part this reflected the creation of the wartime industrial base at Chongqing, which meant that the base level of the metallurgy sector was quite high by 1949. It also reflected the very ambitious nature of the Panzhihua steel project, which did not really come to fruition until the 1980s. The overall effect was that the share of heavy industrial production rose from 43 percent of current price GVIO in 1952, to 59 percent by 1978 (SCZL 1990: 18).

9.1.2. Rural Industrialization in the Maoist Era

Much of the industrial growth of the Maoist era occurred in rural Sichuan, as is demonstrated by the experience of a sample of counties (Table 9.1). The sample is fairly large (there were 155 counties in Sichuan in the early 1980s) but it is not spatially representative. Only one county from the western prefectures of Ya'an, Aba, Liangshan and Ganzi is included, and there are no counties from Yibin and Luzhou in the sample; by contrast, the Chengdu plain is over-represented. However, it is not clear that the sample offers a biased picture of the pace and pattern of rural growth. The median growth rate of the sample differs somewhat from the overall provincial figure, but that is not surprising because the all-Sichuan figure includes urban jurisdictions. Moreover, the sample does include a number of counties which were poor (and industrially-developed), notably Xichong and Kaijiang, and there is nothing here to suggest that their experience was qualitatively different to that of the other counties over the entire Maoist period. As a check on this, data from four poor counties located in Chongqing (but which were part of Sichuan before 1978) were also examined. As the data at the bottom of Table 9.1 show, their experience was of slightly slower growth than the sample median, but not by very much.

The data in Table 9.1 show rapid growth during 1952–57, more so than in any other time period. However, not too much should be read into this: the 1952 industrial base was very low, and therefore much of the growth of the 1950s was simply a process of recovery from the trough of 1945–52. There are also good reasons for supposing that the official data for 1952 under-state true levels of production, whereas those for 1957 are more accurate; this means that growth rates based on official data over-state the true growth rate (Liu and Yeh 1965). The second column of data covers the entire early Maoist period (1952–65). The growth rates for this period are very slow, and even negative in a significant number of cases. This of course reflects the impact of the Great Leap Forward, and the poor growth rates demonstrate the damage inflicted by the iron and steel campaign. Even by 1965, many of Sichuan's counties do not seem to have fully recovered. Counties like Shifang, where a growth rate of well over 15 percent was sustained during all periods—output did collapse in the early 1960s, but it was swiftly made good—were the exception.

By contrast, the rate of rural industrialization was much more rapid in the late Maoist period (1965–78). In all but two of the counties in the sample (three if the Chongqing counties are included), the industrialization rate exceeded 10 percent per year and previous peak levels of industrial output were soon surpassed almost everywhere. To be sure, there is some evidence that the later stages of the Cultural Revolution had a damaging effect on Sichuan's rural economy. Industrial growth rates in almost every case were lower during 1970–78 than they had been in the late 1960s, with 1972 and 1975 being particularly poor years in rural Sichuan. This industrial evidence supports the argument put forward by Walder and Yang (2003) that the Cultural Revolution did impact on rural areas; the political campaigns emphasized by them evidently had economic consequences, and these were felt in the 1970s much more so than in the late 1960s in rural Sichuan. All this helps to explain why so much of the literature on

Table 9.1 Growth of GVIO in a sample of Sichuan counties (percent per annum; counties ranked by growth rates during 1965–78)

County	1952–57	1952–65	1965–78	1970–78
Kaijiang	30.2	7.0	8.3	8.0
Qianwei	18.0	2.9	9.5	6.0
Xinjin	28.3	3.3	11.0	12.4
Pujiang	23.6	3.6	11.9	7.7
Jiajiang	23.0	−1.8	12.1	8.9
Mianzhu	10.9	0	12.1	9.6
Chongqing	20.8	5.7	12.1	13.7
Rongxian	14.9	−0.7	12.2	12.2
Guanxian	16.9	3.4	12.6	10.3
Pengxian	8.9	7.7	13.2	11.8
Xichong	34.9	6.4	13.5	13.3
Nanchong	10.0	−6.0	13.6	9.4
Shehong	10.0	−6.0	13.6	9.4
Santai	−2.3	−7.1	15.4	20.2
Guanghan	18.8	5.0	16.1	11.8
Jingyan	18.7	−0.3	16.2	13.5
Shifang	23.5	15.5	16.9	15.9
Xinlong	n.a.	n.a.	66.5	104.8
Sample median	18.7	3.3	12.9	11.8
All Sichuan	23.4	9.3	11.2	9.3
Chongqing:				
Wushan	11.6	0.5	10.1	11.7
Kaixian	10.2	1.5	9.1	11.6
Nanchuan	26.2	4.0	10.8	5.7
Dianjiang	21.6	1.3	12.2	10.8

Notes: The county data here come from the respective *County Records* and are far from consistent. Wherever possible, I have used GVIO data at 1970 prices (though this does tend to under-state industrial growth in the post-1965 period because it gives a lower weight to the fast-growing heavy industry subsector). Nevertheless, this has not been possible in all cases. Furthermore, the county data are far from consistent in their treatment of industries owned by supra-county levels of government (in some cases they are omitted from the county totals), and in their treatment of commune and brigade industry (brigade industry is often excluded from county GVIO totals because it was officially part of the agricultural sector before 1984). It should also be noted that the GVIO data given in the *xian zhi* are usually for 1952, 1957, 1965, 1970 and 1978, and sometimes for 1962 and 1970, rather than complete time series; missing data have been estimated by linear interpolation.

Sources: Shifang XZ (1988: 13–41); Jiajiang XZ (1989: 212); Kaijiang XZ (1989: 207–8); Peng XZ (1989: 173–5); Xinjin XZ (1989: 97–8); Jingyan XZ (1990: 16–30, 141); Kai XZ (1990: 171–2); Shehong XZ (1990: 283–4); Chongqing XZ (1991: 295); Guan XZ (1991: 315); Nanchuan XZ (1991: 73); Qianwei XZ (1991: 251); Wushan XZ (1991: 193–4); Guanghan XZ (1992: 7); Mianzhu XZ (1992: 376–81); Pujiang XZ (1992: 160–2); Santai XZ (1992: 460–1); Xinlong XZ (1992: 134); Dianjiang XZ (1993: 425–6); Rong XZ (1993: 90); Nanchong XZ (1993: 275–6); Xichong XZ (1993: 306–13).

industrialization in the Sichuan countryside tends to start with 1975. Some of the arguments I have advanced in previous work—suggesting that the economic consequences of the Cultural Revolution in the countryside were negligible—need to be re-thought.

For all that, the positive *long run* impact of the Maoist rural industrialization strategy in Sichuan is not in doubt. Despite the fluctuations of the 1970s, the annual growth rate was impressive. And the very fact that previous peak output was surpassed by the late 1960s, and the trend in growth during the 1970s was firmly upwards, suggests that the process of growth was much more than merely catch-up. Rather, it suggests that a solid industrial foundation had been laid, and that the skills acquired during the Leap may well have produced a long run pay-off.

9.2. Changing Industrial Geography Under Mao

The rural nature of industrialization inevitably meant that the geography of production also changed during the Maoist era. We do not have good data on industrial value-added by prefecture (let alone by county), but the evidence on the growth of GVIO is enough to convey a sense of the changes which occurred across Sichuan (Table 9.2).[4] Three broad geographical patterns are discernible: the beginnings of industrialization in western Sichuan, the development of Chengdu, and the decline of Sichuan's old industrial centres. Of these, the rise of Chengdu was the most important in quantitative terms; it doubled its share of GVIO between 1952 and 1978 to reach 21 percent (whereas Panzhihua, despite its rapid growth, accounted for only 5 percent of provincial GVIO in 1978). To begin with, however, it is worth considering the rise of Sichuan's geographically-disadvantaged western prefectures.

9.2.1. The Rise of Western Sichuan

The growth of Panzhihua is the most arresting feature of Table 9.2. This was intimately connected to the programme of Third Front construction, of which more anon. The industrialization of mountainous Liangshan, the poorest prefecture in Sichuan, is also apparent. It owed much to Front projects such as the development of the rocket facility at Xichang and the construction of the Chengdu-Kunming railway (H. M. Zhu 1992: 119, 126–33). But Liangshan's industrialization rate was more rapid before 1965, when it was second-ranked

---

[4] Data on secondary sector GVA are given in Sichuan tongjiju (1999), but there are no data in this source for industrial GVA. As secondary sector GVA includes construction, it is not a very good measure of industrialization. To give an example of the distortion caused, consider Panzhihua between 1962 and 1965. This was a period of intense construction activity (Panzhihua had just been selected as the centrepiece of Sichuan's Third Front) but it was also one during which industrial production had scarcely begun. During this three year period, GVIO increased 2.1 fold (SCZL 1990: 342) but secondary value-added increased by a factor of 27 (Sichuan tongjiju 1999: 560). Accordingly, secondary value-added provides a highly misleading indicator of the industrial development of Panzhihua in 1965. It is of course true that the main alternative to secondary GVA (which is GVIO) is defective because it does not measure industrial value-added, but this is less of a problem than the impact of the construction boom. This is because the main determinant of the industrial value-added ratio is the balance between light and heavy industry. In fact, those prefectures which show the fastest rates of GVIO growth in Table 9.2—Panzhihua and the Himalayan prefectures—also had the largest shares of heavy industry in 1978 (SCZL 1990). Value-added estimators would therefore only reinforce the pattern of spatial change evident from GVIO trends, and therefore the use of GVIO is easily preferable to the use of secondary GVA.

amongst Sichuan's prefecture. This rapid growth rate partly reflected its low 1952 base; there were only four industrial enterprises in the prefecture at that time, and the only modern one amongst them was a small hydro-electricity plant at Xichang (LYZG 1985: 234). Liangshan's subsequent growth was due mainly to the development of logging (output rose 45 fold between 1952 and 1965), and coal mining (which enjoyed a 30 fold rise in output over the same period). By comparison, total provincial output of these two commodities increased 3.5 fold and 4 fold respectively (SCZL 1990: 36–51). The counties which were to become the Panzhihua municipality also industrialized quickly before 1965 for the same reason. Furthermore, neither Liangshan nor Panzhihua was adversely affected by the Great Leap Forward. GVIO in Sichuan was 10 percent below its 1957 level by 1962, but GVIO was more than twice as large in Liangshan (SCZL 1990: 19, 376).

The topographical obstacles to development further north were, by Chinese standards, truly formidable. Many of the counties of Aba and Ganzi are located on the high Himalayan plateau at altitudes of over 10,000 feet and the transport network is extremely under-developed as a result. This was undoubtedly the main obstacle to the growth of industrial production in the 1980s and 1990s, as Doak Barnett (who visited the region in 1948 and again in 1988) has observed: 'Local leaders were generally realistic, I thought, and openly recognized that the extreme difficulty of transportation in and out of the area was probably the greatest single obstacle to more rapid development' (Barnett 1993: 458). The prefectural *gaikuang* (Surveys) and the *xian zhi* (County Records) published in the 1980s and early 1990s tell the same story.[5] Even in the 1990s, and in the wake of some transport modernization, the roads of the region were tortuous, steep, and jammed with lorries carrying minerals and timber to Chengdu. Transportation in the Anning river valley was somewhat better, partly because of the railway linking Chengdu and Kunming via Panzhihua and Xichang. But even that line is often closed by landslides, and the counties which make up the bulk of Liangshan are to the east of the valley and hence gain little from it. The same is equally true of Muli county to the west. And although logs could be easily 'exported' along the Dadu river corridor via Leshan to Chongqing, or along the upper Yangzi to the east of Xinshizhen, these transport links were much less suited to the shipment of manufactured goods.

But although physical geography conspired against the development of manufacturing in these prefectures, state subsidies and their resource endowments were lavish enough to allow considerable natural resource-based industrialization. The relatively centralized fiscal system ensured that poor counties received significant net transfers, and these under-pinned their industrialization in the pre-1978 period even though—the counties of rural

---

[5] See, for example, AGK (1985); LGK (1985); MGK (1985); MWGK (1985); GGK (1986); Xinlong XZ (1992).

Panzhihua and around Xichang apart—the region benefited little from the Third Front. It also helped that it was comparatively easy to exploit timber and mineral resources in the early days. In both Aba and Ganzi, industrial development was based around heavy industry, in particular the expansion of timber production, the development of hydropower, and the exploitation of the region's extensive mineral deposits. Leather was the most important component of the small light industrial sector (AGK 1985: 153–4, 179–90; GGK 1986: 191–3, 198–201; GZ 1997; AZ 1994). In Sichuan as a whole, the extractive sector contributed slightly over 11 percent of GVIO in 1978.[6] In resource-rich western Sichuan, the figures were much higher. In Liangshan, the share was 33 percent, and it reached 65 and 69 percent in Ganzi and Aba respectively (SCZL 1990). In some counties, extractive industry was even more dominant. In Xinlong (Ganzi prefecture), extractive industry—mainly timber cutting, which accounted for about two thirds of industrial production (Xinlong XZ 1992: 128 and 134)—contributed 96 percent of all industrial production. In Zamtang (Aba), the figure was 93.5 percent in 1978 (SCZL 1990). Indeed, of the 20 counties in which extractive industry contributed over 70 percent of output in 1978, only two (the asbestos-producing county of Shimian in Ya'an, and Yibin county of Yibin prefecture) were to be found outside the three western prefectures.

The second feature of Table 9.2 is the rise of Chengdu.[7] In 1952, its share in Sichuan's industrial production was small, no larger in fact than the combined share of the neighbouring prefectures of Mianyang and Deyang to the north, and light industries dominated production; textiles and food processing together accounted for 63 percent of GVIO. Thereafter, Chengdu's industrialization proceeded apace. Growth throughout the Maoist era was driven by a combination of high levels of state investment, and the construction of three railway lines linking the provincial capital to Kunming (via Panzhihua) in the south, Chongqing to the south-east, and Baoji to the north. The development of these modern transport links was crucial because the railway served as a more than adequate substitute for the river communications that had underpinned the rise of the central riverine zone over the hundred years to 1949. Moreover, the prefecture was critically dependent on other jurisdictions for its supplies of key raw materials, notably coal and timber (CDSZ 1993: 267–8).

The underlying factor at work in the rise of Chengdu was the CCP decision to single out the city as a site for the expansion of heavy industry during the First

---

[6] The phrase 'extractive (*caijue*) sector' is used by China's NBS to refer to the sum of coal mining, lumbering, mining for ferrous and non-ferrous metals, and petroleum extraction (see TJJ 1985: 361).

[7] The prefectural boundaries used here are those of the late 1990s. At that time, Chengdu city proper comprised an urban core of Jinjiang, Qingyang, Wuhou and Chenghua districts, and the suburban districts of Jinniu, Qingbaijiang and Longquanyi. The counties (rural Chengdu) comprised Jintang, Shuangliu, Wenjiang, Pixian, Xindu, Pengzhou (formerly Pengxian), Dujiangyan (formerly Guanxian), Chongzhou (formerly Chongqing), Dayi, Qionglai, Pujiang and Xinjin.

Table 9.2 Growth of GVIO by prefecture, 1952–78 (ranked by growth rate from 1952–78)

	1952–65	1965–78	1952–78
Panzhihua	12.0	43.5	32.2
Chengdu	13.1	10.5	13.2
Ganzi	19.0	10.1	12.3
Liangshan	16.0	11.3	11.5
Deyang	4.6	14.9	10.7
Luzhou	2.8	16.9	10.4
Zigong	8.3	12.8	10.1
Leshan	5.1	15.5	10.1
Mianyang	4.4	12.5	9.0
Yibin	7.5	10.3	8.9
Guangyuan	9.0	12.4	8.6
Chongqing	10.9	6.5	8.5
Ya'an	5.7	11.0	7.4
Aba	17.3	4.0	7.1
Neijiang	2.9	10.6	7.0
Daxian	7.0	11.1	6.9
Nanchong	2.7	11.5	6.3
Suining	0.6	11.5	6.0
Fuling	−1.6	11.4	5.2
Wanxian	2.7	6.5	4.0
Qianjiang	−5.7	12.1	2.4
Median	5.7	11.4	8.6

Notes: The underlying GVIO data (at 1980 constant prices, and including brigade-level industry) are for 1952, 1957, 1962, 1965, 1970, 1975 and 1978 and below; growth rates are estimated by linear interpolation between these years. The prefectural boundaries are those of the late 1980s; the prefectures of Chongqing are included for comparative purposes.

Source: SCZL (1990: 336–77).

5YP. The long run aim was to transform Chengdu from a commercial into an industrial centre, and its rapid growth before 1965 reflected this strategy (Sun 1960; Afanas'yeskiy 1962; CDSZ 1993: 235–7). After 1965, Chengdu's growth slowed as the focus of development shifted to the Third Front; its share in the provincial total declined because Chengdu's industrialization rate was below the median. Industrial production was also much disrupted by the Cultural Revolution: output fluctuated wildly in the 1970s. Thus Chengdu's industrialization rate was faster before 1965 than after, in contrast to the experience of most Sichuan prefectures. For all that, Chengdu's rate of expansion over the entire 1952–78 period was second only to that of Panzhihua. By 1978, indeed, Chengdu was fast approaching a position of parity with Chongqing, and in a sense the creation of Chongqing municipality in 1997 completed the process by enshrining Chengdu as the undisputed centre of industry and government in Sichuan.

The obverse of the rise of western Sichuan and Chengdu was the relative decline of the old industrial centres of Neijiang, Nanchong and Suining. The combined share of these three fell from 17.5 percent in 1952 to only 10 percent in 1978, a massive reversal of fortune.[8] Various forces were at work. One factor was the effective closure of the Yangzi shipping route to foreign trade after 1949; as Sichuan's old centres had developed on the back of trade along the Yangzi and its tributaries, this was a severe blow. Secondly, the modernization of transport across the province weaken the relative position of cities located along the central riverine zone; the coming of the railway—apart from a short line linking Chongqing with coal fields to the immediate north of the city, there was not a single line in the province in the Republican era—had an enormous impact. Thirdly, Maoist emphasis on the development of heavy industry tended to work against light industry-orientated centres such as Nanchong, the heart of Sichuan's silk and silk cloth industry (Dangdai Sichuan congshu bianjibu 1991: 190). Of course these old industrial centres did receive substantial sums to invest in the development of heavy industry, and there is no doubt that production there became much more diversified. In Neijiang, for example, the share of heavy industry in the prefectural GVIO total rose from a mere 12 percent in 1957 to fully 36 percent by 1978 (Neijiang ziyuan 1987: 97). Nevertheless, other parts of the province received a higher priority, and this is reflected in comparative growth rates.

9.2.2. Industrial Geography at the End of the 1970s

The estimates summarized in Table 9.2 provide us with the broad outline of Sichuan's industrial development over time but, because the prefectural totals include urban jurisdictions, they do not provide an adequate picture of the extent of *rural* industrial development. This defect cannot be remedied for pre-1978 because of a lack of county data, but we can at least delineate the outcome of Maoism by using the 1978 data itself. Aggregating GVIO across rural jurisdictions for 1978 reveals that rural Sichuan was still industrially under-developed. GVIO per head averaged 167 *yuan* in rural Sichuan.[9] However, the all-China county average for the same year was 237 *yuan* per head, over 40 percent higher.[10]

---

[8] These figures refer to shares of GVIO in the Sichuan of pre-1997 boundaries. The prefecture which lost out most as a result of reduced international trade was Wanxian, the historic gateway to Sichuan along the Yangzi river but part of Chongqing after 1997. In absolute terms, of course, output increased substantially in the prefecture during the Maoist era: GVIO in 1978 was almost 523 million *yuan* (1980 prices), compared with only 118 million *yuan* in 1952 (SCZL 1990: 358–9). And growth occurred even in its poorest counties. Wushan (astride the Yangzi Gorges and on the border with Hubei province) increased its GVIO from 3.16 million *yuan* in 1952 to 16.72 million *yuan* in 1978 (Wushan XZ 1991: 193–4). In Kaixian—one of the counties in which growth was slowest—GVIO nevertheless increased threefold (Kai XZ 1990: 171–2). For all that, the story of Wanxian is one of relative decline. Whilst its constant price GVIO rose almost fivefold over the Maoist era, its share fell from 7.2 percent in 1952 to only 2.4 percent in 1978.

[9] Measured at current prices (which were virtually identical to 1980 prices for 1982), this figure includes all types of village and sub-village industry. The estimate is calculated from GVIO for 145 of Sichuan's counties; it excludes jurisdictions designated as urban in 1982 (SCZL 1990).

[10] National GVIO in rural areas (at 1980 prices) in 1978 is calculated as total GVIO minus the GVIO of the 232 Chinese jurisdictions designated urban in 1982; see TJNJ (1984: 42–3). GVIO

Table 9.3 Industrial GVA per head in rural Sichuan and Jiangsu, 1978 (*yuan*; county data aggregated by prefecture)

Region	Prefectures	Industrial GVA per head
Western Sichuan	Aba	345
	Ganzi	128
	Liangshan	90
	Ya'an	143
Sichuan Basin and	Chengdu	78
Chengdu Plain	Daxian	33
	Deyang	149
	Guangyuan	37
	Leshan	87
	Luzhou	36
	Mianyang	59
	Nanchong	30
	Neijiang	66
	Suining	47
	Yibin	54
Chongqing municipality	Chongqing	76
(post-1997 boundaries)	Fuling	45
	Wanxian	31
Jiangsu province	Subei	81
	Sunan	245

Notes: Jurisdictions officially classified as urban at the time of the 1982 Population Census are excluded. The data on Sunan, Subei and for the post-1997 prefectures of Chongqing are provided by way of comparison. Prefectural boundaries are those of 1989; see SCTJNJ (1990: 10). Fushun and Rongxian (Zigong city) are included in Neijiang. Miyi and Yanbian counties (part of Panzhihua municipality in 1982) are included in Liangshan. Industrial GVA data are at 1990 constant prices. The all-Sichuan figures for growth and per capita GVA are estimated by aggregating output and population for all 145 counties. Per capita GVA for 1978 is estimated using the 1982 county populations because these are more reliable than the estimates for 1978. The data on Suining county and Guangyuan prefecture are not very reliable, but I have nevertheless included them for comparative purposes. Prefectural averages and growth rates calculated by first summing industrial output and population for the whole prefecture.

Sources: As for Tables 9.6 and 8.5.

The backwardness of the industrial sector in rural Sichuan in 1978 is further evident when county GVA data are aggregated by prefecture. Table 9.3 shows that the most advanced prefectures by 1978 in terms of industrial value-added per head were Deyang (a centre of Third Front production), and the four western prefectures of Ya'an, Ganzi, Aba, and (to a lesser extent) Liangshan, all of which had established a capital-intensive industrial base designed to exploit their mineral and timber resources.[11] The prefecture of Leshan, which (by Sichuan standards) had a fairly well-developed industrial base before 1949 and which had benefited from the Third

includes village level and private industry operating in the countryside, though not all types of sub-village industry.

[11] This fits in well with the national pattern, which shows that the jurisdictions across China with high levels of industrial output per head were usually one of two types: jurisdictions close to big cities, and counties where production was dominated by mining and forestry (Population Census Office 1987: xiv).

Front, was also relatively industrialized. The least industrialized prefectures were mainly to be found in eastern and central Sichuan; industrial output per capita in Nanchong and Daxian prefectures was only about half the provincial average. Older industrial centres such as Yibin, Neijiang and Suining were also characterized by rural under-development in 1978; there, pre-1949 and Maoist industrialization had focused mainly on urban areas. We can also make a direct comparison between industrial GVA per head in rural Sichuan and Jiangsu. For rural Sichuan, the 1978 figure had reached 66 *yuan*, but in Jiangsu's counties it stood at 124 *yuan*.

One surprising feature of these data is that *rural* parts of Chengdu prefecture were relatively backward by 1978.[12] Although per capita output exceeded the provincial mean, and the proportion of the workforce employed in industry was well above the provincial average, rural Chengdu had not been to the fore during the process of rural industrialization before 1978. This was because the Maoist development strategy focused more on Chengdu *city* proper, with the outlying counties regarded as little more than a source of agricultural produce for the urban population. As a result of this urban bias, the disparity between the urban core and rural periphery was stark by the early 1980s. In 1978, per capita GVIO in Chengdu's urban core was 1,487 *yuan* per head measured at 1980 prices, compared with 154 *yuan* in the outlying counties (SCZL 1990).[13] By 1982, GVIO in the city proper was 2,138 *yuan* in 1982, compared with only 127 *yuan* in the counties of Shuangliu and Jintang (TJNJ 1983: 75).[14] Industrial GVA in rural Chengdu prefecture was only 78 *yuan* in 1978, not much better than the provincial average and below the levels of production achieved in the rural areas of Aba, Deyang, Ganzi and Ya'an. Indeed, if we rank the counties by their GVA per capita in descending order in 1978, the best-ranked Chengdu county (Guanxian, now Dujiangyan city) was no better than 25th. This was not because of industrial stagnation after 1965; the median growth rate of industrial production (GVIO) for five of the counties of Chengdu was no less than 12.1 percent per year between 1965 and 1978, which was about the same rate achieved by the urban core.[15] It was the exceptionally rapid growth of the urban core *before* 1965 which was the key factor in the rise of Chengdu city proper.

---

[12] Here, and throughout this chapter, the focus is on Chengdu *prefecture*, a smaller geographical unit than the Chengdu plain. The usual definition of the Chengdu plain includes contemporary Deyang prefecture as well as parts of Leshan prefecture, and excludes Jintang county (which is part of Chengdu prefecture).

[13] County-level data in this source exclude centrally-owned industries. For simplicity, I assume that all such industries were located in Chengdu city proper (which is a fair approximation to the reality) and thus calculate GVIO in the core as the total for the municipality (SCZL 1990: 337) minus the county totals.

[14] These data are at 1980 prices and include centrally-owned SOEs. They exclude *village*-level and sub-*village* industry, but production in these enterprises was not so large in the early 1980s as to alter significantly the comparison.

[15] The data here are from Peng XZ (1989: 173–5); Chongqing XZ (1991: 295); Xinjin XZ (1989: 97–8); Guan XZ (1991: 315); and Pujiang XZ (1992: 160–2).

Rural Chengdu's under-industrialization is emblematic of the outcome of the Maoist development strategy in Sichuan. As has been seen, there is no question that rapid industrial growth occurred across the province between 1952 and 1978, leading to the creation of a substantial industrial base in rural areas by the time of Mao's death: Nevertheless, the province still lagged far behind Jiangsu in the late 1970s. Sunan (at 245 *yuan* per head) was far ahead of every Sichuan prefecture save Aba, and Aba was an oddity because its population was so small relative to its mineral and timber resources. Even Subei (81 *yuan*) was more industrialized than most of Sichuan's prefectures, including Chengdu. Maoism led to the creation of an extensive rural industrial base, but the Sichuan countryside was in no position to challenge the hegemony of the coastal region at the start of the transition era.

9.3. The Engines of Maoist Rural Industrialization

The evidence discussed in the previous section demonstrates that the experience of Sichuan between 1949 and 1978 was similar to that of other Chinese provinces in most respects: rapid industrialization occurred in urban and rural areas alike under Mao, and the engine of growth was heavy industry. In one respect, however, Sichuan's industrialization was unusual: the programme of Third Front construction played a dominant role in the process.

9.3.1. The Commune and Brigade Sector

One indication of the dominance of the Third Front comes from the slow growth of the commune and brigade sector. The value of CBE industrial output increased by only 19 percent between 1966 and 1975; during this same period, industrial output from all types of enterprises doubled across the province (SCZL 1990: 21). This is not to say that all subsectors were unimportant. Small and medium-sized plants produced 84 percent of provincial iron output during 1958–62, even though much of it must have been of poor quality. And the production of iron by the small and medium sector rose from a nadir of 37,000 tonnes per annum during 1963–65 to reach 144,000 during 1971–75, and 340,000 tonnes during 1976–80 (Sichuan zhi 1992: 99). However, the sector as a whole was slow to develop.

The limited contribution of the CBE sector to rural industrialization in Sichuan under Mao reflected the operation of two factors. Firstly, the Third Front was the focus of the developmental effort and, because initial state subsidies were a *sine qua non* for almost all forms of industrial development, this meant that investment in CBEs and county enterprises was crowded-out. It is true that the larger Front projects were funded centrally, but many ancillary projects were not and therefore required appropriations from county budgets.

The second factor hampering the CBE sector was the poor performance of agriculture. Sichuan had been a net exporter of grain during the 1950s (Walker 1984), and this certainly contributed to the scale of the famine in the province after 1958 (Bramall 1993). Thereafter, Sichuan was essentially self-sufficient, but even then its agricultural sector apparently struggled to meet demand (Donnithorne 1984). Accordingly, the provincial government was reluctant to allow communes and brigades to divert labour away from key agricultural tasks, not least the development of irrigation. These constraints on CBE development were further compounded by the spatial impact of the famine. One of the regions worst affected was the Chengdu plain (Bramall 1997), and governments there were most reluctant to neglect agriculture—even though this was the very arena where economic geography were most propitious for the development of CBEs. It is no coincidence that the literature on Sichuan's CBE sector does not even provide data on the sector's pre-1976 output (SCJJDL 1985; SXQS 1988; SSK 1988); there was next to nothing of which to write.

All this began to change in the mid-1970s. The memory of the great famine was beginning to fade and the Third Front was seen as less important following China's rapprochement with the USA. The beginnings of significant CBE growth also owed much to the revival of agriculture, a process driven by the maturation of irrigation networks and the growing availability of both chemical fertilizer and new high yielding varieties (Bramall 1995).[16] Whatever the cause, CBE output quadrupled between 1975 and 1978, and thereafter the sector did not look back.

Yet even though the sector began to grow quickly in the mid-1970s, the backwardness of Sichuan's CBE sector on the eve of the transition era is very apparent. The per capita output of the CBE sector (including all types of enterprises) in Sichuan was only 22 *yuan* in 1978, compared with the national average of 51 *yuan* (at 1970 constant prices). The gap between Sichuan and the coastal provinces was even wider: the comparable figure for Zhejiang was 72 *yuan*, and per capita CBE output in Jiangsu stood at no less than 121 *yuan* per head (SXQS 1988: 89–90). Thus the development of commune and brigade industries in Sichuan under Mao could not have provided much by way of a foundation for the rural growth of the 1980s and 1990s. Insofar as there was a rural industrial legacy from the Maoist era, it was a legacy of Third Front and county-owned industries.

9.3.2. The Third Front

It is the Cultural Revolution which dominates so many accounts of China's experience during the Maoist era. However, the process of economic development

---

[16] The sub-text of many Chinese accounts published in the mid-1980s is that Zhao Ziyang was the pivotal figure and there is no doubt that it was Zhao who, after becoming Party secretary in Sichuan in November 1975, presided over the progressive liberalization of provincial economy in the late 1970s.

was affected far more by the Third Front. Of course much Front construction was concentrated in existing urban centres such as Chongqing, Lanzhou and Shaoguan. Yet the Front was quintessentially a programme of rural industrialization: it sought to create modern industrial enterprises in a rural setting. Nowhere was this more true than in Sichuan.

The Third Front in the province comprised four main components (Gao 1987: 21–8; SCJJNJ 1987: 254–64).[17] Firstly, the development of a steel base at Panzhihua. Secondly, the construction of a railway line linking Chengdu and Kunming between August 1964 and July 1970 (Gao 1987: 73). Thirdly, the development of a conventional weapons production base in the Chongqing area (Wang 1993: 393–6; CSJW 1991: 108–12).[18] Fourthly, the Front programme emphasized the development of a number of industrial subsectors across the province, notably machine-building, metallurgy and chemicals. The construction of the new city of Dukou on the banks of the Jinsha river was the single most important Front project. GVIO in the two counties of Miyi and Yanbian (out of which the Dukou municipality was later to be created) amounted to barely 4 *yuan* per capita in 1952, far below the provincial average of 24 *yuan* and still further behind more developed prefectures such as Leshan (30 *yuan*), Deyang (31 *yuan*) and Luzhou (32 *yuan*) (Sichuan tongjiju 1999: 564, 632; SCTJNJ 1990: 57, 160). But even before the launch of the Front, much had changed; as Table 9.4 demonstrates, industrial output grew at no less than 20 percent per year between 1952 and 1965 as timber and mineral resources started to be developed from what was a very low base level of production. Thereafter, growth was sustained by the decision to create the Panzhihua steel complex, which was designed to serve the needs of the entire south-western region. To be sure, the growth rate of the region slowed after 1965, but it still industrialized as fast as anywhere else in the province between 1965 and 1978. In a sense, this is the classic example of Chinese rural industrialization: Panzhihua was little more than a sleepy rural backwater in the early 1950s, a prefecture where agriculture contributed no less than 84 percent of GDP in 1952. By 1978, the secondary share was 76 percent and Panzhihua's agricultural past was all but forgotten (Sichuan tongjiju 1999: 546, 548, 550).

Yet in many ways it was the fourth element of the Third Front in Sichuan which is of most interest for our purposes because it affected predominantly rural areas in almost every corner of the province (Cui et al. 1985; Gao 1987; Yang 1990). This element of the Front was based on the transfer of plants and

---

[17] Yang (1997: 171) talks of only three constituent parts; this categorization excludes the development of heavy industry subsectors.

[18] The Chongqing weapons base is a misnomer. As well as Chongqing city proper, and counties close to Chongqing such as Jiangjin and Baxian, the base included ten counties along the Jialing and Tuojiang rivers to the north, a group of eight counties along the Changjiang and Wujiang rivers to the east and south-east, and a further group of counties in Yibin prefecture to the west (Gao 1987: 23). It thus spanned the 1997 provincial boundary between Sichuan and Chongqing.

equipment from China's First and Second Fronts to Sichuan, and upon new construction. Its scale was enormous. During the First 5YP, investment in basic construction in Sichuan's industrial sector totalled 1.07 billion *yuan*, of which 321 million *yuan* went into machine-building. During the Third 5YP (1966–70), the totals had increased to 8.01 billion and 2.68 billion *yuan* respectively, rising further to 9.73 billion and 3.01 billion *yuan* during the Fourth 5YP. The development of machine-building also required an expansion of metal production, and here the pace of expansion was even faster. The share of metallurgy in industrial basic construction investment was about 7 percent in the First 5YP, but this climbed to 25 percent during the Third 5YP before dropping back to average 21 percent during the Fourth 5YP (Gao 1987: 418). Taken together, this investment in machine-building and metallurgy accounted for about 55 percent of industrial basic construction during the Third Front period, a colossal volume.[19] Chemical and petroleum production also attracted significant quantities of investment, the former as a means to promote agriculture as well as to satisfy the needs of the military sector. The inevitable concomitant to this focus was a squeeze on light industry. Textiles and food processing combined took barely 1.5 percent of investment in the first phase of the Third Front, dramatically down on the 9 percent share of the First 5YP and, though investment in textiles revived in the early 1970s, the food processing sector remained in the doldrums until the 1980s.

The regions mainly affected by this component of the Front programme seem to have been Fuling, Luzhou, Deyang and, to a lesser extent, Mianyang. In Fuling prefecture, which was part of the Chongqing conventional weapons base (and part of Chongqing municipality after 1997), GVIO had actually fallen between 1952 and 1965 (Table 9.2), but after 1965 it rose annually by more than 11 percent. A further indication of the pace of expansion is provided by the experience of Dianjiang county where heavy industrial production increased by a factor of 7 between 1971 and 1978 compared with a mere doubling of heavy GVIO achieved across the province (SCZL 1990: 19; Dianjiang XZ 1993: 426). In nearby Nanchuan, the share of heavy industry in total GVIO rose from 35 percent in 1970 to a staggering 75 percent in 1975, comfortably in excess of the provincial figure of 54 percent (SCZL 1990: 19; Nanchuan XZ 1991: 73–4). Much of Fuling's growth revolved around the development of its shipping industry. The focal point was Chuandong shipbuilding, an enterprise which expanded rapidly in the 1960s and early 1970s to a point where it managed 20 plants producing internal combustion engines, small military craft and even parts for nuclear submarines (Yang 1990: 184–5; Hessler 2001: 109; Chen 2003: 323).

---

[19] To put this in perspective, the two sectors together accounted for barely more than 30 percent in the early 1980s. By contrast, the combined share of food processing and textiles was up to 14 percent over the same 1981–85 period.

Further to the west, the emphasis in Luzhou prefecture was on developing engineering machinery and (in the 1970s) chemicals. This programme was based around plants newly transferred to the prefecture from Beijing and Fushun (Liaoning province); by 1985 there were no less than 428 machinery enterprises in the prefecture. Luzhou's formidable chemical industry dates from the late 1960s, and during the 1970s its centrepiece was a chemical fertilizer plant imported from the West (Yang 1990: 171). The prefecture alone produced 40 percent of chemical fertilizer output in Sichuan and Chongqing combined by 1978 and, at 16.9 percent per annum, its post-1965 GVIO growth rate was second only to that of Panzhihua amongst Sichuan's prefectures (SCZL 1990: 39, 345; Table 9.5).

More significant, however, were developments in Deyang prefecture to the north-east of Chengdu city. Deyang was relatively industrialized in 1952 when much of its industry centred on agricultural processing. Its most famous enterprise was Shifang Tobacco, established in 1918 and still going strong in the 1980s and 1990s when it employed over 2,000 workers (SCZL 1990: 686; TJJ 2000b: 399). The prefecture's industrial development admittedly lagged behind that of Chengdu prefecture in the early 1950s, but this began to change in 1956 when the state announced preparatory work for the establishment of a Deyang Industrial Zone. Little concrete was achieved before the mid-1960s, but thereafter heavy engineering developed apace. This centred upon Second Heavy Machinery, an enterprise set up in Deyang city during 1965 (Chen 2003: 268). By the late 1980s, it was the second largest machine-producing enterprise in the province, employing more than 17,000 workers. Two other enterprises were also of great significance: the Dongfang electrical machinery plant, established in Deyang city proper in 1966, and employing about 2,000 workers by the late 1980s (SCZL 1990: 698), and the Dongfang steam turbine enterprise in Mianzhu county, where construction started in 1966, and production in 1971. This latter employed over 7,500 workers by 1985 and accounted for about 20 percent of industrial production in the county (Mianzhu XZ 1992: 394). Deyang's growth rate of GVIO thus bears the imprint of the Third Front; at almost 15 percent per year between 1965 and 1978, the prefecture ranked behind only Panzhihua, Luzhou and Leshan—themselves all centres of Third Front endeavour.

Further to the north, considerable energy was expended on developing the production of steel and electronic equipment in Mianyang prefecture (Cui et al. 1985: 192–3; Yang 1990: 202). The focal point was Changcheng Special Steel, which began to be built in 1965 in Jiangyou county (Chen 2003: 259). By 1988, it was employed over 25,000 workers and was the fourth largest enterprise in Sichuan in terms of output value (SCZL 1990: 616, 693). The development of the electronics industry, which was also important for Mianyang, was spread across a wide range of counties including Guangyuan, Wangcang, and Qingchuan. Electronics received a priority equivalent to that granted to Changcheng steel; in all, some 650 million *yuan* was invested in this electronics base between 1966 and 1978, about 22 percent of the national total for the industry during that period (Chen 2003: 283). Yet far more famous, and ultimately more important for the prefecture, was Changhong. It began life as a defence-orientated machinery company in Mianyang city in 1958. In 1972, the enterprise began to shift towards TV production, but even as late as 1978 it was producing only 1,764 sets (SCZL 1990: 348–9). Thereafter, however, its growth was rapid, especially after 1985 under the direction of Ni Runfeng. By the 1990s, Changhong had become one of the largest TV producers in the world; its output stood at around 12 million TVs a year by the turn of the century, and it employed more than 33,000 workers in China (TJJ 2000*b*: 399).

More systematic data on the impact of the Third Front across the province show that Luzhou and Deyang prefectures in particular were massively affected (SCZL 1990: 336–77). In both, heavy GVIO grew by more than 20 percent a year between 1965 and 1978, a figure well in excess of the provincial median of 16 percent. The Third Front was undoubtedly important in both Chongqing municipality and Leshan prefecture as well, but these two already had significant heavy industrial bases; heavy industry therefore grew less quickly there than elsewhere after 1965. Neither Chengdu nor Mianyang—Changcheng and Changhong notwithstanding—seem to have been dramatically affected. In Chengdu's case, heavy industrial production grew by 'only' 12 percent, somewhat below the provincial median. Mianyang, even though much of the literature points to it as a Third Front centre, was much less affected than Deyang to the south. Only after 1978, when Changhong's output began to grow rapidly, did Mianyang began to industrialize quickly.

These prefectural data on the regional impact of the Third Front are broadly confirmed by county data for 1978 on the size of heavy manufacturing, the subsector which expanded most rapidly during the Third Front period. These show heavy manufacturing production averaging 21 *yuan* per head in rural Sichuan in 1978. Despite the Third Front programme, the counties of both Fuling and Luzhou prefectures lagged well behind at 15 and 7 *yuan* respectively. Rural Chengdu stood on a par with the older manufacturing centres of Neijiang and Leshan; output levels were 39 *yuan* per head for Chengdu, and 33 and 37 *yuan* for Neijiang and Leshan respectively. Output per head in Deyang stands in sharp relief at no less than 123 *yuan*, far greater than in any other rural region. To be sure, this comparison is misleading. Deyang was in most respects a city by the late 1970s, even though the jurisdiction was still officially classified as a county and its output is included in the prefectural total. By contrast, Neijiang and Leshan proper were both classified as cities and their output was therefore excluded from the respective prefectural totals. This treatment therefore biases the comparison towards Deyang. However, even if we exclude Deyang 'county', heavy manufacturing production still averaged 54 *yuan* per head, far more than in any other Sichuan prefecture. Given that modern heavy manufacturing was almost negligible in its counties in the early 1950s, Deyang prefecture thus provides a striking illustration of the transformative impact of the Third Front on *rural* areas—a transformation ultimately confirmed by the reclassification of Deyang, Shifang, Guanghan and Mianzhu counties as cities during the 1980s and 1990s.

9.4. Educational Expansion and the Migration of Skilled Labour under Mao

Little is known about levels of education in Sichuan during the Republican twilight, and this makes it harder to assess the true impact of Maoism. However, according to the *Sichuan Statistical Yearbook* published for 1946 by the KMT, the illiteracy rate was 74 percent (Liu 1988: 374). This is lower than the level of illiteracy reported in Buck's 1937 *Land Utilization* study, but the age structure of illiteracy as reported at the 1982 Population Census shows that literacy was rising quite quickly in the late Republican era: amongst those born in 1922 or earlier (and still alive in 1982), the illiteracy rate was 80 percent in 1982, but this had fallen to 53 percent for those born between 1933 and 1937 (Liu 1988: 381). The Buck and KMT estimates are therefore consistent. Nevertheless, illiteracy was still widespread; some 70–80 percent of the metal workers in the province's main plants were illiterate in 1950, and over 80 percent in smaller plants (Sichuan zhi 1992: 237). Accordingly, an overall illiteracy rate of 74 percent at the time of the Revolution is not implausible, and it must have been still higher in rural areas.

We can be more confident about trends after 1952, when school enrolment rates increased steadily (SCTJNJ (1990: 464–5). Most interesting here is the middle school enrolment rate because it was the expansion of this type of education—especially in rural areas—which received so much emphasis in the late Maoist era. Although the rate was volatile (leaping up in 1959, falling back in the early 1960s and then climbing during the late 1960s and across the 1970s) the general trend was firmly upward, suggesting that educational levels in the province were much higher by the time of Mao's death than they had been at the time of the Revolution. By 1982, the literacy rate stood at 62 percent, well up on the 26 percent recorded in the late 1940s (Kua Sichuan 1994: 105). Amongst metal workers, too, the trend was even more marked; the 1979 statistics give an illiteracy rate of only 6 percent (Sichuan zhi 1992: 237). And the province as a whole benefited from the inflow of new universities and colleges; Qinghua, for example, opened a Sichuan campus (*fenxiao*) (Liu 1988: 160–1).

The extent to which the expansion of education contributed to post-1949 industrialization is more debatable. This is perhaps most apparent in the case of western Sichuan where the pace of industrial expansion was as fast as anywhere else in the province. Yet literacy rates improved rather modestly in the region. The average rate even in 1982 was only 41 percent and for

Sichuan's Tibetan population of 900,000 (the majority of whom lived in Ganzi), the 1982 literacy rate was barely 28 percent (Sichuan pucha 1994: 29, 70). Although these rates were substantially higher than at the end of the 1940s, one can hardly claim that this was a noteworthy achievement; the rates compared decidedly unfavourably with the 68 percent recorded in the Sichuan basin. Although a better educational record may well have accelerated the industrialization rate still more in western Sichuan before 1978, it is manifest that rapid educational improvement was by no means a necessary condition for industrial growth.

This evidence on formal education also seems to imply that the migration of skilled labour to rural areas may be a better candidate as an explanation for industrial success. Sichuan 'sent down' no less than 1.43 million young people between 1969 and 1981, principally during 1969 and 1970. The development of forestry in Aba was driven almost entirely by the in-migration of skilled foresters from Mianyang, Wenjiang, Nanchong and Daxian in the 1950s and 1960s, and this provided the foundation for the timber industry. Railway construction also depended upon an influx of skilled workers; this time the migrants were recruited from outside the province. The development of coal and steel production in Jiangyou, Guangyuan and Wangcang during 1958-60 was also driven by an influx of workers; Jiangyou received 115,000 in 1958 alone. However, the permanent impact of this sort of migration was much less; Jiangyou's out-migrants numbered 93,000 in 1960-62.

The Third Front of course was the major factor at work. At the height of construction in 1968, about half a million workers had been transferred into the province from elsewhere (Yang 1997: 168). Dukou was the major beneficiary; in order to construct the steel base at Panzhihua, the municipality received 40,000 new workers from other parts of Sichuan in 1966-67, and these inflow continued during the 1970s. Of a sample of 22,894 workers employed at Pangang in 1979, 4,476 had come from outside the province. This in-migration helped to ensure that the municipality's population grew by nearly 6 percent annually between 1964 and 1982, far ahead of the provincial average of 2.1 percent (Liu 1988: 160-1, 175).

9.5. Rural Industrialization after 1978

It has been demonstrated in previous sections that the pace of industrialization was rapid in Maoist-era Sichuan, that the province's industrial geography markedly altered, and that much of this industrialization occurred in rural areas. The prime mover in this latter process was the Third Front, which at root was a programme of rural industrialization: cities like Panzhihua developed in its wake, but out of the countryside rather than on the sites of existing urban settlements. Hand in hand with this industrial development went an

Table 9.4 The growth of rural industrial GVA and initial conditions (prefectures ranked by growth rates during 1978–2002)

Prefecture	Industrial GVA per head (1990 yuan)		Industrial employment rate (percent)	Literacy rate (percent)	Growth of industrial GVA per head (percent)	
	1978	2002	1982	1982	1978–2002	1978–97
Chengdu	78	3,774	8.4	78	17.5	20.3
Suining	47	820	4.6	67	14.0	15.4
Mianyang	59	1,102	4.3	63	13.2	16.9
Deyang	149	2,602	13.9	67	12.7	16.3
Luzhou	36	630	4.5	66	12.3	14.1
Ya'an	143	1,571	7.4	71	11.7	14.0
Daxian	33	556	2.9	64	11.5	13.2
Guangyuan	37	397	3.9	61	11.4	17.5
Nanchong	30	503	3.4	65	11.3	13.2
Leshan	87	1,138	6.2	61	11.2	12.8
Neijiang	66	829	6.4	69	10.8	12.4
Yibin	54	735	5.4	65	10.2	11.7
Liangshan	90	953	3.9	39	9.5	8.0
Aba	345	894	18.3	49	5.0	5.8
Ganzi	128	268	3.1	33	2.5	4.3
Sichuan	66	1,150	5.4	58	12.6	16.0

Notes: Literacy rates are for the population aged 12 and over. Not much significance should be attached to the reported growth rate for Suining prefecture. It was not only very small (comprising only the counties of Shehong, Pengxi and Suining in 1990), but also the data on Suining county appear very inconsistent for the mid-1990s. The counties of Panzhihua are included in the Liangshan total.

Sources: As for Table 9.6.

expansion in rural education and skills. The result of all this was that Sichuan's manufacturing capability was much higher by the late 1970s than it had been in 1949. In principle, therefore, a foundation for subsequent rural industrialization had been firmly established. It remains to identify the contribution of this rural inheritance to the growth of the transition era.

One thing is not in doubt: the rates of industrial growth achieved across the Sichuan countryside were on a par with those achieved in other parts of China. As Table 9.4 reveals, the growth rate of real industrial GVA per head averaged close to 13 percent per annum between 1978 and 2002, an explosive rate by international standards.[20] Most of Sichuan's prefectures achieved an industrialization rate in the 10 to 14 percent range. There was some variation. Mianyang broke through the 13 percent mark, whereas Yibin only just managed to exceed 10 percent. Given, however, the comparative unreliability of the underlying data, we should probably not read too much into such small differences.

---

[20] Measured at 1990 constant prices. The precise method of calculation is summarized in Appendix Three. Rural Sichuan is defined here as the 144 county jurisdictions of 1982. Some of these counties were of course upgraded to city status during the 1980s and 1990s, but our interest lies with the fate of areas which were rural at the close of the Maoist era.

9.5.1. The Rise of Chengdu

The experience of Chengdu prefecture—the counties to the immediate south and west of the provincial capital—was exceptional. In 1978, the prefecture was ranked only seventh in the province in terms of per capita industrial GVA. However, all that changed in the transition on the back of per capita industrialization rate of over 17 percent per year. No fewer than six of the province's top ten counties in terms of per capita industrial growth were in Chengdu prefecture, with Shuangliu and Pixian at the top with per capita industrial growth rates of about 24 percent per year between 1978 and 2002. As a result of this breakneck growth, Chengdu prefecture was far ahead of the rest of rural Sichuan by the beginning of the new millennium. By 2002, indeed, the prefecture's per capita output was well over three times the provincial average. With Deyang and Mianyang prefectures to the north also industrializing quickly, the province's industrial centre of gravity shifted decisively towards the greater Chengdu region after 1978. By 2002, the combined rural industrial output of Chengdu, Deyang and Mianyang prefectures amounted to nearly 40 percent of the provincial total, even though the three were home to only 15 percent of the province's population.

9.5.2. The Decline of Western Sichuan

Table 9.4 also shows that Western Sichuan was an exceptional region. In 1978, the region enjoyed one of the highest levels of per capita output in the province despite its unfavourable geography. As has been seen, this reflected its above average growth during the Maoist era. The transition era saw a marked reversal of fortune, so much so that, if Sichuan's counties are ranked by their per capita industrial growth rates between 1978 and 2002, the bottom ten were all from western Sichuan (six from Aba, three from Ganzi and one from Liangshan). Liangshan fared best amongst the western prefectures, growing at nearly 10 percent per year. But the median growth rate of Aba's counties was a mere 0.7 percent between 1978 and 1997, well down on the rate achieved during the late Maoist era. Aba as a whole achieved a 5 percent growth rate, but that owed much to the growth of Wenchuan county, an eco-tourism centre located on the edge of the Chengdu plain. Growth there was so rapid (over 14 percent per head) that the county's share in Aba's industrial GVA soared from 15 percent in 1978, to 65 percent by 1997, and to 79 percent in 2002. Ganzi did little better than Aba. Its per capita industrial GVA rose by only 2.5 percent per annum which was by some distance the worst industrialization record of any Sichuan prefecture after 1978.

The poor industrial performance of western Sichuan after 1978 reflects the operation of several factors. One factor was the nature of industrial production. The presence of extractive industry is not a hindrance to growth *per se* because that type of industry is better than nothing; minerals and timber at least offer a resource which can be exploited.[21] This notion is supported by the international evidence; some regions (Montana) and countries (Australia) have become prosperous on the basis of low population densities and high levels of mineral extraction. However, reliance on an exhaustible resource brings with it obvious dangers: the decline of logging and mineral extraction has brought in its wake the decline of Montana (Diamond 2005: 57). Similarly western Sichuan. There, some counties which had prospered under Mao by exploiting minerals and timber found themselves in the 1980s and 1990s with dwindling reserves of both, and hence an industrial infrastructure which was extensive but remarkably ill-suited to the development of manufacturing. Ganzi prefecture provides a good example of both advantages and problems associated with extractive industry. During the good times (1965–78), timber output in the prefecture increased nearly fivefold. Even during the 1980s, some of Ganzi's counties prospered; the exploitation of virgin woodland in Jiulong county allowed timber output to grow 12 fold, and GVIO to rise ninefold, between 1978 and 1988. But for Ganzi as a whole, growth slowed markedly after 1978. Timber output increased over the next decade by only 35 percent as resources were increasingly depleted, and this in turn limited prefectural GVIO to a 2.6 fold increase (SCZL 1990). In neighbouring Aba, the story was similar. Timber production increased from about 0.4 million cubic metres per year in the early 1960s to about 1 million cubic metres by 1980, but beyond that there was little scope for growth; production stagnated at that level in the 1980s and 1990s (SCZL 1990: 372–3; AZ 1994: 1296–7). In fact, timber production aggregated across the whole region appears to have peaked at around 3 million cubic metres in 1980; the growth of the Maoist era (production stood at barely 0.6 cubic metres in 1952) was simply unsustainable. Hydroelectricity generation provides another example of the limits to the exploitation of natural resources. This subsector was a growth area in the 1980s as result of heavy investment. In Ganzi, for instance, almost half of all industrial basic construction investment went into the hydrosector during the 1980s (GZ 1997: 1155–6). In Aba, output increased about fivefold between 1978 and 1989, almost double the rate of increase of GVIO (AZ 1994: 1712–13, 1296–7). But such growth rates were achieved from a very low base, and the nature of hydroelectricity generation meant that they were inherently unsustainable in the 1990s.

---

[21] To test the impact of extractive industry on growth, I included the share of industrial output contributed by the extractive sector as an independent variable in the Sichuan regression for 1978–2002. The coefficient is typically positive (depending on the precise specification) but rarely significant. The common sense explanation for this is that some Sichuan counties gained, but this effect was offset by those counties where natural resources were largely played out. Forestry was a good short and medium term expedient, but it offered little by way of a long term solution. So it was in western Sichuan.

Table 9.5 Counties of Sichuan most severely affected by the logging ban (counties ranked by change in GVIO between 1997 and 2000)

County	Prefecture	GVIO (million *yuan*; current prices)		GVIO index (1997 = 100)
		1997	2000	2000
Baiyu	Ganzi	25.1	1.5	6
Yajiang	Ganzi	22.9	1.4	6
Muli	Liangshan	138.9	8.5	6
Dawu	Ganzi	61.8	6.4	10
Jinchuan	Aba	51.2	6.5	13
Xinlong	Ganzi	46.0	7.5	16
Litang	Ganzi	27.4	5.0	18
Heishui	Aba	54.0	9.9	18
Songpan	Aba	59.7	12.0	20
Zamtang	Aba	27.8	6.2	22
All Sichuan		197,054	261,806	133

Sources: Sichuan tongjiju (1999); SCTJNJ (2001).

The second factor which constrained industrial growth in western Sichuan was government policy, in particular the ban on commercial logging imposed by the central government along the upper Yangzi and in other parts of China in August 1998 in order to reduce soil erosion and flooding (Winkler 2004). Evaluated in its own terms, the ban appears to have been highly successful.[22] Across China, timber output declined from 64 million cubic metres in 1997 to 44 million cubic metres in 2002 (TJNJ 2003: 512). In Sichuan, output collapsed from 4.031 million cubic metres in 1997 to only 0.474 million in 1999, and thence to a paltry 0.032 million cubic metres in 2002 (TJNJ 1998: 470; 2000: 457; 2003: 512). The area which suffered most was the Himalayan plateau and, environmentally desirable though the ban may have been (though even this is in doubt given the evidence suggesting that imported timber from Burma served as substitute), the effects on the local economy were devastating (Table 9.5).

Of the 25 counties hardest hit, 24 were located in one or other of the western prefectures of Ganzi, Aba and Liangshan, and the other county was from neighbouring Ya'an. Xinlong's experience was fairly typical: GVIO there fell from 26.2 million *yuan* in 1999 to 7.5 million in 2000, a figure which was well below its industrial output in 1980 (SCTJNJ 2001: 216; Xinlong XZ 1992; SCZL 1990: 584). The fall was even greater in other counties. In Dawu, output by 2000 was only 10 percent of its 1997 level, and it stood at a mere 6 percent in Yajiang, Baiyu, and Muli. By contrast, current price industrial output was some 33 percent *higher* in rural Sichuan as a whole if we compare 2000 with 1997, reflecting the continuing development of rural manufacturing across the Sichuan basin. Although incomes in the hardest-hit counties were cushioned by the payment

[22] Cutting of timber for subsistence purposes by individual households was still allowed.

of state subsidies, the logging ban effectively brought the entire process of industrialization on the western plateau to a shuddering halt. The problems caused by the ban were compounded by the importance of timber as an input in other parts of the province. Sichuan's Himalayan counties 'exported' 80 percent of timber in the early 1980s, mainly to Chengdu and to Chongqing (SCJJDL 1985: 704).[23] This suggests that Sichuan's overall rate of growth of manufacturing production would have been faster still but for the logging ban.

The third problem faced by western Sichuan after 1978 was its lack of manufacturing capability. A region with a large proportion of its workforce employed in extractive industries is not well-placed to develop manufacturing production because the skills acquired in timber cutting or mineral extraction are essentially low level. Workers employed in resource extraction and processing acquire little experience of a true factory environment; these jobs are much closer in their nature and content to jobs in the agricultural sector. Indeed, as Kaldor famously argued, it is manufacturing which is the engine of industrial growth.[24] From this perspective, the co-existence of a dominant manufacturing sector (the extractive share in GVIO was only 2.3 percent, barely a quarter of the provincial average) and rapid industrial growth on the Chengdu plain was no coincidence.[25] The converse was true for Sichuan's Himalayan counties. Despite high levels of industrial employment, the skills base of the region was weak. In a sense, therefore, western Sichuan provides an example of path dependent industrialization. Extractive industries served it well during the Maoist era but left the region with a legacy which was ill-suited to the development of manufacturing production. In the short term at least, the rational strategy was to continue to invest in extractive industries rather than to diversify into manufacturing.

Nevertheless, this type of path dependency argument should not be pushed too far. History was an obstacle to industrial development in western Sichuan, but the tyranny of distance and the other geographical disadvantages faced by the region were the binding constraints on the development of manufacturing. It is of course true that many of the counties of eastern Sichuan located on the mountainous fringe of the Red Basin also face comparatively high transport costs. However, these obstacles to industrial development are dwarfed by those encountered on the high Himalayan plateau. By all criteria, the counties of Aba, Ganzi and Liangshan were at a marked disadvantage. Even though many of

[23] We have reliable data on domestic trade in timber for the 1980s because most of it was conducted by state-owned companies.
[24] Saudi Arabia is the most obvious exception to Kaldor's 'Law', and there are certainly some who have seen the Tibetan plateau and Xinjiang as likely to follow in the footsteps of Saudi Arabia on account of the vast mineral resources in the area. However, whilst the exploitation of oil reserves may well proceed along comparable lines, it is moot whether the problem of high transport costs which stand as an obstacle to the development of other types of extractive industries can be easily overcome.
[25] The data in SCZL (1990) do not allow us to assess the impact of manufacturing directly because of definitional problems, in particular the treatment of energy supply.

them had established an extensive industrial base during the Maoist era, this did not provide a springboard for sustained industrialization in the 1980s and 1990s because of insuperable transport problems. As the timber and mineral resources which had sustained initial industrialization were run down, so their growth rate faltered. Unable to develop a manufacturing sector, the growth rate of western Sichuan lagged well beyond that of other parts of the province and, in the case of Aba, industrial output per capita fell.

9.6. Sources of Rural Industrial Growth after 1982

The previous section touched upon a number of factors which seemingly conditioned the spatial pattern of growth in the 1980s and 1990s. The counties around Chengdu, whether in Chengdu prefecture itself, Mianyang or Deyang, appear to have benefited from their proximity to Chengdu city. Conversely, western Sichuan's industrialization seems to have been heavily constrained by its geography. However, the validity of these assertions, and the role played by other factors, need to be evaluated more systematically.

9.6.1. The Regression Set-up

The best way to test these hypotheses is to use the unusually complete county-level data for 1978–88 for Sichuan given in SCZL (1990) in conjunction with the data given in successive editions of the *Sichuan Statistical Yearbook* (SCTJNJ) for post-1988.[26] These enable the estimation of per capita industrial GVA growth at 1990 prices for the entire 1978–2002, an approach which mirrors that adopted for Jiangsu in the previous chapter. These growth rates can then be used in conjunction with the initial conditions of 1982 to identify the impact of the initial level of industrial output, the distance of the county from Chengdu or Chongqing, population density, the dependency rate, the literacy rate, the grain yield and the rate of industrial employment.

This regression approach thus mimics that of Chapter 8, except in one respect. In that earlier chapter, distance to the provincial capital was used to simplify the calculation. However, it is plain that Sichuan's counties gained as much (and arguably more) from proximity to Chongqing, the industrial capital of the entire south-west region, as they did from proximity to Chengdu. Chongqing was in no sense equivalent to Beijing or Shanghai, and Chengdu had industrialized rapidly after 1952. Nevertheless, Chongqing in the early 1980s was still a much more significant industrial centre than Chengdu; GVIO was some 40 percent greater in 1982 (TJNJ 1983: 47, 75). Accordingly, the

---

[26] The SCZL (1990) data are nevertheless problematic because, for several localities, they appear to omit industries owned by the provincial government and by central ministries. The problem is most severe for the counties close to Chengdu, which tended to have a relatively higher proportion of such industries. This helps to explain the comparatively poor fit of the estimated equations.

regression uses the proximity of a county to the closest of Chengdu and Chongqing as the 'distance' variable.

9.6.2. Summary Regression Results

Regression results obtained using the framework outlined in the previous section are summarized in Table 9.6. The results produced by estimating

Table 9.6 Regression coefficients for rural Sichuan (dependent variable is growth of industrial GVA per capita)

Variable	Equation (1) 1982–2002		Equation (2) 1982–97
	Unstandardized	Standardized	Unstandardized
Industrial GVA per head, 1982	−0.010 (−1.01)	−0.115	−0.035 (−3.47)
Distance to closest of Chongqing or Chengdu city	−0.040 (−2.63)	−0.226	−0.069 (−4.40)
Dependency rate, 1982	0.085 (1.26)	0.092	−0.040 (−0.58)
Grain yield, 1980	0.065 (3.91)	0.280	0.052 (3.04)
Population density, 1982	0.008 (1.75)	0.188	−0.005 (−1.00)
Rate of industrial employment, 1982	−0.019 (−1.94)	−0.211	0.006 (0.56)
Literacy rate, 1982	0.060 (2.84)	0.282	0.027 (1.25)
Adjusted R^2	0.68		0.56
Number of counties	139		139

Notes: (a) t statistics in parentheses. All variables are in logarithmic form. (b) Equation (1) analyzes the growth of industrial output per head for all counties and all variables for 1982–2002. Equation (2) restricts the time period to 1982–1997 to allow for the impact of the logging ban and because of doubts about data quality for 1997–2002. (c) 'Distance' is the distance to the closer of Chongqing and Chengdu. (d) 'Dependency rate' is the proportion of the population aged under 15 and over 64. (e) 'Grain yield' is output per sown *mu* in 1980. The results are sensitive to the choice of year, but there are good reasons for preferring 1980 data to the alternatives. Our interest is with the effect of initial conditions, and on that basis alone it makes sense to use 1980 data. In addition, examination of trends in the grain yield (SCTJNJ 1990: 139) shows that 1987 was rather a poor year for weather in Sichuan. If the 1987 data are used in the regression, it is therefore not surprising that the grain yield turns out to be insignificant. 1985, for which there are yield data by county, is an equally problematic year because of poor weather, and again yields in that year do not really capture 'initial conditions'. 1980 is admittedly not ideal either because there was considerable flooding in the Min river valley, but weather-induced distortions occur every year and 1980 is therefore probably better than most. (f) 'Population density' is persons per square kilometre. (g) 'Industrial employment' is the proportion of the population employed in industry as a percentage of the total workforce. (h) 'Literacy rate' is for the population aged 12 and over. (i) Industrial GVA is at 1990 prices (see Appendix 2). (j) These data are for jurisdictions identified as counties at the time of the 1982 Census (Panzhihua's counties are included in Liangshan). A number of counties are omitted because of boundary changes (which have generated incomplete or inconsistent data); the counties so excluded are Neijiang, Nanchong, Nanxi and Xichang. Jinkouhe *qu* (district) was part of Leshan city and therefore is excluded. The analysis has been further refined by removing the counties of Guangyuan. These counties are excluded because even a cursory examination of the data shows that the five suffered an abrupt and largely inexplicable decline in their level of industrial production in the late 1990s; industrial value-added in Guangyuan county, for example, fell from 923 million *yuan* in 1998 to 647 million *yuan* in 2002. Closer examination of the data explains this apparent riddle: centrally-owned SOEs seem to have been removed from the data after 1994 (see SCTJNJ 1997). The data on Suining have also been rejected because of inconsistencies. These exclusions leave a total rural population of 58.9 million. (k) The data exclude the counties which belonged to Chongqing municipality after 1997.

Sources: Shouce (1987); Appendix 2 TJJ (1988); NCGY (1989); SCTJNJ (1990, 1993, 1995, 1997, 1999, 2001, 2002 and 2003); SCZL (1990).

equation (1), which includes every one of Sichuan's counties and which covers the entire 1978–2002 time period, are especially interesting for what they tell us about the influence of geography on rates of industrialization. Of those variables which capture the influence of geography, distance to Chengdu/ Chongqing city and the grain yield are statistically significant, and have the expected sign. Literacy also seemingly exerted a powerful effect on industrial growth rates; the low literacy rates of western Sichuan apparently hampered its industrialization rate. Standardized coefficients quantify the importance of geography and literacy. The largest standardized coefficient (0.282) is on literacy, and those on the grain yield (0.28) and distance (−0.226) are almost as large. These figures amount to a change in industrial growth of between 1.7 and 2 percentage points in response to a one standard deviation change in the respective dependent variables. Admittedly population density (itself partly a function of geography) is not statistically significant at the 5 percent level, probably because the experience of counties handicapped by very high population densities (mainly in the Sichuan basin) is matched by that of counties handicapped by labour shortages. Many of the Himalayan counties had very low densities and this imposed significant demand and supply-side constraints on the developments of all types of economic activity.

More generally, these results appear to support the conjecture previously advanced that geographical factors played a critical role in constraining industrialization in western Sichuan. The geography disadvantage suffered by that region is proxied here by distance from the urban centres of Chengdu and Chongqing, and by grain yields. The coefficients on both variables point to the adverse impact of geography on industrialization. It appears that western Sichuan did not enjoy the 'advantages of backwardness' because the geographically-determined constraints upon its development were almost impossible to overcome, even though its human capital base was quite extensive.

Nevertheless, the regression results generated by equation (1) are not very satisfactory. Neither the initial level of per capita output nor the industrial employment rate are statistically significant, and the latter has the 'wrong' sign. At face value, this suggests that the manufacturing capability hypothesis is rejected by the Sichuan evidence. However, it is most unusual for a growth regression to generate an insignificant coefficient on initial output per capita. A Kaldorian might expect a significant positive coefficient because of the operation of cumulative causation; poor counties are locked into a poverty trap by their very backwardness whereas affluent counties are able to use their prosperity to grew even more rapidly. By contrast, an admirer of Abramovitz would expect a significant negative coefficient because of the opportunities for catch-up growth enjoyed by poor counties. And a neoclassical would expect the operation of diminishing returns to labour and capital to produce a negative and significant coefficient. But none would expect the coefficient to be insignificant. This suggests that there is something odd about the regression specification.

9.6.3. Regression Results for 1978–97

One possible explanation for the poor fit of equation (1) is that the data for 1997 to 2002 are distorted. Firstly, there are many more doubts about the reliability of Chinese data for this period than for the first two decades of the post-Mao era (Rawski 2001). It is true that opinion on this is somewhat divided. The NBS re-estimates of national GDP growth rates for 1996–2002 do not significantly alter the pace or pattern of growth (TJJ 2004: 15). According to this re-evaluation, real GDP grew by a total of 57.6 percent between 1996 and 2002, or by 7.8 percent per annum, hardly evidence of prolonged recession.[27] Nevertheless, there is certainly enough anecdotal evidence—not least the marked discontinuity between GDP and unemployment trends—to suggest that we should treat the post-1996 data with suspicion. Furthermore, as Holz (2003) rightly comments, even if there is little evidence of outright falsification at the national level, we do well to recognize the existence of undoubted inconsistencies in the treatment of data across provinces and counties, and the inevitable national accounting problems which must be overcome by a nation in transition to a market-orientated economic system, problems which became increasingly acute in the late 1990s. A second reason for limiting the time period to 1982–97 is the differential impact on the counties of the upper Yangzi of the 1998 logging ban. As has been seen, this had a great effect on the economies of many of the counties of western Sichuan. It also affected a significant number of counties on the periphery of the Sichuan basin, where timber also played an important part in the economy. Their industrial growth rates are all distorted by the inclusion of post-1997 data, and this is probably the best reason for not including post-1997 data.

By restricting the time period to 1982–97, the regression results change substantially (equation (2) of Table 9.6). Firstly, the literacy rate is no longer significant. This finding is not especially surprising given the doubts raised in earlier chapters; it is far from clear that literacy is a necessary condition for rapid industrialization. The fact that the results for literacy are not robust (they vary depending on the precise specification of the estimated equation) largely confirms the theoretical doubts as to its significance. Secondly, and most interestingly, the Sichuan equation now seems more plausible in the sense that the coefficient on the initial value of industrial output per head is significant. However, none of this is sufficient to make the proxy for skills (the level of industrial employment) significant. Does this mean that the capability hypothesis should be rejected for Sichuan, or is there still something awry with the regression specification?

---

[27] The GDP index of 638.2 (where 1978 = 100) given for 1998, the year after the Asian crisis, in TJNJ (1999: 58) has barely changed; the TJJ (2004: 15) volume gives the index for that year as 638.5. The NBS, at least, sees little need to fundamentally re-adjust the Chinese national accounts in the light of more recent data.

9.7. Regression Results for the Sichuan Basin

I have further evaluated this issue of possible mis-specification by considering whether equation (1) of Table 9.6 is distorted by the presence of the counties of western Sichuan. A feature of that regression is that it lumps together the counties of the Sichuan basin and those of western Sichuan, but it is not clear that it really makes sense to group together such disparate counties in the same regression. The counties of western Sichuan, located either in the mountains to the south-west or (still more so) on the high Himalayan plateau, were a world removed from the counties of the Sichuan basin or the Chengdu plain. The incorporation of grain yields, population density and distance to Chengdu/ Chongqing into the regression is simply not enough to pick up the powerful fixed effects generated by location on the Himalayan plateau. The inclusion of these counties simply distorts the regression; it ensures that geography trumps everything else in explaining spatial inequalities in industrialization when we consider the experience of Sichuan as a whole. To put this another way, the Himalayan counties act as outliers—leading to the false inference that geography was the crucial factor for growth, whereas for most of Sichuan it was simply one factor amongst many.

The inclusion of western Sichuan is also problematic because, as previously discussed, a large proportion of its industrial workforce was employed in extractive industry. The essence of the capability hypothesis advanced in this book is that skills acquired by learning-by-doing in *manufacturing* were growth-promoting, not merely that industrial employment *per se* is desirable. From this perspective, rapid industrialization in western Sichuan after 1978 was not possible because its skills legacies from the Maoist era were far less valuable than those inherited in other parts of the province. If the manufacturing capability hypothesis is to be properly tested, we need either to use a measure of manufacturing employment (for which data are unavailable) or to exclude Sichuan's Himalayan counties.

In fact, once the influence of western Sichuan is excluded from the regression, the significance of inherited manufacturing capability becomes apparent. The role of manufacturing capability (as proxied by industrial employment) becomes clear if we re-estimate equation (1) of Table 9.6, but this time restricting its spatial compass to the Sichuan basin, and its temporal scope to 1982–97 (for the reasons discussed in the previous section). These omissions mean that the size of the sample is reduced by no less than 51 counties, leaving a total of 88 to be analysed. Note, however, that this reduction in sample size is much less serious than it appears. The 51 counties excluded had a combined population of only 5 million in 1982, leaving a rump population of 53.9 million in the 88 counties remaining.

The resulting equation (3) in Table 9.7 shows that geography remained an important factor in influencing growth rates; both distance and the grain yield remain statistically significant. Even after the exclusion of the western

Table 9.7 Regression coefficients for the Sichuan basin (dependent variable is growth of industrial GVA per capita)

Variable	Equation (3) 1982–97	Equation (4) 1982–97	
	Unstandardized	Unstandardized	Standardized
Industrial GVA per head	−0.047	−0.044	−0.731
	(−4.19)	(−4.10)	
Proximity to Chongqing or	−0.086	−0.094	−0.625
Chengdu city	(−5.03)	(−5.90)	
Dependency rate	−0.074		
	(−0.83)		
Grain yield, 1980	0.043	0.055	0.342
	(2.11)	(3.11)	
Population density	−0.027	−0.025	−0.462
	(−4.52)	(−4.44)	
Industrial employment rate	0.030	0.032	0.485
	(2.60)	(2.87)	
Literacy rate	0.050		
	(1.03)		
Adjusted R^2	0.42	0.44	
Number of counties	88	88	

Notes: As for Table 9.6, except that the geographical coverage of the regression is restricted to the counties of the Sichuan basin, defined here as rural Sichuan in 1997 less Aba, Ganzi, Liangshan, rural Panzhihua (Miyi and Yanbian), mountainous Ya'an (Shimian and Hanyuan) and Guangyuan. The numbering of the equations follows on from Table 9.6. As before, the data for the independent variables are for 1982 unless otherwise stated. Equation (4) is simply equation (3) without the insignificant variables.

Sources: As for Table 9.6.

prefectures, geography continued to matter: *ceteris paribus*, those counties located close to either Chongqing or Chengdu industrialized much faster than their more distant cousins. The low transport costs enjoyed by those counties close to the provincial capital surely goes far towards explaining the rapid growth experienced in Chengdu prefecture after 1978. More generally, the significance of the geographical variables suggests a clear core-periphery distinction in Sichuan, probably reflecting transport costs across the Sichuan basin which were higher than in many of China's coastal provinces. But geography was not a binding constraint for the counties of the Sichuan basin. It exerted an influence, but it was only one of several factors at work.

The impact of inherited manufacturing capability in determining industrialization rates in Sichuan is also apparent, and the results here therefore accord with those in other chapters. Not only is initial output per head statistically significant and of the right sign, but so also is industrial employment, the proxy for manufacturing capability. This suggests that, for the Sichuan basin (as with the bulk of China), the extent to which counties had developed a skills base was important.[28] The standardized coefficients derived in Equation (4) confirm this

[28] Extending the time period in the opposite direction to encompass 1978–82 (such that the dependent variable is the industrial growth rate for 1978–97, and the independent variables are for 1982 except for the level of industrial GVA, which is for 1978) does not alter these results.

conclusion. A one standard deviation increase in the distance of a county from Chengdu or Chongqing was enough to depress the rate of industrial growth by over 60 percent of a standard deviation, some 2.5 percentage points. And agricultural prosperity, perhaps the best all-round measure of location, also helped growth; a standard deviation rise in the grain yield is associated with an increase in industrial growth of over 30 percent of a standard deviation (1.3 percentage points). But manufacturing capability also mattered. A one standard deviation increase in the initial level of industrial employment was even more important than a corresponding increase in agricultural fertility in spurring the rate of industrial growth, producing a 2 percentage point rise in industrial output growth. Skills may not have been quite as important as distance in influencing industrialization, but they were nevertheless important.

But even the re-specification of the regression does not render statistically significant the literacy rate in the Sichuan basin. This is not very surprising because literacy rates diverged very little across prefectures (Table 9.4). Chengdu prefecture, with a 1982 literacy rate of 78 percent, was an outlier, but for the rest the rate varied across the narrow range between 61 and 71 percent. Only when we include the low literacy prefectures of Liangshan, Aba and Ganzi does the literacy rate become significant. This evidence points to the conclusion that, once a literacy rate of about 50 percent was achieved, further increments did little to raise economic growth. Below that figure, low literacy does seem to have constrained growth.

In sum, the Sichuan evidence broadly supports the national and Jiangsu findings outlined in previous chapters. The initial level of manufacturing capability may not have been the single most important influence upon the growth rate of industrial output, but there is no doubt that it had a powerful positive effect when those parts of the province where geography exerted an overwhelming effect are omitted. There is therefore nothing in the Sichuan evidence to suggest that we can safely neglect the impact of history on the pace and pattern of growth after 1978. In Sichuan, as elsewhere in rural China, rural industrialization depended upon more than favourable geography and a pool of unskilled workers.

9.8. Legacies of the Third Front

All this begs the question of whether the Third Front contributed to rural industrialization after 1978, or whether it was essentially an irrelevance. The development of manufacturing capability certainly helped rural Sichuan according to the regression results of the previous section, but what of the Third Front itself? Was the industrialization of the 1950s, or even the belated development of the CBE sector in the 1970s, more important?

The answer appears to be that the Third Front helped very little. It is true that some of those prefectures most affected by the Front industrialized more rapidly than the norm in the 1980s and 1990s. Mianyang provides a good example. This prefecture was still under-industrialized in 1978 (72 *yuan* per head compared with the provincial average of 75 *yuan*), but the Third Front had not only improved its relative standing but also gave Mianyang an industrial foundation on which to build. Changcheng Special Steel and Changhong, for example, were established as part of the Third Front programme, and both were instrumental in driving post-1978 growth. Given that Changhong had already shifted towards TV production in 1972, it is hard to argue that it was the *gaige kaifang* programme that provided the catalyst for growth.[29] Admittedly Changhong was based in an urban area (Mianyang city proper), but that was not true of Changcheng Special Steel, based in Jiangyou. As Jiangyou county industrialized at a rate of over 13 percent per annum between 1978 and 2002, somewhat above the provincial average (12.5 percent), there are certainly grounds here for arguing that the Third Front did nothing to prevent the rapid rural industrialization of the post-1978 era.

Yet it is hard to be very positive about the long run legacies of the Front. Luzhou, for example, appears to have benefited little from it. Deyang prefecture, which entered the post-Mao era with a massive rural industrial base by Sichuan standards, could do no better than an average rate of industrialization after 1978. A particularly telling demonstration of the limitations of the Front is provided by comparing the counties of Deyang with those of Chengdu prefecture (Table 9.8). Deyang, as we have noted, was one of the centres of Third Front construction. However, Chengdu was not. Per capita industrial production stood at around the provincial average by 1978, but most of Chengdu's industrial expansion occurred *before* 1965 and the inception of the Third Front.[30] The particular usefulness, however, of the Chengdu–Deyang comparison is that it allows a high degree of geographical normalization. Both prefectures lie on the Chengdu plain and therefore face none of the transport costs which hamper industrialization further to the west, and both are close to Chengdu city; Chengdu prefecture lies mainly to the south of the provincial capital of Sichuan, whereas the counties of Deyang are to the north-east. Accordingly, urban proximity offered little relative advantage to either prefecture. Yet despite these geographical similarities, the two prefectures experienced divergent rates of rural industrialization in the 1980s and 1990s. Rural Chengdu industrialized at a per capita rate of 17.5 percent between 1978 and 2002, well in excess of both the provincial average of 12.6 percent and the 12.7 percent rate achieved in Deyang. Indeed, as has been seen, none of Sichuan's prefectures performed as well as Chengdu in the post-Mao era.

[29] But not impossible. An alternative narrative of Changhong's success might point to the agreement signed with Panasonic to develop colour TVs during the early 1980s.

[30] Some Third Front enterprises were established in rural Chengdu including (for example) Xindu Machinery. But the scale of development was far smaller than in neighbouring Deyang prefecture.

Table 9.8 Sources of rural industrialization in Chengdu and Deyang prefectures (counties only)

Variable	Unit	Year	Chengdu	Deyang
Population density	per km²	1982	619	609
Dependency rate	percent	1982	37	35
Literacy rate	percent	1982	78	67
Industrial employment rate	percent	1982	8	14
Industrial GVA per head	1990 *yuan*	1978	96	182
Growth of industrial GVA per capita	percent	1978–2002	17.5	12.7

Note: Prefectural boundaries are those of 1982, excluding officially-designated urban jurisdictions.
Sources: As for Table 9.6.

In fairness, the divergence between the two prefectures may not have been due simply to the Third Front. As Table 9.8 shows, even after normalization for geography, there were significant differences between the two other than in terms of the industrial employment rate (the best proxy for the impact of late Maoism). Deyang may well have lost out because its literacy rate was lower and, perhaps most obviously, because its initial level of per capita output was much higher: it was Chengdu that enjoyed more of the advantages of backwardness. The other important difference between the two prefectures was the relative size of the CBE sector. Rather remarkably, a complete set of data on CBE output by county in Sichuan in 1976 has been published (SXQS 1988: 91–6).[31] This dataset shows that the median GVIO per head of the CBE sector for Sichuan's counties was a meagre 4 *yuan*. However, the median for the counties of Chengdu prefecture was considerably higher (10 *yuan*) and, if we rank counties by commune and brigade GVIO per head in descending order in that year, four of Chengdu's counties (Xindu, Pengxian, Chongqing and Shuangliu) feature in the top ten. Data from 1978 can also be used to estimate the share of the CBE sector in total industrial production by prefecture. The provincial average was 19 percent for Sichuan's counties, and in Deyang it was only 17 percent. In the western prefectures, the shares were 5 percent in Aba, 13 percent in Liangshan and 8 percent in Ganzi. By contrast, the CBE sector accounted for 25 percent of industrial production in rural Chengdu.

Nevertheless, we cannot push these sorts of factors too far as an explanation for Chengdu's exceptionalism. It probably helped that the CBE sector was relatively well developed compared with other types of industry. However, other prefectures boasted an even higher CBE share in 1978. In Wanxian, for example, the share was 34 percent, in Daxian it was 32 percent and in Luzhou it was 31 percent, yet none of these prefectures enjoyed especially rapid industrial growth

---

[31] Probably because using the low base of 1976 makes the growth rate up to 1986 (for which data are also provided in the same source) even more impressive than if 1978 were the base year.

after 1978. Furthermore, the inclusion of the share of GVIO produced by commune and brigade industry in total GVIO for 1978 in the regression does not produce a statistically significant coefficient; the t statistic is only 0.85. In other words, there is little evidence here that CBE industry was much more dynamic or skill-creating than other types of industry. In any case, even if a lack of CBEs helps to explain slow growth in Deyang, the fact remains that it was the emphasis placed on the Third Front that helps to explain the absence of CBEs in the first place.

In addition, the regression results for the Sichuan basin show literacy as insignificant; it is therefore hard to believe that Chengdu's higher literacy rate gave it a decisive advantage over Deyang. Furthermore, although Deyang was handicapped by its higher initial level of per capita industrial output in the late 1970s, the difference was hardly so great to have exerted a major influence on growth. By way of comparison, the counties of Sunan (discussed in the previous chapter) grew very quickly after 1978 even though they started with a much more developed industrial base than Deyang.

It is therefore hard to escape the conclusion that Deyang ought to have done a good deal better if the Front really was so helpful in terms of improving the industrial skills base. The real difference between the two prefectures at the close of the 1970s probably was the *structure* of industrial production, and this in turn reflected the impact of the Third Front.[32] We would expect experience of non-military production to have, *ceteris paribus*, led to the development of more useful skills than involvement in the production of weaponry, and therefore civilian-orientated Chengdu had a great advantage over neighbouring Deyang. The rural Chengdu of the late 1970s may have had a small industrial base in absolute terms, but its skills foundation was arguably more highly-developed than in neighbouring Deyang.

In sum, the Third Front programme played a crucial role in the development of the Deyang-Mianyang manufacturing region, and in shifting the focus of industrialization in Sichuan away from the central riverine zone. Nevertheless, it is not clear that this prior industrialization laid the foundation for the growth of the 1980s. The very fact that Chengdu prefecture industrialized so swiftly after 1978 without a significant Third Front inheritance suggests that the Front was by no means a necessary condition for rapid industrialization. It seems likely that both rural Deyang and rural Chengdu benefited from their proximity to Chengdu city, the focus of so much of the development effort in Sichuan during the 1950s. But rural Chengdu ultimately profited more because, in contrast to neighbouring Deyang, it had no Third Front legacy to shed in the 1980s and 1990s.

---

[32] The prefectural boundaries used here for Chengdu prefecture are those of 1989. At that time, Chengdu city proper comprised the eastern and western inner city districts, as well as Jinniu, Qingbaijiang and Longquanyi. The counties (rural Chengdu) comprised Jintang, Shuangliu, Wenjiang, Pixian, Xindu, Pengxian, Dujiangyan (formerly Guanxian), Chongqing, Dayi, Qionglai, Pujiang and Xinjin.

9.9. The Role of History: Industrial Development in Sichuan before 1949

With the possible exception of Panzhihua and the Anning valley, the Third Front does not appear to have transformed the prospects of Sichuan's rural regions. Can we push this conclusion further and conclude that the meteoric growth experienced in rural Chengdu after 1978 had little to do with Maoism at all? Might it not represent a continuation of growth trends in the Republican period in the sense that *gaige kaifang* removed the shackles imposed during the Maoist era, allowing Chengdu—and other parts of Sichuan—to resume the pattern of growth of the prewar period.[33] If true, that would suggest that the key continuity in Sichuan's industrial history is between the Republican and Dengist eras, with the Maoist period little more than an aberration.

However, one immediate problem with this hypothesis is the limited nature of Chengdu's pre-1949 industrial development. This under-development is partially demonstrated by the population data. On the basis of population density, Skinner (1964–65) and Smith P. J. (1988) have argued that growing commercialization along the Yangzi river trade artery, and the economic development of southern China as a whole, gradually shifted the province's demographic core towards its southern prefectures, and thus away from Chengdu and the northern part of the province (which had historic overland trade routes to Xi'an). This population-based assessment is confirmed by what we know of pre-war industrial production (Zhang and Zhang 1990: 213–94). Sichuan's fledgling industrial sector on the eve of the Second Sino-Japanese war was concentrated in the central riverine zone: the Yangzi river between Chongqing and Xinshizhen, and the lower reaches of the Min, Tuo and Jialing rivers.[33] The Chongqing region had also seen industrial development because of warlordism: Sichuan's provincial militarists took the first steps towards exploiting the minerals in counties such as Jiangbei (which quickly became a centre of coal production). Much of this industrialization was pioneered under the aegis of the Min Sheng shipping company; as part of this process, the company built the province's first railway, a short coal-carrying line in and out of Chongqing city. Silk production was concentrated along the Jialing valley, running from Chongqing via Hechuan to Nanchong, but Leshan was also an important centre. Neijiang prefecture (on the Tuo river) was the centre of sugar processing. Salt mining centred around Zigong, which produced about 50 percent of the province's salt in the 1930s (ZSQ 1985: 212). Other significant commercial

---

[33] Much of the older English- and Chinese-language literature on Sichuan's prewar economy is discussed in Bramall (1993); recent additions include Wright (2000) and Howard (2004). See also Zhang and Zhang (1990) for a relatively complete listing of factories operating in Sichuan on the eve of the war with Japan.

centres along the Yangzi river were Yibin, Luzhou, Fuling and Wanxian, and their prosperity was linked to exports downriver to Shanghai.[34] Some industrial development had occurred in Chengdu itself; the city had become an important centre for silk weaving and for the handicraft leather goods industry. But industrial production on the Chengdu plain was negligible. One survey found that home industry contributed little more than one percent of cash income (Brown and Li 1928) and modern industry was almost non-existent. The Shifang Tobacco Company (as noted above) was a rare exception. Part of the reason for the industrial under-development of the Chengdu plain was its agricultural fertility, which derived from the waters of the fabled Dujiangyan irrigation system. As a result, there was less pressure on households to develop sideline industries, which tended to be better developed in more mountainous areas like Emei (Brown and Li 1926). However, the main reason for Chengdu's backwardness was the cost of transport. This might seen odd given that the Chengdu plain was so named for good reason. However, the railway linking Chengdu to Chongqing was not completed until June 1952, and construction on the rail link north to Baoji was finished only in December 1957 (Yang 1997: 73). In the absence of such modern transport links, traditional water-borne transport was the only viable option, and here Chengdu was disadvantaged because the Min river was not navigable by anything other than small craft north of Leshan.

Industrial production did increase across Sichuan during wartime as skilled labour and factories were transferred from the eastern provinces to the new Nationalist redoubt at Chongqing. Increased demand for foodstuffs helped to galvanize the food processing industry; for example, Anyue county (one of the centres of sugar production), experienced an increase in industrial employment from 24,000 in 1943 to 80,000 in 1945 (NSJSW 1993: 67). However, the wartime boom was short-lived; total industrial production peaked in 1941 and thereafter fell back. For example, salt production rose from 164,000 tonnes in Zigong in 1937 to 263,000 in 1941, before falling to 226,000 tonnes in 1943 (ZSQ 1985: 212). More of the initial gains were dissipated when the seat of the Nationalist government returned to Nanjing. For example, provincial salt production in 1952 stood at 426,000 tonnes (SCZL 1990: 50), and its pre-1949 peak (514,000 tonnes in 1939) was not regained until 1955. The underlying problem was that the backwardness of Sichuan before 1937 was such that the heavy industrial base needed to sustain modern industrial development—especially in terms of energy generation and steel production—was virtually non-existent. In conjunction with the Japanese blockade (which made it almost impossible to import modern machinery), this backwardness effectively ensured that comparatively little modern industrialization occurred even during wartime.

---

[34] One consequence of this was that these regions (though not Sichuan as a whole) were hit by the depression of the 1930s, which impacted severely upon the sericulture sector (Wright 2000).

Insofar as wartime industrialization did occur, it centred on Chongqing, Leshan, and Neijiang, rather than on Chengdu, in order to exploit the mineral resources in these regions.[35] Thus the data assembled by Zhou et al. (1946: 113–14) show that hardly any factories were located on the Chengdu plain even by 1944. Of the 1,926 factories identified across Sichuan, only 155 were based in Chengdu city, compared with 664 in Chongqing. Within Chengdu prefecture, only Chongqing county (with 14), Pengxian (five) and Guanxian (five) had more than one factory. The comparison with Chongqing's rural hinterland is stark: 261 factories were based in Baxian and 210 in Jiangbei county. The macro-data tell the same story. Per capita industrial output in Chengdu prefecture was only about 10 percent of that in rural area around Chongqing and about two thirds of that achieved across the rest of the Sichuan basin (Bramall 1993).[36] Only in the area centred around Deyang did the level of industrialization exceed the provincial average, and even there the degree of development lagged well behind that of Chongqing's rural hinterland.[37]

This evidence that the Chengdu area was industrially under-developed at the close of the Republican era is confirmed by the data on levels of industrial production in the early 1950s, which are undoubtedly far more reliable than those for the early 1940s. That said, it is hard to be sure about the level of per capita industrial production in the Chengdu countryside because the data invariably include Chengdu city in the prefectural totals. However, we can estimate its level using the data given in some of the *xian zhi*, and put this in some sort of context by comparing it with other rural areas (Table 9.9).

The median for the Chengdu counties included in Table 9.9 is 25 *yuan*, and this seems a plausible estimate of production in the Chengdu countryside; it is fairly close to the figure for adjacent Deyang prefecture, which was entirely rural in 1952 and for which the official post-1949 data can therefore be used. Accepting this estimate for rural Chengdu, the comparative data suggest that the prefecture was very much under-developed in 1952. It was certainly more industrialized than Ganzi or Liangshan, and somewhat more so than Subei, but its level of industrial development was barely half that of Sunan.

The central conclusion from this discussion is therefore that little by way of prewar rural industry existed in the Chengdu region. Any notion, then, that post-1978 growth was a natural continuation of the proto-industrial growth of the 1930s, or the industrialization of the war years, appears rather fanciful.

[35] One of the earliest steel plants founded in Sichuan was in Weiyuan county (Neijiang prefecture) during 1941. By that time, work was in progress at two other plants, both in Chongqing (Sichuan zhi 1992: 311).

[36] These comparisons exclude urban centres and do not take full account of handicraft production but, as noted above, there is no evidence that handicraft production was relatively developed in and around Chengdu compared with the rest of the province.

[37] Deyang here refers to the municipal boundaries of the mid-1980s. At that time it comprised Deyang city proper and the counties of Shifang, Guanghan, Zhongjiang (named Luojiang in the pre-1949 period).

Table 9.9 GVIO per head in the Chengdu countryside, 1952 (*yuan*; current prices)

Region/County	GVIO per head
Counties of Chengdu prefecture:	
Pengxian	41
Guanxian	39
Chongqing	27
Pixian	23
Xinjin	20
Pujiang	12
Other Sichuan rural regions:	
Deyang prefecture	31
Liangshan prefecture	7
Ganzi prefecture	3
Wushan county (Wanxian prefecture)	11
Jiangsu rural regions:	
Subei	21
Sunan	52

Notes: The original data on Chongqing, Guanxian, Pengxian and Xinjin are at 1980 prices. These have been converted to 1952 prices using the provincial GVIO deflator (SCTJNJ 1990: 43). The Pixian figure was originally for 1949; I have estimated 1952 GVIO by assuming that the county's GVIO grew at the same rate as the provincial average between 1949 and 1952. The data given for Sichuan's other prefectures are for purely rural areas; none of these prefectures contained any cities in 1952. The Jiangsu data are for counties only. I have converted the Jiangsu data, which are at 1980 prices in Table 8.4, to current prices using the provincial GVIO data at current and 1980 prices given in JSB (1989: 137, 139).

Sources: Peng XZ (1989: 89, 173); Pi XZ (1989: 121, 395); Xinjin XZ (1989: 97, 965); Chongqing XZ (1991: 295); Guan XZ (1991: 315); Wushan XZ (1991: 91, 193); Pujiang XZ (1992: 83, 160); Sichuan tongjiju (1999: 564, 632); Chapter 8: Table 8.4.

Pre-1949 industrialization centred around Leshan, Neijiang, Luzhou and Nanchong and, though these prefectures fared reasonably well after 1978, none of them could match the rates of rural industrialization achieved on the Chengdu plain. The centre of post-1978 industrialization in Sichuan was certainly not the central riverine zone; rather, the industrial centre of gravity seems to have shifted decisively towards the Chengdu region. Therefore 1949 seems to mark a climacteric in the process of rural industrialization in Sichuan: there is clear evidence of change, and very little of continuity across the Revolutionary divide. Insofar as rural Chengdu industrialized quickly after 1978, it owed little to its meagre Republican inheritance.

9.10. Conclusion

Sichuan's experience demonstrates the limits to the manufacturing capability hypothesis advanced in this book. To be sure, the evidence reviewed here suggests that a well-developed capability certainly helped to accelerate the pace of post-1978 industrialization across the Sichuan basin. Nevertheless, the experience of the province taken as a whole is more equivocal. In particular, it is apparent that the Maoist industrial inheritance was powerless in the face of the geographical obstacles in the way of manufacturing development in western Sichuan. In some respects of course it was simply that western Sichuan enjoyed the 'wrong' sort of inheritance; its extractive industry provided much less of a skills base than the manufacturing enterprises that were the norm in most other parts of Sichuan. Nevertheless, it is hard to believe that any sort of skills base would have been enough to ensure rapid manufacturing growth: in western Sichuan at least, geography was destiny.

The evidence on Sichuan also seems to demonstrate the limitations of the Third Front programme. It is perhaps fair to say that the Front was the catalyst for long run transformation in Panzhihua, and other parts of the Anning river valley of Liangshan where geography was relatively favourable; certainly it is hard to believe that industrialization would have occurred in these rural areas without state intervention. Nevertheless, Front legacies were not able to trump extreme geographical disadvantage in other parts of western Sichuan. Most importantly of all, the very fact that a prefecture as well located as Deyang fared much less well than neighbouring Chengdu after 1978 points unerringly to the conclusion that the colossal investment in the Third Front yielded only modest long term benefits in terms of industrial development. The skills generated by participating in defence production were almost as limiting as those acquired via employment in extractive industry; it was employment in civilian sector manufacturing that really seems to have made a difference.

10

Guangdong

The province of Guangdong has been extensively studied, and it has received many accolades in the economic literature for the way in which it fused foreign direct investment and export growth to generate rapid economic expansion.[1] Such plaudits are hardly surprising. Guangdong expanded its industrial production at an annual real rate of over 18 percent between 1978 and 2002, a pace well above the national average and one unmatched by any other Chinese province.[2]

The rate of industrialization was faster in rural than in urban areas. Between 1978 and 1996 (the eve of the Asian financial crisis), the median real annual rate of industrialization in Guangdong's urban jurisdictions was 21 percent.[3] The figure for the median county, however, was 23 percent, and many of the counties located in the Pearl River Delta achieved rates in excess of 30 percent per year.[4] Indeed it says much about Guangdong's experience that a county like Dongguan—written about and acclaimed in equal measure for its pace of industrialization—did not make the top ten.[5] Even the slowest-growing ten

---

[1] The official data on Guangdong are often inconsistent in their treatment of Hainan, which gained provincial status in 1988. For example, Hainan's industrial output is typically included in the Guangdong total pre-1965, but not thereafter (compare TJJ 1990b and GDFZ 1990). For the purposes of this chapter, the Guangdong data consistently exclude Hainan (unless otherwise stated).

[2] By way of comparison, constant price GVA grew at 17.2 percent per year in Zhejiang, 14.4 percent in Jiangsu, 11.7 percent in Sichuan and 12.2 percent nationally (GDTJNJ 2003: 34; JSTJNJ 2003: 58; SCTJNJ 2003: 25; ZJTJNJ 2003: 20; TJNJ 2004: 56, 63).

[3] These urban and rural medians are based on the growth of net industrial output value (NVIO) at 1990 prices, 'rural' being taken to mean all those jurisdictions officially designated as *xian* in 1982, and vice versa. The official data from which these growth rates have been derived (see Table 10.6, below, for their provenance) probably over-state the true industrial growth rate, but lopping even (say) 5 percent off the Guangdong figures still leaves us with exceptionally fast growth rates by international standards.

[4] The term Pearl River delta is used in this chapter to mean the cities and counties of the Zhujiang Delta Open Economic Zone as defined by the State Council in 1987, plus Guangzhou city and the two special economic zones of Shenzhen and Zhuhai. For all the counties and cities included in this definition of the Delta, see Table 10.4.

[5] Dongguan achieved urban status in September 1985 (Yeung 2001: 46) as a result of its ability to attract FDI and because its industrial growth averaged 29 percent per year between 1980 and 1996. As noted in Chapter 2, Dongguan already possessed a significant industrial base by the end

counties in Guangdong achieved annual industrial growth rates of 9 percent, a remarkable record by the standards of other developing countries. In the process, the province attracted a vast pool of migrant labour from the rest of the People's Republic. The remittances paid to their home villages by many of these migrants, and the skills brought back by return migrants, played an important role in reducing poverty in provinces as far afield as Guizhou and Sichuan. In the process, some of the fruits of growth in Guangdong 'trickled down' to the Chinese hinterland.

10.1. Narratives of Growth

Guangdong has attracted more inward investment than the rest of China since 1980, and has seemingly used it to foster exceptionally rapid economic growth via the expansion of export-orientated industries. Small wonder, then, that the term 'Guangdong development model' has been coined to describe this type of approach to economic development.

Guangdong's capacity to attract FDI, and to generate export growth, is usually attributed to three factors. Firstly, post-1978 central government policy favoured it far more than any other province. Three of the four Special Economic Zones were established within its borders at the end of the 1980s, and all received significant central government investment in infrastructure (Kleinberg 1990). In addition, the province received a far more favourable fiscal settlement from central government than (for example) Shanghai or most other provinces (Shirk 1993). In a very real sense, the 'playing field' was tilted towards Guangdong. Nevertheless, and secondly, it is generally acknowledged that this sort of 'state bias' would not have been enough to generate rapid growth in Guangdong but for the province's favourable geography (Bao et al. 2002). For one thing, its semi-tropical climate ensured a much higher level of agricultural productivity than could be achieved on the parched North China plain. For another, the province had the advantage of a long coastline, with all the attendant transport advantages that brought in its train. And, much more importantly, the implementation of the open door policy made Guangdong's proximity to Hong Kong—the key conduit for overseas Chinese investment—of enormous value. Thirdly, Guangdong was industrially under-developed compared with traditional industrial centres like Liaoning and Shanghai, and this encouraged the province to make much more of an effort to implement

of the Maoist era; in 1980, per capita NVIO in the county was 150 *yuan*, 2.5 times greater than the Guangdong rural median (62 *yuan*). However, agriculture still dominated production in many of its communes (Potter and Potter 1990). The experience of Dongguan thus parallels those of Suxichang and the Chengdu plain remarked upon in earlier chapters. Post-1978 industrial growth transformed an essentially rural landscape, but the foundations for that industrialization had been laid prior to the death of Mao.

economic policies which would attract FDI. For Huang (2003: 196, 200), for example,

... regions that pursued efficient economic policies were least endowed with industrial and technical capabilities and, to a lesser extent, with capital resources ... the most competitive firms in China today are located not in traditional industrial strongholds such as Beijing, Shanghai, or Tianjin but in Guangdong, a very rural province at the start of the reforms.

Within Guangdong, Huang points to the success of the famous Kelon refrigerator company, which owed much to the fact that its host county of Shunde was industrially under-developed. Backwardness thus provided an incentive for modernization, as well as the catch-up possibilities emphasized in the more narrowly economic literature (Abramovitz 1986).

In these accounts, therefore, a history of industrialization is at best irrelevant for growth. At worst, it is a handicap: an industrial inheritance discourages innovative economic policy-making, and well-established industrial centres pre-empt valuable reserves of capital and labour which could be used more efficiently elsewhere. Within Guangdong, those parts of the province which did well under Mao, principally the northern prefectures of Shaoguan and Meixian and the southern oil-refining centre of Maoming, failed to prosper after 1978. Moreover, even insofar as a history of industrial development left a favourable legacy, it was trumped by economic geography in the post-Mao era. For the transition era was one in which fiscal decentralization ensured that the traditional geographically-based ascendancy of the Delta and the coastal counties of Shantou re-asserted itself. Globalization merely reinforced the process; in such a world, the proximity of Guangdong's coastal region to Hong Kong, and to the dynamic economies of north-east Asia, was a boon. By contrast, any mountainous county in the interior was at a critical disadvantage. This was as true in a qualitative sense for the counties of Meixian (even though they were located within a coastal province) as it was for Yunnan and western Sichuan. In any case, so the argument goes, post-1978 *rural* industrialization in Guangdong cannot be explained in terms of industrial legacies because these were virtually non-existent. Insofar as industrialization did occur in the province, it was urban-based. The extent of urban and anti-coastal bias was so great that the industrialization process outside the prefectural capitals in areas such as Shaoguan was extremely shallow. Thus 'On the eve of reform, China was basically an agricultural economy ... The economic basis of the coastal regions remained basically unchanged from the prerevolution period' (Bao et al. 2002: 96).

There is much in this grand narrative that is assuredly correct: we cannot explain Guangdong's development without reference to its geography, or its ability to attract foreign direct investment. However, such narratives tell only a part of the story. They under-state the degree of Maoist rural industrialization, and therefore the extent to which rural industrial capability had been developed

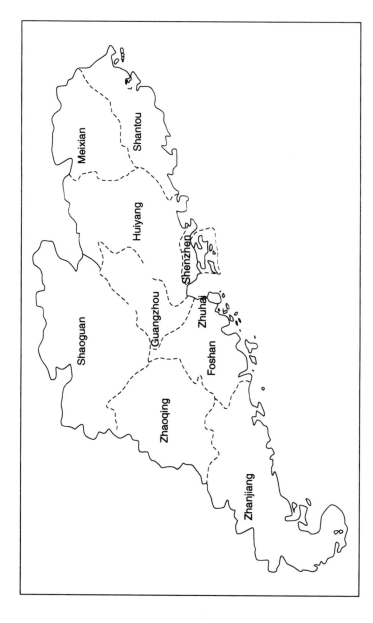

Figure 10.1 The prefectures of Guangdong, early 1980s

by the late 1970s. Secondly, the narratives tend to ignore the abundant evidence pointing to a link running from Maoist industrial legacies to the pace of post-1978 rural industrialization. To be sure, geography and inward investment certainly influenced the pace and pattern of growth. And counties where per capita output was already high in the late 1970s grew less quickly than they might otherwise have done because they enjoyed less scope for catch-up. Nevertheless, these were not the only factors at work; only a part of the spatial pattern of rural industrialization in Guangdong can be explained in these terms. When we normalize for the influence of catch-up, geography and FDI, it is clear that the counties which grew most rapidly were actually those which entered the post-Mao era with a well-developed industrial capability. In Guangdong, as elsewhere in China, it seems that a reservoir of skilled labour was one of the mainsprings of rural industrial success.

10.2. Rural Industry in Guangdong Before 1949

Guangdong was by no means a leading industrial province at the time of the 1949 Revolution, especially when compared with the Manchurian provinces or with Sunan. Some parts of the Delta were comparatively advanced, at least by Chinese standards. In Shunde, for example, per capita GVIO in 1952 stood at 179 *yuan* (Shunde XZ 1996). Nowhere else seems to have attained this sort of level, but there were several Delta counties (such as Panyu, Dongguan, Bao'an and Xinhui) where per capita output stood at more than 40 *yuan*. For Guangdong, as a whole, however, rural GVIO per head averaged only about 20 *yuan* (1980 prices) by 1952.[6] By way of comparison, using the county-level jurisdictional boundaries of 1982 to delineate urban and rural areas, the Jiangsu figure was 28 *yuan* (JSB 1989). The corresponding figure for Sichuan's most industrialized prefectures—such as Deyang, Leshan and Luzhou—was approximately 25 *yuan* (see Chapter 6). In fact, the Guangdong rural average was only a little higher than for backward northern Jiangsu (where it was 18 *yuan*).

Guangdong's small industrial sector was also very traditional, dominated as it was by light industry. For example, cloth contributed 5 percent, grass cloth 9 percent and paper 18 percent of provincial exports during the 1920s (Arnold 1926: 728–9). The largest single industrial sector was food processing, which

---

[6] GVIO per head in Shantou and Guangzhou cities was 213 and 225 *yuan* respectively at 1980 prices (calculated from GZTJNJ 1982: 483; TJJ 1988: 310; Shantou SZ 1999: 54, 1253–5). If we assume that GVIO per head was around 200 *yuan* per head in Guangdong's other less developed cities (which were home to 0.565 million people at the time of the 1953 Population Census—TJJ 1988: 310), that implies an urban GVIO total of 533 million *yuan*. Subtracting this from the provincial total for 1952 (GDFZ 1990) gives rural GVIO of 511 million *yuan* divided across a rural population of 26.66 million (TJJ 1999), giving a figure of 19 *yuan* per head. The median 1952 level of GVIO per head for the counties listed in Appendix 3 is also 20 *yuan*.

alone accounted for about 50 percent of industrial output even as late as the early 1950s (Sun 1959: 88; GDDLZ 1999: 427). Food processing was in turn dominated by the sugar subsector.

Furthermore, there is little real evidence to suggest that a process of industrial take-off was underway in the province during the Republican era. True, sugar production was well-established: traditional handicraft sugar refining had long been well developed in Guangdong and the industry was fed by the sugar cane fields of the Delta counties (Mazumdar 1998). However, the opening-up of China by the British in the early nineteenth century initiated a classical process of de-industrialization in Guangdong which paralleled the fate of traditional cotton textiles in Bengal or Japan. Firstly, handicraft sugar refining was progressively undermined by modern refineries, many of them based in Hong Kong and later in Guangdong itself. Secondly, in Delta counties such as Shunde and Dongguan, sugar cane was increasingly displaced by mulberry cultivation (Mazumdar 1998: 354–5). Instead, the focus of sugar cane production shifted to Shantou, which became a great trading centre in the late nineteenth century. However, Shantou's sugar sector in turn found it hard to compete with the sugar cane produced in Java, Taiwan and the Philippines. Over-supply in the world market led to a collapse in prices after 1905, and thereafter the main Hong Kong-based firms of Jardine and Butterfield Swire '. . . simply stopped buying sugar in Guangdong, turning instead to Java and the Philippines' (Marks 1984: 107). The Guangdong economy was given a fillip by the boom associated with the First World War (A. H. Y. Lin 1997: 84); sugar accounted for about 20 percent of the value of exports going through Shantou according to the Maritime Customs data for 1923 (Arnold 1926: 729). But the 'golden age' quickly came to an end. By the late 1920s, China's imports of refined sugar (of well over 500,000 tonnes) vastly exceeded domestic production, which was little more than 100,000 tonnes in 1930 (Mazumdar 1998: 385). To be sure, the industry did revive during the 1930s. By 1936, it produced around 200,000 tonnes (some of it for export), mostly machine-produced sugar. And sugar production in turn helped to facilitate the development of a range of industries, especially fruit canning. Nevertheless, and despite these emerging linkage effects, there is little to suggest that the Guangdong's sugar industry was in any way comparable to Manchester's cotton textile industry as an engine for modern industrial growth.

The province's textile sector was equally fragile. Little cotton cloth was produced in the province, and post-1949 Chinese accounts uniformly lament the under-developed state of the sector: 'The cotton textile industry cannot meet the needs of the people, so it must be supported by the other provinces' (Sun 1959: 58). In fact, there is some evidence of industrial expansion. Cotton was by no means unimportant in Foshan or in parts of Shantou prefecture. In Haifeng county, for example, handicraft cotton spinning and weaving was largely wiped out by imports and by domestic factory production, but the effects were more than offset by the development of modern textiles mills: '. . . Haifeng's textile industry *per se* was not destroyed by competition from foreign yarns and cloth, only its handicraft form. In fact, textile production had probably increased' (Marks 1984: 118). Nevertheless, cotton was in no sense a leading sector during the 1930s.

Guangdong's key textile industry was silk, and there is no doubt that it was well-established (Faure 1989; Xu 1990; A. H. Y. Lin 1997). The province's first filature was established as early as 1866 (Sun 1959: 100), and by the time of the 1911 Revolution there were 162 filatures operating within the province. This figure climbed during the course of the First World War and the industry reached its apogee in 1926, with 202 filatures and 95,000 machines (Xu 1990: 627). The silk industry was concentrated in the Delta, with 90 percent of raw silk produced in just three counties: Shunde, Zhongshan and Nanhai (Liang 1956: 36; A. H. Y. Lin 1997: 85). Shunde was the epicentre of production. In 1911, the county operated 142 factories employing a total of 64,000 workers, and in 1921 the figures were broadly comparable at 135 factories (81 percent of the provincial total) and 65,000 workers (Shunde XZ 1996: 386–9). Even in 1950, Shunde accounted for 50 percent of mulberry area and 66 percent of silk production (Liang 1956: 36).

Yet the limitations of Guangdong's silk industry in the first half of the twentieth century are readily apparent. Few of Shunde's filatures were steam-powered, and the silk sector was less technologically dynamic than its counter-part in Japan, at least if the productivity data are any indicator (Ma 2004). Furthermore, Guangdong's silk reeling industry was devastated by the Great Depression. By 1936, there were only 36 filatures operating 30,000 machines across the province (Xu 1990: 627). In Shunde's case, the decline was even more pronounced; in 1929 there were 99 factories, but this total had fallen to only nine by 1935 (Shunde XZ 1996: 39). Accordingly, A. H. Y. Lin's (1997: 86) statement that '. . . the entire silk district sank into the abyss of poverty and misery' may only be a small exaggeration. Its decline, at least in the medium term, appears to have been terminal. Despite efforts to revive the industry during the 1950s, output of raw silk reached only 800 tonnes by 1957 (up from 384 tonnes in 1949), a far cry from the 6,000 tonnes produced in the early 1920s (Sun 1959: 101–2).

This evidence on the sugar and silk industries suggests that Guangdong's industrial economy was not on the verge of take-off by the 1930s. The fundamental inefficiency of much of the province's industrial sector is especially apparent from its inability either to penetrate export markets, or to staunch the flow of industrial imports into Guangdong itself. In Delta counties such as Shunde, Dongguan and Bao'an (contemporary Shenzhen), there was an industrial inheritance on which to build at the time of the Revolution, but it was a meagre one.

10.3. Maoist Industrialization in Guangdong

By 1978, Guangdong's industrial economy had been utterly transformed. Its metamorphosis occurred across four dimensions: the absolute level of per capita production was well over ten times higher; a heavy industry subsector had been created; rural industry had expanded dramatically; and the geography of industrial production had been radically altered.

10.3.1. The Growth of Industrial Production, 1952–78

Even during the 1950s, the industrial growth rates registered in Guangdong were unprecedented in the province's history, and of course far out-stripped the rates of advance being achieved in most of the developing world. In that sense, it is hard to talk convincingly of industrial failure in Guangdong during the 1950s. Yet for all that, little concerted effort was made to build on Guangdong's meagre industrial inheritance in the immediate aftermath of the Revolution. In the main this was because the province was seen during the First 5YP as lacking the raw materials needed for the development of heavy industry. As a result, the rate of industrial growth in Guangdong lagged behind the national average during the 1950s (Table 10.1).

The year 1958 proved to be a climacteric in Guangdong's industrial history. By the late 1950s, the pressure to develop heavy industry became intense. Steel was singled out because, 'In the past this province was a blank spot in the relation to the entire country as far as the steel and iron industry was concerned. It produced very little iron. It had never [before 1957] produced as much as even one ton of steel . . .' (Sun 1959: 103). During the Leap the provincial leadership became increasingly radicalized, and under Tao Zhu came to embrace the iron and steel campaign with no little fervour (Chan 2001). One result of this, as

Table 10.1 Growth of secondary sector GVA, 1952–96 (percent per annum)

	Guangdong	China
1952–57	15.3	19.1
1957–65	4.8	1.5
1965–78	13.1	10.7
1952–78	9.6	9.4
1978–96	18.0	12.0

Notes: Growth rates are for urban and rural areas combined and are based on comparable price indices. Guangdong excludes Hainan. Ideally, we would compare the growth of industrial value-added (instead of net material product or secondary value-added), but such data do not seem to exist for Guangdong pre-1978.
Sources: TJJ (1990b); TJJ (1999).

elsewhere in China, was the diversion of farm labour to the industrial sector, leading to food shortages. As a result, the crude death rate in rural Guangdong rose from 8.6 per 1,000 in 1957 to 16 per 1,000 in 1960 (GDRKZ 1995: 61). Nevertheless, partly because of relatively good weather and partly because its pre-Leap level of per capita farm production was so high, Guangdong fared much better during the Leap and its aftermath than many other parts of China. Although the province's rural crude death rate doubled, this was far less than the eightfold rise in the rate recorded in Anhui between 1957 and 1960 (AHSZ 1995: 97). Furthermore, Guangdong's industrial growth rate comfortably exceeded the national average during 1957–65, thus reversing the relative standings of the 1950s. By 1965, in fact, industrial production in the province was almost 50 percent higher than it had been in 1957.

Perhaps more surprisingly, at least in the light of the emphasis placed in much recent literature on the way in which the Third Front programme allegedly shifted the focus of Chinese industrial development from the coast to the interior in the late Maoist era, Guangdong's industrial sector grew faster than the average after 1965. And by 1980, for example, per capita production in Guangdong was still some 60 percent higher than in Third Front-dominated Sichuan (SCZL 1990; GDZL 1991). In part this was because the province had, in Shaoguan, its own Third Front region. By focusing on the 'big' Third Front, too much of the recent literature neglects these types of programmes and their impact. But probably more important was the impact of cumulative causation. As suggested by Kaldor and Krugman, regions which gain an advantage (whether by accident or by virtue of economic geography) are often able to widen the gap between themselves and other less-favoured regions because of the impact of increasing returns. The underlying dynamism of the Guangdong economy was such that even 'state bias' in the allocation of investment towards the interior was enough to reverse the relative standings of Guangdong and Sichuan. Guangdong may have entered the Maoist era with a limited industrial foundation, but it was far better positioned in this regard than western China, and its physical geography helped to lock-in this advantage even in the face of central government subsidies to the western provinces.

Accordingly, any notion that Guangdong was discriminated against between 1949 and 1978 must be based on the failure of the province to achieve its potential, rather than its actual rate of industrial advance. The province might not have been the recipient of massive state investment subsidies, but the fact remains that it increased its share of secondary GVA from 4.7 percent of the national total in 1952 to 5 percent in 1978.[7] Measured in absolute terms, the real

[7] The north-east was the region which lost out during the Maoist era. For example, Liaoning's share of secondary value-added fell from 14.1 percent in 1952 to only 9.3 percent in 1978. Any notion that the southern coastal provinces fared badly is simply a myth; the combined share of Jiangsu, Zhejiang, Fujian and Guangdong rose from 14.4 percent in 1952 to 17.1 percent in 1978 (TJJ 1999: 3, 115).

value-added produced by Guangdong's secondary sector was no less than 14 times greater in 1978 than it had been in 1952 (TJJ 1999: 3, 592, 593). Seen in this light, Bao's claim that its economy was 'basically unchanged' from the Republican era is hard to sustain.

10.3.2. The Development of Heavy Industry

Guangdong's industrial sector was dominated in 1952 by light industry; measured at 1952 prices, the share of light industry was 88 percent of provincial GVIO compared with a national share of 64 percent (TJJ 1985: 19; GDTJNJ 1990: 177). One reason was that the principal mineral deposits were in the relatively inaccessible north of the province and required massive prior investment in transport and other infrastructure.

The dominance of light industry began to come under threat during the First 5YP. Guangdong may not have been in the van of industrialization in the 1950s, but it was not immune to the national emphasis on heavy industry and as a result its machine-building industry in particular began to grow rapidly (Sun 1959: 104–6; Chan 2001). The converse of this was the decline of light industry; for example, the share of food processing in industrial production fell from almost 50 percent in 1952 (nearly double the national average) to only 39 percent by 1957 (GDFZ 1990: 10–11; GDDLZ 1999: 427). By 1960, at the height of the Leap, the food sector's share was down to a mere 22 percent as a result of the expansion of metallurgy, which increased its share from 11 percent in 1957 to 21 percent in 1960. Thereafter, food processing revived somewhat, and by 1965, Guangdong's industrial structure was quite 'traditional' even by Chinese standards; its food processing share was still about double the national average (TJJ 1985: 103; GDFZ 1990: 12). Yet the very fact that the share of this archetypal traditional sector was down to 26 percent, barely half its 1952 share, is an indication of just how far the Guangdong economy had changed by 1965.[8]

After 1964–65, when the cause of Third Front construction was embraced with great fervour by Guangdong's leaders (Bachman 2001: 291–3), the process of industrial transformation accelerated.[9] The Front not only led to the expansion of the defence sector but also, and more importantly, to the development of

---

[8] These data are very sensitive to the set of constant prices used for measurement. The figures cited here are at constant 1957 prices. Valued at 1980 prices, the share of Guangdong's food processing sector in 1965 was no less than 37 percent. These differences in shares result occur because food and textile prices fell very little between 1957 and 1980, whereas the prices of machinery (and many producer goods) fell markedly. For national sectoral shares at 1957, 1970 and 1980 prices, see TJJ (1985: 102–3).

[9] The turning point in perceptions was the Great Leap Forward. Sun's (1959: 104) rather euphoric assessment seems representative: 'This province has very rich iron ore resources which have excellent quality . . . They not only are favourable for the development of steel and iron industries everywhere but also suited to the establishment of larger steel and iron combined enterprises'.

related heavy industries. As a result, the combined share of metallurgy, coal, power, oil and chemicals (at 1980 prices) climbed from 17.5 percent in 1965 to 26.2 percent by 1978. However, the main gainer was the machine-building sector, which increased its share of GVIO from 10 to 20 percent between 1965 and 1978. In so doing, it had developed to the point where it had all but caught up with food processing, which had seen its share decline from 37 to 22 percent by 1978 (GDFZ 1990: 12–15).

As a result of these changes in Guangdong, the share of heavy industry had climbed to almost 43 percent by 1978, compared with 35 percent only eight years before (GDTJNJ 1990: 177). Over the entire 1952 to 1978 period, light industrial output increased by a factor of nine, whereas heavy industrial production increased 58 fold (GDTJNJ 1986: 56–7). Guangdong was still more light industry-orientated than other Chinese provinces in 1978, but there is clear evidence of convergence on the national norm during the Maoist era.

10.3.3. Rural Industrialization in the Maoist Era

The first decade of Maoist rule in Guangdong emphasized the development of urban as much as it did heavy industry. Guangzhou was singled out for attention because in the early 1950s it was essentially a commercial rather than an industrial centre (Vogel 1989: 203). This commercial orientation is clear from its low level of per capita industrial production. To be sure, the city dominated industrial production in the province even in the early 1950s. Guangzhou city proper contributed fully 87 percent of GVIO in Guangzhou prefecture during 1952, and no less than 25 percent of *provincial* GVIO in that year, a staggering figure for a single city (GZTJNJ 1983: 483; GDFZ 1990: 10).[10] However, because the city's population exceeded the 1.5 million mark, per capita GVIO was only about 220 *yuan*, not much higher than in Shunde county or Foshan city, and apparently lower than in Chaozhou. In this regard, Guangzhou had rather more in common with Nanjing (where GVIO per head of 186 *yuan* in 1952) than with Chinese industrial cities such as Suzhou (456 *yuan*) or Wuxi (623 *yuan*) (JSB 1989).

The modelling of the Chinese industrialization strategy of the 1950s on the Soviet development strategy of the Stalinist era led inexorably to an accelerated pace of industrialization in urban centres. In this respect, government efforts to expand industrial production in Guangzhou seem to have borne fruit. GVIO in the city increased by over 13 percent per year between 1952 and 1965, significantly faster than the provincial average of about 10 percent (GZTJNJ 1983: 483; GDFZ 1990: 10–14). By 1978, Guangzhou city's contribution to industrial production in Guangzhou prefecture had actually increased to 94 percent. Elsewhere in Guangdong, industrialization and urbanization advanced hand in

---

[10] Guangzhou prefecture in this comparison is made up of Guangzhou city and the counties of Huaxian, Conghua, Panyu, Zengcheng, Longmen and Xinfeng. GVIO is measured at 1970 constant prices. The provincial total excludes Hainan island.

hand. In Foshan city proper, industry was already comparatively well-established at the time of the Revolution, but industrial output nevertheless grew at 16 percent per year between 1952 and 1965 (Foshan SZ 1994).

Nevertheless, it would be wrong to suppose that *rural* industrial development was neglected in Guangdong. Even before 1965, rural industrialization was underway in most parts of the province. Perhaps the most striking example of rural industrialization is provided by the development of Maoming in south-western Guangdong. A mere county in the early 1950s, Maoming was transformed by the decision to develop it as the centre of oil refining in southern China. The engine of growth was thus the Maoming shiyou gongye gongsi (Maoming Petroleum Industrial Corporation, usually abbreviated as Maoming gongsi), which began to be established in 1955 and which contributed more than 95 percent of GVIO in the jurisdiction (Maoming SZ 1997: 310–11, 487–8). By 1959, the transformation of Maoming had proceeded so far that the county was granted city status (Maoming SZ 1997: 1961), and thereafter its growth continued to be extremely rapid; Maoming city proper achieved an industrial growth rate of no less than 44 percent between 1958 and 1965, far above the provincial average for that period.[11] Precisely because Maoming was only a county prior to the development of oil refining, its experience offers a classic example of the transformative effect of industrialization on an essentially *rural* area. In that regard, its experience has much in common with those of third front centres such as Panzhihua.

More general evidence on rural industrialization in Guangdong is provided in Appendix 3, which brings together industrial output data for a sample of 37 counties and five cities.[12] These growth rates show that the rate of industrialization was rapid in many of Guangdong's counties, and typically faster than in the cities. Growth was particularly rapid in Huazhou, Wengyuan and Ruyuan, but many of the counties in this sample did better than the provincial average. Indeed Guangzhou city, partly because it entered the Maoist era with such an extensive industrial base, languished towards the bottom of the list. After 1965, the pattern of industrialization was increasingly balanced between rural and urban areas. In no small measure, this was because the growth rates of all three cities included in the Appendix 3 sample slowed dramatically. In Guangzhou's case, the growth rate of GVIO slowed from 13.3 percent during 1952–65 to 9.3 percent during 1965–78. In consequence, the city's share in the GVIO of Guangzhou prefecture began to decline, albeit very slowly, during the 1970s (GZTJNJ 1983: 483). The slowdown in Foshan and Maoming was even more abrupt.

At the same time, the rate of industrialization in rural areas held up rather well despite the higher levels of industrialization which had been attained by the

[11] At 1980 prices. The original Maoming figure for 1965 was at 1957 prices, which has been converted to 1980 prices using the all-industry deflator.

[12] This sample is representative of the province as a whole, as is evident from the similarity between the (median) sample growth rate and the average provincial rate.

early 1970s. As Appendix 3 shows, the rural median declined only marginally if we compare 1952–65 with 1965–78. The sustained pace of rural industrialization appears to reflect the accelerated development of the CBE sector. Between 1965 and 1978, brigade and below industry averaged an annual growth rate of 11.1 percent, somewhat above the provincial average (GDFZ 1990: 10–11). However, this comparison disguises the acceleration underway in the early 1970s. For although output grew at only 1.2 percent per year between 1965 and 1972, it soared thereafter to average no less than 28 percent between 1972 and 1978. Take Shaoguan prefecture. There, CBE industrial output tripled between 1970 and 1978 (Shaoguan SZ 2001: 1043, 1053). In Wengyuan, for example, CBE gross income increased 2.7 fold between 1970 and 1980, and brigade-level income increased 3.6 fold (Wengyuan XZ 1997: 244). In Lechang, the share of central and provincial-owned SOEs declined from 61 percent in 1965 to 48 percent by 1976 as local industry began to develop (Lechang XZ 1994: 204–5). The same sort of rapid expansion occurred in Maoming prefecture, where brigade-level industrial output increased ninefold between 1965 and 1978 (Maoming SZ 1997: 550). In the Delta, too, the commune and brigade sector grew quickly. In Shunde, for example, commune-level GVIO increased twofold between 1962 and 1970, but between 1970 and 1978 it increased nearly fivefold (Shunde XZ 1996: 379). A further sign of rural industrialization was the expansion of coal production by commune and brigade enterprises across the province; output increased from 147,000 tonnes in 1965 to 2.8 million tonnes by 1978 (GDFZ 1990: 96).

The pace of rural industrial growth was certainly not uniform. It appears, for example, that commune and brigade industry was slow to develop in desperately poor Meixian prefecture.[13] Meixian itself did rather well, with commune-level output increasing fivefold between 1970 and 1977, thus matching more favourably located Shunde (Mei XZ 1994: 372). Wuhua's rural industry fared equally well, especially after the establishment of a CBE bureau in 1977 (Wuhua XZ 1991: 175–6). But elsewhere in Meixian, the growth rate was much slower. In Dapu, for example, the output of the CBE sector was only about 50 percent higher in 1978 than it had been in 1965 (Dapu XZ 1992: 213). And in Jiaoling, output increased less than threefold between 1970 and 1980 (Jiaoling XZ 1992: 265). More generally, rural industry did not enjoy a position of ascendancy in Guangdong by 1980. Far from it. Despite being home to 84 percent of the population, Guangdong's counties produced only 44 percent of industrial output in 1980. To put this another way, urban GVIO exceeded 1500 *yuan* per head, whereas the average for rural jurisdictions was a mere 200 *yuan* (GDFZ 1990; TJJ 1990*b*).

---

[13] This was in part a consequence of limited infrastructural development. A railway link between Meizhou and Shenzhen/Shantou was only completed in June 1996.

And yet, despite the low *level* of rural industrialization achieved by 1978, the notion that Guangdong 'walked on two legs' is less of a myth than suggested by the Chinese conventional wisdom in the 1980s and 1990s. The rural sector had far to go to close the gap between itself and Guangdong's cities, but its very growth rate shows that it had begun the process of catching up. It is perhaps fanciful to talk of rural industrial 'take-off' in Guangdong in the 1970s, but there is no doubt that the growth process was underway well before the 1978 watershed.

10.3.4. Changing Industrial Geography

The fourth feature of industrial development in Guangdong during the Maoist era was the changing geography of production, a process of change driven as much by defence as by narrowly economic considerations. Thus the Maoist era saw the eclipse of much of the coastal region, the traditional centre of Guangdong's industry.[14] Its converse was the rise of the mountainous region to the north-east of the provincial capital, a process driven by 'little' Third Front programmes explicitly designed to re-locate industry away from the coastal prefectures (the Delta region, Huiyang and Shantou) and towards the mountainous prefectures of Shaoguan and Meixian. For all that, industry collapsed in no part of the province before 1978. As was true of other Chinese provinces, Guangdong entered the transition era with an industrial base that was infinitely more developed than that it inherited in 1949.

(A) COASTAL ECLIPSE: RELATIVE DECLINE IN THE DELTA AND SHANTOU

During the 1950s and early 1960s, parts of the Delta fared comparatively well. Guangzhou prefecture grew more quickly than the provincial average, increasing its share of provincial GVIO to 49 percent, well above the 40 percent recorded in 1952 (Table 10.2). After 1965, and as the Maoist development strategy gave increasing weight to rural industrialization and to the Third Front, the position of the Delta deteriorated. As a result, Guangzhou's share in GVIO fell back, such that by 1978 it was no higher than in 1949. Indeed, as Table 10.2 shows, Guangzhou's growth rate was well below those achieved in Maoming, Meixian and Shaoguan after 1965.

Foshan, home to many of the Delta counties and the most affluent of Guangdong's prefecture at the start of the Maoist era, fared much less well even before 1965. Its growth rate in the early Maoist era (10 percent per annum) was hardly disappointing when viewed in international perspective, or when compared with Shantou or Meixian before 1965. In part this was because the First 5YP provided for the establishment of modern state-owned sugar refineries, the

---

[14] Strictly speaking, the coast-interior dichotomy is an over-generalization; the coastal prefectures of Zhanjiang and Maoming in the south-west of the province fared relatively well.

Table 10.2 Rural industrialization in Guangdong's prefectures, 1952–78 (median industrial growth rates of GVIO)

Prefecture	1952–65	1965–78
Guangzhou	11.5	8.1
Foshan	10.2	10.8
Shaoguan	16.0	14.3
Maoming	13.8	10.2
Meixian	9.5	11.3
Shantou	5.8	8.0

Notes: The medians for each prefecture are for rural jurisdictions only and are based on the counties listed in each prefecture in Appendix 3. Data are at 1980 constant prices.
Source: Appendix 3.

five largest of which were all located in the Delta (Liang 1956: 41–3). Nevertheless, Foshan's industrialization was not fast enough to prevent its share in provincial GVIO declining from 24 percent in 1952 to a mere 16 percent in 1965. Several factors seem to have been at work. For one thing, the Revolution led to the disruption of the pre-1949 trade in sugar and raw silk between Foshan and Hong Kong. Secondly, the First 5YP gave priority to the development of heavy industry in Guangzhou city, rather than to the Delta's rural hinterland. Thirdly, Foshan prefecture was held back by the emphasis placed on developing lower value-added sugar cane production (to meet growing consumer demand) at the expense of mulberries and silkworms during the 1950s. In Shunde, for example, the share of mulberry bushes in county cultivated area seems to have fallen from 96 percent in the mid-1920s to 43 percent in 1950 and to only 18 percent in 1955. Over the same period, the area given over to sugar cane increased from almost nothing to 52 percent (Sun 1959: 129–30). Liang (1956: 55) makes the same point:

Shunde county, which was mainly a mulberry-silk producing locality, suddenly became a sugar cane growing area . . . In the early years immediately after liberation, when planning work was not yet strengthened, sugar cane acreages were blindly expanded.

As a result of these processes, the structure of the Delta's agricultural economy increasingly reverted back to that of the 1840s, when limited opportunities for trade led to an emphasis on the production of food (sugar) rather than cash crops (silk). In both the late eighteenth century and in the 1950s and 1960s, China's relative isolation ensured a pattern of agricultural development which was led by sugar in the Pearl River Delta.

After 1965, Foshan's fortunes revived somewhat because of the shift in national emphasis towards rural industry. By 1978, the prefecture's share in GVIO was back at 18 percent, well below its 1952 level but significantly up on the nadir of 1971. For all that, Foshan was deemed too vulnerable to serve as a centre for defence industrialization, and its share in state investment after 1965 was curtailed accordingly. The result of this is clear from the composition of GVIO. Whereas Guangdong's heavy industry share in GVIO was 43 percent in 1978, Foshan city proper recorded only 32 percent (Foshan SZ 1994: 774–7). The figure for Xinhui county was much the same at 34 percent in 1975 (Xinhui XZ 1995: 247) but in Shunde it was only 24 percent (Shunde XZ 1996: 379). In short, location worked to Foshan's disadvantage. The trade links it had developed before the Revolution were largely severed, and its vulnerability to attack ruled out its selection as a Third Front centre. Its industrial sector did not collapse, but the prefecture was not an engine of growth in the Maoist era.

The relative decline of Shantou prefecture was much more marked. Shantou (Swatow) itself had long been a centre of commerce and light industrial production, in no small measure because of its Treaty Port status. Indeed its contribution of 12 percent to provincial industrial production in 1952 placed it ahead of all of Guangdong's other prefectures save Guangzhou and Foshan. However, its vulnerability to attack and lack of mineral resources meant that Shantou received little investment in the Maoist era. And precisely because international trade was more important there than anywhere else in Guangdong before 1949, self-sufficiency hit the prefecture hard, as is evident from the data (Table 10.2). In combination with Shantou's relative high population density, the result was that per capita industrial output was only 57 *yuan* in 1980, well below Guangdong's rural average (80 *yuan*) and only about one third of the level enjoyed by Foshan (GDZL 1991).

To be sure, industrialization was still possible. The aim of the Leap in Shantou, as elsewhere in China, was to create a heavy industrial sector. Furthermore, industry was identified as the motor for growth in the late 1960s in accord with the national slogan to 'take agriculture as the base and industry as the leading sector'. In the Fourth 5YP period, one of the central objectives was to establish a chemical fertilizer plant in every county as part of a more general campaign to promote rural industrial development. In the late 1970s, too, some attempts were made to develop power generation in order to help the modernization of agriculture (Shantou SZ 1999: 1233–4). In short, Shantou may have lagged behind other Guangdong prefectures, but we do well to note that its industrial growth rate in the Maoist era surpassed that of most developing countries.

(B) THE RISE OF MAOMING, MEIXIAN AND SHAOGUAN

The main beneficiaries of the Maoist industrialization strategy in Guangdong were the predominantly rural prefectures of Shaoguan and Meixian in the north-west—seven of the eight fastest-growing counties in the 37 county sample for 1965–78 (Appendix 3) were to be found in Shaoguan, Meixian or northern Huiyang—and Zhanjiang in the south-west of the province (Table 10.2). Zhanjiang's rise was driven mainly by the decision to develop Maoming as a centre of oil refining in the mid-1950s. In 1952, Zhanjiang prefecture accounted for less than 5 percent of provincial GVIO and this had increased to only 6 percent in 1957. By 1965, however, its GVIO share was up to 10 percent of the provincial total, or about double its 1952 share. The development of oil refining generated momentum of its own, so much so that Maoming's growth continued to be rapid even in the face of the anti-coastal bias inherent in the Third Front programmes of the late 1960s and 1970s. As Appendix 3 shows, two of the fastest-growing jurisdictions in the 42 county and city sample were Maoming city and nearby Xinyi county, and thus Zhanjiang's share in the provincial total continued to climb, reaching 12.5 percent by 1978. The process culminated in the creation of the municipality of Maoming in 1983 out of the northern part of Zhanjiang—an affirmation of the startling transformation of an area which in the 1950s had been little more than a rural backwater.

The experience of Shaoguan offers a further illuminating example of accelerating *rural* industrialization well before the 1978 watershed.[15] In a strict sense, the growth of the prefecture dates back to World War II, when it was the centre of anti-Japanese resistance by the provincial Guangdong government; the wartime population of Shaoguan city increased no less than fivefold (Vogel 1989: 230). However, the real expansion occurred after 1949. Central to this process was the exploitation of the region's economic geography. Shaoguan is well-endowed with mineral resources such as coal, iron ore, uranium (Bachman 2001: 284), and tungsten (Sun 1959: 109, 164–5). This worked to the prefecture's advantage during the Great Leap Forward, when a decision was taken to develop Shaoguan as a heavy industrial base, and to expand the size of the city by a factor of five (Sun 1959: 168, 174–5).

The key step was the establishment of Shaoguan Iron and Steel in 1958, which later became one of the mainstays of the prefecture's industrial production. This expansion made possible a sevenfold real GVIO increase in the prefecture between 1952 and 1965 (Shaoguan SZ 2001: 362, 482–3 and 487–8), whereas the provincial increase was fourfold (TJJ 1990*b*: 629). By 1965, the prefectural share of heavy industry in GVIO was already as high as 55 percent, compared with a provincial share of 24 percent (GDTJNJ 1990: 177; Shaoguan SZ 2001: 487–8).[16] Of course this rapid development was not surprising in a statistical sense; Shaoguan's industrial base was almost non-existent in 1952. Nevertheless, it is clear that industrialization in the prefecture dates from the 1950s, and equally evident that heavy industry was the engine of growth. This latter makes Shaoguan's experience unusual by international standards; the Rostowian

---

[15] Shaoguan here refers to those jurisdictions included within the prefecture in the early 1980s. These were Shaoguan city proper and the counties of Qujiang, Lechang, Renhua, Nanxiong, Shixing, Wengyuan, Fogang, Yingde, Qingyuan, Yangshan, Lianshan, Liannan, Lianxian and Ruyuan.

[16] Shares are calculated in both cases at 1980 prices. The provincial data in the original source are at 1957 prices. I have converted these to 1980 prices using the provincial GVIO deflator (TJJ 1990*b*: 629) and the national heavy industry deflator (TJNJ 1985: 309). The use of 1957 prices would raise the heavy industry share for both province and prefecture. In both cases, the GVIO data are for commune-level enterprises and above.

'textiles first' route is the recommended strategy, especially for a poor rural area. In Maoist China, however, Shaoguan's experience was almost the norm.

Further impetus was provided to Shaoguan's development when the prefecture was singled out as the centre for the province's little Third Front after 1964, and indeed as a key part of the Huanan heavy industrial base (Vogel 1989: 229–32; Bachman 2001; Shaoguan SZ 2001: 477–8). Its selection reflected both Shaoguan's mineral base and, as importantly, the military advantages inherent in its mountainous topography. By the mid-1960s, this new phase of industrialization was well underway. A number of Delta-based factories were moved to Shaoguan, and a big increase in investment designed to create infrastructure and to develop new factories took place; some 1.4 billion *yuan* was invested in basic construction between 1967 and 1975 (Shaoguan SZ 2001: 467). The result was a continuing expansion of industrial production in this previously backward prefecture. Between 1965 and 1978, industrial output increased almost fivefold. Once again, heavy industry was in the van of the advance, so much so that its share in GVIO had risen to a remarkable 73 percent by 1978. This was well above the median for China's provinces, and on a par with the shares being recorded in Ningxia, Heilongjiang and Liaoning provinces. Shaoguan had not quite reached the heights achieved in Gansu (where the 1978 share of heavy industry was a heady 82 percent), but it is very evident that the prefecture was one of the pre-eminent centres of heavy industry during the Maoist era.[17] By 1978, indeed, the prefecture was producing 39 percent of Guangdong's iron and steel, 29 percent of electricity, 55 percent of its coal and 17 percent of its cement. Shaoguan Iron and Steel alone accounted for about a quarter of the province's steel-making capacity by 1978 (GDFZ 1990: 94–9, 108–22, 130). Any notion, then, that Guangdong was essentially unaffected by Maoist industrialization is flatly contradicted by the Shaoguan evidence.

It would be equally wrong to assume that Shaoguan's industrialization was confined to its urban core. To be sure, Shaoguan city was the single most important centre of industrial production in the prefecture (Table 10.3). In 1980, the city's GVIO per head stood at 2,811 *yuan*, some 15 times the county average; with only 6 percent of the prefecture's population, Shaoguan city nevertheless produced 49 percent of prefectural output (GDZL 1991). However, one of the salient features of Maoist industrialization in the prefecture

[17] Metallurgy was the largest single industrial subsector in Shaoguan by 1978 (contributing 24 percent of GVIO), followed by machinery (16 percent). The main loser in percentage terms during the Maoist era was the food processing industry, which saw its share decline from 32 percent in 1957 to 10 percent in 1978. For all that, the fastest-growing subsector between 1965 and 1978 was actually textiles. Its share in GVIO was only 6 percent in 1978, but its output increased by a factor of 18 between 1965 and 1978 compared with an overall industrial increase which was sixfold. Admittedly this was in part because textile prices declined very little in the 1960s and 1970s, but the trend is still clear enough to conclude that even Shaoguan's light industrial sector experienced considerable modernization in the late Maoist era (Shaoguan SZ 2001: 486–7).

Table 10.3 Rural industrialization in Maoist Shaoguan

	Growth of real GVIO 1965–78 (percent; 1980 prices)	GVIO per capita in 1980 (*yuan*; 1980 prices)	Share of heavy industry (percent)
Nanxiong	8.1	142	43
Wengyuan	12.9	110	48
Qingyuan	8.1	160	38
Liannan	15.6	171	75
Lechang	15.6	391	47
Ruyuan	16.0	258	77
Shaoguan counties	n.a.	188	54
Shaoguan city	n.a.	2,811	76
All Shaoguan	14.3	347	65

Notes: The aggregate figures for Shaoguan's counties refer here to all counties in the prefecture and not just those in the sample. GVIO growth rates calculated by OLS.

Sources: Nanxiong XZ (1991: 124); GDZL (1991); Lechang XZ (1994: 204–5); Qingyuan XZ (1995: 307); Liannan XZ (1996: 273–4); Ruyuan XZ (1997: 311); Wengyuan XZ (1997: 119–20); Shaoguan SZ (2001: 482–3).

was the development of rural industry. The very fact that the data in Table 10.3 show that the six counties industrialized as rapidly as the prefectural average demonstrates that Shaoguan's growth was not driven merely by its urban core. The source of this rural dynamism was the Third Front. There are many examples. In Ruyuan, industrialization focused on the expansion of power generation, and this subsector contributed over 50 percent of the county's GVIO by the late 1970s (Ruyuan XZ 1997: 311). In Lechang, much of the impetus for industrialization came from the re-location of factories producing weapons, agricultural machinery and metal products, and which were owned by central government ministries or the provincial government, into the county; almost half of all GVIO in Lechang was produced in these factories by 1976. An even more telling indication of the growing dominance of heavy industry in Lechang is that the output of the Second Light Industry Bureau increased by only about 20 percent between 1965 and 1976, whereas total GVIO increased 5.5 fold over the same period (Lechang XZ 1994: 201, 204–5).[18]

Not every county grew as quickly as Ruyuan or Lechang. Table 10.3 shows that the rates of industrialization achieved in Nanxiong and Qingyuan were almost funereal by comparison, seemingly because of limited heavy industrial growth. For example, Qingyuan's economy was much more light industry orientated than the norm: the share of light industry in its GVIO was fully 62 percent in 1978, little changed from 67 percent share recorded in 1965 and by some way the highest of any county in the sample (Qingyuan XZ 1995: 307).[19] Nanxiong's

---

[18] The Ministry of Handicraft Industry was re-named as the Second Ministry for Light Industry in the mid-1960s to reflect the progressive technological upgrading of the handicraft industries under its jurisdiction.

[19] In some respects, Qingyuan had more in common with the counties of the Delta, and it was in fact classified by the State Council as belonging to the Greater Delta in November 1987. Not

industrial production was also dominated by consumer good production. In the Republican era, the county was Guangdong's second-biggest tobacco producer (Remick 2004: 47–8) and the production of tobacco and cigarettes dominated industrial output in the Maoist era. Booming consumer demand helped the county after 1978, but its relatively undiversified and light industry-geared industrial sector put it at a disadvantage in the 1960s and 1970s. Only those counties singled out as centres for heavy industry prospered in the late Maoist period, whether in Shaoguan or elsewhere.

Meixian prefecture, home to a large Hakka population, was by some distance the poorest region within Guangdong in 1949. In an advanced Delta county like Shunde, industrial output stood at about 25 percent of agricultural output in 1952. In Meixian county itself, and in nearby Dapu, the figure was not very different (Dapu XZ 1992: 119; Mei XZ 1994: 371–2).[20] But the figures were much lower elsewhere in the prefecture. In Jiaoling, for example, the industry share was just 20 percent, and it was only 10 percent in Pingyuan; in Wuhua, the share was barely 18 percent even as late as 1957 (Wuhua XZ 1991: 112; Jiaoling XZ 1992: 118–19; Pingyuan XZ 1993: 781–2).

All this began to change after 1952. Although Meixian is portrayed by Vogel (1989: 245) and Ku (2003) as having experienced little industrialization in the Maoist era, the data reveal a different story. Between 1952 and 1965, for example, the industrial growth rate averaged close to 10 percent, a phenomenal figure by international standards (Table 10.2). Much of the impetus came from the Great Leap Forward, when work began on the construction of an iron and steel base (Sun 1959: 159). Thereafter, the focus of development remained on heavy industry, with the output destined mainly for consumption in Shantou (to which Meixian prefecture previously belonged). Not surprisingly, therefore, the data reveal very big increases in the production of cement, timber and coal. Output of the latter, concentrated in Meixian, Jiaoling and Wuhua, was in fact so large that the prefecture was producing almost a quarter of provincial output by 1978 (GDFZ 1990: 112). Power generation, based on coal and hydropower, also expanded quickly.

Thus, although Shaoguan was undoubtedly the centre of heavy industrial production in the province, Meixian was also a significant producer by the late 1970s.[21] It did not grow as quickly as Shaoguan, but its industrial sector certainly

only was it light industry-orientated but also its location (close to Guangzhou city) made it a much less suitable centre for Third Front production. These locational and historical factors help to explain why Qingyuan—along with several other counties (Yingde, Fogang, Lianshan, Liannan, Lianxian and Yangshan) located in southern and south-western Shaoguan—was detached to form a new Qingyuan prefecture in the mid-1980s.

[20] This was one reason why part of Meixian was removed from the county to create Meizhou city.

[21] There is also evidence of industrialization in northern Huiyang, the very poor region which became Heyuan prefecture in the late 1980s. In Longchuan, one of the poorest counties in the whole province, industrial GVIO increased at a rate of nearly 19 percent per year between

out-performed those located in Foshan, Maoming and rural Guangzhou. The scale of industrialization is also apparent from the relative decline of agricultural production; as a percentage of GVAO, gross industrial output had climbed to 51 percent in Pingyuan, 58 percent in Wuhua, 97 percent in Dapu and 140 percent in Jiaoling. By 1980, the prefecture's level of industrialization was still below the provincial average (and less than half that achieved in Foshan), but Meixian had nevertheless made significant strides in the Maoist era.

The net effect of these herculean efforts was a significant alteration in Guangdong's industrial geography. Production in Shantou and in the Delta did not stagnate, but the Maoist era was evidently one during which the locus of industrial growth shifted firmly towards Guangdong's previously under-developed periphery: Zhanjiang and Maoming on the province's west wing, and Shaoguan and Meixian to the east, were the main gainers from the process.[22]

10.3.5. Maoist Industrial Legacies

It is important not to exaggerate the extent of Guangdong's industrial develop-ment under Mao. Industrial employment rates in rural areas tell part of the story; with a rate of 11.6 percent in 1982, the province lagged behind neighbour-ing Fujian (14.4 percent), the Manchurian provinces (all of which exceeded 16 percent), Jiangsu (19.1 percent) and, most striking of all, Zhejiang province (25.9 percent). Furthermore, the spatial transformation of industrial production accomplished under Mao was rather limited. Despite their neglect during much of the Maoist era, the coastal prefectures of Shantou, Guangzhou, Foshan and Huiyang still accounted for 76 percent of industrial value-added in 1980, despite being home to only 56 percent of the province's population. This imbalance in part reflected the continuing dominance of Guangzhou city itself. However, even the county-level jurisdictions of the Delta, which were home to only 30 percent of Guangdong's population, contributed fully 46 percent of provincial industrial production. Rural Foshan alone produced 28 percent of industrial value-added even though it accounted for only 14 percent of total population. The converse of the high level of development achieved in the Delta was the continuing under-development of much of Guangdong's periphery. Despite the Third Front, the Meixian-Heyuan-Shaoguan-Shantou region remained very

1965 and 1978, the fastest of any county in the sample of counties in Appendix 3. In one sense this is misleading because the rapid growth rate reflected the construction of a vast hydropower complex at Gangshuba, the second largest in the province in 1974. Nevertheless, this one project undoubtedly had the effect of vastly improving the prospects of the county in the longer run. In the late 1970s, Longchuan was an extremely poor county; distributed collective income was below 50 *yuan* in every year between 1975 and 1979 (Longchuan XZ 1994: 487). By the new millennium, however, Longchuan was no longer officially classified as one of China's 592 poor counties.

[22] This 'west wing' (*xiyi*) and 'east wing' (*dongyi*) terminology features prominently in recent government publications.

poor by national standards. The national list of officially-designated poor counties drawn up for the province in 1986 by the State Council's *Office of the Leading Group for Economic Development in Poor Areas* reflected this. Every one of the seven Meixian counties were included in this list of 24 counties as being poor, and a further five were located in and around Heyuan, the area adjacent to Meixian. Five of Shaoguan's counties were also on this list, as were three counties located in Shantou (NCGY 1989: 639–43; OLG 1989). In short, 21 of Guangdong's 24 poor counties were in the northern part of the province, the very region which had been the focus of Third Front construction. Neither Maoist development (nor the agricultural miracle of 1976–84) had served to eradicate poverty on Guangdong's east wing.

And yet the degree of progress made under Mao was palpable. Firstly, and in stark contrast to the situation in 1949, a heavy industrial base was well-established in the province. Guangdong's production was still more orientated towards light industry than elsewhere in China, but its industrial structure was very different to that of 1949. Secondly, Guangdong's little Third Front programme did have the effect of altering the spatial distribution of industrial production. The share of the northern and central coastal region (Shantou, Huiyang and the Delta) declined from 80 percent of provincial GVIO in 1965 to 74 percent in 1980, whereas the significance of the northern mountainous region (Meixian and Shaoguan) increased from 7 to 10 percent (GDFZ 1990).[23] The coastal region continued to dominate industrial production, but its dominance was much less than it had been in the early 1950s. Thirdly, rural industrialization was firmly underway by the late 1970s. Early Maoist industrialization may have focused on the development of urban industrial sectors but industrial growth accelerated across rural Guangdong after the mid-1960s. This process affected not only the Delta counties, the pre-Revolutionary centre of Guangdong's rural industry (such as it was), but also those of the peripheral mountainous region where rural industry was often barely established in the early 1950s. State-owned industry was typically the mainstay of the rural industrialization process, but commune and brigade industry assumed increasing importance by the mid-1970s. Finally, Guangdong's rate of rural industrial employment in 1982 placed it well ahead of provinces such as Guizhou (3.5 percent), Gansu (4.8 percent) and Henan (4.1 percent). Guangdong was not China's most industrialized province at the time of Mao's death, but it entered the post-Mao era with a substantial industrial base, not least in rural areas. Any notion, therefore, that rural industrial development in Guangdong only began in a serious way after 1978 is contradicted by the evidence.

---

[23] The coastal share of net industrial output was approximately the same as its GVIO share. Although value-added was higher in heavy than in light industry, the dominance of heavy industry in Guangzhou city proper offset the dominance of light industry in Foshan and Shantou. However, the heavy industry orientation of the north raised its share from 10 percent of GVIO to 12 percent of provincial NVIO in 1980 (estimated from GDZL 1991).

10.4. The Expansion of Rural Education and Skills

The development of industry across Guangdong was paralleled by an expansion of education, such that the level of education amongst Guangdong's rural population was not only higher than in Zhejiang and Jiangsu, but one of the highest in China by the time of the 1982 Population Census (TJJ 1988). At 77.2 percent, the average literacy rate for Guangdong's counties was higher than for every Chinese province except Liaoning (80 percent). In this sense at least, rural Guangdong entered the transition era with an immeasurable advantage over other parts of the People's Republic. Furthermore, the official data suggest that this increase in literacy was very much a post-1949 phenomenon. In 1952, barely 12 percent of the population had a primary education or better, whereas by 1982 the figure was around 65 percent (GDRKZ 1995: 90, 109). Enrolment data show a similar upward trend. In 1957, the provincial enrolment rate for the cohort of children of school age stood at almost 60 percent; by 1982, this had increased to 96 percent by 1978 (GDRKZ 1995: 94).

A more detailed examination of post-1949 trends suggests that substantial progress was made by poor prefectures such as Meixian and Shaoguan. In Wuhua county (Meixian), the number of those with an upper middle school education increased from 8,800 in 1964 to 64,000 in 1982 (Wuhua XZ 1991: 582). In Dapu, the number increased from 6,000 to 42,000 over the same period (Dapu XZ 1992: 101). By 1982, Meixian was actually one of the leading prefectures in the country in terms of education. At 83 percent, its literacy rate was substantially above the 77 percent rural average for Guangdong, even though its per capita industrial output was comparatively low (65 *yuan* compared with the provincial average of 80 *yuan*). In terms of formal education at least, Meixian entered the transition era well placed, and according to Peterson (1994*a*: 937), this was primarily because 'Poverty drove Meixian villagers to seek livelihoods through education.'

Neighbouring Shaoguan also appears to have made considerable progress. In Qingyuan county, the total number of illiterates aged 12 and over fell from 283,000 in 1947 to 221,000 in 1964, and to 162,000 by 1982; over the same time period, the county's total population almost doubled (Qingyuan XZ 1995: 140, 147). In Lechang, the proportion of illiterates fell from 36 percent in 1964 to 21 percent in 1982, far below the 1947 rate of 53 percent (Lechang XZ 1994: 109). In Ruyuan, the number of illiterates declined from 71,000 in 1941 to 49,000 by 1982 (Ruyuan XZ 1997: 173–4). The more systematic data available in the *Municipal Records* (Table 10.4) point firmly in the same direction: every county in Shaoguan recorded a large reduction in illiteracy between the 1964 and 1982 Censuses.

Detailed consideration of these Shaoguan data, however, points to a more complex story. For one thing, the county-level data are hard to interpret. The pre-1949 figures typically do not specify which age group is referred to, and

Table 10.4 Illiteracy rates in Shaoguan prefecture, 1964–82 (counties ranked by 1964 illiteracy rate)

	1964 (percent)	1982 (percent)	Change (percentage points)
Shaoguan city	25	9	−16
Qujiang	29	18	−11
Wengyuan	31	17	−14
Shixing	32	17	−15
Lianshan	32	15	−17
Lianxian	33	17	−16
Renhua	35	18	−17
Lechang	36	21	−15
Nanxiong	36	23	−13
Yingde	36	21	−15
Qingyuan	37	18	−19
Liannan	38	19	−19
Yangshan	39	21	−18
Ruyuan	41	23	−18
All Shaoguan	35	19	−16
Shaoguan Counties	35	20	−15

Note: The rates here are calculated as illiterates aged 12 and over as percentage of total population. These figures therefore under-state the true illiteracy rate because they use total population as the denominator, rather than the population aged 12 and over (for which no county-level data are available).

Sources: Qingyuan XZ (1995: 145, 147); TJJ (1988: 358–60, 638–43); Shaoguan SZ (2001: 369, 410–11).

the post-1949 data in several of the *County Records* contrast a 12 and over illiteracy rate in 1964, with a 15 and over illiteracy rate in 1982. In any case, even the official data show that the rate of increase of literacy in Shaoguan was only a little better than the provincial average. As a result, the average illiteracy rate amongst Shaoguan's counties (25 percent) was still above the provincial average of 23 percent in 1982 (TJJ 1988). This is a rather surprising outcome given that per capita net industrial output in the prefecture was well above the provincial average. It suggests that the emphasis placed on developing Shaoguan as a centre of Third Front industry did not extend to levels of education. Education was not ignored, but it is clear that the Maoist emphasis in Guangdong was on industrialization, rather than development broadly conceived.

A second more general qualification centres on the under-statement of the pre-1949 educational inheritance in Maoist accounts. As Peterson (1994*a*: 928) points out, there were no less than 30,000 modern primary schools in the province in 1949 and the rate of enrolment achieved was second only to Hebei and Shandong. Although only 30 percent of the cohort were enrolled in primary school, a similar number seem to have been enrolled in *sishu*, the traditional private schools. As is pointed out by Pepper (1996: 77): '. . . Statistics . . . never included data on such schools. They were synonymous with the Dark Ages for early modernizing intellectuals and ignored by the creators of the new school system'. The true extent of educational attainment pre-1949 was thus higher than modernizing intellectuals and CCP officials were prepared to admit. One clear implication is that the apparent improvement in enrolment rates in the Maoist era reflected little more than a substitution of modern primary education for traditional *sishu* education, rather than an increase in the total volume of education. One might even argue that the *minban* (local community or people's schools) were little more than *sishu* schools teaching a Communist rather than a Confucian orthodoxy.

A third problem relates to the quality of post-1949 schooling. Peterson (1994*a*, *b*) argues that the focus in Guangdong, as elsewhere in China, was on the promotion of a narrowly vocational education in rural areas, one which was designed to equip students with the skills needed to run a production team but little else. For example, collectivization increased the demand for education but at the same time skewed that pattern of demand towards a very narrow curriculum. This in turn, he argues, limited the social mobility of the rural population—and, by implication, may not have provided the wider education needed to manage and develop rural industry. These general problems were intensified in Guangdong's case by central attempts to privilege Mandarin Chinese over both local dialects and Cantonese. Particular problems arose over whether children should be taught dialect-based *pinyin* or *hanyu pinyin* (Peterson 1994*b*: 933–4). In practice, social and political advancement required a knowledge of *hanyu pinyin* and this tended to penalize poor rural areas where it was easier to teach dialect-based *pinyin*. It has also been suggested that, because private commerce and industry in the Delta counties increased the demand for education before 1949, the suppression of the private sector under Mao actually discouraged educational participation. For Peterson (1994*a*: 937–40), however, this decline was offset by the increased demand for education generated by inter-prefectural trade.

Of course the development of human capital within Guangdong was not confined to the expansion of formal education. The *shangshan xiaxiang* campaign also had a significant effect in rural areas. Between 1962 and 1974, some 580,000 young people were 'sent down' from urban centres to the countryside, with 1968 (176,000) being the peak year. These newcomers supplemented the ranks of the 29,000 cadres sent to the countryside between 1966 and 1970 (GDRKZ 1995: 67–8). The poorest regions within Guangdong were the principal beneficiaries. Indeed without an influx of skilled labour, the industrialization of Shaoguan would have been impossible.

We are left with the conclusion that Guangdong's record on educational development between 1949 and 1978 was rather mixed. The province entered the transition era with one of the highest levels of attainment of any province, and a clear implication is that this prior expansion of primary education may help to explain why Guangdong outpaced other parts of China in its development of rural industry during the 1980s and 1990s. However, there is also evidence of significant regional variation; insofar as policy aimed at reducing spatial inequalities, the inequalities to be narrowed were those in per capita income rather than educational outcomes. For all the attempts to develop Shaoguan, it was to be Meixian and the Delta counties—alike in the neglect they suffered under Mao—which entered the transition era with a far superior educational foundation.

10.5. Rural Industrialization after 1978

It has been demonstrated in the previous section that Guangdong inherited an extensive industrial legacy from the Maoist era. By dint of an extraordinary mobilization of the labour force, and high levels of investment in both education and Third Front programmes, Guangdong possessed a significant manufacturing capability at the dawn of the 1980s. It remains to evaluate the significance of these legacies for subsequent growth.

On this point, the literature is rather dismissive. Four lines of criticism feature in the writings of scholars such as Bachman (2001) and Vogel (1989). Firstly, it is argued, much of the industry established in northern Guangdong was inefficient. For example, Shaoguan's steel plants were almost all loss-making in the late 1970s. They therefore constituted a drain on resources, rather than a springboard for expansion. Secondly, insofar as industrial capability had developed in areas like Shaoguan and Meixian, the inheritance was quickly dissipated by the out-migration of skilled labour. This reflected both the reversal of the sending down process and the development of labour markets in the Delta and in Guangdong's cities. Such labour migration ensured that post-1978 rural industrialization in the province was not path dependent in any meaningful sense; the interior prefectures very quickly suffered the dissipation of their inheritance. Thirdly, *gaige kaifang* offered Delta counties such as Dongguan and Shunde new markets for textiles, garments and electronics. As all these goods could be produced with unskilled labour and because the Delta was an attractive destination for unskilled peasant labour resident in central and western China, the absence of a significant Maoist inheritance of heavy industry was no impediment to industrial growth. A labour force skilled in defence and heavy industrial production was if anything a handicap in exploiting these lucrative market opportunities. Fourthly, the proximity of Hong Kong and the ability of the province to attract FDI ensured an alternative supply of skills and technologies. If a Guangdong county had not developed industrial capability under Mao, it could be imported; in that sense, history did not matter.

Some of these arguments contain an element of truth, but most of them are over-stated. Take migration. One of the difficulties with the proposition that out-migration denuded the interior of Guangdong of the skilled labour it needed to develop industry is that much Chinese internal migration, especially from the countryside to the cities, has been temporary rather than permanent. Initial migration out of Chinese counties in the 1980s was largely seasonal until contacts and connections had been established. Even then, there is considerable evidence that the average stay of a migrant in a city like Shanghai was no more than four years (Murphy 2002: 44). A combination of pull factors such as culture, the desire to own property or to exploit investment opportunities, and push factors such as linguistic difficulties—a real issue for many Mandarin-speaking migrants to predominantly Cantonese-speaking Delta counties (Guldin 2001)—legal obstacles and outright discrimination persuaded a majority to return home. Moreover, return migrants may well have enhanced the industrial capability of their home town by bringing back with them skills, capital and a knowledge of urban markets. Furthermore, in so far as prefectures such as Shaoguan and Meixian lost skilled workers to the Delta, these workers may have been replaced by an influx of workers from other parts of China. Shaoguan and Meixian may have been poor by Guangdong standards but they were more affluent than many parts of the Chinese interior and their markets were arguably easier to enter than the crowded and competitive Delta labour market for a migrant from Anhui or Sichuan. In other respects, too, the conventional wisdom is problematic. Shaoguan's enterprises may have been inefficient in the 1970s, but this does not preclude the possibility of longer run learning-based transformation; static inefficiency of itself offers no good test of the infant industry hypothesis. Furthermore, as discussed in a previous chapter, there is much evidence to suggest that industrial productivity was positively correlated with skills, such that skilled labour was much more important for the industries of the Delta than is sometimes suggested.

Ultimately, however, it is an empirical issue as to whether the legacies of the Maoist era acted as a spur to growth; the debate on the extent and impact of labour migration, for example, can only be resolved by recourse to the evidence, not along *a priori* theoretical grounds. And the place to begin any evaluation of the impact of Maoist legacies is with the prefectural evidence.

10.5.1. Patterns of Prefectural Growth after 1978

Even a cursory examination of the prefectural data reveals that the geography of rural industrial expansion was very different after 1978 to that which occurred during the late Maoist era (Table 10.5). Whereas the epicentre of post-1965 industrial growth had been Shaoguan and Maoming, it was the Delta that assumed centre-stage after 1978. In fact, as Table 10.5 shows, Shaoguan's share in provincial NVIO plummeted from 13.5 percent in 1980 to barely 3 percent in 1996. Part of the reason was the out-migration of skilled labour. By 1981, 28,000 of the 29,000 cadres originally sent down into the Guangdong countryside between 1966–70 had already returned to their original work unit (GDRKZ 1995: 68). In Qingyuan county, net out-migration soared from 7,662 in 1997 to 11,589 in 1978 and to 14,425 in 1979, before falling back to around 7,000 by 1982 (Qingyuan XZ 1995: 142). Zhanjiang also suffered a marked decline, and the fall from grace suffered by desperately poor Meixian was equally dramatic. Taken together, this evidence suggests that Maoist industrialization provided little by way of a springboard for future growth.

By contrast, Foshan's share increased by 8 percent points and that of rural Guangzhou by 6 percentage points. Taken as a whole, the share of the Inner Delta counties increased from 37 percent in 1980 to fully 50 percent by 1996, reflecting an industrial growth rate of a remarkable 27 percent. The counties of the Outer Delta industrialized even more rapidly—despite the lack of investment there during the Maoist era.

We need, however, to be careful before concluding that this sort of prefectural evidence demonstrates some form of economic failure in northern Guangdong. For one thing, the rate of industrialization achieved in the northern prefectures even after 1978 was fast enough, and sustained for long enough, to ensure that the worst of the poverty of the late 1970s was eliminated. The Office of the Leading Group identified 24 Guangdong counties as being poor in 1986, but the 2004 classification by the renamed OLG for Poverty Alleviation and Development—which identified 592 poor counties across China—did not include a single Guangdong county in its list (OLG 2004). Whether this was simply a reflection of changes in the poverty line is unclear; a document issued as late as March 1996 by the provincial government identified 28 poverty-stricken counties, of

Table 10.5 Rural industrial growth rates by prefecture in Guangdong, 1980–96 (ranked by growth rates of NVIO per head)

Prefecture	Share in provincial NVIO (percent)		Growth of NVIO per head, 1980–96 (percent per annum)	NVIO per head, 1980 (*yuan*)
	1980	1996		
Guangzhou	6.5	12.8	29.3	94
Foshan	28.1	36.0	27.2	155
Huiyang	10.7	13.2	27.2	75
Zhaoqing	7.8	8.4	27.0	61
Shantou	15.1	16.8	25.2	57
Zhanjiang	11.8	8.1	21.5	51
Meixian	6.6	1.8	17.0	65
Shaoguan	13.5	2.9	13.9	98
Inner Delta	36.5	50.1	27.4	147
Outer Delta	9.1	14.6	28.8	70
The Rest	54.4	35.3	22.0	62
All counties	100.0	100.0	25.0	80

Notes: Prefectural boundaries are those of 1982, and prefectural totals are calculated by summation of county values; cities are excluded. The Inner Delta is defined here as Dongguan, Doumen, Enping, Gaoming, Heshan, Kaiping, Nanhai, Panyu, Sanshui, Shunde, Taishan, Xinhui, Zengcheng and Zhongshan. The Outer Delta counties comprised Boluo, Conghua, Gaoyao, Guangning, Huaxian, Huidong, Huiyang, Qingyuan, and Sihui. The excluded urban jurisdictions located in the Delta were Foshan, Jiangmen, Zhaoqing and Huizhou. Note that Shenzhen, Zhuhai and Guangzhou city are excluded from the official 1987 definition of the Delta. Bao'an, which was incorporated into Shenzhen, is also excluded because the time series data available on its industrial output are inconsistent.
Sources: As for Table 10.7.

which 16 were listed as requiring 'all-out' support (Guangdong Party Commission 1996). But taken at face value (and even the 1996 document stated an expectation that poverty in these counties would be overcome by 1997), the OLG evidence suggests that the policies of the 1980s and 1990s were remarkably effective in alleviating poverty in mountainous areas. Insofar as the Guangdong hinterland suffered decline after 1978, it was only by way of comparison with the extraordinary growth achieved in the Delta. By international standards, even the rate of industrialization attained in Shaoguan was extraordinary.

Secondly, any criticism of the legacy of Maoist industrialization in the north of Guangdong based purely on spatial differences in growth rates is problematic because it ignores the constraints on development imposed by geography: most obviously, the Shaoguan-Heyuan-Meixian region is mainly mountainous and thus enormously disadvantaged relative to the counties of the Delta. It also ignores the statistical handicap imposed by Shaoguan's comparatively well-developed industrial base. To put this another way, Shaoguan and other prefectures might well have grown more slowly still but for their inherited industrial base. Only by normalizing for geography, base levels of per capita industrial production and other factors can we properly isolate the effect of history on post-1978 industrial performance.

The significance of Maoist human capital and industrial legacies in rural Guangdong becomes more apparent when growth rates are explicitly set against initial conditions for rural areas (Table 10.6). At first glance, these growth differentials do not appear capable of explanation in terms of the legacies of the Maoist era. In particular, the industrial employment and literacy rates enjoyed by the fastest ten were only marginally greater than those of the slowest-growing ten. Indeed it appears that the fastest-growing Guangdong counties benefited more from their very industrial backwardness in 1980 (as measured by

Table 10.6 Fast and slow-growing counties in Guangdong, 1978–96

Group	NVIO per capita growth, 1980–96 (percent per year)	Industrial employment, 1982 (percent)	Literacy rate, 1982 (percent)	NVIO per capita, 1980 (yuan)
Slowest ten counties	9	6	74	111
Fastest ten counties	32	9	81	58
Shaoguan prefecture	15	7	75	93
Foshan prefecture	27	13	83	155
Shantou prefecture	25	12	68	57
Rural median	25	8	80	79

Notes: NVIO is measured at 1990 constant prices by aggregating all county values and then dividing by population. Literacy and industrial employment rates are for the median county in each group. The slowest-growing ten counties (bottom up) were Ruyuan, Lianshan, Xuwen, Yingde, Yangshan, Shixing, Longchuan, Heyuan, Lianxian and Liannan. The top ten (the fastest first) were Gaoming, Heshan, Zengcheng, Yunfu, Haifeng, Huidong, Puning, Kaiping, Sanshui and Enping.
Sources: GDZL (1991); GDTJNJ (1992, 1993, 1994, 1995 and 1997).

per capita NVIO) than from their human capital inheritance. Geography also appears to have been more closely correlated with growth than Maoist legacies. Of the bottom ten counties, no fewer than seven were located in mountainous Shaoguan, two in mountainous northern Huiyang (Heyuan and Longchuan) and one (Xuwen) in the extreme south of the province, far removed from Guangzhou city, Hong Kong and Shenzhen. By contrast, seven of the fastest-growing counties were located in the Delta. Kaiping offers a fairly typical example. Although the county benefited from its inherited industrial base, the mainspring of growth appears to have been foreign capital and links with Hong Kong (Remick 2004: 152–3). Of the fast-growing counties outside the Delta, Haifeng is a coastal county, Puning is close to the Shantou special economic zone, and Yunfu benefited both from being a marble producer and its proximity to Zhaoqing city.

The significance of geography and human capital becomes more apparent when we compare the industrialization trajectories of (delta) Foshan, (coastal) Shantou and (mountainous) Shaoguan prefectures. Although Foshan was disadvantaged by its high level of per capita industrial output in 1980, it was favourably placed in terms of both human capital and location to grow quickly after 1978. By contrast, Shaoguan was handicapped. Its human capital endowment was less than the provincial average, it had a relatively high level of industrial output per head, and it was unfavourably located in the mountainous region in the northern part of the province. In addition, the emphasis on the development of capital-intensive heavy industry meant only a comparatively small proportion of its population had gained experience of industrial employment. Taken together, this constellation of factors explains why Shaoguan grew less quickly than Foshan after 1978. The Maoist development strategy may have improved Shaoguan's standing, but it was not enough to *transform* its prospects.

As for Shantou, its experience after 1978 suggests *inter alia* that Maoist emphasis on the expansion of rural education was of little instrumental significance. This is because Shantou achieved rapid industrialization even though it entered the transition era with the lowest literacy rate of any Guangdong prefecture. More precisely, other factors seem to have trumped education. In Shantou's case, its coastal location attracted export-orientated inward investment. Secondly, and more importantly, Shantou's high rate of industrial employment meant that it possessed a deep reservoir of skilled labour by the early 1980s. Shantou city proper and Chaozhou city both had large manufacturing sectors. 36 percent of Shantou's workforce was employed in manufacturing and no less than 58 percent in the case of Chaozhou. But many of Shantou's counties also had large manufacturing workforces despite the Maoist neglect of the prefecture. Of Chao'an labour force 39 percent was employed in manufacturing in 1982, and the rate exceeded 20 percent in four other Shantou counties (Shantou SZ 1999: 465). In short, Shantou's workers may not have been producing much, but a large number of them had experience of industrial employment at the start of the transition era. Shantou's well-developed light industrial sector, and the high rates of employment this involved, thus gave it an advantage over heavy industry-orientated Shaoguan. That the prefecture did not grow as quickly as Foshan despite enjoying a much lower base level of output suggests that Shantou was locationally disadvantaged. The prefecture was home to a special economic zone and enjoyed a coastal location, but the evidence here suggests that proximity to Hong Kong and Guangzhou were much more important.

This type of prefectural-level analysis tells us a good deal. It suggests that formal education was less important for industrial development in rural Guangdong than either the level of industrial employment, or the initial level of industrial output per head. However, the most obvious feature of Table 10.6 is the apparent correlation between growth rates and geography. Even if human capital legacies assisted the growth process, it seems from these data that it was geography which was decisive.

10.5.2. Analysis

The analysis offered in the previous section is, however, far too aggregated to be conclusive; we need to examine the county data more systematically. More importantly, we need to normalize for all other variables to identify the impact of any one of them, and that points to a need for more formal regression analysis using the complete Guangdong dataset.

Table 10.7 summarizes the regression results for Guangdong county-level data. Here the set-up mirrors that of previous chapters. The independent variables initially employed are level indicators in order to avoid exogeneity problems, and the central aim is to test whether Maoist industrial and human capital legacies contributed positively to growth when geographical factors are allowed for. I then widen the analysis to incorporate inward investment, a variable which cannot really be ignored in Guangdong's case even though it creates endogeneity problems. The time period chosen (1980–96) reflects two considerations. Firstly, systematic county-level data for 1978 on industrial output have proven to be unobtainable, whereas comprehensive data exist for every year from 1980 to 1989. These have been supplemented for subsequent years by the data contained in successive issues of the provincial *Statistical Yearbook*, thus producing a complete time series on industrial output. Secondly, there is no doubt that the Asian crisis of 1997–98 had an important but differential impact across the province, and that the inclusion of data for these years would distort the underlying pattern of growth. For this reason it seems appropriate to take the analysis no further than 1996.

The first set of results for Guangdong is shown under equation (1). The results accord with those observed in previous chapters. For example, the grain yield had an insignificant influence on rural industrialization, whereas both the initial level of industrial output per head and proximity to the provincial capital

Table 10.7 Regression results for Guangdong, 1980–96 (dependent variable is growth of net industrial output per capita)

Variable	Equation			
(1982 unless stated)	(1)	(2)	(3)	
			Unstandardized	Standardized
NVIO per head (1980)	−0.073	−0.078	−0.078	−0.721
	(−6.90)	(−7.95)	(−9.06)	
Industrial employment rate	0.021	0.026	0.044	0.416
	(1.73)	(2.26)	(5.10)	
Dependency rate	−0.192	−0.172		
	(−1.74)	(−1.69)		
Literacy rate	0.039	0.031		
	(0.81)	(0.71)		
Grain yield	0.025	0.030		
	(0.68)	(0.91)		
Distance (Shenzhen)	0.006	0.007		
	(0.29)	(0.39)		
Distance (Guangzhou)	−0.076	−0.058	−0.054	−0.356
	(−3.95)	(−3.20)	(−4.72)	
Population density	0.027	0.008		
	(2.67)	(0.71)		
Capital inflow (1986–90)		0.011	0.015	0.424
		(3.63)	(5.51)	
Adjusted R²	0.67	0.72	0.69	0.69
Number of counties	74	74	74	74

Notes: (a) t statistics in parentheses. All variables are in logarithmic form. (b) Equation (1) is for all rural jurisdictions (as defined in the 1982 Population Census) and all independent variables except foreign capital. Equation (2) repeats equation (1) but adds foreign capital. Equation (3) re-computes equation (2), but excludes those variables which were obviously insignificant in equation (2). (c) 'Dependency rate' is the proportion of the population aged under 15 and over 64. (d) 'Grain yield' is output in 1982 divided by grain sown area in 1982. For some counties, the 1982 data in the *Liangshi zhi* seem unreliable. They appear to show an increase in grain-sown area between 1982 and 1987 (which is not very plausible) as well as very different yields when compared with the *Gaiyao* 1987 data. In such cases, 1982 output data have been used with 1987 grain sown area. However, the overall results are not sensitive to changes in the year used for the grain yield; the data for neither 1982 nor 1987 are significant. (e) 'Population density' is persons per square kilometre. (f) 'Industrial employment rate' is the proportion of the population employed in all types of industry as a percentage of the total workforce. (g) 'Literacy rate' is for the population aged 12 and over. (h) NVIO per head is net industrial output value at 1990 prices and has been calculated using 1993 value-added ratios. These ratios are consistent (though rather lower) than those for township and above independent accounting enterprises at the time of the 1985 Industrial Census. NVIO includes all types of industry after 1983 but omits (as is the case with almost all Chinese data) sub-village industries for 1983 and earlier; however, production in the sub-village subsector was small during this period. Experimentation reveals that the results are not sensitive to the use of 1980 or 1982 as the base year. I have used 1980 as the base because it gives a longer time series for the growth rate. (i) 'Foreign capital inflow' is the median value of actual (not contracted) capital inflow for 1986–1990 measured in US$. This measure includes all types of foreign capital, not just FDI (for which separate data are not readily available). The use of the median value avoids the distortion caused by year-on-year fluctuations; these were typically large for Guangdong's least developed counties. The choice of 1986–1990 is a little arbitrary. There is no case for using pre-1986 data because FDI flows prior to that year are both small and highly volatile. But whether we use 1986–1990 or post-1990 data does not seem to matter much because the spatial pattern of FDI flows was essentially the same; the bulk of FDI went into the Delta counties in both sub-periods. (j) Bao'an, Lechang and Huiyang counties are excluded from all equations because of data distortions caused by boundary changes.

Sources: Shouce (1987); TJJ (1988); NCGY (1989); GDZL (1991); GDTJNJ (1992: 476–8; 1994: 425–33, 446–9; 1997: 290, 558–61); GDLSZ (1996).

are significant and have the expected (negative) sign. It is interesting that proximity to Guangzhou was more important than proximity to the Shenzhen Special Economic Zone as a factor influencing growth even though this latter was the focus of inward investment. This result no doubt reflects the sheer size of the provincial capital; Guangdong's population was ten times that of Shenzhen's in the early 1980s, and the differential in per capita industrial output was similar. By contrast, though largely in line with the results in previous chapters, literacy played little of a growth-inducing role; the ascendancy of the Delta in the post-Mao era was not based upon the prior development of primary education. This supports what has been previously noted in the case of Shantou, and the contention of those, like Peterson, who have argued that Maoist attempts to promote the expansion of a rather narrowly defined notion of literacy did little to promote development.

There are, however, some unexpected results in Table 10.7. The first is that the level of industrial employment is not significant as a determinant of industrial growth in rural Guangdong: equation (1) shows that the coefficient has the right (positive) sign but it is not significant. This result does not appear to have been driven by the factors discussed in the earlier chapter on Jiangsu. The *kotadesa* argument is less strong on *prima facie* grounds for Guangdong than for Jiangsu because the distinction between rural and urban areas was much clearer in Guangdong. In any case, the inclusion of officially-designated urban jurisdictions in the sample does not alter the results; initial industrial employment remains insignificant. I have also experimented with the removal of prefectures from the sample to determine whether any of Guangdong's prefectures operated as an outlier, but here too the results obtained in equation (1) are not sensitive to these exclusions. The finding that initial industrial employment was not a significant determinant of subsequent industrial growth in Guangdong thus appears robust, and as such contradicts the results summarized elsewhere in this book.

However, the apparent insignificance of industrial employment is not borne out by closer analysis. In fact, the insignificance of the variable seems to stem from the mis-specification of equation (1). That there is a mis-specification is hinted at by the apparent significance of population density in the equation. Previous regressions determined that it was either insignificant (the all-China regression), or had a negative influence on the growth rate (in the cases of Jiangsu and Sichuan). It could of course be that Guangdong was unusual in this regard, but it is unlikely; a large number of econometric studies on the relationship between population density and economic growth have concluded that there is no causal relationship between the two, and there is no good reason to suppose that Guangdong is unique. The most plausible explanation for Guangdong's anomalous status is probably that the population density variable is picking up the effect of other factors. In particular, population density in equation (1) may well be serving as a proxy for the impact of foreign capital, which tended to flow to high density jurisdictions because they offered both a large market and, perhaps more importantly, a large labour force. This suggests that, even though there is a potential exogeneity problem—does industrial growth cause foreign capital inflow, or foreign capital inflow cause industrial growth?—the mis-specification dangers caused by excluding it may be even greater.

This argument for the inclusion of foreign capital in the Guangdong regression is of course reinforced by its scale. Whereas other Chinese provinces attracted modest amounts of inward investment, this was certainly not true of Guangdong. Of all foreign capital flowing into China 45 percent went to Guangdong in 1990, 29 percent in 1993 and 28 percent even in 1996 (TJJ 1995: 288–9; TJNJ 1997: 608). With the province accounting for only about 6 percent of the national population, Guangdong's position as a magnet for capital inflows is very evident. Furthermore, many scholars have pointed to the role played by FDI in driving growth in Guangdong, not least because it provided the basis for the creation of an export-orientated industrial sector. Whereas the impact of capital inflow up to the mid-1990s in most Chinese provinces must have been limited simply because the quantities involved were so small, we can make no such simplifying assumption for Guangdong.

This conclusion that FDI is simply too important to ignore in Guangdong's case is supported by the finding that, if we exclude population density (and continue to exclude inward investment), industrial employment becomes a much more significant influence on growth rates. In other words, in the absence of population, it is industrial employment which picks up the impact of foreign capital inflow. This is as one might expect (inward investment would be attracted to jurisdictions with a large industrial workforce). However, this is conjecture. A better method is to include foreign capital as an independent variable in its own right, and this is the approach taken in equation (2), which includes the median value of foreign capital inflow by county for 1986–90 as an independent variable.

The result obtained by estimating equation (2) are very much in line with those obtained in previous chapters. When we control for capital inflows, the initial level of industrial employment in the early 1980s emerges as a statistically significant positive influence on the pace and pattern of industrial growth in the 1980s and 1990s. That equation (1) was mis-specified is now very apparent. Once we include capital inflow, population density is no longer a statistically significant influence on rural industrialization rates. More generally, the results generated by the estimation of equation (2) are remarkable. Despite massive movements of migrant labour, and equally massive flows of inward investment, there is clear evidence that the Maoist legacy of manufacturing capability played a statistically significant role in driving the growth of Guangdong during the 1980s and 1990s. To be sure, foreign capital inflows were a growth-promoting factor, but it seems to be the *combination* of foreign capital inflow, proximity to the provincial capital (which is one measure of 'geography') and inherited industrial skills which explains spatial differences in growth rates. And once we clear away the statistically insignificant variables, the role played by these factors becomes even clearer, as equation (3) shows. Taken together, the independent variables incorporated into equation (3) seem to explain some 70 percent of the variation in rural industrial growth rates (as measured by the standardized coefficients).

This econometric evidence thus suggests that the long run impact of the expansion of manufacturing capability during the Maoist era in Guangdong was profound. Favourable geography, the ability to attract FDI and a low base level of per capital industrial output all played their part in Guangdong's post-1978 industrial success. Nevertheless, as the standardized coefficient on the 1982 industrial employment rate shows, the prior development of rural industry mattered enormously. Dongguan offers an excellent example. It attracted an enormous volume of inward investment, and that alone seems superficially to offer a complete explanation of growth. Yet it must also be remembered that Dongguan already boasted an industrial employment rate of over 21 percent at the time of the 1982 Population Census, a rate which was far above the provincial average. It was not inward investment that created manufacturing capability in Dongguan: such capability already existed. Rather, it was the combination of inward investment with prior learning-by-doing which was decisive. In short, there is nothing here to suggest that rural industrialization in Guangdong under Mao was in vain. Much of that rural industry may have been inefficient by conventional criteria, but the clear inference from the regression results is that more extensive prior industrialization would have allowed more rapid growth after 1978, and hence a faster pace of poverty alleviation.

10.5.3. Qualifications: The Third Front and Fruit Processing

For all that, an inherited industrial skills base was not a sufficient condition, nor even an absolutely necessary condition for rural industrialization in the Guangdong of the 1980s and 1990s. For one thing, and echoing the results for Sichuan province, Third Front investment in Shaoguan did not lay the foundations for future prosperity. Even though a number of Shaoguan's counties had quite high industrial employment rates in 1982, none of them grew especially quickly thereafter. Renhua is a particularly good example. Despite an industrial employment rate of over 24 percent, the county's industrial output grew annually by only 13 percent—a good performance by most standards, but far below the Guangdong rural average for 1980–96. This almost certainly reflects the orientation of much Third Front investment towards mineral extraction and simple resource processing industries, which provided few of the skills needed to exploit the market opportunities of the 1980s and 1990s. The Guangdong evidence thus tends to support the conclusion reached in the earlier Sichuan chapter: Third Front industrialization was a cul-de-sac because it led to a rather limited development of industrial capability. It succeeded in increasing industrial output but did relatively little to enhance skills. By contrast, traditional light industry seems to have been rather more effective in creating a foundation for subsequent industrial advance. To put this more generally, some types of industrial employment generated more learning-by-doing than others.

Secondly, the Guangdong evidence demonstrates that it was certainly possible to industrialize quickly without much of a skills inheritance. In fact, a number of Guangdong counties seem to have taken advantage of their climate and economic geography to embark upon a process of rapid industrialization which bore no resemblance to the development processes of their Maoist or Republican past. The best example of this is rural Maoming. There, the counties of Gaozhou, Huazhou and Xinyi moved rapidly to establish themselves as producers of fruit (such as lychees and bananas) and vegetables for both the north China and overseas markets. With the Delta counties increasingly geared towards textile production in the 1980s, this left a market opportunity for the Maoming counties, which they were able to exploit via the Hong Kong–Beijing railway and the port facilities offered by Maoming city. By the mid-1990s, all three ranked amongst the top hundred fruit-producing counties in China, and Gaozhou was in fact the national leader. On the base of this expansion of agriculture, all three counties developed extensive food processing industries. The most remarkable feature of this development was that the three had virtually no industry to speak of in the early 1980s. If we rank Guangdong's counties by their rate of industrial employment in 1982, Xinyi was second to bottom, Gaozhou was third from bottom and Huazhou was eighth from bottom. In all three, the industrial employment rate was less than half the provincial average—and yet the three achieved industrial output growth per head of between 24 and 27 percent which exceeded the Guangdong rural average. Maoming's experience is in a sense the exception that proves the rule. The prior development of manufacturing capability was usually an essential desideratum for rapid industrialization, but a favourable constellation of other factors occasionally rendered it unnecessary.

10.6. Conclusion

Guangdong's industrial base by the late 1970s was more rural, less geographically concentrated, and less dominated by traditional light industry than it had been at the time of the Revolution. Above all, its reservoir of essential industrial skills was much deeper. This expansion of manufacturing capability in rural Guangdong provided the province with a solid foundation for the industrialization of the 1980s and 1990s. But skills did not operate in isolation. The spatial pattern of growth across the province bears the imprint of Guangdong's economic and physical geography. Moreover, inflows of foreign investment undoubtedly helped to promote growth; it would have been remarkable indeed if capital flows on the scale enjoyed by Guangdong had not induced such an effect. And those parts of the province which grew most rapidly were those regions where output levels in the early 1980s were low. Nevertheless, the pivotal role played by Guangdong's Maoist inheritance is apparent. Even in a province where the flows of foreign capital and migrant labour were enormous, inherited industrial capability was a key influence on the rural industrial growth rate.

11

Conclusion

The growth of rural industry in China is one of the most dramatic changes that has occurred in the developing world over the last 25 years: rural industrialization has truly transformed the Chinese countryside. But its most profound consequence has been to engineer a remarkable reduction in the level of absolute poverty. By the end of the century, close to 200 million rural citizens were employed within the rural non-farm sector, and many of these new industrial workers had been lifted out of (income) poverty in the process. They may not have been affluent by the time of Hu Jintao's accession in December 2002, but most had achieved what was by Chinese standards a 'comfortable' (*xiaokang*) standard of living. It is this ascent from poverty which demarcates the China of the new millennium from the economies of sub-Saharan Africa and south-Asia. Identifying the reasons for successful Chinese rural industrialization is therefore a task of great importance. If it can be properly explained, perhaps it can also be replicated.

11.1. The Process of Rural Industrialization, 1949–2006

The first step to understanding this process is to appreciate that rural industrialization was already well advanced by 1978 in many parts of China. For all the attention lavished on the process of rural industrial development in the 1980s and 1990s, we need to recognize that industrial production surged ahead in those parts of the People's Republic singled out for Third Front construction as early as the mid-1960s. The Front was quintessentially a programme of rural industrialization: it was the development of industry which transformed the prospects of rural areas as far afield as Panzhihua in Sichuan, and Shaoguan in Guangdong. Moreover, the Front was no mere exercise in regional policy. It encompassed not only the provinces of western China, but also the hinterland of coastal provinces such as Zhejiang and Guangdong. The Third Front was thus a truly national development programme.

This process of rural industrial development begun under the auspices of Third Front construction continued during the early 1970s. In part it was driven by the continuation of the (greater) Third Front programme, which extended its reach into western Hunan and Hubei during the early 1970s. More important, however, was the expansion of county-level state-owned industries, and the launch of the five small industries programme. As a result of this latter, the growth rate of commune and brigade industrial output during 1971–78 was more than double that achieved during the 1960s. The mass of data released on rural industrial growth in the various provincial compilations and the *County Records* testifies amply to the extent of change across rural China. Accelerating rural industrial growth therefore substantially pre-dates the 1978 watershed.

This conclusion that rural industrialization began during the late Maoist era is not new: almost all the literature recognizes its truth. Nevertheless, most scholars understate both the pace and extent of the industrial transformation underway in the Chinese countryside before 1978. In large measure, this is because the definition of 'rural' used is far too limiting. By classifying state and collectively-owned industry at the county level as urban, the conventional wisdom does great damage to Chinese realities. This definitional bias is emblematic of a more general malaise in the analysis of Chinese development. Any rural area which is successful is re-classified as urban, and its urban status determines how it is viewed for analytical purposes. In consequence the rural-urban income divide never closes: how could it when any area which successfully industrializes is automatically re-classified as urban? The reality is that 'urban' and 'rural' are not used to denote location, but rather as pseudonyms for 'successful' and 'failed'. Only, therefore, when we look at the *original* status of locations do we obtain a proper understanding of the impact of the process of development. So it is with rural industrialization. We need to look at Panzhihua through the rural lens of the 1960s, not through the urban lens of the 1980s. Only by doing that can we obtain a true measure of the extent of rural industrialization in the late Maoist era. And yet, for all that, it is hard to argue that industrial take-off occurred in the Maoist era. Only during the transition era did the growth of rural industry become self-sustaining, and labour productivity rise at a rapid pace. The average level of labour productivity attained in the new enterprises was still well below that long since achieved in many countries but, in combination with real wage rates that were far below the world average, many of China's rural industries were globally competitive by the dawn of the new millennium. It is this which demarcates the rural industrialization of the 1990s from that of the 1970s.

Transition-era rural industrialization was driven by the TVE sector. In the late 1970s, non-agricultural TVEs employed a little over 20 million workers. By the mid-1990s, employment was nudging towards the 130 million mark. Even though these figures are not precise—the re-definition of the sector in 1984 enlarged its scope—this was a remarkable pace of growth. With a quarter of the rural workforce employed in the TVE sector by the end of the 1990s, its significance for the rural economy was manifest. Furthermore, real labour productivity in the TVE sector increased at annual rate of over 16 percent between 1984 and 2002; not only was the sector larger, it was also vastly more efficient. Nevertheless, rural industrialization was about more than just the growth of township, village, private and household enterprises even after 1978. Employment in county-based SOEs, whether run by county governments themselves or by higher administrative jurisdictions, certainly grew less quickly than in TVEs. In 1978, however, the county sector was no less important than the CBE sector (as it then was); enterprises owned by counties alone employed over 20 million workers. Even in the late 1990s, county-based SOEs were still home to over 30 million workers. Accordingly, whilst much of the reduction in rural poverty was caused by the development of the TVE sector, rural SOEs continued to play a vital role. Had the rural state sector simply withered away after 1978, China's ascent from poverty would have been long delayed.

11.2. The Agency Agenda

Conventional scholarship, as represented by the work of Wong (1991*a*), Sachs and Woo (1994) or Whiting (2001), assigns a dominant role to private ownership, both foreign and domestic, as the driving force behind rapid Chinese post-1978 rural industrialization. The rural industries of the late Maoist era, so the story goes, were inefficient precisely because they were owned and managed by China's communes and brigades, instead of by private entrepreneurs. They muddled on beyond the 1978 watershed because the costs of closure were perceived to be too high; only in the mid-1990s was it recognized that their losses had escalated to such an extent that the costs of closure were smaller than those incurred in continuing to provide subsidies. By then, the dismantling of loss-making public industries mattered much less than at the start of the transition era because a vibrant private industrial sector had been established under the aegis of foreign capital and private sector entrepreneurship.

These accounts are unconvincing because they exaggerate the significance of private entrepreneurship, and the contribution of inward investment. In so doing, orthodox scholars understate the critical role played by township and village governments across China in driving the industrialization process via the creation and management of publicly-owned enterprises. The orthodoxy also errs in characterizing public enterprises as uniformly inefficient. There is no question that Chinese rural industry was highly competitive in international markets during the 1980s and 1990s; the ability of the sector to gain market share, not trends in profitability or productivity, is the clearest indicator of its underlying efficiency. To be sure, Chinese industry was not operating at the world technological frontier during the post-Mao era. But that is no reason to condemn it; the very fact that per capita GDP increased so dramatically shows that China's industrialization strategy was correct in its essentials during the

1980s and 1990s. The 'right' development strategy is that which maximizes per capita GDP (and measures of human development), not one that achieves international comparable levels of industrial productivity but which has an industrial sector which is too small to ensure full employment. A handful of oil refineries or tobacco plants will provide the basis for operating on the world production possibility frontier but only a flimsy foundation for sustained increases in well-being for the whole population.

The account of post-1978 rural industrialization offered by Oi (1999) is altogether more plausible. She rightly identifies the public sector as the driving force behind post-1978 rural industrialization, just as it had been in the late Maoist era. A private sector emerged to supplement it during the 1980s and 1990s, but it played only a marginal role. More significantly, Oi recognizes that Chinese rural industrialization was not path dependent. Rather, the inefficient public sector industries of the late Maoist era were transformed by fiscal decentralization. By hardening the budget constraints faced by local government, China's central government was able to force township and village officials to create profitable rural industries in order to generate the revenue needed to finance public works, local economic development and the local government itself.

Nevertheless, for all the force of Oi's analysis, her revisionism shares the orthodoxy's view that we must look to changes in the incentive structure in order to explain rural industrial growth. And this emphasis on agency and incentives is the principal flaw in the fiscal decentralization hypothesis. Oi's claim is that counties lacked the incentive to develop extrabudgetary income, and that these incentives were only put in place after 1978. However, the evidence suggests that the incentives for rural industrialization were rather strong by the early 1970s: the fiscal system was already relatively decentralized. Why, then, did rural industrial take-off fail to occur in the 1970s?

11.3. The Learning Hypothesis

The most plausible explanation for the absence of rural industrial take-off in the period between 1958 and 1978 is that there was a lack of industrial capability. Rural China enjoyed the advantages of backwardness in the 1950s, and the state was committed—in both word and deed—to the promotion of rural industrialization. Neither agency nor incentive were lacking in the 1960s and 1970s. Take, for example, the failure of the Great Leap Forward. One can hardly argue that the Chinese fiscal system was other than highly decentralized by the late 1950s. And the pressure exerted by central government on commune and provincial officials alike to expand iron and steel production in 1958–59—the central objective of the Second Five Year Plan—was so great that one cannot argue that these officials lacked for incentive. Yet the rural industrialization programme failed.

One possible explanation for this failure is that the *specific* policies of 1958 were misconceived. And they undoubtedly were: the focus on iron and steel production was far too narrow and the sheer scale of investment was altogether too large to sustain. But there was more to it than that, as the failure of the state to create efficient rural industries in the 1960s and 1970s suggests. For although the 'five small industries' programme launched after the fiscal decentralization of 1970 worked in the sense that the growth rate accelerated, it failed to create efficient industries. Of course the campaigns associated with the Cultural Revolution during the early 1970s did not help the industrialization cause. But we need to distinguish between these short run factors, and long run policy. There is no question that rural industrial development was one of the central goals of policy-making in the late 1960s and 1970s. And therefore the very fact that industry was so obviously promoted—yet under-performed—suggests that there was some other constraint upon rural industrial growth in the 1970s, one which transcended mere incentive and agency. For neither agency nor incentive were wanting: if government action alone had been a sufficient condition for rural industrialization, then China would have experienced successful rural industrial development during the late Maoist era. We need a better explanation.

The learning hypothesis offers precisely that. Its essence is that the absence of take-off in rural China between 1958 and 1978 reflected a lack of manufacturing skills and competencies ('capability'). For one thing, the countryside had limited access to the advanced technologies and new goods increasingly available to China's cities. For another, the ability of rural workers to utilize the technologies and know-how (even if they had been available) was strictly limited. Levels of formal education were low. Few workers had experienced modern manufacturing, and therefore industrial skill levels were low. Thus the ability of the rural sector to make use of more advanced technology—its absorptive capacity—was strictly limited. In such circumstances, it is hardly surprising that the Great Leap Forward, with its focus on the development of iron and steel production in the countryside, was such a failure. The pre-conditions for the successful development of a metallurgy simply did not exist in the Chinese countryside in the late 1950s. A lack of manufacturing capability was the binding constraint on Chinese rural industrialization, not some failure of incentive or agency.

The historic contribution of the late Maoist era was to break that constraint. It did so in three ways. Firstly, manufacturing capability in rural China was enhanced by the expansion of formal education. Late Maoism may not have initiated the development of rural education—the credit for that properly lies with the May 4th movement—but the promotion of mass primary and secondary education transformed the rural landscape. Secondly, the transfer of educated youth and skilled workers to the countryside proved an important conduit for the transfer of skills from urban to rural areas. China's farm workers no longer needed to learn in isolation. Thirdly, and most importantly, the act of rural industrialization itself set in train a cumulative process of learning. China's farmers had learnt a good deal from iron and steel production during the Leap. But by the mid-1960s, China's rural industrialization strategy had evolved into much more of a classical 'big push' strategy characterized by the development of a wide range of heavy industries. Learning—the development of manufacturing capability—was the result. Chinese farmers learnt about manufacturing by the sheer act of working in rural industry. And their learning progressed apace because of the progressive introduction of new goods and new production processes into the countryside. These new goods—even machinery was new for many peasants—and process innovation generated the sort of learning often discussed in the international literature on the effects of introducing new goods into a previously closed economy. China's rural workforce learnt how to run successful rural industries via learning-by-doing in unsuccessful infant industries first.

This type of alternative approach is lent ready support by what we know of the limited reach of the open door. Parts of Jiangsu, Zhejiang, Fujian and especially Guangdong were transformed by inward investment, but these areas along China's Pacific seaboard were the exception rather than the rule. As S. Wei (2000) has suggested, the challenge is to explain why China attracted so *little* FDI until the late 1990s, rather than so much. Secondly, and in the light of the discussion in the previous chapter, it is difficult to see how successful rural industrialization could have been accomplished without an extensive skills base. Some foreign-funded and domestically-funded firms employed large numbers of unskilled workers, frequently young women, in garment and electronic assembly work. Even there, however, a body of skilled workers was needed for high skill tasks and for the maintenance of machinery. The corollary is clear: the acceleration in rural industrial growth in China after 1978 reflected at least as much the gradual creation of industrial capability during the Maoist era as it did the favourable incentives faced by local government, or the contribution of the open door. Only by the late 1970s had the capability of China's rural industrial sector evolved to such an extent that the process of industrial take-off was able to begin in earnest. Maoist industrial development may have been a failure in the short term: the rural industries created were often inefficient. But the development programme was a long term success because the very act of setting up and running rural industries led to a process of learning and thence to the enhancement of manufacturing capability.

In many respects, therefore, late Maoism may accurately be portrayed as an extended process of learning during which many of the formal and informal skills necessary for the development of rural industry were acquired. By the late 1970s, China's rural communities had vastly enhanced their capability to run, develop and sustain rural industry. Worker and cadre alike had the necessary skills and competencies as a result of learning-by-doing. By then, indeed, the process of learning has gone so far that industrial production was beginning to grow quickly in many parts of the countryside. The fact that such acceleration was underway—well before the inception of *gaige kaifang*—goes far towards confirming that a learning process was underway, one which gradually ignited rural industrialization across the whole of China. Of course the learning process was far from complete at the close of the 1970s, and many of China's rural industries were inefficient. However, they were becoming increasingly less so. Rural industry was maturing, and in the process the foundations for the break-neck industrialization of the 1980s and 1990s had been well and truly laid. Just as Adam Smith did not foresee Britain's Industrial Revolution when writing *The Wealth of Nations* in 1776, so Deng Xiaoping and other critics of the Maoist regime failed to recognize the extent to which the manufacturing capability necessary for industrial catch-up already existed in the Chinese countryside by 1978.

11.4. The National Evidence

One way to test this learning hypothesis is to use county-level data and to determine if—after normalization for geography, initial per capita output and population factors—there is any relationship between levels of inherited human capital and rural growth during the 1980s and the 1990s. With over 2,000 county-equivalents across China, this approach allows an exhaustive test of the hypothesis, and is superior to the use of provincial-level data because Chinese provinces contain urban as well as rural centres: provincial data hide much more than they reveal. The county is not an ideal analytical unit because it too includes citizens who are recognizably urban in outlook and attitude. Nevertheless, the overwhelming majority of those resident in the towns of China's counties during the 1970s and 1980s had far more in common with the Chinese peasantry than with the citizens of its great urban centres.

An ideal test of the hypothesis that the pace of Chinese rural industrialization owed much to initial conditions would start with data on the growth rates of county-level per capita *industrial* output between 1970 (when rural industrial output growth started to accelerate) and some point during the first decade of the new millennium. These rates would then be compared against county data on population density, dependency, education, and skills acquired by learning-by-doing. In addition, we would want to look at the effect of the initial level of per capita industrial output, and include measures proxying the impact of *gaige kaifang*, such as foreign trade, and changes in ownership. In practice, however, the data impose a number of limitations. The most obvious is that there are no comprehensive county-level data for the 1970s on either output growth or the desired independent variables. Even if there were, we would be sceptical of their value; the State Statistical Bureau virtually ceased to function during the 1960s and 1970s, and those data which were collected were based upon small-scale surveys rather than censuses. For reliable empirical work, therefore, the base year needs to be 1982, the year of the first post-Mao population census. That census collected and assembled a wide range of social and economic data. This gives us data on initial conditions, and we can use them in conjunction with data for the late 1990s to estimate rates of county-level output growth.

These data paint a clear picture. They show that the growth of per capita GDP (a good proxy for the growth of per capita rural industrial output) during 1982–2000 is positively related to the 1982 literacy rate, the 1982 industrial employment rate, and the grain yield achieved by counties in the mid-1980s (which serves as one proxy for physical geography). Conversely, per capita growth was negatively related to the initial level of per capita GDP, the dependency rate, and distance to provincial capitals and the great metropolitan centres of Shanghai, Beijing and Hong Kong. In all these cases, the coefficient estimated is statistically significant at the usual 5 percent level. Indeed, of the variables tested, only population density emerges as insignificant. Of course statistical significance is not the same as economic or substantive significance. To evaluate the latter, we need to consider the size of the coefficients: to what extent did the variables considered have a large effect on the growth rate? This test shows that literacy, grain yields and proximity to the provincial capital had only very modest (albeit statistically significant) effects on growth rates. By contrast, all the other variables were important. In particular, a one standard deviation increase in the rate of industrial employment in 1982—the best proxy for skills at the close of the Maoist era—appears to have been enough to raise a county's per capita growth rate over the next two decades by about one quarter of a standard deviation. Moreover, these inherited skills were as important as any other factor in affecting the growth rate of any particular county: there is no evidence that physical geography, or proximity to an urban centre, trumped skills as a determinant of county-level growth rates.

Such national-level results cannot be viewed as decisive because of the rather rough and ready nature of the national dataset employed. There are two potential problems with it: the employment of crude GDP estimates as a substitute for industrial value-added data, and reliance on endpoint rather than complete time series data to calculate output trends. As a minimum we need to experiment with different time periods and with industrial GVA data to see if the national results are robust. In practice this means that we need to use county level evidence for a number of provinces to see if the national results are replicated for smaller samples of Chinese counties.

11.5. Tales from the Provinces

The three provinces looked at in more detail were Guangdong, Jiangsu and Sichuan. In part this is because there are relatively good time series data on county-level industrial growth in all three; that makes for a more reliable assessment of the sources of industrial development than if we use endpoint GDP data. More importantly, these three provinces demonstrate the range of industrialization processes at work. Sichuan was the centre of the Third Front construction before 1978, and therefore offers a test of the hypothesis that the Front laid the foundations for subsequent growth. Jiangsu, and in particular Sunan, was home to a vast range of commune and brigade industries in the Maoist era, and to the rapid expansion of the TVE sector after 1978. Its experience therefore allows us to investigate the influence of the Maoist CBE legacy on the rural industrialization of the transition era. In addition, precisely because proto-industry was well-developed in Jiangsu before 1949, we can also evaluate the long run impact of China's proto-industrial legacies. Guangdong attracted far more foreign direct investment than any other province. We can therefore look directly at whether Guangdong's post-1978 growth was driven by its Maoist industrial legacies—not least its small Third Front programme in Shaoguan prefecture—or by capital inflows from abroad.

In fact, and for all the limitations of the national dataset, it quickly becomes apparent from an examination of the provincial data that the results obtained in Chapter 7 are generally robust. Indeed one reading of the evidence from the three provinces is that their experience fully supports the learning hypothesis. This is because, in all three cases, the level of industrial employment at the start of the transition era emerges as a statistically significant determinant of the growth rate of industrial output. More importantly, initial industrial employment had substantive significance: a one standard deviation increase in the level of industrial employment is estimated to have increased industrial output growth per head by about 0.4 of a standard deviation in Guangdong and Sichuan, and by 0.9 of a standard deviation in Jiangsu.

Furthermore, the provincial evidence points even more firmly than the national evidence to the conclusion that history exerted a more powerful influence than geographical factors on growth rates. Whereas the initial level of per capita industrial output and the level of industrial employment were significant in all three provinces as determinants of industrial growth, the results for the geographical variables are much less robust. The grain yield was significant in not a single case, very much suggesting that agricultural prosperity was neither sufficient not necessary as a condition for rapid industrialization. This is very much at odds with the bulk of the literature which has tended to argue that an agricultural revolution is a necessary pre-condition for industrialization. The evidence implies instead that the advantages of agricultural prosperity (a large surplus) was offset by its disadvantages (prosperous farming communities had less need to develop rural industry). The other geographical proxies do little better. Proximity to the provincial capital spurred growth in Sichuan and Guangdong, but it did not do so in Jiangsu, where even Shanghai appears to have exerted little significant effect. It is hard to be absolutely certain as to what this result means, but the implications are probably that proximity to the key urban centre mattered little for growth if transport costs were low, or where there were multiple urban centres or growth poles. That proximity to Guangzhou did matter in Guangdong suggests that transport was relatively under-developed outside the Pearl River core, and that peripheral regions such as Shaoguan or Zhanjiang could not easily market their output outside the province. The limited impact of geography is also attested to by the manner in which high population density hindered growth in Sichuan and Jiangsu, but exerted no significant influence in Guangdong. This evidence seems broadly in line with those international studies which suggest that population does not have a significant impact on development processes.

The provincial evidence further suggests that proto-industrial legacies were rather less important than Maoist industrialization in creating the conditions for industrial take-off after 1978. The entire proto-industrial hypothesis is problematic at a theoretical level because it assumes both that skills were long lived (or trans-generational) and that they were relevant to the market and technological conditions of the 1980s and 1990s. The evidence tends to invalidate these assumptions. In Sichuan's case, this is apparent from the geography of industrialization. Before 1949, the focus of industrialization was the central riverine zone linking Leshan, Nanchong, Luzhou, Neijiang and Chongqing. In the 1980s and 1990s, however, the focus had shifted decisively to the region around Chengdu. In Jiangsu, the industries of the transition era sprung up in the same places as pre-1949 proto-industry. However, although there was a proto-industrial renaissance in Sunan in the early 1980s, the character of growth was very different in that it was reliant upon modern technology and the development of heavy industry, rather than traditional textile products. Similarly Guangdong: there, the proto-industrial legacy of sugar processing and silk production provided little by a way of a foundation for modern industrial development. Textiles certainly revived in the Delta after 1978, but the rapid modernization of counties such as Shunde was driven much more by electronics and machine-building. And many of the post-1978 growth centres had little tradition of industrial production before 1949; Dongguan's growth, for example, is not explicable in proto-industrial terms.

For all that, the experience of Sichuan, Jiangsu and Guangdong casts doubt on several aspects of the learning hypothesis. For one thing, there is little convincing evidence that high literacy levels in 1982 stimulated growth. The literacy rate was not statistically significant at the usual five percent level for either Jiangsu or Guangdong. Admittedly, there is some suggestion that literacy mattered in Sichuan: the regression results for that province show that literacy was positively correlated with industrial growth and that the western ethnic minority prefectures in particular were hampered by their very low literacy rates. Furthermore, the growth differential between fast-growing Chengdu and slow-growing Deyang prefecture appears at least partly due to the higher literacy rate in the former. Nevertheless, any inference drawn from all this is necessarily undermined by the finding that literacy was not statistically significant for the Sichuan basin, home to the bulk of the provincial population. It may be that we need a better measure of formal education than literacy, but experimentation with other measures in the case of Jiangsu yields little improvement in significance. Given that literacy had very limited substantive significance even in the national sample, these results suggest that formal education may not have been very important beyond some sort of threshold; once counties had achieved a literacy rate of 40 to 50 percent, further increases appear to have generated little by way of a growth premium, not perhaps an entirely surprising conclusion for poor rural jurisdictions using relatively unsophisticated technologies.

The provincial evidence also shows that geographical factors, though less important in general than historical legacies, cannot be entirely discounted in explaining rural industrialization. On the contrary. In those parts of China where physical geography was especially inhospitable, the development of manufacturing was very hard. A good demonstration is provided by Sichuan, where initial industrial employment levels mattered only when we excluded the geographically-disadvantaged prefectures of Aba, Ganzi and Liangshan from the regression. They were not helped by the nature of their industrialization; mineral and timber processing generated many fewer skills than manufacturing, and many of these natural resources (which had provided the basis for their industrialization during the Maoist era) had been depleted by 1978. But ultimately the binding constraint on industrial development across the Himalayan plateau was the high cost of transportation. Geography was not destiny for most of the Chinese countryside, but it fatally hampered the development of manufacturing in some parts of western China.

The evidence on Jiangsu, Sichuan and Guangdong further suggests that the type of industry promoted in the Maoist era was important. Manufacturing was the engine of growth, but some types of manufacturing were more effective than others. Just as the development of Kerala seems to have been constrained by over-investment in chemicals (Thomas 2005), so long run industrialization in China was handicapped by the emphasis placed on expanding the military sector. The defence-orientated industries of the Third Front in particular did not provide an adequate foundation for future growth. Take Sichuan. Deyang, Ya'an and Mianyang benefited from the Maoist industrialization strategy in the short run: all three were singled out as centres of Third Front production. But precisely because of the defence-orientated nature of their industrial production, it provided a limited basis for post-1978 growth. This seems to explain why Deyang—despite other favourable conditions, most notably proximity to Chengdu city itself—could industrialize no more rapidly than the provincial average in the years after 1978. Of course Deyang was hampered by its very success in developing industrial production before 1978; its level of per capita industrial GVA was higher than that achieved in any other Sichuan county by

1978. But the emphasis placed on Third Front construction was not conducive to future growth. By contrast, the counties of Chengdu prefecture grew quickly after 1978 because much of their industry was civilian in orientation.

The evidence on Shaoguan, home to Guangdong's little Third Front programme, points towards the same conclusion. The prefecture received massive investment during the late Maoist era aimed at developing iron and steel production and a range of defence products. As a result, the prefecture provided about 14 percent of Guangdong's industrial output by 1980. But Shaoguan's industrial base provided little by way of a springboard. Between 1980 and 1996, per capita industrial production grew at less than half the rate achieved in the Delta counties, and its share in the provincial total plummeted to a mere 3 percent by 1996. Doubtless physical geography played a role, but it has to be said that the obstacles to industrial production in northern Guangdong are altogether less formidable than those encountered in western Sichuan. The clear conclusion from this Guangdong evidence is that defence industrialization was a burden. As in Sichuan, the Third Front fell far short of providing a sufficient foundation for the expansion of rural industrial production in the years after Mao's death. Panzhihua's long run success is the exception, not the rule.

An additional finding from the provincial evidence is that foreign direct investment played an important role in spurring rural industrialization in the coastal provinces. This is not an especially surprising conclusion: it would be odd if inflows of new ideas and goods did not help development. More surprising, however, is the way in which FDI appears to have interacted with initial skill levels; when FDI was added to the regressions for Jiangsu and Guangdong, the coefficients on 1982 industrial employment became more significant for both. This suggests that FDI was attracted to those areas where industrial skills were already well-developed, and as we might expect. Foreign companies brought new technologies and management expertise in their wake, but a skilled indigenous labour force was a necessary complement. Insofar as there was a rural economic miracle in Jiangsu and Guangdong, it was driven by a combination of Maoist legacies and inward investment.

11.6. Towards an Encompassing Explanation of Rural Industrialization

Long run economic development depends first and foremost upon the creation of a successful manufacturing sector.[1] And in order to be successful, a manufacturing sector must be efficient, in the sense of being able to meet the full employment

---

[1] A basic needs approach (designed to expand capabilities such as life expectancy and educational attainment) offers a viable medium term development strategy, but its long run utility is questionable. As Kerala, Sri Lanka and Cuba have all discovered, catch-up only appears to be possible on the basis of industrialization.

demand for manufactures without compromising the need to simultaneously secure balance of payments equilibrium and a stable rate of inflation.

The central conclusion advanced in this book is that the development of such a sector, particularly in the countryside, is a long, slow and painful process. Efficient rural industry cannot be created overnight, as Vietnam and the countries of south Asia and sub-Saharan Africa have discovered. This is because much knowledge and learning is tacit rather than formal, and can only be acquired by a process of learning-by-doing. Access to the global economy is not enough. Physical capital travels easily across international frontiers, and so too a limited range of managerial skills, but the barriers to the acquisition of skilled labour via in-migration are formidable. Even when entry can be successfully negotiated and social obstacles overcome, the sheer scale of the in-migration required to transform the prospects of poor countries with high population densities is daunting. In all these senses, the options open to modern developing countries are far more limited than were those of the Atlantic economies in the late Victorian era.

The need for learning-by-doing thus circumscribes development choices. In particular, governments in poor countries need to recognize that the creation of efficient industries in the long run requires that their societies must countenance—and subsidize—necessarily inefficient infant industries in the short term whilst the learning process is taking place. The resources for such a programme needed to be extracted from the agricultural sector, either via taxation, or (better) the manipulation of the internal terms of trade. To advise that efficient rural industries can be created easily, or that the agricultural sector need carry no extra burden, is to counsel perfection, not to advance a viable development strategy.

China after 1949 embarked upon a journey along this road. The late Maoist era is properly regarded as an extended process of learning-by-doing, and inevitably there were failures along the way: the Great Leap Forward is but the most egregious example. Development was also constrained by external factors. The perceived threat offered by the USA and the Soviet Union to the very survival of the People's Republic circumscribed China's ability to develop, and skewed its industrialization towards a more militarily-orientated approach than might otherwise have been the case. Nevertheless, the late Maoist era in China was remarkable for the persistent promotion of rural industry. As a result, extensive learning occurred in the countryside, and manufacturing capability expanded apace. The transition era saw the Chinese countryside enjoying the fruits of this learning process.

None of this is to claim that the evolution of manufacturing capability was enough to guarantee industrial take-off after 1978. Changes to the incentive structure faced by local government also contributed to industrial success, not least because of the pivotal role played by the local Chinese state in driving industrialization. However, 1970 was the real turning-points; fiscal decentralization did increase after 1978, but the system was already relatively decentralized by then. But successful rural industrialization in China, as elsewhere, was predicated upon more than mere agency and incentive. It also depended upon the prior development of skills and competencies. A 1987 OECD publication puts the general point with admirable clarity: 'Over the longer term, economic growth arises from the interplay of *incentives* and *capabilities* [original emphasis]. The capabilities define the best that can be achieved; while the incentives guide the use of the capabilities and, indeed, stimulate their expansion, renewal or disappearance' (in Lall 1992: 169). By over-playing the contribution of incentive and agency in rural China, orthodox and revisionist scholars alike provide only a partial explanation of the process of rural industrialization. We need to combine capability with incentive and agency for a complete explanation.

It would be equally wrong to claim that all Maoist attempts to develop rural industry were successful in promoting learning-by-doing. The Third Front in particular appears to have been a failure in the sense that it led to little long run learning: Front programmes in locations as far afield as Deyang and Shaoguan provided little by way of foundation for industrial take-off. Whatever the merits of the Third Front from a strategic viewpoint, it was a failure as a programme of long run rural industrial development. Furthermore, the evidence discussed in this book suggests that Maoist educational programmes were not especially effective as instruments for the promotion of industrialization. Investment in rural education generated enormous intrinsic benefits, but learning-by-doing was far more important for industrial development. This suggests the rather unpalatable conclusion that policy-makers face an uncomfortable choice between investing in education, and expanding industry, during the early stages of development.

China's experience also sheds a good deal of light on the desirability of labour migration. One consequence of learning-by-doing under Mao was that the knowledge base in those rural regions of China (such as Sunan) which had pioneered the production of new manufacturing goods was much broader than that in other regions by 1978. This in turn made for marked regional variation in industrial productivity. Moreover, although the Maoist programme of rural industrialization may have laid a skills foundation in rich and poor rural areas alike, its long run impact was necessarily much greater in more prosperous regions precisely because of the emphasis placed on the production of skill-intensive new goods. After 1978, prior learning-by-doing meant that industrialized regions found it easier to produce the new types of goods, and utilize the new types of technologies introduced via the open door. As the Chinese economy became more open during the late 1970s and 1980s, so industrialized rural regions could use their pre-existing knowledge base to exploit the new technologies which became available, and to produce new types of goods. By contrast, regions with a limited knowledge base found it hard to develop the production of old goods, let alone new ones, leading to a process of regional divergence after 1978.

Regional divergence reflects the fact that the Chinese labour market, like other markets, does not work to reduce spatial inequalities. This is not primarily because of the *hukou* system, often singled out as the key rigidity in the literature: there was no *hukou* system in nineteenth century Britain, and yet real wage gaps and capital market failure were pervasive (Williamson 1991). Labour markets work badly across the world because of imperfect information, transaction costs and the operation of increasing returns in affluent regions; together these prevent the attainment of labour market equilibrium (or produce an inefficient equilibrium). Increasing returns in combination with chance events lead to regional concentrations of production which are largely independent of physical geography and which persist over long periods of time; the core-periphery distinction is often an enduring one (Krugman 1991, 1995). Physical geography acts as a binding constraint on the development of some mountainous and land-locked regions, but (contra Sachs 2005) it offers little by way of a general theory of regional development. As Fujita et al (1999: 2) say '. . . the dramatic spatial unevenness of the real economy is surely the result not of inherent differences among locations but of some set of cumulative processes, necessarily involving some form of increasing returns, whereby geographic concentration can be self-reinforcing'.

Inequalities in rural industrial development and income were held in check during the Maoist era by the presence of barriers to labour migration. Of course labour migration was by no mean uncommon even before 1978. However, the bulk of it was state-sponsored rather than spontaneous, and its main direction was from east (high wage regions) to west (low wage regions), the opposite of what would have happened if the flows had been market-driven. This lack of a national labour *market* tended to help the development of infant industries in poor areas. By preventing the out-migration of skilled workers, it encouraged local governments to invest in skill development and ensured that local spillover effects were captured locally rather than dissipated. In this way, firms were able to appropriate many of the benefits of expenditure on training. This is not to say that there were no economic costs to controls on labour migration. Even putting aside the restrictions on freedom involved, barriers to migration cut poor regions off from the remittance flows and return migration that were features of the post-1978 era. Still, the very fact that regional inequalities have increased across China since 1978 despite a massive increase in the scale of migration suggests that the economic costs may well be much greater than the benefits. In a second best world, the erection of barriers to labour migration in combination with subsidies to infant industries in poor areas is likely to be a better way of promoting the development of manufacturing capability and reducing spatial inequality.

The GDP Regression: Estimation and Sources

This Appendix outlines the procedure used to estimate county-level GDP per head for 1982 and summarizes the nature and sources of the data used in the regression analysis of Chapter 7.

A1.1. Coverage

In the 1982 Population Census, 2,059 separate county-level jurisdictions are identified including the counties administered by Beijing, Tianjin and Shanghai (see TJJ 1988: 556–699). This total treats the *zhen* (banners) of Nei Menggu and agricultural *qu* as county-equivalents. The total excludes those jurisdictions officially identified as cities proper or urban *qu* in the 1982 Population Census. For example, in the case of Hebei province, the jurisdictions of Shijiazhuang, Tangshan, Handan, Xingtai, Baoding, Zhangjiakou, Chengde, Qinghuangdao, Langfang, Cangzhou and Hengshui were all classified as cities in 1982 and are therefore excluded from the rural sample. Rural jurisdictions which were re-classified from county to city between 1982 and 2000 (Shulu/Xinji in Hebei is a well-known example) remain as counties for the purpose of this analysis: our interest lies with the fate of those areas which were rural at the beginning of the 1980s.

Of the 2,059 county-level jurisdictions, it has proven impossible to calculate growth rates for 49. This is almost invariably because these counties had been absorbed by the neighbouring urban jurisdiction, and no longer had an independent existence by the late 1990s. For example, the Bao'an county of 1982 has been absorbed into Shenzhen, Zhenhai by Ningbo and Xichang county (Sichuan) by Xichang city. It is therefore impossible to disaggregate out their GDP. This leaves a national dataset of 2,010 county-equivalents for which we can calculate GDP growth rates between 1982 and 1999/2000.

A1.2. Estimation of GDP for Each County

The primary source for the county level GDP data is TJJ (1988: 556–99). This provides data from the 1982 Census on population and the sectoral composition of employment, as well as the gross value of agricultural and industrial output (GVAIO) at 1980 prices, for each of China's cities and counties in 1982. The main problem is to convert estimates GVAIO per capita into estimates of GDP per capita. This is undertaken for each county and city as follows:

1. Total agricultural employment is the product of total population, the share of the population in employment, and the share of the employed workforce in agriculture.

2. Output per agricultural worker is estimated as follows. Firstly, average output per worker for each province is calculated by dividing provincial gross agricultural output (GVAO)—from TJJ (1990b)—by the provincial agricultural workforce as given by the 1982 Census. Secondly, to allow for differences in agricultural productivity between counties, 1985 GVAO per member of the rural population by county as a proportion of provincial 1985 GVAO per rural inhabitant is used to adjust the provincial average for each county in 1982. The 1985 figures are from NCGY (1989).

3. County GVAO is estimated by multiplying (1) and (2).

4. County gross industrial output value (GVIO) is calculated by subtracting (3) from GVAIO. In a handful of cases, this produces a negative figure for GVIO (because the estimate of GVAO in poor counties is based on an exaggerated level of labour productivity in agriculture); this is avoided by setting GVAO equal to GVAIO, thus making GVIO zero (which is not such a bad assumption for many poor counties for the early 1980s). We therefore have estimates of GVAO and GVIO by county at 1980 prices.

5. County GVAO and GVIO at 1980 prices are next converted into current price GVAO and GVIO. The provincial ratios of current to constant price GVAO and GVIO are used for this conversion. These provincial data are from TJJ (1990b).

6. Next, GVAO and GVIO are converted to a GDP-basis by multiplying county values by (respectively) the ratio of provincial value-added in the primary sector to GVAO, and the ratio of provincial value-added in industry to GVIO. Provincial data here are from TJJ (1997). This gives value-added in industry and agriculture by county.

7. The seventh step is to calculate the size of the workforce in 'services' (i.e. all sectors apart from agriculture and industry). To do this, I first calculate the share of 'service' employment in total employment as 1—(share of agricultural employment + share of industrial employment).

8. The service workforce is then obtained by multiplying together total population, the share of the population in employment and the share of the employed workforce in services.

9. Service value-added per worker (GDP basis) is provincial GDP—(agricultural value-added + industrial value-added), divided by the provincial workforce employed in services. Provincial data here from TJJ (1997).

10. Total value-added in services by county is (8) multiplied by (9).

11. Total GDP by county is (10) plus (6). Dividing by population gives per capita GDP.

Per capita GDP data for 1999 and 2000 come principally from two sources. The 1999 figures are taken from the on-line data published by the National Bureau of Statistics (TJJ 2000b). These data are for 1992, 1995 and 1999, but GDP data are only given for 1999. The 2000 data for each county are taken from XSNJ (2001). I have then averaged the 1999 and 2000 data, a procedure which both reduces volatility, and expands the range of counties included in the dataset because neither the 1999 nor the 2000 datasets are complete. In addition, I have obtained data on a small number of counties which were re-designated cities after 1982 from the *Chinese Urban Yearbooks* for 1999 and 2000 (CSNJ 1999, 2000).

A1.3. Sources for Independent Variables

A1.3.1. Population Density, Industrial Employment Rates and Literacy Rates

Data are available directly by county from TJJ (1988). The literacy rate is for the population aged 12 and over. The data on industrial employment by county include construction and mining; this is clear by comparing the totals with the more disaggregated data usually published in the various *County Records*.

A1.3.2. Dependency Rate

This is the proportion of county's population aged 14 and under, and 65 and over. Percentages on these two are given separately in TJJ (1988) and they are summed to give the total dependency rate.

A1.3.3. Grain Yields

The grain yield serves as a proxy for geographical conditions in each county. Grain yields used are those for 1987; earlier data (1980 and 1985) exist, but are too badly affected by weather. The data suggest that 1987 yields were at least on a par with 1984 (Xin nongye 2000: 40) i.e. not too badly affected by weather. In cases where 1987 yields are implausibly low i.e. well below even 1980 and 1985 levels (e.g. Zhangjiakou prefecture in Hebei), I have used 1985 yield data. Where grain data are missing, I have used those of a neighbouring county. For big cities (e.g. Beijing), the figure for the highest yielding county is used. If there are grain data for a small city but not for its neighbouring county (usually they have the same name), the city data are used and vice versa.

A1.3.4. Distance and Proximity to Provincial Capitals

This is the distance from a county to the nearest of Beijing-Tianjin, Shenzhen or Shanghai. For each county, distance is calculated using the latitude and longitude of a county (given in Shouce 1987) in relation to metropolitan centres and provincial capitals. The procedure is admittedly crude; for example, some of the counties of northern Guizhou would have benefited far more from their proximity to Chongqing than to Guiyang. On the other hand, Guiyang was the centre of government for Guizhou's counties, and therefore its significance cannot be ignored. On balance, it seems preferable to focus exclusively on distance to the provincial capital, rather than to adopt a more ad hoc and qualitative approach designed to identify the nearest 'important' provincial-level city.

Estimation of Industrial GVA in Sichuan

A2.1. Estimating the Growth of Industrial Gross Value-Added by County

The procedure used to estimate industrial value-added was to start with the published data on GVIO. Complete county sets are available for 1978, 1980, 1985–88, 1989 and 1991–2002. Missing years were estimated by linear interpolation. The data are relatively consistent and, although there are some sharp year-on-year fluctuations, these are smoothed out in calculating the growth rate. The most suspect time series seems to be that for Guangyuan prefecture in the late 1990s; it appears that the output of many state-owned enterprises has been omitted from the data. For this reason (as discussed in Chapter 9), I have omitted Guangyuan from some of the regression calculations. I have also omitted Suining from the analysis because industrial production there seems to fall for no good reason in the mid-1990s. Most fundamentally (and discussed in Chapter 9), many of the industrial output data for rural Chongqing municipality (comprising Chongqing proper as well as the prefectures of Wanxian and Fuling), whether in SCZL (1990) or in CQTJNJ (1989), are inconsistent and too unreliable to include in most of the analysis.

The industry definition used includes all types of industry, including village-level and below. Note that the county-level data published in the 1985 Industrial Census for 1980 and 1985 volumes are not comprehensive because they exclude many small-scale enterprises. In those instances where data on the output of village-level industry is unavailable for 1978 and 1980 (48 counties are involved), the provincial growth rate was applied to 1985 village output levels to estimate it.

Value-added data for industry are available for 2000–02. For 1978–85, I have used the ratio of GVIO to GVA for independent-accounting enterprises given for each county in SCZL (1990) in 1985. Although value-added ratios are given for 1978 and 1980, these ratios are implausible for many of the counties, especially in western Sichuan. The 1985 value-added ratios are more reliable because they were estimated during the 1985 Industrial Census. For 1986–89, I have used the ratio of GVIO to GVA for independent-accounting enterprises for each county given in SCZL (1990) for each year. GVA for 1989–99 is estimated as a weighted average of county value-added ratios in 1988 and in 2000; the weighting for the early 1990s is dominated by the value-added ratio of 1988, and vice versa.

Value-added data are all expressed at 1990 prices. The data for the 1980s are given in 1980 constant prices, and the provincial industry deflator was used to convert these to 1990 constant prices. The provincial deflator was also used to convert current to constant 1990 price data for the data for each county for all subsequent years.

Per capita industrial output growth was estimated by calculating population growth rates between the endpoints of 1982 and 1997, and 1982 and 2002. The use of per capita data helps to eliminate the more pernicious boundary changes. The data for 1982 used in the regressions, the grain yield figures for 1987, and the distance of counties from Chengdu and Chongqing, were taken from the sources discussed in Chapter 7.

A2.2. The Reliability and Coverage of the Sichuan County Data

The apparent under-development of the rural hinterland of Chengdu in the late 1970s does not appear to be an artefact resulting from the exclusion of industrial enterprises owned by central ministries or by the provincial government. It is evident from a comparison between the data in SCZL (1990)—the main source for the industrial data for the early 1980s—and the data in some of the *xian zhi*, that the SCZL data include all types of industrial enterprises. See for example Chongqing XZ (1991: 417), Shifang XZ (1988:13–41) or Dianjiang XZ (1993: 304, 426) and compare with the SCZL (1990) data. It is true that, if we sum *xian* and *qu* GVIO for Chengdu prefecture, the aggregate of the parts is far less than the prefectural whole. In 1978, for example, GVIO for Chengdu (counties and *qu*) is 1283 million *yuan* by aggregation, but given separately as 4,531 million *yuan* (SCZL 1990: 337, 399–415). However, this difference reflects not omissions from the county totals, but a vast understatement of GVIO in Chengdu city proper. In 1984, for example, GVIO in Chengdu city proper was 6,664 million *yuan* (TJNJ 1985: 93), whereas the SCZL (1990) figure for the city proper obtained by aggregating output in the various *qu* comes to only 1,093 million *yuan* for 1985. In the 1990s and after, the development of special economic zones of one form or another has added to the problem. These are usually administered directly by the municipality and their output omitted from data for the districts. Again, however, this is a distortion to the level of output in Chengdu city proper, rather than the outlying counties which are our focus. Nor can the under-development of *rural* Chengdu be explained in terms of defence-related anomalies. The Chongqing area was a key centre of weapons production, but the same is not true of Chengdu prefecture. Accordingly, it seems reasonable to accept the data on rural industrialization in the Chengdu region for the late 1980s at face value.

County GVIO and NVIO in Guangdong

A3.1. Growth Rates for County Industrial Output, 1952–78

Growth rates for GVIO in many of Guangdong's counties and cities are cited in Chapter 10. The full list of growth rates is given in Table A3.1. The data from which these growth rates are estimated in several cases use a range of constant prices (1957, 1970, 1980 and 1990 prices). I have converted the figures to 1980 prices in all cases using the provincial GVIO deflators. It should be recognized that the county data are not entirely consistent because *village* (team)-level industry and below is included for some counties but not for others. This tends to distort growth rates in the 1970s, when the village and below subsector began to grow quite quickly in many Guangdong counties. Nevertheless, this subsector was still such a small component of overall GVIO that the extent of the distortion is not especially great.

A3.2. The Estimation of Net Industrial Output Value, 1980–96

The regression analysis and many of the tables summarizing county-level industrial growth after 1980 used in Chapter 10 focus on net industrial output value (NVIO). NVIO is preferred to GVIO because differences in value-added by county mean that GVIO exaggerates the gap between Guangdong's most industrialized counties (where value-added is typically lower because the dominance of light industry), and its less industrialized counties (where heavy industry tends to be the key sector). For example, the value-added ratio in 1993 was 23 percent in Shunde but 54 percent in Ruyuan.

In order to estimate NVIO by county for 1980–90, I have started with GVIO data at 1980 prices by county; these data include village-level industry and below. I have then converted GVIO at 1980 prices to GVIO at 1990 prices using individual county deflators. GVIO in 1990 is available by county in both 1990 prices (GDTJNJ 1992: 476–8) and in 1980 prices (GDZL 1991). These GVIO data are then converted to NVIO using the ratio of NVIO to GVIO by county in 1993 (GDTJNJ 1994: 425–33). The ideal would be to use value-added ratios for each year, but these are either not available or inconsistent. In order to prevent the growth of NVIO being driven by inconsistent fluctuations in value-added, I have simply used the 1993 ratio for every year. Differences in these ratios between counties (for example, value-added is higher in the heavy industry-dominated counties of Shaoguan than in the Delta) in 1993 broadly correspond with those apparent in the 1985 Industry Census. However, I have not used these Census ratios because they cover only township-level industry and above. For 1991–96, GVIO data covering all types of industry are available at 1990 prices. As with the 1980–90 data, I have used 1993 value-added ratios by county to estimate NVIO.

Table A3.1 Growth of industrial production in Guangdong's counties, 1952–78 (percent per annum at constant prices; ranked by 1965–1978 growth rates)

County/City	Prefecture	Growth of GVIO, 1952–65	Growth of GVIO, 1965–78
Maoming city	Maoming	44.1	20.2
Longchuan	Huiyang	7.6	18.9
Xinyi	Maoming	15.2	18.1
Ruyuan	Shaoguan	21.4	16.0
Liannan	Shaoguan	18.6	15.6
Lechang	Shaoguan	13.4	15.6
Meixian	Meixian	6.1	15.3
Jiaoling	Meixian	11.4	13.0
Wengyuan	Shaoguan	48.0	12.9
Conghua	Guangzhou	11.8	12.3
Taishan	Foshan	15.2	12.1
Huili	Shantou	5.8	11.9
Wuhua	Meixian	21.9	11.3
Jixi	Shantou	6.8	11.2
Foshan city	Foshan	16.0	11.1
Shunde	Foshan	3.7	10.8
Gaozhou	Maoming	12.3	10.7
Longmen	Guangzhou	11.1	10.4
Xinhui	Foshan	10.2	9.9
Jianying	Shantou	4.5	9.9
Dianbai	Maoming	7.4	9.7
Pingyuan	Meixian	9.5	9.6
Huazhou	Maoming	24.8	9.4
Dongguan	Huiyang	6.4	9.4
Guangzhou city	Guangzhou	13.3	9.3
Zijin	Huiyang	7.9	9.1
Xinfeng	Guangzhou	14.2	8.4
Raping	Shantou	8.9	8.3
Qingyuan	Shaoguan	11.2	8.1
Nanxiong	Shaoguan	8.5	8.1
Chenghua	Shantou	3.5	8.0
Huaxian	Guangzhou	16.8	7.8
Shantou city	Shantou	11.0	7.7
Chaozhou city	Shantou	9.2	7.7
Shaoyang	Shantou	6.0	7.3
Nana's	Shantou	4.0	7.0
Puning	Shantou	10.7	6.6
Dapu	Meixian	6.8	6.2
Huiyang	Huiyang	7.4	6.2
Panyu	Guangzhou	7.8	5.6
Zengcheng	Guangzhou	10.3	5.5
Bao'an	Foshan	9.0	3.8
Urban median		13.3	9.3
Rural median		9.5	9.7
Rural and urban median		10.3	9.7
All Guangdong		10.2	10.1

Notes: The Guangdong growth rate includes village and sub-village industries as well as all urban centres but excludes Hainan. The Shantou data are from the Shantou SZ (1999) except for the counties of Raping, Jianying, Jixi and Shaoyang, for which the respective *County Record* data are used.

Sources: GZTJNJ (1983: 483); GDFZ (1990: 10–14); Nanxiong XZ (1991: 170); Wuhua XZ (1991: 112); Dapu XZ (1992: 213); Deng (1992: 240–1); Jiaoling XZ (1992: 118–19); Jieyang XZ (1993: 229–31); Pingyuan XZ (1993: 781–2); Foshan SZ (1994: 774–7); Jiexi XZ (1994: 121–3); Lechang XZ (1994: 204–5); Longchuan XZ (1994: 203–4); Mei XZ (1994: 228–9); Raoping XZ (1994: 223); Zijin XZ (1994: 197); Dongguan SZ (1995: 353–4); Qingyuan XZ (1995: 307); Xinhui XZ (1995: 242–3); Liannan XZ (1996: 273–4); Shunde XZ (1996: 379); Bao'an XZ (1997: 149); Chaoyang XZ (1997: 241); Maoming SZ (1997: 310–11); Ruyuan XZ (1997: 311); Wengyuan XZ (1997: 119–20); Taishan XZ (1998: 225–6); Shantou SZ (1999: 54).

The Definition of Rural Industry

The classification of industry in China in the late 1970s was made more straightforward than in other countries by the virtual absence of private and foreign-owned enterprises. This left two main categories. State-owned enterprises (SOEs) were owned by higher level administrative jurisdiction—central ministries, provinces and provincial-level cities, prefectures and prefectural-level cities, counties and county-level cities—and they were 'owned' in the sense that residual profits (after any agreed retentions for investment and wages, and after the payment of taxes) accrued to the owning jurisdiction. Collectively-owned enterprises (COEs) were enterprises where residual profits notionally accrued to the workers and managers of the enterprise, instead of the owning level of government. The category thus covered central ministry-owned, city-owned and county-owned collectives (*jiti gongye qiye*), enterprises owned by communes (*gongshe*) and brigades (*dadui*), usually abbreviated as *shedui* enterprises (CBEs), and enterprises owned by towns located within counties (*zhen*).[1]

This distinction between the state and collective enterprises was misleading in two respects. Firstly, most urban collective enterprises were little different to SOEs in scale, level of technology and way in which they were administered.[2] They were, for example, often fully incorporated into the Plan, and any residual profits were remitted upwards to the owning level of government. Indeed some collective enterprises were more tightly controlled by upper levels of government than the SOEs operating alongside them (Blecher and Shue 1996). Secondly, CBEs were collective in name only. As communes and brigades were organs of government, it is more appropriate to view CBEs as state enterprises also. The distinction between them and other SOEs can best be thought of in terms of the level of government which owned them; CBEs were owned by local (i.e. sub-county) government, whereas other enterprises were owned by higher level jurisdictions.

[1] However, the industrial output of brigade and sub-brigade industries was included in agricultural production (GVAO), rather than in industrial production (GVIO), before 1984 (*zhen* or town industry was typically included in GVIO as *zhen* were regarded as equivalents of communes). Many of the statistical publications of the late 1980s and 1990s have rectified this, and have produced time series data for GVIO which include the output of the brigade sector going back to 1949. But most pre-1988 publications do not, and the same is true of some of the *County Records* published in the 1990s.

[2] This was not the case in the 1950s, when COEs were less technologically advanced than SOEs. Many of them were created out of pre-1949 handicraft industries (Donnithorne 1967; Riskin 1987: 98), whereas most SOEs were either foreign companies which had been nationalized, or new industries established with imported Soviet technology. Some of the handicraft cooperatives/collectives in turn became the foundation for commune industries during the Great Leap Forward (Riskin 1971: 264–5).

A4.1. The Re-definition of the Commune Sector

The main post-1978 change in classification was caused by the re-organization of local government in March 1984 (set out in the Central Committee's document no. 4 of 1 March 1984), whereby *xiang* (townships) and *zhen* (*xiang*-level towns) replaced communes, and *cun* (villages) replaced production brigades; production teams (*dui*) retained their name but lost their political and administrative functions.[3] As a result, the ownership of CBEs was transferred to the new *xiang* and *zhen*; the industries thus remained (at least initially) under the ownership of the local state.

However, the new category of *xiangzhen qiye* (literally township and town, but usually translated as township and village) was broader than the old CBE category. It included smaller *cun yi xia bian qiye* (sub-village enterprises) as well as the old commune and brigade industries; these smaller enterprises were owned by *dui* (teams), *lianying* (cooperatives) and *geti* (individual or self-employed households). These three enterprise types had been included in the sideline sub-sector of agriculture before 1984—that is, they contributed to agricultural rather than to industrial production in the Chinese national accounts. The 1984 change included them in the TVE category, and thus re-classified their output as industrial instead of agricultural. The coverage of TVE sector was further expanded to include private (*siying*) enterprises after their legalization in 1988.[4] In addition, industrial TVEs included industry owned by *zhen* because many of the *zhen* were seen as little different to *xiang*. *Zhen*-owned industry is often therefore often included in the *xiang* category in Chinese statistical publications. The term *xiangcun* industry also appears in Chinese materials. In general this differs from TVE because it excludes below-*cun* industry and *zhen* industry, and it is often used to refer to the public component of the TVE sector.

Before 1984, we are justified in regarding CBEs as enterprises *owned* by local government. From 1984 to about 1996, however, we should think of the successor TVEs as being *subordinated* to local government. Private enterprises were by definition not owned by the *xiang*, *zhen* or *cun* governments. Further, as a number of writers have pointed out, some enterprises used the term 'collective' as a flag of convenience to describe themselves and thus have 'red hat' status. They were *de facto* private enterprises but wished to insure

---

[3] A typical Chinese county of the mid-1980s was divided into *xiang* (townships), *zhen* (towns) and a county seat (*chengzhen*). Townships and towns were in turn divided into *cun* (villages) and (confusingly) smaller towns (*zhen*). Kunshan county in Jiangsu, for example, in 1987 comprised 13 *xiang*, 6 *zhen* and the county seat (Kunshan XZ 1990: 90). *Zhen* were typically so designated because they were seen as more 'developed' than *xiang*, and thus prosperous counties tended to have more *zhen* than poor counties. For example, prosperous Cangnan county in Zhejiang was divided into 19 *zhen* and 16 *xiang* in 2000, whereas (poor) Wencheng county was divided into 25 *xiang* and only 7 *zhen* (WZTJNJ 2001:15). Sichuan's prosperous Deyang municipality (made up of 5 county-level administrative units) comprised 128 *zhen* and 33 *xiang*, whereas poor Liangshan (16 county equivalents) numbered only 74 *zhen* against its 542 *xiang* in 2001 (SCTJNJ 2002: 3). At the opposite end of the scale, Yixing in Sunan had small city status by 1996, and this was reflected in its having 31 *zhen* and only 13 *xiang*. In neighbouring Xishan city (formerly Wuxi county), there was not a single *xiang* (Wuxi tongjiju 1997: 115–17). Nevertheless, standard measures of income, per capita industrial output and the proportion of the workforce classified as non-agricultural often show little real difference between the development levels of *zhen* and *xiang*. In Yixing, the *xiang* with the highest GDP per head was more prosperous than 26 of the 31 *zhen* (Wuxi tongjiju 1996: 115–16). Evidently, then, the difference in status between the two types of jurisdiction was determined by considerations that were not purely economic.

[4] A *siying* (private) enterprise is one employing more than seven workers. A *geti* (individual) enterprise is so classified if it employs seven workers or less. Both types are of course private enterprises; the difference between them is only one of size.

Table A4.1 The township and village sector in the mid-1980s (number of enterprises; millions)

	1983	1984	1985	1986
Township (*xiang/zhen/she*)	0.34	0.40	0.42	0.43
Village (*cun/dadui*)	1.01	1.25	1.15	1.09
Team (*dui*)	n/a	0.21	0.28	0.21
Cooperative (*lianhu*)	n/a	0.91	1.12	1.09
Self-employed (*geti*)	n/a	3.30	9.25	12.33
Total	1.35	6.07	12.22	15.15

Note: These data include all types of TVEs; 240,000 of them were involved in agricultural activities in 1986. The *geti* figure is a residual. The township figure here includes towns.
Source: Nongye bu (1989: 290–1).

themselves against both a change in the political wind, and continued hostility towards the private sector within the Chinese Communist Party. In addition, collective status exempted them from the taxes levied on the private sector. After 1996, TVEs comprised a dwindling number of public enterprises because of the rapid privatization of *xian*, *zhen* and *cun* enterprises; most enterprises included in the TVE category after 2000 were certainly private. Nevertheless, we are probably justified in using the phrase 'subordinated to' local government for these enterprises during the bulk of the 1980s and 1990s. Even the private sector was subject to what might be called indicative planning during these two decades; it was a brave entrepreneur indeed who ignored the wishes of local government given the extra-juridical power it was able to wield in respect of finance, taxation and the regulation of the labour force.

The size of the industrial TVE sector by the mid-1980s is set out in Table A4.1. It is clear that most of the dramatic increase of the mid-1980s was driven by re-definition, namely the inclusion of small self-employed household businesses from 1984 onwards. Not surprisingly, the contribution of *xiang* and *cun* enterprises to total TVE output and employment was much larger than suggested by the number of enterprises. In 1986, in fact, *xiang* and *cun* enterprises together employed 55 percent of all TVE workers and contributed 69 percent of gross output value, even though they accounted for only 10 percent of enterprises (Nongye bu 1989: 290–5).

A4.2. The Limitations of the *Shedui* and *Xiangzhen* Categories

It is conventional to define the rural industrial sector of the late Maoist era (1958–78) as encompassing industrial commune and brigade enterprises (CBEs), and that of the post-Mao era as encompassing township and village industrial enterprises (TVEs). However, there are five problems with this approach which I will outline in turn. Two are relatively minor: the omission of household sidelines, and the inclusion of agricultural enterprises in the TVE category. The third and more serious problem is that it is often unclear whether CBE includes (or is even meant to include) industries owned by production teams. Fourthly, the CBE category excludes industries owned by town (*zhen*) governments. These last two criticisms do not apply to the *xiangzhen* concept (which includes *zhen* and all types of small-scale industries except sidelines), but is a weakness in the CBE approach. The fifth problem—and by far the most serious—is that both TVE and CBE categories exclude industries owned by the county (and higher levels of government) but based within county boundaries.

A4.2.1. Household Handicraft Sidelines

Even the TVE definition excludes household handicraft sidelines (*nongmin jiating jianying shougongye*). Insofar as household handicrafts were sideline products rather than the main products of households, they continued to be classified as sidelines in 1984, and continued to be so treated after the sideline subsector was itself incorporated into farming in 1993. They have therefore been consistently classified as a component of agricultural output in the Chinese accounts, even though it is arguable that they ought to be classified as a type of rural industry. Of course one might argue on the contrary that, precisely because such handicrafts are sideline products of households engaged primarily in agricultural production (and often closely related to agricultural products), they should be classified as part of agricultural production.[5] But none of these issues are especially worrying because the subsector is simply not large enough to distort trends. Although the absolute value of rural handicraft sidelines was large—17.2 billion *yuan* (1980 prices) in 1986 (Nongye bu 1989: 122), and 36.5 billion *yuan* (1990 prices) in 1992 (NCTJNJ 1993: 67)—these sidelines contributed only 4.2 percent of net peasant income in 1978, 3.1 percent in 1988 and 2.7 percent in 1999 (Xin nongye 2000: 75, 85). It is hard to get excited over these sorts of magnitudes.

A4.2.2. Agricultural Enterprises

The second problem with the TVE category as a measure of rural industry is that it includes some farm enterprises. If we wish to identify the number of TVE *industrial* enterprises (*xiangzhen gongye qiye*), we need to exclude farm TVEs. In 1978, agricultural enterprises made up around one third of all *xiang* and *cun* enterprises and employed 22 percent of the *xiangcun* workforce. Thereafter, their decline was rapid in both absolute and relative terms; agricultural *xiangzhen* employment was only about a third of its 1978 level by 1986, and its share in the employment total was 3 percent (Nongye bu 1989: 290–2). Their inclusion in the TVE category matters even less by the end of the 1990s; only 165,000 of the 20.7 million TVEs were agricultural in 1999 and they contributed only 1.4 percent of value-added (NYNJ 2000: 246, 250). For the late 1970s and 1980s, however, we need to strip out farm enterprises from the CBE total to track the development of rural industry. Fortunately, these sorts of disaggregated data are usually available.

A4.2.3. Sub-brigade Industry

The third, and more serious, problem relates to the coverage of CBE industry. Some accounts use CBE to include team (*dui*), cooperative (*lianhe*), individual (*geti*) enterprises and even *siying* (private) enterprises. The expanded use of CBE in this way in effect applies the coverage of the term TVE to the industries of the Maoist era and thus ensures a degree of consistency of treatment.

However, the data which appear in most publications and which are labelled *shedui* usually do not include these small enterprises. In fact, there are no consistent national data

---

[5] In some counties, these sidelines were of great importance. A case in paper is handicraft paper production in Jiajiang, which provided about half of all rural industrial jobs in the late 1990s (Eyferth 2004: 78).

on non-agricultural enterprises operating below the brigade level before 1984—see for example Nongye bu (1989: 291) or He (2004: 39). Some Chinese jurisdictions have revised the late Maoist data, re-labelling commune and brigade industry as township and village industry, and expanding the coverage of the series to include team-level industry and below. However, this is probably true of only a minority. Brigade-level production is often omitted from the CBE category in most *County Record* data, and small-scale enterprises are often just ignored. In part this is because the data do not exist; these were usually regarded as little more than agricultural sidelines. However, this type of omission also reflects a continuing reluctance to acknowledge the existence of private industry in the Maoist era.

Irrespective of the coverage of the CBE category in Chinese sources, any plausible definition of rural industry must include team, cooperative, individual and private industry. For example, private industries existed in rural China during the early 1960s, and re-emerged in the mid-1970s in provinces such as Zhejiang, Guangdong and Anhui; it would be wrong to ignore their existence, or that of the more numerous industries owned by production teams. As far as possible, therefore, the usage of the term 'rural industry' in this book covers all types of sub-brigade industry.

A4.2.4. Towns

A fourth definitional problem relates to industry operating within towns (*zhen*). Here there are two separate questions. Firstly, should this type of industry be classified as rural? Secondly, was *zhen* industry included in the CBE aggregates?

Consider first the treatment and designation of towns in the 1980s and 1990s. One use of *zhen* is to describe relatively small towns located *within xiang*. These are usually the seat of the *xiang* government, just as they were the seat of commune government in the late Maoist era. Such towns are often called *jizhen* (market towns) and are clearly sub-*xiang* economic entities. In that sense, their industrial production clearly features within *xiang* aggregates and therefore causes few problems. However, there were other *zhen* within Chinese counties that had genuine administrative status, and therefore the term TVE industry has been used after 1984 to cover industries owned by designated towns (*jianzhi zhen* or simply *zhen*), county towns (*xianzhen*) and townships (*xiang*). These first two need some explanation.

Firstly, consider county towns. They existed because the seat of government in almost all Chinese counties was designated a *zhen*. Such towns have a variety of names across China e.g. *xiao chengzhen* (small city), *xiancheng* (county city) or *xianzhen* (county town); all owned industries of various types. Some of these industries were owned directly by the *zhen*. Others were owned by *jiedao* (neighbourhood or district) committees in instances where the town was comparatively large. *Jiedao* industries in some ways therefore correspond to brigade enterprises in township or communes.

The second category is that of designated towns (*jianzhi zhen*). In many poor counties, especially during the early 1980s, the county town was often the only jurisdiction bearing the *zhen* appellation. Indeed Fei (1986: 103) noted that this was true even for many of the counties of northern Jiangsu. However, it was certainly not true of more prosperous Chinese counties, many of which were home to a number of towns that were approximately equivalent in status to communes; these *zhen* are often known as *jianzhi zhen* (designated town). After the 1984 re-organization of local government, which saw the communes renamed as *xiang*, industries located in these *zhen*—as well as industries in the county town—were included in the *xiangzhen* category. More precisely, according to the set of rules published in November 1984, a *xiang* jurisdiction was up-graded to *zhen* status if it was the seat to the county government, or if it was the seat for the government of a *xiang* (proved that the *xiang* had a population of less than 20,000 and more than 2,000 non-agricultural persons resident in it), or if it had a population of more than 20,000 and a non-agricultural population of more than 10 percent), or if it were special in some other way (e.g. a mining area) (Gong'an bu 1985: 102). In the case of Jiangsu province's Suzhou municipality, there were 17 *zhen* scattered across the five counties which made up the municipality (Shazhou, Taicang, Kunshan, Wuxian and Wujiang) (Gong'an bu 1985: 27). By 1995, the rules had changed substantially. As a result, all five of Suzhou's counties had become cities (*shi*) and every one of their *xiang* had been abolished or upgraded, leaving a total of 152 *zhen* (Suzhou tongjiju 1996: 12). The total non-agricultural population certainly increased over this period but not at a rate sufficient to justify the re-classification of *xiang* as *zhen*. In other words, in Suzhou, and elsewhere in China, most of the *zhen* which existed by the mid-1990s were not true urban jurisdictions but essentially *xiang*-level rural units.

For the post-1983 era, therefore, we can be confident that the *xiangzhen* category included industry based in all types of jurisdictions called *zhen*, irrespective of whether they were *xianzhen* or *jianzhi zhen*. A case could be made for categorizing *xianzhen* industry as urban, but even county seats—especially in the early 1980s—had a profoundly rural character to them. One thinks here of the absence of pavements, and frequently unmetalled roads. As for the *jianzhi zhen*, most of them were upgraded to *zhen* status in the 1980s and 1990s simply by administrative fiat. Until the mid-1990s at least, few deserved the name. For these reasons, it is clear that the industries classified as *xiangzhen* genuinely deserve to be called rural.

What of the Maoist era? Some accounts steer around this problem by simply assuming that the only jurisdiction which existed immediately under the county in the late Maoist period was the commune. This no doubt partially reflects the tendency in Chinese for the term *zhen* to be pressed into service in a variety of contexts (see for example Mo 1987: 16), and the terminology here is very confusing. Nevertheless, it is very clear that a considerable number of towns existed as administrative units directly under counties in the late Maoist era. In Kunshan county (Jiangsu), there were 21 communes and three towns in 1963 (Kunshan XZ 1990: 87). Pengxian in Sichuan was home to seven *zhen* and 30 *xiang* (later communes) in 1963, and to six *zhen* and 32 communes in 1981 (Peng XZ 1989: 31). Much poorer Wushan county in the Yangzi Gorge region was divided into seven *qu* (districts) in 1963 and the one *zhen* and 64 communes were allocated to one or other of the *qu* (Wushan XZ 1991: 41). The presence of a single town in Wushan thus replicated the type of pattern found in northern Jiangsu, and the *qu* also appears as an intermediate level in other counties; for example, Zhejiang's Linhai county was divided into districts and was home only to two *zhen* even in 1982 (Linhai XZ 1989: 90). Ningxian (Gansu) seems to have been an even more extreme case. It had no administrative towns, simply 22 communes, in 1978 (Ning XZ 1988: 54).

The industrial production of enterprises owned by these towns played an important role in the local economy in late Maoist China, and cannot simply be ignored. We can glean an impression of its significance from those *County Records* which have explicitly distinguish between *zhen* and commune enterprises. Of the 482 brigade-level and above industrial enterprises operating in 1980 in Gansu's Tianshui municipality—the city proper plus the counties under its jurisdiction—208 were *xiang* enterprises and 41 were *zhen* enterprises (Tianshui tongjiju 1989: 524). A fuller accounting is provided for Taicang

Table A4.2 The structure of county industrial production in 1978 (percentages of county GVIO)

	Taicang	Taixing
State-owned	46	30
County collectives	13	12
Zhen	9	9
She	21	30
Dui	10	19

Source: Taicang (1991: 270); Taixing XZ (1993: 266).

and Taixing counties in Jiangsu (Table A4.2). These data show that in both cases the *zhen* subsector accounted for nearly 10 percent of all industrial production in 1978. Jiangsu was probably unusual in that it had more town-owned enterprises than most other provinces, but it is nevertheless clear that the *zhen* sector cannot be ignored in any proper accounting.

The significance of *zhen* industry means that it is galling that the coverage of the CBE category is so imprecise for most counties in the Maoist era: the data published for Taicang and Taixing are unusual. However, it is likely that the CBE category often omits *zhen* industry, thereby ignoring industry which was both important and rural in character. CBE industry is therefore too narrow a definition of Maoist rural industry.

A4.2.5 Re-thinking the Status of County SOEs and COEs

The most serious problem with both CBE and TVE definitions of rural industry is that they omit SOEs and COEs located within county-level jurisdictions, whether *xian* (counties) or county-level cities (*xianji shi*).[6] Most of these industrial enterprises were located in either the county town or in another town within the county (few were located in communes) during the late 1970s.

Some scholars have argued that the exclusion of such a large number of essentially rural enterprises from the definition of rural industry distorts underlying Chinese realities. Mo (1987: 16), in his well-known study of TVEs in Jiangsu, was explicit in contending that rural industry was a broader entity: '*Xiangzhen* industry is only a component part of rural industry'. Christine Wong (1991a: 321), in arguing that much supposedly self-sufficient rural industrialization during the Cultural Revolution was actually state-funded, includes agriculturally-orientated SOEs at county and prefectural level in her definition: 'In this chapter "rural industry" will include industrial enterprises run by people's communes and production brigades, as well as state-owned industries at the county and prefectural levels that are oriented toward agriculture'. She delineated the rural industrial sector even more broadly in an earlier paper, her justification for the inclusion of local SOEs and COEs in the rural category being that 'These enterprises are mostly small-scale and operate largely free of state control' (Wong 1989: 39). On the basis of this approach, the rural sector contributed 25 percent of national GVIO in 1983; large and small collectives owned

---

[6] At the time of the 1982 Census, there were 236 cities and 2,136 counties (Population Census Office 1987: xv). By the end of 2001, there were 2,053 counties and 393 county-level cities in China, reflecting both growing urbanization and the re-designation of some counties as cities (TJNJ 2002: 3).

by counties and prefectures contributed 3–5 percentage points, state-owned enterprises at the county level contributed 13–15 and CBEs a further 7 points (Wong 1989: 38–41). Thus the CBE sector made up only about a third of the rural industrial sector. Riskin (1978*a*: 77) also preferred a broader definition: ' "Rural industries" refers to those industries run by the rural communes and their production brigades, and state industries at the sub-provincial level, chiefly those operated by the *hsien*'.[7]

The essential problem with the official classification in the eyes of Mo, Riskin and Wong is that many of the county-owned SOEs and COEs operating in county towns and other larger towns within China's counties had more of an affinity with the rural than the urban sector. The county towns of the 1980s had little in common with China's big cities in terms of infrastructure or facilities. We can thus apply the logic of the previous section. *Zhen* enterprises fall within the TVE definition of rural industry. Given that most SOEs and COEs were also located within these towns, it makes sense to classify these too as rural enterprises. Furthermore, local-level COEs and SOEs were integrated into the rural economy in three respects. Firstly, a considerable part of enterprise revenue entered the county budget and was therefore available to finance a range of rural projects. Secondly, much of the expenditure by enterprise employees went on goods sold in local markets and produced by the local farm population. Thirdly, a proportion of the SOE and COE workforce in the 1970s and 1980s was made up of 'temporary' contract workers (*linshi hetong gong*) whose *hukou* was agricultural and who in fact were not temporary but long stay workers.[8] These workers were recruited from the communes to fill labour shortages in SOEs and COEs; they were attractive to these enterprises because their *hukou* status was in the countryside, and thus the enterprises did not have to provide the housing and educational facilities which were the norm for contracted SOE and COE workers.

If we accept that county-*owned* SOEs and COEs are rural, a logical extension of the argument is that SOEs and COEs owned by higher level jurisdictions (central ministries, provinces, prefectures and municipalities) but located *within* counties should also be classified as rural. These enterprises were by no means unimportant, especially in the 1980s before the explosive growth of the *xiangzhen* sector.[9] Moreover, there is a case for

[7] Many of China's state and collective industries are self-evidently urban enterprises. The largest state-owned industries were located in cities, subordinated to the governance of ministries, provincial and municipal governments, and were a world removed from the rural sector. Much the same applies to enterprises owned by urban collectives (*chengzhen jiti suoyouzhi*), many of the enterprises so classified being little different in terms of operation, location and governance to their cousins in the state sector. It is the treatment of enterprises located within county boundaries that creates most of the debate (though, as the quotation from Wong makes clear, some would argue that there is a case for also treating prefectural SOEs and COEs as rural enterprises).

[8] In Shulu county studied by Blecher and Shue (1996: 110), there were more temporary contract workers than regular workers in county enterprises in 1976 and even in 1990 temporary workers made up over 25 percent of the regular workforce. There were also a large number of temporary contract workers in southern Jiangsu. In the town of Zhenze in Wujiang county, about 20 percent of the workforce were 'peasant workers' (Fei 1986: 200).

[9] In Jiangsu's affluent Kunshan county in 1987, for example, there were 205 companies operating jointly with Shanghai enterprises, 21 cooperating with enterprises based elsewhere in China and five joint ventures with foreign funding (Kunshan XZ 1990: 262–3). In poor Wushan county in Sichuan, five of the 18 SOEs were run by higher-level jurisdictions in 1985 (Wushan XZ 1991: 193). In Santai, also in Sichuan, three of the 52 SOEs were centrally-run; these three employed 3,599 workers (7 percent of all county industrial workers) and produced about 15 percent of gross output value in 1987 (Santai XZ 1992: 454, 460–1).

arguing that they should be classified as rural enterprises on the grounds that their workers contributed to the local economy on the demand side, and that these enterprises also recruited temporary workers from the agricultural sector. Still, the argument is less clear-cut than in the case of county-owned industries. The enterprises owned by supra-county jurisdictions were much less obviously rural than those which fell under the control of China's counties. They were typically located in county towns rather than in ordinary *zhen*, employed few temporary workers, contributed little (if anything) to the county budget, used more sophisticated technologies, and produced outputs which were usually unrelated to agriculture. For all that, it is hard to regard these enterprises as having much in common with the large and relatively sophisticated enterprises which were the mainstay of industrial production in China's large cities. They were more similar to the *xiangzhen qiye* and county-owned SOEs, than to the industrial enterprises of Beijing, Shanghai and Daqing.

It therefore seems most appropriate to classify all SOEs and COEs based within county boundaries—irrespective of level of ownership—as rural enterprises. The decisive factor here is their treatment in the Chinese national accounts. For example, the provincial statistical yearbooks published in the 1980s and 1990s provide data on industrial output by county, and these data include the production of all enterprises located within the county boundaries. Similarly, the Population Census data for 1982 on industrial employment within counties cover all types of industries, irrespective of their ownership. It therefore appears reasonable to follow suit, and to put together all the industries located within a county together, rather than to distinguish between them on the grounds of ownership.

A4.3. The Role of the Hukou

The main disadvantage of classifying COEs and SOEs located within a county rural enterprise is that the approach re-classifies urban citizens residing in the county (i.e. those with a non-agricultural *hukou*), and working in the COEs and SOEs, as rural.[10] The same problem applies to those working in *zhen* enterprises and also having a non-agricultural *hukou*. This does some violence to Chinese realities because these employees are officially urban (unless they were temporary contract workers). These employees are included in the urban surveys (*chengzhen*) of income and expenditure because of their *hukou* status rather than their place of residence.[11]

The jurisdictions principally affected are county towns where the bulk of the county population with a non-agricultural *hukou* resided.[12] In Wushan county (Sichuan), 56 percent of the non-agricultural population lived in the county town in the mid-1980s (Wushan XZ 1991: 100). In Santai, also in Sichuan, the figure for 1987 was very similar

---

[10] A further controversial aspect of the equating county with rural and city with urban is that farmers working in (say) Shanghai classify as urban citizens. But in many ways this makes sense; they possessed an urban *hukou* and their lifestyle was far more urban than that of farmers working in (say) Henan.

[11] These surveys distinguish between households resident in large cities (*chengshi*) and in county cities (*xiancheng*), but all are classified as urban to distinguish them from rural (*nongcun zhumin*) households.

[12] Of course the reclassification of *xiang* as *zhen* did not affect the status of citizens living within the affected jurisdictions. Their status attached to their person and depended upon their *hukou*, rather than their place of residence. For that reason, peasant migrants from *zhen* working in (say) Beijing and Shanghai continue be classified as peasants unless their *hukou* status is changed.

Table A4.3 The non-agricultural population living in China's towns, end 1984

Province	Total town population (millions)	Non-agricultural town population (millions)	Non-agricultural share (percent)
Hebei	7.911	1.588	20.1
Jilin	7.277	3.447	47.4
Jiangsu	4.519	2.629	58.2
Fujian	5.772	1.584	27.4
Henan	6.466	2.592	40.1
Guangdong	5.597	4.073	72.8
Sichuan	6.027	4.165	69.1
Shaanxi	5.730	1.603	28.0
Xinjiang	1.647	1.044	63.4
All China	134.474	52.283	38.9

Source: Gong'an bu (1985: 1).

(Santai XZ 1992: 129). In the more prosperous county of Kunshan in Jiangsu, the non-agricultural population residing in the county town was 62 percent of the county total (Kunshan XZ 1990: 141). Or, to take a Zhejiang example, 21,152 out of Tonglu county's non-agricultural population of 55,490 (38 percent) in 1985 lived in the county town (Tonglu XZ 1991: 81).

Nevertheless, it was rare for more than a minority of the population living in county towns to have possessed a non-agricultural *hukou* in the mid-1980s.[13] The Sichuan basin was an exception; there, the non-agricultural population exceeded 75 percent of the population of the county town in virtually every county. The proportions were also high in peri-urban Shanghai and in Guangdong. In North China, however, the figures were much lower. In none of the county towns of Xingtai prefecture in Hebei (the prefecture was divided into 14 counties at the end of 1984) did the figure come even close to 50 percent. Of Shijiazhuang prefecture's 15 counties, the non-agricultural ratio exceeded 50 percent only in Shulu (which was one reason why the county was upgraded to a city in the 1980s). In Jiangsu's prosperous Wujin county, fully 64 percent of those living in the county town at the time of the 1990 Population Census had an agricultural *hukou* (Wujin pucha 1992: 12), though this is rather misleading because Changzhou city was in effect the county town for Wujin and therefore home to most of those without an agricultural *hukou*.

The national picture is apparent in Table A4.3, which lists the non-agricultural population of *all* towns in a selection of China's provinces at the end of 1984, and which

[13] For counties taken as a whole, the non-agricultural population was only a small part of the total population in the 1980s and even in the 1990s. In Santai in Sichuan, for example, the non-agricultural population (*fei nongye renkou*) was 6.1 percent in 1987 (Santai XZ 1992: 125). In Wushan, one of Sichuan's least prosperous counties at the time (it is now part of Chongqing), the corresponding figure was 5.4 percent in 1985 (Wushan XZ 1991: 100). The average for the five county-level jurisdictions within Suzhou in 1995 was 19.4 percent (Suzhou tongjiju 1996: 53). In the four relatively prosperous counties of Changsha municipality in Hunan, the non-agricultural population accounted for 8.2 percent of the total in 1990 (HNTJNJ 1991: 309). The figures were substantially higher by the end of the 1990s. But of course this is the very reason why rural industrialization has attracted so much interest, and in any case the pace of urbanization did not justify the wholesale re-classification of *xiang* as *zhen*. For our purposes, the issue is how to classify industries and populations at the beginning of the 1980s. If we wish to argue that rural areas have been transformed by industrialization, we need to be clear that they were rural in the first place.

shows that the non-agricultural population was in a minority in China's towns in the early 1980s. These data are particularly useful because, although they cover more than just county towns, those jurisdictions designated as urban in 1984 were much more obviously 'urban' than the new creations (*jianzhi zhen*) of the late 1980s. In other words, even the most obviously 'urban' settlements within China's counties in the early 1980s were not really urban, at least in terms of the *hukou* status of the bulk of their population. In the absence, therefore, of large truly urban settlements within Chinese counties, it is reasonable to regard counties as predominantly rural and, by implication, the industrial enterprises located within their boundaries as rural also.

A4.4. Summary

For these various reasons, the approach adopted in this book is to adopt a wider definition of rural industry than is the norm in the literature. Instead of using either the CBE or TVE definition, I classify all Chinese jurisdictions designated counties (*xian*) as rural, and designate all county-level *shi* (cities) as urban. It follows that all types of industrial enterprises operating within a Chinese county, irrespective of ownership and size, should be regarded as being rural industries.

Two final observations. Firstly, any distinction between urban and rural areas, whether for the Maoist or post-Mao eras, is ultimately arbitrary. In the Asian context, it has been argued by McGee and others that modernization in many rice-based regions has not led to the 'classical' Western process of urbanization. Rather, the distinction between urban and rural areas has been blurred. Small towns have sprung up instead of urban agglomerations, the economically-active members of individual households are engaged in both farm and industrial production, and much industrial production is seasonal. The phenomenon has been labelled as *kotadesasi*, and it is argued to be widespread in parts of China, and especially in Jiangsu and Guangdong (Ginsburg et al. 1991; Ho 1994); the Chinese phrase *litu bu lixiang* ('leave the land but not the countryside') aptly summarizes the process.[14] Precisely because of the existence of *kotadesasi*, we need to be aware that variations in definition might lead to different results and, as a corollary, to different conclusions on the impact of Maoist programme upon rural industrial development after 1978. Accordingly, the econometric analysis in this book is subjected to sensitivity analysis on this point to see if the inclusion of officially-designated cities in the samples influences the conclusions to be drawn.

Secondly, although any definition of urban and rural cannot be time invariant, it must recognize the on-going process of urbanization which has taken place across China since 1949. For example, many county-level jurisdictions were upgraded during the Maoist era to city status. This upgrading particularly affected areas picked out for Third Front construction (such as Panzhihua in Sichuan or Shiyan in Hubei), or for the development of port or oil-refining facilities (such as Maoming in Guangdong). Should such up-graded jurisdictions be classified as rural (their status at the beginning of, or at least early on in, the Maoist era) or as urban (their status at the close of the 1970s)?

There is no straightforward answer but, given that our interest lies primarily in the extent to which industry developed in rural areas, it makes sense to use the initial status of

---

[14] *Kota* (city), *desa* (village), *si* (process) is Indonesian in origin (Ginsburg et al. 1991: xvii). *Kotadesasi* and *desakota* are used inter-changeably in the literature.

a jurisdiction to define the nature of the industrialization process therein. That of course still leaves open the question of 'initial status when'? However, given that (by any definition) rural industrialization did not really get underway until the late 1950s, and that jurisdictional boundaries fluctuated wildly during the Leap, it is logical to use the 1964 Population Census delineation of jurisdictional status. In discussing Maoist rural industrialization, I therefore tend to use 1964 status to determine whether a process of industrialization is urban or rural. The industrial development of Daqing is thus an urban process; the city of Daqing was only created in 1979 but the oil industry developed in Anda, a jurisdiction officially classified as urban in 1964. Conversely, the industrialization of Panzhihua classifies as rural industrial development because the complex was created on a site which was officially classified as rural in 1964. The 1964 cut-off date does have the important implication that we should regard much of the Third Front construction of the 1960s as a programme of *rural* industrialization (because most Front county-level jurisdictions were officially rural in the early 1960s). However, that is hardly inappropriate. After all (see Chapter 2), the explicit aim of the Front programme was to bring about industrial growth in relatively backward, inaccessible and predominantly rural areas. It does, however, mean that the way in which we usually think about the scope of Maoist rural industrialization needs to be revised.

At the same time, it make little sense to view the continuing industrialization of jurisdictions such as Panzhihua in the 1980s as a process of rural industrialization. By then, Panzhihua was a city and its industry was manifestly developing in an urban location. On the other hand, it makes little sense to use the jurisdictional categories of the late 1990s. Many counties were upgraded to city status in the late 1980s and 1990s even though upgrading was hardly warranted by the size of their non-agricultural populations. In some cases, of course, the change in designation was justified; the transformation wrought by the growth of the non-farm rural sector was so profound that it made little sense to regard such places as rural jurisdictions any longer. However, such jurisdictions were manifestly rural at the start of the 1980s and that is how we should classify them: we are interested, after all, in the extent and impact of rural industrialization and therefore we need to look at areas which were initially rural, irrespective of their end-period status. Kunshan in Jiangsu is an example of an essentially rural landscape transformed by industrialization, and it is now (rightly) viewed as a city. Nevertheless, its growth since the early 1980s is properly regarded as the transformation of rural to an urban landscape via industrialization. The obvious year to pick for the identification of status is 1982 because that was the year of a Population Census and therefore the data used to identify cities—occupation of the population, *hukou* status etc.—was reliable. The national-level econometrics employed in this book therefore uses the term 'rural' to refer to jurisdictions officially classified as counties at the time of the 1982 Population Census.

Bibliography

I have used the name of a county followed by XZ or SZ in the text to refer to the County or City Records (*xian zhi or shi zhi*) for that jurisdiction.

Abramovitz, M. (1986). 'Catching Up, Forging Ahead and Falling Behind'. *Journal of Economic History*, 46(2): 385–406.

—— and David, P. (1996). 'Convergence and Deferred Catch-up: Productivity Leadership and The Waning of American Exceptionalism', in R. Landau, T. Taylor and G. Wright (eds.) *The Mosaic of Economic Growth*. Stanford: Stanford University Press.

Acemoglu, D., Johnson, S. and Robinson, A. (2001). 'The Colonial Origins of Comparative Development'. *American Economic Review*, 91: 1369–401.

——, —— and —— (2002). 'Reversal of Fortune: Geography and Institutions in the Making of the Modern World Income Distribution'. *Quarterly Journal of Economics*, 117: 1231–94.

AD (1981). *Administrative Divisions of the People's Republic of China*. Beijing: Cartographic Publishing House.

Afanas'yeskiy, Y. A. (1962). *Szechwan*. New York: JPRS Translation No. 15308 (originally published in Russian by the Publishing House of Oriental Literature, Moscow).

Aghion, P. and Howitt, P. (1998). *Endogenous Growth Theory*. Cambridge, MA: MIT Press.

AGK (Aba Zangzu zizhizhou gaikuang bianxiezu; Editorial Group for 'A Survey of Aba Prefecture') (1985). *Aba Zangzu zizhizhou gaikuang* (A Survey of Aba Tibetan Autonomous Prefecture). Chengdu: Sichuan minzu chubanshe.

AHSQ (Anhui sheng renmin zhengfu banggongting; General Office of the Anhui People's Government) (ed.) (1987). *Anhui sheng qing* (Conditions in Anhui), 3 vols. Hefei: Anhui renmin chubanshe.

AHSZ (Anhui sheng difang zhi bianji weiyuanhui; Editorial Committee for the Local Records of Anhui Province) (ed.) (1995). *Anhui sheng zhi—Renkou zhi* (Anhui Provincial Records—Population Records). Hefei: Anhui renmin chubanshe.

Amsden, A. H. (1989). *Asia's New Giant*. Oxford: Oxford University Press.

—— (2001). *The Rise of the Rest*. Oxford: Oxford University Press.

Anhui tongjiju (Anhui Statistical Bureau) (various years). *Anhui tongji nianjian 1997* (Anhui Statistical Yearbook). Beijing: Zhongguo tongji chubanshe.

Arnold, J. (1926). *China: A Commercial and Industrial Handbook*. Washington, DC: Government Printing Office.

Arrow, K. (1962). 'The Economic Implications of Learning by Doing'. *Review of Economic Studies*, 29: 155–73.

Arthur, B. (1989). 'Competing Technologies, Increasing Returns, and Lock-In by Historical Events'. *Economic Journal*, 99: 116–31.

AZ (Aba Zangzu zizhizhou weiyuanhui; Aba Prefecture Editorial Committee) (1994). *Aba Zangzu zizhizhou zhi* (Records for Aba Tibetan Autonomous Prefecture). Chengdu: Minzu chubanshe.

Bachman, D. (2001). 'Defence Industrialization in Guangdong'. *China Quarterly*, 166: 273–304.

Bakken, B. (1998). *Migration in China*. Copenhagen: Nordic Institute of Asian Studies.

Baldwin, R. E. (1969). 'The Case Against Infant Industry Tariff Protection'. *Journal of Political Economy*, 77(3): 295–305.

Bao, S. M., Chang, G. H., Sachs, J. D. and Woo, W. T. (2002). 'Geographic Factors and China's Regional Development under Market Reforms, 1978–1998'. *China Economic Review*, 13: 89–111.

Bao'an XZ (*Bao'an xian zhi*) (Bao'an County Records) (1997). Guangzhou: Guangdong renmin chubanshe.

Baoying XZ (*Baoying xian zhi*) (Baoying County Records) (1994). Nanjing: Jiangsu renmin chubanshe.

Barnett, A. D. (1993). *China's Far West*. Boulder, CO: Westview.

Barro, R. (1997). *Determinants of Economic Growth*. Cambridge, MA: MIT Press.

—— (2001). 'Human Capital and Growth'. *American Economic Review*, 91(2): 12–17.

—— and Sala-i-Martin, X. (1995). *Economic Growth*. New York: McGraw-Hill.

Beasley, W. G. (1990). *The Rise of Modern Japan*. London: Weidenfeld and Nicolson.

Becker, G. S. (1974). *Human Capital*. New York: National Bureau of Economic Research.

Bell, L. S. (1999). *One Industry, Two Chinas*. Stanford: Stanford University Press.

Benhabib, J. and Spiegel, M. M. (1994). 'The Role of Human Capital in Economic Development'. *Journal of Monetary Economics*, 34(2): 143–73.

Bergère, Marie-Claire (1989). *The Golden Age of the Chinese Bourgeoisie*. Cambridge: Cambridge University Press.

Bernhofen, D. M. and Brown, J. C. (2005). 'An Empirical Assessment of the Comparative Advantage Gains from Trade: Evidence from Japan'. *American Economic Review* 95(1): 208–25.

Bernstein, T. P. (1977). *Up to the Mountains and Down to the Villages*. New Haven: Yale University Press.

BFT (Bureau of Foreign Trade) (1933). *China Industrial Handbooks—Kiangsu*. Shanghai: Ministry of Industry.

Birdsall, N., Kelley, A. C. and Sinding, S. W. (eds.) (2001). *Population Matters*. Oxford: Oxford University Press.

Blecher, M. (1991). 'Development State, Entrepreneurial State', in G. White (ed.) *The Chinese State in the Era of Economic Reform*. London: Macmillan.

—— and Shue, V. (1996). *Tethered Deer*. Stanford: Stanford University Press.

Blomstrom, M. and Kokko, A. (1998). 'Multinational Corporations and Spillovers'. *Journal of Economic Surveys* 12(2): 1–31.

Bloom, D. and Williamson, J. G. (1998). 'Demographic Transition and Economic Miracles in Emerging Asia'. *World Bank Economic Review*, 12(3): 419–55.

Bloom, D. E. and Sachs, J. D. (1998). 'Geography, Demography and Growth in Africa'. *Brookings Papers on Economic Activity*, 2: 207–95.

—— Canning, D. and Sevilla, J. (2003). 'Geography and Poverty Traps'. *Journal of Economic Growth*, 8: 355–78.

Borensztein, E., De Gregorio, J. and Lee, J. W. (1998). 'How Does Foreign Direct Investment Affect Economic Growth'? *Journal of International Economics*, 45: 115–35.

Boserup, E. (1981). *Population and Technology*. Oxford: Basil Blackwell.

Bosworth, B. P. and Collins, S. M. (2003). 'The Empirics of Growth: An Update'. *Brookings Papers on Economic Activities*, 2: 113–206.

Bowles, P. and Dong, X. Y. (1999). 'Enterprise Ownership, Enterprise Organisation, and Worker Attitudes in Chinese Rural Industry'. *Cambridge Journal of Economics*, 23: 1–20.

Bowlus, A. J. and Sicular, T. (2003). 'Moving towards Markets? Labor Allocation in Rural China'. *Journal of Development Economics*, 71: 561–83.

Bowman, M. J. and Anderson, C. A. (1963). 'Concerning the Role of Education in Development', in C. Geertz (ed.) *Old Societies and New States*. New York: Free Press.

Bozhou qing (Bozhou shi qing diaochazu; Survey Team for Conditions in Bozhou City) (1993). *Baixianshi jingji shehui diaocha: Bozhou juan* (Survey of the Economy and Society in One Hundred Counties and Cities: Bozhou Volume). Beijing: Zhongguo dabaike quan shu chubanshe.

Bramall, C. (1989). *Living Standards in Sichuan, 1931–1978*. London: Contemporary China Institute Research Notes and Studies no. 8.

—— (1993). *In Praise of Maoist Economic Planning*. Oxford: Clarendon Press.

—— (1995). 'Origins of the Agricultural "Miracle": Some Evidence from Sichuan'. *China Quarterly*, 143: 731–55.

—— (1997). 'Living Standards in Prewar Japan and Maoist China'. *Cambridge Journal of Economics*, 21(4): 551–70.

—— (2000). *Sources of Chinese Economic Growth, 1978–1996*. Oxford: Oxford University Press.

—— (2003). 'Path Dependency and Growth in Rural China since 1978'. *Asian Business and Management*, 2(3): 301–22.

—— (2004). 'Chinese Land Reform in Long Run Perspective and in the Wider Asian Context'. *Journal of Agrarian Change*, 4(1, 2): 107–41.

Brandt, L. and Zhu, X. D. (2000). 'Redistribution in a Decentralized Economy'. *Journal of Political Economy*, 208(2): 422–39.

Brean, D. J. S. (ed.) (1998). *Taxation in Modern China*. London: Routledge.

Brömmelhörster, J. and Frankenstein, J. (eds.) (1997). *Mixed Motives, Uncertain Outcomes*. London: Lynne Rienner.

Brown, G. P. (1998). 'Budgets, Cadres and Local State Capacity in Rural Jiangsu', in F. Christiansen and J. Z. Zhang (eds.) *Village Inc.* Richmond: Curzon.

Brown, H. and Li, M. L. (1926). 'A Survey of 25 Farms on Mount Omei'. *Chinese Economic Journal*, 1(12): 1059–76.

—— and —— (1928). 'A Survey of 50 Farms on the Chengtu Plain'. *Chinese Economic Journal*, 2(1): 43–73.

Brun, J. F., Combes, J. L. and Renard, M. F. (2002). 'Are There Spillover Effects Between Coastal and Noncoastal Regions in China'? *China Economic Review*, 13: 161–9.

Buck, J. L. (1937). *Land Utilization in China*. Oxford: Oxford University Press.

Burns, J. P. (1981). 'Rural Guangdong's Second Economy, 1962–74'. *China Quarterly*, 88: 629–44.

Byrd, W. A. and Lin Q. S. (eds.) (1990). *China's Rural Industry*. Oxford: Oxford University Press.

Byron, R. P. and Manoloto, E. Q. (1990). 'Returns to Education in China'. *Economic Development and Cultural Change*, 38(4): 783–96.

Cai, F. and Wang, D. W. (2003). 'Migration as Marketization'. *China Review*, 3(2): 73–93.

Caizheng bu (Ministry of Finance) (2000). *Quanguo dishixian caizheng tongji ziliao 1996* (Statistical Materials on Finance in China's Counties and Cities). Beijing: Caizheng jingji chubanshe.

Cantwell, J. (1995). 'The Globalisation of Technology'. *Cambridge Journal of Economics*, 19: 155–74.

Cao, M. G. (1987). *Zhongguo renkou—Jilin fence* (China's Population—Jilin). Beijing: Zhongguo caizheng jingji chubanshe.

Cao, Y. and Shen, K. (1997). 'Rural Enterprises in Jiangsu Province'. *China Business Review*, 27–40.

Cao, Y. Z., Qian, Y. Y. and Weingast, B. (1999). 'From Federalism, Chinese Style to Privatization, Chinese Style'. *Economics of Transition*, 7(1): 103–31.

CDSZ (Chengdu shi difang zhi bianzuan weiyuanhui; Committee for the Compilation of Chengdu's Records) (1993). *Chengdu shi zhi: Dili zhi* (Chengdu City Records: Geographical Records). Chengdu: Chengdu chubanshe.

Chai, J. C. H. (1998). *China—Transition to a Market Economy*. Oxford: Clarendon Press.

Chan, A. O. (2001). *Mao's Crusade*. Oxford: Oxford University Press.

Chan, K. W. (2004). 'Internal Migration', in Hsieh and Lu (eds.) *Changing China*. Oxford: Westview.

—— Hu, Y. (2003). 'Urbanization in China in the 1990s'. *China Review*, 3(2): 49–71.

Chan, A., Unger, J. and Madsen, R. (1992). *Chen Village*. Berkeley: University of California Press.

Chang, J. (1991). *Wild Swans*. London: HarperCollins.

Chang, H-J. (2002). *Kicking Away the Ladder*. London: Anthem.

Changshu XZ (*Changshu xian zhi*) (Changshu County Records) (1990). Shanghai: Shanghai renmin chubanshe.

Chaoyang XZ (*Chaoyang xian zhi*) (Chaoyang County Records) (1997). Guangzhou: Guangdong renmin chubanshe.

Chen, J. Y. (ed.) (1988). *Xiangzhen qiye moshi yanjiu* (Research on Township and Village Enterprise Models). Beijing: Zhongguo shehui kexue chubanshe.

Chen, H. Y. (ed.) (1989). *Chongman shengji de Wenzhou* (Vibrant Wenzhou). Wenzhou: Wenzhou tongji chubanshe.

Chen, D. L. (2003). *Sanxian jianshe* (Third Front Construction). Beijing: Zhonggong zhongyang dangxiao chubanshe.

Chen, C. and Wang, X. G. (eds.) (1986). *Zhongguo xianshi zhengqu ziliao shouce* (Handbook of Materials on China's County and City Administrative Divisions). Beijing: Ditu chubanshe.

Chen, K., Jefferson, G. H., Rawski, T., Wang, H. C. and Zheng, Y. X. (1988). 'New Estimates of Fixed Investment and Capital Stock for Chinese State Industry'. *China Quarterly*, 114: 243–66.

Cheng, J. Y. S. (ed.) (1998). *The Guangdong Development Model and Its Challenges*. Hong Kong: City University of Hong Kong Press.

Cheng, L. K. and Kwan, Y. K. (2000). 'The Location of Foreign Direct Investment in Chinese Regions', in T. Ito and A. Krueger (eds.) *The Role of Foreign Direct Investment in East Asian Economic Development*. Chicago: Chicago University Press.

Chongqing tongjiju (Chongqing Statistical Bureau) (1989). *Chongqing jianshe sishinian* (A Decade of Construction in Chongqing). Beijing: Zhongguo tongji chubanshe.

Chongqing XZ (*Chongqing xian zhi*) (Chongqing County Records) (1991). Chengdu: Sichuan renmin chubanshe.

CQTJNJ (Chongqing tongjiju; Chongqing Statistical Bureau) (various years). *Chongqing tongji nianjian 1997* (Chongqing Statistical Yearbook). Beijing: Zhongguo tongji chubanshe.

Coale, A. J. and Hoover, E. M. (1958). *Population Growth and Economic Development in Low Income Countries*. Princeton: Princeton University Press.

Cooper, E. (1998). *The Artisans and Entrepreneurs of Dongyang County*. Armonk, NY: M. E. Sharpe.

Cornwall, J. (1977). *Modern Capitalism*. London: Martin Robertson.

Crafts, N. F. R. (1985). *British Economic Growth During the Industrial Revolution*. Oxford: Clarendon Press.

Crawcour, E. S. (1988). 'Industrialization and Technological Change, 1885–1920', in P. Duus (ed.) *The Cambridge History of Japan*, vol. 6. Cambridge: Cambridge University Press.

CSJW (Chongqing shi jihua weiyuanhui) (Chongqing City Planning Committee) (ed.) (1991). *Chongqing shi jingji zonghe zhi* (Summary of Chongqing's Economic Records). Chongqing: Chongqing chubanshe.

CSNJ (Zhongguo chengshi fazhan yanjiusuo; Chinese Urban Development Research Institute) (various years). *Zhongguo chengshi nianjian 1999 and 2000* (Chinese Urban Yearbook). Beijing: Zhongguo chengshi nianjian shechushe.

Cui, X. H., Shi, Z. K., Fan, G. Z. and Xiong, Z. Y. (1985). *Sichuan chengshi jingji* (Sichuan's Urban Economy). Chengdu: Sichuan kexue jishu chubanshe.

Dangdai Sichuan congshu bianjibu (Editorial Committee for the Series 'Contemporary Sichuan') (1991). *Sichou mingcheng Nanchong* (The Famous Silk City of Nanchong). Chengdu: Sichuan renmin chubanshe.

Dantu XZ (*Dantu xian zhi*) (Dantu County Records) (1993). Nanjing: Jiangsu kexue jishu chubanshe.

Danyang XZ (*Danyang xian zhi*) (Danyang County Records) (1992). Nanjing: Jiangsu renmin chubanshe.

Dapu XZ (*Dapu xian zhi*) (Dapu County Records) (1992). Guangzhou: Guangdong renmin chubanshe.

Dasgupta, P. and Weale, M. (1992). 'On Measuring the Quality of Life'. *World Development*, 20(1): 119–31.

David, P. (1985). 'Clio and the Economics of QWERTY'. *American Economic Review*, 75: 332–7.

De Long, B. and Summers, L. H. (1993). 'How Strongly do Developing Economies Benefit from Equipment Investment'? *Journal of Monetary Economics*, 32(4): 395–415.

Démurger, S. (2001). 'Infrastructure Development and Economic Growth'. *Journal of Comparative Economics*, 29(1): 95–117.

—— Sachs, J. D., Woo, W. T., Bao, S. M. and Chang, G. (2002). 'The Relative Contribution of Location and Preferential Policies in China's Regional Development'. *China Economic Review*, 13: 444–65.

Deng, X. M. (ed.) (1992). *Kaifa Zhong de Daya wan* (The Opening Up of China's Daya Bay). Guangzhou: Guangdong renmin chubanshe.

Deng, X. P. ([1987] 1994). 'We Shall Speed Up Reform', in Central Committee (ed.) *Selected Works of Deng Xiaoping*, vol. III. Beijing: Foreign Languages Press.

360

Deqing XZ (*Deqing xian zhi*) (Deqing County Records) (1992). Hangzhou: Zhejiang renmin chubanshe.

Diamond, J. (2005). *Collapse*. London: Penguin.

Dianjiang XZ (*Dianjiang xian zhi*) (Dianjiang County Records) (1993). Chengdu: Sichuan renmin chubanshe.

Dong, F. R. (1992). *Industrialization and China's Rural Modernization*. London: Macmillan.

Dong, X. Y. and Putterman, L. (1997). 'Productivity and Organization in China's Rural Industries'. *Journal of Comparative Economics*, 24(2): 181–201.

—— Bowles, P. and Ho, S. P. S. (2002). 'State Ownership and Employee Attitudes'. *Journal of Comparative Economics*, 30: 812–35.

Dongguan SZ (*Dongguan shi zhi*) (Dongguan City Records) (1995). Guangzhou: Guangdong renmin chubanshe.

Donghai XZ (*Donghai xian zhi*) (Donghai County Records) (1994). Beijing: Zhonghua shuju chubanshe.

Donnithorne, A. (1967). *China's Economic System*. New York: Praeger.

—— (1972). 'China's Cellular Economy'. *China Quarterly*, 52: 605–19.

—— (1976). 'Centralization and Decentralization in China's Fiscal Management'. *China Quarterly*, 66: 328–40.

—— (1984). 'Sichuan's Agriculture: Depression and Revival'. *Australian Journal of Chinese Affairs*, 12: 59–86.

Drèze, J. and Sen, A. (1995). *India: Economic Development and Social Opportunity*. Oxford: Clarendon Press.

Du, W. Z. (1987). *Zhongguo renkou—Jiangsu fence* (China's Population—Jiangsu). Beijing: Zhongguo caizheng jingji chubanshe.

Du, H. Y. (1990). 'Causes of Rapid Rural Industrial Development', in W. A. Byrd and Q. S. Lin (eds.) *China's Rural Industry*. Oxford: Oxford University Press.

Du, Y. (2000). 'Rural Labor Migration in Contemporary China', in West and Zhao (eds.) *Rural Labor Flows in China*. Berkeley: University of California.

Easterly, W. (2001). *The Elusive Quest for Growth*. Cambridge, MA: MIT Press.

Eatwell, J. (1982). *Whatever Happened to Britain?* London: Duckworth.

Edin, M. (1998). 'Why Do Chinese Local Cadres Promote Growth'? *Forum for Development Studies*, 1: 97–127.

—— (2003). 'State Capacity and Local Agent Control in China'. *China Quarterly*, 173: 35–52.

Ellman, M. (1989). *Socialist Planning*. Cambridge: Cambridge University Press.

Endicott, S. (1988). *Red Earth*. London: I. B. Tauris.

Enos, J. L. (1984). 'Commune- and Brigade-Run Industries in Rural China', in K. Griffin (ed.) *Institutional Reform and Economic Development in the Chinese Countryside*. London: Macmillan.

Enright, M. J., Scott, E. E. and Chang, K. M. (2005). *The Greater Pearl River Delta and the Rise of China*. Singapore: John Wiley.

Eyferth, J. (2003). 'De-industrialization in the Chinese Countryside'. *China Quarterly*, 173: 53–73.

—— (2004). 'How not to Industrialize: Observations from a Village in Sichuan', in J. Eyferth, P. Ho and E. B. Vermeer (eds.) (2004). *Rural Development in Transitional China*. London: Frank Cass.

Fagerberg, J. (1994). 'Technology and International Differences in Growth Rates'. *Journal of Economic Literature*, XXXII(3): 1147–75.

Fan, C. C. (1999). 'Migration in A Socialist Transitional Economy'. *International Migration Review*, 33(4): 954–87.

—— (2003). 'Rural-Urban migration and Gender Division of Labor in Transitional China'. *International Journal of Urban and Regional Research*, 27(1): 24–47.

—— (2004*a*). 'Out to the City and Back to the Village', in A. M. Gaetano and T. Jacka (eds.) *On the Move*. New York: Columbia University Press.

—— (2004*b*). 'Gender Differences in Chinese Migration', in C. M. Hsieh and M. Lu (eds.) *Changing China*. Oxford: Westview.

—— and Li, L. (2002). 'Marriage and Migration in Transitional China'. *Environment and Planning*, 34: 619–38.

Faure, D. (1989). *The Economy of Pre-Liberation China*. Hong Kong: Oxford University Press.

Fei, X. T. ([1939] 1980). *Peasant Life in China*. London: Routledge.

—— (1983). *Chinese Village Close-Up*. Beijing: New World Press.

—— (ed.) (1986). *Small Towns in China*. Beijing: New World Press.

Feltenstein, A. and Iwata, S. (2005). 'Decentralization and Macroeconomic Performance in China'. *Journal of Development Economics*, 76: 481–501.

Fengyang XZ (*Fengyang xian zhi*) (Fengyang County Records) (1999). Beijing: Difangzhi chubanshe.

Fforde, A. and de Vylder, S. (1996). *From Plan to Market*. Boulder, CA: Westview.

Findlay, C., Watson, A. and Wu, H. X. (eds.) (1994). *Rural Enterprises in China*. Basingstoke: Macmillan.

Finnane, A. (1993). 'The Origins of Prejudice'. *Comparative Studies in Society and History*, 35(2): 211–38.

Fleisher, B. and Chen, J. (1997). 'The Coast-Noncoast Income Gap, Productivity and Regional Economic Policy in China'. *Journal of Comparative Economics*, 25: 220–36.

Foreman-Peck, J. and Millward, R. (1994). *Public and Private Ownership of British Industry, 1820–1990*. Oxford: Clarendon Press.

Forster, K. (1998). *Zhejiang in Reform*. Sydney: Wild Peony.

Foshan SZ (*Foshan shi zhi*) (Foshan Municipality Records) (1994). Guangzhou: Guangdong renmin chubanshe.

Francks, P. (1992). *Japanese Economic Development*. London: Routledge.

Fu, X. L. and Balasubramanyam, V. N. (2003). 'Township and Village Enterprises in China'. *Journal of Development Studies*, 39(4): 27–46.

Fujita, M., Krugman, P. and Venables, A. J. (1999). *The Spatial Economy*. Cambridge, MA: MIT Press.

Gaetano, A. M. and Jacka, T. (eds.) (2004). *On the Move*. New York: Columbia University Press.

Gao, Y. T. (ed.) (1987). *Dangdai Sichuan jiben jianshe* (Capital Construction in Contemporary Sichuan). Chengdu: Sichuan sheng shehui kexueyuan chubanshe.

Gao, M. B. (1999) *Gao Village*. London: Hurst and Company.

Gao, T. (2005). 'Labor Quality and the Location of FDI: Evidence from China'. *China Economic Review*, 16: 274–92.

Gaoyou XZ (*Gaoyou xian zhi*) (Gaoyou County Records) (1990). Nanjing: Jiangsu renmin chubanshe.

Garnaut, R. and Song, L. G. (eds.) (2003). *China's Third Economic Transformation: The Rise of the Private Economy*. London: Routledge.

—— —— Tenev, S. and Yao, Y. (2005). *China's Ownership Transformation*. Washington: World Bank.

Gates, H. (1996). *China's Motor*. Ithaca: Cornell UP.

GDDLZ (Guangdong sheng difang shizhi bianzuan weiyuanhui; Committee for the Compilation of Guangdong's Historical Records) (1999). *Guangdong sheng zhi: Dili zhi* (Guangdong Provincial Records: Geographical Records). Guangdong: Guangdong renmin chubanshe.

GDFZ (*Guangdong sheng tongjiju;* Guangdong Statistical Bureau) (1990). *Guangdong sheng guomin jingji he shehui fazhan tongji ziliao 1949-89* (Statistical Materials on the Economic and Social Development of Guangdong). Guangzhou: Guangdong tongji chubanshe.

GDJYZ (Guangdong sheng difang shizhi bianzuan weiyuanhui; Committee for the Compilation of Guangdong's Historical Records) (ed.) (1995). *Guangdong sheng zhi—Jiaoyu zhi* (Guangdong Provincial Records—Educational Records). Guangzhou: Guangdong renmin chubanshe.

GDLSZ (Guangdong sheng difang shizhi bianzuan weiyuanhui; Committee for the Compilation of Guangdong's Historical Records) (ed.) (1996). *Guangdong sheng zhi—Liangshi zhi* (Guangdong Provincial Records—Grain Records). Guangzhou: Guangdong renmin chubanshe.

GDRKZ (Guangdong sheng difang shizhi bianzuan weiyuanhui; Committee for the Compilation of Guangdong's Historical Records) (1995). *Guangdong sheng zhi: Renkou zhi* (Guangdong Provincial Records: Population Records). Guangdong: Guangdong renmin chubanshe.

GDTJNJ (Guangdong tongjijul; Guangdong Statistical Bureau) (various years). *Guangdong tongji nianjian 1986, 1990, 1992, 1994, 1997, 1999 and 2003* (Guangdong Statistical Yearbook). Beijing: Zhongguo tongji chubanshe.

GDZL (*Guangdong sheng tongjiju;* Guangdong Statistical Bureau) (1991). *Guangdong sheng xian (qu) guomin jingji tongji ziliao 1980-1990* (Statistical Materials on the Economy of the Counties and Districts of Guangdong). Guangzhou: Guangdong tongji chubanshe.

Gerschenkron, A. (1962). *Economic Backwardness in Historical Perspective*. Cambridge, MA: Harvard University Press.

GFYZ (Guowuyuan fazhan yanjiu zhongxin) (State Council Research Centre for Development) (1992). *Zhongguo diqu fazhan shuju shouce* (Data Handbook on the Development of China's Regions). Beijing: Zhongguo caizheng jingji chubanshe.

GGK (Ganzi Zangzu zizhizhou gaikuang bianxiezu; Editorial Committee for 'A Survey of Gansu Prefecture') (1986). *Ganzi Zangzu zizhizhou gaikuang* (A Survey of Ganzi Tibetan Autonomous Prefecture). Chengdu: Sichuan minzu chubanshe.

Gilley, B. (2001). *Model Rebels*. Berkeley: California University Press.

Ginsburg, N., Koppel, B. and McGee, T. G. (eds.) (1991). *The Extended Metropolis*. Honolulu: University of Hawaii Press.

Glaeser, E. L., La Porta, R., Lopez de Silanes, F. and Shleifer, A. (2004). 'Do Institutions Cause Growth'? *Journal of Economic Growth*, 9: 271–303.

Gong'an bu (Ministry of Public Security) (1985). *Zhongguo chengshi renkou ziliao shouce* (Handbook on China's Urban Population). Beijing: Ditu chubanshe.

Goodman, D. and Feng, C. Y. (1994). 'Guangdong', in D. S. G. Goodman and G. Segal (eds.) *China Deconstructs*. London: Routledge.

Görg, H. and Greenaway, D. (2004). 'Much Ado about Nothing? Do Domestic Firms Really Benefit from Foreign Direct Investment?' *World Bank Research Observer*, 19(2): 171–97.

Gray, J. (1974). 'Politics in Command'. *Political Quarterly*, 45(1): 37–8.

—— (2006). 'Maoism in Retrospect'. *China Quarterly*, September, 187.

GSNJ (Gansu nianjian bianweihui; Gansu Yearbook Editorial Committee) (1997). *Gansu nianjian 1997* (Gansu Yearbook). Beijing: Zhongguo tongji chubanshe.

GSSQ (Zhonggong Gansu sheng wei yanjiushi; Research Unit of the Gansu Committee of the CCP) (ed.) (1988). *Gansu sheng qing* (Conditions in Gansu Province). Lanzhou: Gansu renmin chubanshe.

Gu, Z. C. (1985). 'Sichuan gongye jiegou de tedian yuji gaishan de tujing' (Peculiarities in Sichuan's Industrial Structure and Ways to Improve It), in Sichuan sheng shehui kexueyuan jingji yanjiusuo (Economic Research Institute of the Sichuan Academy of Social Sciences) (ed.) *Zhongguo shehuizhuyi jingji yanjiu* (Research on China's Socialist Economy). Chengdu: Sichuan sheng kexueyuan chubanshe.

Guangdong Party Commission (1996). 'Several Policies and Provisions Concerning Further support to Mountainous Areas to Quicken Economic Development'. Issued 11 March at http://www.getgd.net/gd (Accessed May 2005).

Guangdong sheng wei—Guangdong tongjiju (Guangdong Statistical Bureau) and Zhonggong Guangdong sheng wei (Guangdong Committee of the CCP) (eds.) (1992). *Zhujiang sanjiaozhou guomin jingji tongji ziliao 1980–1991* (Statistical Materials on the Economy of the Pearl River Delta). Guangzhou: Zhonggong Guangdong sheng wei.

Guanghan XZ (*Guanghan xian zhi*) (Guanghan County Records) (1992). Chengdu: Sichuan renmin chubanshe.

Guannan XZ (*Guannan xian zhi*) (Guannan County Records) (1995). Nanjing: Jiangsu guji chubanshe.

Guan XZ (*Guan xian zhi*) (Guan County Records) (1991). Chengdu: Sichuan renmin chubanshe.

Guizhou tongjiju (Guizhou Statistical Bureau) (1984). *Guizhou jingji shouce* (Guizhou Economic Handbook). Guiyang: Guizhou renmin chubanshe.

—— (1997). *Guizhou tongji nianjian 1997* (Guizhou Statistical Yearbook). Beijing: Zhongguo tongji chubanshe.

Guldin, G. E. (2001). *What's A Peasant To Do?* Boulder, CO: Westview.

GYPC (Disanci quanguo gongye pucha bangongshi; Office of the Third National Industrial Census) (1997). *Zhongghua renmin gongheguo 1995 nian gongye pucha ziliao huibian* (Summary of Materials on the 1995 National Industrial Census). Beijing: Zhongguo shehui kexue chubanshe.

GZ (Ganzi Zangzu zizhizhou weiyuanhui; Ganzi Prefecture Editorial Committee) (1997). Ganzi *Zangzu zizhizhou zhi* (Records for Ganzi Tibetan Autonomous Prefecture). Chengdu: Sichuan renmin chubanshe.

GZJ (Guizhou juan bianji weiyuanhui; Guizhou Volume Editorial Committee) (1995). *Zhongguo nongye quanshu—Guizhou juan* (A Compendium of Chinese Agriculture—Guizhou Volume). Beijing: Zhongguo nongye chubanshe.

GZSQ (Guizhou sheng qing bianji weiyuanhui; Guizhou sheng qing Editorial Committee) (1986). *Guizhou sheng qing* (Conditions in Guizhou Province). Guiyang: Guizhou renmin chubanshe.

GZTJNJ (*Guangzhou tongji nianjian 1982, 1983;* Guangzhou Statistical Yearbook). (1982, 1983). Guangzhou: Guangzhou tongji nianjian wei chubanshe.

Haimen XZ (*Haimen xian zhi*) (Haimen County Records) (1996). Nanjing: Jiangsu kexue jishu chubanshe.

Haining SZ (*Haining shi zhi*) (Haining City Records) (1995). Shanghai: Hanyu dacidian chubanshe.

Haiyan XZ (*Haiyan xian zhi*) (Haiyan County Records) (1992). Hangzhou: Zhejiang renmin chubanshe.

Han, D. P. (2000). *The Unknown Cultural Revolution*. New York: Garland Publishing.

—— (2001). 'The Impact of the Cultural Revolution on Rural Education and Economic Development'. *Modern China*, 27(1): 59–90.

Han, S. S. and Pannell, C. (1999). 'The Geography of Privatisation in China 1978–1996'. *Economic Geography*, 75(3): 272–96.

Hanjiang XZ (*Hanjiang xian zhi*) (Hanjiang County Records) (1995). Nanjing: Jiangsu renmin chubanshe.

Hare, D. and West, L. (1999). 'Spatial Patterns in China's Rural Industrial Growth and Prospects for the Alleviation of Regional Income Inequality'. *Journal of Comparative Economics*, 27(3): 475–97.

Hayami, A., Saito, O. and Toby, R. P. (eds.) (2004). *Emergence of Economic Society in Japan 1600–1859*. Oxford: Oxford University Press.

HBGK (Hubei sheng difangzhi bianji weiyuanhui; Editorial Committee for Hubei's Provincial Records) (ed.) (1984). *Hubei shixian gaikuang* (A Survey of Hubei's Cities and Counties). Wuhan: no publisher.

He, R. F. (ed.) (1987). *Wenzhou jingji geju* (The Structure of Wenzhou's Economy). Hangzhou: Zhejiang renmin chubanshe.

He, K. (ed.) (2004). *Zhongguo de xiangzhen qiye* (China's Township and Village Enterprises). Beijing: Zhongguo nongye chubanshe.

He, J. S. and Pooler, J. (2002). 'The Regional Concentration of China's Interprovincial Migration Flows, 1982–90'. *Population and Environment*, 24(2): 149–82.

Heckman, J. (2003). 'China's Investment in Human Capital'. *Economic Development and Cultural Change*, 51(4): 795–804.

Helpman, E. (2004). *The Mystery of Economic Growth*. Cambridge, MA: Harvard University Press.

Henan yanjiushi (Henan sheng renmin zhengfu diaocha yanjiushi; Research Unit of the People's Government of Henan Province) (1987). *Henan sheng qing* (Conditions in Henan Province). Zhengzhou: Henan renmin chubanshe.

Hershatter, G. (1986). *The Workers of Tianjin*. Stanford: Stanford University Press.

Hessler, P. (2001). *River Town*. London: John Murray.

HNQH (Hunan sheng nongye quhua weiyuanhui; Editorial Committee for Hunan Province Agricultural Districts) (ed.) (1989). *Hunan sheng nongye quhua*, vol. 5 (Agricultural Districts of Hunan Province). Changsha: Hunan kexue jishu chubanshe.

HNSQ (Hunan tongjiju; Hunan Statistical Bureau) (1989). *Hunan sheng qing* (Conditions in Hunan Province). Changsha: Hunan renmin chubanshe.

HNTJNJ (Hunan tongjiju; Hunan Statistical Bureau) (various years). *Hunan tongji nianjian 1982, 1986 1987, 1989, 1991* (Hunan Statistical Yearbook). Beijing: Zhongguo tongji chubanshe.

HNXZ (Henan sheng difang shizhi bangongshi; Office of Historical Records for Henan Province) (ed.) (1995). *Henan sheng zhi—Xiangzhen qiye zhi* (Henan Provincial Records—Township and Village Enterprise Records). Zhengzhou: Henan renmin chubanshe.

Ho, S. P. S. (1994). *Rural China in Transition*. Oxford: Clarendon Press.

—— and Kueh, Y. Y. (eds.) (2000). *Sustainable Economic Development in South China*. Basingstoke: Macmillan.

—— Bowles, P. and Dong, X. Y. (2003). 'Letting Go of the Small: An Analysis of the Privatisation of Rural Enterprises in Jiangsu and Shandong'. *Journal of Development Studies*, 39(4): 1–26.

Holz, C. (2003). 'Fast, Clear and Accurate: How Reliable are Chinese Output and Economic Growth Statistics'? *China Quarterly*, 173: 122–63.

Hong, L. J. (1997). 'Sichuan', in D. S. G. Goodman (ed.) *China's Provinces in Reform*. London: Routledge.

—— (2004). 'Chongqing'. *China Quarterly*, 178: 448–66.

Honig, E. (1986). *Sisters and Strangers: Women in the Shanghai Cotton Mills, 1919–49*. Stanford: Stanford University Press.

—— (1992). *Creating Chinese Ethnicity: Subei People in Shanghai, 1850–1980*. New Haven: Yale University Press.

—— (1996). 'Native Place and the Making of Chinese Ethnicity', in G. Hershatter, E. Honig, J. Lipman and R. Stross (eds.) *Remapping China*. Stanford: Stanford University Press.

Howard, J. H. (2004). *Workers at War*. Stanford: Stanford University Press.

Hsiao, K. H. (1987). *The Government Budget and Fiscal Policy in Mainland China*. Taipei: Chung-hua Institute for Economic Research.

Hsieh, C. M. and Lu, M. (eds.) (2004). *Changing China*. Oxford: Westview.

Hsueh, T. T. and Li, Q. (eds.) (1999). *China's National Income 1952–1995*. Boulder, CA: Westview.

Hu, H. Y. (1987). *Zhongguo renkou—Shanghai fence* (China's Population—Shanghai). Beijing: Zhongguo caizheng jingji chubanshe.

Hu, A. and Jefferson, G. H. (2002). 'FDI Impact and Spillover: Evidence from China's Electronic and Textile Industries'. *World Economy*, 25(8): 1063–76.

Huang, X. L. (1988). *Zhongguo renkou—Guangxi fence* (China's Population—Guangxi). Beijing: Zhongguo caizheng jingji chubanshe.

Huang, P. C. C. (1990). *The Peasant Family and Rural Development in the Yangzi Delta 1350–1988*. Stanford: Stanford University Press.

Huang, Y. S. (1996). *Inflation and Investment Controls in China*. Cambridge: Cambridge University Press.

—— (2003). *Selling China*. Cambridge: Cambridge University Press.

Huber, R. J. (1971). 'Effect on Prices of Japan's Entry into World Commerce after 1858'. *Journal of Political Economy*, 79(3): 614–28.

Huenemann, R. W. (1984). *The Dragon and the Iron Horse: The Economics of Railroads in China 1876–1937*. Cambridge, MA: Harvard University Press.

Hutton, W. (1995). *The State We're In*. London: Jonathan Cape.

Imai, K. I. (2003). *Beyond Market Socialism*. Tokyo: Institute of Developing Economies.

Ishikawa, S. (1967). *Economic Development in Asian Perspective*. Tokyo: Kinokuniya Co.

—— (1988). 'Patterns and Processes of Intersectoral Resource Flows', in G. Ranis and T. P. Schultz (eds.) *The State of Development Economics*. Oxford: Basil Blackwell.

Jacobs, J. B. (1999). 'Uneven Development', in H. Hendrischke and Feng C. Y. (eds.) *The Political Economy of China's Provinces*. London: Routledge.

—— and Hong, L. J. (1994). 'Shanghai and the Lower Yangzi Valley', in D. S. G. Goodman and G. Segal (eds.) *China Deconstructs*. London: Routledge.

Jefferson, G. H. and Rawski, T. G. (1994). 'Enterprise Reform in Chinese Industry'. *Journal of Economic Perspectives*, 8(2): 47–70.

—— and Singh, I. (1999). *Enterprise Reform in China*. Oxford: Oxford University Press.

—— Hu, A. G. Z., Guan, X. J. and Yu, X. Y. (2003). 'Ownership, Performance and Innovation in China's Large- and Medium-Size Industrial Enterprise Sector'. *China Economic Review*, 14: 89–113.

—— Rawski, T. G. and Zheng, Y. X. (1992). 'Growth, Efficiency and Convergence in China's State and Collective Enterprises'. *Economic Development and Cultural Change*, 40(2): 239–66.

—— —— and —— (1996). 'Chinese Industrial Productivity'. *Journal of Comparative Economics*, 23(2): 146–80.

Jiajiang XZ *(Jiajiang xian zhi)* (Jiajiang County Records) (1989). Chengdu: Sichuan renmin chubanshe.

Jiang, Y. R. (1998). *Zhongguo nongye quanshu—Jiangsu juan* (A Compendium of Chinese Agriculture—Jiangsu Volume). Beijing: Zhongguo nongye chubanshe.

Jiang, H. (1999). *The Ordos Plateau of China*. New York: United Nations University Press.

Jiang, Y. R. and Ashley, D. (2000). *Mao's Children in the New China*. London: Routledge.

Jiangpu XZ *(Jiangpu xian zhi)* (Jiangpu County Records) (1995). Nanjing: Hehai daxue chubanshe.

Jiangshan SZ *(Jiangshan shi zhi)* (Jiangshan City Records) (1990). Hangzhou: Zhejiang renmin chubanshe.

Jiangsu tongjiju (Jiangsu Statistical Bureau) (1992). *1992 nian Jiangsu shixian jingji* (The Economy of Jiangsu's Cities and Counties in 1992). Beijing: Zhongguo tongji chubanshe.

Jiangyin XZ *(Jiangyin xian zhi)* (Jiangyin County Records) (1992). Shanghai: Shanghai renmin chubanshe.

Jiaoling XZ *(Jiaoling xian zhi)* (Jiaoling County Records) (1992). Guangzhou: Guangdong renmin chubanshe.

Jiashan XZ *(Jiashan xian zhi)* (Jiashan County Records) (1995). Shanghai: Sanjian shudian.

Jie, X. W. and Wang, W. Y. (2001). 'Sichuan xiangzhen qiye erci chuangye zhong de jiegou tiaozheng yu kongjian buju' (The Structural Adjustment and Layout of Sichuan's Township and Village Industries during the Second Transformation). *Jingji tizhi gaige* (Reform of the Economic System), 4: 25–34.

Jiexi XZ *(Jiexi xian zhi)* (Jiexi County Records) (1994). Guangzhou: Guangdong renmin chubanshe.

Jieyang XZ *(Jieyang xian zhi)* (Jieyang County Records) (1993). Guangzhou: Guangdong renmin chubanshe.

Jingjiang XZ *(Jingjiang xian zhi)* (Jingjiang County Records) (1992). Nanjing: Jiangsu renmin chubanshe.

Jingyan XZ *(Jingyan xian zhi)* (Jingyan County Records) (1990). Chengdu: Sichuan renmin chubanshe.

Jinhu XZ *(Jinhu xian zhi)* (Jinhu County Records) (1994). Nanjing: Jiangsu renmin chubanshe.

Jinjiang XZ (*Jinjiang xian zhi*) (Jinjiang City Records) (1994). Shanghai: sanlian shudian.

Jintan XZ (*Jintan xian zhi*) (Jintan County Records) (1993). Nanjing: Jiangsu renmin chubanshe.

JNSZ (Shanghai shehui kexueyuan jingji yanjiusuo; The Economic Research Institute of the Shanghai Academy of Social Science) (1991). *Jindai Jiangnan sizhi gongye shi* (A History of the Silk Industry in Modern Jiangnan). Shanghai: Shanghai renmin chubanshe.

Johnson, G. and Woon, Y. F. (1997). 'Rural Development Patterns in Post-Reform China'. *Development and Change*, 28: 731–51.

JSB (Jiangsu tongjiju; Jiangsu Statistical Bureau) (ed.) (1989). *Jiangsu sishinian 1949–1989* (Forty Years in Jiangsu). Beijing: Zhongguo tongji chubanshe.

JSJJZ (Jiangsu sheng difangzhi bianzuan weiyuanhui; Compilation Committee for Jiangsu Provincial Records) (ed.) (1999). *Jiangsu sheng zhi—Jingji zonghe zhi* (Jiangsu Provincial Records—Summary Economic Records). Beijing: Difang chubanshe.

JSJYZ (Jiangsu sheng difangzhi bianzuan weiyuanhui; Jiangsu Records Editorial Committee) (2000). *Jiangsu sheng zhi: Jiaoyu zhi*, vol. 2 (Jiangsu Provincial Records: Education). Nanjing: Jiangsu guji chubanshe.

JSK (Jiangsu shehui kexueyuan; Jiangsu Academy of Social Science) (1987). *Jiangsu sheng gongye diaocha tongji ziliao* (Statistical Materials from Jiangsu Industrial Surveys). Nanjing: Nanjing gongxueyuan chubanshe.

JSSXGK (Jiangsu shixian gaikuang weiyuanhui; Jiangsu shixian gaikuang Editorial Committee) (1989). *Jiangsu shixian gaikuang* (A Survey of Jiangsu's Cities and Counties). Nanjing: Jiangsu jiaoyu chubanshe.

JSTJNJ (Jiangsu tongjiju; Jiangsu Statistical Bureau) (ed.) (various years). *Jiangsu tongji nianjian 1988, 1994, 1997, 1998, 1999, 2002 and 2003* (Jiangsu Statistical Yearbook). Beijing: Zhongguo renmin chubanshe.

JSXZ (Jiangsu sheng difangzhi bianzuan weiyuanhui; Compilation Committee for Jiangsu Provincial Records) (ed.) (2000). *Jiangsu sheng zhi—Xiangzhen gongye zhi* (Jiangsu Provincial Records—Township and Village Industry Records). Beijing: Difang chubanshe.

Ju, F. T. and Wu, D. S. (1986). 'The Formation and Development of the Silk Town Shengze', in X. T. Fei (ed.). *Small Towns in China*. Beijing: New World Press.

JXTJNJ (Jiangxi tongjiju; Jiangxi Statistical Bureau) (1990). *Jiangxi tongji nianjian 1990* (Jiangxi Statistical Yearbook). Beijing: Zhongguo tongji chubanshe.

JYNJ (*Zhongguo jiaoyu nianjian 1949–1981, 1995 and 1997*; Chinese Educational Yearbook) (1984, 1995 and 1997). Beijing: Zhongguo renmin chubanshe.

Kaijiang XZ (*Kaijiang xian zhi*) (Kaijiang County Records) (1989). Chengdu: Sichuan renmin chubanshe.

Kai XZ (*Kaixian zhi*) (Kai County Records) (1990). Chengdu: Sichuan daxue chubanshe.

Kaldor, N. (1957). 'A Model of Economic Growth'. *Economic Journal*, 67(3): 591–624.

—— ([1961] 1989). 'Capital Accumulation and Economic Growth', in F. Targetti and A. P. Thirlwall (eds.) *The Essential Kaldor*. London: Duckworth.

—— ([1966] 1989). 'Causes of the Slow Rate of Economic Growth in the United Kingdom', in F. Targetti and A. P. Thirlwall (eds.) *The Essential Kaldor*. London: Duckworth.

—— (1970). 'The Case for Regional Policies'. *Scottish Journal of Political Economy*, 17(3): 337–48.

Karshenas, M. (1995). *Industrialization and Agricultural Surplus*. Oxford: Oxford University Press.

Kemp, M. C. (1960). 'The Mill-Bastable Infant Industry Dogma'. *Journal of Political Economy*, LXVIII: 65–7.

Keng, S. and Chen, C. W. (2005). 'Farewell to the Developmental State: Government and Business in the Kunshan Miracle', unpublished ms.

Keynes, J. M. (1936). *The General Theory of Interest, Money and Employment*. London: Macmillan.

Kikeri, S. and Nellis, J. (2004). 'An Assessment of Privatization'. *World Bank Research Observer*, 19(1): 87–118.

Kitson, M. and Michie, J. (1996). 'Manufacturing Capacity, Investment, and Employment', in J. Michie and J. Grieve Smith (eds.) *Creating Industrial Capacity*. Oxford: Oxford University Press.

—— and —— (eds.) (2000). *The Political Economy of Competitiveness*. London: Routledge.

Kleinberg, R. (1990). *China's Opening to the Outside World*. Boulder, CA: Westview.

Knight, J. and Song, L. N. (1993). 'Workers in China's Rural Industries', in K. Griffin and R. W. Zhao (eds.) *The Distribution of Income in China*. London: Macmillan.

—— and —— (1999). *The Rural-Urban Divide*. Oxford: Oxford University Press.

—— —— and Jia, H. B. (1999). 'Chinese Rural Migrants in Urban Enterprises', in S. Cook and M. Maurer-Fazio (eds.) *The Workers' State Meets the Market*. London: Frank Cass.

Köll, E. (2003). *From Cotton Mill to Business Empire*. Cambridge, MA: Harvard University Press.

Kremer, M. (1993). 'Population Growth and Technological Change'. *Quarterly Journal of Economics*, CVIII: 551–75.

Krueger, A. O. and Tuncer, B. (1982). 'An Empirical Test of the Infant Industry Argument'. *American Economic Review*, 72(5): 1142–52.

Krugman, P. (1991). *Geography and Trade*. Cambridge, MA: MIT Press.

—— (1993a). 'Protection in Developing Countries', in R. Dornbusch (ed.) *Policymaking in the Open Economy*. Oxford: Oxford University Press.

—— (1993b). 'The Current Case for Industrial Policy', in D. Salvatore (ed.) *Protectionism and World Welfare*. Cambridge: Cambridge University Press.

—— (1995). *Development, Geography, and Economic Theory*. Cambridge, MA: MIT Press.

—— (1996). *Pop Internationalism*. Cambridge, MA: MIT Press.

Ku, H. B. (2003). *Moral Politics in a South Chinese Village*. Lanham, MD: Rowman and Littlefield.

Kua Gansu (Kua shiji de Zhongguo renkou bianweihui; Editorial Committee for 'China's Population Towards the Twenty-First Century') (1994). *Kua shiji de Zhongguo renkou—Gansu juan* (China's Population Towards the Twenty-First Century—Gansu). Beijing: Zhongguo tongji chubanshe.

Kua Sichuan (Kua shiji de Zhongguo renkou bianweihui; Editorial Committee for 'China's Population Towards the Twenty-First Century') (1994). *Kua shiji de Zhongguo renkou—Sichuan juan* (China's Population Towards the Twenty-First Century—Sichuan). Beijing: Zhongguo tongji chubanshe.

Kueh, Y. Y. and Ash, R. F. (1996). 'The Fifth Dragon', in B. Hook (ed.) *Guangdong: China's Promised Land*. Hong Kong: Oxford University Press.

Kumar, A. (1994a). 'Economic Reform and the Internal Division of Labour in China', in D. S. G. Goodman and G. Segal (eds.) *China Deconstructs*. London: Routledge.

—— (1994b). *China: Internal Market Development and Regulation*. Washington, DC: World Bank.

Kunshan XZ (*Kunshan xian zhi*) (Kunshan County Records) (1990). Shanghai: Shanghai renmin chubanshe.

Lall, S. (1992). 'Technological Capabilities and Industrialization'. *World Development*, 20(2): 165–86.

—— (2001). 'Competitiveness Indices and Developing Countries'. *World Development*, 29 (9): 1501–25.

—— and Albaladejo, M. (2004). 'China's Competitive Performance'. *World Development*, 32(9): 1441–66.

Lardy, N. R. (1976). 'Centralization and Decentralization in China's Fiscal Management'. *China Quarterly*, 66: 340–54.

—— (1978). *Economic Growth and Distribution in China*. Cambridge: Cambridge University Press.

Lau, L. J., Qian, Y. Y. and Roland, G. (2000). 'Reform Without Losers: An Interpretation of China's Dual-Track Approach to Transition'. *Journal of Political Economy*, 108(1): 120–43.

Lavely, W., Xiao, Z. Y., Li, B. H. and Freedman, R. (1990). 'The Rise in Female Education in China', *China Quarterly*, 121: 61–93.

Layard, R., Nickell, S. and Jackman, R. (1991). *Unemployment*. Oxford: Oxford University Press.

LDNJ (Zhongguo guojia tongjiju; National Bureau of Statistics) (various years). *Zhongguo laodong tongji nianjian 1990, 1997, 2001, 2003 and 2005* (Chinese Statistical Yearbook of Labour). Beijing: Zhongguo tongji chubanshe.

Lechang XZ (*Lechang xian zhi*) (Lechang County Records) (1994). Guangzhou: Guangdong renmin chubanshe.

Lee, C. K. (1995). 'Engendering the Worlds of Labor'. *American Sociological Review*, 60(3): 378–97.

Lee, P. K. (2000). 'Into the Trap of Strengthening State Capacity'. *China Quarterly*, 164: 1007–24.

Leeming, F. (1985). *Rural China Today*. London: Longman.

Leibenstein, H. (1957). *Economic Backwardness and Economic Growth*. New York: Wiley.

Lewin, P. (ed.) (2002). *The Economics of QWERTY*. Basingstoke: Palgrave.

Lewis, W. A. (1954). 'Economic Development with Unlimited Supplies of Labour'. *Manchester School of Economic and Social Studies*, 22: 139–91.

Lewis, J. W. and Xue, L. T. (1988). *China Builds the Bomb*. Stanford: Stanford University Press.

Li, J. G. (1988). 'Wenzhou jingji de fazhan' (The Development of the Wenzhou Economy) in *Nongcun jingji qingkuang* (The Rural Economic Situation), 6: 6–28.

Li, L. C. L. (1997). 'Provincial Discretion and National Power: Investment Policy in Guangdong and Shanghai, 1978–1993'. *China Quarterly*, 152: 778–804.

Li, P. (1997). 'Report on the Work of Government, 1997'. *Beijing Review*, 40(13): 1–20.

Li, B. Z. (1998). *Agricultural Development in Jiangnan, 1620–1850*. Basingstoke: Macmillan.

Li, C. R. (1992). *A Study of China's Population*. Beijing: Foreign Languages Press.

Li, H. B. and Rozelle, S. (2000). 'Saving or Stripping Rural Industry: An Analysis of Privatization and Efficiency in China'. *Agricultural Economics*, 23: 241–52.

—— and —— (2004). 'Insider Privatization with a Tail: The Screening Contract and Performance of Privatized Firms in Rural China'. *Journal of Development Economics*, 75: 1–26.

Li, J. X., Zhang, G. H. and Lian, S. Q. (eds.) (1999). *Zhongguo shichang yingxiao huanjing nianjian 1998* (Chinese Market and Business Environment Yearbook). Beijing: Zhongguo tongji chubanshe.

Li, X. Y., Liu, X. M. and Parker, D. (2001). 'Foreign Direct Investment and Productivity Spillovers in the Chinese manufacturing sector'. *Economic Systems*, 25: 305–21.

Liang, R. C. (1956). *Guangdong jingji dili* (Beijing: Academia Sinica). Translated (1958) as *Economic Geography of Kwangtung*. New York: Joint Publications Research Service, JPRS/DC-389.

Liang, H. (1996). 'Zhangjiagang: A Miracle of Urban Development'. *Beijing Review*, 39(8, 9) at http://www.china.or.cn/bjreview/february/96-8-13.html (accessed 31 October 1997).

Liannan XZ (*Liannan xian zhi*) (Liannan County Records) (1996). Guangzhou: Guangdong renmin chubanshe.

Lianshui XZ (*Lianshui xian zhi*) (Lianshui County Records) (1990). Nanjing: Jiangsu guji chubanshe.

Lin, G. Z. (ed.) (1992). *Zhejiang sheng jingji dili* (An Economic Geography of Zhejiang). Beijing: Xinhua chubanshe.

Lin, A. H. Y. (1997). *The Rural Economy of Guangdong 1870–1937*. Basingstoke: Macmillan.

Lin, G. C. S. (1997). *Red Capitalism in South China*. Vancouver: University of British Columbia Press.

—— (2001*a*). Metropolitan Development in a Transitional Socialist Economy'. *Urban Studies*, 38(3): 383–406.

—— (2001*b*). 'Evolving Spatial Forms of Urban-Rural Interaction in the Pearl River Delta, China'. *Professional Geographer*, 53(1): 56–70.

—— (2002). 'The Growth and Structural Change of Chinese Cities'. *Cities*, 19(5): 299–316.

Lin, M. X. (2002). 'Guoyou qiye gaige yu tuokun de shizheng yanjiu' (Research on the Reform and Elimination of Losses in State-Owned Enterprises). *Dangdai jingji yanjiu* (Research on the Contemporary Economy), 1: 32–5.

Lin, J. Y. F. and Liu, Z. Q. (2000). 'Fiscal Decentralization and Economic Growth in China'. *Economic Development and Cultural Change*, 49(1): 1–22.

—— and Yao, Y. (2001). 'Chinese Rural Industrialization in the Context of the East Asian Miracle', in J. E. Stiglitz and S. Yusuf (eds.) *Rethinking the East Asian Miracle*. Oxford: Oxford University Press.

—— Cai, F. and Li, Z. (1996). *The China Miracle*. Hong Kong: Chinese University Press.

Linhai XZ (*Linhai xian zhi*) (Linhai County Records) (1989). Hangzhou: Zhejiang renmin chubanshe.

Lishui XZ (*Lishui xian zhi*) (Lishui County Records) (1997). Nanjing: Jiangsu guji chubanshe.

Liu, H. K. (1988). *Zhongguo renkou—Sichuan fence* (China's Population—Sichuan). Beijing: Zhongguo caizheng jingji chubanshe.

Liu, Z. (ed.) (1990). *Dangdai Zhongguo de Hunan* (Contemporary China: Hunan). Beijing: Zhongguo shehui kexue chubanshe.

Liu, Y. L. (1992). 'Reform From Below: The Private Economy and Local Politics in the Rural Industrialization of Wenzhou'. *China Quarterly*, 130: 293–316.

Liu, X. F. (1993). 'Employment, Output and Structure in China's Rural Non-Farm Sector,' unpublished PhD dissertation, University of Cambridge.

Liu, Z. Q. (2002). 'Foreign Direct Investment and Technology Spillover'. *Journal of Comparative Economics*, 30: 579–602.

—— (2003). 'The Economic Impact and Determinants of Investment in Human and Political Capital in China'. *Economic Development and Cultural Change*, 52(2): 369–94.

Liu, S. N. and Wu, Q. G. (1986). *China's Socialist Economy*. Beijing: Beijing Review Press.

Liu, T-C. and Yeh, K-C. (1965). *The Economy of Mainland China*. Princeton: Princeton University Press.

Liu, Y., Chew, S. B. and Li, W. (1998). 'Education, Experience and Productivity of Labor in China's TVEs: The Case of Jiangsu'. *China Economic Review*, 9(1): 47–58.

Long, G. Y. and Ng, M. K. (2001). 'The Political Economy of Intra-Provincial Disparities in Post-Reform China'. *Geoforum*, 32(2): 215–34.

Longchuan XZ (*Longchuan xian zhi*) (Longchuan County Records) (1994). Guangzhou: Guangdong renmin chubanshe.

Lou, B. B., Zheng, Z. X., Connelly, R. and Roberts, K. D. (2004). 'The Migration Experiences of Young Women from Four Counties in Sichuan and Anhui', in A. M. Gaetano and T. Jacka (eds.) *On the Move*. New York: Columbia University Press.

Lucas, R. E. (1988). 'On The Mechanics of Economic Development'. *Journal of Monetary Economics*, 22: 3–42.

—— (1993). 'The Making of a Miracle'. *Econometrica*, 61(2): 251–72.

Lyons, T. P. (1994). *Poverty and Growth in a South China County*. New York: East Asia Program, Cornell University.

LYZG (Liangshan Yizu zizhizhou gaikuang bianxie; Editorial Committee for 'A Survey of Liangshan Prefecture') (1985). *Liangshan Yizu zizhizhou gaikuang* (A Survey of the Liangshan Yi Minority Autonomous Region). Chengdu: Sichuan minzu chubanshe.

LYZW (Liangshan Yizu zizhizhou weiyuanhui) (Party Committee of the Liangshan Yi Minority Autonomous District) (ed.) (1993). *Liangshan wenshi ziliao xuanji*, vol. 11 (Selected Materials on the History and Culture of Liangshan). No publisher.

Ma, X. D. (2000). 'Insider and Outsider Community Strategies toward Migrant Workers', in L. A. West and Y. H. Zhao (eds.) *Rural Labour Flows in China*. Berkeley: University of California.

Ma, D. B. (2004). 'Why Japan, Not China, was the First to Develop in East Asia: Lessons from Sericulture, 1850–1937'. *Economic Development and Cultural Change*, 52(2): 369–94.

Mako, W. P. and Zhang, C. L. (2003). *Management of China's State-Owned Enterprise Portfolio*. Beijing: World Bank.

Mallee, H. (2000). 'Agricultural Labor and Rural Population Mobility', in L. A. West and Y. H. Zhao (eds.) *Rural Labor Flows in China*. Berkeley: University of California.

Mankiw, N. G. (1995). 'The Growth of Nations'. *Brookings Papers on Economic Activity*, 1: 275–326.

—— Romer, D. and Weil, D. N. (1992). 'A Contribution to the Empirics of Economic Growth'. *Quarterly Journal of Economics*, CV11(2): 407–37.

Mao, Z. D. (1964). 'Talk on the Third Five Year Plan', 6 June 1964. In Maoist Documentation Project, *Long Live Mao Zedong Thought*. Available at http://www.maoism.org/msw (accessed 22 December 2003).

—— (1966a). 'Talk at Enlarged Meeting of the Political Bureau', 20 March 1966. In Maoist Documentation Project, *Long Live Mao Zedong Thought*. Available at http://www.maoism.org/msw (accessed 22 December 2003).

—— (1966*b*). 'Notes on the Report of Further Improving the Army's Agricultural Work by the Rear Service Department of the Military Commission', 7 May 1966. In Maoist Documentation Project, *Long Live Mao Zedong Thought*. Available at http://www.maoism.org/msw (accessed 22 December 2003).

Mao, K. S. (1987). *Zhongguo renkou—Hunan fence* (China's Population—Hunan). Beijing: Zhongguo caizheng jingji chubanshe.

Maoming SZ (*Maoming shi zhi*) (Maoming Municipality Records) (1997). Henan: Sanlian shudian chushe.

Marks, R. B. (1984). *Rural Revolution in South China*. Madison: Wisconsin University Press.

Marton, A. M. (2000). *China's Spatial Economic Development*. London: Routledge.

Mazumdar, S. (1998). *Sugar and Society in China*. Cambridge, MA: Harvard University Press.

McCloskey, D. (1985). 'The Loss Function Has Been Mislaid: The Rhetoric of Significance Tests'. *American Economic Review* (supplement), 75(2): 201–5.

—— (2002). *The Secret Sins of Economics*. Chicago: Prickly Paradigm Press.

—— and Ziliak, S. (1996). 'The Standard Error of Regressions'. *Journal of Economic Literature*, March: 97–114.

McCombie, J. S. L. and Thirlwall, A. P. (1994). *Economic Growth and the Balance of Payments Constraint*. London: Macmillan.

McNally, C. (2004). 'Sichuan'. *China Quarterly*, 178: 426–47.

Megginson, W. L. and Netter, J. M. (2001). 'From State to Market: A Survey of Empirical Studies on Privatization'. *Journal of Economic Literature*, 39(2): 321–89.

Mei XZ (*Meixian zhi*) (Meixian County Records) (1994). Guangzhou: Guangdong renmin chubanshe.

Mendels, F. F. (1972). 'Proto-industrialization'. *Journal of Economic History*, 32(1): 241–61.

Meng, X. (1990). 'The Rural Labour Market', in W. A. Byrd and Q. S. Lin (eds.) *China's Rural Industry*. Oxford: Oxford University Press.

—— (2000). 'Rural Wage Gap, Information Flow, and Rural-Urban Migration', in L. A. West and Y. H. Zhao (eds.) *Rural Labor Flows in China*. Berkeley: University of California.

MGK (Muli Zangzu zizhixian gaikuang bianxie; Editorial Committee for 'A Survey of Muli County') (1985). *Muli Zangzu zizhixian gaikuang* (A Survey of Muli Tibetan Autonomous County). Chengdu: Sichuan minzu chubanshe.

MSJZB (Mianyang shi jinrong zhi bangongshi) (Office for the Banking Records of Mianyang City) (ed.) (1993). *Mianyang shi jinrong zhi* (Mianyang City Banking Records). Chengdu: Sichuan cishu chubanshe.

Mianzhu XZ (*Mianzhu xian zhi*) (Mianzhu County Records) (1992). Chengdu: Sichuan kexue jishu chubanshe.

Mitch, D. (1993). 'The Role of Human Capital in the First Industrial Revolution', in J. Mokyr (ed.) *The British Industrial Revolution*. Boulder, CA: Westview.

Mo, Y. R. (1987). *Jiangsu xiangzhen gongye fazhan shi* (A History of the Development of Township and Village Industry in Jiangsu). Nanjing: Nanjing gongxueyuan chubanshe.

Mokyr, J. (ed.) (1985). *The Economics of the Industrial Revolution*. London: Allen and Unwin.

Mood, M. S. (2005). 'Opportunists, Predators and Rogues: The Role of Local State Relations in Shaping Chinese Rural Development'. *Journal of Agrarian Change*, 5(2): 217–50.

Murphy, R. (2002). *How Migrant Labor is Changing Rural Labour*. Cambridge: Cambridge University Press.

Murphy, R., Shleifer, A. and Vishny, R. (1989). 'Industrialization and the Big Push'. *Journal of Political Economy*, 97: 1003–26.

MWGK (Maowen Qiangzu zizhixian gaikuang bianxie; Editorial Committee for 'A Survey of Maowen County') (1985). *Maowen Qiangzu zizhixian gaikuang* (A Survey of Muli Qiang Autonomous County). Chengdu: Sichuan minzu chubanshe.

Myrdal, G. (1957). *Economic Theory and Under-Developed Regions*. London: Duckworth.

Nakamura, J. (1966). *Agricultural Production and the Economic Development of Japan*. Princeton, NJ: Princeton University Press.

Nanchong XZ (*Nanchong xian zhi*) (Nanchong County Records) (1993). Chengdu: Sichuan renmin chubanshe.

Nanchuan XZ (*Nanchuan xian zhi*) (Nanchuan County Records) (1991). Chengdu: Sichuan renmin chubanshe.

Nanxiong XZ (*Nanxiong xian zhi*) (Nanxiong County Records) (1991). Guangzhou: Guangdong renmin chubanshe.

Naughton, B. (1988). 'The Third Front'. *China Quarterly*, 115: 351–86.

—— (1991). 'Industrial Policy during the Cultural Revolution: Military Preparation, Decentralization and Leaps Forward', in W. A. Joseph, C. P. W. Wong and D. Zweig (eds.) *New Perspectives on the Cultural Revolution*. Harvard: Harvard University Press.

—— (1995). *Growing Out of the Plan*. Cambridge: Cambridge University Press.

—— (1997). 'Fiscal and Banking Reform', in M. Brosseau, H. C. Kuan and Y. Y. Kueh (eds.) *China Review 1997*. Hong Kong: Chinese University Press.

—— (2001). 'Provincial Economic Growth in China', in M. F. Renard (ed.) *China and Its Regions*. Cheltenham: Edward Elgar.

NBS (National Bureau of Statistics) (2005). 'Statistical Communiqué of the PRC on 2004 National Economic and Social Development'. Available at http://www.stats.gov.cn, 28.2.2005 (accessed 18 August 2005).

NCGY (Zhongguo tongjiju; National Bureau of Statistics) (1989). *Zhongguo fenxian nongcun jingji tongji gaiyao 1980–1987* (An Outline of Rural Economic Statistics by County in China).

—— (1990). *Zhongguo fenxian nongcun jingji tongji gaiyao 1988* (An Outline of Rural Economic Statistics by County in China).

—— (1991). *Zhongguo fenxian nongcun jingji tongji gaiyao 1989* (An Outline of Rural Economic Statistics by County in China).

—— (1992). *Zhongguo fenxian nongcun jingji tongji gaiyao 1990* (An Outline of Rural Economic Statistics by County in China).

—— (1993). *Zhongguo fenxian nongcun jingji tongji gaiyao 1991* (An Outline of Rural Economic Statistics by County in China).

NCTJNJ (Zhongguo guojia tongjiju; National Bureau of Statistics) (1993). *Zhongguo nongcun tongji nianjian 1993* (Chinese Rural Statistical Yearbook). Beijing: Zhongguo tongji chubanshe.

Neijiang ziyuan (Neijiang shi guotu ziyuan bianxiezu) (Editorial Committee for 'Natural Resources of Neijiang City') (1987). *Neijiang shi guotu ziyuan* (Natural Resources of Neijiang City). Chengdu: Sichuan kexue jishu chubanshe.

NSJSW (Neijiang shi jihua shengyu weiyuanhui) (Neijiang City Family Planning Committee) (1993). *Neijiang diqu renkou zhi* (Population Records for Neijiang Prefecture). Beijing: Zhongguo renkou chubanshe.

Nei Menggu tongjiju (Inner Mongolia Statistical Bureau) (1999). *Huihuang de Nei Menggu* (Brilliant Inner Mongolia). Beijing: Zhongguo tongji chubanshe.

Nelson, R. (1956). 'A Theory of the Low Level Equilibrium Trap in Underdeveloped Economies'. *American Economic Review*, 46: 894–908.

—— and Phelps, E. (1966). 'Investment in Humans, Technological Diffusion and Economic Growth'. *American Economic Review*, 56(1–2): 69–75.

—— and Winter, S. G. (1982). *An Evolutionary Theory of Economic Change*. Cambridge, MA: Harvard University Press.

Nicholas, S. and Oxley, D. (1993). 'The Living Standards of Women during the Industrial Revolution, 1795–1820'. *Economic History Review*, XLVI(4): 723–49.

Ning XZ (*Ning xian zhi*) (Ning county Records) (1988). Lanzhou: Gansu renmin chubanshe.

Ningyuan qing (Ningyuan xian qing diaochazu) (Survey Team for Conditions in Ningyuan County) (1993). *Baixianshi jingji shehui diaocha: Ningyuan juan* (Survey of the Economy and Society in One Hundred Counties and Cities: Ningyuan Volume). Beijing: Zhongguo dabaike quan shu chubanshe.

Nolan, P. (1983). *Growth Processes and Distributional Change in a South China Province: The Case of Guangdong*. London: School of Oriental and African Studies.

—— and Dong, F. R. (eds.) (1990). *Market Forces in China*. London: Zed.

Nongcun fazhan yanjiusuo (Rural Development Research Institute) (2004). Zhongguo nongcun jingji xingshi fenxin yu yuce (Analysis and Forecast of the State of the Rural Chinese Economy). Beijing: Shehui kexue wenshu chubanshe.

Nongye bu (Ministry of Agriculture) (1985). *Zhongguo nongye nianjian 1985 (Chinese Agricultural Yearbook)*. Beijing: Zhongguo nongye chubanshe.

—— (1989). *Zhongguo nongcun jingji tongji daquan* (Complete Statistics on the Chinese Rural Economy). Beijing: Nongye renmin chubanshe.

Nurkse, R. (1953). *Problems of Capital Formation in Underdeveloped Countries*. Oxford: Oxford University Press.

Nyberg, A. and Rozelle, S. (1999). *Accelerating China's Rural Transformation*. Washington, DC: World Bank.

NYNJ (Nongye bu) (Ministry of Agriculture) (various years). *Zhongguo nongye nianjian 2000, 2005* (Chinese Agricultural Yearbook). Beijing: Zhongguo nongye chubanshe.

NYTJZL (Nongye bu) (Ministry of Agriculture) (various years). *Zhongguo nongye tongji ziliao 1987, 1988, 1989, 1990, 1991, 1992, 1994* (Statistical Materials on Chinese Agriculture). Beijing: Nongye chubanshe.

O'Connor, D. (1998). 'Rural Industrial Development in Vietnam and China'. *OECD Development Centre Technical Paper*, no. 140. Paris: OECD.

Odgaard, O. (1992). *Private Enterprise in Rural China*. Aldershot: Avebury.

OECD (Organization for Economic Cooperation and Development) (2002). *China in the World Economy*. Paris: OECD.

Ogilvie, S. C. (1997). *State Corporatism and Proto-Industry*. Cambridge: Cambridge University Press.

—— and Cerman, M. (eds.) (1996). *European Proto-Industrialization*. Cambridge: Cambridge University Press.

Ohkawa, K. and Rosovsky, H. (1973). *Japanese Economic Growth: Trend Acceleration in the Twentieth Century*. Stanford: Stanford University Press.

Oi, J. C. (1992). 'Fiscal Reform and the Economic Foundations of Local State Corporatism in China'. *World Politics*, 45(1): 99–126.

—— (1999). *Rural China Takes Off*. Berkeley, CA: California University Press.

Oi, J. C. and Walder, A. G. (1999). *Property Rights and Economic Reform in China*. Stanford: Stanford University Press.

Oksenberg, M. and Tong, J. (1991). 'The Evolution of Central-Provincial Fiscal Relations in China, 1971–1984'. *China Quarterly*, 125: 1–32.

OLG (Office of the Leading Group of Economic Development in Poor Areas under the State Council) (1989). *Outline of Economic Development in China's Poor Areas*. Beijing: State Council.

—— (2004). 'List of Key Counties for National Poverty Reduction and Development'. Available at http://en.cpad.gov.cn/item/2004–05–24/50003.html (accessed 24 May 2005).

Pack, H. (2001). 'Technological Change and Growth in East Asia', in J. E. Stiglitz and S. Yusuf (eds.) *Rethinking the East Asian Miracle*. Oxford: Oxford University Press.

Pan, Z. F. (1988). *Zhongguo renkou—Guizhou fence* (China's Population—Guizhou). Beijing: Zhongguo caizheng jingji chubanshe.

Panzhihua tongjiju (Panzhihua Statistical Bureau) (2001). *Panzhihua tongji nianjian 2001* (Panzhihua Statistical Yearbook). Beijing: Zhongguo tongji chubanshe.

Parente, S. L. and Prescott, E. C. (1994). 'Barriers to Technology Adoption and Development'. *Journal of Political Economy*, 102: 298–321.

Park, A. and Shen, M. G. (2003). 'Joint Liability Lending and the Rise and Fall of China's Township and Village Enterprises'. *Journal of Development Economics*, 71: 497–531.

—— and Wang, S. G. (2001). 'China's Poverty Statistics'. *China Economic Review*, 12: 384–98.

—— Rozelle, S., Wong, C. P. W. and Ren, C. Q. (1996). 'Distributional Consequences of Reforming Local Public Finance in China'. *China Quarterly*, 147: 751–78.

Peng XZ (*Peng xian zhi*) (Peng County Records) (1989). Chengdu: Sichuan renmin chubanshe.

Pennarz, J. (1998). 'Adaptive Land-Use Strategies of Sichuan Smallholders', in F. Christiansen and J. Zhang (eds.) *Village Inc—Chinese Rural Society in the 1990s*. London: Curzon.

People's Government of Guangdong (1996). 'Several Policies and Provisions of the CCP Commission and the People's Government of Guangdong Province Concerning Further Support to Mountainous Areas to Quicken Their Economic Development'. Available at htt://www.getgd.net/gd-poli/english/01-1-1.htm (accessed 24 May 2005).

Pepper, S. (1996). *Radicalism and Education Reform in Twentieth Century China*. Cambridge: Cambridge University Press.

Perkins, D. H. (1998). 'Have China's Economic Reforms Stalled'? in G. W. Wang and J. Wong (eds.) *China's Political Economy*. Singapore: Singapore University Press.

Peterson, G. (1994a). 'The Struggle for Literacy in Post-Revolutionary Guangdong'. *China Quarterly*, 140: 926–43.

—— (1994b). 'State Literary Ideologies and the Transformation of Rural China'. *Australian Journal of Chinese Affairs*, 32: 95–120.

Piek, H. (1998). *Technology Development in Rural Industries*. London: Intermediate Technology.

Pi XZ (*Pi xian zhi*) (Pi County Records) (1989). Chengdu: Sichuan renmin chubanshe.

Pingding XZ (*Pingding xian zhi*) (Pingding County Records) (1992). Beijing: Shehui kexue wenxian chubanshe.

Pinghu XZ (*Pinghu xian zhi*) (Pinghu County Records) (1993). Shanghai: Shanghai renmin chubanshe.

Pingyuan XZ (*Pingyuan xian zhi*) (Pingyuan County Records) (1993). Guangzhou: Guangdong renmin chubanshe.

Pollin, R. (1995). 'Financial Structures and Egalitarian Economic Policy'. *New Left Review*, 214: 26–61.

Population Census Office (1987). *The Population Atlas of China*. Oxford: Oxford University Press.

Potter, S. H. and Potter, J. M. (1990). *China's Peasants*. Cambridge: Cambridge University Press.

Pritchett, L. (2001). 'Where Has All the Education Gone'? *World Bank Economic Observer*, 15(3): 367–91.

Pu, X. R. (ed.) (1986). *Sichuan zhengqu yange yu zhidi jin shi* (An Account of the Evolution of the Current Administrative Divisions of Sichuan). Chengdu: Sichuan renmin chubanshe.

Pujiang XZ (*Pujiang xian zhi*) (Pujiang County Records) (1992). Chengdu: Sichuan renmin chubanshe.

Putterman, L. (1997). 'On the Past and Future of China's Township and Village-Owned Enterprises'. *World Development*, 25(10): 1639–55.

Qianwei xian zhi (Qianwei County Records) (1991). Chengdu: Sichuan renmin chubanshe.

Quingyuan XZ (*Qingyuan xian zhi*) (Qingyuan County Records) (1995). Guangdong, no publisher.

Qu, G. P. and Li, J. C. (1994). *Population and Environment in China*. Boulder, CO: Lynne Rienner.

Raoping XZ (*Raoping xian zhi*) (Raoping County Records) (1994). Guangzhou: Guangdong renmin chubanshe.

Ravallion, M. and Chen, S. H. (2004). 'China's Uneven Progress Against Poverty'. *World Bank Policy Research Working Paper*, 3408. Washington, DC: World Bank.

Rawski, T. G. (2001). 'What is Happening to China's GDP Statistics'? *China Economic Review*, 12: 347–54.

Remick, E. (2004). *Building Local States*. Cambridge, MA: Harvard University Press.

Riskin, C. (1971). 'Small Industry and the Chinese Model of Development'. *China Quarterly*, 46: 245–73.

—— (1978*a*). 'China's Rural Industries'. *China Quarterly*, 73: 77–98.

—— (1978*b*). 'Political Conflict and Rural Industrialization in China'. *World Development*, 6: 681–92.

—— (1987): *China's Political Economy*. Oxford: Oxford University Press.

RKNJ—Zhongguo shehui kexueyuan renkou yanjiusuo (Population Research Institute of the Chinese Academy of Social Sciences) (ed.) (various years). *Zhongguo renkou nianjian 1985, 1986, 1992* (Chinese Population Yearbook). Beijing: Jingji guanli chubanshe.

Rodrik, D. (ed.) (2003). *In Search of Prosperity*. Princeton, NJ: Princeton University Press.

—— Subramanian, A. and Trebbi, F. (2004). 'Institutions Rule: The Primacy of Institutions Over Geography and Integration in Economic Development'. *Journal of Economic Growth*, 9: 131–65.

Rogers, M. (2004). 'Absorptive Capability and Economic Growth'. *Cambridge Journal of Economics*, 28(4): 577–96.

Romer, P. M. (1986). 'Increasing Returns and Long-Run Growth'. *Journal of Political Economy*, 94(5): 1002–37.

Romer, P. M. (1990). 'Endogenous Technological Change'. *Journal of Political Economy*, 98(5): S71–S102.

—— (1993). 'Idea Gaps and Object Gaps in Economic Development'. *Journal of Monetary Economics*, 32: 543–73.

Rong XZ (*Rong xian zhi*) (Rong County Records) (1993). Chengdu: Sichuan daxue chubanshe.

Rosenstein-Rodan, P. N. (1943). 'Problems of Industrialization of Eastern and South-Eastern Europe'. *Economic Journal*, 25: 202–11.

Rowthorn, R. and Coutts, K. (2004). 'Deindustrialization and the Balance of Payments in Advanced Economies'. *Cambridge Journal of Economics*, 28(5): 767–90.

Rowthorn, R. E. and Wells, J. R. (1987). *De-Industrialization and Foreign Trade*. Cambridge: Cambridge University Press.

Rozelle, S. (1994). 'Rural Industrialization and Increasing Inequality'. *Journal of Comparative Economics*, 19(3): 362–91.

—— Li, G., Shen, M. G., Hughart, A. and Giles, J. (1999). 'Leaving China's Farms'. *China Quarterly*, 158: 367–93.

Ruf, G. A. (1998). *Cadres and Kin*. Stanford: Stanford University Press.

Ruyuan XZ (*Ruyuan xian zhi*) (Ruyuan County Records) (1997). Guangzhou: Guangdong renmin chubanshe.

Sachs, J. D. (2005). *The End of Poverty*. London: Penguin.

—— and Woo, W-T. (1994). 'Structural Factors in the Economic Reforms of China, Eastern Europe and the Former Soviet Union'. *Economic Policy*, 18: 101–46.

—— and —— (1997). 'Understanding China's Economic Performance'. *NBER Working Paper*, 5935.

—— McArthur, J., Schmidt-Traub, G. et al. (2004). 'Ending Africa's Poverty Trap'. *Brookings Papers on Economic Activity*, 1: 117–240.

Saggi, K. (2002). 'Trade, Foreign Direct Investment and International Technology Transfer'. *World Bank Research Observer*, 17(2): 191–235.

Saha, B. (2000). 'Emerging MNCs from China'. *Economic and Political Weekly*, 25, November 4234–45.

Saito, O. (1996). 'The Rural Economy: Commercial Agriculture, By-employment and Wage Work', in M. B. Jansen and G. Rozman (eds.) *Japan in Transition: From Tokugawa to Meiji*. Princeton: Princeton University Press.

—— and Tanimoto, M. (2004). 'The Transformation of Traditional Industries', in A. Hayami, O. Saito and R. P. Toby (eds.) *Emergence of Economic Society in Japan 1600–1859*. Oxford: Oxford University Press.

Sanderson, M. (1991). *Education, Economic Change and Society in England 1780–1870*. London: Macmillan.

Santai XZ (*Santai xian zhi*) (Santai County Records) (1992). Chengdu: Sichuan renmin chubanshe.

Sargesson, S. and Zhang, J. (1999). 'Reassessing the Role of the Local State'. *China Journal*, 42: 45–74.

Schultz, T. W. (1960). 'Capital Formation by Education'. *Journal of Political Economy*, December 68(6).

Scott, M. FG. (1989). *A New View of Economic Growth*. Oxford: Clarendon Press.

SCJJDL (*Sichuan sheng jingji dili*) (An Economic Geography of Sichuan Province) (1985). Chengdu: Sichuan kexue jishu chubanshe.

SCJJNJ (Sichuan jingji nianjian bianji weiyuanhui) (Editorial Committee for the Sichuan Economic Yearbook) (1987). *Sichuan jingji nianjian 1986* (Sichuan Economic Yearbook). Chengdu: Sichuan kexue jishu chubanshe.

SCTJNJ (Sichuan tongjiju) (Sichuan Statistical Bureau) (various years). *Sichuan tongji nianjian 1990, 1992, 1993, 1994, 1995, 1997, 1999, 2001, 2002 and 2003* (Sichuan Statistical Yearbook). Beijing: Zhongguo tongji chubanshe.

SCZL (Sichuan gongye qiye zonglan bianji weiyuanhui) (Editorial Committee for A Summary Account of Sichuan's Industrial Enterprises) (ed.) (1990). *Sichuan gongye qiye zonglan* (A Summary Account of Sichuan's Industrial Enterprises). Beijing: Zhongguo tongji chubanshe.

Seeberg, V. (1990). *Literacy in China*. Bochum: Brockmeyer.

Shang, J. C. (ed.) (1989). *Dangdai Zhongguo de Zhejiang* (Contemporary China: Zhejiang). Beijing: Zhongguo shehui kexue chubanshe.

Shanton SZ (*Shantou shi zhi*) (Shantou Municipality Records) (1999). Beijing: Xinhua chubanshe.

Shaoguan SZ (*Shaoguan shi zhi*) (Shaoguan Municipality Records) (2001). Beijing: Zhonghua shuju chubanshe.

Shapiro, J. (2001). *Mao's War Against Nature*. Cambridge: Cambridge University Press.

Shazhou XZ (*Shazhou xian zhi*) (Shazhou County Records) (1992). Nanjing: Jiangsu renmin chubanshe.

Shehong XZ (*Shehong xian zhi*) (Shehong County Records) (1990). Chengdu: Sichuan daxue chubanshe.

Shen, Y. M. and Tong, C. Z. (1992). *Zhongguo renkou qianyi* (Population Migration in China). Beijing: Zhongguo tongji chubanshe.

Sheng, Y. M. (1993). *Intersectoral Resource Flows and China's Economic Development*. London: Macmillan.

Shifang XZ (*Shifang xian zhi*) (Shifang County Records) (1988). Chengdu: Sichuan renmin chubanshe.

Shimbo, H. and Saito, O. (2004). 'The Economy on the Eve of Industrialization', in A. Hayami, O. Saito and R. P. Toby (eds.) *Emergence of Economic Society in Japan 1600–1859*. Oxford: Oxford University Press.

Shirk, S. L. (1993). *The Political Logic of Economic Reform in China*. Berkeley: University of California Press.

Shouce, W. Y. (1987). *Zhongguo shixian shouce* (Handbook of China's Counties and Cities). Hangzhou: Zhejiang jiaoyu chubanshe.

Shunde XZ (*Shunde xian zhi*) (Shunde County Records) (1996). Guangzhou: Guangdong renmin chubanshe.

SDFGJYK (Sichuan daxue fei guoyouzhi jingji yanjiu ketizu) (Sichuan University Economic Research Group on the Non-Public Sector) (2001). 'Dali fazhan fei gongyouzhi qiye cujin Sichuan jingji de kuayue shi fazhan' (Energetically Develop the Non-public Enterprise Sector in Order to Promote Sichuan's Economic Development). *Jingji tizhi gaige* (Reform of the Economic System) 6: 115–19.

Sichuan pucha (Sichuan sheng renkou pucha bangongshi) (Office for the Population Census in Sichuan) (1994). *Sichuan Zangzu renkou* (Sichuan's Tibetan Population). Beijing: Zhongguo tongji chubanshe.

SSK (Sichuan shehui kexueyuan) (Sichuan Academy of Social Science) (ed.) (1988). *Sichuan shehui jingji qingshi zonghe kaocha ji fazhan duice yanjiu* (A Summary Study of

Sichuan's Economy and Society, and Research on How to Develop Them). Chengdu: Sichuan sheng shehui kexueyuan.

Sichuan tongjiju (1999). *Sichuan wushinian* (Fifty Years in Sichuan). Beijing: Zhongguo tongji chubanshe.

Sichuan zhi (Sichuan sheng difang zhi bianzuan weiyuanhui) (Committee for the Compilation of Sichuan's Records) (ed.) (1992). *Sichuan sheng zhi—Yejin zhi* (Sichuan Provincial Records—Metallurgy Records). Chengdu: Sichuan kexue jishu chubanshe.

Sigurdson, J. (1977). *Rural Industrialization in China*. Cambridge, MA: Harvard University Press.

Simon, J. J. (1981). *The Ultimate Resource*. Princeton: Princeton University Press.

Singh, A. (1977). 'UK Industry and the World Economy: A Case of Deindustrialisation'? *Cambridge Journal of Economics*, 1: 113–36.

Siu, H. F. (1989). *Agents and Victims in South China*. New Haven: Yale University Press.

Skinner, G. W. (1964–65). 'Marketing and Social Structure in Rural China'. *Journal of Asian Studies*, 24(1, 2 and 3), 3–43, 195–228 and 363–99.

Smil, V. (1993). *China's Environmental Crisis*. Armonk, NY: M. E. Sharpe.

Smith, T. C. (1959). *The Agrarian Origins of Modern Japan*. Stanford: Stanford University Press.

—— (1988). *Native Sources of Japanese Industrialization, 1750–1920*. Berkeley: University of California Press.

Smith, P. J. (1988): 'Commerce, Agriculture and Core Formation in the Upper Yangzi, 2 AD to 1948'. *Late Imperial China*, 9(1): 1–78.

Smyth, R. (1999). 'Rural Enterprises in Jiangsu Province, China'. *Development Policy Review*, 17: 191–213.

Solinger, D. (1999). *Contesting Citizenship in Urban China*. Berkeley: University of California Press.

Solow, R. M. ([1970] 1988). *Growth Theory*. Oxford: Oxford University Press.

Song, N. G. (1987). *Zhongguo renkou—Nei Menggu fence* (China's Population—Nei Menggu). Beijing: Zhongguo caizheng jingji chubanshe.

Song, Z. X. (1987). *Zhongguo renkou—Liaoning fence* (China's Population—Liaoning). Beijing: Zhongguo caizheng jingji chubanshe.

Songjiang XZ (*Songjiang xian zhi*) (Songjiang County Records) (1991). Shanghai: Shanghai renmin chubanshe.

Spence, M. (1976). 'Competition in Salaries, Credentials, and Signaling Prerequisites for Jobs'. *Quarterly Journal of Economics*, 90(1): 51–74.

SSDSB (Shandong sheng difang shizhi bangongshi) (Office of Historical Records for Shandong Province (ed.) (1997). *Shandong sheng zhi—Xiangzhen qiye zhi* (Shandong Provincial Records—Township and Village Enterprise Records). Jinan: Shandong renmin chubanshe.

Stiglitz, J. E. and Yusuf, S. (eds.) (2001). *Rethinking the East Asian Miracle*. Oxford: Oxford University Press.

Stokey, N. (1988). 'Learning by Doing and the Introduction of New Goods'. *Journal of Political Economy*, 96(4): 701–17.

Su, R. Y. (1988). *Zhongguo renkou—Gansu fence* (China's Population—Gansu). Beijing: Zhongguo caizheng jingji chubanshe.

Succar, P. (1987). 'The Need for Industrial Policy in LDCs: A Re-statement of the Infant Industry Argument'. *International Economic Review*, 28(2): 521–34.

Sun, J. Z. (ed.) (1959). *Huanan diqu jingji dili*. Beijing: Kexue chubanshe. (Trans. 1962 as *Economic Geography of South China*. New York: Joint Publications Research Service, JPRS no. 14,954.)

Sun, C. C. (1960). *Economic Geography of Southwestern China*. New York: Joint Publications Research Service trans. No. 15069 from the original *Xinan diqu jingji dili* (Beijing: Kexue chubanshe).

Sun, Y. (1995). *The Chinese Reassessment of Socialism 1976-1992*. Princeton: Princeton University Press.

Suqian SZ (*Suqian shi zhi*) (Suqian City Records) (1996). Nanjing: Jiangsu renmin chubanshe.

Sutton, A. C. (1973). *Western Technology and Soviet Economic Development, 1917-1965*. Stanford: Hoover Institute.

Suzhou tongjiju (Suzhou Statistical Bureau) (1996). *Suzhou tongji nianjian 1996* (Suzhou Statistical Yearbook). Beijing: Zhongguo tongji chubanshe.

SXQS (*Sichuan xiangzhen qiye shinian*) (Ten Years of Sichuan's Township and Village Enterprises) (1988). Chengdu: Sichuan renmin chubanshe.

SXTJNJ (Shanxi tongjiju) (Shanxi Statistical Bureau) (1985). *Shanxi tongji nianjian 1985* (Shanxi Statistical Yearbook). Taiyuan: Shanxi renmin chubanshe.

Taicang XZ (*Taicang xian zhi*) (Taicang County Records) (1991). Nanjing: Jiangsu renmin chubanshe.

Taira, K. (1978). 'Factory Labour and the Industrial Revolution in Japan', in P. Mathias and M. Postan (eds.) *The Cambridge Economic History of Europe*, VII, pt. 2. Cambridge: Cambridge University Press.

Taishan XZ (*Taishan xian zhi*) (Taishan County Records) (1998). Guangzhou: Guangdong renmin chubanshe.

Taixing XZ (*Taixing xian zhi*) (Taixing County Records) (1993). Nanjing: Jiangsu renmin chubanshe.

Tan, G. K. (1994). *Zhongguo nongye quanshu—Guangdong juan* (A Compendium of Chinese Agriculture—Guangdong Volume). Beijing: Zhongguo nongye chubanshe.

Tang, H. L. (1988). *Shanxi sheng jingji dili* (An Economic Geography of Shanxi Province). Beijing: Xinhua chubanshe.

Tao, Y. Z. (1988). *Sunan moshi yu zhengfu zhidao* (The Sunan Model and Governance). Shanghai: Shanghai kexue chubanshe.

Targetti, F. and Thirlwall, A. P. (eds.) (1989). *The Essential Kaldor*. London: Duckworth.

Temple, J. and Johnson, P. (1998). 'Social Capability and Economic Growth'. *Quarterly Journal of Economics*, 113(3): 965–90.

Thant, M., Tang, M. and Kakazu, H. (eds.) (1994). *Growth Triangles in Asia*. Hong Kong: Oxford University Press.

Thomas, J. J. (2005). 'Kerala's Industrial Backwardness'. *World Development*, 33(5): 763–83.

Thompson, E. P. (1968). *The Making of the English Working Class*. London: Pelican.

Thirlwall, A. P. (2002). *The Nature of Economic Growth*. Cheltenham: Edward Elgar.

Tianshui shi tongjiju (Tianshui Statistical Bureau) (ed.) (1989). *Tianshui sishinian* (Forty Years in Tianshui). Beijing: Zhongguo tongji chubanshe.

TJJ (Zhongguo guojia tongjiju) (National Bureau of Statistics) (1985). *Zhongguo gongye jingji tongji ziliao 1949-1984* (Economic Statistics on Chinese Industry). Beijing: Zhongguo tongji chubanshe.

—— (1988). *Zhongguo renkou tongji nianjian 1988* (Chinese Population Statistics Yearbook). Beijing: Zhongguo tongji chubanshe.

TJJ (Zhongguo guojia tongjiju) (National Bureau of Statistics) (1989). *Zhongguo laodong gongzi tongji ziliao 1978–1987* (Statistical Materials on the Chinese Labour Force and Wages). Beijing: Zhongguo tongji chubanshe.

—— (1990*a*). *Zhongguo chengshi sishinian* (Forty Years of Urban China). Beijing: Zhongguo tongji xinxi zixun fuwu zhongxin.

—— (1990*b*). *Quanguo gesheng zizhiqu zhixiashi lishi tongji ziliao huibian* (Collection of Historical Statistical Materials on China's Provinces, Autonomous Regions and Centrally-Administered Cities). Beijing: Zhongguo tongji chubanshe.

—— (1992). *Zhongguo renkou tongji nianjian 1992* (Chinese Population Statistics Yearbook). Beijing: Zhongguo tongji chubanshe.

—— (1993). *Zhongguo renkou tongji nianjian 1993* (Chinese Population Statistics Yearbook). Beijing: Zhongguo tongji chubanshe.

—— (1995). *Zhongguo duiwai jingji tongji nianjian 1994* (Chinese Foreign Economic Relations Statistical Yearbook). Beijing: Zhongguo tongji chubanshe.

—— (1997). *Zhongguo guonei shengchanzongzhi jisuan lishi ziliao 1952–1995* (Historical Materials on Chinese Gross Domestic Product). Dalian: Dongbei caizheng daxue chubanshe.

—— (1999). *Xin Zhongguo wushinian tongji ziliao huibian* (Collection of Statistical Material on Fifty Years of New China). Beijing: Zhongguo tongji chubanshe.

—— (2000*a*). *Zhongguo nongcun pinkun jiance baogao 2000* (Chinese Rural Poverty Monitoring Report). Beijing: Zhongguo tongji chubanshe.

—— (2000*b*). *Zhongguo gongye jiaotong nengyuan wushinian tongji ziliao huibian* (Collection of Statistical Materials on Chinese Industry, Transport and Energy over the Last Fifty Years). Beijing: Zhongguo tongji chubanshe.

—— (2000*c*). *Xianshi shehui jingji zhuyao zhibiao* (Main Economic and Social Indicators for China's Counties and Cities). Available at http://www.stats.gov.cn/sjjw/qtsj/ xianshi (accessed March 2001).

—— (2001). *Zhongguo renkou tongji nianjian 2001* (Chinese Population Statistics Yearbook). Beijing: Zhongguo tongji chubanshe.

—— (2003*a*). *Zhongguo nongcun pinkun jiance baogao 2003* (Chinese Rural Poverty Monitoring Report). Beijing: Zhongguo tongji chubanshe.

—— (2003*b*). *Zhongguo nongcun zhumin diaocha nianjian 2003* (Chinese Rural Household Survey 2003). Beijing: Zhongguo tongji chubanshe.

—— (2004). *Zhongguo guonei shengchan zongzhi jisuan lishi ziliao 1996–2002* (Data on Chinese Gross Domestic Product). Beijing: Zhongguo tongji chubanshe.

TJNJ (Zhongguo guojia tongjiju) (National Bureau of Statistics) (various years). *Zhongguo tongji nianjian 1981, 1983–2005* (Chinese Statistical Yearbook). Beijing: Zhongguo tongji chubanshe.

Tong, W. H. (1997). *Zhongguo nongye quanshu—Fujian juan* (A Compendium of Chinese Agriculture—Fujian Volume). Beijing: Zhongguo nongye chubanshe.

Tonglu XZ (*Tonglu xian zhi*) (Tonglu County Records) (1991). Hangzhou: Zhejiang renmin chubanshe.

Tongshan XZ (*Tongshan xian zhi*) (Tongshan County Records) (1993). Beijing: Zhongguo shehui kexue chubanshe.

Tsurumi, E. P. (1990). *Factory Girls*. Princeton: Princeton University Press.

UNDP (United Nations Development Programme) (2000). *Policies for Poverty Reduction in China*. Beijing: UNDP.

van de Walle, D. and Cratty, D. J. (2004). 'Is the Emerging Non-Farm Market Economy the Route out of Poverty in Vietnam'? *Economics of Transition*, 12(2): 237–74.

Veeck, G. (1991). 'Regional Variations in Employment and Income in Jiangsu Province', in N. Ginsburg, B. Koppel and T. G. McGee (eds.) *The Extended Metropolis*. Honolulu: University of Hawaii Press.

Vogel, E. F. (1989). *One Step Ahead in China*. Cambridge, MA: Harvard University Press.

von Tunzelmann, G. N. (1978). *Steam Power and British Industrialization to 1860*. Oxford: Oxford University Press.

—— (1994). 'Technology in the Early Nineteenth Century', in R. Floud and D. McCloskey (eds.) *The Economic History of Britain since 1700*. Cambridge: Cambridge University Press.

Wade, R. (1990). *Governing the Market*. Princeton, NJ: Princeton University Press.

Wagner, D. B. (1995). 'The Traditional Chinese Iron Industry and Its Modern Fate'. *Chinese Science*, 138–61.

Walder, A. G. (ed.) (1998). *Zouping in Transition*. Cambridge, MA: Harvard University Press.

—— and Yang, S. (2003). 'The Cultural Revolution in the Countryside'. *China Quarterly*, 173: 74–99.

Walker, K. R. (1984). *Food Grain Procurement and Consumption in China*. Cambridge: Cambridge University Press.

Walker, K. L. M. (1999). *Chinese Modernity and the Peasant Path*. Stanford: Stanford University Press.

Wang, M. Y. (1987). *Zhongguo renkou—Hebei fence* (China's Population—Hebei). Beijing: Zhongguo caizheng jingji chubanshe.

Wang, S. J. (1988). *Zhongguo renkou—Zhejiang fence* (China's Population—Zhejiang). Beijing: Zhongguo caizheng jingji chubanshe.

Wang, W. (ed.) (1993). *Dangdai Zhongguo de bingqi gongye* (The Ordnance Industry in Contemporary China). Beijing: Dangdai Zhongguo chubanshe.

Wang, F. L. (1998). *From Family to Market*. Oxford: Rowman and Littlefield.

Wang, S. G. and Hu, A. G. (1999). *The Political Economy of Uneven Development*. Armonk, NY: M. E. Sharpe.

—— and —— (2001). *The Chinese Economy in Crisis*. Armonk, NY: M. E. Sharpe.

Wei, S. J. (2000). 'Why Does China Attract so Little Foreign Direct Investment'? in T. Ito and A. Krueger (eds.) *The Role of Foreign Direct Investment in East Asian Economic Development*. Chicago: University of Chicago Press.

Wei, Y. H. D. (2000a). *Regional Development in China*. London: Routledge.

—— (2000b). 'Fiscal Reforms, Investment and Regional Development in Jiangsu Province'. *Issues and Studies*, 36(2): 73–98.

—— and Fan, C. C. (2000). 'Regional Inequality in China'. *Professional Geographer*, 52(3): 455–69.

—— and Kim, S. W. (2002). 'Widening Inter-County Inequality in Jiangsu Province, China, 1950–1995'. *Journal of Development Studies*, 38(6): 142–64.

Weitzman, M. and Xu C. G. (1994). 'Chinese Township-Village Enterprises and Vaguely Defined Cooperatives'. *Journal of Comparative Economics*, 8(2): 121–45.

Wengyuan XZ (*Wengyuan xian zhi*) (Wengyuan County Records) (1997). Guangzhou: Guangdong renmin chubanshe.

Wenshi ziliao weiyuanhui (Historical and Cultural Materials Committee) (1993). *Liangshan wenshi ziliao xuanji* (Selected Materials on the History and Culture of Liangshan), vol. XI. Xichang, no publisher.

Wenzhou tongjiju (various years). *Wenzhou tongji nianjian 1985, 1989 and 2001* (Wenzhou Statistical Yearbook). Beijing: Zhongguo tongji chubanshe.

West, L. A. and Zhao, Y. H. (eds.) (2000). *Rural Labor Flows in China*. Berkeley: University of California.

Whiting, S. H. (2001). *Power and Wealth in Rural China*. Cambridge: Cambridge University Press.

Williamson, J. G. (1991). 'Did English Factor Markets Fail During the Industrial Revolution?' in N. Crafts, N. Dimsdale and S. Engerman (eds.) *Quantitative Economic History*. Oxford: Clarendon Press.

—— (2001). 'Demographic Change, Economic Growth, and Inequality', in N. Birdsall, A. C. Kelley and S. W. Sinding (eds.) (2001). *Population Matters*. Oxford: Oxford University Press.

Winkler, D. (2004). 'Forest Use and Implications of the 1998 Logging Ban in the Tibetan Prefectures of Sichuan', in Z. Jiang, M. Centritto, S. Liu and S. Zhang (eds.) *The Ecological Basis and Sustainable Management of Forest Resources. Informatore Botanico Italiano*, 134: 2.

Wirtschaffer, R. M. and Shih, M. (1990). 'Decentralization of China's Electricity Sector'. *World Development*, 18(4): 505–12.

Wong, C. P. W. (1982). 'Rural Industrialization in the People's Republic of China', in Joint Economic Committee, US Congress (ed.) *China under the Four Modernizations*. Washington, DC: US Government Printing Office.

—— (1988). 'Interpreting Rural Industrial Growth in the Post-Mao Period'. *Modern China*, 14(1): 3–30.

—— (1989). 'Between Plan and Market', in S. Gomulka, Y. C. Ha and C. O. Kim (eds.) *Economic Reforms in the Socialist World*. London: Macmillan.

—— (1991*a*). 'The Maoist Model Reconsidered', in W. A. Joseph, C. P. W. Wong and D. Zweig (eds.) *New Perspectives on the Cultural Revolution*. Cambridge, MA: Harvard University Press.

—— (1991*b*). 'Central Planning and Local Participation under Mao', in G. White (ed.) *The Chinese State in the Era of Economic Reform*. London: Macmillan.

—— (ed.) (1997). *Financing Local Government in the People's Republic of China*. Hong Kong: Oxford University Press.

Wong, R. B. (1997). *China Transformed*. Ithaca: Cornell University Press.

Wong, C. P. W., Heady, C. and Woo, W. T. (1995). *Fiscal Management and Economic Reform in the People's Republic of China*. Oxford: Oxford University Press.

Woo, W. T. (1997). 'Crises and Institutional Evolution in China's Industrial Sector', in Joint Economic Committee (ed.) *China's Economic Future*. Armonk, NY: M. E. Sharpe.

—— (1998). 'Chinese Economic Growth', in M. Fouquin and F. Lemoine (eds.) *The Chinese Economy*. London: Economica.

—— Parker, S. and Sachs, J. D. (1997). *Economies in Transition*. Cambridge, MA: MIT Press.

World Bank (1988). *China: Growth and Development in Gansu Province*. Washington, DC: World Bank.

—— (1993). *The East Asian Miracle*. Oxford: Oxford University Press.

—— (2000). *World Development Report 2000/2001*. Oxford: Oxford University Press.

—— (2001*a*). *China: Overcoming Rural Poverty*. Washington, DC: World Bank.

—— (2001*b*). *China: Air, Land and Water*. Washington, DC: World Bank.

—— (2004). *World Development Indicators 2004*. Oxford: Oxford University Press.

Wright, T. (1984). *Coal Mining in China's Economy and Society, 1895–1937*. Cambridge: Cambridge University Press.

—— (2000). 'Distant Thunder: The Regional Economy of Southwest China and The Impact of the Great Depression'. *Modern Asian Studies*, 34(3): 697–738.

Wu, N. K. (1993). *A Single Tear*. London: Hodder and Stoughton.

Wu, H. X. (1994). 'The Rural Industrial Enterprise Workforce', in C. Findlay, A. Watson and H. X. Wu (eds.) *Rural Enterprises in China*. Basingstoke: Macmillan.

Wu, J. L. (2005). *Understanding and Interpreting Chinese Economic Reform*. Mason, OH: Thomson.

Wuhua XZ (*Wuhua xian zhi*) (Wuhua County Records) (1991). Guangzhou: Guangdong renmin chubanshe.

Wujiang XZ (*Wujiang xian zhi*) (Wujiang County Records) (1994). Nanjing: Jiangsu kexue jishu chubanshe.

Wujin pucha (Wujin xian renkou diaocha bangongshi) (Population Census Office of Wujin County) (1992). *Jiangsu sheng Wujin xian 1990 nian renkou pucha ziliao* (Materials from the 1990 Population Census in Wujin County, Jiangsu). Beijing: Zhongguo tongji chubanshe.

Wushan XZ (*Wushan xian zhi*) (Wushan County Records) (1991). Chengdu: Sichuan renmin chubanshe.

Wuxi tongjiju (Wuxi Statistical Bureau) (1997). *Wuxi tongji nianjian 1997* (Wuxi Statistical Yearbook). Beijing: Zhongguo tongji chubanshe.

Wuxian GZ (Wuxian jingji weiyuanhui) (Wuxian Economic Committee) (ed.) (1993). *Wuxian gongye zhi* (Wuxian Industrial Records). Shanghai: Shanghai shehui kexue chubanshe.

Wuxian zhi (Wuxian Records) (1994). Shanghai: Shanghai guji chubanshe.

WXG (Wuxi xian jingji weiyuanhui) (Wuxi County Economic Committee) (ed.) (1990). *Wuxi xian gongye zhi* (Industrial Records for Wuxi County). Shanghai: Shanghai renmin chubanshe.

Xiangshui XZ (*Xiangshui xian zhi*) (Xiangshui County Records) (1996). Nanjing: Jiangsu guji chubanshe.

Xiangzhen qiyeju (Township and Village Industry Bureau) (2005). '2004 quanguo xiangzhen qiye yunxing qingkuang' (Changes in the Situation of Chinese Township and Village Enterprises during 2004). Available at http://zw.cte.gov.cn/tjxx, 4 February 2005 (accessed 3 January 2006).

Xichong XZ (*Xichong xian zhi*) (Xichong County Records) (1993). Chongqing: Chongqing chubanshe.

Xinhui XZ (*Xinhui xian zhi*) (Xinhui County Records) (1995). Guangzhou: Guangdong renmin chubanshe.

Xinjin XZ (*Xinjin xian zhi*) (Xinjin County Records) (1989). Chengdu: Sichuan renmin chubanshe.

Xinlong XZ (*Xinlong xian zhi*) (Xinlong County Records) (1992). Chengdu: Sichuan renmin chubanshe.

Xin nongye (Guojia tongjiju nongcun shehui jingji diaocha zongdui) (Rural Economic and Social Survey Team of the National Bureau of Statistics) (2000). *Xin Zhongguo wushinian nongye tongji ziliao* (Statistical Materials on Fifty Years of New China's Agriculture). Beijing: Zhongguo tongji chubanshe.

XSNJ (Zhongguo guojia tongjiju) (National Bureau of Statistics) (various years). *Zhongguo xianshi shehui jingji tongji nianjian 2001, 2002, 2003 and 2004* (Statistical Yearbook on the Economy and Society of China's Counties and Cities). Beijing: Zhongguo tongji chubanshe.

Xu, D. X. (ed.) (1982). *China's Search for Economic Growth*. Beijing: New World Press.

Xu, X. W. (1988). 'The Struggle of the Handicraft Cotton Industry against Machine Textiles in China'. *Modern China*, 14(1): 31–50.

—— (ed.) (1990). *Zhongguo jindai saosi gongye shi* (A History of the Silk Reeling Industry in Modern China). Shanghai: Shanghai renmin chubanshe.

Xu, B. (2000). 'Multinational Enterprises, Technology Diffusion and Host Country Productivity Growth'. *Journal of Development Economics*, 62: 477–93.

Xue, M. Q. (1981). *China's Socialist Economy*. Beijing: Foreign Language Press.

XZNJ (Zhongguo xiangzhen qiye nianjian bianji weiyuanhui) (Editorial Committee for the Chinese Township and Village Enterprise Yearbook) (various years). *Zhongguo xiangzhen qiye nianjian 2002, 2003* (Chinese Township and Village Enterprise Yearbook). Beijing: Zhongguo nongye chubanshe.

—— (1989). *Zhongguo xiangzhen qiye nianjian 1978–1987* (Chinese Township and Village Enterprise Yearbook 1978–1987). Beijing: Zhongguo nongye chubanshe.

Yamazawa, I. (1990). *Economic Development and International Trade*. Honolulu: Resource Systems Institute.

Yang, C. (ed.) (1990). *Dangdai Zhongguo de Sichuan* (Contemporary China: Sichuan). Beijing: Zhongguo shehui kexue chubanshe.

—— (ed.) (1997). *Dangdai Sichuan jianshi* (A Short History of Contemporary Sichuan). Beijing: Dangdai Zhongguo chubanshe.

Yang, R. (1997). *Spider Eaters*. Berkeley: California University Press.

Yang, G. Q. and Tao, T. (ed.) (1988). *Dangdai Zhongguo de huaxue gongye* (Contemporary China: Chemical Industry). Beijing: Zhongguo shehui kexue chubanshe.

Yang, Q. H. and Guo, F. (1996). 'Occupational Attainments of Rural to Urban Temporary Economic Migrants in China, 1985–1990'. *International Migration Review*, 30(3): 771–87.

Yeung, G. (2001). *Foreign Investment and Socio-Economic Development in China: The Case of Dongguan*. Basingstoke: Palgrave.

Yixing XZ (*Yixing xian zhi*) (Yixing County Records) (1990). Shanghai: Shanghai renmin chubanshe.

YNTJNJ (Yunnan tongjiju) (Yunnan Statistical Bureau) (various years). *Yunnan tongji nianjian 1990* (Yunnan Statistical Yearbook). Beijing: Zhongguo tongji chubanshe.

Young, A. (1991). 'Learning by Doing and the Dynamic Effects of International Trade'. *Quarterly Journal of Economics*, 106(2): 369–405.

—— (2000). 'The Razor's Edge: Distortions and Incremental Reform in the People's Republic of China'. *Quarterly Journal of Economics*, CXV(4): 1091–135.

Young, S. and Yang, G. (1994). 'Private Enterprises and Local Government in Rural China', in C. Findlay, A. Watson and H. X. Wu (eds.) *Rural Enterprises in China*. Basingstoke: Macmillan.

Yu, D. C. (1989). *Quanguo baicun laodongli qingkuang diaocha ziliaoji* (Collected Materials from a National Multi-Village Survey of the Situation of the Labour Force Across China). Beijing: Zhongguo tongji chubanshe.

ZGZ (*Zhangye gongye zhi*) (Zhangye Industrial Records) (1993). Beijing: Zhongguo chengshi chubanshe.

Zhang, Z. Y. (1988). *Zhongguo jiage jieshou yanjiu* (Research on the Structure of China's Prices). Taiyuan: Shanxi renmin chubanshe.

Zhang, K. H. J. (2001). 'How Does Foreign Direct Investment Affect Growth in China?' *Economics of Transition*, 9(3): 679–93.

Zhang, X. B. and Li, G. (2003). 'Does *Guanxi* Matter to Nonfarm Employment'? *Journal of Comparative Economics*, 31: 315–31.

Zhang, S. D. and Hou, Z. Y. (ed.) (1990). *Dangdai Zhongguo de Henan* (Contemporary China: Henan). Beijing: Zhongguo shehui kexue chubanshe.

Zhang, H. Y. and Ming, L. Z. (1999). *Zhongguo siying qiye fazhan baogao* (Report on the Development of China's Private Enterprises). Beijing: Zhongguo shehui kexue chubanshe.

Zhang, X. J. and Zhang, L. H. (1990). *Sichuan jindai gongye shi* (A History of Industry in Modern Sichuan). Chengdu: Sichuan renmin chubanshe.

Zhang, T. and Zou, H. F. (1998). 'Fiscal Centralization, Public Spending and Economic Growth in China'. *Journal of Public Economics*, 67: 221–40.

Zheng, B. X. (1987). *Gansu sheng jingji dili* (An Economic Geography of Gansu). Beijing: Xinhua chubanshe.

Zheng, Y. L. and Gao, B. H. (1987). *Zhongguo renkou—Anhui fence* (China's Population—Anhui). Beijing: Zhongguo caizheng jingji chubanshe.

Zhou, H. L. (1994). *Suxichang fazhan baogao* (A Report on the Development of Suxichang). Beijing: Renmin ribao chubanshe.

Zhou, K. X. (1996). *How the Farmers Changed China*. Boulder, CA: Westview.

Zhou, L. S., Hou, X. D. and Chen, S. Q. (eds.) (1946). *Sichuan jingji dituji shuoming* (An Annotated Economic Geography of Sichuan). Beibei: Zhongguo dili yanjiusuo.

Zhu, H. M. (1992). *Dangdai Liangshan* (Contemporary Liangshan). Chengdu: Bashu shushe chubanshe.

Zhu, R. (ed.) (1992). *Dangdai Zhongguo de nongye* (Contemporary China: Agriculture). Beijing: Dangdai Zhongguo chubanshe.

Zijin XZ (*Zijin xian zhi*) (Zijin County Records) (1994). Guangzhou: Guangdong renmin chubanshe.

Ziliak, S. and McCloskey, D. (2004). 'Size Matters: The Standard Error of Regressions in the *American Economic Review*'. *Journal of Socio-Economics*, 33: 527–46.

ZJJ (Zhejiang juan bianji weiyuanhui) (Zhejiang Volume Editorial Committee) (1997). *Zhongguo nongye quanshu—Zhejiang juan* (A Compendium of Chinese Agriculture—Zhejiang Volume). Beijing: Zhongguo nongye chubanshe.

ZJTJNJ (Zhejiang tongjiju) (Zhejiang Statistical Bureau) (various years). *Zhejiang tongji nianjian 1989, 1995, 1996, 1999, 2001 and 2003* (Zhejiang Statistical Yearbook). Beijing: Zhongguo tongji chubanshe.

Zong, H. W. (1989). *Years of Trial, Turmoil and Triumph*. Beijing: Foreign Languages Press.

Zou, Q. Y. and Miao, W. J. (1989). *Zhongguo renkou—Yunnan fence* (China's Population—Yunnan). Beijing: Zhongguo caizheng jingji chubanshe.

ZSDSWY (Zhonggong Shandong sheng wei yanjiushi) (Research Office of the Shandong Committee of the Chinese Communist Party) (1989). *Shandong sishinian* (Forty Years of Shandong). Jinan: Shandong renmin chubanshe.

ZSQ (Zigong shi jingji yanjiusuo) (Zigong City Economic Research Institute) (1985). *Zigong shi qing* (Conditions in Zigong City). Zigong, no publisher.

Zweig, D. (1997). *Freeing China's Farmers*. Armonk, NY: M. E. Sharpe.

Zysman, J. (1983). *Governments, Markets and Growth*. London: Martin Robertson.

ZYSWZY (Zhonggong Yunnan sheng wei zhengce yanjiushi) (Policy Research Office of the Yunnan Province Party Committee) (1986). *Yunnan sheng qing* (Conditions in Yunnan Province). Kunming: Yunnan renmin chubanshe.

Index

Index

Index

Sichuan 7, 13, 19, 24, 25, 41–2, 80, 113, 171, 179 n., 198, 236, 244–84, 287, 319
  constant price GVA 285 n.
  development of industries 12, 143
  discrimination/prejudice against native workers 158
  emergence of new cities 33
  employment in household and private enterprises 77 n.
  entrepreneurial local governments 83
  ethnic minority prefectures 65
  extrabudgetary income from county-run enterprises 110
  family farming in mountainous parts 48
  famine (late 1950s) 22
  GVIO 16, 250, 252, 254, 256, 259–62, 267, 268, 269, 270, 278, 289
  illiteracy 263
  important role in reducing poverty 286
  industrial GVA estimation 340–1
  large construction 10
  lending to collective industries 21
  literacy 264, 272, 276
  migration from 154, 159 n.
  negative influence on growth rate 317
  non-public sector share 77
  papermaking 8
  party membership 157
  poorest prefecture in 250
  post-1978 growth 3
  privatization 52
  railway construction linking Yunnan, Guizhou and 14
  ratio of extrabudgetary to budgetary spending 114
  relative isolation and adverse physical geography 173
  slowest-growing counties 188
  Third Front 17, 92, 143, 146, 246 n., 250, 252, 253, 255–64, 276–80, 284, 293, 322
  Tibetan population 264
  TVEs 60, 62, 85
  urban manufacturing 155
  wages directly related to seniority and skills 163
  xiafang 150, 264
  see also Chengdu; Nanchong
sideline industries 57, 175
  less pressure on households to develop 281
  suppression of 145
Sigurdson, J. 20
silk 130, 132, 133, 150, 166, 167, 209–14, 254, 280, 281
  see also mulberry cultivation
sinecures 73
Singapore 70
Singh, A. 95–6, 98, 99

Sino-Japanese war (1937–45) 146, 246, 280
sishu (private) schools 308, 309
Siu, H. F. 21, 143, 150
Sixty Articles 9
siying (private) enterprises 66, 77
skilled labour 6, 49, 73, 92, 160, 184
  availability in fast-growing counties 202
  barriers to migration of 174
  deep reservoir of 314
  exodus of 136, 200
  importance for development 157
  lack of 161, 164
  locally-available, premium attached to 201
  lost 202, 311
  migration of 208, 263–4, 310
  misallocated 200 n.
  persistent net flow of 136
  prevented from leaving 200
  reservoir of 289
  rural industrialization erected upon an edifice of 165
  shortages of 123, 128, 129, 163
  supply of 183
  transferred 281
skills 129, 133, 174–5
  acquired 168, 201
  complementary 135
  drain of 242
  enhancement of 118, 121
  expansion of 307–10
  foreign 6, 45, 74, 180
  general demand for 135
  handicraft 215
  industrial productivity positively correlated with 311
  informal 4, 160
  inherited 211
  lack of 163
  link between education and 154–64
  low 100, 160
  management 164
  manufacturing 134
  passed from generation to generation 6
  prior 195
  readily codifiable 140
  tacit 160
  traditional 209
skills acquisition 4, 142
  advanced general 144
  extensive process of 5
  important element in 140
  learning-by-doing 139, 140
  requisite 122
skills diffusion 135, 142, 144–54
  promotion of 165
skills transfers 100, 123, 146, 150, 180
  intergenerational 215

Index